BLACKSTONE'S GUIDE TO

The Financial Services and Markets Act 2000

SECOND EDITION

BLACKSTONE'S GUIDE TO

The Financial Services and Markets Act 2000

SECOND EDITION

Edited by
Michael Blair QC

With contributions by
Andrew Henderson, Paul Kennedy, Alex Kuczynski,
Helen Marshall, David Simpson,
and Emma Vick

OXFORD
UNIVERSITY PRESS

OXFORD

UNIVERSITY PRESS

Great Clarendon Street, Oxford OX2 6DP

Oxford University Press is a department of the University of Oxford.
It furthers the University's objective of excellence in research, scholarship,
and education by publishing worldwide in

Oxford New York

Auckland Cape Town Dar es Salaam Hong Kong Karachi
Kuala Lumpur Madrid Melbourne Mexico City Nairobi
New Delhi Shanghai Taipei Toronto

With offices in

Argentina Austria Brazil Chile Czech Republic France Greece
Guatemala Hungary Italy Japan Poland Portugal Singapore
South Korea Switzerland Thailand Turkey Ukraine Vietnam

Oxford is a registered trade mark of Oxford University Press
in the UK and in certain other countries

Published in the United States
by Oxford University Press Inc., New York

British Library Cataloguing in Publication Data

Data available

Library of Congress Cataloging-in-Publication Data

Data available

Typeset by Glyph International Private Ltd, Bangalore, India
Printed in Great Britain
on acid-free paper by
Clays Ltd, St Ives plc

ISBN 978-0-19-957633-3

1 3 5 7 9 10 8 6 4 2

Preface to the Second Edition

When the first edition of this Guide appeared in early 2001, I little thought that, within the same decade, the Financial Services and Markets Act 2000 (FSMA) would be so substantially amended as to require a rewritten further edition of the Guide.

But so it has proved, contrary to my expectation. At least in the years since 2005, some major changes have been made to the FSMA, and large parts of the original edition of this book are now sadly dated.

The main reason for my belief at the time was that the FSMA was written as a high-level 'framework', with general provisions calling for much of the detail to be filled in by the Treasury or by the Financial Services Authority (FSA). While that remains true of many parts of the FSMA, the purity of the structure has not, overall, held up as firmly as might have been expected. The reasons for this are perhaps three:

- the activities of the European Community institutions under the Financial Services Action Plan have been substantial;
- development of domestic policy has also led to change at the primary level as well as in the lower two tiers; and
- international financial and economic events over the last two years have provoked further changes to the UK way of doing things in the regulatory field and in related areas; indeed that process of change is still underway.

The areas that have undergone the most profound change at primary level are:

- Part 6 (see Chapter 8) dealing with official listing: this was changed to accommodate the Prospectus Directive in 2005 and the Transparency Obligations Directive in 2006;
- Part 8 (see Chapter 10) dealing with market abuse, was overhauled to comply with the Market Abuse Directive in 2005;
- various Parts (3 on Authorisation, 13 on Incoming Firms, 18 on Exchanges, and 28 (Miscellaneous (trade matching) and a new Part 18A on Suspension from Trading) underwent change to cater for the Markets in Financial Instruments Directive in 2007;
- Part 12 (in Chapter 14) has been rewritten in 2009 so as to adapt the regime for vetting controllers of authorised firms to fit the Acquisitions Directive;
- Part 15 (see Chapter 17) on the Financial Services Compensation Scheme has been amended by the Banking Act 2009 in the wake of recent difficulties about paying depositors promptly after the collapse of a bank; and
- Part 16 (see Chapter 18) on the Financial Ombudsman Scheme (FOS) now reflects the decision to expand the jurisdiction of FOS into the consumer credit field.

There have been many other changes, consequent on outlying legislation such as the Enterprise Act 2002 and the Companies Act 2006. However, it should be noted that some reviews of specific parts of the FSMA (for example, on enforcement, FOS, and financial promotion) have not led to any change to the FSMA itself; changes made have instead been accommodated within the framework of the FSMA.

The field is still subject to possible further change, particularly in relation to financial stability and 'macro-prudential regulation'. Further substantive initiatives are being pursued, both domestically and on the international plane, and both on the substance and on the institutional framework for financial services regulation.

As with the first Edition, this Guide is in the nature of an introductory description of the FSMA, and does not attempt to be exhaustive even at the level of the primary legislation. Space does not permit full treatment of the underlying Treasury legislation and the FSA Rules. For a more detailed analysis of the subject, including the secondary material, the reader is referred to two more substantial works published by the Oxford University Press. These are *Financial Services Law*, (now in its second edition, published in March 2009, and edited by myself, Professor George Walker, and Robert Purves), and *Financial Markets and Exchanges Law* (published in February 2007 and edited by myself and Professor George Walker).

This Guide contains a copy of the FSMA, up to date as at 31 July 2009, with footnotes to aid in an understanding of the historical development of the legislation. As to the chapters themselves, the book begins with four fairly general chapters (which should set the scene as it is today and which between them cover the first two parts of the FSMA). Thereafter the treatment generally follows in chapters following the order of presentation in the FSMA itself. So, for example, *Discipline*, which is one of the passages looked at most frequently, and which appears in the FSMA at Part 14, is described in Chapter 16.

None of the authors of individual chapters is to be taken to be representing the views of any firm or institution with which he or she is linked by employment or partnership.

The publishers and I both hope that this second edition will be of value to those who need either to grasp what the general shape of financial regulation now is, or to look quickly at one or more of the relevant components of the subject. Undergraduate and graduate students, and new entrants to the financial services industry, or to allied professions (compliance, accountancy, and law), should find the Guide of particular use in coming to grips with the field.

Michael Blair QC
3 Verulam Buildings
Gray's Inn
London WC1R 5NT
August 2009

Preface to the First Edition

The Financial Services and Markets Act 2000 has finally been produced after a prolonged and innovative parliamentary process. Its central tenet, that there should be integrated financial regulation based on clear objectives, proportionality and fairness, has attracted general support, though there has been much contention round the edges. The Act creates a fresh start for the oversight of this crucially important sector of the United Kingdom economy, and is being widely studied elsewhere in the world. A centrepiece of this new government's legislation agenda over the last two years, it provides the framework for a more detailed working out of its principles and requirements that is yet to be finalised.

The focus now shifts from Parliament itself to the Treasury and to ministers, who have to put in place a layer of secondary legislation, and to the Financial Services Authority, which is planning and consulting on its *Handbook* to contain the rules and guidance needed to make the Act into a fully workable system.

This book is largely focused on the new Act, and has gone to press without waiting for certainty or completeness in either of these supporting layers. In particular, it does not analyse in any depth the crucially important Regulatory Activities Order and Financial Promotion Order, on which the Treasury proposes further consultation in the autumn of 2000. Nor is it able to grapple with issues about transition or commencement, which also depend on policy development in the Treasury.

Nonetheless the authors hope that an early account and analysis of the Act itself may be useful to the very many people who will be affected by the legislation when it commences, and to those who are preparing to advise them.

The financial services industry is innovative and fast-moving. The systems for regulation of it have to be effective and fast-moving too. No sooner had the ink dried on the Act but it was already in need of amendment. The Credit Institutions Directive (2000/12/EC) of 20 March 2000 entered into force on 15 June, the day after royal assent to the Bill, and rendered out of date some parts of Sch 3 on EEA passport rights. In this work we have sought to be as up to date as we can in a rapidly evolving world.

Two of the authors are employees of the Financial Services Authority, and I have recently retired as general counsel to its board. None of us should be taken as writing on behalf of, or as expressing any view of, the Authority in this work.

The publishers envisage a possible further and expanded edition of this book when more of the underlying detail has been settled. Meanwhile the law is stated as at 6 July 2000.

Michael Blair QC
3 Verulam Buildings
Gray's Inn
London WC1R 5NT
July 2000

Acknowledgements

Andrew Henderson would like to thank Jodie Griffiths, Muna Motaleb and Max Rohrig, all of Clifford Chance LLP, for their assistance in preparing his contributions to this book.

Helen Marshall would like to thank Michelle Kelly, Chris Leonard, Emma Simmonds, Claire Simpson and Achala Siriwardhane, all of Bingham McCutchen (London) LLP, for their assistance in preparing her contributions to this book.

Contents—Summary

Contents—Detailed

Table of Cases

Table of Legislation

EC legislation

Biographies

Editor

Michael Blair QC is a specialist on financial services and financial services regulation. He joined commercial Chambers (3 Verulam Buildings, Gray's Inn) in 2000 after serving as General Counsel to the Board of the Financial Services Authority from 1998 to 2000, and as head of the legal function in its predecessor body, the Securities and Investments Board from 1987 to 1997. Before that he had served from 1982 to 1987 as an Under Secretary in the home civil service (Lord Chancellor's Department), latterly taking responsibility for the criminal and civil legal aid schemes in England and Wales as well as for the higher courts and matters affecting the legal profession.

His practice is largely advisory though he has appeared before the Chancery Division, the Financial Services and Markets Tribunal and the Financial Services Authority's Regulatory Decisions Committee. He sits judicially as a Member of the Competition Appeal Tribunal, and was the Chairman of SWX Europe Ltd until the Swiss blue-chip equities trading was returned to Zurich from London in mid-2009. He has been a Board member of the Dubai Financial Services Authority since 2004, and was Master Treasurer of the Middle Temple, his Inn of Court, in 2008.

He is the author or editor of a number of works mainly in the financial services field and mainly for Oxford University Press.

Contributors

Andrew Henderson is of counsel and the head of Clifford Chance LLP's Middle East financial services regulation and risk management group. He advises banks, broker-dealers, investment advisers and managers on risk and governance, entering new markets (particularly, emerging and frontier markets), financial services mergers and acquisitions, the regulatory aspects of equity and debt capital markets transactions, market regulation, financial products (including OTC and exchange traded financial and commodities derivatives), the structuring and offering of private funds and retail funds and structured products (including Exchange Traded Funds and Exchange Traded Commodities) and the regulation of Islamic financial institutions and *Sharia*-compliant products. He has also advised public authorities, including regulators and exchanges in the United Kingdom, United States, Abu Dhabi, Dubai, Qatar, Botswana, and Singapore.

Before joining Clifford Chance, Andrew worked as a regulatory and corporate lawyer in a leading international law firm in London, having focused on regulatory investigations and financial services disputes prior to that. He has been seconded twice to the Financial Services Authority, to the General Counsel's Division and Enforcement Division, respectively, and to the compliance department of a leading international investment bank.

Andrew is a member of the Securities and Investment Institute and the ISDA CE-EMEA Committee. He holds a PhD in public law from the University of Cambridge where he taught (part-time) for three years. He has had various articles published in professional and academic journals on financial services markets and regulation and contributed, most recently, to *Financial Services Law* (OUP, Second Edition, March 2009).

Paul Kennedy is a specialist in the regulation of financial services, corporate reporting and the professions. A qualified actuary and accountant, he worked for Prudential and then Coopers & Lybrand before training as a barrister at 11 Stone Buildings, and practised at Warwick House Chambers. In 1999 he joined the FSA's legislation team, which he led from 2000 to 2004. He was a part-time secondee to the HM Treasury Bill and implementation teams for FSMA from 1999 to 2002, and led FSA input to the Treasury's two-year review of FSMA in 2003–4. From 2004 to 2006 he was responsible for oversight of the Financial Ombudsman Service and the Financial Services Compensation Scheme. He is a former member of Council of the Institute of Actuaries and was a part-time secondee from the FSA to the Morris Review of the Actuarial Profession, which recommended in 2005 that the FRC should assume responsibility for setting actuarial standards and overseeing the actuarial profession. He subsequently joined the FRC in 2006. He contributed to *Financial Services Law* (OUP, Second Edition, March 2009).

Alex Kuczynski is the General Counsel for the Financial Services Compensation Scheme (FSCS). The FSCS is established in the UK as the single compensation scheme for regulated financial services, protecting claims for deposits, investments, insurance and insurance mediation, and mortgage business.

As General Counsel, Alex is involved in the present work in the UK on reform of the FSCS's framework to deal with the failure of banks, as well as the reviews of FSCS's role and scope more generally. The FSCS is a member of the European Forum of Deposit Insurers, and Alex works with EFDI and overseas compensation schemes.

Previously, Alex worked for the Investors Compensation Scheme, and before that was a lawyer in private practice.

Helen Marshall is a solicitor and partner in the Financial Services Regulatory practice at Bingham McCutchen (London) LLP. She focuses her practice on advising clients in connection with all aspects of the financial regulatory framework in the UK. Clients include major financial institutions such as banks, brokerages, insurance companies, investment advisors, and regulatory bodies.

During her nine years at the lead regulator, first at the Securities and Investments Board (SIB) and latterly at the Financial Services Authority (FSA), Helen was employed in a number of senior roles. She was head of enforcement law and policy during 2000 and 2001 and head of forensic investigation from 2001 to 2003. Helen had particular responsibility for investigations in the fund management and broking sector, and she was responsible for a number of major disciplinary cases brought against financial institutions and individuals. She was also heavily involved in helping to shape and develop many of the FSA's own practices and procedures under the Financial Services and Markets Act of 2000.

Since re-entering private practice in 2003, Helen has acted on a wide range of regulatory investigations, enforcement and disciplinary proceedings as well as advised on all aspects of the financial services regulatory framework. As well as being a regular speaker on financial services regulatory matters, Helen is an editor and contributor for *Butterworths* Financial Regulation Service, a member of *The Times* Law Panel and a former member of *Complinet's* Editorial Board. She is also a regular speaker on financial services regulatory matters.

David Simpson is a barrister in 3 Verulam Buildings. He advises on all aspects of the regulation of insurance, banking, and investment. He has been instructed in claims relating to unauthorised collective investments scheme, negligent investment advice, SCARPs (precipice bonds), structured products, endowment mis-selling and appointed representatives. He also has extensive experience of working for regulators. He was seconded to the General Counsel Division of the FSA in 2005 and subsequently involved in drafting Handbook text implementing the Capital Requirements Directive and as part of the project to simplify the Conduct of Business Rules. He has recently represented the FSA in a number of Part VII transfer hearings. He was retained as a consultant to the Qatar Financial Centre Regulatory Authority and appeared on behalf of the Dubai Financial Services Authority in a recent application for an injunction in support of an investigation into suspected market abuse.

Emma Vick was until recently Deputy CEO of SWX Europe, the London-based exchange for the larger Swiss equities, with responsibility for all aspects of regulation and compliance at SWX Europe (formerly virt-x). She was also responsible for corporate governance obligations, risk management, and key aspects of business continuity management.

Prior to SWX Europe, Emma worked for the London Stock Exchange where she had been Head of Membership and Settlement Regulation and later Chief Risk Officer.

In November 2008, SIX Swiss Exchange announced that trading of Swiss blue chips was to be reunified in Zurich by mid-2009. Emma led the winding down of SWX Europe's business in London and is now director of Coriastus Limited which was formed recently to provide management consultancy and executive coaching.

1

THE POLICY BACKGROUND

Paul Kennedy

A. INTRODUCTION

As this edition goes to press, the outlook for the Financial Services and Markets Act   1.01
2000 (FSMA) appears uncertain, with all political parties proposing radical change, and
the opposition Conservative Party promising outright abolition of the Financial Services
Authority (FSA), the single regulator for financial services in the UK. Particular controversy surrounds the role of the central bank, the Bank of England, in prudential regulation; and the related question of whether prudential and conduct of business regulation
should be undertaken by a single institution or separately—the so-called 'twin peaks'
approach. Nevertheless, whatever the eventual institutional arrangements, much of the
overall and detailed policy framework underlying the FSMA seems likely to remain,
including the need for:

(a) a framework capable of providing consistent but targeted regulation for a wide range
of financial markets and services, including banking, securities, and insurance
business;

(b) a powerful and independent regulator (or regulators) with a full range of statutory
rule-making, supervisory and enforcement tools capable of delivering effective
regulation;

(c) a framework capable of addressing both conduct of business and prudential
aspects of regulation, so as to deliver financial stability, consumer protection and
market confidence, but also encourage firms to manage their own affairs, compete
and innovate;

(d) effective accountability mechanisms, including clear objectives and incentives for regulatory institutions and their staff, and safeguards to ensure that decision-making is proportionate, transparent and fair;

(e) effective co-ordination of financial services regulation with the work of other agencies and government departments responsible for business, consumer protection, and competition (including the Office of Fair Trading (OFT)); crime prevention; and financial stability, monetary policy and economic management (the Bank of England and the Treasury); and

(f) a credible framework and institutions capable of promoting and representing British interests abroad, and delivering on international commitments, particularly to implement European legislation.

1.02   This chapter considers the policy background and objectives which led to the establishment of the FSA, and the extent to which the new regulatory system has been successful in meeting those objectives and responding to new challenges, particularly the banking crisis of 2007–8. Finally, there is a discussion of the proposals for future consolidation and reform.

B. BACKGROUND TO THE ESTABLISHMENT OF THE FSA

1.03   The proposal to establish a single regulator for financial services took many practitioners and commentators by surprise when it was announced by the incoming Labour government in May 1997. The Party's policy handbook, *New Labour, New Life for Britain* had, perhaps deliberately, been vague about the new government's plans for financial regulation. It promised only to 'reform and strengthen the regulatory system' and 'to simplify both the structure and the nature of the system so that it commands the confidence of both the public and the industry'. While the FSMA is consistent with both these statements, it goes much further than many observers had expected, which suggests that it also struck a chord with internal Treasury thinking at the time.

1.04   In the first edition of this book, Michael Taylor explained how the FSMA could be seen as the product of a long process of evolution, reflecting the UK's experience of financial regulation since the late 1970s, when the Wilson Committee had observed three quite separate streams, which exhibited significant differences in the style and nature of regulation, especially in the balance between statutory and self-regulation. These were the 'primary' banking sector, monitored and supervised by the Bank of England; the organised markets in the City, such as the Stock Exchange and Lloyd's, which operated largely on the basis of separation of functions and self-regulation; and the rest of the financial sector, including building societies and insurance companies and licensed securities dealers, which were subject to largely reactive statutory regulation.

1.05   By 1997, many of these distinctions had broken down as a result of the impact of legislative changes directed at encouraging greater innovation and competition (for example, the City's Big Bang in 1986) coupled with measures to enhance consumer protection (as advocated by the Gower Report and implemented in the Financial Services Act 1986), increasing globalisation, cross-ownership of institutions, and the impact of single market directives.

A number of commentators, such as Michael Taylor in his report *Twin Peaks:*   1.06
A Regulatory Structure for the New Century (Centre for the Study of Financial Innovation)
argued that industry convergence required regulatory convergence if the latter was to
remain effective. The time was therefore right for a complete overhaul and consolidation
of financial services regulation. As Rt Hon Gordon Brown MP, then Chancellor of the
Exchequer, said in announcing the creation of the FSA:

[I]t is clear that the distinctions between different types of financial institution—banks, securities
firms and insurance companies—are becoming increasingly blurred. Many of today's financial
institutions are regulated by a plethora of different supervisors. This increases the cost and reduces
the effectiveness of supervision.

Although the blurring of boundaries argument was undoubtedly influential, other   1.07
factors were equally, if not more, important in giving the FSMA its final shape. At least
as important as the desire to bring the regulatory structure up to date were three other
considerations: the decision to award the Bank of England greater independence in the
formulation of monetary policy; the government's desire to end what it described as
'City self-regulation' and especially to respond to what it regarded as the scandal of the
mis-selling of personal pensions; and the long-standing desire on the part of the regulators, strongly supported by the new government, to obtain greater powers to combat
financial crime.

1. Central bank independence

Like the decision to create a single 'super-regulator', the decision to grant the Bank of   1.08
England autonomy in monetary policy did not feature in the Labour Party's election
manifesto. The intellectual ground for this surprise move had been laid well in advance
by a number of influential supporters of the case for central bank independence, including several former Conservative Chancellors of the Exchequer, and it had been proposed
by the centrist Liberal Democrat Party. Nevertheless, one issue that had received comparatively little prior attention was whether the Bank of England, as an independent
central bank, should also conduct banking supervision. The evidence of other countries
provided two different possible models.

The first, Federal Reserve, model stresses the synergies between the conduct of mon-   1.09
etary policy and banking supervision. In particular, since banks are the conduit through
which changes in short-term interest rates are transmitted to the wider economy, the
central bank needs to be concerned about their financial soundness as a precondition for
an effective monetary policy. A subsidiary argument stresses the synergies which exist
between the information needed for monetary policy purposes and that needed to assess
the soundness of the banking system. The alternative, Bundesbank, model stresses
instead the risks to the central bank of it directly conducting banking supervision.[1] First,
a central bank which is also responsible for supervision may err on the side of laxity if it
fears that tight monetary conditions may lead to bank failures. Second, bank failures
inevitably will occur and when they do they will be blamed on the supervisor. If the

---

[1] The Bundesbank itself lost its role in setting German monetary policy to the European Central Bank as a
result of European Monetary Union in 1998.

supervisor is the central bank, its credibility will be undermined, and with it its credibility in the conduct of monetary policy. Thus the Bundesbank model stresses that the relationship between the central bank and the banking supervisor should be sufficiently distant to limit the scope for such 'reputational contagion'.

1.10   The arguments for combination or separation of function were therefore finely balanced, and in practice the different arrangements are found in approximately equal measure in countries with independent central banks.[2] However, in the British case two factors seem to have been decisive. First, the Labour Party had a long history of being unimpressed by the Bank of England's capability as a bank regulator. This dated back to the debates on the first UK Banking Act, in 1979, but was subsequently reinforced by episodes like BCCI (1991) and Barings (1995), although neither episode resulted in a firm policy commitment to remove banking supervision from the Bank. Second, the Bank of England Act 1998 presented an opportunity to effect a first transfer of powers under the Banking Act from the Bank to the FSA,[3] the new single regulator which had itself emerged from the Securities and Investments Board (SIB). The 1998 Act permitted the government to change the regulatory arrangements in a way which supported its general objective of modernising the system, but without the immediate need to establish a new regulatory agency. Given the circumstances of a crowded legislative timetable, such an opportunity must have seemed very attractive to Treasury ministers. Thus, shortly after the Bank of England was granted monetary policy independence, the government announced that it would also lose responsibility for banking supervision to what subsequently became the FSA. Nevertheless, recognising the role of both the FSA and the Bank of England in maintaining financial stability, the government announced the establishment of a tri-partite committee, consisting of the Treasury, the Bank and the FSA to co-ordinate their activities, supported by a Memorandum of Understanding. This is discussed further in Chapter 2.

1.11   Surprisingly, the decision to opt for a single regulator rather than the 'twin peaks' approach of separate prudential and conduct of business regulators (as in Australia), attracted little controversy, except from academics. Many of the existing regulators, such as the SIB (see below), had in effect both prudential and conduct of business functions, and the clinching argument seems to have been that where these conflicted they needed to be resolved by a single body, in possession of all the facts, in the public interest. The alternative would be an unseemly row between two regulatory bodies, which would undermine confidence in the system.

2. An end to 'self-regulation'

1.12   Although 'self-regulation' in its truest sense had long ceased to exist in the City, Labour Party spokesmen had criticised the decision in 1986 not to create a statutory securities commission in the UK, and continued to insist that in the absence of such a body the resulting system remained largely 'self-regulatory'. Bryan Gould, the Party's then

---

[2] Article 105(5)–(6) of the EC Treaty further envisages that either the European Central Bank or the European System of Central Banks (ECBS) might be given prudential responsibilities in the supervision of banks.

[3] See Michael Blair *et al*, *Blackstone's Guide to the Bank of England Act 1998* (London: Blackstone Press, 1998).

spokesman on City affairs, said in a parliamentary debate on the Bill for the Financial Services Act 1986 that 'failure to put in place a proper independent statutory commission will be regretted by the government and is already being regretted by the City', and he also criticised the then Conservative government for its failure to bring Lloyd's within the framework provided for by the Bill. The characterisation of the arrangements brought in by the 1986 Act as 'self-regulatory' provided ammunition for opposition spokesmen as evidence emerged of various regulatory failings by the new agencies established under it, and the emerging scandals at Lloyd's in the early 1990s cast doubt on the wisdom of exempting the insurance market from the 1986 Act's scope.

Of the various scandals that afflicted the regulators under the 1986 Act, none had a greater impact than that of pensions mis-selling. The mis-selling issue concerned the way in which personal, portable pensions, introduced by the Conservative government in the mid-1980s, were marketed and sold. These pensions were provided through the life insurance companies, and were intended to be an alternative to occupational pensions which, it was argued, led to rigidities in the labour market by encouraging workers to remain with the same employer for long periods of time. The protection of individuals against the sale of unsuitable pension plan products was to have been provided by the regulatory framework established by the Financial Services Act 1986, which was completing its parliamentary passage at the same time as the legislation for the new portable pensions. In the words of Sir John Major, then a junior minister concerned with the introduction of the new system, the 1986 Act would 'safeguard people against the unscrupulous overselling of personal pensions'.

Approximately eight million personal pensions were sold in the UK between 1988 and 1995. Some were sold to people who were in occupational schemes and who were advised to transfer out of these schemes and to take out personal pensions in their place. For those prospective pensioners who were in well-funded schemes and where the prospective pension was protected against inflation, as was the case with many public-sector employees, it would be very difficult to argue that it was good advice to leave those schemes in favour of personal pensions with no employer contribution and an uncertain return. In at least some cases this mis-selling seems to have been due to the fact that insurance company salesforces were poorly controlled and were remunerated on a commission-only basis, thus leading to high-pressure sales tactics. These sales practices continued, notwithstanding a regulatory regime that included as its key concepts 'best advice' and 'suitability', both of which had been introduced into the regulatory framework as a way of regulating the sale of complex, packaged financial products such as pensions.

The essence of the government's response to the mis-selling episode was to attribute it to the failings of self-regulation. The reason that mis-selling had not been detected and dealt with by regulators at a sufficiently early stage, it was argued, was because the Self-Regulating Organisations (SROs) under the 1986 Act failed to take adequate enforcement action. This was because they were hamstrung by their industry-dominated boards. Meanwhile, the SIB lacked sufficient enforcement powers to ensure that appropriate regulatory actions were taken. The SIB possessed only the power to 'derecognise' an SRO, an option that was too draconian to be an effective basis for intervention. In the absence of the kinds of intervention powers available to the United States Securities and Exchange Commission (SEC) in its dealings with its SROs, the SIB was thus constrained from ensuring that the SROs regulated in the public interest.

1.16　　While this analysis can be disputed in a variety of ways, it formed the basis for the Labour Party's conclusion, while in opposition, that the complex two-tier system of the SIB and SROs needed to be replaced by a single, statutory body responsible for the regulation of all securities and investments business. Although the model most often cited was that of the US SEC, this overlooked the fact that the latter body itself made substantial use of SROs. Instead, a completely unitary system was proposed in which the functions of the existing SROs would be absorbed into a reformed and enhanced SIB, reconstituted as a proper statutory body. This proposal formed the nucleus for what has subsequently become the FSA, although the latter has gained the important additions of banking, building society and insurance regulation, as well as the function of acting as the competent authority for listing which was transferred to the FSA from the London Stock Exchange in May 2000. Moreover, the FSA, which the SIB became, remains a private company discharging a public function, and hence the proposal for a 'statutory commission' has never in fact been enacted.

3. Dealing with financial crime

1.17　The third influential factor behind the new regime derives from a long-standing sense on the part of the financial services regulators that they lacked adequate powers to combat financial crime, especially market manipulation and insider dealing. For several years in speeches made by its then chairman, Sir Andrew Large, the SIB argued that there were serious shortcomings in the investigation and disposal of cases of insider dealing and market abuse. In part these shortcomings were due to fragmented jurisdictions, with the SIB having no powers over market abuse resulting from the conduct of individuals who were not authorised persons under the Financial Services Act 1986. In part they were also due to the fact that such cases could only be prosecuted under the criminal law, with a criminal rather than a civil burden of proof. As Sir Andrew remarked in a speech delivered on 29 October 1996:

> . . . under the criminal system the evidential and public interest hurdles to be cleared before commencing a successful prosecution in the criminal courts are, quite correctly, high. But, as a result, activities which take place outside the scope of the regulators, whether the actions of company directors or end users of markets, may finish up not being taken to court. And since there is no sufficient civil alternative, what we would deem unacceptable actions from a regulatory viewpoint, and which we could often deal with if entered into by someone who was subject to regulation, can currently go unchallenged.

1.18　　In often complex cases, with evidence that could only be interpreted on the basis of specialist knowledge, this meant that the number of prosecutions brought for market abuse was very small and the number of convictions even smaller. The regulators spent several years pressing for a revision to the law that would permit them to dispose of cases of market abuse through civil rather than criminal channels. Significantly, this was one aspect of UK regulatory reform where its proponents seem to have drawn direct inspiration from US law and practice. This is the basis for the FSA's Code of Market Conduct and the provisions of the FSMA relating to its powers in relation to individuals who breach that code.

1.19　　This aspect of the FSMA also proved to be the most controversial initially. It resulted in the draft Bill being criticised in an opinion of Lord Lester of Herne Hill QC, commissioned by a Joint Committee of the Lords and Commons that had been established to scrutinise it, on the grounds that the proposed new regime was incompatible with the European Convention on Human Rights. In consequence the government introduced a number of important amendments, most notably to the proceedings of the Financial Services and Markets Tribunal which would hear cases involving a breach of the Code of Market Conduct at first instance. Moreover, the regime lost its 'civil' tag, which counsel's opinion had strongly argued was something of a misnomer.

C. DELIVERING THE POLICY OBJECTIVES

Although the practical mechanics of implementing the new framework were far from easy, and took more than four and a half years, the idea of a single regulator for financial services was welcomed by industry and consumer bodies alike. The Bill, when it emerged, attracted cross-party support, although there was considerable debate over the FSA's powers and accountability (discussed in Chapter 2). Unification of the various bodies was implemented smoothly and successfully under the FSA's first chairman, Sir Howard Davies, so that it had already been operating as a single regulator for nearly two years when the FSMA came into force at N2 (that is, on 1 December 2001).   1.20

The FSA rapidly became the suggested repository for a number of new responsibilities, including mortgage providers, pre-paid funeral plans,[4] and UK listing authority (on the demutualisation of the London Stock Exchange). Further regulation was to follow, including mortgage and insurance intermediaries (also implementing the insurance mediation directive), and other types of home finance arrangement as well as payment services. The regulation of intermediaries expanded the FSA's remit enormously, so that by 31 March 2009 there were over 27,000 directly regulated firms, and over 166,000 approved individuals.   1.21

The main areas which have so far remained largely outside FSA regulation are consumer credit, occupational pensions, corporate governance and reporting, the control of takeovers, hedge funds and credit rating agencies, all of which nevertheless have clear links to the FSA. There are proposals to expand the FSA's role in some of these as well.   1.22

The FSA has also taken an interest in other activities because of its responsibility for consumer education and the Financial Ombudsman Scheme (FOS—see Chapter 18). Like the FSA, the FOS replaced a number of sectoral ombudsman and other adjudication schemes which had been established in banking, financial services and insurance. The FOS's jurisdiction extends to a number of areas, particularly in banking and consumer credit, which go beyond the scope of the FSA's jurisdiction.   1.23

Early concerns that FSA regulation would be unduly burdensome or would stifle competition were largely allayed, and the FSA appeared to enjoy wide support at least from the larger institutions. The UK was also highly regarded internationally, particularly compared to the US following the passing of the Sarbanes-Oxley Act in response to the Enron and WorldCom scandals. Indeed the Treasury's review of the FSMA after   1.24

---

[4] Pre-paid funeral plans were included primarily to force plan providers to introduce consumer safeguards which enable them to avoid the need for FSA regulation. See Chapter 3.

two years concluded that it was working well and recommendations could be incorporated either in changes to secondary legislation, including deregulatory amendments to the FSMA through an order under the Regulatory Reform Act 2006, or in changes to the FSA's (and where appropriate the FOS's) procedures.

1.25 Another area which has proved less controversial than expected is the FSA's regulation of markets, including cases for market abuse. After a slow start, and an initial setback (*FSA v Davidson and Tatham*), the FSA is now seen as a successful and effective regulator of the markets, taking action, for example, to curb short selling as part of the credit crunch (see Chapter 10).

D. INTERNATIONAL INFLUENCES

1.26 The FSMA's framework structure was intended to allow further European single market directives to be accommodated without the need for significant free-standing legislation. Nevertheless, the volume of European law requiring implementation grew enormously as a result of the European Commission's Financial Services Action Plan, which was launched in 1998, with the aim of achieving a 'single deep and liquid capital market' in Europe.

1.27 The Financial Services Action Plan consisted of 42 regulatory measures which aimed to deliver a single market in financial services by 2005. Specific measures are considered in individual chapters of this book. However, a number of general features have limited the FSA's room for manoeuvre as a national rule-maker.

1.28 First, there was the introduction of the Lamfalussy process for improving the delivery and implementation of European laws. This established a four-level structure of regulation:

Level 1: Principle-based legislation approved by the Council and the European Parliament, which also defines the scope for implementing measures.

Level 2: Detailed implementing measures (in effect, secondary legislation) under an accelerated procedure involving technical advice from a committee of European regulators.[5]

Level 3: Enhanced co-operation between supervisors to ensure proper implementation of Level 1 and Level 2 measures.

Level 4: Commission enforcement of implementation.

1.29 Although the FSA has been well placed to influence the work of the relevant committees, 'comitology' has inevitably involved a closer degree of harmonisation with other regulators than would otherwise be the case. Following the banking crisis (see below), there have also been calls for greater co-ordination worldwide, including the establishment of regulatory authorities for the single market to replace comitology (following the de Larosière report in March 2009).

1.30 Second, a number of measures, such as the Prospectus Directive and the Markets in Financial Instruments Directive, have imposed maximum harmonisation restrictions, which limit the ability of Member States to introduce additional host country requirements for the 'general good'. In practice, many of the Directives have required changes

---

[5] CESR (Committee of European Securities Regulators), CEIOPS (Committee of European Insurance and Occupational Pensions Supervisors), CEBS (Committee of European Banking Supervisors).

to the FSMA itself, including the Transparency Directive, the Market Abuse Directive, which resulted in a slight narrowing of the market abuse regime (see Chapter 10), and the Acquisitions Directive (see Chapter 14).

Third, the practice of adding additional domestic requirements to European direc-   1.31
tives when they are implemented in the UK ('gold plating') is now actively discouraged by the Cabinet Office following concerns about over-regulation. For example, a number of consumer protection measures have been introduced which apply across all business activities and not just in financial services, such as the Unfair Commercial Practices Directive. The FSA has chosen not to implement this directive through its own conduct of business rules, but will exercise its functions as a designated enforcement body under the Enterprise Act 2002, in consultation with the OFT.

E. EARLY CHALLENGES

The regulatory system faced a succession of challenges, ahead of the banking crisis of   1.32
2007–8, which although they led to criticisms of the FSA at the time, were largely attributed to the regulatory regimes which had preceded the FSMA, or the absence of full regulation. Indeed their resolution has sometimes been seen as a validation of the new regulatory approach under the FSMA.

1. Insurance regulation

The FSA became responsible for prudential insurance regulation in January 1999,   1.33
initially exercising delegated functions under the Insurance Companies Act 1982. In December 2000, the Equitable Life Assurance Society, the largest UK mutual life insurer, collapsed after the House of Lords[6] ruled that it could not reduce its bonus commitments to holders of policies with annuity guarantees (for which it had made inadequate provision), and it failed to find a buyer.[7] Subsequent reviews by Lord Penrose and the Parliamentary Ombudsman were heavily critical of the supervision which had preceded FSA involvement, but also criticised the FSA's handling of the crisis it inherited, and particularly its failure to close the insurer to new business at an earlier stage.

In May 2001, Independent Insurance collapsed following the discovery of fraudulent   1.34
reporting of outstanding claims and reinsurance. Company failures in the general insurance field were not new, and this was soon picked up by the Policyholders Protection Board, which became part of the Financial Services and Compensation Scheme (FSCS) in 2001. However, questions were raised about whether the FSA should have spotted the concerns earlier.

The FSA was heavily criticised for its part in the failures of both institutions. Although   1.35
much of the criticism was directed at the predecessor regime, questions were asked about the adequacy of its supervision. In the case of the Equitable, there were also questions about its ability to balance the interests of different policy groups when undertaking both conduct of business and prudential regulation.

---

[6] The House of Lords is superseded by the Supreme Court as of 1 October 2009.
[7] *Equitable Life Assurance Society v Hyman* [2000] UKHL 39.

1.36   The stock market fall in 2002 presented the FSA with fresh challenges. A large number of life insurers, which had large holdings in shares, found themselves unable to comply with the FSA's prudential rules, which replicated requirements under the Insurance Companies Act 1982, or were forced to sell shares, thus driving the stock market still lower (procyclicality). Some of the insurers had issued policies with annuity or other guarantees, like the Equitable (although it had fortuitously been forced to sell its shares before the crisis). The FSA was forced to issue hundreds of waivers of its rules to insurers to allow them to continue operating.

1.37   Criticisms were largely directed at the procyclicality of the existing rules. The FSA responded to these concerns by undertaking a review of insurance regulation, with a specific review of the regulation of with-profits business. The development of new market-consistent reserving requirements, and a new approach to policyholder protection based on the principle of 'treating customers fairly' rather than the 1982 Act's trigger of 'policyholders' reasonable expectations', were generally hailed as a vindication of the new regulatory approach established under the FSMA.

2. Treating customers fairly

1.38   'Treating customers fairly' (TCF) is a key requirement in the FSA's Principles for Businesses (see Chapter 12), and soon became a major theme of retail regulation. The fall in market values in 2002 had led to retail consumers suffering unexpected losses on a number of investment products which in some cases appeared to have been mis-sold, at least to the extent that the investment risks associated with those products had not been explained.

(a) *Pensions mis-selling.* Most of the cases arising from the pensions mis-selling scandal had now been settled, but the compensation paid obviously did not reflect the latest losses. A number of consumers sought to re-open these cases, although largely unsuccessfully.

(b) *Mortgage endowments.* The fall in share prices had a significant impact on mortgage endowments, life assurance policies which had been sold (often with a commission incentive to the salesman) to mortgage borrowers as an investment product which would repay their original loan. The policies had often been sold on the basis of optimistic assumptions about investment returns. However, in the light of lower interest rates and investment losses, it became apparent that many of these would fail to repay the original loan.

(c) *Market value reductions.* The fall in share prices led insurers carrying on with-profits business to impose 'market value reductions' on policyholders who wished to terminate (or surrender) their policies early, since it would mean selling the underlying investments at a loss. Many policyholders complained that the risks had not been properly explained, or that the reductions were excessive.

(d) *Split-capital investment trusts (splits).* These investment companies, although nominally controlled by their shareholders, were often in effect controlled and marketed by their fund managers, to which they paid large management charges, and had been encouraged to take on additional gearing to boost performance during the long stock market boom. Many trusts had increased their gearing (and the management charges) by cross-investing in each others' shares. When the underlying investments fell in value, many investors suffered large or even total losses on investments which had been marketed as safe, or as tax planning vehicles.

(e) *Precipice bonds.* A number of investment products, often relying on derivatives marketed by investment banks, offered guaranteed returns unless underlying investments fell by a certain margin. The scale of the falls in 2002 exceeded these levels causing substantial losses to investors.

The resolution of these problems has often been long and messy, requiring a combination of regulatory tools, centred around TCF and enforcing the complaints-handling obligations of firms, and backed up by independent 'fair and reasonable' determinations by the FOS. While these cases arguably demonstrate the effectiveness of the regulatory system in identifying and eventually resolving cases of mis-selling and other unfair treatment, the FSA has sometimes struggled to demonstrate that it is dealing with the issues, which has led many commentators to express frustration.   1.39

Systemic problems have often placed a heavy burden on the FOS, which the FSA has worked hard to resolve through a combination of supervisory and enforcement measures, as well as industry guidance, and voluntary settlements in the case of splits. However, the FSA suffered an early setback in using enforcement as a tool,[8] which has made it more cautious. The process has been slow and has often lacked transparency, which the FSA and the FOS have tried to improve through a 'wider implications' process, although with mixed success.   1.40

3. Banking conduct

Many of these products were sold by banks, which were also found to have mis-sold payment protection insurance on credit cards and other credit products. The conduct of most retail banking business was, until 2009, excluded from regulation, with reliance instead being placed on the voluntary Banking Code.[9]   1.41

However, as interest rates have fallen, banks have increasingly turned to explicit charges for accounts which have become overdrawn or for late payments, triggering large numbers of complaints to the FOS under both its compulsory jurisdiction (which applies to authorised persons including banks) and its consumer credit jurisdiction (for firms which are licensed under the Consumer Credit Act 2004). The OFT, which regulates consumer credit, has taken the lead in dealing with these complaints. However, following its assumption of responsibility for home finance and payment services, and concerns raised in the banking crisis of 2007–8 (see below), the FSA has confirmed its willingness to regulate the conduct of banking business.[10]   1.42

---

[8] *Legal & General Assurance Society Ltd v Financial Services Authority* [2005] UKFSM012 (FSMT).

[9] Issued by the Banking Code Standards Board, which will be renamed the Lending Standards Board on 1 November 2009.

[10] In particular, the FSA's Banking Conduct of Business Sourcebook (*BCBS*) will come into effect on 1 November 2009.

4. Retail distribution

1.43 The FSA's increasing responsibility for intermediaries across a wide variety of investment categories, including investments, insurance and mortgages, has prompted it to undertake a number of reviews of its approach to retail distribution. A long-standing concern, going back to the Financial Services Act 1986, when there was a requirement for sales staff to state whether they were independent or tied to the product (polarisation), has been the influence of commission and other inappropriate sales incentives. These have been blamed for many instances of mis-selling in the past, as well as the subject of training and skills of sales staff.

1.44 A number of measures have been suggested, including the introduction of low-charge 'stakeholder' products, and the availability of cheap products on the internet has begun to reduce the dependency on commission-driven selling. The FSA has now announced the prohibition of commission from 2010, which is likely to lead to a further restructuring of retail distribution.

F. THE BANKING CRISIS OF 2007–8

1.45 The origins of the banking crisis have been widely discussed, including in an influential report in March 2009 by Lord Turner, who became chairman of the FSA in the midst of the crisis. Although the global liquidity and credit crunch which precipitated the crisis largely originated in the US, most of the major UK banks, including several recently demutualised building societies, had left themselves exposed as a result of heavy lending to retail consumers, secured on inflated house prices, and a policy of expansion, including acquisitions of other banks.

1.46 From early August 2007, conditions in credit markets deteriorated sharply and Northern Rock plc, which relied on wholesale market funding to finance most of its mortgage lending activities, experienced increasing difficulty in securing funding. On 13 September 2007, it was forced to reveal that it had received emergency funding from the Bank of England. Although the FSA tried to reassure depositors, and the FSCS provided 90 per cent protection for up to £35,000 of their savings with any institution, only the first £2,000 was guaranteed in full. The period from Friday 14 February to Monday 17 September 2007 saw the first run on the retail deposits of a United Kingdom bank since Victorian times, which was only ended when the government announced that it would guarantee its debts. In February 2008, after failing to find a buyer, Northern Rock was taken into public ownership.

1.47 Criticisms of the regulatory system's response to this first crisis inevitably focused on the role of the tripartite arrangements between the Treasury, the FSA, and the Bank of England, which were supposed to ensure financial stability. The Treasury Select Committee, in its report, *The Run on the Rock* (January 2008), was heavily critical of these arrangements and, while not calling for their abolition, recommended major changes.

1.48 There were also criticisms of the delay and uncertainty which preceded the rescue, largely because, unlike in insurance, there was no resolution mechanism for banks which got into difficulty. The Banking (Special Provisions) Act 2008, which was put on a permanent basis in the Banking Act 2009, was enacted to enable the rescue, and gave the Bank of England a specific role in future rescues.

Further difficulties arose during 2008, which became a full-blown banking crisis in   1.49
September 2008, with the collapse of Lehman Brothers Inc. in the US, and the failure
of a number of Icelandic banks with branches in the UK. Bradford & Bingley plc was
taken into public ownership and another leading mortgage lender, Halifax Bank of
Scotland plc (HBOS) was in effect rescued by Lloyds Bank plc in the same month,
giving it nearly one third of the UK market in savings deposits. In October 2008, the
government was forced to inject £37bn into three UK banks—Lloyds, HBOS and Royal
Bank of Scotland plc—effectively nationalising them.

Subsequent revelations about the excessive risks taken by the banks concerned, which   1.50
had previously been regarded as models of prudence, shocked the public, and inevitably
attention was turned to the incentives and remuneration of the individuals involved.
The Treasury Select Committee, for example, has called for a total overhaul of the City's
bonus culture, which the FSA has accepted.

The Turner Review in March 2009 accepted that there had been regulatory failings,   1.51
including a failure of the regulatory architecture to address macro-prudential risks, with
FSA supervisors focusing on individual firms and the central bank on monetary policy
and interest rates; a procyclical prudential and accountancy regime; and an inadequate
depositor protection regime and bank resolution mechanism. There had also been a
failure of market discipline and corporate governance within the institutions concerned.
However, it rejected the 'twin peaks' approach, pointing out that regulators needed a
comprehensive view of the risks involved. It said there was no evidence that a 'twin
peaks' approach would have dealt any better with the crisis.

G. PROPOSALS FOR REFORM

The Turner Review proposed 28 major reforms, both to the FSA's own procedures and   1.52
to wider domestic and international arrangements, including co-ordinated action to
tackle procyclicality in accounting and reserving requirements and supervision of credit
rating agencies. In the UK, it proposed an enhanced supervisory approach to banks and
other key institutions, which involved greater challenge to their business models, strate-
gies and remuneration policies. It also called for closer co-operation between the FSA
and the Bank of England on macro-prudential issues, and expansion of its own capabilities in this area.

Meanwhile, the FSA has signalled a new enforcement-led approach to regulation,   1.53
backed up by 'intensive supervision' and a new more 'credible deterrence philosophy'
with increased penalties. In a speech in March 2009, the FSA's Chief Executive,
Mr Hector Sants, said:

There is a view that people are not frightened of the FSA. I can assure you that this is a view I am
determined to correct. People should be very frightened of the FSA.

July 2009 saw the publication of two alternative proposals by the government and the   1.54
opposition Conservative Party. The government's White Paper, *Reforming financial
markets*, accepted the analysis in the Turner Review. It proposed an amendment to the
FSA's statutory objectives, discussed in Chapter 2, to specifically include financial stability, alongside a similar mandate for the Bank, and new powers to support this objective.
There would be a new statutory Council for Financial Stability, chaired by the Chancellor,

with increased Parliamentary accountability, and a re-examination of the role and governance of the FOS and the FSCS.

1.55   The Treasury also consulted on additional measures to help consumers, such as the appointment of consumer advocates and an expansion of the FSA's ability to require an industry-wide review of past sales under s 404, without the need for a Treasury order or to demonstrate breaches of its rules. The FSA would also be given wider information-gathering powers, for example, to tackle market abuse.

1.56   While most of these measures were welcomed as far as they went, many commentators, including the Treasury Select Committee, have described the proposals as cosmetic, particularly on financial stability, and as failing to clarify the responsibilities of the Treasury, the FSA and the Bank.

1.57   The Conservative Party's response, *From Crisis to Confidence: Plan for Sound Banking*, proposed a radical solution to that problem, which re-opened the debate about 'twin peaks' and the role of the central bank in regulation. It advocated the abolition of the FSA and the transfer of its prudential functions to the Bank of England, which would be given full responsibility for regulating banks and other significant entities such as insurers. The Bank would have an independent Financial Stability Committee, in parallel with its Monetary Policy Committee, to oversee its new functions.

1.58   The FSA's consumer protection powers, including the licensing of intermediaries, would be exercised by a new Consumer Protection Agency (CPA), which would also pick up consumer credit, leaving the OFT to focus on competition and markets issues. A further proposal on which the Conservatives said they would consult would be to merge the FSA's markets and listing division with the Takeover Panel and the Financial Reporting Council, so as to establish in effect a UK version of the US Securities and Exchanges Commission.

1.59   Initial responses to this radical proposal have been cautious. Concerns have been raised about inevitable disruption, and uncertainty about the FSA's ability to deliver effective regulation in the meantime.

1.60   There is some recognition that a stand-alone CPA untroubled by prudential supervisory responsibilities might be a lot tougher and more transparent than the FSA, but this is unlikely to please firms. Meanwhile, consumer groups fear that a CPA wielding primarily enforcement powers will have less ability to influence firms' behaviour than the FSA through thematic work such as Treating Customers Fairly. Questions were also asked about which agency would take over responsibility for tackling financial crime.

1.61   Doubts have been raised too about the appetite of the Bank of England to resume direct supervisory functions, and its ability to focus on macro-prudential issues whilst also addressing micro-prudential regulation of individual firms. The Liberal Democrats' Treasury Spokesman, Rt Hon Vince Cable MP, has suggested a compromise arrangement in which the FSA would retain its responsibilities for prudential supervision; but the Bank of England would be given a lead role, and statutory responsibility, for financial stability issues, with powers to require the FSA to address its concerns.

1.62   Pending resolution of these issues, the FSA has said it will continue to pursue its reform agenda. Given that its performance may be a significant factor at the general election which must take place by the summer of 2010, the FSA seems likely to find itself at least temporarily subject to an additional level of scrutiny, going well beyond the accountability arrangements established under the FSMA. These accountability arrangements are considered next in Chapter 2.

2

ACCOUNTABILITY AND OBJECTIVES OF THE FSA

Paul Kennedy

A. INTRODUCTION

This chapter is concerned with the mechanisms for ensuring the Financial Services 2.01
Authority's (FSA's) accountability in the broadest sense. Two distinct strands of Part 1 of
the Financial Services and Markets Act 2000 (FSMA) put in place a framework for the
FSA's accountability: the first creates institutional mechanisms for accountability by
specifying a series of provisions relating to the FSA's constitution and governance
arrangements. The second specifies a number of objectives and principles that the FSA
must observe in the exercise of its functions. These represent the criteria according to
which the FSA's performance of the functions conferred on it may be judged. This chapter explains the background to both these aspects of the arrangements for the FSA's
accountability, before a final section which considers the way they have operated in
practice. However, it begins with a brief section considering the reasons for the FSA
having been established with a rather unusual constitutional status, as a private company
discharging a public function.

B. A PRIVATE COMPANY DISCHARGING A PUBLIC FUNCTION

The arrangements for the regulation of the financial sector under the FSMA are some- 2.02
what unusual, although not unprecedented. In conferring regulatory powers on a body

corporate (s 1), the FSMA departed from earlier practice adopted in the UK for the regulation of most other industrial sectors.[1] Vesting these powers in a private company has a number of important consequences. In the first place the FSA is not to be regarded as acting on behalf of the Crown, and its members, officers and staff are not Crown servants (Sch 1, para 13). This is a status that they share in common with the staff of the Bank of England, who are similarly not Crown servants, although the Bank is a public, rather than private, corporation.

2.03　　Secondly, it avoids the personalised approach to regulation that had been a feature of the approach adopted for utilities like water, electricity, gas and telecommunications. The regulation of each of these sectors was initially entrusted to a Director General in whom powers were vested personally by statute.[2] However, as discussed elsewhere in this book, the range of powers conferred on the FSA by the FSMA is very extensive; arguably it creates the most powerful regulatory body for financial services anywhere in the world. It would be obviously inappropriate for such a broad range of powers to be vested personally in a single individual, especially as the way that the more limited powers of the utilities regulators have been exercised has itself been the subject of much criticism. These factors argue for a much less personalised approach to the regulatory arrangements for financial services than would have been inevitable had the Director General model been adopted.

2.04　　The most commonly discussed alternative to individual appointments is to establish the regulatory body as a multi-member commission. In the UK this administrative arrangement has been adopted for a variety of regulatory and quasi-judicial functions. Despite a passing interest in the concept while in opposition, the Labour Party in government has not been disposed significantly to extend the use of regulatory commissions, although in many other countries they are widely used for the regulation of financial services as well.[3] As discussed in Chapter 1, there has also been a renewed interest in the concept of an appointed committee to oversee financial stability issues affecting the Treasury, the FSA and the Bank of England, as already adopted for monetary policy.

2.05　　In theory, a multi-member commission has a number of advantages compared with vesting powers in a single individual. It arguably leads to greater consistency of decision-making over time and may also result in greater regulatory independence from either government or the industry. On the other hand, it is sometimes urged against the multi-member commission that it is not well-adapted to speedy decision-making, which can be of the essence in the regulation of financial services, especially when responding to a possible systemic crisis.

2.06　　Vesting powers in a body corporate represents a departure from either of the main administrative forms used for the regulation of other industries and in other countries of the world. Nonetheless, it has been argued that this arrangement is able to combine the best elements of the Director General and multi-member commission models discussed above. The FSA's governance arrangements display aspects of both approaches and the

---

[1] It is worth noting, however, that subsequent legislation has tended to favour the use of corporations governed by a board on the model of the FSA.

[2] Again, most of these have now been replaced by a board structure as discussed at 2.06.

[3] For example, it is the organisational form of the United States Securities and Exchange Commission and Federal Deposit Insurance Corporation.

FSMA requires that its constitution provides both for a board of directors and a chairman, who is also a member of the governing body (Sch 1, para 2(2)). This arrangement, it has been argued, provides a balance between the need for rapid decision-making informed by special expertise (provided by the chairman and executive members of the board) while maintaining an element of collegiality in the decision process as well as a degree of independent oversight (provided by the non-executive members). A further advantage claimed for the board arrangement is that it enhances the transparency and accountability of regulatory bodies, and this was one of the primary reasons cited for adopting the same governance arrangements for the Office of Fair Trading (OFT) and the utilities.

2.07 Nonetheless, an early controversy related to the issue of whether or not the roles of chairman and chief executive should be combined, as they were initially with the first chairman, Sir Howard Davies, or split as at present. Many concerns were expressed about the power that a combined role confers on a single individual. Although the government strenuously opposed any prescription on this matter, it ultimately accepted a compromise amendment tabled in the Lords that:

In managing its affairs, the [FSA] must have regard to such generally accepted principles of good corporate governance as it is reasonable to regard as applicable to it (s 7).

In the Combined Codes on corporate governance the separation of roles is recommended, although not mandated.[4]

2.08 Although unusual, the decision to vest regulatory powers in a body corporate was not entirely unprecedented in the UK. As noted in the previous chapter, many of the 'governmental' functions under the Financial Services Act 1986 (FSA 1986) were delegated to the Securities and Investments Board (SIB), which was established as a company limited by guarantee. The exercise of statutory powers by a private-sector body was there adopted in an effort to ensure that regulation remained rooted in the financial markets; in theory a private-sector body would be more alert to the concerns of the industry, especially regarding the regulatory burden, than a government department or agency would be. The decision to vest powers in a body corporate in the successor to FSA 1986 may also have been influenced by similar considerations, although administrative expediency may have played at least as great a part in the decision to adopt this form. A new governmental agency could not have become operational until it had been legislated into existence; this would have necessitated a long delay in setting up the new regulatory arrangements for the financial sector. By vesting powers in a body corporate rather than a new governmental agency the considerable logistical and administrative problem of merging nine separate regulatory agencies into one was significantly eased since an existing regulatory body, the SIB, could be made the core of the new arrangements, starting when it changed its name by special resolution to the Financial Services Authority in October 1997.

---

[4] The issue has largely disappeared since the roles were split, and the FSA's annual report includes a statement of compliance with the Codes.

C. INSTITUTIONAL MECHANISMS FOR ACCOUNTABILITY

2.09   Vesting such a broad range of powers in any body, whether a governmental agency or a private company, places a special premium on ensuring that they are used in a responsible and accountable manner. The need for accountability has to be balanced by the need to ensure that the regulatory body is independent of improper influence, whether exercised on it by politicians or by the industry it regulates; the necessity of such independence as a prerequisite for effective regulation is a common theme throughout the various international statements of regulatory best practice.[5] The task of ensuring a proper balance between regulatory independence on the one hand and accountability on the other is a complicated one, and proved to be one of the most controversial aspects of the FSMA.

2.10   The model of accountability adopted is closely aligned with that applied to public corporations, like the Bank of England, notwithstanding that the FSA's legal form is that of a private company. Indeed, there are some important parallels between the accountability arrangements established by the FSMA and those put in place by the Bank of England Act 1998. At the same time there are also significant differences.

2.11   In both cases, the accountability arrangements reflect the traditional constitutional doctrine that incorporated bodies should not be directly answerable to Parliament, and that it is for ministers to answer for the exercise or non-exercise of whatever powers they may possess. Thus for both the Bank and the FSA the primary line of accountability is to HM Treasury. The Treasury has four main mechanisms for holding the FSA to account. The first is the power of appointment or dismissal of the FSA's board and chairman, powers reserved to the Treasury by the FSMA, para 2(3) of Sch 1. However, there are two main differences from the appointment of the Bank of England's governor and court. Firstly, the latter are formally Crown appointments, whereas the FSA board appointments are not. Secondly, the FSMA does not specify any formal criteria for the appointment or dismissal of members of the governing body, other than they cannot be currently serving members of Parliament or of the Northern Ireland Assembly. Unlike the governor of the Bank of England, for example, the chairman of the FSA does not have a statutory fixed term in office. In this respect, the FSMA is less prescriptive than the Bank of England Act 1998, which contains a number of provisions relating to the terms of office, the qualifications for appointment, and conditions for the dismissal of the Bank's governor and court of directors (Bank of England Act 1998, Sch 1, paras 1–8). Accordingly, there are fewer statutory requirements for ensuring the security of tenure, independence and appropriate qualifications of appointees to the FSA's governing board than for the Bank of England's court. On the other hand, appointments to the FSA board are in practice governed by the principles set out by the Nolan Committee on Standards in Public Life which provides a degree of non-statute-based transparency to the appointments process.

---

[5] For example, Basel Committee on Banking Supervision, *Core Principles for Effective Banking Supervision* (2006) and International Organisation of Securities Commissions (IOSCO), *Objectives and Principles of Securities Regulation* (2003).

In addition to the power of appointment and dismissal of the members of the FSA's   2.12
governing body, the FSMA confers on the Treasury three other mechanisms for holding
the FSA to account. In the first place, the FSA must submit to the Treasury, at least once
each year, a report covering such matters as the FSA's discharge of its functions; the
extent to which its objectives have been met; the extent to which it has complied with
the principles that should govern the discharge of its functions set out in s 2(3); and
any other matters the Treasury may direct (Sch 1, para 10(1)). This report is to be
accompanied by a report from the non-executive directors of the governing body (Sch 1,
para 10(2)) and will be laid before Parliament (Sch 1 para 10(3)).

In addition, the Treasury is empowered—by ss 12 to 18 of the FSMA—to commis-   2.13
sion reviews and inquiries into aspects of the FSA's operations. A review is to be conducted by a person who appears to the Treasury to be independent of the FSA (s 12(7))
and is confined to considering the economy, efficiency and effectiveness with which the
FSA has used its resources in discharging its functions (s 12(1)). The merits of the FSA's
general policies and principles are explicitly excluded from such reviews (s 12(3)). They
are thus, in broad terms, equivalent to a 'value for money' review conducted by the
National Audit Office (NAO), for which they are intended to be substitutes (see below).
These reports must also be laid before Parliament (s 12(5)(a)) and the Treasury may
decide on the extent of further publication (s 12(5)(b)).

By contrast, inquiries under s 14 relate to specific, exceptional events occurring within   2.14
the FSA's range of regulatory responsibilities. If events concerning a collective investment scheme or the activities of a person carrying out an authorisable activity (whether
or not authorised to do so) either could have posed a grave risk to the financial system
or caused or risked causing significant damage to the interests of consumers, and these
events might not have occurred but for a serious failure either in the regulatory system
or its operation, then the Treasury is empowered to commission an independent inquiry
into those events (s 14(2)). Similar powers may be exercised where the event concerns
listed securities or the issuer of listed securities which caused or could have caused significant damage to holders of listed securities and when those events might not have
occurred but for a serious failure in the regulatory system for listing (or in the operation
of that system) (s 14(3)). The Treasury may also decide on whether the report of such an
inquiry is published, in whole or in part (s 17(2)). If any report or part of a report is
published then it must be laid before Parliament (s 17(5)). Hence, unlike reviews, it is
not automatic that the report of an inquiry will be laid before Parliament.

The FSMA, therefore, places the Treasury clearly at the centre of the FSA's account-   2.15
ability arrangements. Several other accountability mechanisms are envisaged by the
FSMA. An important element in the FSA's accountability is provided by the requirement
that a majority of the members of the governing body should be non-executive (Sch 1,
para 3(1)(a)). The FSMA gives a statutory role to the non-executive members of the
Board, similar to the arrangements introduced for the Bank of England under the Bank
of England Act 1998. There is a committee of the governing body, consisting solely of
non-executive members, with a chairman appointed by the Treasury. This committee is
charged with a special role in respect of the FSA's efficiency, internal controls and determining the remuneration of the chairman and the executive members of the board.

A second, company-like aspect of the FSA's accountability is that it is obliged to hold   2.16
an annual meeting, analogous to a shareholders' meeting for a public limited company,
but in the present case open to any interested parties. The annual public meeting must

be held within three months of the report under Sch 1, para 10, being made to the Treasury, and the purpose of the meeting is to permit the report to be considered by facilitating a general discussion of its contents and by providing an opportunity for questions to be put to the FSA about any of its acts or omissions in the discharge of its functions (Sch 1, para 11(2)). The FSA must prepare and publish a report of the meeting no later than one month after the meeting's conclusion (Sch 1, para 12).

2.17 The FSA's accountability to two further important stakeholder groups—consumers and practitioners—is achieved through a general duty to consult under s 8 of the FSMA, and the establishment of two statutory bodies, a Consumer Panel and a Practitioner Panel (originally Forum), both of which were initially established on a non-statutory basis in November 1998, together with a non-statutory Smaller Businesses Practitioner Panel. The Consumer Panel advises the FSA on the interests and concerns of consumers and reports on the FSA's effectiveness in meeting its objectives, particularly those relating to consumer protection and public awareness statutory objectives (see below.) This Panel can raise its own concerns, initiate research and publish its own reports. The Practitioner Panel's membership comprises senior representatives of the businesses that are regulated by the FSA. Both Panels may make representations to the FSA, and the FSA must 'have regard' to such representations. By s 11, if the FSA disagrees with the view expressed or proposal made in the representation it must give the panel a statement in writing of its reasons for disagreeing, and this statement may be made public. The membership of both statutory panels is determined by the FSA itself,[6] albeit on an arm's length basis, although the Treasury's approval is required for the appointment and dismissal of the chairmen of these Panels (s 9(3) and s 10(3)).

2.18 The only explicit mention of accountability to Parliament in the FSMA is the requirement that the FSA's report to the Treasury, and the reports commissioned under s 12, should be laid before Parliament, and inquiries commissioned under s 14 may be so laid. Although reflecting a traditional constitutional doctrine, the absence of a more formal mechanism of parliamentary accountability formed the subject of much debate during debates on the Bill. The House of Lords Delegated Powers and Deregulation Committee argued that if ministers were to exercise the same kind of rule-making power that the FSMA vests in the FSA, there would undoubtedly be a case for parliamentary control. The Joint Committee on Financial Services and Markets also recommended that a parliamentary committee should scrutinise the FSA's annual report and take regular evidence from a broad section of consumers and practitioners. In addition, a number of expert commentators argued for a 'dual-key' approach to appointments of the FSA's chairman and board, with nominations by ministers being subject to confirmation hearings by Parliament.[7] However, as already discussed, the FSMA does not envisage a substantial role for parliamentary accountability and cleaves to the traditional constitutional doctrine of accountability through ministers. Furthermore, because the FSA is funded by a levy on the financial services industry rather than by public funds, the government

---

[6] Subject to a power for the Secretary of State to direct the FSA to appoint a non-executive member of the National Consumer Council (now part of Consumer Focus) under s 10(5A)–(5C).

[7] As proposed, among others, by Robert Laslett and Michael Taylor in *Independence and Accountability: Tweaking the Financial Services Authority* (London: Centre for the Study of Financial Innovation, 1998) and by Tyrie and McElwee in *Leviathan at Large: The New Regulatory for the Financial Markets* (London: Centre for Policy Studies, 2000).

held that there was no case for making it subject to oversight by the NAO, including NAO 'value for money' reviews, on the grounds that no public money was involved. Hence involvement of the NAO, which traces the use of public money and reports to the Public Accounts Committee of the House of Commons, would be inappropriate. The commissioning of reviews by the Treasury, discussed above, has been adopted as an alternative to NAO oversight.

Judicial review and scrutiny of the FSA's actions were also expected to be an important accountability mechanism.[8] Although established as a private company, the FSA is subject to judicial review and to the panoply of administrative law since it clearly performs a public function and is empowered to do so by statute. On the other hand, the FSMA applies a number of largely subjective criteria to the way in which the FSA is required to discharge its tasks: for example, the FSA is required to act in a way which is compatible with the regulatory objectives and in a way which is most appropriate for meeting them. But, while the former of these (compatibility) is not subjective, the latter refers to the way which the FSA considers most appropriate for meeting the objectives (s 2(1)(b)). It has been argued that the introduction of such a personalised criterion constrains, to some degree, the scope for judicial review.

Moreover, the FSMA confers on the FSA a broadly drafted immunity from suit. Although the importance of ensuring that individual officers of the FSA are immune from suit for actions taken in furtherance of their official duties is widely recognised, that of the FSA as a body corporate has been much more controversial. The FSA has immunity from suit for all its acts except those taken in bad faith or in breach of the Human Rights Act 1998 (Sch 1, para 19). This broad immunity was also enjoyed by a number of the regulatory agencies that the FSA replaced, but became more controversial given the concentration of powers in the FSA's hands, making it a much more powerful body than those it replaced. In these circumstances, it was argued, such a broadly drafted immunity from suit needed to be accompanied by a strong and independent complaints procedure. By Sch 1, para 7, the FSA is required to establish a complaints scheme for dealing with any complaints arising from the discharge of its functions, or the failure to discharge its functions (other than its legislative functions). The FSMA also provides for an investigator who can act independently of the FSA (Sch 1, para 7(1)(b)). The complaints procedure is necessary to give some redress to regulated businesses and individuals who are damaged by the FSA's maladministration. However, serious doubts were expressed in debates on the Bill about the adequacy of the arrangements provided for under the FSMA, and this remained a controversial feature of it. In agreeing not to disturb the substance of a late amendment the government accepted that the scheme must confer power on the independent investigator to recommend compensatory payments, payable by the FSA, to a justified complainant (Sch 1, para 8(5)).

D. OBJECTIVES AND PRINCIPLES

In addition to the institutional arrangements for holding the FSA to account, the FSMA contains a number of regulatory objectives and principles that are intended to provide

2.19

2.20

2.21

---

[8] Judicial review has not been much used in practice; see 2.59 below.

criteria by which the FSA's performance of its functions may be judged. Giving such prominence to the FSA's objectives is intended to help to ensure that regulation is effective and appropriate and that the FSA can be held accountable for the way in which its functions are exercised. In this respect, the FSMA crystallises the experience gained by a number of regulatory agencies since the 1980s in defining more clearly their role and functions.

2.22   While the approach of the FSMA greatly contributes to the clarity of regulation and establishes an entity which should enjoy a firm understanding of its aims and purposes, the very broad range of financial activities regulated by the FSA has required careful balancing in the formulation of these objectives. A balance has had to be struck across two different dimensions: the first involves developing a single set of objectives that can embrace the different aims and purposes of banking, securities and insurance regulation. The second has involved finding a regulatory middle way between, on the one hand, the demands of consumers for security and protection, and the need to maintain and promote suitably high industry standards, and, on the other, the recognition that unnecessarily burdensome regulation can stifle innovation and competition in financial markets, and that regulation should not aim to absolve individuals from the responsibility for making their own financial decisions.

2.23   The statutory objectives that define the FSA's overall purpose are four in number: maintaining market confidence; promoting public awareness; protecting consumers; and reducing financial crime. The FSMA applies these objectives, together with the associated principles of regulation, directly to the FSA's general functions, including rule-making, the preparation and issuing of codes, and the general policies which guide its work. As the competent authority under Part 6 (the 'UK Listing Authority') the FSA also has a specific general duty, under s 73, which is similar to but not quite the same as the principles of regulation laid down in s 2(3). However, in its capacity as the listing authority the FSA does not have fixed objectives that are equivalent to those in s 2(2) that apply to its regulatory functions. This issue is considered further in Chapter 8.

1. Market confidence

2.24   The FSA's market confidence objective is defined as 'maintaining confidence in the financial system' (s 3(1)), including financial markets and exchanges, regulated activities and connected activities. The term 'confidence' is generally used in the context of the regulation of securities markets, where the purpose of regulation is often said to be to provide investors and potential investors with confidence in the integrity and orderly conduct of the market. In the words of the IOSCO *Objectives and Principles*, the aim is to ensure that markets are 'fair, efficient and transparent'. Markets with these characteristics are ones in which the process of price discovery will operate on the basis of the information available to all investors. To guard against the risk that market prices may be distorted by insiders exploiting their superior information, market integrity regulation embraces such matters as the authorisation of exchanges, ensuring a reliable price formation process, and the prevention of improper trading practices including market manipulation and insider dealing. Thus market integrity regulation at one extreme shades off into dealing with conduct that falls within the purview of the criminal law, while at the other extreme it is concerned with ensuring that markets operate efficiently. Market integrity regulation, combined with regulation of the disclosure of information in securities offerings (discussed below), has formed the core of the traditional functions of securities regulators throughout the world.

However, the objective as formulated in the FSMA goes beyond this relatively limited conventional sense in which regulation is concerned with market confidence. The objective refers to confidence 'in the financial system', which indicates a comparatively extended meaning. An important element in this extended meaning is the *stability* of the financial system, which the Treasury and the FSA itself have made clear that they regard as being integral to the market confidence objective. As the FSA explained in its document *A New Regulator for the New Millennium* (2000, referred to as '*New Millennium*'), maintaining confidence 'involves . . . preserving both actual stability in the financial system and the reasonable expectation that it will remain stable' (Ch 1, para 2). 2.25

It is consistent with the existence of financial stability that individual firms should fail; this is the natural consequence of a competitive market economy in which investors incur risks in response to the prospective returns of their risk-taking. When a financial firm miscalculates the trade-off between risk and return, investors and its creditors (including depositors) may lose money. Thus the users of financial services need also to understand that different types of investment carry different levels of risk, and it is not the purpose of financial regulation to remove risk from the financial system altogether. As the FSA remarked in the *New Millennium* document, a regime that attempted to eliminate all risks for users of financial services would be excessively burdensome and uneconomic, and would encourage excessive levels of risk taking. Hence the 'market confidence' objective contemplates the possibility of the failure of individual firms (*New Millennium*, Ch 1, para 6). 2.26

By contrast, *financial instability* can be thought of as arising where financial distress in one financial institution is communicated to others. Contagion may occur as a result of problems in one institution triggering a crisis of customer confidence in other institutions; alternatively it may occur because the failure of one institution to settle its obligations causes the failure of other, fundamentally sound, institutions. Traditionally, the risk of this type of contagion was thought to be highest among banks, that is deposit-taking institutions. This is because of the inherent difficulty of the financial service they provide, which is to transform illiquid assets (loans) from and into liquid liabilities (deposits). A commitment to pay a depositor can be met in normal times, because customers' demand for access to their funds is reasonably predictable and liquid assets can be held to meet this demand. However, when a sufficiently large number of customers demand convertibility at the same time, the bank's commitment to provide them with liquid funds cannot be met without some form of outside assistance. Since all deposit-takers suffer from the same potential weakness, and it can be difficult for depositors to distinguish between a sound bank and an unsound one, a crisis of confidence in one entity can quickly spread to others that are perceived to share the same characteristics. Further, the nature of the weakness is such that concern about insolvency, whether or not well-founded, may be sufficient actually to cause insolvency if assets have to be liquidated at reduced prices ('fire sale prices') to meet the demands of withdrawing depositors. 2.27

A further source of potential contagion among banks is that they participate in the payments system, where obligations are settled between financial intermediaries. The failure of one participant in that system to meet its obligations can have serious implications for the ability of other participants to meet their own obligations. Disruption to the payments system can in turn precipitate a wider economic crisis. Arguably, it is in the 2.28

core of the payments system that the greatest systemic risk arises. However, other elements of the financial system infrastructure, including settlements and clearing systems, also contain the potential to act as a transmission mechanism for contagion between financial institutions. Hence the FSA has also stressed that its concern with financial sector stability is not limited to ensuring the financial soundness of the banking system, but is also concerned with other elements of the financial system—including clearing houses and settlement systems—that are a vital part of the system's infrastructure.

2.29   In view of the overarching importance attached, and recently re-emphasised, to systemic stability, it is surprising that it was only implicit in the market confidence objective in s 3 of the FSMA. This was the view of the Joint Committee on Financial Services and Markets which proposed that the 'market confidence' objective be amended to refer explicitly to systemic risk, so that the FSA's objectives would include 'maintaining confidence *in the soundness* of the financial system' (emphasis added). The committee was also of the view that some reference to the FSA's role as a crisis manager, in collaboration with the Treasury and the Bank of England, should be incorporated in this objective. However, ministers were not persuaded by this argument. The government's position on the systemic protection objective was that public and market confidence in the financial system clearly requires confidence in the soundness of the system as a whole. However, other aspects are also relevant, notably maintaining confidence in the effective prudential supervision of individual institutions. Singling out one aspect could throw doubt on the FSA's role in this area and narrow its remit. The government agreed with the committee that co-operation with the Bank of England and the Treasury is very important, but claimed that this had been adequately covered in a published memorandum of understanding (MoU, updated in 2006).

2.30   The MoU divides responsibility for systemic stability between the Bank and the FSA on the following lines: the Bank is responsible for 'the overall stability of the financial system as a whole' (para 2) which involves, *inter alia*, the financial system infrastructure (in particular the payments system) and the 'broad overview' of the system (para 2 (iii)). By contrast, the FSA's responsibilities are primarily institution-specific, relating to individual firms, markets, and clearing and settlement systems (para 3). However, within this broad distinction, the Bank is also permitted to undertake official financing operations in 'exceptional circumstances' in order to 'limit the risk of problems in or affecting particular institutions spreading to other parts of the financial system' (para 2(iv)).

2.31   Paragraph 11 of the MoU states that the Bank and the FSA 'would immediately inform and consult each other' if either should become aware of a potentially systemic problem, while para 12 envisages the appointment of a 'lead institution' to manage the situation and to co-ordinate the authorities' response in the event that a problem develops. There is no presumption that the 'lead institution' should be the Bank and para 3(iii)(b) of the MoU would appear to envisage that in at least some cases the FSA will take on a crisis resolution role, at least as it relates to an individual institution, and may assume the role of attempting to broker a private-sector solution that has previously been the exclusive preserve of the central bank.

2.32   The first edition of this chapter predicted that the respective roles of the Bank and the FSA would not become entirely clear until the crisis management arrangements were tested in practice, as they were in the banking crisis of 2007–8. As discussed in Chapter 1, this revealed a failure by any of the bodies to focus properly on the threats to financial stability. While the opposition Conservative Party's response is to give this responsibility to the Bank of England as part of a break-up of the FSA, the government has proposed, in *Reforming financial services* (July 2009), that the FSA (as well as the Bank[9]) should be given a formal objective of maintaining financial stability in addition to market confidence, and both should be overseen by a statutory Financial Stability Council chaired by the Chancellor.

The proposal would also give the FSA powers to support this objective, such as an ability to make general rules to support financial stability as well as to protect the interests of consumers, which is the current scope of s 138. While this extension is likely to be welcomed as focusing greater attention on financial stability, it should, at least in theory, be unnecessary, because of the wide definition of 'consumer' which has been used in s 138 and indeed the consumer protection objective. General rules made to protect the interests of consumers may already be used, and in practice have been used, directly to maintain financial stability and market confidence, by protecting the interests of consumers who are not customers of the authorised persons concerned, and by protecting both market counterparties and trust beneficiaries (see Chapter 12). 2.33

2. Public awareness and consumer protection

Although as we have seen none of the objectives are mutually exclusive, these two objectives are conveniently considered in parallel since they are in practice closely related. The public awareness objective is defined as 'promoting public understanding of the financial system' (s 4(1)), which includes both awareness of the benefits and risks associated with different kinds of investment and financial dealing and the provision of appropriate information and advice (s 4(2)). By contrast, the consumer protection objective refers in quite general terms to 'securing the appropriate degree of protection for consumers' (s 5(1)). Both these objectives are concerned with the problem of correcting the imbalances of information between producers and consumers of financial services. 2.34

Economists refer to such information imbalances as 'information asymmetries'. If a market is to function well, buyers must have adequate information to be able to evaluate competing products. They must be able to identify the range of buying alternatives and understand the characteristics of the buying choices they confront. However, these conditions are often absent from the market for retail financial products. The essence of a financial contract is that it involves a promise: money is exchanged today for an (often vague) promise of money in the future. Most ordinary consumers have only a limited ability to assess the extent to which the promisor (that is, the supplier of the financial contract) is in a position to make good the promise made to them. Moreover, the fact that the nature of a financial contract involves a promise, means that transactions of this type are especially vulnerable to fraud and the exploitation of the unwary. It was in the context of these types of information imbalance that the father of the Financial Services Act 1986, Professor Jim Gower, used his now famous phrase about the purpose of regulation being 'to prevent reasonable people from being made fools of'. 2.35

---

[9] See s 238 of the Banking Act 2009, which introduces a financial stability objective ('to contribute to protecting and enhancing the stability of the financial systems of the United Kingdom') and a financial stability committee for the Bank at ss 2A and 2B of the Bank of England Act 1998.

2.36   The traditional method for correcting these information imbalances has been to institute regulatory requirements for firms to disclose information to their clients. This type of disclosure is intended both to alert users and potential users of financial services to the risks of the transactions into which they may enter and also to inform them of such matters as costs and terms and conditions. This type of regulation is explained in the IOSCO *Objectives and Principles of Securities Regulation* as follows:

> The most important means for ensuring investor protection is the requirement of full disclosure of information material to investors' decisions. Investors are, thereby, better able to protect their own interests.

In other words, the essence of this type of regulation is to ensure that investors are placed in a position to make a fully informed judgement of the costs and potential risk and return characteristics of a financial contract. Beyond this, regulation does not seek to absolve them of responsibility for the decisions taken on the basis of the information so disclosed, and in this sense it might be described as a form of *caveat emptor*—let the buyer beware. However, a more accurate description of this principle is 'freedom with disclosure', and it has long been a central pillar in Britain of the regulation of many forms of financial contract, dating back at least to the Joint Stock Companies Act 1844. It leaves the producer and the consumer free to enter into transactions subject to the important proviso that the consumer does so on the basis of full and accurate disclosure. The principle of freedom with disclosure is also closely related to other forms of regulation, for example, the labelling of foods so that potential consumers can judge for themselves whether they wish to consume the contents. Indeed, the connection between disclosure regulation of securities and food labelling was explicitly made by the American Justice Louis D. Brandeis in his 1914 book *Other People's Money*:

> [I]t is now recognised in the simplest merchandising, that there should be full disclosures . . . The law has begun to require publicity in aid of fair dealing. The Federal Pure Food Law does not guarantee quality or prices; but it helps the buyer to judge of quality by requiring disclosure of ingredients. Among the most important facts to be learned for determining the real value of a security is the amount of water it contains.

2.37   Nonetheless, in recent years there have been many who have argued that the complexity of financial products like pensions and life assurance means the doctrine of freedom with disclosure cannot reasonably be applied to them, and that some higher degree of consumer protection is required than mere disclosure. Disclosure might provide the consumer with a good deal of information, but the consumer might then be unable to interpret it properly or to understand the significance of what he or she was being told. This thinking informed the concepts of 'best advice' and 'suitability' as they appeared in the rulebooks of the SROs that operated under the Financial Services Act 1986. Thus Rule 5.1 of the SIB's Conduct of Business Rules required that the firm should not effect for a customer any transactions which the firm believed to be unsuitable for the customer, and the 'know your customer' requirements of the SRO rule books placed heavy emphasis on the firm's need to obtain sufficient detailed information regarding a customer and his current investment and financial position to ensure that the proposed investment was appropriate and affordable and that the customer fully understood the nature and risks of the product. These concepts represented a partial shift away from the freedom-with-disclosure regime, since they placed an obligation on the provider of financial services to offer the consumer products that were appropriate to the consumer's financial needs. To continue the food analogy, it is equivalent to requiring a shopkeeper or a waiter to recommend a certain food to a customer—other than one who positively insists on making his own choice—based on a detailed assessment of his needs, tastes and financial resources. Failure to observe these requirements was a breach of regulatory rules and also provided the consumer with a cause of action.

The suitability and best advice regime was clearly ineffective in preventing the mis-selling of personal pensions (see Chapter 1). This led some observers to argue for a more restrictive approach, usually referred to as product regulation. This type of regulation seeks to guarantee that a financial product meets certain government-prescribed minimum quality standards; and it would also ban certain types of product from sale altogether. Although product regulation has a long history on the Continent of Europe, where it is now being gradually phased out as the result of deregulation, this type of regulation has been relatively rare in Britain. While the introduction of basic products such as 'stakeholder pensions' has moved Britain more in the direction of product regulation, the consensus of opinion is still against a significant extension of this type of regulation. It is argued that it would excessively lower customers' standards of care and would reduce competition and innovation to the ultimate detriment of consumers. 2.38

The FSMA attempts to strike a careful balance between the range of possible responses to information imbalances between firms and their customers. The first draft of what is now s 5(2) was very close to the principle of freedom with disclosure in that it emphasised the 'general principle that consumers should take responsibility for their decisions'. As the Joint Committee noted in its report on the draft Bill, 'This is a version of the time-honoured principle, *caveat emptor*, "Let the buyer beware"'. This initial formulation of the statutory objective was controversial. On the whole it was welcomed by representatives of the industry, particularly on the grounds that it avoided raising public expectations about what the regulatory system could reasonably be expected to deliver. On the other hand, it met with a good deal of criticism from representatives of organised consumer interests. The National Consumers Council (NCC, now Consumer Focus) argued for the principle of *caveat emptor* to be disapplied from non-business customers or at least strongly qualified; the FSA's own consumer panel proposed deleting the *caveat emptor* principle altogether. In evidence to the Joint Committee, Sir Howard Davies (the FSA's chairman) acknowledged fears that the provision as drafted might be taken not merely to qualify the consumer protection objective, but to negate it entirely. The government responded to concerns about the possible negation of consumer protection by the principle of *caveat emptor* by inserting a new paragraph (c) in s 5(2). This provision now requires the FSA, in considering what is the appropriate degree of protection, to take into account the need that consumers may have for advice and accurate information. Thus section 5 taken as a whole strikes a balance between what consumers may reasonably expect, and their responsibility for decisions in the context of this expectation. 2.39

This balance was further developed in the FSA's *New Millennium* document, which distinguished between a number of different risks, including what it terms 'prudential risk', 'bad faith risk', 'complexity/unsuitability risk' and 'performance risk'. The FSA argued that it has a role to play in reducing the first three of these risks, but that regulation is not intended to guard against 'performance risk', that is, the risk 'that investments do not deliver the hoped-for returns'. Hence regulation could reasonably be expected to protect the consumer against the risks of firm collapse, fraud, misrepresentation or deliberate mis-selling and the risk that consumers are sold a product that is unsuitable for their needs, but not the inherent risks of investing. 2.40

2.41   Despite the careful balance that has been struck in the formulation of the consumer protection objective, one factor that is not directly recognised in section 5 is the role of competition in ensuring that consumers are provided with high-quality, good-value products. Although, as we have seen, the proper functioning of a market depends on consumers' ability to assess the products they are being offered, to the extent that this condition can be met, a greater degree of competition is to be preferred to a lesser one. The role of competition as a partial substitute for regulation was recognised by the Cruickshank report on the British banking industry. Nonetheless, this important observation does not form part of the FSA's objectives as formulated. Indeed, as will be discussed below, the extent to which the promotion of competition should feature among the FSA's objectives was one of the most controversial issues in their formulation.

2.42   A final issue that arose in the context of this objective was the precise nature of the 'consumers' who require protection. Information imbalances between a firm and unsophisticated retail investors are obviously acute. At the other extreme, financial intermediaries, which deal with each other frequently and which employ teams of specialist traders, lawyers and other experts might be reasonably expected to be able to protect their own interests. Hence the traditional UK approach for distinguishing between retail and wholesale business, including disapplying conduct of business rules designed for retail transactions to those that only involve financial intermediaries.

2.43   The degree to which the distinction between the professional and retail investor should be enshrined in statute became a controversial matter during the drafting of the Bill. The experience of the Financial Services Act 1986 regime, in which unnecessary and burdensome conduct of business rules had been initially applied to interprofessional markets, had made the industry wary of a repeat performance under the FSMA. Even representatives of organised consumer interests were inclined to support such a distinction. For example, the NCC proposed that language akin to that of a 'business customer' from the Unfair Contract Terms Act 1977 could be adopted in the FSMA, to exempt this category of user of financial services from FSMA's protections. However, against this proposal it was urged that there were certain categories of business customer (for example, small businesses) which might also need a high degree of protection from improper sales practices by financial intermediaries. This point illustrates the difficulty of defining the wholesale/retail distinction in a way that can accommodate the varying degrees of sophistication of a wide range of users of financial services. In addition, as discussed under market confidence, a wide definition of 'consumer' was used in order for the FSA to be able to use its consumer protection powers to support its other objectives, including market confidence and financial stability. Ultimately, therefore, the argument that this distinction was best captured in the rules and codes promulgated by the FSA prevailed over the argument that it was sufficiently important to ensure that there was a clear statutory basis for applying a different, less onerous conduct-of-business regime to markets in which professional investors deal only with other professionals.

2.44   As a result, the FSMA does not formally incorporate the wholesale/retail distinction, although the requirement in s 5(2)(b) that in determining what is an appropriate level of consumer protection the FSA should have regard to 'the differing degrees of experience and expertise that different consumers may have in relation to different kinds of regulated activity' clearly reflects this thinking. Section 5(2)(a) also requires the FSA to have regard to the different degrees of risk in different kinds of investment or other transaction. The FSA's gloss on its statutory objectives reflects the important issue that the necessary degree of regulatory protection for consumers depends in part on their degree of sophistication. The *New Millennium* document stated that the level of protection provided would depend on the sophistication of the consumer, and that professional counterparties need (and want) much less protection than the retail consumer.

While the FSA must pursue the objective of an 'appropriate' level of consumer protection, the public awareness objective provides it with an alternative basis on which to address the information imbalances that are characteristic of financial markets. Well-informed, knowledgeable consumers will obviously be in a better position to understand and evaluate the characteristics of different types of financial products as well as their own financial needs. Thus the FSA's second statutory objective (s 4) requires it to promote 'public understanding of the financial system'. The prominence of this objective in the FSA's statutory responsibilities suggests that the government assigns it a very high priority. It is argued that if markets are to function efficiently consumers also need to become more financially literate, especially if they are to be able to make proper provision for their old age and periods of unemployment in a time of a diminishing role for the State.

2.45

The FSA stated in its *New Millennium* document that it would pursue two main aims under this objective. It would endeavour to promote a higher level of general financial literacy and aim to improve the information and advice available to consumers. The second aim clearly involves significant overlap with the consumer protection objective. Thus the FSA proposed to make greater use of league tables and relative performance indicators, which a number of the previous regulatory bodies had also sought to develop under their consumer protection remit; it would appear that the FSA's intention is to extend this work. However, the promotion of financial literacy does involve a significant new departure and the FSA has stated that it interprets this aim as involving the provision of programmes to enable consumers to acquire the knowledge and skills they require to become better-informed consumers. This would also involve it in fostering public understanding of retail financial products, in particular on the part of vulnerable or inexperienced consumers.

2.46

Assigning a role to the FSA in promoting consumer understanding of the financial system also represents an innovation in the sense that this type of regulation serves a social purpose as well as contributing to the efficient working of financial markets. Regulation in Britain has been overwhelmingly concerned with ensuring market efficiency and other social objectives have generally been promoted by the use of government spending programmes rather than regulatory action. (From an economic perspective even the prevention of fraud and other types of financial crime promotes market efficiency.) This contrasts with the situation in some other countries where regulation has been used to serve social ends.[10]

2.47

Although this type of social regulation has been rare in Britain, the issue of whether it should be extended by incorporation in the FSA's statutory objectives was considered during the public consultation exercise on the draft Bill. The NCC requested the Treasury to add to the list of objectives 'the need for reasonable access to financial

2.48

---

[10] An example is the community service obligation embodied in the Community Reinvestment Act of 1977 (12 USC § 2901–2906) in the United States; the purpose of this Act is to ensure that the supply of credit is not cut off to particular communities, especially in low-income areas.

services for those who have difficulty in getting access to products appropriate to their needs'. The House of Commons Treasury Select Committee also suggested that the FSA could become involved in matters of financial and social exclusion. However, the government, supported by the report of the Joint Committee of the Houses of Lords and Commons, resisted calls for the FSA's objectives to be amended to include these explicitly 'social' objectives. As the Joint Committee commented, the addition of such an objective 'would make life excessively difficult for a regulator responsible for prudential supervision, and would damage lines of accountability'. It recommended instead that if the government wished to impose social obligations on financial firms it should do so directly. With the exception of the public understanding role of the FSA, therefore, an extension of regulation as a means to promote certain 'social' objectives has not been significantly extended.

3. The reduction of financial crime

2.49   The fourth of the statutory objectives is the 'reduction of financial crime', which means 'reducing the extent to which it is possible for a business carried on by a regulated person to be used for a purpose connected with financial crime' (s 6(1)). In this context financial crime includes 'misconduct in, or misuse of information relating to, a financial market'. Hence one intention of this objective is to provide statutory underpinning to market integrity regulation, especially that aspect of it that shades off into combating certain forms of criminal conduct (for example, insider dealing).

2.50   In addition, the financial crime objective covers a number of other functions previously discharged by the FSA's predecessor agencies. These include the important function of protecting consumers of financial services from fraud or dishonesty; as noted earlier, financial transactions are especially prone to this type of abuse since their essence is a promise to pay a sum of money at some future date. Thus financial crime is defined (by s 6(3)(a)) as including any criminal offence involving 'fraud or dishonesty'. The prevention of money laundering has also become an issue on which regulators have been expected to play an enhanced role in recent years. This has important linkages with certain prudential issues, most notably the adequacy of a firm's systems and controls, of which controls on money laundering are an element. Moreover, as the FSA noted in the *New Millennium* paper, the exposure of a financial firm to being used for criminal purposes may also damage public confidence in that institution and possibly in the wider financial system. Hence there is a clear sense in which the financial crime objective also links with the first statutory objective of maintaining public confidence in the financial system.

E. PRINCIPLES OF REGULATION

2.51   In discharging its objectives under the FSMA, the FSA must have regard to obligations set out in s 2(3). These 'principles of good regulation' are intended to provide the FSA with guidance on the way in which Parliament expects it to discharge its duties.[11]

---

[11] These are more specific than the government's five 'principles of good regulation' (transparent, accountable, proportionate, consistent and targeted), which all regulators including the FSA are expected to follow, although understandably they are sometimes confused.

The first principle (s 2(3)(a)) refers to the way in which the FSA allocates and deploys   2.52
its resources. The FSMA requires it to do so in 'the most efficient and economic way'. In
the *New Millennium* paper the FSA undertook that in deference to this principle it
would go beyond the statutory requirement to consult on fees and would also consult on
its budget. Moreover, the FSA would also seek to develop a 'thematic' and risk-based
approach to regulation, in which resources are allocated according to what are perceived
as being the institutions and sectors that pose the greatest risk to consumers and users of
financial services and the wider financial system.

The second principle concerns the corporate governance of financial firms, and espe-   2.53
cially the role of management (s 2(3)(b)). A long-standing matter of concern in Britain
and in many other countries is that a regulatory regime might result in a shifting of
responsibility from the firms' management to the supervisory authorities. No supervision, however effective, could—or should—ever replace sound management in the firm.
It is important that supervisors and regulators do not become a kind of superior management board, and that sound corporate governance remains consumers' first and most
important protection. In recognition of this important point, the FSMA's second principle of good regulation requires the FSA to have regard to 'the responsibilities of those
who manage the affairs of authorised persons'. The FSA initially interpreted this to mean
that senior management are to be held responsible for risk management and controls
within firms, and that as a regulator it should not be too intrusive into firms' commercial
decisions (*New Millennium*, p 10). However, following the banking crisis of 2007–8, the
FSA has signalled that it will take a much more questioning and intrusive approach.[12]

The third principle requires the FSA's regulation to be 'proportionate to the benefits,   2.54
considered in general terms, which are expected to result' from it (s 2(3)(c)). In having
regard to this principle, the FSA takes into account the costs incurred by firms and consumers, including extensive use of cost/benefit analysis of proposed regulatory requirements. The proportionality of regulation is also relevant to distinction between wholesale
and retail consumers referred to earlier in this chapter. Cost-benefit analysis is similar,
but not identical, to the impact assessments which government and other public regulators are required to undertake, and some studies have concluded that the FSA's approach
is broadly equivalent. Although the FSA has been active in publishing its approach to
cost-benefit analysis, and has embraced wider economic concepts such as market failure
analysis, opinions vary on its effectiveness; and the need to justify additional safeguards
through cost-benefit analysis was seen by some as having inhibited effective regulation
of banks. In *Reforming financial services*, the government has proposed further changes
to ensure that the FSA takes into account wider economic impacts, including the costs
of failure to act.

The remaining principles can be considered together since they are closely related,   2.55
and are often confused. The fourth principle requires the FSA to have regard to the
desirability 'of facilitating innovation in connection with regulated activities'; the fifth
principle requires the FSA to have regard to the 'international character of financial
services and markets' and the desirability of 'maintaining the competitive position of the

---

[12] See the Turner Review (March 2009), discussed further in Chapter 1 and at 2.65 below. The Treasury
Select Committee (July 2009) has suggested that 'The solution lies in making sure that the regulator does
enough to insulate the taxpayer and small depositor from the impact of a firm's failure whilst avoiding treading
on the shoes of those with responsibility for a firm's stewardship'.

United Kingdom'; while the sixth and seventh principles encourage the FSA both to facilitate competition and minimise adverse impacts of its regulation on competition.

2.56 The prominence given to competition and competitiveness in the principles of regulation reflects their prominence in the debate on the formulation of the FSA's objectives. Many industry commentators were concerned that creating such a powerful regulatory agency, with a clear focus on consumer protection, would in time prove to be a recipe for over-regulation. These concerns were heightened by the widespread belief that historically the City of London had flourished as a financial centre in part because it has enjoyed a relatively light regulatory burden.[13] This sense of unease found expression in the argument that the promotion of competition (as a proxy for competitiveness) should explicitly feature as one of its statutory objectives, a position that found many influential supporters in the City. The primary justification for an explicit statutory objective was the belief that it would provide a needed counterbalance to the pressures the FSA would inevitably face to expand its consumer protection remit. Despite suggestions at certain stages of the legislative process that the government was minded to accept their arguments, ultimately the concern that an additional objective (duplicating the role of the competition authorities) would make the FSA's task impossibly complex, appears to have prevailed. Nonetheless, the government went some way towards meeting these concerns: first, by strengthening the role of the competition authorities in scrutinising FSA regulation; and second, by incorporating competition and competitiveness as principles to which the FSA must have regard.

F. THE ACCOUNTABILITY MECHANISMS IN PRACTICE

2.57 The FSA has always taken its accountability seriously and actively engages with its stakeholders and with the public, primarily through its website. Despite the formal exclusion of any direct accountability of the FSA to Parliament, the Treasury Select Committee has been one of the most active bodies in seeking and challenging evidence from the FSA and its senior staff, and outspoken in making recommendations to it, particularly in relation to its handling of the banking crisis of 2007–8. The practitioner panels and the consumer panel have also been active in commenting on the FSA's activities, both privately and in public.

2.58 By contrast, the debate about splitting the roles of chairman and chief executive was quickly resolved when the roles were separated on the retirement of Sir Howard Davies in 2003. As part of its review of the FSMA after two years, the Treasury asked the OFT to undertake a review of the impact of FSMA on competition, which was a commitment given to Mr Don Cruickshank in 1999. The Treasury also answered those who had wanted the NAO to review the FSA, by appointing the NAO to undertake the first value for money review of the FSA under s 12.[14]

---

[13] An argument advanced, for example, in the City Research Project's *Final Report* (March 1995).
[14] April 2007: <http://www.nao.org.uk/pn/06-07/0607500.htm>.

The FSA has been subject to very limited judicial challenge,[15] indeed even less than   2.59
the Financial Ombudsman Service (FOS). A bigger source of legal challenge, outside the
Financial Services and Markets Tribunal, has related to questions of disclosure, following
the Freedom of Information Act 1998, which have reflected the tension between the
FSA's expressed desire to be open and transparent, and the need for confidentiality under
the FSMA. The FSA has been criticised for its lack of transparency on a number of
matters, and has recently consulted on the use of transparency as a regulatory tool.

The FSA's complaints scheme has been reasonably active, and the independent   2.60
complaints commissioner, who deals with cases where complainants are dissatisfied with
the FSA's response, received 163 allegations or complaints in the year from 1 April 2008
to 31 March 2009, although very few have been upheld. The Parliamentary Ombudsman
did however make findings of maladministration against the FSA in relation to its supervision of the Equitable Life Assurance Society under the Insurance Companies Act 1982,
and also against the government for consumer literature, intended to warn consumers
about the dangers of opting out of their occupational pension scheme, which described
scheme benefits as 'guaranteed'. A similar complaint had been made against the FSA,
but fell outside the Parliamentary Ombudsman's jurisdiction.

Given that it already produces a statement of compatibility with the regulatory objec-   2.61
tives when it consults on its Handbook provisions, the FSA has conspicuously struggled
with its obligation to report on the extent to which, in its opinion, the statutory objectives have been met or on its consideration of the so-called principles of good regulation
in s 2(3). In some years, the FSA has reported its activities instead under three 'strategic
aims': 'promoting efficient, orderly and clean markets' (corresponding to the market
confidence and financial crime objectives), 'helping retail consumers achieve a fair deal'
(corresponding to the consumer protection and public awareness objectives), and
'improving our business capability and effectiveness' (corresponding to the principles of
good regulation). The FSA nevertheless takes the outcomes of its regulation seriously.
It has developed an Outcomes Performance Report (OPR), but has conceded that evalu-
ating its performance will always be challenging.[16]

There has been a clearer focus on the regulatory objectives in the FSA's reports since   2.62
the start of the banking crisis, following which it accepted that there had been a dramatic
collapse in confidence, implying serious mistakes by all those involved. Senior FSA staff
have also signalled that considerations under s 2(3) such as innovation in financial services and even senior management responsibility, both of which have been blamed for
some of the excesses which led to the banking crisis, may need to be sacrificed for a more
questioning and intrusive supervisory approach in order to meet the regulatory objectives. The FSA's non-executive committee has also reported on its scrutiny of the FSA's
economy and efficiency, but has generally raised no concerns. Indeed, the extra costs of
FSA fees and regulation required to deal with the aftermath of the banking crisis appear
to have been largely accepted by the industry. Financial Services Compensation Scheme

---

[15] See, for example, *R (Davis) v Financial Services Authority* [2003] 1 WLR 1284, Lightman J; [2004] 1
WLR 185 (Court of Appeal), and *R (Yukos Oil) v. FSA and Stock Exchange* [2006] EWHC 2044.
[16] *Our approach to performance evaluation* (FSA, 2002); *How we evaluate our performance—the Outcomes
Performance Report and developments in our approach since 2002* (FSA, 2007).

(FSCS) levies arising from the banking crisis, and defaults by intermediaries following mis-selling, are probably a bigger concern for firms.

2.63   The Treasury has not so far exercised their formal power to direct the FSA to include specific matters in its report, presumably relying instead on informal liaison over the contents of the FSA's report. In *Reforming financial markets*, however, the Treasury announced that the FSA will be expected to include a separate chapter on competition in future reports, thus responding to earlier concerns about the impact of regulation on access to financial services.

2.64   Perhaps surprisingly, there has been no formal use of the Treasury's power to order an inquiry under s 14 of the FSMA, either in the case of split-capital investment trusts or the banking crisis. The Treasury appointed Lord Penrose to investigate the events leading to the collapse of the Equitable Life Assurance Society, but most of the events considered were before the passing of the FSMA, and so the power was not used. The Treasury has preferred to arrange informal reviews of relevant matters instead; and the activity of the Treasury Select Committee has to some extent filled the gap.

2.65   In response to the banking crisis, the Treasury asked the FSA to provide a report, undertaken by its internal audit department, on its own supervision of Northern Rock plc, and subsequently a broader review by the FSA's new chairman, Lord Turner, on the causes of the crisis more generally. Although the FSA's reports were praised for their frankness, the Treasury Select Committee has criticised this approach as inadequate, with some commentators suggesting that the failure to order an inquiry may have been motivated by sensitivity about the Treasury's own role. This serves as a reminder that the operation of many accountability mechanisms will continue to be dominated by political considerations. At the same time, the Treasury Select Committee has reiterated that the FSA is an independent body, established in statute, and does not need 'permission' from politicians to regulate financial institutions properly:[17]

It is easy now for the FSA to promise to be more invasive in its supervision, because public and political opinion has swung behind such an approach. However, we firmly believe that it is not the job of the supervisor to be popular and merely follow political fads. The FSA must develop sufficient self-reliance to stick to its guns in the face of criticism from industry or politicians, because ultimately, the job of the FSA may be to make unpopular decisions from time to time.

---

[17] *Banking Crisis: regulation and supervision*, July 2009.

3

REGULATED AND PROHIBITED ACTIVITIES

Paul Kennedy

A. INTRODUCTION

Part 2 of the Financial Services and Markets Act 2000 (FSMA) sets the basic scope of   3.01
Financial Services Authority (FSA) regulation by prohibiting persons who are not authorised (or exempt) from:

(a) carrying on regulated activities in the United Kingdom (the 'general prohibition':
    s 19); and
(b) falsely claiming to be authorised or exempt (s 24).

Part 2 contains two further prohibitions which are not described in this chapter. First,   3.02
it prohibits an authorised person from carrying on regulated activities without permission (s 20), as described in Chapter 6. Second, it restricts the communication of financial promotions by an unauthorised person (s 21), as described in Chapter 4.

Consistent with the FSMA being framework legislation, the detail of the regulated   3.03
activities is left to secondary legislation, and in particular the Financial Services and
Markets Act 2000 (Regulated Activities) Order 2001 SI 2001/544 (Regulated Activities
Order), as frequently amended. Further information may be found in the FSA's Perimeter
Guidance manual (PERG).

B. THE GENERAL PROHIBITION

1. Elements of the general prohibition

3.04   The general prohibition is as follows (s 19(1)):

No person may carry on a regulated activity in the United Kingdom, or purport to do so, unless he is—

(a) an authorised person; or

(b) an exempt person.

3.05   To decide if a person's activities breach the general prohibition, the following principal elements need to be considered, each of which is described in more detail later in this chapter:

(a) Is the person carrying on regulated activities, that is, activities specified as regulated activities in the Regulated Activities Order?

(b) If so, are those activities carried on by way of business?

(c) If so, is the person carrying them on in the United Kingdom?

(d) If so, is the person an exempt person or can the person benefit from another exemption?

(e) If not, the person contravenes the general prohibition unless he is an authorised person.

3.06   As the general prohibition covers purporting to carry on a regulated activity as well as actually carrying one on, it is clear that an unsuccessful attempt to carry on a regulated activity is within the scope of the prohibition.

2. Authorised persons

3.07   The routes to authorisation are described in Chapter 5. An authorised person cannot breach the general prohibition, even if the authorised person's permission (see Chapter 6) does not include the regulated activity in question. This 'single perimeter' will be of assistance in avoiding problems of defining the boundaries between different regulated activities. An authorised person carrying on a regulated activity without permission will contravene s 20 and may be subject to FSA enforcement action as well as an action for damages if the Treasury so prescribe (s 20(3)). But an authorised person need not be concerned about the criminal offence and potential unenforceability of agreements that result from contravention of the general prohibition (s 20(2)).

3. Exempt persons and other exemptions

3.08   'Exempt persons' are appointed representatives (s 39(1)), recognised investment exchanges (s 285(2)), recognised clearing houses (s 285(3)) and persons exempt as a result of a s 38(1) exemption order (s 417(1)). But a person is only an 'exempt person' in relation to a regulated activity to which the exemption relates (s 417(1)). So an exempt person carrying on a regulated activity outside the scope of the relevant exemption will contravene the general prohibition. There are also specific exemptions from the general prohibition in Part 19 (Lloyd's names and former Lloyd's names) and Part 20 (members of certain professions carrying on limited regulated activities incidental to professional services). A person benefiting from one of these specific exemptions is not an 'exempt person'. This is important in view of the many particular dispensations for exempt persons, such as exemptions from the restriction on financial promotion (see Chapter 4).

C. REGULATED ACTIVITIES

1. Treasury's power to specify the regulated activities

The Treasury specifies what is a 'regulated activity' by order (s 22) and this power is used   3.09
to make and update the Regulated Activities Order. Generally, a regulated activity must be described in terms of a specified activity relating to a specified investment (s 22(1)(a)), which can be any asset, right or interest (s 22(4)), for example, the specified activity of dealing as agent relating to the specified investment of shares. However, the Treasury may also specify an activity which does not relate to any investment, but rather is carried on in relation to property of any kind (s 22(1)(b)). Section 22(1)(b) has been used, for example, to specify that the activity of operating a collective investment scheme is a regulated activity irrespective of the type of property to which the collective investment scheme relates. There are no express limitations on this power although, under rules of statutory interpretation, the long title of the Act may set an outer limit. Both the first order specifying the regulated activities and further orders which, in the opinion of the Treasury, extend the meaning of regulated activity are subject to the affirmative resolution procedure and therefore require approval by resolutions of both Houses of Parliament (Sch 2, para 26).

Schedule 2 to the Act describes the Treasury's power in more detail, but without   3.10
limiting it (s 22(2) and (3)). In particular:

(a) it lists in general terms particular activities (Sch 2, Part 1) and investments (Sch 2, Part 2) which may be specified for the purposes of s 22(1);
(b) it permits the Regulated Activities Order to include exemptions (Sch 2, para 25(1)(a)), which are generally treated as exclusions from the main activity so that the activity in question is not treated as a regulated activity at all;
(c) it empowers the Treasury to give itself or the FSA discretionary decision-making powers in the Regulated Activities Order (para 25(1)(b)), and powers to make rules or regulations or to provide information or documents relating to the definition of regulated activity (para 25(1)(c) to (e)). Examples of functions given to the FSA under the Order include certification of certain issuers within an exclusion for issuing electronic money (arts 9C–9L), and of newspapers and other media within an exclusion for advising on investments (art 54(3)); and registration of persons carrying on insurance mediation activities (arts 93–96). Transitional provisions may be included, such as grandfathering of existing regulated firms or interim authorisation for existing practitioners, when a new regulated activity is introduced.

2. Regulated activities and European Directives

3.11 Various European Directives[1] in the financial services area and under the Single Market Programme set a minimum level for the scope of the general prohibition. These Single Market Directives require each European Economic Area (EEA) State, including the United Kingdom, to introduce in its national law an authorisation requirement for persons established in that State who carry on specified financial services. But EEA States are permitted to extend the authorisation requirement to other activities (except where a Directive imposes 'maximum harmonisation' restrictions); and the scope of the authorisation requirement of the FSMA, as set out in the Regulated Activities Order, goes well beyond the Directives in many respects where the government has perceived a need to protect consumers or regulate markets in other areas.

3. The Regulated Activities Order

3.12 Tables 3.1 and 3.2 at the end of this chapter contain a summary of the regulated activities and the principal exclusions in the Order.

3.13 The Order picks up and in some cases extends the activities which were regulated under the predecessor legislation to the FSMA, namely:

(a) *Accepting deposits* (art 5) by banks, building societies and credit unions (which were initially exempt);

(b) *Effecting and carrying out contracts of insurance* (art 10) by insurers and friendly societies, as well as insurance and syndicate management and advice activities undertaken at Lloyd's (arts 56–58), which is itself an authorised person (see Chapter 21); and

(c) *Investment business activities*, including dealing, arranging, administration and advice in relation to securities (shares, debentures, etc, as defined in art 3) and contractually based investments (options, futures, contracts for differences, and qualifying contracts of insurance with an investment element, as defined in art 3), as well as activities relating to the management of assets generally.

3.14 In addition, several major activities have been added by the government in response to domestic or international developments:

(a) *Home finance activities*

The government has progressively introduced regulation of activities relating to mortgage contracts, home purchase plans, home reversion plans, and sale and rent-back plans, as well as corresponding contracts recognised under Sharia law, in response to concerns about the scope for consumer detriment. The activities covered include advice and arranging, as well as effecting transactions. Many of the institutions concerned, such as banks and building societies, are already authorised, as are intermediaries concerned with investments and insurance. However, the inclusion of arranging and advice has significantly expanded the number of firms which are subject to FSA regulation, either

---

[1] Principally the Markets in Financial Instruments Directive (2004/39/EC), the banking Directives now consolidated as the Banking Consolidation Directive (2006/48/EC) and various Directives in the life and non-life insurance areas.

as authorised firms or as appointed representatives of authorised firms, to include, for example, many estate agents, surveyors and professional firms.

(b) *Insurance mediation and long-term care*

Many of the existing investment business activities relating to arranging and advice on qualifying contracts of insurance with an investment element have been extended or replicated for other insurance contracts, as a result of the Insurance Mediation Directive (2002/92/EC). As with home finance activities, the effect of bringing insurance mediation into regulation was to extend enormously the number of businesses potentially affected, including those concerned with travel and transport, property and health. However, the exclusions in the Order permit many firms to undertake these activities as appointed representatives or professional firms subject to a registration requirement. At the same time, the government took the opportunity to extend the definition of qualifying contracts of insurance to include arranging and advice on long-term care contracts, so as to enhance consumer protection for vulnerable individuals.

(c) *Pre-paid funerals*

Pre-paid funeral plans have many similarities to insurance, and concerns about their regulatory status and consumer safeguards prompted the government to include them in the Order subject to two major exclusions for trust-based and insurance-based plans (art 60). The majority of plan providers rely on one of these exclusions, and self-regulation by the Funeral Planning Authority. So far no firm has obtained permission from the FSA to undertake regulated funeral plan activities as an authorised person.

(d) *Stakeholder and pension products*

Following the Sandler Review, which recommended a range of low-risk, low-cost 'stakeholder' contracts to be marketed without the full range of FSA conduct of business rules, the Treasury has specified a separate activity of providing 'basic advice on stakeholder products' (art 52B). This activity does not reflect an extension of FSA regulation, but is essentially a means of identifying this activity to facilitate less regulation. The greater variety of permitted personal pension vehicles, including self-invested pension plans (SIPPs), is also reflected in the Order (arts 52 and 82).

(e) *Multilateral trading facilities*

The responsibilities of home and host regulators are now governed by the Markets in Financial Instruments Directive (2004/39/EC) in relation to many investments. The Regulated Activities Order identifies a separate category of activity relating to facilities for trading investments covered by the Directive (art 25D).

Further extensions are planned, although these will not necessarily result in additional   3.15
regulated activities. To implement the Payment Services Directive (2007/64/EC), which covers money transmission services, the Treasury has chosen to establish a parallel authorisation regime for payment institutions other than credit institutions and electronic money issuers, which is largely outside the FSMA and introduces exclusions from regulated activities.[2]

---

[2] The Payment Services Regulations 2009 SI 2009/209.

D. ACTIVITIES CARRIED ON 'BY WAY OF BUSINESS'

3.16   For an activity to be a regulated activity, it must be carried on 'by way of business' (s 22(1)). 'By way of business' is not defined in the FSMA, but the Treasury has the power by order to specify circumstances in which a regulated activity is or is not to be regarded as carried on by way of business (s 419). The explanatory notes to the Act explain that this power may be used for the purposes of s 22(1). The effect of this order is as follows:

(a) Accepting deposits is not treated as carried on by way of business if deposits are not held out as accepted on a day-to-day basis and are accepted only on particular occasions.

(b) Investment business and home finance activities are carried on by way of business only by persons who carry on the business of engaging in one or more such activities.

(c) Insurance mediation activities are carried on by way of business only if taken up or pursued for remuneration.

(d) Trustees of occupational pension schemes may be treated as carrying on the regulated activity of managing investments unless all day-to-day decisions are delegated to a person who is authorised or exempt in relation that activity, or involve pooled investments on the advice of an authorised person.

3.17   There is much case law in other contexts on the word 'business', but in general it seems that its interpretation depends on the context in which it is used. Two factors that are likely to be particularly relevant to a determination of whether an activity is carried on by way of business are frequency and commercial purpose. However it seems that, for an activity to be carried on 'by way of business' is a lower hurdle than for the carrying on of it to *be* a business. In interpreting the meaning of 'by way of business' in the context of the Financial Services Act 1986, s 63 (whether a gaming contract was entered into by way of business), it was held[3] that there was:

no reason . . . to place a narrow meaning on the word 'business'. It clearly should not be given a technical construction but rather one which conforms to what in ordinary parlance would be described as a business transaction as opposed to something personal or casual.

3.18   Further, the court added:

Regularly entering into a certain type of transaction for the purpose of profit is a good indication that the party . . . is doing so by way of business. But it is equally possible that the very first time it enters into such a contract it is doing so by way of business because it is doing so as part of its own overall business activities.

3.19   It is important to distinguish the 'by way of business' test in s 22(1) from that relating to financial promotion (s 21(1)), which restricts communicating financial promotions 'in the course of business'. This seems to be an even lower hurdle, and s 21(1) seems merely to require that the person be engaged in a business (of any sort) in the course of

---

[3] In *Morgan Grenfell and Co Ltd v Welwyn Hatfield District Council* [1995] 1 All ER 1 at p 13.

which the financial promotion is communicated; there is no need to consider whether the communication itself is made 'by way of business'. So advice about a pension scheme given by an employer to its employees might arguably not be given 'by way of business' but a financial promotion relating to it would be communicated 'in the course of business'.

E. TERRITORIAL SCOPE OF THE GENERAL PROHIBITION

The territorial scope of the general prohibition has three elements. First, the requirement in s 19(1) that a regulated activity must be carried on in the United Kingdom, for which no further definition is given so that interpretation will depend on the general law. Second, s 418 extends the application of the general prohibition in cases where it might otherwise not apply under the general law: this extends the *outward* application. Third, the Regulated Activities Order cuts back the *inward* application of the general prohibition for overseas persons. It is convenient to look separately at activities *within*, *outward* from and *inward* into the United Kingdom, although this approach may not be appropriate in complex cases involving, say, multiple parties or multiple jurisdictions.   3.20

1. Regulated activities within the United Kingdom

Where both the person carrying on the regulated activity and the client or counterparty are located in the United Kingdom, and all aspects of the activity are carried on here, it is clear that the regulated activity is carried on in the United Kingdom. That is the case even if the person has no establishment in the United Kingdom but acts through an agent here, whether a permanently established UK agent or an employee on a temporary visit here. But an overseas person acting through an agent in the United Kingdom may be able to take advantage of exemptions or exclusions for overseas persons in the Regulated Activities Order.[4]   3.21

2. Regulated activities outward from the United Kingdom

Where a person performs an activity from a UK location, but the client or counterparty is outside the United Kingdom, the territorial application of the general prohibition is less clear. It is necessary to analyse this situation by reference to the general law. The approach taken under English law is as follows: 3.22

(a) For the regulated activities of establishing etc a collective investment scheme, arranging deals for another, making arrangements enabling or facilitating deals, safeguarding and administering investments and managing investments, the general approach is to regard these as, by their nature, carried on where the firm is, rather than the client. This appears to be the appropriate treatment for managing the underwriting capacity of a Lloyd's syndicate as well.

---

[4] See further *3. Regulated activities inward into the United Kingdom* below.

(b) Advice is generally regarded as given where it is received by the client, and this appears to be the appropriate treatment for the proposed regulated activities of investment advice and advice on syndicate participation at Lloyd's.

(c) For accepting deposits, 'accepting' is defined as assuming the liability to repay the deposit (Regulated Activities Order, art. 2(1)). Such liability is generally regarded as assumed when (and where) the deposit is first received by the acceptor or its agent. In practice, for non-cash transactions, the currency of the deposit has been regarded as significant because the first receipt by the acceptor (or its agent) is often only in the United Kingdom where UK sterling payment facilities are used.

(d) For the other regulated activities, the law of contract may be of assistance.

Where communication is instantaneous, transactions are normally treated as entered into where and when the acceptance of the offer to enter into the transaction is received by the offeror. Where communication is not instantaneous, for example, by post, the transaction is treated as entered into when the acceptance is posted, and so probably where the offeree is located. The position can become even more complicated where agents receive and pass on orders, as is commonly the case in relation to the effecting of insurance contracts.

3.23   Where a person might not otherwise be regarded as carrying on a regulated activity in the United Kingdom, FSMA, s 418, provides that the person is to be so regarded in five cases, which are particularly relevant to activities outward from the United Kingdom. In each of these cases, the person will require authorisation or exemption under the general prohibition (s 19(1)) and, if an authorised person, permission under s 20. The first two cases seem to be intended to implement the requirement for 'home State' authorisation under the Single Market Directives (see Chapter 5). The first three cases apply to a person who has a registered office (or head office, where it does not have a registered office) in the United Kingdom, and provide that the person is to be regarded as carrying on a regulated activity in the United Kingdom if:

(a) Under the *first case*, the person is entitled to exercise passport rights under a Single Market Directive and is carrying on a regulated activity to which that Directive applies in another EEA State.

(b) Under the *second case*, the person is the manager of a fund which is entitled to passport rights and persons in another EEA State are invited to become participants in the fund.[5]

(c) Under the *third case*, the day-to-day management of a regulated activity is the responsibility of the person's registered or head office or another establishment maintained by the person in the United Kingdom. The meaning of 'day-to-day management' is unclear and this case seems to represent a potential widening of the authorisation requirement under all of the existing regimes, where activities of a non-UK office are under the day-to-day management of a UK office. On the other hand, it seems that activities of a UK person carried on from a UK office but under the day-to-day management of an overseas office would not fall under any of these three cases, and whether they are carried on 'in the United Kingdom' will depend on the general law.

---

[5] Currently, this would cover funds within the scope of the UCITS Directive (85/611/EEC).

The *fourth case* applies to a firm which does not have its head office in the United 3.24
Kingdom; the firm will be regarded as carrying on a regulated activity in the United Kingdom
if it is carried on from an establishment maintained by it in the United Kingdom. The
fifth case applies (following the Electronic Commerce Directive) in any other case where
a firm provides an information society service (such as communications over the internet) to persons in another EEA State from an establishment in the United Kingdom.

The judicial interpretation of *establishment* includes tests or indications based on 3.25
'exclusive occupation of premises', 'some degree of permanence' and 'some organisation
on the premises'[6] and an 'established place of business' is 'some more or less permanent
location not necessarily owned or even leased by the company, but at least associated
with the company and from which habitually or with some degree of regularity business
is conducted'.[7] There is considerable European case law on the meaning of establishment, but as this provision does not seem to be intended to implement a requirement of
a Single Market Directive this is unlikely to be relevant. The establishment must also
be maintained by the firm. Clearly, the payment of rent or other overheads would be
regarded as maintaining the establishment. But it seems that 'maintained' should be
interpreted more broadly than this to include other forms of use, provided there is some
sort of responsibility for or control over the establishment. On the other hand, it seems
that a place of business of an agent or subsidiary of a firm would not be 'maintained' by
the firm without something more.

3. Regulated activities inward into the United Kingdom

The analysis of the general law position for activities outward from the United Kingdom 3.26
is applicable also in relation to activities carried on from overseas with a client or counterparty in the United Kingdom. But where an activity would be regarded as carried on
in the United Kingdom under the general law, it may still be outside the scope of the
general prohibition because of a 'by way of business' exemption for an overseas person
(that is, broadly, a person who does not carry on a regulated activity from an establishment maintained by the person in the United Kingdom). The Regulated Activities
Order also provides exclusions for an overseas person applicable to particular regulated
activities, and for almost all incoming information society services.

F. FALSE CLAIMS TO BE AUTHORISED OR EXEMPT

Section 24 of the Act creates an offence of falsely describing oneself, or holding oneself 3.27
out, as an authorised or exempt person in relation to a particular regulated activity. It is
a defence for the accused to prove that all reasonable precautions were taken and all due
diligence exercised to avoid committing the offence.

---

[6] *Lord Advocate v Babcock and Wilcox (Operations) Ltd* [1972] 1 WLR 488 at p 492 per Lord Morris of
Borth-y-Gest.
[7] *Re Oriel Ltd* [1985] 3 All ER 216 at p. 219 per Oliver LJ.

G. SANCTIONS FOR BREACH OF THE GENERAL PROHIBITION

3.28　The sanctions for breach of the general prohibition are potentially severe, namely, criminal liability, unenforceability of agreements, compensation and action by the FSA or the Secretary of State to obtain an injunction and restitution.

1. Criminal sanctions

3.29　Breach of the general prohibition is an offence punishable by up to two years' imprisonment and an unlimited fine (s 23). It is a defence for the accused to prove that all reasonable precautions were taken and all due diligence exercised to avoid committing the offence (s 23(3)). For example, in determining whether a defendant took 'all reasonable precautions and exercised all due diligence' a court might take into account whether the defendant acted reasonably in accordance with legal advice or FSA guidance that activities did not amount to carrying on regulated activities in the United Kingdom.

2. Unenforceability of agreements and compensation

3.30　There are two ways in which contravention of the general prohibition may lead to an agreement being unenforceable (neither is applicable if the regulated activity is 'accepting deposits', see below):

(a) An agreement made by an *unauthorised person* in the course of carrying on any regulated activity in contravention of the general prohibition, the making or performance of which constitutes or is part of the regulated activity, is unenforceable against the other party (s 26). Section 26 does not apply if the unauthorised person is an EEA firm with a right to passport under any of the Single Market Directives.[8]

(b) An agreement made by an *authorised person* is unenforceable against the other party if it is made in the course of carrying on a regulated activity but in consequence of action by an *unauthorised person* which contravened the general prohibition (s 27). It is irrelevant whether the authorised person was acting within or outside the scope of his permission. Section 27 does not apply to an agreement made by an exempt person acting as principal within the scope of the exemption. It also does not apply if the unauthorised person is an EEA firm with a right to passport under a Single Market Directive (Sch 3, para 16(3)).

3.31　Subject to the above, the FSMA makes it clear that agreements are not illegal or invalid as a result of a contravention of the general prohibition (s 28(9)). This ensures that the innocent party to the agreement may continue to enforce it against the other party, notwithstanding that performance of the agreement may be a criminal offence. In addition, since ss 26 to 29 provide civil remedies for a contravention of the general prohibition, even if the general prohibition were to be regarded as a 'duty', it seems that

---

[8] Sch 3, para 16(2); see Chapter 5 for further details relating to passporting.

no action may be brought under the tort of breach of statutory duty in accordance with the general principles of that tort.[9]

Under both ss 26 and 27, the innocent party to the agreement may recover money or property transferred under the agreement as well as compensation for any loss sustained as a result of having parted with it, but not profits made by the other party (ss 26(2) and 27(2)). The compensation is in the amount agreed between the parties or determined by the court (s 28(2)); how remote the recoverable losses can be is not expressly provided for. If property transferred under the agreement has passed to a third party (seemingly even one aware of the circumstances), the third party is not affected by the rescission of the agreement (s 28(8)) although equitable remedies may still be available. The innocent party is entitled instead to recover the value of the property at the time of its transfer, even if that value has since increased. If the innocent party elects not to be bound by the agreement or recovers money under these provisions, money or property already received by the innocent party under the agreement must be returned (s 28(7)). 3.32

The court has a discretion to allow an agreement to be enforced or assets transferred under the agreement to be retained if it is satisfied that this is 'just and equitable' (s 28(3)).[10] The FSMA sets out issues that the court must have regard to in exercising this discretion, but which are not preconditions to a court allowing enforcement, namely: 3.33

(a) In the case of an agreement within s 26, the court must have regard to whether the *unauthorised person* reasonably believed that he was not contravening the general prohibition (s 28(5)). 'Reasonable belief seems to be a lower hurdle for the unauthorised person than the defence against the criminal offence described above (s 23(3)).

(b) In the case of an agreement within s 27, the court must have regard to whether the *authorised person* knew that the *unauthorised person* was contravening the general prohibition (s 28(6)). Actual knowledge appears to be required so that an authorised person is not under an obligation to exercise reasonable diligence in checking, for example, the authorised status of an adviser who introduces clients.

Section 28(9) expressly provides that a contract which is unenforceable as a result of ss 26 or 27 is not otherwise illegal or invalid. So, for example, while there is now no express provision (as there was in the predecessor legislation) that contravention of the authorisation requirement for insurance business would not affect the validity of a reinsurance contract entered into in respect of an unenforceable insurance contract, that seems to be the result of the general words in section 28(9). 3.34

3. Accepting deposits in breach of the general prohibition

The sanction of unenforceability of agreements and compensation does not apply in relation to the regulated activity of 'accepting deposits' in contravention of the general prohibition (ss 26(4) and 27(4)). 'Accepting deposits' is not defined but presumably, by virtue of ss 22(1), means the regulated activity of that description in the Regulated 3.35

---

[9] *Lonrho Ltd v Shell Petroleum Co Ltd (No 2)* [1982] AC 173, per Lord Diplock.

[10] This would seem to include potential recovery of fees due under an engagement letter: *Watersheds Ltd v da Costa* 2009 All ER (D) 140, which also considered the scope of the arranging activity in art 25(2) of the Regulated Activities Order.

Activities Order. The logic appears to be that the depositor should be able to recover the deposit pursuant to the terms under which it was accepted. Section 29 provides a remedy against an *unauthorised person* accepting deposits in contravention of the general prohibition: where the depositor is not entitled under the agreement to recover the deposit without delay, he may apply to the court for an order directing its return. As under s 28, the court need not make such an order if this is 'just and equitable' and the court must have regard to whether the deposit-taker reasonably believed that he was not contravening the general prohibition. Section 29 does not apply if the unauthorised person is an EEA firm with a right to passport under any of the Single Market Directives (Sch 3, para 16(4)).

4. Further powers to restrain contraventions

3.36 The FSA has published on its website a number of injunctions it has obtained to restrain contraventions of the general prohibition and orders to disgorge profits and require restitution of losses arising from such contravention (ss 380 and 382).[11] The FSA maintains published lists of firms and individuals (presumably having some connection with financial services) who it is aware are not authorised to carry out regulated activities, and who it knows or suspects may be in breach of the general prohibition. This is in addition to its public register of authorised and other regulated persons which is kept under s 347. See Chapters 25 to 27.

---

[11] See also the court's power to order a winding up on the 'just and equitable' ground under s 367(3)(b) of FSMA: Re The Inertia Partnership LLP (2007) 1 BCLC 739.

Table 3.1

Table 3.1 Regulated activities and the investments to which they relate. The Table is based on the Financial Services and Markets Act 2000 (Regulated Activities) Order 2001 (as amended), and is subject to change.

Investment	Accepting deposits (art 5)	Issuing electronic money (art 9B)	Effecting and carrying out contracts of insurance (art 10)	Dealing in investments as principal (art 14)	Dealing in investments as agent (art 21)	Arranging deals in investments (art 25)	Arranging deals in home-finance contracts (arts 25A-25C, 25E)	Operating a multilateral trading facility (art 25D)	Managing investments (art 37)	Assisting in the administration and performance of a contract of insurance (art 39A)
Any assets										X
Rights to or interests in investments (art 89)				X	X	X		X	X	X
Home finance contracts (arts 88-88C)							X			
Funeral plan contracts (art 87)									X	
Lloyd's syndicate capacity and syndicate membership (art 86)						X				
Contracts for differences (art 85)				X	X	X		X	X	
Futures (art 84)				X	X	X		X	X	
Options (art 83)				X	X	X		X	X	
Pension rights (art 82)				X	X	X		X	X	
Units in a collective investment scheme (art 81)				X	X	X		X	X	
Certificates representing securities (art 80)				X	X	X		X	X	
Instruments giving entitlement to securities (art 79)				X	X	X		X	X	
Government securities (art 78)				X	X	X		X	X	
Debt instruments (arts. 77-77A)				X	X	X		X	X	
Shares etc (art 76)				X	X	X		X	X	
Qualifying contracts of insurance (art 75)			X	X	X	X			X	X
Non-qualifying contracts of insurance (art 75)			X	X	X	X			X	X
Electronic money (art 74A)		X								
Deposits (art 74)	X									

Regulated activities

47

Table 3.1

Table 3.1 *Continued*

Investment	Safeguarding and administering investments (art 40)	Sending dematerialised instructions (art 45)	Establishing etc a collective investment scheme (art 51)	Establishing etc a pension scheme (art 52)	Advising on investments, including basic advice on stakeholder products (arts 52B and 53)	Advising on home finance contracts (arts 53A–53D)	Activities relating to Lloyd's (arts 56–58)	Entering into funeral plan contracts (art 59)	Entering etc into home finance contracts (arts 61, 63B, 63F, 63L)	Agreeing to carry on specified kinds of activity (art 64)
Any assets	X*		X							Depends on the kind of activity to which it relates. (Does not apply to articles 5, 9B, 10, 25D, 51, or 52.)
Rights to or interests in investments (art 89)	X	X			X					
Home finance contracts (arts 88–88C)						X			X	
Funeral plan contracts (art 87)	X	X			X			X		
Lloyd's syndicate capacity and syndicate membership (art 86)							X			
Contracts for differences (art 85)	X	X			X					
Futures (art 84)	X	X			X					
Options (art 83)	X	X			X					
Pension rights (art 82)	X	X		X	X					
Units in a collective investment scheme (art 81)	X	X			X					
Certificates representing securities (art 80)	X	X			X					
Instruments giving entitlement to securities (art 79)	X	X			X					
Government securities (art 78)	X	X			X					
Debt instruments (arts. 77–77A)	X	X			X					
Shares etc (art 76)	X	X			X					
Qualifying contracts of insurance (art 75)	X	X			X					
Non-qualifying contracts of insurance (art 75)	X	X					X			
Electronic money (art 74A)	X									
Deposits (art 74)										

Regulated activities

*In particular circumstances.

Table 3.2 Exclusions and their application to the regulated activities. The table is based on the Financial Services and Markets Act 2000 (Regulated Activities) Order 2001. Many of the exclusions are subject to conditions and limitations or apply in different ways to different regulated activities or investments. Reference should therefore be made to the full text of the exclusion in each case.

Regulated activities	Exclusions								
	Deals with or through authorised persons (various)	Trustees, nominees and personal representatives (art 66)	Course of profession or non-investment business (arts 67, 72C)	Sale of goods or supply of services (arts 68, 72B)	Groups and joint enterprises, including enterprise capital funds (arts 69, 72E)	Sale of body corporate (art 70)	Employee share schemes (art 71)	Overseas persons, incoming information society services and overseas risks (arts 72, 72A, 72D)	Other specific exclusions
Accepting deposits (art 5)								art 72A	arts 6–9A
Issuing electronic money (art 9B)								art 72A	art 9C
Effecting and carrying out contracts of insurance (art 10)								art 72A	arts 11–12
Dealing in investments as principal (art 14)	arts 15–16	art 66		art 68	art 69	art 70	art 71	arts 72, 72A, 72D	arts 17–19
Dealing in investments as agent (art 21)	art 22		art 67	arts 68, 72B	arts 69, 72E	art 70	art 71	arts 72, 72A, 72D	art 23
Arranging deals in investments (art 25)	art 29	art 66	arts 67, 72C	arts 68, 72B	arts 69, 72E	art 70	art 71	arts 72, 72A, 72D	arts 26–28, 29, 30–33, 34–35

Table 3.2 *Continued*

Regulated activities	Exclusions								
	Deals with or through authorised persons (various)	Trustees, nominees and personal representatives (art 66)	Course of profession or non-investment business (arts 67, 72C)	Sale of goods or supply of services (arts 68, 72B)	Groups and joint enterprises, including enterprise capital funds (arts 69, 72E)	Sale of body corporate (art 70)	Employee share schemes (art 71)	Overseas persons, incoming information society services and overseas risks (arts 72, 72A, 72D)	Other specific exclusions
Arranging deals in home-based contracts (arts 25A-25C, 25E)	arts 29, 29A, 33A	art 66	art 67					arts 72, 72A	arts 26–27, 28A, 29A, 33, 33A
Operating a multilateral trading facility (art 25D)								art 72	
Managing investments (art 37)		art 66	art 72C	art 68	arts 69, 72E			art 72A	art 38
Assisting in the administration and performance of a contract of insurance (art 39A)		art 66	arts 67, 72C	art 72B				arts 72A, 72D	art 39B
Safeguarding and administering investments (art 40)	arts 41, 42	art 66	arts 67, 72C	art 68	arts 69, 72E		art 71	arts 72, 72A, 72D	arts 50, 51, 52, 58

Table 3.2

Table 3.2

Activity							
Sending dematerialised instructions (art 45)		art 66			art 69		art 72A	arts 46–49
Establishing etc a collective investment scheme (art 51)							art 72A	
Establishing etc a pension scheme (art 52)							art 72A	
Advising on investments, including basic advice on stakeholder products (arts 52B and 53)		art 66	art 67	arts 68, 72B	arts 69, 72B	art 70	arts 72, 72A, 72D	art 54
Advising on home-based contracts (arts 53A-53D)		art 66	art 67				arts 72, 72A, 72D	arts 54, 54A
Activities relating to Lloyd's (arts 56-58)							art 72A	
Entering into funeral plan contracts (art 59)							art 72A	art 60
Entering etc into home-based contracts (arts 61, 63B, 63F, 63J)	arts 62, 63, 63C, 63D, 63G, 63H, 63K, 63L	art 66	art 67				arts 72, 72A	
Agreeing to carry on specified kinds of activity (art 64)	Depends on the kind of activity to which it relates. (Does not apply to articles 5, 9B, 10, 25D, 51 or 52.)						arts 72, 72A	

4

FINANCIAL PROMOTION

Paul Kennedy

A. INTRODUCTION

This chapter describes the restriction on financial promotion by unauthorised persons in   4.01
s 21 of the Financial Services and Markets Act 2000 (FSMA) and the consequences of
contravening this restriction. It also briefly describes how financial promotion by authorised persons is regulated, and how it fits in with other provisions of the FSMA. Further
information may be found in the Financial Services Authority's (FSA's) Perimeter
Guidance manual (PERG).

The principal elements of the financial promotion regime are as follows: 4.02

(a) The restriction on financial promotion in s 21 applies to unauthorised persons only.
Financial promotion by authorised persons is primarily regulated by the FSA's rules,
although there are restrictions on financial promotion of unregulated collective
investment schemes by authorised persons in Part 17.
(b) An unauthorised person may communicate a financial promotion only if an exemption applies or if the content of the financial promotion has been approved by an
authorised person. This approval is regulated by the FSA's rules, so that the authorised person will have to ensure that relevant disclosures are included and take
responsibility for the accuracy of the promotion, thereby giving the recipient a right
of redress and the FSA a right to bring enforcement action.

(c) The financial promotion regime is built around a wide restriction in s 21 subject to exemptions which the Treasury may make in secondary legislation to cut back the scope of the restriction to workable proportions. The primary source of these exemptions is the Financial Services and Markets Act 2000 (Financial Promotion) Order 2005 (SI 2005/1529 as amended) (referred to in this chapter as the Financial Promotion Order, or FPO).

(d) The financial promotion regime covers communications in any form or medium, including written advertisements, telephone calls, visits, letters, faxes, e-mails, broadcasts and Internet websites. The FPO distinguishes between *real-time communications*, which in turn may be *solicited* or *unsolicited*, and other forms of financial promotion.

(e) The FPO contains broad exemptions for financial promotions relating to deposits and non-qualifying insurance (insurance with a limited investment element), which is consistent with there being less regulation of the conduct of deposit-taking and general insurance business than of investment business.

4.03   The government's stated intention in developing the financial promotion regime was to modernise and streamline the legislative framework applying to financial promotion in the UK, 'to ensure that the UK is best placed to reflect . . . the opportunities of new and rapidly evolving communications technology' and

[T]o create a regime that is capable of standing up to the developments of modern technology while remaining effective against the more traditional methods of promoting financial services.[1]

The legislation does not use the phrase 'financial promotion' other than in the title of s 21 (and in empowering the FSA to make 'financial promotion rules' in s 145). In this chapter, 'financial promotion' has been used as a shorthand term to refer to an invitation or inducement of the type restricted by s 21.

B. OTHER UK LEGISLATION RELEVANT TO FINANCIAL PROMOTION

4.04   This section describes the other principal UK legislation that is relevant to financial promotions.

1. General advertising regulation

4.05   Most advertising targeted at UK consumers is subject to self-regulatory mechanisms through the Advertising Standards Authority and relevant codes of practice.[2] There are also statutory controls on advertising. The Trade Descriptions Act 1968 makes it an offence to offer goods using a false trade description and gives enforcement powers to local weights and measures inspectors. There are specialist regimes, such as the statutory regulation of consumer credit and consumer hire advertisements, and the media-specific controls for

---

[1] HM Treasury, *Financial Promotion—Second Consultation Document*, October 1999; *Hansard* HC Standing Committee A, 22 July 1999.

[2] Such as the Banking Code, and the British Code of Advertising, Sales Promotion and Direct Marketing.

commercial television, cable and radio, as well as the Investment Recommendation (Media) Regulations 2005 (SI 2005/382).

The Consumer Protection from Unfair Trading Regulations 2008[3] establish a general   4.06
duty not to trade unfairly and seek to ensure that traders act honestly and fairly towards their customers, including in advertising. The FSA is an enforcement authority in respect of these and other regulations under the Enterprise Act 2002, and takes responsibility for enforcement against authorised persons, appointed representatives and certain other firms under a concordat with the OFT (effective 26 May 2008).

2. Electronic commerce

The Electronic Commerce (EC Directive) Regulations 2002,[4] have the effect of impos-   4.07
ing home State control[5] of electronic communications, subject to suitable control over content and disclosures. This is a move away from the Single Market Directives which permitted host States to impose their own marketing rules on services cross-border where these are in the interest of the 'general good'.

3. Data protection and privacy

Restrictions on the use of telecommunications equipment for cold calling are imposed   4.08
by the Privacy and Electronic Communications (EC Directive) Regulations 2003.[6] In summary, unsolicited communications to individuals transmitted by automated calling mechanisms or by fax are prohibited without prior consent. Other forms of unsolicited telecommunications to individuals (eg telephone calls and e-mails) are permitted without consent, unless the individual has notified the caller that he or she does not wish to receive such calls or if the individual's name is recorded on a public register maintained by the Office of Communications (Ofcom). The Information Commissioner has enforcement powers under these regulations as well as under the Data Protection Act 1998, for example, in relation to the inappropriate processing of personal data.

C. OTHER PARTS OF THE FSMA RELEVANT TO FINANCIAL PROMOTION

1. Listing particulars and prospectuses

The FSMA, Part 6, makes it an offence (under section 85) to offer transferable securities   4.09
to the public in the UK, unless an approved prospectus has been made available. Where a prospectus is prepared in accordance with prospectus rules, it will benefit from an exemption from the restriction on financial promotion (FPO, art 71), but other financial promotions connected with the offer must still comply with the restriction. Where the offer falls under the exemption in section 86, the restriction on financial

---

³ SI 2008/1277, implementing the Unfair Commercial Practices Directive, 2005/29/EC.

⁴ SI 2002/2013, implementing the Electronic Commerce Directive, 2000/31/EC.

⁵ Strictly, the Directive gives control to the State of origin, which would also apply where the message comes from a branch in another Member State.

⁶ SI 2003/2426, implementing the Privacy and Electronic Communications Directive, 2002/58/EC.

promotion will still apply, and any offering document must be communicated or approved by an authorised person or fall under an exemption from the restriction. In general, however, there are corresponding exemptions under the FPO. For offers to be officially listed, listing particulars or a prospectus is required under the FSMA, Part 6, and there is an exemption for such documents (art 70).

2. Unregulated collective investment schemes

4.10 FSMA, Part 17, contains restrictions on authorised persons who communicate or approve financial promotions relating to unregulated collective investment schemes.

3. Financial promotion and regulated activities

4.11 Persons engaged in financial promotion need to consider whether they are carrying on a regulated activity, potentially in contravention of the general prohibition (s 19). The most relevant regulated activities are investment advice and arranging.

4. Offences and market abuse

4.12 The communication of financial promotions could potentially amount to market abuse (Part 8) or an offence under s 397 (misleading statements and practices).

D. WHY IS A FINANCIAL PROMOTION REGIME NEEDED AT ALL?

4.13 Why are the general advertising and marketing controls not sufficient for financial services? Although general controls have been significantly enhanced over the last ten years, there is still a strong consumer protection case for a separate and additional regulatory regime on the grounds that promoting financial services can lead consumers into making significant, long-term and sometimes high-risk commitments. Statutory controls can go beyond ensuring the accuracy of advertising to requiring the disclosure of risks associated with an investment and also full disclosure of terms and charges. Controls have arguably become more important with the increase in direct sales of financial services through off-the-page, telephone and Internet marketing, without the consumer receiving advice from an intermediary.

4.14 In addition, reliance on the general prohibition on carrying on regulated activities is arguably not sufficient. This is, first, because of the probable link between the financial promotion regime and the territorial scope of the general prohibition through the overseas persons exclusions and, second, because the promotion of regulated activities is often concerned with the stage before any regulated activities are actually carried on, enabling the FSA to take preventative action. This is particularly true given that an unauthorised person contravenes the general prohibition only at the stage of 'agreeing' to carry on a regulated activity and not before. Nevertheless, the wide scope of the financial promotion regime has made it controversial with many practitioners, regulated and unregulated. Its development has been the subject of numerous requests for exemptions, and much legislative effort by the Treasury and the FSA, including as part of the review of the FSMA two years after N2.

E. RESTRICTION ON FINANCIAL PROMOTION

1. Elements of the restriction on financial promotion

Subsections (1) and (2) of s 21 are the keystones of the regime. They provide that: 4.15

(1) A person (A) must not, in the course of business, communicate an invitation or inducement to engage in investment activity.
(2) But subsection (1) does not apply if—
    (a) A is an authorised person; or
    (b) the content of the communication is approved for the purposes of this section by an authorised person.

To decide if person A is contravening the restriction on financial promotion, the   4.16
following elements need to be considered, each of which is described in more detail later in this chapter:

• Is A acting 'in the course of business'?
• If so, is A 'communicating' anything, which includes 'causing a communication to be made' (s 21(13))?
• If so, is the communication an 'invitation or inducement'?
• If so, is it an invitation or inducement to 'engage in investment activity'?
• If so, is the content of the communication 'approved' by an authorised person?
• If not, is the communication within the territorial scope of the restriction?
• If so, does an exemption apply?
• If not, A is contravening the restriction unless A is an authorised person.

2. In the course of business

The restriction on financial promotion is contravened only when a person communi-   4.17
cates 'in the course of business'. Communications between private individuals in a personal capacity are therefore not restricted. Under s 21(4), the Treasury has the power, by regulations, to define the circumstances in which a person acts in the course of business for this purpose, but have not so far chosen to do so.

Chapter 3 contains a discussion of the interpretation of the requirement that an activ-   4.18
ity be 'carried on by way of business' to be a regulated activity under s. 22(1), and what constitutes a 'business'. Section 21(1) seems merely to require that the person be engaged in a business (of any sort) in the course of which the financial promotion is communicated; there is no need to consider whether the communication itself is made 'by way of business' or whether making such communications constitutes a business of the person. During debate on s 21,[7] the Minister said:

It seems reasonable to regulate people promoting investments or investment services in the course of their business, whether or not such services are carried on as a business. A company might, for instance, promote its own shares in the course of business, but it would not necessarily be carrying on the business of selling those shares.

---

[7] *Hansard* HC Standing Committee A, 20 July 1999.

4.19   For a communication to be 'in the course of' a business, it seems that there must be some connection between the business and the communication such that the person potentially derives a direct or indirect financial benefit from the communication. An example of a financial promotion that is likely to be regarded as communicated in the course of business, but which might not immediately be obvious as such, is an employer's leaflet promoting a group personal pension scheme to its employees.

3. Communicate

4.20   'Communicate' seems to encompass both the activity of physically transmitting or giving information to another person and the activity of imparting information. Under s 21(13), 'communicate' includes causing a communication to be made, which confirms that pre-transmission activities are potentially caught by the restriction on financial promotion. It appears that all of the following are potentially within the restriction:

(a) A person transmitting his or her own financial promotions. Examples of this are making a telephone call, holding a face-to-face conversation and handing over a leaflet.

(b) A person transmitting a financial promotion without being aware of its contents or being involved in the preparation of its intellectual content. Examples of this are a person distributing leaflets prepared by another person, a broadcaster transmitting a television or radio advertisement, a telephone company transmitting a telephone call, an Internet service provider transmitting an e-mail, a direct mail firm distributing advertisements and a newspaper publishing an advertisement. The Treasury has established exemptions for 'mere conduits' (FPO, arts 18, 18A).

(c) A person involved at a stage prior to the transmission of the communication who instigates its communication. Examples are a person who submits an advertisement to a newspaper for publication or to a broadcaster for broadcasting. But it appears that a person who does not personally transmit a financial promotion must directly cause it to be communicated to be caught by the restriction. Taking the example of a television advertisement, the advertising agency which creates the intellectual content of a television advertisement, the production company which records the advertisement and the company which maintains the transmitter which transmits it are unlikely to contravene the restriction when the financial promotion is communicated, unless otherwise involved with the financial promotion.

4.21   It is clear that more than one person can potentially contravene the restriction in relation to a single communication. Continuing the example of a television advertisement, it would appear that the advertiser communicates it (that is, causes it to be communicated), the television station which determines whether and when the advertisement will be transmitted communicates it (either by transmitting or causing transmission by others) and the cable company down whose cables it is transmitted also communicates it.

4.22   It is arguable that all persons who communicate (including causing the communication) of a financial promotion need to be authorised persons, unless an authorised person approves the content of the financial promotion or an exemption applies. The involvement of an authorised person in communicating the financial promotion or causing it to be communicated would not appear to prevent unauthorised persons from contravening the restriction in relation to the same financial promotion. Although s 25(2)(a) provides a defence to the criminal offence if the person concerned believed on reasonable grounds that the content of the communication was '*prepared*, or approved' by an authorised person (emphasis added), there is no equivalent defence against an agreement being treated as unenforceable as a result of an unlawful communication. Of course, if the authorised person who communicates the financial promotion also approves its content, this relieves other persons involved in the communication from potentially contravening s 21(1).

4. Invitation or inducement

The phrase 'invitation or inducement' is a departure from the previous legislation which used alternative formulations based on whether an advertisement contains an invitation or information intended or calculated to lead to the relevant activity. The dictionary definitions of 'invitation' suggest that it includes a request or solicitation. An 'inducement' would seem to be a wider concept, and some dictionary definitions suggest that no promotional intent is necessary—something can be an inducement if it merely brings something about or causes it to happen. In the Race Relations Act 1976, 'to induce' was held to mean 'to persuade or to prevail upon or to bring about'.[8] The fact that purposive wording has been used in conjunction with the word 'inducing' in FSMA, s 397(2) might support this interpretation. But to apply this wide interpretation of 'invitation or inducement' in this context would extend the restriction to many types of communication which the existing legislation does not restrict. To require an unauthorised person to obtain approval from an authorised person for non-promotional correspondence and conversations seems potentially unworkable. 4.23

Pressed on this matter during the passage of the Bill, the minister confirmed the government's stated policy was 'to capture promotional communications only', that '"inducement", in its Bill usage, already incorporates an element of design or purpose on the part of the person making the communication' and that 'design or purpose is implicit in this context'.[9] 4.24

If that is right, it seems that non-promotional materials are not caught. In the same debate, the minister said that the restriction: 4.25

will not catch . . . public announcements, exchange of draft share purchase agreements in corporate finance transactions or cases in which the recipient of a communication simply misunderstands its contents and engages in investment activity as a result.

---

[8] *Commission for Racial Equality v Imperial Society of Teachers of Dancing* [1983] ICR 473 at p 476.

[9] *Hansard* HL, 18 May 2000, cols 387 and 388. It seems likely that a court would have regard to these clear statements under the rule in *Pepper v Hart* [1993] AC 593. Under that rule, a court may have regard to certain classes of material contained in *Hansard* where an enactment is obscure or ambiguous, or where its literal meaning would lead to an absurdity (meaning, in this context, a result which is unworkable, impracticable or productive of a disproportionate counter-mischief).

But that is not to say that it is necessary for a communication to contain a recommendation for it to be an 'invitation or inducement'. A selection of factual information that would tend to influence a recipient's decision may be an inducement, although factual information that is provided in a fair and balanced way may not. In the context of actionable misrepresentation at common law it has been held that, although mere incompleteness might not make a communication into an inducement, an omission that makes the communication one-sided so as to amount to a travesty and not an accurate summary may do so.[10] Some communications that fall within the definition of the regulated activity of investment advice are likely to be inducements.

4.26   Must actual promotional intent on the part of the communicator be proved, or may an objective test be applied? An objective test appears appropriate for whether a communication is an 'invitation' and it seems reasonable to assume that an objective test may be applied to 'inducement' as well. To quote the minister again, whether something is an inducement 'will depend on the actual or perceived intent behind the communication'. So all the circumstances of the communication are likely to be relevant to a determination of whether it is an invitation or inducement, including its content, its character, its context and the experience, both general and particular, of the recipients. The restriction on financial promotion looks to the act of communication rather than any result flowing from it, so there is no need for any investment activity to be engaged in as a result of the communication, nor for the communication to be actually received by anyone. On the other hand, it is clear that the restriction cannot be contravened without a communication being made, even if there is some duty to make a disclosure.

5. Engage in investment activity

4.27   'Engaging in investment activity' is defined in s 21(8) as:

(a) entering or offering to enter into an agreement the making or performance of which by either party constitutes a controlled activity; or

(b) exercising any rights conferred by a controlled investment to acquire, dispose of, underwrite or convert a controlled investment.

4.28   An important question is whether non-specific or 'image' financial promotions are caught. It seems that they are, and that the references in s 21(8) to 'an agreement' and 'a controlled investment' should not be regarded as relating to a *particular* agreement or investment. This interpretation is supported by the references to 'particular investment' in the exemption for generic promotions (FPO, art 17) and in the definition of 'advising on investments' (Regulated Activities Order, art 51).

4.29   For an agreement to fall within limb (a) of the definition in FSMA, s 21(8), it does not matter whether the recipient of the communication is to enter the agreement by acceptance of an offer or by making an offer which is accepted by the other party (who need not be the communicator). Making or performing the agreement must constitute a 'controlled activity', but it does not matter whether the controlled activity is conducted by the recipient (for example, by purchasing a share) or the other party

---

[10] *Oakes v Turquand and Harding* (1867) LR 2 HL 325 at p 342 per Lord Chelmsford.

(for example, by managing the recipient's assets). But a communication that induces the recipient not to take action (for example, a defence document in a takeover bid) is not a financial promotion. A communication falls within limb (b) if it promotes the exercise of certain rights conferred by an investment. Examples include a notice inducing the recipient to exercise a warrant or option. But inducing the exercise of voting rights is not restricted.

The Treasury has the power to specify what is a controlled activity and a controlled investment in secondary legislation, and to confer certain certification functions on the FSA, just as they can specify what is a regulated activity for the purposes of the general prohibition (see Chapter 3). In the FPO, the controlled activities track the regulated activities almost exactly. The principal difference is that the exclusions applicable to regulated activities do not apply to the controlled activities. For example, an overseas broker whose dealing services would not contravene the general prohibition because it can benefit from the overseas persons exclusions could still contravene the restriction on financial promotion if it promotes those services to UK persons.

6. Approval of financial promotions by authorised persons

The restriction on financial promotion does not apply to a communication if 'the content of the communication is approved for the purposes of this section by an authorised person' (FSMA, s 21(2)(b)). The words 'for the purposes of this section' make it clear that the approval must be specifically for the purposes of enabling the financial promotion to be communicated by unauthorised persons free of the restriction on financial promotion. For example, if a solicitor who is an authorised person approves an advertisement for legality generally, that would not suffice unless the solicitor does so specifically for the purposes of s 21 as well. Further, approval for the purposes of communication by the authorised person itself, rather than by unauthorised persons, would not suffice. An unauthorised person would therefore be well advised to obtain specific confirmation of the purposes of an approval before relying on it. The requirement is for the 'content of the communication' to be approved. Where an invitation or inducement forms part of a larger communication, does this mean that the entire communication needs to be approved or just the part constituting an invitation or inducement (for example, an advertisement in a newspaper or parts of a website)? Although it is not completely clear, it seems that 'communication' in s 21(2)(b) means the invitation or inducement communicated (compare s 21(13)).

An authorised person must comply with FSA rules when approving financial promotions for communication by others (COBS 4.10). The steps to be taken by an authorised person in approving a financial promotion (in particular, as to the disclosures to be included in an approved communication and ensuring that it is not misleading) are broadly similar to those required if the communication was made by the authorised person, and require the authorised person to take responsibility for the accuracy of the financial promotion. An unauthorised person who communicates a financial promotion does not contravene the restriction on financial promotion merely because the authorised approver contravenes the rules (there is an exception regarding unregulated collective investment schemes in s 240(2)). But the authorised person may face an action for damages (s 150) and FSA enforcement action.

4.33   The application of the approval process to all forms of financial promotion could lead to some areas of major difference when compared to existing regimes, as follows:

Oral financial promotions
In theory, oral financial promotions by unauthorised persons do not contravene the restriction on financial promotion if the content of the communication is approved, but given the difficulty in controlling the content of real-time oral communications, this may not always be practicable. In recognition of this, the FSA has prohibited approvals of financial promotions to be made in the course of a personal visit, telephone conversation or other interactive dialogue (COBS 4.10.4R).

Deposits and insurance
Financial promotions relating to deposits and non-qualifying insurance contracts (typically those without an investment element) may be approved, although they also benefit from wide exemptions in the Financial Promotions Order.

Unregulated collective investment schemes
Investment advertisements relating to unregulated collective investment schemes may generally be issued by authorised persons only.[11] Section 240 includes a mechanism whereby an authorised person may approve such financial promotions if it would be permitted to communicate the financial promotion itself under s 238. Importantly, contravention of this condition leads to the approval being invalid and to the unauthorised person contravening the restriction in s 21.

F. TERRITORIAL SCOPE

4.34   Under the FSMA, the restriction on financial promotion has an unlimited territorial scope, subject to a restriction in s 21(3) for promotions originating outside the United Kingdom. The Treasury has proposed cutting back the territorial scope in the FPO.

4.35   Financial promotions *within the United Kingdom*, that is, that originate within the United Kingdom and are communicated to persons in the United Kingdom, are within the territorial scope of the restriction. The Financial Promotions Order provides no exemptions for *outward financial promotions*. This is despite concerns about dual regulation of financial promotions by UK persons into other jurisdictions which impose their own requirements on incoming promotional material. The Treasury's view was that these concerns were outweighed by the need for the FSA to be able to take action against a UK promoter in support of an overseas regulator which was facing inappropriate promotions. The restriction on *inward financial promotions* applies only if a communication which originates outside the UK is 'capable of having an effect in the United Kingdom' (s 21(3)). This phrase seems to be open to a wide interpretation and to include any invitation or inducement which is capable of resulting in a UK person engaging in investment activity. The intention of the communicator to promote to UK persons seems to be irrelevant. However, the Financial Promotions Order contains an exemption for a

---

[11]   See the exemptions order made under s 238(6), SI 2001/1060.

financial promotion communicated from a place outside the UK and not *directed at* persons in the UK. It includes a number of (non-exhaustive) tests for interpreting what is 'directed at' and a safe harbour if all tests are satisfied. The exemption does not apply to financial promotions relating to deposits or general insurance contracts.

A particular feature of the territorial scope of the restriction on financial promotion is   4.36
the Electronic Commerce Directive (2000/31/EC). The Directive adopts, as a starting point, home State (or State of origin) control of electronic commerce, so that a European Economic Area (EEA) State from whose jurisdiction an electronic communication is sent regulates the communication's content and use and obliges disclosure of the country of origin. This recognises the difficulty of regulating electronic services being offered from overseas and broadly follows the recommendation of an IOSCO report.[12] The Treasury has implemented this home State approach through art 20B of the FPO. The government has agreed that 'the UK must be prepared to relinquish regulation of inward promotions in favour of a move to home-state regulation when the latter is provided for in the future by EC legislation or other multilateral agreements'.[13]

G. INTRODUCTION TO THE FINANCIAL PROMOTION ORDER

The Treasury has a wide power, under FSMA, s 21(5), to make exemptions from the   4.37
restriction on financial promotion in secondary legislation (subject to an affirmative resolution procedure). The power has been exercised several times, including as part of a review of the FSMA two years after N2, and the current version of the FPO was remade in 2005. The following paragraphs discuss the main features of the FPO, other than in relation to territorial scope, which is discussed above. Table 4.1 at the end of this chapter contains a tabular summary of the exemptions under the FPO, and their application to different types of communications.

1. Types of communications

The FPO draws a distinction between *real-time communications* and *non-real-time*   4.38
communications and between *solicited* and *unsolicited real-time communications*. These distinctions are important and many of the exemptions apply differently to different types of communication. But no distinction is drawn between solicited and unsolicited non-real-time communications. The terminology does not lend itself to instant under-standing—as a rule of thumb, the distinction between real-time and non-real-time com-munications broadly replicates that between advertisements and telephone calls, but in a technology-neutral way, and the distinction between solicited and unsolicited real-time communications broadly replicates that between solicited and unsolicited calls.

---

[12] *Securities Activity on the Internet—a Report by the Technical Committee*, International Organisation of Securities Commissions, September 1998.

[13] HM Treasury, *Financial Promotion — Second Consultation Document*, October 1999, part 2, para. 2.14.

2. Application of the exemptions to real-time communications

4.39   The exemptions in the FPO apply in different ways to real-time communications. The principal features are as follows.

Deposits and non-qualifying insurance.
The restriction on financial promotion does not apply to real-time communications which relate to deposits or general insurance contracts.

Solicited real-time communications.
Most solicited real-time communications (for example, solicited calls) are exempt.

Unsolicited real-time communications
Some exemptions apply to unsolicited real-time communications only, some do not distinguish between real-time and non-real-time communications and some do not apply to unsolicited real-time communications. However, concerns about cold-calling mean that unsolicited real-time communications have more restricted exemptions than other communications.

3. Exemptions for deposits and general insurance contracts

4.40   In addition to exempting all real-time communications relating to deposits or general insurance contracts, non-real-time communications relating to those investments are exempt provided that they contain certain disclosures relating to the deposit-taker or insurance company concerned.

4. Exemptions for other investments

4.41   There are extensive but elaborate exemptions in the FPO for financial promotions that relate to investments other than deposits and general insurance contracts.

H. SANCTIONS

4.42   The sanctions for breach of the restriction on financial promotion are potentially severe, namely, criminal liability, unenforceability of agreements, compensation, and action by the FSA or the Secretary of State[14] to obtain an injunction and restitution.

1. Criminal sanctions

4.43   Contravention of the restriction on financial promotion is an offence punishable by up to two years' imprisonment and an unlimited fine (FSMA, s 25). There are two defences for the accused to prove. The first is that the accused believed on reasonable grounds that the content of the communication was prepared or approved by an authorised person.

---

[14] Originally at the Department of Trade and Industry (DTI), now Business, Innovation and Skills (BIS).

For example, a newspaper publisher or website operator who undertakes reasonable enquiries to ascertain that an advertiser is an authorised person should be able to rely on this defence. But it should be noted that there is no equivalent of the 'prepared' limb of this defence in relation to the other sanctions. The second defence is that the accused took all reasonable precautions and exercised all due diligence to avoid committing the offence, which is identical to the defence under the general prohibition (see Chapter 3 for further details).

2. Unenforceability of agreements and compensation

Civil sanctions apply for contravention of the restriction on financial promotion. They are available to a person entering a 'controlled agreement', or exercising rights conferred by a controlled investment, 'as a customer', 'in consequence of an unlawful communication' (s 30(2) and (3)). The controlled agreement, or obligation to which the customer is subject, is unenforceable against the customer and the customer can recover amounts transferred under the agreement or obligation as well as compensation for losses that resulted from having parted with those amounts. A 'controlled agreement' is an agreement, the making or performance of which by either party constitutes a controlled activity (s 30(1)). 'As a customer' is not defined and seems to depend on all the circumstances such as the nature of the relationship and whether one party is using the services of the other rather than merely being a counterparty.   4.44

The words 'in consequence' suggest that the unlawful communication must be a direct cause of the agreement being entered into. But the agreement need not be with the person who communicated the unlawful financial promotion. So it would be possible, subject to the court's discretion discussed below, for there to be no connection between the communicator and the person who is unable to enforce the agreement. It seems that, in such circumstances, both the communicator and the person entering into the agreement with the customer could be required to pay compensation for the customer's losses.   4.45

The court has a discretion under the FSMA to allow an agreement to be enforced or assets transferred under the agreement to be retained if it is satisfied that this is 'just and equitable' (s 30(4)). Issues that the court must have regard to in exercising this discretion are set out in s 30(5), (6) and (7). They are: 4.46

(a) if the other party to the agreement made the unlawful communication, whether he reasonably believed that he was not making such a communication;
(b) if some other person made the unlawful communication, whether the other party to the agreement knew that the agreement was entered into in consequence of an unlawful communication.

These conditions are very similar to those applicable in relation to the general prohibition (see Chapter 3 for further details).   4.47

3. Further sanctions against contraventions

The FSA and the Secretary of State are entitled to seek injunctions to restrain antici-   4.48
pated contravention of the restriction on financial promotion and orders to disgorge

profits and require restitution of losses arising from such contravention (ss 380 and 382).[15]

I. FINANCIAL PROMOTION BY AUTHORISED PERSONS

4.49 The restriction on financial promotion in FSMA, s 21, does not apply to authorised persons. In communicating a financial promotion, an authorised person must comply with the following:

(a) Rules on financial promotions made by the FSA. Broadly, authorised persons may communicate financial promotions subject to certain due diligence and disclosure requirements. The rules adopt many of the concepts used in the FSMA, so that the analysis of those concepts in this chapter applies.

(b) Restrictions on communicating and approving financial promotions relating to unregulated collective investment schemes in Part 17 of the FSMA, and exemptions from those restrictions in any Treasury regulations made under s 238(6) and in the FSA's rules.

(c) The FSA's Principles for Businesses (PRIN) and other high-level standards, including Principle 7 (Communications with customers: A firm must pay due regard to the information needs of its clients, and communicate information to them in a way which is clear, fair, and not misleading).

(d) The other UK legislation relevant to financial promotions referred to earlier in this chapter. As the FSA has increasingly chosen (or been required by s 145(3)–(3B) and directives imposing home State supervision) to carve requirements out of its own rules, it can be expected to make significantly greater use of its non-FSMA enforcement powers in future.

---

[15] However, the FSA can usually rely on contravention of the general prohibition in s 19 instead.

Table 4.1

Table 4.1 Categories of exemption under the FPO, and their availability for non-real-time and real-time communications.

Exemption	Non-real time communications	Solicited real-time communications	Unsolicited real-time communications
Exemptions in relation to deposits and insurance			
Deposits	art 22*	art 23	art 23
Non-qualifying insurance (limited investment element)	arts 24*, 25	art 26	art 26
Exemptions for specific types of communication			
Follow-up communications	art 14	art 14	—
Introductions to authorised persons	art 15*	arts 15*, 28B*	arts 15*, 28B*
Generic promotions	art 17	art 17	art 17
Causing communication by an authorised person	art 17A	art 17A	art 17A
Incoming electronic commerce	art 20B*	art 20B (in theory)	art 20B (in theory)
One-off	art 28*	art 28*	art 28A*
Statutory (non-FSMA), redress	arts 29 (not home finance), 56	arts 29, 56	arts 29, 56
Relating to markets	arts 37, 41, 67, 68, 69	arts 37, 41, 67, 68, 69	—
Corporate reporting	art 59	—	—
Relating to sale of a body corporate	art 62	art 62	art 62
Relating to takeovers of relevant unlisted companies	arts 64*, 65, 66	arts 64*, 65	arts 64*, 65
Listing particulars, prospectuses for unlisted securities	arts 70, 71	—	—
Exemptions for communications by specific communicators			
By customers	art 13	art 13	art 13
By exempt persons	art 16(1)	art 16(1)	art 16(2)* appointed representatives only
By mere conduits, electronic commerce providers	arts 18, 18A	arts 18, 18A	arts 18, 18A
By journalists	art 20*	—	—
By company directors (broadcast)	art 20A (but must be spoken)	art 20A	art 20A
By overseas communicators, nationals of other EEA states	arts 31, 36	arts 30, 36	arts 32*, 33*
By governments, central banks	art 34	art 34	—

Table 4.1

Table 4.1 *Continued*

Exemption	Non-real time communications	Solicited real-time communications	Unsolicited real-time communications
By industrial and provident societies	art 35	art 35	—
By joint enterprise participants, group companies	arts 39, 45	arts 39, 45	arts 39, 45
By trustees, settlors and beneficiaries	arts 53, 54	arts 53, 54	arts 53, 54
By members of professions	arts 55, 55A*	art 55	art 55
By managers of residential premises	art 58	art 58	—
By operators of an employee share scheme	art 60	art 60	art 60
By suppliers of other goods and services	art 61	art 61	—
By employers offering pension products	art 72*	art 72	art 72
By advice centre staff	art 73*	art 73*	art 73*
Further exemptions for communications to specific recipients			
To overseas recipients	art 12*	art 12*	art 12* (from outside the UK)
To investment professionals, high net worth and sophisticated investors	arts 19*, 48*, 49*, 50*, 50A*, 51	arts 19*, 48*, 49*, 50*, 50A*, 51	arts 19*, 48*, 49*, 50*, 50A*, 51
To persons placing promotional material, or in the business of dissemination	arts 38, 47	arts 38, 47	arts 38, 47
To members and creditors of a corporate body or common interest group, participants in a recognised collective investment scheme	arts 40, 42, 43, 44, 52*	arts 40, 42, 43, 44, 52*	—
To bodies corporate in relation to qualifying credit	art 46	art 46	art 46

*subject to restrictions, including required disclosures.

5

AUTHORISATION AND EXEMPTION

David Simpson

A. INTRODUCTION

Part 3 of the Financial Services and Markets Act 2000 (FSMA) sets out who has autho- 5.01
risation to carry on the regulated activities within its scope and how that authorisation
ends, how firms from other European Economic Area (EEA) States can obtain authorisation by exercising rights under European law and how UK firms can exercise rights
in other EEA States. It gives the Treasury power to exempt persons, by order, from the
general prohibition. It also provides an exemption for appointed representations of
authorised persons.

B. AUTHORISATION

1. What is authorisation?

The FSMA creates a single authorisation regime for the regulated activities within its 5.02
scope. This contrasts with the predecessor legislation, under which persons wishing to
carry on different kinds of financial services activities needed to be authorised under
more than one statute; for example, the Banking Act 1987 for deposit-taking, and the
Financial Services Act 1986 for investment business.

Authorisation under the FSMA brings a person inside the criminal perimeter in the 5.03
sense that an authorised person cannot commit the criminal offences in Part 2, which are
contravention of the general prohibition (ss 19 and 23), contravention of the restrictions

on financial promotions (ss 21 and 25) and falsely claiming to be authorised or exempt (s 24). Instead, the ability of an authorised person to carry on regulated activities is controlled through the permission regime (Chapter 6) and by the Financial Services Authority's (FSA's) rules.

5.04 Being authorised confers a number of rights, in addition to the ability to carry on regulated activities in the United Kingdom lawfully, including the ability to approve financial promotions under s 21 and the ability to appoint appointed representatives under s 39. But authorisation brings with it a host of obligations. In particular, authorised persons have to comply with the FSA's rules, pay fees to the FSA and, in most cases, contribute to the compensation scheme.

2. Who is authorised?

5.05 Section 31 sets out the following four routes to authorisation:

(a) *Part 4 permission*
A person with a 'Part 4 permission' is an authorised person. This covers:

(1) A person who applies for and is given permission by the FSA under Part 4 to carry on one or more regulated activities (s 31(1)(a)).
(2) A person who received a Part 4 permission because his authorisation under predecessor legislation was grandfathered under transitional provisions made by the Treasury under ss 426 and 427.

(b) *EEA firms*
A person established in another EEA State who exercises passport rights to carry on activities in the United Kingdom under a Single Market Directive is an authorised person (s 31(1)(b) and Sch 3). Such a person is referred to in the Act as an 'EEA firm' (the definition in Sch 3, para 5) and the rights exercised are commonly called a 'passport'. See further under 'Passport Rights under the Single Market Directives' later in this chapter.

(c) *Treaty firms*
5.06 A person established in another EEA State who exercises rights under the EC Treaty is authorised (s 31(1)(c) and Sch 4). These are rights anterior and in addition to those governed by the Single Market Directives. A person who seeks to exercise such rights is referred to in the Act as a 'Treaty Firm' (the definition in Sch 4, para 1). See further Section D. Treaty Rights later in this chapter.

(d) *Others*
5.07 Persons may be otherwise authorised under FSMA (s 31(1)(d)). This covers:

(1) The Society of Lloyds, which is an authorised person by virtue of s 315(3).
(2) UCITS qualifiers under Schedule 5, that is, the operator, trustee and depositary of a collective investment scheme constituted in another EEA state, where the scheme has been 'recognised' pursuant to section 264 of the FSMA.
(3) Investment Companies with Variable Capital (ICVCs). An open-ended investment company, authorised under the OEIC Regulations 2001 made under s 262, is an

authorised person with permission to operate the scheme and carry on other connected activities, which would include marketing (Sch 5, paras 1(3) and 2(2)). Such firms are called 'ICVCs' or 'investment companies with variable capital' in the FSA Handbook. Authorisation of an ICVC as an authorised person, in addition to its 'product' authorisation under Part 17, is necessary as it is a separate legal entity carrying on regulated activities in its own right, unlike a unit trust. The automatic authorisation of an ICVC does not extend to its authorised corporate director, which must seek authorisation by an alternative route.

3. Can a person be authorised by more than one route?

It is possible for a person authorised through one of these routes to be authorised to carry on regulated activities by other routes. A person is either an authorised person or it is not, so it would not be correct to regard a person as having more than one authorisation. But authorisation through more than one route may result in a person having more than one permission to carry on regulated activities in the United Kingdom (see Chapter 6). Since 2000, a doctrine has developed that a person only ever has one permission—but that permission may have several aspects or elements. 5.08

4. Authorisation of partnerships and unincorporated associations

FSMA 2000, s 32, makes particular provision for partnerships and unincorporated associations. Such a firm may be authorised under the Act, in which case it is authorised to carry on regulated activities in the name of the firm (s 32(1)(a)). This clarifies the position of a firm without separate legal personality; for example, an English partnership. 5.09

Section 32(1)(b) provides that the authorisation of the firm is not interrupted by changes in its membership. If a firm is dissolved through a change of partners in a partnership or a change of membership in an unincorporated association, its authorisation continues to have effect in relation to any individual or firm which succeeds to the whole, or substantially the whole, of the business of the dissolved firm (s 32(2) and (3)). 5.10

Section 32 does not apply to a partnership constituted under the law of any place outside the United Kingdom which is a body corporate. What is a 'body corporate' will be determined under the general law, as the inclusive definition in s 417(1) is of little assistance in interpretation. 5.11

C. PASSPORT RIGHTS

FSMA Sch 3 gives effect in UK law to European single markets in banking, investment services and insurance. The Directives concerned (referred to in the Act as the Single Market Directives) are: 5.12

(a) the Banking Consolidation Directive (2006/48/EC) (BCD);
(b) the First, Second and Third non-life insurance directives (73/239/EC, 88/357/EC, and 92/49/EC) and the Life assurance consolidation directive (2002/83/EC);
(c) the Reinsurance Directive (2005/68/EC) (RID);
(d) the Insurance Mediation Directive (2002/92/EC) (IMD);

(e) the UCITS Directive (85/611/EC); and

(f) the Markets in Financial Instruments Directive (2004/39/EC) (MiFID).

1. What is a passport?

5.13 Under the Single Market Directives, certain firms (referred to as 'EEA firms') which are established and authorised under the laws of one EEA State have the right to carry on certain activities in other EEA States without the need to obtain a further authorisation in those other EEA States. These Directive rights are referred to in the Act as 'EEA Rights' (Sch 3, para 7) and commonly known as a 'passport'. The State where a passporting firm is established is commonly known as its 'home state'.

2. Which firms are entitled to a passport?

5.14 The following types of EEA firm are entitled to a passport:

(a) investment firms, as defined in MiFID, which are authorised by their home state regulators;

(b) credit institutions, as defined in the BCD, which are authorised by their home state regulators;

(c) financial institutions, as defined in the BCD, that is, unauthorised subsidiaries of credit institutions authorised under the BCD;

(d) life or non-life insurers, as defined in the various insurance directives, which are authorised under those directives by their home state regulators;

(e) reinsurers, as defined in the Reinsurance Directive, which are authorised under that directives by their home state regulators;

(f) insurance and reinsurance intermediaries, as defined in the IMD, which are authorised under that directive by their home state regulators; and

(g) management companies, as defined in the UCITS Directive, which are authorised under that directive by their home state regulators.

5.15 If a firm is not incorporated in an EEA State (or, if an unincorporated association, does not have its head office in the EEA), it will not be entitled to a passport under the Single Market Directives, even if it is authorised in an EEA State. For example, a branch of a US corporation authorised in the United Kingdom does not have a passport. In addition, a firm may be unable to have a passport because it does not carry on activities in a way specified under the Directive, or because it falls within an exemption under the Directive.

3. Exercise of passport rights by incoming EEA firms

5.16 The route to authorisation will depend upon which activities are performed by the EEA firm and whether it wishes to exercise its passport rights by establishing a branch in the UK or by providing cross-border services into the UK.

5.17 An EEA pure reinsurer wishing either to establish a branch or to provide cross-border services qualifies for authorisation automatically, provided that its home state has fully implemented the Reinsurance Directive, failing which it must satisfy the FSA that at least the prudential requirements of that directive have been implemented in its home state.

An EEA firm wishing to establish a branch in the UK under the IMD need merely 5.18
inform its home state regulator of its intention so to do and await that regulator's confirmation that it has notified the FSA of the firm's intention, one month after which it is
entitled to use its passport (paragraph 13(1A) of Part 2 of Sch 3 of the FSMA).

An EEA firm wishing to establish a branch in the UK under any other Single Market 5.19
Directive must first obtain the consent of its home state regulator and that regulator
must notify the FSA of its consent (and the scope thereof). Authorisation is then automatic after a specified period of time, or may happen sooner if the firm receives notification within that time period (paragraph 13(1) of Part 2 of Sch 3 to the FSMA).

An EEA firm wishing to provide cross-border services into the UK (that is, to do business 5.20
in the UK without establishing a branch there) must first notify its home state regulator
and may then have to wait for one or more things to happen (depending upon which
type of EEA firm it is), namely (a) for its home state regulator to send a 'regulator's
notice' to the FSA; (b) for that regulator to inform it that such notice had been sent; and
(c) for one month to pass after it was so informed (paragraph 14 of Part 2 of Sch 3 to the
FSMA).

An investment firm wishing to use a tied agent in the UK is treated as if it were 5.21
establishing a branch in the UK and must comply with the establishment conditions at
paragraph 13(1) of Part 2 of Sch 3 to the FSMA.

4. What activities are covered by the passport?

An EEA firm that qualifies for authorisation under one of the above routes has permis- 5.22
sion to carry on the activities identified in the various notifications involved in the passporting process. This permission will reflect any requirements or limitations imposed on
the firm by its home state regulator. The permission may include activities that are not
regulated activities in the UK, because not all of the activities within the scope of the
Single Market Directives are regulated activities in the UK.

The only qualification to this relates to EEA firms establishing a branch in the UK 5.23
with a view to marketing collective investments schemes in the UK. There the FSA has
the power to restrict the firm from doing this if the way in which it intends to market
the scheme does not comply with UK law (paragraph 15A of Part 2 of Sch 3 to the
FSMA). The FSA must inform the firm of the rules that it must comply with.

Where an incoming EEA firm wishes to carry on a regulated activity in the UK for 5.24
which it has no EEA Right (either because the activity falls outside the scope of the
Single Market Directives, or because the activity is within the scope of the directive but
not covered by the firm's home state authorisation) the firm may apply to the FSA for a
'top-up' permission. This involves making the same application process as a UK firm
would make for a similar permission.

5. Exercise of passport rights by outgoing UK firms

A firm whose head office is in the UK and which is entitled to carry on an activity in 5.25
another EEA State by virtue of the Single Market Directives is referred to in the
FSMA as a 'UK firm'. This term includes financial institutions, as defined in the BCD.
A UK firm wishing to exercise its EEA Right to establish a branch or provide cross-
border services into another EEA State must first satisfy conditions set out in Part 3 of

Schedule 3 to the FSMA. Failure to do so will generally result in disciplinary action by the FSA under Part 14 of the FSMA, although a financial institution will also commit an offence by doing so (paragraph 21 of Part 3 of Sch 3).

5.26   The procedures set out in the FSMA for UK firm to exercise their EEA Rights mirror those in respect of incoming EEA firms.

5.27   UK pure reinsurers have automatic passport rights on the basis of their authorisation by the FSA under the Reinsurance Directive (paragraph 19(5ZA) of Sch 3 to the FSMA).

5.28   A UK firm wishing to establish a branch in another EEA State under the IMD must inform the FSA of its intention to establish such branch and await the FSA's confirmation that it has notified the host state regulator of the firm's intention, one month after which it is entitled use its passport (paragraph 19(5)(a) of Sch 3 to the FSMA).

5.29   A UK firm wishing to establish a branch in another EEA State under any other Single Market Directive must first obtain the consent of the FSA and the FSA must notify the host state regulator of its consent. Authorisation is then automatic after two months starting from the date of the FSA's consent, or may happen sooner if the firm (of the FSA) receives certain notification from the host state regulator (paragraph 19(5)(b) of Sch 3 to the FSMA).

5.30   A UK firm wishing to provide cross-border services into another EEA State must first notify the FSA of its intention, identifying the cross-border services that it wishes to provide and supplying specified other information (paragraph 20(1) of Sch 3 to the FSMA).

(a) The FSA must then, within one month, send to the host state regulator a copy of the UK firm's notice of intention (for firms passporting under MiFID, the BCD, or the UCITS Directive, or the IMD if the host state has requested such notification) or its own consent notice (for firms passporting under the Insurance Directives) (paragraphs 20(3), (3A) and (3B) of Sch 3 to the FSMA respectively).

(b) UK firms passporting under the Insurance Directives, MiFID or the IMD (where notification is requested) cannot start providing cross-border services until the FSA confirms that it has given the relevant notice to the host state regulator (paragraph 20(4B) of Sch 3 to the FSMA), and firms passporting under the IMD must wait a further month after that (paragraph 20(3B)(c) of Sch 3 to the FSMA).

5.31   The FSA may withhold consent to a UK firm establishing a branch in another EEA State if (in the case of firms passporting under the BCD, MiFID, UCITS and Insurance Directive) it doubts the adequacy of the firm's resources and administrative structure (paragraph 19(7B) of Sch 3 to the FSMA), or (additionally in respect of firms passporting under the Insurance Directives) it questions the reputation, qualifications or experience of the directors or managers of the UK firm or its proposed authorised agent (paragraph 19(7B) of Sch 3 to the FSMA).

5.32   The EEA Passport Rights Regulations (SI 2001/2511) contain further detailed provisions relating to the contents of the various notifications required in the passporting process along with procedures to be followed in the event of the cancellation or amendment of an incoming EEA firm or outgoing UK firm's passport.

5.33   Determining whether a branch is established or services are provided cross-border may be difficult, particularly in the case of cross-border services. EEA regulators have taken different views on this question. Some have adopted a 'solicitation test', under which a firm is regarded as providing services to a resident of that State if a particular transaction, or the relationship under which the transaction is conducted, was solicited by the firm. The United Kingdom has generally adopted a less expansive view of when services should be regarded as provided cross-border.

The European Commission has published interpretative communications providing   5.34
its own interpretation of the rules on freedom to provide services in the banking sector (97/C209/04) and insurance sector (C(99)5046 and 2000/C43/03). It has not yet published any equivalent communication on the MiFID, the IMD, the RID, or the UCITS Directive.

In the banking sector, the Commission has favoured a 'characteristic performance' test   5.35
which broadly treats a service as provided in the place with which the service is most closely connected. The FSA takes the view that a similar test should be applied to credit institutions and MiFID investment firms.

In the insurance sector the determinative factor is the location of the risk or commit-   5.36
ment. Thus the provision of insurance services via the internet does amount to the provision of insurance services into the EEA State where the risk is situated.

D. TREATY RIGHTS

Schedule 4 to the FSMA gives effect in UK law to the rights of establishment and to   5.37
provide services cross-border under arts 43 and 55 of the EC Treaty which go beyond the passport rights covered by FSMA, Sch 3. These 'Treaty rights' permit a person, established and authorised under the law of one EEA State (its 'home State'), to carry on an activity in other EEA States ('host States') so long as the law of its home State provides equivalent protection to that of the host State or meets EU harmonised minimum requirements applicable in that area of law. These rights are given specific effect for many financial services firms through the Single Market Directives. However, as explained above, the Directives do not cover the full range of financial services or financial service providers. Schedule 4 provides a mechanism for EEA persons to exercise Treaty rights in the UK in the absence of passport rights. The Act contains no equivalent mechanism for a UK firm to exercise Treaty rights in another EEA State; this is a matter for the local law in that State.

Schedule 4 does not define the extent of Treaty rights, which are the subject of develop-   5.38
ing case law in the EU, but sets the conditions that must be met for authorisation by this route. The FSA must receive confirmation from the Treaty firm's home State regulator that it has authorisation in the home State for the regulated activities that it seeks to carry on in the United Kingdom. The laws of the home State must provide equivalent protection—a certificate from the Treasury to this effect is conclusive evidence of that fact. Alternatively, those laws must satisfy EU harmonised minimum requirements applicable in that area of law. If the regulated activities that the firm is seeking to carry on are covered by the firm's passport rights under Sch 3, then those rights must be exercised instead of Treaty rights. A Treaty firm is also required to give notice of its intention to exercise its Treaty rights and to provide such information as the FSA may require. Failure to give proper notice may be a criminal offence. On qualifying for authorisation, a Treaty firm has permission to carry on each regulated activity which it sought to carry on under Sch 4.

E. ENDING OF AUTHORISATION

5.39   The ending of a person's authorisation results in the provisions of the FSMA, and the FSA's rules, applicable to authorised persons ceasing to apply to that person, with certain exceptions. For example, some of the FSA's information-gathering and investigation powers under Part 11 continue to apply even after a person's authorisation has ended. The compensation scheme (Part 15) and the ombudsman scheme (Part 16) will continue to apply with respect to activities carried on while authorised. The method of ending authorisation depends on the route through which authorisation was obtained. If a person is authorised under more than one of the routes under s 31 (for example, if it is an EEA firm authorised under Sch 3 and has a top-up permission under Part 4), then the person will cease to be an authorised person only when authorisation under each of those routes ends (ss 34(3), 35(3) and 36(2)).

F. EXEMPTION ORDERS

5.40   Section 38 of the FSMA gives the Treasury the power to make orders exempting specific persons or classes of person from the general prohibition in s 19 and, therefore, from the need to be authorised. Section 38(2) provides that a person with a Part 4 permission may not benefit from such an exemption, and so cannot have the status of both an authorised person and an exempt person.

5.41   The Treasury has exercised this power to exempt persons in four broad categories specified in the Exemption Order (SI 2001/1201). The first category of persons are exempt from the general prohibition in so far as they are carrying out any regulated activity apart from effecting or carrying out contracts of insurance; persons in this category are generally supranational bodies of which the UK or another EEA State is a member. The second category of persons is exempt in respect of accepting deposits; these persons include municipal banks, local authorities, charities, and industrial and provident societies. The third category is exempt in respect of investment business; persons in this category are generally bodies subject to control or oversight by the government. The fourth category are exempt in respect of particular activities specific to each body; such persons include enterprise schemes, trade unions and the electricity and gas industries.

G. EXEMPTION OF APPOINTED REPRESENTATIVES

5.42   Section 39 of the FSMA creates a particularly significant exemption from the general prohibition. This is for appointed representatives of authorised persons. The exemption applies only if:

(a) the appointed representative is a party to a contract with an authorised person referred to as the principal, which permits the appointed representative to carry on regulated activities; and

(b) the principal has accepted responsibility in writing for the conduct of those regulated activities.

The contents of the appointed representative's contract with its principal must comply with prescribed requirements found in the Appointed Representatives Regulations (SI 2001/1217). These regulations also limited the activities in respect of which an appointed representative is exempt to specified administrative and advisory functions relating to investments, home finance transactions and insurance. 5.43

If an appointed representative is also a 'tied agent' within the meaning of the MiFID then it is not exempt unless and until it is recorded in the register maintained by either the FSA or, where relevant, another EEA regulator (s 39 (1A)). 5.44

Any person may become an appointed representative, including a body corporate, a partnership, and an individual in business on his own account. It is not, however, possible for an authorised person to be an appointed representative. The FSMA does not prevent an appointed representative from acting for more than one principal, although the FSA prohibits this in respect of certain activities. 5.45

In general the FSA's rules apply to the principal only, not to the appointed representative. But any business conducted by an appointed representative for which the principal has accepted responsibility will be treated as having been done by the principal (s 39(3) and (4)). So the principal must have permission for any such business that is a regulated activity. Further, the authorised principal may be liable to FSA enforcement action or a claim for damages in respect of any action or omission of the appointed representative in carrying on the regulated activities which would amount to a contravention of the FSA's rules if carried on by the principal. So the principal will have an interest in ensuring compliance by the appointed representative with those rules. In addition, certain of the FSA's powers, including information-gathering and investigation powers under Part 11, apply directly in relation to an appointed representative. There is, however, a limitation on the responsibility of the principal in respect of criminal offences, when the knowledge and intentions of the appointed representatives are not attributed to the principal in most circumstances (s 39(6)). 5.46

6

PERMISSION TO CARRY ON REGULATED ACTIVITIES

David Simpson

A. INTRODUCTION

Having dealt with the requirement for authorisation in Chapter 5, the Financial Services   6.01
and Markets Act 2000 (FSMA) moves on, in Part 4, to deal with the closely related
concept of permission.

B. WHAT IS PERMISSION?

Under the FSMA, the two concepts of authorisation and permission are designed to   6.02
work together to achieve a single integrated regime. The key to understanding the two is
in ss 19 and 20. It is a breach of the general prohibition, and thus a criminal offence, for
a person to carry on a regulated activity in the United Kingdom without being an authorised person. (The separate category of exempt person is not relevant to permission.)
That results from s 19, which is dealt with in Chapter 3. Under s 20, an authorised
person who carries on a regulated activity in the United Kingdom without permission is
taken to have contravened a requirement imposed by the Financial Services Authority
(FSA) under the Act. This means that the permission is not in itself relevant for criminal
prosecution purposes. And the only people who have permission are authorised persons.
While acting outside a permission is deemed to be a contravention of a requirement
imposed on the person by the FSA, that deemed contravention does not adversely affect

related transactions, or give rise to an action for breach of statutory duty, though the Treasury has the power, under s 20(3), to make a contravention of s 20 actionable by persons who suffer loss as a result, rather like breach of the FSA's rules (s 150).

6.03 An authorised person will in the ordinary way have only one permission under Part 4 to carry on regulated activities under the Act. Colloquially, it may be convenient for a firm to be described as having a permission to carry on deposit taking, and another to carry on fund management business, etc. But, technically, each firm will have its own permission, and will have one only. The only exception to this is what might be described as 'top-up' permission. If an incoming firm, which is entitled to carry on certain regulated activities pursuant to its 'passport', or under the Treaty or the UCITS Directive, wishes to be able to carry on other non-passportable regulated activities in the United Kingdom, it will need to apply to the FSA for that purpose. It will then have its authorisation and permission under Part 3, and its permission under Part 4 to carry on the additional activities. That permission under Part 4 will in turn lead to a separate basis for the person's authorisation under s 31(1)(a), though the Act does not contemplate multiple authorisations as such.

6.04 To underline this conceptual approach, s 40(2) prevents an authorised person from applying for permission if he already has extant permission under Part 4. Instead, an application to vary the permission is the way ahead. Further, an 'EEA firm' (a firm of the European Economic Area), as defined in para 5 of Sch 3 to the Act, may not apply for permission under Part 4 to carry on any regulated activity which it is or would be entitled to carry on in exercise of an EEA right (as defined in para 7 of Sch 3). This applies whether the EEA firm is seeking to operate through a branch in, or by providing cross-border services into, the United Kingdom. Interestingly, there is no equivalent prohibition for so-called Treaty firms, that is, those relying on the Treaty alone and not on any of the relevant single market directives.

6.05 For most firms, the means of becoming authorised for the purposes of the Act is, ignoring European and transitional aspects, the obtaining of a Part 4 permission to carry on one or more regulated activities: see s 31(1). The application to the FSA will therefore technically be an application for permission, and the granting of permission will lead to the status of authorised person. An application for permission, under s 40, may be made by an individual, a body corporate, a partnership or an unincorporated association.

6.06 The FSA may, under s 42(2), give permission for the applicant to carry on the regulated activity or activities concerned. If the FSA gives permission, it must, under s 42(6), specify the permitted regulated activity or activities, described in such manner as the FSA considers appropriate. Generally, the FSA's description of a firm's permission will refer to regulated activities and specified investments as defined in the Regulated Activities Order. However, the FSA sub-divides certain of those activities and investments in order to concentrate regulatory attention on types of business deemed high-risk—for example, advising on pension transfers and opt-outs and investment business involving spread bets.

6.07 Under s 347, the FSA must maintain a publicly accessible record of every authorised person, and the record must include information about the services which each authorised person holds himself out as able to provide: so, though the language of permission is not used in Part 23, the record itself tracks the permission granted to UK authorised persons.

6.08 The procedure on an application for permission is set out in ss 51 to 53. An application must be determined before the end of six months from receipt of the completed application. If an application is incomplete, the deadline is 12 months, though incomplete applications can nevertheless be determined without requiring them to be perfected. If an application is to be refused, a warning notice (as to which see Chapter 28) has to be served. This gives an unsuccessful applicant the FSA's reasons and an opportunity to make representations to the FSA though not, in this case, access to evidence relied on by the FSA in reaching its decision. The disappointed applicant will also have the opportunity to have the matter referred to the Financial Services and Markets Tribunal if a subsequent decision notice is served, refusing the application.

C. CONDITIONS, LIMITATIONS, AND REQUIREMENTS

It is convenient now to deal with three other concepts relevant to the permission regime. The first is the so-called 'threshold conditions' dealt with in s 41 and Sch 6. The second is the limitations which may be included in a permission under s 42(5). And the third is the selection of requirements that may be included in a permission under s 43.

6.09

1. Threshold conditions

The threshold conditions are dealt with in s 41. When giving or varying permission, or imposing any requirement under s 43, the FSA is obliged by s 41(2) to ensure that the person concerned will satisfy and continue to satisfy the threshold conditions in Sch 6. The test is to be applied in relation to all the regulated activities for which that person has or will have permission. The particular conditions will be described later in this chapter.

6.10

2. Limitations

The inclusion of *limitations* is specifically enabled by s 42(7)(a), which enables the FSA to incorporate in the description of regulated activity for which permission is given such limitations as it considers appropriate. An example given in the paragraph itself is a limitation as to the circumstances in which the activity may, or may not, be carried on. In practice the type of limitations may restrict the type or number of clients with whom a firm may deal, the type of specified investments in respect of which a firm may undertake designated investment business, and the type of insurance business that a firm may undertake. The limitation may be incorporated at the outset or when a variation is applied for (s 44(5)). The limitations envisaged will be of permanent effect unless the permission is varied (see below). Under s 52(6) a proposal to incorporate a limitation attracts the warning and decision notice procedure, but, as with an application for permission, on the basis that the FSA does not have to offer access to used and unused material (this is because s 52(6) does not appear in the lists in s 394(a) or (b)).

6.11

3. Requirements

The FSA is also enabled, by s 43, to include in a Part 4 permission such requirements as the FSA considers appropriate. Whilst limitations are related to specific activities or investments, restrictions relate to all, or a number, of the activities that a person

6.12

carries on. Requirements may be positive or negative, that is, requiring the person concerned to take specified action, or not to take action. Requirements may extend to activities which are not in themselves regulated activities. They can also cope with the issues confronting the firm as a member of a group, where appropriate.

6.13   Examples of the way in which restrictions are used in practice include:

(a) defining the scope of a number of regulated activities carried on by a firm in order that a particular differentiated regulatory regime applies; for example, the regime relating to oil market participants;

(b) defining the prudential category into which a firm will fall;

(c) requiring a firm to obtain additional capital within a particular time following the granting of the permission, (or to secure an undertaking from a parent company to supply capital when required);

(d) prohibiting a firm from holding client money or from taking on a particular director or significant member of staff;

(e) imposing requirements in respect of non-regulated activities such as holding or controlling client money, ISA, PEP, or Child Trust Fund management, operating an investment trust savings scheme and managing a broker fund; and

(f) imposing financial requirements such as a requirement that the firm obtain the FSA's approval before paying a dividend.

6.14   It appears from s 43(5) that the requirements may be permanent or of limited duration, though, by s 43(6), the FSA may vary the permission under s 44 or s 45 after the expiry of the period. Accordingly, a prime purpose of the requirements is to act as a temporary expedient to assist an applicant in the early months or years following authorisation, though, as with a limitation, a requirement may be varied, indeed imposed afresh, where a variation of permission is applied for (s 44(1)(e) and (5)).

6.15   For a particular form of requirement, 'an assets requirement', see s 48 and the discussion on it below. Section 52(6) provides for the warning notice and decision notice procedure described above to be used in the case of a proposed requirement.

D. THE THRESHOLD CONDITIONS

6.16   The FSA is obliged to ensure that applicants for permission satisfy the threshold conditions on a continuing basis. The test is to be applied in relation to all the regulated activities concerned.

6.17   If the applicant is an incoming firm applying for top-up permission, or for a variation of its existing top-up permission, then the FSA is obliged only to consider threshold conditions 1, 3, 4, and 5 as relevant to the regulated activities for which the firm will have its top-up permission.

6.18   Under section 185(2) of the FSMA, the FSA will also have regard to the threshold conditions in deciding whether or not to impose conditions on its approval of an acquisition or increase of control over an authorised firm.

6.19   Loosely described as the 'fit and proper' requirements, Sch 6 in fact contains rather more substance, though the fit and proper concept, known as 'suitability', is the most significant of the conditions.

In Sch 6, there were originally five conditions concerning permission under Part 4 (s 40); however, a sixth condition, numbered 2A, was added in 2002 as part of the implementation of a directive on Motor Insurance. There are three more threshold conditions relating to incoming passport holders and foreign insurers which are not dealt with further in this work. The six general threshold conditions are as follows: 6.20

(1) legal status;
(2) location of offices;
(2A) appointment of claims representatives;
(3) close links;
(4) adequate resources; and
(5) suitability.

(1) *Legal status*

The first threshold condition (Sch 6, para 1) deals with required legal status for insurance business, deposit taking and issuing electronic money. To carry on insurance business, an authorised person must be a body corporate, registered friendly society, or a member of Lloyd's. Deposit takers and issuers of electronic money must be bodies corporate or partnerships.   6.21

(2) *Location of offices*

Paragraph 2 of Sch 6, as amended, implements requirements of the Post BCCI Directive, the IMD, and MiFID. The requirements depend upon whether the firm is a body corporate and, if it is a body corporate, whether or not it has a registered office.   6.22

The rules for bodies corporate established under the law of any part of the UK are as follows: If the firm is carrying out investment services and activities and it does not have a registered office, then it must carry on business in the UK. If the firm is carrying on insurance mediation activities, then it must have its registered office, or if it has no registered office, its head office, in the UK. For all other firms, the firm's head office and registered office (if it has one) must be in the UK.   6.23

The rules for persons which are not bodies corporate are as follows: If the person's head office is in the UK then it must carry on business in the UK. If the person is carrying on insurance mediation activities, then he will be treated as having a head office in the UK if his residence is in the UK.   6.24

The difficulty with these rules is that none of the directives from which they derive actually define 'head office'. The FSA has indicated in its own guidance (COND 2.2.3G) that this is not necessarily the firm's place of incorporation or the place where its business is wholly or mainly carried on. The key issue is the location of the firm's central management and control, ie the location of the firm's directors and senior management who make decisions relating to the firm's central direction, and the material management decisions of the firm on a day-to-day basis; and the central administrative functions of the firm, such as central compliance and internal audit.   6.25

(2A) *Claims representatives*

Any person seeking to carry on, or carrying on, motor vehicle liability insurance business is required to have a claims representative in each EEA State other than the UK.   6.26

This applies whether or not the insurer is carrying on insurance business in any of those EEA States; the purpose is to assist driver and passengers in the event of an accident abroad. A claims representative is a person with responsibility for handling and settling claims arising from accidents. FSA rules on the appointment and responsibilities of claims representatives are to be found in ICOBS 8.2.

(3) Close links

6.27 Paragraph 3 of Sch 6 makes a threshold condition for the grant of permission which deals with problems brought to prominence in the BCCI case, which arise when persons seeking authorisation here have close links with another person of such a kind as to prevent the FSA from supervising the applicant effectively. The lead test in the paragraph is that, if there are close links (see below) with another person, then two tests must be satisfied:

(a) those links are not likely to prevent effective supervision by the FSA; and
(b) if the person to whom the applicant is linked is himself regulated outside the EEA, then that foreign regulation does not prevent effective supervision of the applicant.

6.28   Close links are defined at para 3(2) in classic company law terms, involving the concept of parent undertakings, subsidiary undertakings and 20 per cent control.

(4) Adequate resources

6.29 The fourth threshold condition concerns the adequacy of the resources of the applicant in relation to the regulated activity to be carried on. The resources may be taken to include:

(a) the provision which the applicant makes in respect of liabilities (including contingent and future liabilities); and
(b) the means by which the applicant manages the incidence of risk in connection with his business.

6.30   *Resources* is thus to be construed in a broad way as substantially more than capital and guarantees, etc. The reference to risk management in particular indicates that the real test is not the simplistic one of amount of capital, but rather a subjective assessment of the probability of the firm concerned surviving any particular level of disturbance or shock. In applying this test the FSA considers both the financial and non-financial resources of a firm, including its human resources. It takes into account the competence of persons who exert influence over the firm, such as the firm's directors and partners, and expects a firm applying for a Part 4 permission to present a well constructed business plan with a level of detail commensurate to the complexity of the proposed activities of the firm.

(5) Suitability

6.31 The fifth general threshold condition is the so-called 'fit and proper' test. The applicant has the burden of satisfying the FSA that he is a fit and proper person having regard to all the circumstances. The paragraph specifically includes as relevant to the circumstances the connection which the applicant has with any person, the nature of the regulated activity concerned and the need to ensure that affairs are conducted soundly and prudently.

6.32   The reference in para 5 to connection overlaps to some extent with the close links issue discussed above, though here the existence of individuals is much more prominent than in the case of para 3 (close links). A 'connection' is undefined, though s 49(1) makes it plain that the FSA may regard as connected for this purpose any person in or likely to be in a 'relationship' with the applicant. So this will include connected persons in the company law sense as well as others who might be thought to be bad apples capable of infecting a barrel. There is also an overlap with the Approved Persons regime (set out in SUP 10) under which the FSA assesses the suitability of each person performing a controlled function within the firm (see further in Chapter 7).

In its own guidance relating to this condition, the FSA indicates that it will have regard to all relevant matters, wherever arising, that go to a firm's suitability. These include, but are not limited to, whether the firm (1) conducts or will conduct its business with integrity and in compliance with proper standards; (2) has, or will have, a competent and prudent management; and (3) can demonstrate that it conducts, or will conduct, its affairs with the exercise of due skill, care and diligence (COND 2.5.4G).   6.33

When assessing this threshold condition in relation to an EEA firm, the FSA is required by the Financial Groups Directive to consult other competent authorities with respect to the suitability of the firm's shareholders and the reputation and experience of directors involved in the management of another entity in the same group.   6.34

1. Protection of consumers

The topic of threshold conditions would not be complete without referring to FSMA, s 41(3). The FSA's obligation to ensure that the threshold conditions will be satisfied does not prevent it from taking such steps as it considers are necessary, in relation to a particular authorised person, in order to secure its regulatory objective of the protection of consumers. Parliament here seems to be saying that, as long as the FSA pays due regard to the threshold conditions, it does not need to be enslaved by them if it needs to take action, for instance, by an own-initiative variation of permission, in order to protect consumers. The most obvious way in which this might be relevant could be where the FSA concluded that the firm's resources were not adequate, under para 4 of Sch 6, but then decided not to cancel the permission straight away, because of the need to allow some time for positions to be unwound or transactions to be completed.   6.35

E. VARIATION AND CANCELLATION OF PERMISSION

Section s 44 to 46 of the FSMA deal with two quite separate cases of variation or cancellation of permission.   6.36

Section 44 deals with the natural tendency of firms to expand their range of activities, or to contract them. The initiative, under s 44, rests with the authorised person concerned. It proposes, and the FSA disposes. If the FSA proposed to refuse an application to reshape the permission, it would have to apply the tests of adverse effect on the interests of consumers, or desirability in the interests of consumers.   6.37

The second class of variation is quite different. Here the initiative is with the FSA and its power to take regulatory action can be triggered by one or more of three preconditions set out in s 45(1). These are, broadly speaking, breach or anticipated breach of the threshold conditions, not carrying on a regulated activity for a year or more, and protection of the interests of consumers or potential consumers. Under an amendment   6.38

introduced by the Banking Act 2009, the FSA may impose a variation on a firm's permission in order to protect the interests of consumers or potential consumers of other authorised persons as well as those of the firm itself. The FSA's powers on an own-initiative basis are to vary the permission or cancel it.

6.39   A further power in s 45(2A) was introduced to reflect MiFID and permits the FSA to cancel the Part 4 permission of an investment firm if the firm has failed to carry on an investment service or activity in the last six months, is found to have obtained its permission by making a false statement or by other irregular means, no longer satisfies certain authorisation conditions found in Chapter 1 of Title II to MiFID, or has seriously and systematically infringed operating conditions found in Chapter 2 of Title II to MiFID.

6.40   There is in s 46 an additional, free-standing power to 'intervene' where the trigger event is more restricted, but where the test for 'intervention' is much lower. If the FSA considers that a person has acquired control over a UK-authorised person with a Part 4 permission and it appears to the FSA that the likely effect of the acquisition of control on the authorised person or on any of its activities is uncertain, then the FSA has an immediate power to impose or vary a requirement under s 43 as if the authorised person were applying afresh for permission.

6.41   Because an own-initiative variation (other than that under s 46) is akin to disciplinary or enforcement action, there is procedure for review of the FSA's decision. If the FSA proposes to cancel the permission, the full warning notice and decision notice procedure is available (s 54). In this case, the FSA must also, under s 394, allow the firm to have access to FSA material relevant to the decision. If, however, the proposal is to vary the permission, but not cancel it altogether, there is one procedure for urgent cases (where the variation can take effect immediately or on a stated date) and another for less urgent cases.

6.42   Either way s 53 requires written notice (known as a 'supervisory notice'—see s 395(2)) with details of the variation, reasons and an offer to consider representations made about the proposal. If, having considered those representations, the FSA decides to go ahead (or not to rescind an immediate variation), then there must be written notice of the decision which informs the person of his right to refer the matter to the Tribunal. The procedure in s 53 is similar to but not the same as the more usual warning notice and decision notice procedure.

6.43   The exercise of own-initiative power with immediate effect (or on a stated date) and without allowing the time for prior representations and tribunal proceedings is available only if the FSA reasonably considers that it is necessary to do so having regard to the ground on which it is acting (s 53(3)). However, the FSA has to give written notice, including the reasons for its decision on timing, and the authorised person has a chance to make representations to the FSA either after the variation takes effect or, if the timing permits, beforehand. Either way the authorised person has the right to refer the matter to the Tribunal, which will be able to test the reasonableness of the FSA decision to proceed with immediate or near-immediate effect.

6.44   The scheme of the Act also contemplates that the person concerned can refer the matter to the Tribunal straightaway, on receipt of the first supervisory notice, whenever there is actual, as opposed to proposed, exercise of the own-initiative power (s 55(2) and s 53(5)(c) and (e); see also s 133(1)(a)).

F. ASSETS REQUIREMENTS

Under s 48 of the FSMA, the FSA has a special power, either at the outset, when giving   6.45
a permission to an authorised person, or thereafter, when varying it, to impose an 'assets
requirement' on the person. Assets requirements are defined in s 48(3) as a special sort
of requirement which either prohibits the person from dealing or places restrictions on
his dealing with his assets, or which requires some or all of those assets, or customer
assets held by that person, to be transferred to and held by a trustee approved by the
FSA.

Under s 48(5), the consequence of a requirement addressed to the person concerned   6.46
has legal effect in relation to that person's bank and other places where the person keeps
an account. The bank or other institution is relieved of any relevant contractual obligations to that person, and is made liable to the FSA if it acts in breach of the requirements
after it has had notice of them.

While the requirement to transfer assets to a trustee does not have immediate legal   6.47
effect, but depends upon compliance with the requirement by the authorised person,
nonetheless s 48(7) renders void any charge created by that person over any assets of his
which are held in accordance with the requirement. Accordingly, while the trusteeship
direction depends upon the person concerned executing the transfer, the Act prevents
subversion of the transfer by charges over any beneficial interest.

Compliance with the regime for assets requirements is enforceable under Part 14   6.48
(disciplinary measures), etc, though s 48(9) creates a special criminal offence to support
the provision securing that assets held by the trustee may be released or dealt with only
with the FSA's consent. The trustee may well not be an authorised person, and thus not
open to the disciplinary measures in Part 14.

G. OVERSEAS REGULATORS

There remains one section in Part 4 of the FSMA to deal with. This is s 47, which specifies   6.49
the power of the FSA to vary or cancel permission on its own initiative, but at the
request of an overseas regulator of a kind prescribed by the Treasury in the Own-initiative
Power (Overseas Regulators) Regulations 2001/2639. The background to this section,
plainly enough, is the obligation in the Single Market Directives on home State regulators to take measures relating to the home State authorisation if properly requested to do
so by the host State regulator. Accordingly, if a United Kingdom firm has a branch in
Portugal, and the Portuguese regulator (assuming that it is prescribed by the Treasury
under s 47) requests the taking of measures in relation to the UK firm because of impro-
prieties of a prudential character in the Portuguese branch, then s 47 provides the
machinery, powers and conditions upon which that intra-European co-operation is to
take place. The own-initiative power becomes exercisable at the request, or in order to
assist, the Portuguese regulator even if Part 13 (incoming firms: intervention by FSA) is
not available. So the s 47 powers are available for Portuguese purposes even in respect of
a United Kingdom firm. The section divides into two parts, depending on whether there
is a need to comply with a Community obligation.

6.50   If there is such a need, that criterion for action appears to be sufficient on its own and to replace the other tests in s 45(1) (breach of threshold conditions etc). The FSA has to act at its own expense in that case (s 47(6)).

6.51   If not, s 47(4) empowers the FSA to take into account factors such as reciprocity, the nature of the foreign law or requirement that may have been broken, extraterritorial jurisdiction, seriousness of the case and the public interest. The list is virtually the same as that in s 195(6). Here, too, the criteria for action in s 45(1) appear to be displaced: this emerges not from s 47 itself or from s 45(5) but from the fact that the s 195 criteria appear to justify intervention even if the criteria in s 194(1) are not available (see s 195(2)).

6.52   In this case, where there is no Community obligation, the FSA may expect the requesting regulator (if a request has been made) to contribute to the costs involved.

7

PERFORMANCE OF REGULATED ACTIVITIES

David Simpson

A. INTRODUCTION

Part 5 of the Financial Services and Markets Act 2000 (FSMA), in contrast with almost   7.01
all of the rest of the Act, focuses its attention on individuals, whether within the financial
services industry or on its fringes. It contains two quite separate forms of control in
relation to individuals, one 'negative' and the other 'positive'. The negative one, effectively prohibiting a person from staying in or entering the financial services industry,
is in ss 56 to 58. The positive one, under which certain people carrying on specific activities in financial services firms have to be positively vetted and approved, is in ss 59 to 71.
The negative power bears directly upon the individual, though there are consequential
obligations on firms (see s 56(6)): the positive one, however, is fashioned so as to impinge
on individuals through firms and relates to the individual when acting for the firm in a
particular specified capacity. Technically, the positive power can impinge on corporate
persons (and on externally employed contractors) as well, but the main focus is on individuals in or working for firms.

B. PROHIBITION ORDERS

Sections 56 to 58 of the FSMA deal with the negative form of control. If it appears to   7.02
the Financial Services Authority (FSA) that an individual is not fit and proper, it can
prohibit him or her from the industry, either totally or in part. A prohibition order

under FSMA, s 56, leads to criminal sanctions for breach (s 56(4)) and authorised persons must take reasonable care to avoid any function of theirs being performed by someone who is prohibited in relation to the function in question (s 56(6)). Section 56 may be use punitively, in respect of past misconduct, as well as preventively in respect of future activities; it may be used by the FSA in respect of past misconduct even where its disciplinary powers under s 66 are time-barred; and may be invoked even if the person concerned has no present intention to carry on the functions prohibited. A list of prohibited persons is available from the FSA's website.[1] In recent years the list has been swelled by a number of mortgage brokers targeted by the FSA's enforcement division in connection with the mis-selling of self-certified mortgages.

7.03   If an authorised person is in breach of s 56(6), a private person who suffers loss as a result of that contravention has a right of action against the authorised person under s 71. That section is built on similar lines to its equivalent in relation to contravention of an FSA rule in s 150(1). The Treasury has exercised its power under s 71(3) to define 'private person' in the Rights of Action Regulations 2001 (SI 2001/2256). Broadly, the definition includes any individual unless he suffers the loss in the course of carrying on a regulated activity, and any person who is not an individual, unless he suffers the loss in the course of carrying on business of any kind. These Regulations also confer a right of action under s 71 on a person who is acting in a fiduciary or representative capacity on behalf of a private person. Sections 57 and 58 provide the necessary machinery for adjudication and subsequent variation in this context.

C. POSITIVE POWER OF APPROVAL

7.04   Section 59 of the FSMA establishes a fundamental principle that when an authorised person enters into an arrangement in relation to carrying on a regulated activity, any person performing a 'controlled function' under the arrangement needs to be approved by the FSA to perform that function. This requirement depends, crucially, on the definition of controlled function, and s 59 goes on to set the framework for establishing which functions in firms are to be controlled functions. Section 59(2) deals with the problems that can arise in the commercial world when a person working for a firm is not necessarily doing so under an arrangement entered into between him or her and the firm, but under an arrangement entered into by a person who has contracted with the firm to provide services. Consultants, matrix management and, indeed, appointed representatives (as to which see s 39) are all within the scope of this extended form of control over individuals.

7.05   A controlled function is a function of a description specified by the FSA in rules (s 59(3)). And, in order for the rules to be validly made, the FSA has to fit the descriptions of functions into one or more of three conditions. These are broadly as follows (my emphasis):

(a) the 'management' condition (s 59(5)), which is that the function is likely to enable the person responsible to exercise a significant influence on the conduct of the firm's affairs;

---

[1] <http://www.fsa.gov.uk/register/prohibitedIndivs.do>.

(b) the 'customer-relations' condition (s 59(6)), which is that the function will involve the person dealing with customers of the authorised person and

(c) the 'customers' property' condition (s 59(7)), which is that the function will involve the person dealing with property of customers.

All three conditions have to relate to the regulated activity, and in the second and third conditions there has to be a substantial connection with that activity.   7.06

In rules in Chapter 10 of the FSA's Supervision Manual (SUP), the FSA states that the following persons are performing controlled functions (please note that certain numbered functions have been taken off the list):   7.07

Those exercising 'governing functions', namely: directors (CF1); non-executive directors (CF2); chief executives (CF3) of firms that are bodies corporate; partners (CF4) of firms that are partnerships; directors of firms that are unincorporated associations (CF5); and persons responsible for directing the affairs of small friendly societies (CF6).   7.08

Those exercising 'required functions', namely: persons responsible for apportioning responsibilities among directors and senior managers and for overseeing the establishment and maintenance of systems and controls (CF8); persons responsible for overseeing compliance with the regulatory system (CF10); persons responsible for making reports required by the money laundering rules (CF11); and three types of actuary (CF12, 12A and 12B).   7.09

Those exercising the 'systems and controls function'. This category embraces any employee who reports to the governing body or audit committee of the firm in relation to its financial affairs, setting and controlling its risk exposure and adherence to internal systems and controls, procedures and policies.[2]   7.10

Those exercising a 'significant management function'—namely: senior managers of significant business units (CF29).   7.11

Those exercising a 'customer function', namely all persons dealing with clients, or with clients' property, in a manner substantially connected with the carrying on of a regulated activity by the firm (CF30).   7.12

Sections 60 to 62 deal with the machinery whereby approval can be obtained for the performance by an individual of a particular controlled function in a firm. The application is made by the firm (and s 60(6) deals with the case where the applicant firm is not yet authorised at the time when it needs to make its application). The test for granting the application, in s 61(1), is that the FSA is satisfied that the so-called 'candidate' is a fit and proper person to perform the function to which the application relates. Ancillary tests such as qualification, training and competence are mentioned in s 61(2). The FSA has, by s 61(3), three months in which to determine whether to grant the application or to start the statutory machinery enabling review of a proposed refusal. The three-month period is interrupted during any time when the firm is responding to a request by the FSA to provide further information. The FSA has indicated that it expects to process 85 per cent of applications within two, four or seven days, depending upon the nature of the application.   7.13

Section 62 provides the machinery for a warning notice on a proposal to refuse, and a decision notice on a refusal of an application: rights to have the matter referred to the Financial Services and Markets Tribunal then ensue for firm and individual alike.   7.14

---

[2] SUP10.8.1R

Equally, if the FSA is minded to withdraw an individual approval given under Part 5, on the grounds that the person is not fit and proper, then there has to be the warning notice and decision notice procedure followed by a right to refer the matter to the Tribunal (s 63).

D. STATEMENTS OF PRINCIPLE ON THE CONDUCT OF APPROVED PERSONS

7.15   Sections 64 and 65 provide for statements of principle to be issued by the FSA, coupled with a code of practice, relating to the conduct expected of approved persons. The purpose of the code is to help to determine whether or not a person's conduct complies with the statement of principle.

7.16   The statements of principle issued by the FSA are found in Chapter 2 of the FSA's Approved Persons Regime rulebook (APER) and are as follows:

(a) An approved person must act with integrity in carrying out his controlled function.

(b) An approved person must act with due skill, care and diligence in carrying out his controlled function.

(c) An approved person must observe proper standards of market conduct in carrying out his controlled function.

(d) An approved person must deal with the FSA and with other regulators in an open and cooperative way and must disclose appropriately any information of which the FSA would reasonably expect notice.

(e) An approved person performing a significant influence function must taken reasonable steps to ensure that the business of the firm for which he is responsible in his controlled function is organised so that it can be controlled effectively.

(f) An approved person performing a significant influence function must exercise due skill, care and diligence in managing the business of the firm for which he is responsible in his controlled function.

(g) An approved person performing a significant influence function must take reasonable steps to ensure that the business of the firm for which he is responsible in his controlled function complies with the relevant requirements and standards of the regulatory system.

7.17   These statements of principle are different in character from the so-called FSA principles for businesses. The latter are rules, made under Part 10; that are addressed to firms and breach of them leads to all the consequences set out in the Act for breach of a rule. Statements of principle made under s 64, however, are addressed to approved persons and a special code of discipline is set up at ss 66 to 69 (see further below) to enforce them against the individual personally.

7.18   The statements of principle are coupled with codes of practice (found in Chapters 3 and 4 of APER) which have evidential value in helping to determine whether or not the person is in breach of the principle. The machinery relating to these codes of practice is markedly similar to that provided in s 122 for the code of market conduct, though there are some differences. Essentially, in the context of individual approval, a code may be relied on in so far as it tends to establish:

(a) that the conduct complies with a statement of principle; or

(b) that the conduct is in contravention of a statement of principle.

In the market abuse context, however, the effect of s 122(1) and (2) is that (a) and (b)   7.19
above apply, but subject to the proviso that behaviour described in the market abuse
code as not amounting to market abuse is *conclusively* taken not to be market abuse.

The procedural requirements in s 65 for making statements and codes are not unlike   7.20
those relating to rules, as to which see Chapter 12.

E. DISCIPLINARY POWERS

Sections 66 to 69 provide a special disciplinary system in relation to the enforcement of   7.21
the statements of principle and the code. The central concept, in s 66(1) and (2), is
'guilty of misconduct'. That misconduct is either:

(a) failure to comply with a statement of principle; or
(b) being knowingly concerned in a contravention by the firm of a requirement imposed
    on the firm.

This definition of misconduct therefore requires approved persons to comply with the   7.22
statements of principle, and also to avoid any knowing participation in a breach by the
firm of any requirement imposed upon it. Individuals who do not require approval
cannot be disciplined for 'knowing concern' in a firm's contravention of a rule, etc,
except in a case where the FSA takes proceedings for injunctions or restitution under
Part 25 (see Chapter 27). This underlines the importance of the borderline to be drawn
between those functions which require Part 5 approval and those which do not.

The sanctions available against approved persons are, by s 66(3), an unlimited penalty   7.23
of a financial character, or a statement of misconduct. These are similar to, though dealt
with in a different order from, the financial penalties and public censure sanctions
available against firms under Part 14. Section 66 contains, however, a provision not to
be found in Part 14, namely that, once the FSA has become aware of misconduct, it
has two years in which to begin proceedings against the individual, after which the disciplinary powers cease to be exercisable, although the court-based powers in Part 25
remain at least technically available. Section 67 deals with the rights to a warning notice,
decision notice and reference to the Financial Services and Markets Tribunal.

Part 5 (like s 123 for market abuse penalties) does not actually specify that the penal-   7.24
ties are payable to the FSA, though ss 91(5) and 206(3) so provide for other penalties
payable by issuers of securities and by firms: but the implication of Part 3 of Sch 1 to the
Act is that penalties under s 66 (and s 126) are indeed payable to the FSA.

F. STATEMENT OF POLICY

Part 5 of the FSMA deals with one other adjectival matter concerning approved persons   7.25
and discipline of them. Under s 69(1) the FSA is obliged to prepare and issue a statement of its policy about penalties payable by approved persons, dealing with the imposition and with their amount. This section is one of a number in the Act which require the
FSA to produce statements of policy relating to disciplinary matters: others are at s 93
(listing), s 124 (market abuse) and s 210 (general discipline). Certain elements of that
required policy are laid down by s 69(2), including the seriousness of the misconduct,
the question of deliberate or reckless misconduct and (thus emphasising that approved

persons do not have to be individuals) whether the approved person is an individual. The meat of the section is in subsection (8), which requires the FSA to have regard to the statement of policy in force at the time of the misconduct (not of the decision-making) in taking decisions about penalties. The FSA has issued the required statement in Chapter 6 of its DEPP handbook.

8

OFFICIAL LISTING

Andrew Henderson

A. INTRODUCTION

Part 6 of the Financial Services and Markets Act 2000 (FSMA) governs official listing. **8.01** It facilitates the operation of the capital markets, which is essential to the efficient and orderly operation of any developed economy. The capital markets provide a mechanism through which securities, such as shares, bonds, depositary receipts, and units in collective investment schemes can be offered to the public and the public can share in the growth of the value of those securities or receive an income. This in turn allows companies to raise funds in the primary market and for the securities to be traded in the secondary market.[1]

1. The European basis for Part 6

Part 6 has undergone much change since the FSMA was first enacted. This is mainly due **8.02** to the implementation of various EU directives and regulations in Part 6, although, in some places, the UK has imposed further requirements not based on EU law. Prior to 1 July 2005, the main European Directives relevant to Part 6 were:

(a) the Consolidated Admissions and Reporting Directive (CARD),[2] which dealt with the requirements for admission to official listing and continuing obligations of listed

---

[1] For discussion of the context in which Part 6 operates, see, for example, Ferran *Principles of Corporate Finance Law* (2008: OUP), pp 409 to 421.

[2] Directive 2001/34/EC.

companies. Much of CARD is repealed but provisions dealing with eligibility for listing survive; and

(b) the Public Offers Directive,[3] which covered public offers of securities both listed and unlisted. This has been superseded.

8.03 Since 1 July 2005, the key directives relevant to Part 6 are:

(a) The Prospectus Directive (PD),[4] which governs the contents, approval and publication of prospectuses in connection with applications for admission to a regulated market and offers of securities to the public;[5]

(b) The Market Abuse Directive (MAD),[6] which governs insider dealing, market manipulation and the disclosure of inside information; and

(c) The Transparency Directive (TD),[7] which deals with other ongoing disclosure obligations of, and relating to, issuers.

8.04 In addition, the audit committee requirement of the Statutory Audit Directive[8] and the corporate governance statement requirement of the Company Reporting Directive[9] are also relevant to corporate governance rules made under Part 6.[10]

2. Interaction with other regimes

8.05 The legal and regulatory issues which arise in the context of official listing may not necessarily be restricted to Part 6. Other parts of the FSMA may be relevant. For example, the provisions governing financial promotion in s 21 will be relevant in the context of advertisements and other communications.[11] In this respect, the various exemptions contained in articles 68 to 71 of the FSMA (Financial Promotion) Order 2005[12] (hereafter referred to as the Financial Promotion Order, or FPO) may be particularly relevant. However, the provisions of Article 15 of the PD governing advertisements, in respect of which the exemption in Article 70 of the FPO (Promotion included in listing particulars etc) will not apply, should be noted. [13]

8.06 The provisions governing market abuse in Part 8 of the FSMA may also be relevant.[14] In addition to the issues arising with respect to disclosure obligations, where Part 6 forms part of the implementation of the MAD, the market abuse regime may be relevant in the context of false statements made in listing particulars or a prospectus or failures or breaches of disclosure and transparency obligations.[15]

---

[3] Directive 89/298/EEC.

[4] Directive 2003/71/EC.

[5] The Prospectus Directive Regulation ((EC) No 809/2004) (PDR) which sets out, amongst other things, the detailed contents requirements for prospectuses is also of key importance. See paragraph 8.34 below.

[6] Directive 2003/6/EC.

[7] Directive 2004/109/EC.

[8] Directive 2006/43/EC.

[9] Directive 2006/46/EC.

[10] FSMA, s 73A(6) and s 89O.

[11] See Chapter 4.

[12] 2005/1529.

[13] FPO, art 70(1)(d). See also Prospectus Rule (PR) 3.3 (advertisements).

[14] See Chapter 10.

[15] See FSMA, s 118(7).

The provisions in s 397 of the FSMA, which make it a criminal offence to make an   8.07
intentionally misleading or reckless statement, promise, or forecast or to dishonestly
conceal any material facts for the purpose of inducing another person to buy, sell, or
exercise any rights conferred by a relevant investment, and ss 2 and 3 of the Fraud Act
2006, which make it a criminal offence either to make false representations or to fail to
disclose information when there is a duty to do so, would be relevant in the context of
false statements made in listing particulars or a prospectus or failures or breaches of
disclosure and transparency obligations.

B. PART 6 AND THE FSA

1. The FSA as Competent Authority

The functions conferred on the competent authority by Part 6 are exercised by the   8.08
Financial Services Authority (FSA).[16] When carrying out its duties as competent authority, the FSA is referred to as the UK Listing Authority (UKLA).

A set of general functions with regard to listing is specified in similar terms to those in   8.09
s 2(4) for the FSA's other functions. These include: its function of making rules under
Part 6; its function of giving general guidance in relation to Part 6; and its function of
determining the general policy and principles by reference to which it performs particular functions under Part 6.[17] However, only six of the seven principles of good regulation in s 2(3) are relevant to the FSA's discharge of these general functions, the missing
requirement being s 2(3)(b) (responsibility of managers).[18] The principles in s 73(1)(c)
(the desirability of facilitating innovation) and s 73(1)(f) (the desirability of facilitating
competition) were amended to extend their coverage to regulated markets in other
European Economic Area (EEA) states.[19] The scope of the same two principles is extended
to any market where the functions relate to transparency rules.[20] Certain amendments
to other provisions of the FSMA are set out in Sch 7 to apply where the FSA acts as
competent authority.[21]

2. The FSA's power to make rules

As a result of the implementation of the PD and MAD, the FSA was given the power to   8.10
make Part 6 Rules which included listing rules, disclosure rules and prospectus rules.[22]
This was extended to include transparency and corporate governance rules.[23] The FSA's
responsibilities and powers are no longer restricted to listed issuers and the FSA has

---

[16] FSMA, s 72(1).

[17] FSMA, s 73(2).

[18] FSMA, s 73(1).

[19] FSMA (Market Abuse) Regulations 2005 (2005/381) (MAR 2005), reg 4, Sch 1, para 1.

[20] FSMA, s 73(1A) inserted by the Companies Act 2006 (CA), s 1272, Sch 15, Pt 1, paras 1 and 2.

[21] The Treasury is given power by s 72(3) to transfer these functions by order to another person in accordance with the provisions set out in Sch 8.

[22] FSMA, ss 73A and 101. See the FSMA (Market Abuse) Regulations 2005 (2005/381) (MAR 2005),
reg 4, Sch 1, para 2 and Prospectus Regulations 2005 (2005/1433) reg 2(1), Sch 1, para 1.

[23] FSMA, s 73A(6) inserted by the Companies Act 2006, s 1272, Sch 15, Pt 1, paras 1 and 3.

made a new Block of the FSA Handbook containing three new modules which comprise the following:[24]

(a) Listing Rules (LR), which contain rules and guidance for issuers of securities admitted to or seeking admission to the official list and focus on eligibility for listing, and continuing obligations of the issuers of listed securities and sponsors.

(b) Prospectus Rules (PR), which contain the rules and guidance setting out the circumstances in which a prospectus is required, the contents and format of a prospectus, the approval and publication of a prospectus, issues relating to third party issuers and miscellaneous provisions such as those relating to qualified investors and persons responsible for a prospectus.[25]

(c) Disclosure Rules, which form part of the Disclosure and Transparency Rules (DTR) in the FSA Handbook and contain the rules and guidance in relation to the publication and control of 'inside information', insider lists and the disclosure of transactions by persons discharging managerial responsibilities and their connected persons.[26]

(d) Transparency Rules, which form part of the DTR and contain rules and guidance in relation to continuing financial reporting, the disclosure of major shareholdings, information that issuers must provide to holders of their securities, and wider access to information about issuers and securities.[27]

(e) Corporate Governance Rules, which form part of the DTR and contain rules and guidance in relation to audit committees and the corporate governance statement of listed companies.[28]

8.11 Despite the important role of the various EU directives in making Part 6 Rules, the FSA's powers to make Part 6 Rules are not limited by the directives. For example, the provisions in the LR relating to the 'Listing Principles' in LR 7 and sponsors in LR 8 are 'super-equivalent', meaning that the FSA has made the relevant rules included despite there being no requirement under any EU directive to do so, thereby imposing duties in addition to those under the directives.

3. Controlling the FSA's powers

8.12 As a public body, the FSA will be subject to judicial review by the courts.[29] In addition, specific decisions regarding listing, prospectuses, and transparency may give rise to a right of referral to the Financial Services and Markets Tribunal (Tribunal).[30] Furthermore, the FSA is subject to Treasury oversight. The Treasury is empowered to order the regulating provisions and practices of the FSA to be kept under review having regard to possible significant adverse effects on competition.[31]

---

[24] <http://fsahandbook.info/FSA/html/handbook/>.
[25] See also FSMA, s 84 and paragraph 8.25 to 8.45 below.
[26] See also FSMA, s 96A and paragraph 8.50 to 8.55 below.
[27] See also FSMA, s 89A and paragraph 8.56 to 8.62 below.
[28] See also FSMA, s 89O and paragraph 8.63 below.
[29] See Henderson 'Judicial Review and FSMA'[2001] *Judicial Review* 255.
[30] These are discussed below.
[31] FSMA, s 95(1) and (2).

4. Exemption from liability in damages

Section 102(1) contains a general exemption from liability and damages for the FSA and its staff in connection with anything done or omitted in the discharge, or purported discharge, of its functions as competent authority under the Act.[32] This will not apply to acts or omissions shown to have been in bad faith or awards in connection with unlawful acts or omissions under s 6(1) of the Human Rights Act 1998.[33]

8.13

C. LISTING

1. The Official List

In addition to its general functions set out above, the FSA is responsible for the maintenance of the official list and may admit to the official list such securities and other instruments as it considers appropriate and which the Treasury permits.[34]

8.14

Although the FSA is responsible for the admission of securities to listing, the London Stock Exchange and the other exchanges in the UK retain responsibility for the admission of securities to trading. Listing is therefore confined to the admission of securities to the official list, which means that they have satisfied the requirements set with regard to structure, content and presentation and are, in effect, eligible to be considered by the Stock Exchange or other exchange for admission to trading. Admission to trading is confined to the admission of securities to dealing on a particular exchange. This may or may not involve approved or listed securities. For example, there is no requirement for the securities of an issuer which wishes to join the Alternative Investment Market (AIM), the London Stock Exchange's international market for smaller growing companies, to be admitted to the official list.[35]

8.15

2. Applications for listing

The LR specify the requirements for applications to be admitted to the official list.[36] The FSA must be satisfied that the requirements of the listing rules and any other requirements imposed are satisfied.[37] The requirements for listing all securities are set out in LR 2 while additional requirements for the listing of equity securities, closed ended investment funds, open ended investment companies, debt and specialist securities, global depositary receipts ('certificates representing certain securities'), and securitised derivatives are set out in LR 6, 15, 16, 17, 18 and 19, respectively. An application may be refused if the FSA considers that granting it would be detrimental to the interests of investors, but only having regard to factors relating to the issuer.[38] Applications can be

8.16

---

[32] FSMA, s 102(1).
[33] FSMA, s 102(2).
[34] FSMA, s 74. The requirements for listing applications are set out in LR 3.
[35] See <http://www.londonstockexchange.com>.
[36] FSMA, s 75(1).
[37] FSMA, s 75(4).
[38] FSMA, s 75(5).

made only by or with the consent of the issuer of the securities.[39] If the securities are already officially listed in another EEA State, an application may be refused if the issuer fails to comply with any relevant obligations relating to that listing.[40]

8.17 The FSA's decision must be notified to the applicant within six months of the original date of receipt of the application or the date on which any further information requested has been provided.[41] If due notice is not given, the application will be deemed to have been refused.[42] Once admitted, however, the admission may not be challenged on the ground that any relevant requirement or condition had not been satisfied.[43]

8.18 The listing of any securities may be discontinued where there are special circumstances which preclude normal regular dealings as provided for in or in accordance with the LR.[44] The FSA may exercise this power on its own initiative or on the application of the issuer.[45]

8.19 Where securities are delisted, the issuer may refer the matter to the Tribunal.[46] A detailed procedure concerning the discontinuance or suspension of listing generally is set out in s 78 and discontinuance or suspension of listing at the request of the issuer is set out in s 78A. These generally provide for notice which must contain specified material including details and date of effectiveness, reasons for suspension or discontinuance, the right to make representations, and the relevant period as well as the right to refer the matter to the Tribunal. This is, however, without prejudice to the right of the FSA to delist with immediate effect.

3. Listing particulars

The distinction between listing particulars and a prospectus

8.20 Listing Rules may provide that securities of a kind specified in the rules may not be admitted to the official list unless appropriate listing particulars have been submitted to and approved by the FSA and published or such other document as may be required has been published.[47] The Listing Rules may not specify securities of a kind for which an approved prospectus is required as a result of s 85.[48] This highlights the important distinction between listing particulars and a prospectus, in respect of which there is a different regime set out in ss 84 to 87, discussed below.

Contents and persons responsible

8.21 The requirements for listing particulars require a document in such form and containing such information as may be specified in the Listing Rules.[49] The requirements for listing particulars for the professional securities market and certain other securities are set out

---

[39] FSMA, s 75(2).
[40] FSMA, s 75(6).
[41] FSMA, s 76(1).
[42] FSMA, s 76(2).
[43] FSMA, s 76(7).
[44] FSMA, s 77(1) and (2).
[45] FSMA, s 77(2A).
[46] FSMA, s 77(5).
[47] FSMA, s 79(1).
[48] FSMA, s 79(3A)
[49] FSMA, s 79(2).

in LR 4. The persons responsible for listing particulars are to be determined in accordance with regulations issued by the Treasury.[50] The FSMA (Official Listing of Securities) Regulations 2001[51] (OLSR) identify these persons and include the issuer of the securities to which the particulars relate and, where the issuer is a body corporate, each person who is a director of that body at the time when the particulars are submitted to the FSA.[52] The OLSR also set the limits with respect to such responsibility.

The general duty of disclosure in listing particulars

Section 80(1) imposes a general duty of disclosure in relation to listing particulars. Listing particulars are to contain all such information as investors and their professional advisers would reasonably require or expect to find there for the purpose of making informed assessments of the assets and liabilities, financial position, profits and losses and prospects of the issuer and of the rights attaching to the securities. In considering what information it would be reasonable to require, regard must be had to:
8.22

- the nature of the securities and their issuer;
- the nature of the persons likely to consider acquiring them;
- the fact that certain matters may reasonably be expected to be within the knowledge of professional advisers of a kind which persons likely to acquire the securities may reasonably be expected to consult; and
- any information available to investors or their professional advisers as a result of requirements imposed on the issuer of the securities by a recognised investment exchange, by listing rules or by or under any other enactment.[53]

This is without prejudice to any specific information required by the Listing Rules or by the FSA.[54] This only relates, however, to information within the knowledge of the person responsible for the listing particulars or which it would be reasonable for him to obtain by making enquiries.[55]

Supplementary listing particulars

Supplementary listing particulars must be issued where there has been any significant change to the matters set out in the original particulars.[56] There is no duty to issue supplementary particulars unless the issuer is aware of the change or new matter or is notified of it by a person responsible for the listing particulars.[57]
8.23

Exemptions from disclosure

The FSA may permit certain information to be omitted from the listing particulars on various grounds, including where its disclosure would be contrary to the public interest.[58]
8.24

---

[50] FSMA, s 79(3).
[51] SI 2001/2956.
[52] See FSMA (Official Listing of Securities) Regulations 2001 (2001/2956), reg 6.
[53] FSMA, s 80(4).
[54] FSMA, s 80(2).
[55] FSMA, s 80(3).
[56] FSMA, s 81(1).
[57] FSMA, s 81(3).
[58] FSMA, s 82(2).

The Secretary of State or the Treasury may issue a certificate confirming that the disclosure of certain information would be contrary to the public interest.[59]

D. OFFERS TO THE PUBLIC

1. The requirement to have a prospectus

Offers of transferable securities and requests for admission to trading

8.25 By identifying two prohibitions, s 85 of the FSMA specifies the two situations in which an approved prospectus is required: firstly, it is unlawful for transferable securities to be offered to the public in the UK unless an approved prospectus has been made available to the public before the offer is made.[60] Secondly, it is unlawful to request the admission of transferable securities to trading on a regulated market situated or operating in the UK unless an approved prospectus has been made available to the public before the request is made.[61]

8.26 An 'offer of transferable securities to the public' is defined in the PD as 'a communication to persons in any form and by any means, presenting sufficient information on the terms of the offer and the securities to be offered, so as to enable an investor to decide to purchase or subscribe to these securities'. This definition shall also be applicable to the placing of securities through financial intermediaries.'[62] This is implemented in s 102B of the FSMA which makes it clear that, for domestic purposes, an offer of transferable securities is limited to the UK. 'Transferable securities' are defined in s 102A(3) of the FSMA to have the same meaning as transferable securities under art 4(18) of MiFID, but excluding money market instruments which have a maturity of less than 12 months, and include shares in companies.

8.27 Therefore, any Initial Public Offering (IPO) will require a prospectus, including any offer of securities relating to an AIM listing. However, the mere admission to trading on AIM will not require a prospectus because AIM is not a regulated market. Disclosure requirements under the AIM Rules for Companies would, however, apply.[63]

8.28 A breach of the prohibitions in s 85(1) or (2) has two consequences: a person who contravenes them is criminally liable,[64] and the contravention is actionable at the suit of a person who suffers loss as a result.[65]

Transactions which do not require a prospectus

8.29 Transferable securities may be offered without a prospectus if:

• the offer is made to or directed to 'qualified investors' only;

---

[59] FSMA, s 82(3).
[60] FSMA, s 85(1).
[61] FSMA, s 85(2).
[62] Prospectus Directive, art 2.1(d).
[63] See Ferran, n 1, p 430.
[64] FSMA 2000, s 85(3).
[65] FSMA 2000, s 85(4). This is subject to the defences and other incidents applying to actions for breach of statutory duty.

- the offer is made to or directed at fewer than 100 persons, other than qualified investors, per EEA State;[66]
- the minimum investment required is at least 50,000 euros (or equivalent);
- the securities are denominated in amounts of at least 50,000 euros (or equivalent); or
- the total consideration for the transferable securities being offered does not exceed 100,000 euros or an equivalent amount in foreign currency.[67]

The PD defines what is meant by a 'qualified investor' and includes legal entities which are authorised or regulated to operate in the financial markets, various governmental and supranational bodies and natural persons who ask to be treated as qualified investors and satisfy two of the criteria in art 2.2 of the PD.[68] The FSA must establish and maintain a register of qualified investors. An individual may not be entered in the register unless he is resident in the UK and meets at least two of the criteria in art 2.2 of the PD and a company may not be entered unless its registered office is in the UK and it falls within the meaning of 'small and medium-sized enterprises' in art 2.1 of the PD.[69]   8.30

Election to have a prospectus

Section 87 of the FSMA permits an issuer, whose home state is the UK, to elect to have a prospectus if he wants to issue, make an offer of, or request the admission to a regulated market of non-equity transferable securities issued by various government or supranational bodies, credit institutions in certain circumstances and the other types of transferable securities falling within Sch 11A of the FSMA identified in FSMA, s 87(4). The PR will apply to such securities but the LR will not.[70]   8.31

2. The prospectus

The format and contents of a prospectus

The FSA may not approve a prospectus unless it is satisfied that: the UK is the home state of the relevant issuer, the prospectus contains the 'necessary information', and all applicable requirements imposed by or in accordance with Part 6 of the FSMA or the PD have been complied with.[71]   8.32

The prospectus must be presented in a form which is comprehensible and easy to analyse, having regard to the particular nature of the securities and their issuer, and include a summary conveying briefly and in non-technical language the essential characteristics of and risks associated with the issuer, the securities, and any guarantor.[72]   8.33

---

[66] For these purposes, the trustees of a trust, members of a partnership in their capacity as such or two or more persons jointly will be treated as a single person (FSMA, s 86(3)).

[67] FSMA, s 86(1). The 100,000 euro limit applies on a rolling 12-month basis, meaning that each offer of securities will be aggregated with any other offer of securities of the same class made by the same person within the previous 12 months (FSMA, s 86(4)). FSMA, s 86(5) and (6) deals with the calculation of an 'equivalent amount'.

[68] PD, art 2(1)(e).

[69] FSMA, s 87R.

[70] FSMA, s 87(2) and (3).

[71] FSMA, s 87A(1).

[72] FSMA, s 87A(3) to (5). See PR 2.1.2 *et seq* which deals with the summary.

Where the prospectus does not include the final offer price or the amount of transferable securities to be offered to the public, the applicant must provide that information in writing as soon as this is finalised.[73]

8.34 The prospectus must comply with the format requirements set out in the PR which, following the PD, permit a prospectus to be drawn up as a single document or separate documents comprising a registration document, securities note and summary.[74]

'Necessary Information' and Materiality

8.35 For the purposes of s 87A(1), the 'necessary information' means the information necessary to enable investors to make an informed assessment of the assets and liabilities, financial position, profits and losses, and prospects of the issuer of the securities and of any guarantor and the rights attaching to the securities.[75]

8.36 The duty to provide 'necessary information' highlights the principle of mandatory prospectus disclosure.[76] The duty underpins the more specific requirements set out in the PR. In practice, what is meant by the 'necessary information' is determined by provisions in the PR, App 3, that it, the 'Schedules and Building Blocks and Table of Combinations of Schedules and Building Blocks', which are copied from the PD. So, for example, the prospectus for an offer of debt securities would need to contain the information in Annex 1, Annex II (where the issuer wishes to rely on Pro forma financial information) and Annex IV of the PR, App 3.

8.37 Section 87A(4) of the FSMA states that the 'necessary information must be prepared having regard to the particular nature of the transferable securities and their issuer.' In this respect, it adds an element which is similar to that of materiality under US securities regulation, in particular Rule 10b–5 made under the Securities Exchange Act 1934, which prohibits material misstatements and omissions as well as fraudulent acts in connection with purchases and sales of securities. The US courts have defined materiality in the context of Rule 10b–5 in terms of the type of information that a reasonable investor would consider significant in making an investment decision. The test of materiality does not depend on the literal truth of individual statements but is based on the total mix of information available. Therefore, when, for example, there is adequate cautionary language warning investors as to certain risks, optimistic statements are not materially misleading.[77]

Exemptions from disclosure in a prospectus

8.38 The FSA may allow an issuer to omit information from a prospectus on various grounds, including where disclosure would be contrary to the public interest.[78] The Secretary of State or the Treasury can issue a public interest certificate but this does not bind the FSA.[79]

---

[73] FSMA, s 87A(7).

[74] See PR 2.2. The PR also permit an issuer of non-equity securities, in certain circumstances, to use a 'base prospectus'.

[75] FSMA, s 87A(2).

[76] See Ferran, n 1, p 429.

[77] See Hazen *Principles of Securities Regulation* (2005: Thomson West) Ch 12.

[78] FSMA, s 87B(1). See PR 2.5 which deals with omissions of information.

[79] FSMA, s 87B(2).

The approval process

The FSA must tell the applicant of its decision on an application for approval of a pro-   8.39
spectus before the end of the period for consideration.[80] This is normally 10 days from
receipt of the application, but 20 days for new issuers and seven days for a supplementary prospectus or when a request for further information is complied with.[81] Requests
for information must be made within the period for consideration and must be reasonable.[82] Missing the deadline is not treated as automatic approval of the prospectus.

The FSA must issue a written notice if it approves, refuses to approve, or proposes to   8.40
refuse to approve a prospectus or supplementary prospectus.[83] In the case of an actual or
proposed refusal, the notice must give reasons and inform the applicant of his right to
refer the matter to the Tribunal.[84] The FSMA gives the FSA the power to impose various
requirements, including an obligation to include information necessary for investor
protection.[85]

The FSMA also contains provisions dealing with transfers of applications for approval   8.41
from the FSA to a competent authority in another EEA state and vice versa.[86]

The supplementary prospectus

If, between the closure of the offer and the start of trading in securities covered by a   8.42
prospectus or supplementary prospectus, a significant new factor arises or a material
mistake or inaccuracy is found in the prospectus, the applicant for approval must submit
to the FSA for approval a supplementary prospectus containing details of the new factor
or inaccuracy and must provide sufficient information to correct the problem.[87]

Passporting

Where a competent authority of an EEA State other than the United Kingdom (EEA   8.43
Regulator) provides the FSA with a certificate of approval which confirms that a prospectus has been drawn up in accordance with the PD, then the prospectus will be
treated as an approved prospectus for the purpose of offering the securities in the UK.[88]
The FSMA requires the FSA to provide a certificate of approval for a prospectus which
the FSA has approved where an issuer wishes to rely on that prospectus to offer securities
in the jurisdiction of an EEA Regulator.[89]

The powers of the FSA

The FSMA gives the FSA the powers to suspend or prohibit an offer to the public or the   8.44
admission of transferable securities to trading on a regulated market situated in the UK
and publicly censure an issuer where the issuer is failing or has failed to comply with his

---

[80] FSMA, s 87C(1).
[81] FSMA, s 87C(2) and (9).
[82] FSMA, s 87C(5), (6) and (8).
[83] FSMA, s 87D(1), (2), (4) and (7).
[84] FSMA, s 87D(3), (5) and (6).
[85] FSMA, s 87J.
[86] FSMA, ss 87E and 87F.
[87] FSMA, s 87G. See also PR 3.4.
[88] FSMA, s 87H.
[89] FSMA, s 87I.

obligations under an applicable provision.[90] The FSMA sets out the procedure for a suspension or prohibition including the requirement to give written notice and the right of the recipient of the notice to make representations and refer the matter to the Tribunal.[91] The FSA may exercise these powers at the request of an EEA Regulator.[92]

Withdrawal rights

8.45   The FSMA gives a purchaser or subscriber for securities the right to withdraw from transactions where the original prospectus does not include information about the price and volume of the securities.[93] The purchaser or subscriber can withdraw his acceptance between the date of that acceptance and the second working day after the FSA is given the information regarding the price and volume as required by FSMA, s 87A(7).[94] Where a supplementary prospectus has been published prior to publication, anyone who has agreed to buy or subscribe prior to publication can withdraw his acceptance before the end of two working days beginning on the first working day after the date on which the supplementary prospectus was published.[95]

E. SPONSORS

8.46   The sponsors' regime is designed to ensure that primary listed companies and applicants seeking primary listings (new applicants) understand the regulatory framework imposed on them under Part 6 of the FSMA and to provide the FSA with written assurance that primary listed companies and/or new applicants are complying with the regulatory framework.[96] Sponsors are not required by any Directive; they simply allow the FSA to be confident that issuers of securities are being properly prepared for listing. Typically, the role is performed by an investment bank who may also act as underwriter on the IPO in respect of which it is acting as sponsor.

8.47   Under the FSMA, a sponsor means any person approved by the FSA for the purpose of the LR.[97] The LR may require any person to make arrangements with a sponsor for the carrying out of certain specified services and for the maintenance of a list of relevant sponsors and conditions for listing.[98] The sponsors' obligations are contained in LR 8, which underwent significant amendment in February 2009.

8.48   The Act also includes provisions by way of warning notices and decision notices and the right to apply to the Tribunal where an application for approval as a sponsor is to be refused or an existing approval cancelled.[99] The Enforcement Guide (EG) 18 deals with

---

[90] FSMA, ss 87K to 87M. See also PR 5.6.3.
[91] FSMA, ss 87N to 87O.
[92] FSMA, s 87P.
[93] FSMA, s 87Q(1).
[94] FSMA, s 87Q(2) to (3).
[95] FSMA, s 87Q(4).
[96] See *Sponsors Regime—a Targeted Review*, CP 08/05, p 4.
[97] FSMA, s 88(2).
[98] FSMA, s 88(3).
[99] FSMA, s 88(4) to (7).

the cancellation of approval as a sponsor.[100] The FSA may also, under special provisions in the LR, proceed against the sponsor for breach of a requirement imposed on him or her under the rules.[101] This would result in a public censure of the sponsor, again subject to notice and the right to apply to the Tribunal.[102] Third parties who could be prejudiced by the proposed discipline are given appropriate due process rights.[103]

F. CONTINUING OBLIGATIONS

1. Continuing obligations generally

An issuer's regulatory duties are not confined to the listing and offering process; its status as a publicly listed company brings with it special obligations, both to existing and potential investors. FSMA, s 96 empowers the FSA to make listing rules governing these continuing obligations. In this regard, the FSA has made LR 9 which set out a list of general requirements, including compliance with the DTR[104] and Model Code, which imposes dealing restrictions on the securities of a listed company.[105] The LR also deal with an issuer's continuing obligations with respect to existing shareholders; certain documents, such as those relating to employee share schemes, which require prior shareholder approval; certain transactions, such as rights issues; notifications, preliminary statements of annual results, statements of dividends and half-yearly reports; and annual financial reports.[106]

8.49

2. Disclosure obligations

Section 96A of the FSMA requires the FSA to make rules imposing continuing disclosure obligations on issuers trading on a regulated market in the UK. Section 96B deals with the definition of 'a person discharging managerial responsibilities within an issuer'. Both implement the MAD. Relying on ss 96A and 96B, the FSA has made DTR 2 and DTR 3.

8.50

Under DTR 2, an issuer is required to notify a Regulated Information Service of any inside information which directly concerns the issuer.[107] 'Inside information' has the same meaning as it does under the market abuse regime,[108] which highlights the role of the disclosure requirement as one of the two basic regulatory responses to dealing with inside information, the other being the prohibitions on dealing and other types of

8.51

---

[100] See *Strata Technology* FSA Final Notice 30 January 2004 for an example of where the FSA refused an application for approval as a sponsor.

[101] FSMA, s 89(1). See also LR 8.7.19.

[102] FSMA, s 89(2) to (4).

[103] FSMA, ss 392 to 393.

[104] See paragraph 8.50 to 8.55 and 8.56 to 8.62 below.

[105] LR 9.2. The Model Code is contained in LR 9, Annex 1.

[106] LR 9.3 to 9.8.

[107] DTR 2.2.1 R and MAD, art 6(1). DTR contains detailed guidance on identifying inside information and when to disclose it.

[108] FSMA, s 103. The definition is contained in s 118C. See Chapter 10 below.

conduct relating to inside information contained in FSMA, s 118, Part 5 of the Criminal Justice Act 1993 and instruments such as the City Code on Takeovers and Mergers.

8.52 The FSA has fined various issuers for not disclosing inside information. In, for example, *Woolworths*,[109] the inside information in question was a variation in a supply contract that was likely to reduce the annual profit by about 10 per cent for 29 days. When this was announced, it resulted in a fall in the share price.

8.53 As an important qualification to the duty to disclose inside information, the DTR specify the circumstances in which an issuer may delay the disclosure of inside information in order not to prejudice its 'legitimate interests', which include the situation where the issuer is conducting negotiations.[110] The delay is only permitted where it will not mislead the public, any person who receives the information owes the issuer a duty of confidentiality, and the issuer is able to ensure the confidentiality of the information.[111] The DTR also impose obligations with respect to matters such as the control of inside information and 'insider lists'.[112]

8.54 Under DTR 3, 'persons discharging management responsibility', that is, directors or certain senior executives,[113] and their 'connected persons' within the meaning of the Companies Act 1985, s 346, must notify the issuer in writing of all transactions for their own account.[114] The issuer is, in turn, required to disclose such information and other information specified in the DTR.[115]

8.55 In case of a breach of the disclosure rules, the FSA may suspend trading in the financial instrument in question.[116]

3. Transparency obligations

8.56 Section 89A of the FSMA gives the FSA the power to make rules implementing the TD. The purpose of the TD is to enhance the amount and quality of information available about issuers, making it easier for existing and prospective investors to make informed investment decisions with respect to securities of an issuer, that is to buy, hold or sell those securities.

8.57 Relying on s 89A, the FSA has made DTR 4, which deals with financial reporting and sets out the requirements for annual financial reports,[117] half-yearly financial reports,[118] interim financial statements,[119] and the exemptions from these requirements.[120] In the context of financial reporting, FSMA s 90A is also important: s 90A imposes civil liability

---

[109] FSA Final Notice, 8 June 2008.
[110] See DTR 2.5.3R.
[111] DTR 2.5.1R and MAD, art 6(2) and (3). DTR 2.5.6 deals with the position where there is selective disclosure.
[112] DTR 2.3 to 2.4 and 2.6 to 2.8.
[113] FSMA, s 96B.
[114] DTR 3.1.2R and MAD, art 6(4).
[115] DTR 3.1.4.
[116] FSMA, s 96C.
[117] DTR 4.1. See TD, art 4.
[118] DTR 4.2. See TD, art 5.
[119] DTR 4.3. See TD, art 6.
[120] DTR 4.4. See TD, art 8.

on issuers in relation to reports and statements published in response to requirements under provisions implementing TD, arts 4, 5, and 6.[121]

FSMA, ss 89B to 89E give the FSA the power to make rules requiring: the notification of voteholder information to the issuer or the public, an issuer to publicise information or to notify the FSA, the notification of voting rights in itself held by an issuer, and the notification of amendments to an issuer's constitution. Relying on these powers and FSMA s 89A, the FSA has made DTR 5 and 6.

8.58

DTR 5 sets out the voteholder and notification rules. It contains provisions governing: the notification of the acquisition or disposal of major shareholdings and major proportions of voting rights and notifications of voting rights arising from the holding of certain financial instruments. [122] The notification thresholds for a UK issuer, that is, where the percentage of voting rights reaches, falls or exceeds the relevant amount as a result of an acquisition or disposal of shares or financial instruments, are three per cent and each one per cent threshold thereafter up to 100 per cent.[123] For these purposes, direct and indirect holdings will be relevant, as will holdings subject to an agreement with a third party as to the exercise of voting rights, the temporary transfer of voting rights, shares held as collateral, voting rights held through a corporate entity, and voting rights held through a nominee or trust arrangement.[124] DTR 5 also sets out provisions governing the aggregation of managed holdings;[125] acquisitions and disposals by issuers of shares;[126] disclosures by issuers;[127] notifications of combined holdings;[128] and the various procedures associated with these notifications.[129]

8.59

DTR 6 governs the obligations of issuers to provide information on their shares and debt securities and includes requirements to notify proposed amendments to its constitution and to ensure equality of treatment of shareholders.[130]

8.60

The FSMA gives the FSA the power to call for information from various persons, including an issuer in respect of whom the DTR have effect, a voteholder or an auditor of an issuer or voteholder where such information is reasonably required by the FSA in connection with the transparency rules.[131] The FSA can establish requirements as to form and verification/authentication, and can ask for explanations as to the content of documents.[132] The FSMA also gives the FSA powers with respect to publication.[133]

8.61

The FSA has various powers which it can exercise in the case of the infringement of a transparency obligation, including the power to censure an issuer or to suspend or prohibit trading in its securities.[134]

8.62

---

[121] For discussion, see Ferran, n 1, pp 467 to 470.
[122] DTR 5.1 to 5.3. See TD, arts 9 to 11.
[123] DTR 5.1.2R and TD, art 9(1) and (2).
[124] DTR 5.1.2R and TD, art 10(a) to (h).
[125] DTR 5.4. See TD, arts 10, 12 and 23.
[126] DTR 5.5.
[127] DTR 5.6.
[128] DTR 5.7.
[129] DTR 5.8 to 5.11.
[130] DTR 6.1. See TD, arts 16 to 19.
[131] FSMA, s 89H.
[132] FSMA, s 89I. See, for example, DTR 5.8.10 and DTR 5.10.1.
[133] FSMA, s 89J.
[134] FSMA, ss 89K to 89N.

4. Corporate governance

8.63   Section 89O of the FSMA empowers the FSA to make corporate governance rules in connection with any community obligation relating to the corporate governance of issuers admitted or seeking admission to trading on a regulated market. Relying on s 89O, the FSA has made DTR 7 which governs the requirement for an issuer to appoint an audit committee,[135] and the requirement to include a corporate governance statement containing specific information in its directors' report.[136] Any rules made under s 89O may not impose greater burdens on foreign-traded issuers than those imposed under these rules and the listing rules on issuers admitted or seeking admission to trading on a regulated market in the UK.[137]

G. COMPENSATION, PENALTIES, AND INVESTIGATIONS

1. Compensation

8.64   Any person responsible for listing particulars or a prospectus is liable to pay compensation to any person who has acquired securities to which the particulars or prospectus apply and has suffered loss as a result of any untrue or misleading statement in the particulars or prospectus or the omission of any matter which should otherwise have been set out in the particulars or prospectus.[138]

8.65   For listing particulars, the persons responsible are set out in the OSLR.[139] For a prospectus, the persons responsible are identified in PR 5.5 and include the issuer, anyone assuming responsibility in the prospectus, and each person who has authorised the contents of the prospectus.[140]

8.66   The claim is open not only to original subscribers but also to subsequent purchasers provided that they can show that there is a causal link between the particulars or prospectus and the loss.[141]

8.67   Any claim is subject to certain exceptions, which include the person responsible for the listing particulars or prospectus reasonably believing that the listing particulars or prospectus was accurate.[142]

8.68   These statutory liabilities are without prejudice to any other liability that may arise.[143] In this respect, a person responsible for a prospectus may also be liable to a claim for rescission and claims in contract and tort.[144]

---

[135] DTR 7.1. The relevant obligations are contained in the Audit Directive (2006/43/EC), art 41.

[136] DTR 7.2. The relevant obligations are contained in the Fourth Company Law Directive (78/660/EEC), art 46a.

[137] FSMA, s 89O(3) and (4).

[138] FSMA, s 90.

[139] See paragraph 8.21 above.

[140] See PR 5.5.4 R.

[141] See Ferran, n 1, pp 450 to 452.

[142] FSMA, Sch 10.

[143] FSMA, s 90(6).

[144] See Ferran, n 1, pp 445 to 450.

2. Penalties

Penalties may be imposed by the FSA on any person (issuer or applicant for listing) who has breached any Part 6 rule.[145] This includes present and former directors who have been knowingly involved in such a breach.[146] Penalties are to be paid directly to the FSA. No proceedings for a penalty may be started after two years from the date on which the FSA knew of the contravention or of the circumstances from which the contravention could reasonably be inferred.[147] 8.69

Where a penalty is to be imposed, the FSA must follow the warning and decision notice procedures and the person affected by the penalty may refer the matter to the Tribunal.[148] 8.70

The FSA's policy with regard to the imposition of penalties and amount is set out in DEPP 6. Criteria on amount include the seriousness of the contravention, the mental element (deliberate or reckless) and whether the person was an individual. The penalty is otherwise unlimited, and, once paid to the FSA, has to be applied for the benefit of issuers of listed securities.[149] 8.71

3. Investigations

The FSA may appoint one or more persons to conduct an investigation where it considers that there has been a breach of the Listing Rules or requirements of the FSMA with regard to registration or publication of prospectuses or the advertising rules.[150] This may include situations where a director of an issuer or applicant company has been involved with a breach of the rules.[151] 8.72

---

[145] FSMA, s 91(1).
[146] FSMA, s 91(2).
[147] FSMA, s 91(6).
[148] FSMA, s 92. FSMA, ss 93 to 94 deal with the FSA's policy on penalties.
[149] FSMA, s 100(2).
[150] FSMA, s 97.
[151] FSMA, s 92(1)(b) and (c).

9

CONTROL OF BUSINESS TRANSFERS

David Simpson

A. Introduction	9.01
B. Control of Business Transfers	9.02

A. INTRODUCTION

Part 7 of the Financial Services and Markets Act 2000 (FSMA) provides a scheme for 9.01
effecting, with the approval of the court, transfers of insurance business (that is, rights
and liabilities under contracts of insurance), or of banking business (that is, rights and
liabilities of deposit takers to depositors). Section 104 provides that no such transfer
is to have effect unless the court has sanctioned it by order made under s 111(1). This
section has only been brought into force for the purpose of insurance business transfers.[1]
However, banks have the option of effecting transfers of banking business through the
same procedures and may find it simpler to do so.

B. CONTROL OF BUSINESS TRANSFERS

'Insurance business transfer' is defined in section 105. Essentially, it involves any scheme 9.02
to transfer the whole or part of a firm's insurance business to another firm where (a) the
transferor is a UK authorised person and the business is carried one in one or more
European Economic Area (EEA) states, or (b) the business is reinsurance carried on in
the UK, or (c) the business is carried on in the UK and the transferor is neither a UK
authorised person nor an EEA firm. Five excluded cases are specified including schemes
where the authorised person is a friendly society (where transfers are governed by Part 8
and Sch 15 of the Friendly Societies Act 1992), transfers of pure reinsurance business
to which each affected policyholder has consented (provided that a certificate of post-
transfer solvency is obtained from the relevant authority), and compromises or arrangements to which Part 27 of the Companies Act 2006 applies. Section 232 of the FSMA
and the Financial Services and Markets Act 2000 (Control of Transfers of Business Done

---

[1] SI 2001/3538, art 2(1)(2).

at Lloyd's) Order 2001 (SI 2001/3626) apply Part 7, with some modifications, to transfers of business from members of Lloyds.

9.03   'Banking business transfer' is defined in s 106. Essentially, this involves a transfer of the whole of part of the banking business of either (a) a UK authorised firm to any other body whether or not the transferor carries on the business in the UK, or (b) an authorised person that is not a UK authorised person to another body that will carry it on in the UK. Schemes involving building societies and credit unions are excluded, as are compromises or arrangements to which Part 27 of the Companies Act 2006 applies.

9.04   Section 107(2) permits an application be made by either or both of the transferor and transferee. Usually both apply to the Court by way of Part 8 Claim Form.

9.05   Under powers granted by Section 108, the Treasury has imposed certain procedural requirements on applicants for business transfers.[2] Thus applicants are required (subject to any waiver of the rules by the court) to publicise the intended transfer in various newspapers and to provide various documents to the Financial Services Authority (FSA) and to any person who requests them.

9.06   Insurance business transfer applications must be accompanied by a 'scheme report' whose author and form have been approved by the FSA (s 109). SUP 18 contains guidance on the skills and experience expected of the author (referred to as the 'independent expert') and guidance on the form of the scheme report.

9.07   The FSA and any person who alleges that he may be adversely affected by the scheme have a right to be heard on the application (s 110). In practice, the FSA participates in almost all insurance business transfer hearings and has, on one occasion, voiced opposition to the granting of the scheme on the grounds of inadequate disclosure to policyholders.[3] Schedule 12 of the FSMA requires the applicants to obtain certificates of solvency and of consent/non-objection from the FSA and/or relevant EEA regulators.

9.08   Once all of the above formalities are complied with, the court may sanction the transfer if, 'in all the circumstances of the case' it is 'appropriate' to do so: section 111(1). The court thus considers 'whether the scheme as a whole is fair as between the interests of the different classes of persons affected'; however, it does not need to be satisfied that 'no better scheme could have been devised'.[4]

9.09   The effect of sanctioning the scheme is to transfer the relevant business to the transferee; policyholders or depositors are thereafter treated as if they had always been the customers of the transferee. The court has power to make ancillary orders under section 112 to give practical effect to the transfer by, for example, ordering that legal proceedings brought against the transferor are to be continued against the transferee.

---

    [2] Financial Services and Markets Act 2000 (Control of Business Transfers) (Requirements on Applicants) Regulations 2001.
    [3] Re Windsor Life Assurance Company Ltd [2007] EWHC 3429 (Ch); Folio 6958 of 2007.
    [4] Re London Life Association Limited 21 February 1989 (unreported) per Hoffman LJ at paragraphs 6 and 7; applied by Evans-Lombe J in Re Axa Equity & Law Life Assurance Society plc and Axa Sun Life plc [2001] 1 All ER (Comm) 1010—considering the similar discretion previously exercised under Schedule 2C of the Insurance Companies Act 1982.

10

PENALTIES FOR MARKET ABUSE

Helen Marshall

A. INTRODUCTION

One of the most innovative and controversial aspects of the Financial Services and Markets Act 2000 (FSMA) was the inclusion of provisions concerning market abuse.   10.01

Financial markets must be protected from abuse or malpractice. Otherwise, their effective operation would be significantly damaged. Liquidity and efficiency would be undermined and the stability and continued development and prosperity of the economy as a whole threatened.   10.02

In attempting to control abusive practice, the interests of legitimate market participants in the conduct of normal trading operations must also be fully protected. Without the maintenance of a free and open market place, competition and innovation would be constrained. A correct balance must accordingly be secured between the prohibition of illegitimate market activity and the protection of normal trading practices. It is in achieving this balance that most of the difficulties surrounding the introduction of the market abuse regime arose during its drafting.   10.03

The market abuse provisions are set out in Part 8 of the FSMA. Their objective is to make the operation of the markets more open, transparent and fair through the penalisation of various forms of behaviour considered to constitute market abuse or malpractice.   10.04

B. MARKET OFFENCES

10.05   The introduction of penalties for market abuse was considered necessary to correct the perceived omissions in the earlier legislative framework which existed in the United Kingdom. The original objective was to create a new civil regime to parallel the various criminal controls which were already in place. The market abuse regime was intended to include a greater number of abuses while at the same time allowing a wider range of more relevant penalties to be imposed, correcting the perceived deficiencies in the patchwork of criminal offences which previously dealt with market abuse.

10.06   It was not intended that the FSMA would repeal all of the existing criminal provisions which apply to market conduct and market offences. Indeed, the practical effect of many of the criminal provisions has been extended by allowing the Financial Services Authority (FSA) to undertake criminal prosecutions itself. The objective of the market abuse measures is to create a new parallel quasi-civil regime to act as a complement or supplement to the criminal provisions in operation.

C. DRAFTING AND REVISION

10.07   The history of the drafting of what is now Part 8 of the FSMA reflects the difficulties which arise in attempting to establish an appropriate level of control over abusive practices in the financial services area.

10.08   The provisions in the original Bill were materially amended, in particular, in response to concerns with regard to legal certainty and to compliance with the European Convention on Human Rights. Other critics questioned the basic idea of creating a new civil regime and suggested that the only change needed was to revise and extend the existing criminal provisions, but this was rejected by the government.

10.09   A Joint Committee on Financial Services and Markets was then set up to consider a number of the provisions in the Bill, which it did in its First and Second Reports. These were followed by the government response document of June 1999. In its First Report of 27 April 1999 (House of Commons Papers, Session 1998–99, 328), the Joint Committee questioned the perceived lack of certainty of the proposed regime, in particular, with regard to the general drafting of the original clause 56, the absence of any intent requirement and the lack of any statutory safe harbour for conduct in compliance with the FSA's proposed Code of Market Conduct which was to be issued under the FSMA. The report also doubted the fairness of the new regime and its compatibility with the European Convention on Human Rights.

10.10   The possibility of infringement of the European Convention on Human Rights was considered separately in a joint opinion by Lord Lester of Herne Hill QC and Javan Herberg to the Joint Committee. Incorporation of the Convention into United Kingdom law by the Human Rights Act 1998 means that from October 2000, the courts were required to construe legislation in a manner compatible with the Convention as far as possible and that the FSA will be potentially liable in damages for any breach of Convention rights (FSMA, Sch 1, para 19).

10.11   Although the draft Bill had attempted to classify the disciplinary and market abuse offences as civil, the report of the Joint Committee considered that most, if not all, would, in fact, be criminal in nature for the purposes of the Convention. Article 6 would then require that there had to be an independent and impartial court and a fair trial, involving equality of arms, the right to proper legal assistance and full protection of the presumption of innocence and privilege against self-incrimination. Article 7 also requires that the offence charged must be clearly defined in law, while art 4 of Protocol 7 (which is not incorporated into UK law by the Human Rights Act 1998) may prevent dual prosecution under the criminal law and the market abuse provisions of the FSMA.

The government subsequently took advice from Sir Sidney Kentridge QC and   10.12
James Eadie and announced a series of changes to the Bill to increase certainty and reduce the possibility of a successful challenge under the Convention. Following further review and amendments, the market abuse regime contained within the FSMA came into effect.

Significant changes were made to Part 8 of the FSMA in 2005, to align it with the   10.13
European Market Abuse Directive[1] and its implementing measures. These changes were brought in through the Financial Services and Markets Act 2000 (Market Abuse) regulations 2005.[2] When implementing the Directive, the government retained the definition of a 'regular user' of the market and the two UK super-equivalent provisions which went beyond the scope of the Directive, but made them subject to a 'sunset clause' with an expiry date of 30 June 2008. Following a consultation process in 2008, these provisions have been retained until 31 December 2009.[3] There is also to be a European Commission review of the Directive, expected to report in 2009.

D. FRAMEWORK FOR MARKET ABUSE REGIME

The statutory definition of market abuse is set out in FSMA, s 118(1).   10.14

While drafted as seven behaviours (FSMA, s 118(2) to (8)), the concept of market   10.15
abuse is essentially based on the failure to uphold relevant standards in the two particular areas of activity referred to in FSMA, s 118. The first of these (FSMA, s 118(2) to (4)) will generally apply to information misuse (such as insider trading or improper disclosure), and the latter (FSMA, s 118(5) to (8)) to most instances of market manipulation (such as manipulating transactions). The first can also be considered to be more use based or passive in operation while the second involves some more immediate or direct form of active market manipulation. The seven behaviours are developed further in the FSA's Code of Market Conduct (the Code) which is considered further below.

The FSA is empowered to impose penalties under FSMA, s 123(1) on persons who   10.16
are or have engaged in market abuse.

The FSA may impose a penalty on any person who either is or has engaged in market   10.17
abuse (FSMA, s 123(1)(a)) or has required or encouraged another to do so by taking or refraining from taking any particular action (FSMA, s 123(1)(b)). In determining whether a penalty is to be imposed, account must be taken of the extent to which the

---

[1] Directive 2003/6/EC of the European Parliament and the Council of 28 January 2003.
[2] SI 2005/385.
[3] SI 2008/1439 The Financial Services and Markets Act 2000 (Market Abuse) Regulations 2008. FSMA, s 118(9).

person (or persons) believed, on reasonable grounds, that their behaviour did not amount to market abuse or to requiring or encouraging another to behave in that way (FSMA, s 123(2)(a)), or took all reasonable precautions and exercised all due diligence to avoid engaging in market abuse or requiring or encouraging another to do so (FSMA, s 123(2)(b)). The FSA may issue a public censure rather than impose a financial penalty (FSMA, s 123(3)). The imposition of a penalty under Part 8 will not render any transaction void or unenforceable (FSMA, s 131).

10.18   While the purpose or objective of the conduct may be taken into account to determine whether a defence may be available under FSMA, s 123(2), the abusive behaviours specified under FSMA, s 118 do not require the person engaging in the behaviour to have intended to commit market abuse (MAR 1.2.3G). As such, consideration of alleged market abuse is conducted on an objective rather than subjective basis looking to effect rather than intent.

1. Code of Market Conduct

10.19   Section 119(1) of the FSMA requires the FSA to prepare and issue a code for the purpose of determining whether or not particular behaviour amounts to market abuse.

10.20   The Code sets out the standards of conduct expected of those using prescribed markets. The purpose is to assist market participants to identify relevant standards of conduct which, if complied with, will avoid market abuse and to assist persons to determine whether they are required by SUP 15.10 to report a transaction to the FSA as a suspicious one (MAR 1.1.2G).

10.21   Although it was originally intended that the Code would only have evidentiary weight, the government subsequently decided, in response to parliamentary pressure, that compliance would constitute a full defence against any allegation of market abuse. This is now provided for in FSMA, s 122(1). The status of these MAR provisions is designated as 'C' (that is, 'conclusive' status).

10.22   The Code sets out a number of activities which the FSA considers will constitute market abuse. The Code is, however, neither conclusive nor exhaustive. Whether a particular activity constitutes market abuse is for the FSA to determine on a case-by-case basis, subject to recourse to the Financial Services and Markets Tribunal and possibly to the courts. Conduct not set out in the Code may still amount to market abuse for the purposes of the FSMA. FSMA, s 122(2) accordingly provides that the Code may be relied on insofar as it indicates whether or not behaviour should be taken to amount to market abuse. The Code is thus only evidential with regard to breaches (FSMA, s 122(2)), but conclusive with regard to exemptions (FSMA, s 122(1)).

10.23   The Code begins by defining the application of the Code (MAR1.1) and providing guidance on the scope of the market abuse regime (1.2). It then provides detailed guidance on the seven behaviours constituting market abuse (MAR 1.3 to MAR 1.9).

2. Scope of Market Abuse Regime

10.24   Section 118(1) of the FSMA sets out the broad scope of the market abuse regime. Key aspects of the scope of the market abuse regime are expanded on elsewhere in Part 8 of the FSMA and the Code and are described below.

(a) *Scope of investments*

The scope of the market abuse regime is limited to behaviour in relation to a specific 10.25
class of investments. Section 118(1) of the FSMA specifies that behaviour in relation to
qualifying investments traded on a prescribed market or qualifying investments for
which a request for admission to trading on such a market has been made are captured
by the market abuse regime. With regard to the insider trading/improper disclosure
provisions in ss 118(2) and (3), the FSMA specifies that investments which are related
investments to qualifying investments are also included in the regime.

Prescribed markets and qualifying investments are defined in the Financial Services 10.26
and Markets Act 2000 (Prescribed Markets and Qualifying Investments) Order 2001.
Prescribed markets include regulated UK Recognised Investment Exchanges and the
OFEX market (now PLUS[4]). Qualifying investments are defined by reference to the
definition of 'financial instrument' in the Market Abuse Directive (for example, transferable securities and units in collective investment undertakings).

(b) *Behaviour*

Behaviour includes any action or inaction (FSMA, s 130A(3)). FSA guidance states that 10.27
failure to act will be indicative of 'behaviour', if it involves failing to discharge a legal or
regulatory obligation or if the person's representations have created a reasonable expectation of him acting in a particular manner, those representations are no longer correct,
and he has failed to inform people whom he is under a duty or obligation to inform that
the representations are no longer correct (MAR 1.2.6E).

Market abuse may be behaviour by one person alone or with one or more other per- 10.28
sons either acting jointly or in concert (FSMA, s 118(1)). Under FSMA, s 123(1), market
abuse may also be committed directly or by requiring or encouraging others to do so.
The Code provides some guidance with regard to determining whether a person's conduct or inaction amounts to requiring or encouraging (MAR 1.2.23G). Behaviour may,
for example, amount to market abuse where a director of a company instructs an
employee to deal in qualifying investments or relevant products. Likewise, market abuse
may occur where a person recommends or advises a friend to engage in behaviour which,
if he himself engaged in it, would amount to market abuse.

The FSA also elaborates that behaviour occurring prior to a qualifying investment 10.29
being admitted to trading (see FSMA, s 118(1)(a)(ii)), will generally be caught by the
market abuse regime if a request for admission is subsequently made and if the behaviour continues to have an effect once an application has been made for the qualifying
investment to be admitted for trading (MAR 1.2.5E).

(c) *Territoriality*

Behaviour will be taken into account only if it occurred in the United Kingdom or in 10.30
relation to qualifying investments on a market which is situated in the United Kingdom
or accessible electronically in the United Kingdom (FSMA, s 118(5)).

---

[4] PLUS Markets plc is the correct name of the Recognised Investment Exchange, although the SI has not
been amended.

(d) *Regular user*

10.31   The concept of the regular user is used to define the standard by which misuse of information (FSMA, s 118(4)), and misleading and distortive behaviour is judged under
the market abuse regime (FSMA, s 118(8)). Its meaning and use are developed further
in the Code.

10.32   The regular user is defined in FSMA, s 130A as a reasonable person who regularly
deals on a particular marketing in investments of the kind in question. FSMA, s 118(9)
provides that this definition will cease to have effect on 31 December 2009.[5] The Code
clarifies that the regular user is a hypothetical person, and the standard is an objective
one (while retaining some subjective features of the markets for the investments in
question) (MAR 1.2.21G).

E. BEHAVIOURS CONSTITUTING MARKET ABUSE

10.33   If the threshold criteria regarding type of investments, territoriality, and so on, are met,
conduct must fall within one of the seven behaviours set out in FSMA, s 118(2) to (8)
to constitute market abuse. The seven behaviours are alternative rather than cumulative
for the purposes of the Act and a particular course of conduct may fall within more than
one category. The fundamental elements of each behaviour are described below.

1. Insider dealing

10.34   The first type of activity which constitutes market abuse is insider dealing, which is set
out in FSMA, s 118(2). It is the first of three behaviours which can be broadly described
as information misuse. The provision is elaborated on in MAR 1.3.

10.35   Insider dealing is defined as behaviour 'where an insider deals, or attempts to deal, in
a qualifying investment or related investment on the basis of inside information relating
to the investment in question'.

10.36   The concepts of 'insiders', 'inside information' and acting 'on the basis of' inside information are central to the scope of insider dealing.

(a) *Inside information*

10.37   Inside information is defined as information of a precise nature regarding qualifying
investments, or the issuers of qualifying investments, which is not generally available
and would have a significant effect on the price of either the qualifying investments or
related investments, if generally available (FSMA, s 118C(2)).

10.38   The definition of inside information is in turn dependent on three concepts which are
defined in the FSMA:

• *Precise information.* Information is considered 'precise' if it indicates circumstances
that exist or may reasonably be expected to come into existence (or an event which has
occurred or may reasonably be expected to occur), and, is specific enough to enable a

---

[5] SI 2008/1439 The Financial Services and Markets Act 2000 (Market Abuse) Regulations 2008.

conclusion to be drawn about the possible effect of those circumstances on the price of qualifying investments (or related investments) (FSMA, s 118C(5)).

• *Generally available information.* Section 118C(8) of the FSMA indicates that information which can be obtained by research or analysis conducted by, or on behalf of, users of a market will be 'generally available' for the purposes of the market abuse regime, and therefore is not considered to be inside information. MAR 1.2.12E elaborates on this, providing further factors which will be material to whether or not information is generally available (for example, it is available on the internet or has been disclosed to a prescribed market).

• *Information likely to have a significant effect on price.* The Code defines this as information of a kind which a reasonable investor would be likely to use as part of the basis of his investment decisions (FSMA, s 118C(6)).

The FSMA clarifies that where a person is charged with execution of orders concerning qualifying investments or related investments, inside information includes information conveyed by a client and related to the client's pending orders which relates to one or more issuers of the qualifying investments (FSMA, s 118C(4)). The definition of inside information is modified in respect of commodity derivatives (see FSMA, s 118C(7)).   10.39

(b) *Insider*

An insider is defined in FSMA, s 118B as a person who has inside information as a result of: his membership of an administrative, management or supervisory body of an issuer of qualifying investments; his holding in the capital of an issuer of qualifying investments; or having access to information through the exercise of his employment, profession or duties; or as a result of his criminal activities.   10.40

An insider also includes a person who has obtained inside information by means other than the ones described and which he knows, or could be reasonably expected to know, is inside information (FSMA, s 118B (e)). The Code elaborates on the definition of insider in MAR 1.2.8E.   10.41

(c) 'On the basis of'

A critical aspect of behaviour constituting insider dealing is that the insider deals (or attempts to deal) 'on the basis of' inside information. The Code clarifies that it will be indicative of behaviour 'on the basis of' inside information, where the inside information is the reason for, or a material influence on, the decision to deal/attempt to deal (MAR 1.3.4E).   10.42

The Code also indicates that an insider will not be acting on the basis of inside information, if the decision to deal/attempt to deal was prior to the person possessing the inside information or if the person is dealing to satisfy a legal or regulatory obligation which came into being before he possessed the inside information (MAR 1.3.3E(1) and (2)).   10.43

The Code clarifies that an organisation will not be dealing on the basis of inside information, if none of the individuals with possession of the inside information had any involvement in the decision to deal, behaved in such a way as to influence the decision to deal, or had any contact with those who were involved in the decision to deal (MAR 1.3.3E(3)).   10.44

(d) *Behaviour indicating insider dealing*

10.45   The Code specifies that dealing on the basis of inside information that is not trading information (see safe harbour for market makers at MAR 1.3.7C[6]) or 'front running' will constitute insider dealing (MAR 1.3.2(1) and (2)). 'Front running' occurs where a transaction is executed for a person's own benefit, ahead of an order which he is to carry out with or for another where the order constitutes inside information (and is likely to have a significant effect on price). The transaction intends to take advantage of the anticipated impact of the order on the market price.

10.46   The Code also specifies that certain behaviours in the context of a takeover bid will constitute market abuse (MAR 1.3.2(3) and (4)). The first of these is where an offeror/potential offeror, enters into a transaction in a qualifying investment on the basis of inside information concerning the proposed bid, that provides an economic exposure to movements in the price of the target company's shares (for example, a spread bet on the target company's share price). The second is where a person who acts for the offeror/potential offeror deals for his own benefit in qualifying investments or related investments on the basis of information concerning the proposed bid which is inside information.

(e) *Safe harbours*

10.47   The Code specifies a number of scenarios where dealing on the basis of inside information will not constitute market abuse (safe harbours). These are:

- *Market makers.* A transaction by a person that may lawfully deal in qualifying investments or related investments on their own account (for example market makers), will not of itself amount to insider dealing, where he is pursuing the legitimate business of such dealing (including entering into an agreement for the underwriting of an issue of financial instruments) (MAR 1.3.7C). This safe harbour applies even if the person possesses trading information which is inside information (MAR 1.3.8G). Indicators of whether or not a person's behaviour is in pursuit of a legitimate business are described in MAR 1.3.10E and 1.3.11E (including whether the person's transaction has no significant effect on price, or whether the person acted in contravention of a relevant legal, regulatory or exchange obligation).

- *Execution of client orders.* MAR 1.3.12C states that dutiful carrying out (or arranging for the carrying out) of an order on behalf of clients (including as portfolio manager) will not in itself amount to insider dealing by the person carrying out the order. The FSA has indicated that where inside information held by a person executing client orders is not limited to trading information, this will be indicative that the behaviour is not dutiful carrying out of an order on behalf of a client (MAR 1.3.14E).
  Indicators of whether a person's behaviour is dutiful execution of an order on behalf of another are set out in MAR 1.3.15E (for example, where behaviour is in compliance with FSA conduct of business obligations or equivalent rules in another jurisdiction or where the behaviour was with a view to facilitating or ensuring the effective carrying out of the order).

---

[6] 'Trading information' is a defined term in the FSA Handbook Glossary.

- *Takeover and merger activity.* The Code indicates that behaviour based on inside information for the purposes of gaining control of the target company or effecting a merger
with that company, will not of itself amount to insider dealing under certain circumstances. The Code also clarifies that inside information in this context relates to
information that an offeror or potential offeror is considering/going to make an offer
for a company or alternatively, information gained through due diligence by the offeror (MAR 1.3.18G).

Indicators that behaviour does not constitute insider dealing in relation to takeover
and merger activity are set out in MAR 1.3.17C (for example, where an irrevocable
undertaking or expression of support to accept an offer is sought from holders of securities issued by the target).
Examples of insider dealing are contained in MAR 1.3.20G to 1.3.23G.

2. Improper disclosure

Improper disclosure is the second of the market abuse behaviours which can be broadly   10.48
described as information misuse (FSMA, s 118(3)). Improper disclosure is defined as
behaviour where 'an insider discloses inside information to another person otherwise
than in the proper course of the exercise of his employment or profession or duties'
(FSMA, s 118(3)). It is distinct from insider dealing in that no dealing is required to
constitute the offence. The mere fact of disclosure of inside information in specified
circumstances is sufficient to constitute market abuse.

(a) *Behaviour indicating improper disclosure*
The Code indicates that disclosure of inside information by the director of an issuer to   10.49
another in a social context or the selective briefing of analysts (that is, not whole market
disclosure) by directors of issuers or persons discharging managerial responsibilities, will
amount to improper disclosure (MAR 1.4.2E).

(b) *Safe harbours*
The Code indicates that disclosures made to a government department or regulatory   10.50
body (including the Bank of England, Competition Commission, and Takeover Panel)
for the purposes of fulfilling a legal or regulatory obligation or in connection with the
performance of the functions of that body will not constitute improper disclosure
(MAR 1.4.3C). Similarly, any disclosure required or permitted under Part 6 Rules of the
FSMA (Official Listing) or similar regulatory obligation will not constitute improper
disclosure (MAR 1.4.4C). Examples of improper disclosure are set out in MAR 1.4.6G
to MAR 1.4.7G.

The Code sets out factors which will indicate that a person has made a disclosure in   10.51
the proper course of the exercise of his employment, profession or duties, and therefore
has not engaged in behaviour which constitutes market abuse (MAR 1.4.5E to 1.4.5AG).
These include where the disclosure is permitted by the rules of a prescribed market, of
the FSA or the Takeover Code (MAR 1.4.5(1) E), where confidentiality agreements
are imposed on the person to whom the information has been disclosed in certain circumstances (for example, seeking advice from professional advisers) (MAR 1.4.5(2)E),

and where disclosure is made in relation to the disposal or acquisition of an investment from the person receiving the information in certain circumstances (MAR 1.4.5(3)E).

3. Misuse of information

10.52 Section 118 (4) of the FSMA sets out the market abuse behaviour of misuse of information. The scope of the provision is expressly drafted to capture behaviour which does not fall within the definition of insider dealing or improper disclosure and acts as a catch-all for behaviour which is of the same nature as insider dealing or improper disclosure.[7]

10.53 Misuse of information is behaviour which is based on information which is not generally available but which, if available to a regular user of the market, would be relevant when deciding the terms on which transactions should be effected and is likely to be regarded by a regular user of the market as a failure to observe the standard of behaviour expected of a person in his position.

10.54 The meaning of the phrases 'generally available' and 'based on' (equivalent to 'on the basis of') are the same as those set out in MAR 1.2.12E to MAR 1.2.13E, and MAR 1.3.3E to MAR 1.3.5E, respectively (MAR 1.5.4E and MAR 1.5.5E).

(a) *Behaviour indicating misuse of information*

10.55 The Code indicates that behaviour which does not amount to insider dealing (for example, information that does not fall within the definition of inside information) will instead constitute misuse of information where dealing or arranging deals in qualifying investments is based on 'relevant information'[8], which is not generally available and relates to matters that a regular user would reasonably expect to be disclosed to users of the particular prescribed market (MAR 1.5.2E(1)).

10.56 The Code also indicates that behaviour which does not amount to improper disclosure will constitute misuse of information where a director giving relevant information, which is not generally available and relates to matters which a regular user would reasonably expect to be disclosed to users of the particular prescribed market, to another otherwise than in the proper course of the exercise of his employment or duties (MAR 1.5.2E(2)).

10.57 MAR 1.5.3G outlines other behaviours which are 'capable' of amounting to misuse of information.

10.58 The requirement of whether a regular user would reasonably expect the relevant information to be disclosed to users of the particular prescribed market, is elaborated on in MAR 1.5.7E and is generally where there is a legal or regulatory requirement to disclose to the market or it is usual for this information to be the subject of a public announcement.

---

[7] Section 118(4) retains the definition of market abuse which is broader than that in Directive 2003/6/EC. SI 2008/1439 The Financial Services and Markets Act 2000 (Market Abuse) Regulations 2008 ensure that this and ancillary provisions remain in force until 31 December 2009.

[8] The definition of relevant information is set out in MAR 1.5.6E and is broader than that of inside information.

(b) *Safe harbours*

MAR 1.5.8G states that behaviour falling within the descriptions of behaviour that does not amount to insider dealing (MAR 1.3.6C, MAR 1.3.7C, MAR 1.3.12C and MAR 1.3.17C), also do not amount to misuse of information, if the references in those descriptions to inside information included a reference to relevant information. 10.59

Examples of misuse of information are contained in MAR 1.5.10E. 10.60

4. Manipulating transactions

The first market manipulation offence under the FSMA is referred to as 'manipulating transactions' and is set out in s 118(5). This behaviour consists of 'effecting transactions or orders to trade other than for legitimate reasons and in conformity with accepted market practices on the relevant market', which manipulate the market in one of two ways. The first is where the transactions give a false or misleading impression as to the supply of, or demand for, or as to the price of one or more qualifying investments. The second is where the transactions secure the price of one or more qualifying investments at an abnormal or artificial level. 10.61

(a) *Legitimate reasons*

The concept of transactions not being for 'legitimate reasons' is a fundamental element of a manipulating transaction. MAR 1.6.5E specifies that transactions will not be for legitimate reasons where the person's purpose behind the transaction is to induce others to trade in, or to position or move the price of, a qualifying investment; the person has another, illegitimate, reason behind the transactions or order to trade; or if the transaction was executed in a particular way with the purpose of creating a false or misleading impression. 10.62

Indicators of where transactions will be for legitimate reasons are set out in MAR 1.6.6E (for example, where the transaction is pursuant to a prior legal or regulatory obligation owed to a third party). 10.63

The Code also clarifies that normal self interested behaviour and volatility in the markets will not of themselves be indicative of manipulating transactions (MAR 1.6.7G and MAR 1.6.8G). 10.64

(b) *Behaviour indicating manipulating transactions*

The Code indicates that the following trading will constitute manipulating transactions which give a false or misleading impression when engaged in other than for legitimate reasons (MAR 1.6.2E): buying or selling qualifying investments at the close of the market with the effect of misleading investors who act on the basis of closing price; sale or purchase of a qualifying investment where there is no change in beneficial interest or market risk (wash trades); entering into a series of transactions that are shown on a public display for the purpose of giving the impression of activity or price movement in a qualifying investment (painting the tape); and entering orders into an electronic trading system above or below the previous offer, and withdrawing them before they are executed, in order to give a misleading impression of the demand for/supply of the qualifying investment at that price. 10.65

The Code indicates that the following trading will constitute manipulating transactions, in relation to giving a false or misleading impression about the price of an 10.66

investment other than where they are entered into for legitimate reasons (MAR 1.6.4E): transactions that secure a dominant position over the supply of or demand for a qualifying investment and which have the effect of fixing—directly or indirectly—purchase or sale prices or creating other unfair trading conditions; simultaneous buy/sell transactions of a security at the same price by the same party/colluding parties which offset market risk; entering small orders into an electronic trading system, at prices which are higher than the previous bid or lower than the previous offer, in order to move the price of the qualifying investment; an abusive squeeze;[9] parties with holdings in a primary offering, purchasing further holdings to force up the price of the investments and attract interest from other investors before selling the qualifying investments; transactions employed so as to create obstacles to the price falling below a certain level; and trading on one market or trading platform with a view to improperly influencing the price of the same or a related qualifying investment that is traded on another prescribed market.

10.67   MAR 1.6.9E and MAR 1.6.10E set out a number of factors which will indicate whether or not manipulating transactions have occurred (for example, whether transactions lead to a beneficial change in ownership, or the extent to which orders to trade given or transactions undertaken are concentrated within a short time span in the trading session and lead to a price change which is subsequently reversed).

10.68   Examples of manipulating transactions are set out in MAR 1.6.15 to MAR 1.6.16E.

5. Manipulating devices

10.69   Behaviour constituting use of manipulating devices is set out in FSMA, s 118(6) and covers transactions effected or orders to trade which employ fictitious devices or any other form of deception or contrivance.

(a) *Behaviour indicating use of manipulative devices*

10.70   The Code indicates that the following behaviours will constitute use of manipulating devices (MAR 1.7.2E): voicing an opinion in the media about a qualifying investment, while having previously taken positions on that qualifying investment and profiting from the impact of the opinions voiced on the price of that instrument without having disclosed the conflict of interest properly; a transaction or series of transactions that are designed to conceal the underlying ownership of a qualifying investment, so that disclosure requirements are circumvented (not including nominee holdings); taking a long position in a qualifying investment and then disseminating misleading positive information about the qualifying investment with a view to increasing its price ('pump and dump'); and taking a short position in a qualifying investment and then disseminating misleading negative information about the qualifying investment, with a view to driving down its price ('trash and cash').

---

[9] An abusive squeeze occurs where a person has a significant influence over the supply of, or demand for, or delivery mechanisms for a qualifying investment related investment; has a position in an investment under which quantities of the qualifying investment (or related investment) are deliverable and engages in behaviour with the purpose of positioning at a distorted level the price at which others have to deliver, take delivery or defer delivery to satisfy their obligations in relation to a qualifying investment. See MAR 1.6.11E to 1.6.13G for further factors in relation to an abusive squeeze.

MAR 1.7.3E sets out the factors to be taken into account in determining whether manipulating devices have been used (for example, whether transactions entered into by persons are preceded or followed by the dissemination of false information, or research or investment recommendations which are erroneous or biased).

10.71

6. Dissemination of false or misleading information

Section 118 (7) of the FSMA defines the market abuse behaviour of dissemination of false or misleading information as behaviour constituted by the dissemination of information by any means which gives, or is likely to give, a false or misleading impression as to a qualifying investment by a person who knew or could reasonably be expected to have known that the information was false or misleading. There is no requirement for the person to profit from the dissemination of information.

10.72

Section 118A(4) of the FSMA clarifies that a journalist who disseminates false or misleading information is to be assessed by the codes governing his profession unless he derives any advantage or profits from the dissemination of the information.

10.73

(a) Behaviours indicating dissemination of false or misleading information

MAR 1.8.3E indicates that spreading false or misleading information about a qualifying investment through the media/RIS or undertaking a course of conduct which will give a false or misleading impression about a qualifying investment, will amount to dissemination of false or misleading information.

10.74

The Code indicates that it will be indicative of dissemination of false and misleading information if a 'normal and reasonable person' would know or should have known that the behaviour was false and misleading (MAR 1.8.4). Conversely, where the knowledge that the information being disseminated was false or misleading could only be determined by crossing an information barrier within an organisation (for example, a Chinese wall), it will be indicative that the behaviour was not dissemination of false or misleading information.

10.75

Examples of disseminating false or misleading information are set out in MAR 1.8.6E.

10.76

7. Misleading behaviour and distortion

'Misleading behaviour' and 'distortion' have been enacted expressly to cover any residual cases of market manipulation that do not fall within the other specified market abuse behaviours.

10.77

Section 118(8) of the FSMA[10] sets out that where behaviour does not fall within the manipulating transactions, manipulative devices and dissemination of false or misleading information behaviours, it may still constitute misleading behaviour or distortion. The FSMA states that behaviour will constitute 'misleading behaviour' where it is likely to give a regular user of the market, a false or misleading impression as to the

10.78

---

[10] FSMA, s 118 (8) retains a definition of market abuse which is broader than that in Directive 2003/6/EC. SI 2008/1439 The Financial Services and Markets Act 2000 (Market Abuse) Regulations 2008 provides that FSMA, s 118(8) and ancillary provisions will remain in force until 31 December 2009.

supply of, demand for, or price or value of qualifying investments. Alternatively, behaviour will constitute distortion where it would be regarded by a regular user of the market as behaviour that could distort or would be likely to distort the market in such an investment.

10.79 For behaviour to constitute 'misleading behaviour' or 'distortion', it is also necessary that the behaviour is likely to be regarded by a regular user of the market to be a failure to observe the standard of behaviour reasonably expected of someone of that position in the market.

(a) *Behaviour indicating misleading behaviour*

10.80 MAR 1.9.2E indicates that the movement of physical commodity stocks or the movement of an empty cargo ship will constitute misleading behaviour, if it might create a false or misleading impression as to the supply of, or demand for, or the price or value of a commodity or deliverable into a commodity futures contract.

10.81 As a result of market turmoil in 2008, several provisions were introduced into the Code to address concerns that short selling would drive down the price of vulnerable securities. MAR 1.9.2AE indicates that behaviour will constitute misleading behaviour if there is failure to give adequate disclosure that a person has reached or exceeded a disclosable short position (0.25 per cent of the issued capital of a company) during a rights issue period, where the short position relates to securities which are the subject of a rights issue. The requirements for adequate disclosure are elaborated on in MAR 1.9.2BR.

10.82 At the peak of the global financial crisis in September 2008, the FSA, along with a number of financial regulators around the world, introduced emergency provisions to prevent short selling in financial sector companies. The FSA version of these restrictions was to prohibit the taking up or increase of short positions in UK financial sector companies (MAR 1.9.2CE). This prohibition expired on 15 January 2009, however there is still a requirement to provide adequate ongoing disclosure of a disclosable short position in a UK financial sector company (MAR 1.9.2DE). Non compliance with the requirement will constitute misleading behaviour. Ongoing disclosure requires disclosure to be made each time a short position reaches, exceeds or falls below 0.25, 0.35, 0.45, 0.55 per cent and each additional one per cent thereafter.

10.83 MAR 1.9.4E sets out factors which will indicate whether or not behaviour which is likely to give a regular user a false or misleading impression as to the supply of, demand for or price or value of qualifying investments or related investments (for example, the legal and regulatory requirements of the market concerned and the extent and nature of the visibility/disclosure of the person's activity).

10.84 MAR 1.9.5E sets out the factors to be taken into account in determining whether or not behaviour has also failed to meet the standard expected by a regular user (for example, whether the transaction is pursuant to the legal and regulatory obligations owed to a third party or if the individuals responsible could only have known that they had created a false or misleading information by breaching a Chinese wall).

8. Statutory exceptions

10.85 Statutory exceptions from the market abuse regime are set out in MAR 1.10. Compliance with an exception will mean that the behaviour does not amount to market abuse.

The first exception is in relation to buy-back and stabilisation measures, which allow   10.86
certain activity to support the market price of relevant securities for a predetermined
period of time, under certain circumstances (for example, where a security is under selling pressure) (MAR 1.10.1G). These measures are elaborated on in MAR 1 Annex 1 and
MAR 2.

The second exception is in relation to the control of information rule contained in   10.87
SYSC 10.2.2R (that is, effective segregation of inside information from other parts of an
organisation's activities through information barriers such as Chinese walls), and behaviour conforming with rules relating to Official Listing rules (for example, requirement
around timing, dissemination, announcements, release of information) (MAR 1.10.2G).
Finally, the Code clarifies that behaviour conforming with certain rules of the Takeover
Code will not, of itself, constitute market abuse (MAR 1.10.3G to 1.10.6C).

The statutory exceptions are distinct from the immunity from a penalty created where   10.88
a person has either reasonably believed that behaviour did not constitute market abuse
or took all reasonable precautions and due diligence to avoid engaging in market abuse
(FSMA, s 123(2)(a) and (b)). MAR did previously contain material on this aspect, but
this has been removed.

F. PROCEDURE

Where the FSA proposes to impose a penalty, it must first provide a warning notice,   10.89
which must, in particular, state the amount of the penalty or proposed censure statement
(FSMA, s 126(1), (2) and (3)). This initiates the procedure set out in Part 16 of the Act
(see Chapter 28). If the FSA decides to take action, it must issue a decision notice which
must again state the amount of the penalty or content of the statement (FSMA, s 127(1),
(2) and (3)). This is subject to reference of the matter to the Financial Services and
Markets Tribunal (under FSMA, s 127(4)), which is considered further in Chapter 11.

The FSA may direct any Recognised Investment Exchange or Recognised Clearing   10.90
House to terminate, suspend or limit the scope of any existing inquiry where it considers
it desirable or expedient to do so (FSMA, s 128(1)).

The FSA may also apply to the court under ss 381 or 383 to consider whether the   10.91
circumstances are such that an injunction should be issued to restrain the market abuse
or a restitution order should be made.

G. PENALTIES

On finding that market abuse has occurred, the FSA may impose a financial penalty   10.92
(FSMA, s 123(1)), publish a public censure (FSMA, s 123(3)), apply to the court for an
injunction (FSMA, s 381) or restitution order (FSMA, s 383), or itself order restitution
(FSMA, s 384).

The FSA may apply for an injunction where there is a reasonable likelihood that a   10.93
person may engage in market abuse or where a person has already engaged in market
abuse and there is a reasonable likelihood of him continuing to do so (FSMA, s 381(1))
or where steps could be taken to remedy or mitigate the market abuse (FSMA, s 381(2)

and (6)). A court may also restrain a person from disposing of or otherwise dealing in any assets (FSMA, s 381(3) and (4)).

10.94   A court may order a person to pay to the FSA such sum as may be considered just having regard to the profits accrued or loss or other adverse effect suffered as a result of market abuse (FSMA, s 383(4)). The FSA is to pay the amounts received to such qualifying persons as the court may direct (FSMA, s 383(5)). A qualifying person is a person to whom the profits would otherwise have been attributable or who has suffered the loss or other adverse effect (FSMA, s 383(10)). The court may also require such accounts or other information to be supplied as it may require (FSMA, s 383(6)). The accounts and information may also have to be verified in such manner as the court may direct (FSMA, s 383(7)).

10.95   While the FSA is not obliged to impose any particular penalty in respect of market abuse under FSMA, s 123, it is required to issue a statement of policy with regard to the imposition and amount of penalties and the operation of at least the main basis of the exception regime provided in respect of reasonable belief or reasonable precaution (FSMA, s 124(1) and (3)). The general approach of the FSA to enforcement is considered in Chapters 16, 27, and 29.

10.96   The FSA's proposed approach to sanctions for market abuse is now set out in section 6.2 to 6.5 of its Decision Procedure and Penalties Manual (DEPP). DEPP 6.2 sets out a non-exhaustive list of factors which the FSA will consider in deciding whether to impose sanctions for a general breach of requirements. These include: the nature, seriousness, and impact of the suspected breach; the conduct of the person after the breach; the previous disciplinary record and compliance history of the person; FSA guidance and other published materials; and action taken by the FSA or other regulators in similar cases (DEPP 6.2.1G). For market abuse cases, the FSA will also consider the degree of sophistication of the users of the market in question, the size and liquidity of the market, the susceptibility of the market to market abuse, and the impact that any financial penalty or public censure may have on the financial markets or on the interests of consumers (DEPP 6.2.2G).

10.97   In addition to the general factors, the FSA cannot impose a penalty for market abuse where it is satisfied that there are reasonable grounds on which the person believed his behaviour did not amount to engaging in, requiring or encouraging market abuse, or that he took all reasonable precautions and exercised due diligence (FSMA, s 123(2)). The FSA will consider the factors listed in DEPP 6.3.2G when making this assessment, which include whether: the behaviour was analogous to behaviour described in MAR 1; the person followed published FSA guidance on the behaviour; the behaviour complied with the rules of a prescribed market or other regulatory requirements (including the Takeover Code); the level of knowledge, skill, and experience of the person; the person can demonstrate that the behaviour was engaged in for a legitimate purpose; the behaviour was undertaken following internal consultation/escalation (for example, discussion with line manager); legal or professional advice was sought; and market authorities were consulted.

10.98   If the FSA decides that a penalty is required following the assessment outlined in DEPP 6.2 and 6.3, it will consider the factors in DEPP 6.4 and 6.5 in determining whether a public censure or financial penalty is more appropriate.

Where the same course of conduct may give rise to both a criminal offence and a   10.99
breach of the market abuse provisions, the FSA will consider the factors set out in section 12.8 of the Enforcement Guide (EG) in deciding which is the appropriate course
to pursue. These include: the seriousness of the misconduct; whether there are victims
who have suffered a loss; the extent and nature of the loss; the effect of the misconduct
on the market; the extent of any profits gained or losses avoided by the conduct; whether
the misconduct is likely to be continued or repeated; the person's disciplinary history
for market misconduct; the extent to which reparation has already been made to victims
and systems and controls defects have been rectified; and whether there is a better chance
of reparation to victims through a criminal prosecution.[11]

---

[11] Where a criminal prosecution for market abuse has already commenced or will commence the FSA will
consider the factors in EG 12.4 in deciding whether to take any civil action.

11

HEARINGS AND APPEALS

Helen Marshall

A. INTRODUCTION

Part 9 of the Financial Services and Markets Act 2000 (FSMA) establishes the Financial   11.01
Services and Markets Tribunal (the Tribunal),[1] which is fully independent of the Financial
Services Authority (FSA) and run by the Ministry of Justice. The Tribunal hears cases
referred to it by those who wish to contest the FSA's decisions to issue them with decision
notices and supervisory notices, for example to discipline authorised firms and approved
persons, to vary a firm's permission to conduct certain or all regulated activities, or to
withdraw individual approval.

The FSMA deals with the conduct of Tribunal proceedings in a number of different   11.02
places. First, the Lord Chancellor, who is now the head of the Ministry of Justice, is given
power (under FSMA, s 132(3)) to make rules about the conduct of proceedings before
the Tribunal. The Lord Chancellor of the day exercised this power by way of the Financial
Services and Markets Tribunal Rules 2001[2] (the FSMT Rules). FSMA, Sch 13 and s 133
also make provision about Tribunal proceedings, which to varying degrees are subject to
rules made under FSMA, s 132(3).

Being an independent and impartial tribunal established by law, with full first instance   11.03
jurisdiction, the Tribunal is the principal mechanism in the FSMA for ensuring that

---

[1] See s 132 of the FSMA.
[2] SI 2001/2476 (FSMT Rules).

the administrative-based enforcement process satisfies the requirements of art 6 of the European Convention on Human Rights. The Tribunal is, of course, itself subject to the provisions of the Human Rights Act 1998.

B. COMPOSITION OF THE TRIBUNAL

11.04 FSMA, Sch 13 provides that the Lord Chancellor must appoint a panel of persons to serve as chairmen of the Tribunal, who must be lawyers with a seven-year general qualification in England and Wales or equivalent professional qualifications in Scotland or Northern Ireland (Sch 13, para 3). From that panel, the Lord Chancellor must appoint one person to be President and may appoint one to be Deputy President (FSMA, Sch 13, para 2). The President and Deputy President (if one is appointed) must have 10-year legal qualifications or equivalent.

11.05 The Lord Chancellor must also appoint a lay panel of persons, who appear to him to be 'qualified by experience or otherwise to deal with matters of the kind that may be referred to the Tribunal' (FSMA, Sch 13, para 3(4)). In practice, it appears that the lay panel members have been selected to provide coverage for the Tribunal across a broad range of financial services sectors.

11.06 The terms on which Tribunal members are appointed (including remuneration and expenses) are matters for the Lord Chancellor, who may remove them on the ground of incapacity or misbehaviour (FSMA, Sch 13, paras 4 and 5).

11.07 The Lord Chancellor may appoint staff for the Tribunal to be paid from his own budget (FSMA, Sch 13, para 6).

C. REFERENCES TO THE TRIBUNAL

1. Time limits for references

11.08 FSMA, s 133 and Rule 4(2) of the FSMT Rules provide that a reference to the Tribunal must be made within 28 days of the date a decision notice or supervisory notice is given, or such other period as may be specified in rules of procedure made under FSMA, s 132(3). The period may be extended by the Tribunal, if there is nothing in the rules to the contrary (FSMA, s 133(2)).

2. The FSA's role after the issue of a decision notice

11.09 The FSA must not take the action specified in a decision notice, for example, to impose a penalty, during the period within which the matter could be referred to the Tribunal (FSMA, s 133(9)(a)). If the matter is so referred, the FSA must wait until the matter has been determined by the Tribunal and, if appropriate, any appeal from the Tribunal's decision has been finally determined (FSMA, s 133(9)(b)). This provision does not apply to supervisory notices, some of which can have effect in advance of the decision of the Tribunal.

D. PROCEEDINGS BEFORE THE TRIBUNAL

1. Constitution of the Tribunal

The President of the Tribunal is to make standing arrangements for the selection of 11.10
persons to act as members of the Tribunal for the purposes of a reference (FSMA,
Sch 13, para 7(1)). On any reference at least one member must be from the panel of
chairmen (FSMA, Sch 13, para 7(2)). Where it appears to the Tribunal that a matter
involves a question of fact of special difficulty, it may appoint one or more experts to
assist it (FSMA, Sch 13, para 7(4)).

2. Tribunal procedure

Paragraph 9 of Sch 13 of the FSMA sets out the matters for which rules made under 11.11
s 132(3) may make provision. Practice directions about the Tribunal's procedures are set
out in the FSMT Rules, pursuant to FSMA, Sch 13, para 10. Rule 17(2) of the FSMT
Rules requires that all hearings shall in be public unless the conditions set out in
Rule 17(3) are applicable, which are that the Tribunal is satisfied that a private hearing
is necessary in the interests of morals, public order, national security, the protection of
the private lives of the parties, or due to any unfairness to the applicant or prejudice to
the interests of consumers that might result from a hearing in public.

3. What evidence may the Tribunal consider?

FSMA, s 133(3) states that the Tribunal may consider any evidence relating to the sub- 11.12
ject matter of the reference, whether or not it was available to the FSA at the material
time. Rule 19(3) of the FSMT Rules also states that evidence may be admitted by the
Tribunal whether or not it would be admissible in a court of law and whether or not it
was available to the FSA when taking the referred action.

The Tribunal may summon any person to give evidence or produce documents to it 11.13
(FSMA, Sch 13, para 11(1)) and FSMT Rule 12(1)). Evidence may be taken on oath
(FSMA, Sch 13, para 11(2)). A person who fails to comply with a Tribunal summons or
who interferes with or suppresses documentary evidence is guilty of an offence (FSMA,
Sch 13, para 11(3)). Less serious cases may be dealt with by magistrates imposing the
maximum fine available to them (which is £5,000) (FSMA, Sch 13, para 11(4)). A conviction in the Crown Court may result in a term of up to two years' imprisonment and/
or an unlimited fine (FSMA, Sch 13, para 11(5)).

4. Legal assistance before the Tribunal: coverage of the scheme

Part 9 of the FSMA provides that the Lord Chancellor may by regulations establish a 11.14
scheme governing the provisions of legal assistance in connection with proceedings
before the Tribunal (FSMA, ss 134 and 135). The Lord Chancellor has exercised this
power by way of the Financial Services Markets Tribunal (Legal Assistance) Regulations

2001 (SI 2001/3632) (the Legal Assistance Regulations) and the Financial Services and Markets Tribunal (Legal Assistance) Regulations 2001 (SI 2001/3633).

11.15   There is only one category of person for whom the scheme can make provision, namely, an individual who has, pursuant to FSMA, s 127(4), referred to the Tribunal an FSA decision to impose a penalty or publish a statement in respect of that individual's market abuse under FSMA, s 123 (see FSMA, s 134(3) and Rule 3(2)(b) of the Legal Assistance Regulations). Rules 8–36 of the Legal Assistance Regulations further set out criteria that must be met for the scheme to apply.

5. Legal assistance before the Tribunal: funding the scheme

11.16   The funding arrangements for legal assistance before the Tribunal are contained in s 136 of the FSMA.

11.17   Whilst the Lord Chancellor uses money provided by Parliament, he is able to issue demands to the FSA from time to time to cover the actual or anticipated cost of the scheme. The FSA pays that money to him and he pays it into the Consolidated Fund. In this way, the scheme is effectively self-financing in that the industry rather than the taxpayer can be made to pay for it.

11.18   The FSA has power to make rules requiring authorised firms (or a subset of them) to pay for the scheme. Whilst the market abuse regime applies to authorised and unauthorised market abusers, and is designed to reinforce market confidence as a whole, the costs of the legal assistance scheme are borne only by the authorised community. Indeed, the FSA has discretion to limit the funding to a class of authorised firms.

E. DECISIONS OF THE TRIBUNAL

1. What is the Tribunal's role?

11.19   FSMA, s 133(4), provides that it is for the Tribunal to determine what, if any, is the appropriate action for the FSA to take in relation to the referred matter. It is not for the Tribunal to take the action itself. On determining a reference, the Tribunal must remit the matter to the FSA with such directions as the Tribunal considers appropriate for giving effect to its determination. Under s 133(8), the Tribunal may, on determining a reference, also make recommendations as to the FSA's regulating provisions or its procedures. Whilst the FSA is not bound to follow any such recommendations, they would be bound to carry significant weight.

2. Extent of the Tribunal's determinations

11.20   Given that the Tribunal has full jurisdiction to hear all matters of fact, it might be expected that it can order the FSA, following a reference, to take any action which it is open to the FSA to take under the FSMA. However, the Tribunal's powers of determination are somewhat narrowed by FSMA, s 133(6) and (7).

11.21   To understand these provisions it is necessary first to recall that decision notices may be issued under various provisions of the Act. They may relate to penalties for market abuse, for example. In those cases, the government has decided, as a matter of policy, to apply the protections of the European Court of Human Rights relating to criminal proceedings, limiting what use can be made of compelled statements and providing free or subsidised legal assistance in cases of hardship. However, decision notices may relate to disciplinary penalties which do not attract these protections. The FSA may issue a decision notice under one Part of the Act only if the warning notice which preceded it was issued under the same Part (see Chapter 28). In turn, FSMA, s 133(6) prevents the Tribunal from going further than the FSA could. For example, in hearing a case about a disciplinary penalty, the Tribunal is prevented from concluding that a market abuse penalty should be imposed. This is designed to reduce further the possibility that any relevant Convention rights have not been afforded during the process.

Furthermore, different procedures apply prior to the issue of decision notices and supervisory notices, notably in relation to the disclosure of evidence and in relation to third-party rights. FSMA, s 133(7) ensures that these procedures cannot be circumvented. It does this by precluding the Tribunal, when the reference follows a supervisory notice, from directing the FSA to do something which would have otherwise required the giving of a decision notice. 11.22

3. Form of decision

A decision of the Tribunal must be committed to writing, signed by the chairman, and must state the reasons for the decision and whether it was unanimous or by majority (FSMA, Sch 13, para 12(2)). The decision must be communicated to each party, and the written reasons sent as soon as reasonably practicable to each party and any authorised person concerned (if not a party) (FSMA, Sch 13, para 12(3)). The Treasury must also be sent a copy (FSMA, Sch 13, para 12(4)). All decisions must be published (FSMT Rules 20(1)). If all or part of the hearing was held in private, the Tribunal will consider whether it would be desirable to publish all or part of its decision (Rule 20, FSMT Rules). 11.23

4. Costs

FSMA, Sch 13, para 13(1) provides that the Tribunal may order costs against any party if it considers that the party has behaved vexatiously, unreasonably, or frivolously. Such order may extend to all or part of the costs or expenses of other parties in connection with the proceedings. 11.24

There is also provision in FSMA, Sch 13, para 13(2), for the FSA to be ordered to pay costs or other expenses of other parties if the FSA's decision which is the subject of the reference was unreasonable. 11.25

5. The FSA's role in response to a determination

The FSA must act in accordance with the Tribunal's determination and any directions it gives (FSMA, s 133(10)). It may revise its regulating provisions or its procedures following any recommendation which accompanies the determination, but has to follow the ordinary statutory procedures, including consultation, before doing so. Indeed, the criticisms of enforcement procedures levelled at the FSA by the Tribunal in *Legal & General* 11.26

Assurance Society Limited v The Financial Services Authority (case 011, 2005), to some degree prompted the FSA's Enforcement Process Review later in 2005.

6. How may the Tribunal's order be enforced?

11.27 The FSMA provides that the Tribunal's order may be enforced as if it were an order of a county court or an order of the Court of Session in Scotland (FSMA, s 133(11)).

F. APPEALS

11.28 Appeals from decisions of the Tribunal are to the Court of Appeal (or the Court of Session in Scotland) on a point of law only (FSMA, s 137(1)). Such appeals may only be brought with the permission of the Tribunal or the relevant appellate court (FSMA, s 137(1) and (2)). Moreover, the point must arise from a decision of the Tribunal disposing of the reference (FSMA, s 137(1)). The FSA has appealed on two occasions; one of which was subsequently withdrawn by the FSA after separate action resulted in the cancellation of the person's permission.[3] In the only appeal that has been heard by the Court, the FSA won the appeal, which overturned the Tribunal's decision.[4]

11.29 Where the appellate court decides that the Tribunal's decision was wrong in law, it may remit the matter to the Tribunal for a rehearing and determination, or itself make a determination (FSMA, s 137(3)). There are no provisions corresponding to FSMA, s 133(5) to (11) which describe how the FSA is to respond to any determination of the appellate court and how any order of that court is to be enforced. It may perhaps be assumed that the intention was to enable the appellate court to do anything the Tribunal could have done and to require the FSA to act accordingly. Rules made under FSMA, s 132 can deal with matters related to these appeals (FSMA, s 137(6)).

11.30 Appeals from the Court of Session and the Court of Appeal lie, with leave, to the House of Lords[5] (FSMA, s 137(4) and (5)).

---

[3] See FSA statement regarding *Salman Khan* Tribunal Decision, 20 January 2009.
[4] *Financial Services Authority v Fox Hayes* [2009] EWCA Civ 76 (17 February 2009).
[5] The House of Lords is superseded by the Supreme Court as of 1 October 2009.

12

RULES AND GUIDANCE

Andrew Henderson

A. INTRODUCTION

Part 20 of the Financial Services and Markets Act 2000 (FSMA) gives the Financial   **12.01**
Services Authority (FSA) its principal rule-making powers for authorised persons.
In addition, it gives the FSA power to issue guidance on regulatory matters. It also sets
out the procedures that the FSA must follow in exercising its rule-making powers,
including those conferred in other Parts of the FSMA, and the procedures for competition scrutiny of the exercise of those powers.

B. RULES

The making of rules and giving of guidance is central to the functioning of the FSA,   **12.02**
being two of its general functions set out in the FSMA.[1] It is constitutionally unusual
for a private company like the FSA to be given powers to make secondary legislation,
and therefore these powers have been conferred within a defined framework of responsibilities and accountability arrangements. These include the constitutional accountability framework in FSMA, Part 1, which includes the requirement for the FSA to
act compatibly with its regulatory objectives set out in s 2(2) and the principles of good
regulation in s 2(3). In addition, the FSA is subject to the procedural constraints, including
those in ss 152 to 155 specific to the making of rules.

---

[1] FSMA, s 2(4)(a) and (c).

12.03   As well as the express constraints set out in the FSMA, the FSA's rule-making powers, as powers to make secondary legislation, are subject to the principles of good administration imposed by the common law.[2] As such, the FSA's making of rules is subject to control by the courts in the form of judicial review.[3] In making rules, the FSA will need to ensure that: (a) it acts in conformity with EU law, the European Convention on Human Rights and common law rights; (b) the rules are not certain, unreasonable, or made in bad faith;[4] (c) there are no procedural errors; and (d) the FSA adheres to the principle against sub-delegation, ie that a power conferred by Parliament on A must be exercised by A and not by B.[5] Both by reason of this doctrine, and the express constraints in the FSMA, the FSA's ability to modify the application of its rules on an individual basis is limited, except where permitted by FSMA.[6]

1. The FSA Handbook[7]

12.04   The FSA exercises its power to make rules in Part 20 through the FSA Handbook of Rules and Guidance (FSA Handbook). In practice, it is the FSA Handbook that dictates the manner in which authorised firms should act and, as such, is the main legal instrument to which those in authorised firms, charged with ensuring that the firms act in compliance with the regime under the FSMA, will refer on a day-to-day basis. The FSA Handbook is also the best articulation of the policy and principles of the FSA by which it discharges its particular functions. The FSA is obliged to publish its rule making instruments, which it does by publishing them on its website and it is these instruments which contain the definitive rules.[8]

12.05   Although the majority of the rules in the FSA Handbook are made under Part 20, the FSA also has other legislative powers under the FSMA which it has exercised in making parts of the FSA Handbook. For example, s 64 gives the FSA the power to issue the Statements of Principle and Code of Practice for Approved Persons (APER);[9] s 73 gives the FSA the power to make Part 6 Rules, which the FSA has used to make the Listing Rules, Prospectus Rules and Disclosure and Transparency Rules;[10] and s 119 gives the FSA the power to issue the Code of Market Conduct (MAR).[11]

---

[2] See, for example, Wade and Forsyth *Administrative Law* (10th Ed), p 732 *et seq.*

[3] See Henderson 'Judicial Review and FSMA' [2001] *Judicial Review* 255.

[4] But see FSMA, s 56 which states that FSA rules may apply in different ways to different persons or activities. They cannot, therefore, be struck down as unreasonable merely because they are unequal in their operation between different classes. (See *Kruse v Johnson* [1898] 2 QB 91).

[5] Wade and Forsyth *Administrative Law*, n 2, pp 745 to 758.

[6] See FSMA, s 148 discussed at 12.29 below.

[7] For detailed discussion see Blair, Walker and Purves *Financial Services Law* (2nd Ed) p 203 *et seq.*

[8] FSMA, s 152 states that the FSA must notify the Treasury in writing when a new rule is made or an existing rule is modified.

[9] See Chapter 7.

[10] See Chapter 8.

[11] See Chapter 10.

The FSA Handbook is divided into multiple 'blocks' which are divided into individual 'blocks' as follows:[12]   12.06

Block	Topic	FSA Abbreviation
High-Level Standards	Principles for Businesses	PRIN
	Senior Management Arrangements, Systems and Controls	SYSC
	Threshold Conditions	COND
	Statements of Principle and Code of Practice for Approved Persons	APER
	The Fit and Proper Test for Approved Persons	FIT
	General Provisions	GEN
	Fees Manual	FEES
Prudential Standards	General Prudential Sourcebook	GENPRU
	Prudential Sourcebook for Banks, Building Societies and Investment Firms	BIPRU
	Prudential Sourcebook for Insurers	INSPRU
	Prudential Sourcebook for Mortgage and Home Finance Firms and Insurance Intermediaries	MIPRU
	Prudential Sourcebook for UCITS firms	UPRU
	Interim Prudential Sourcebook for Banks	IPRU(BANK)
	Interim Prudential Sourcebook for Building Societies	IPRU(BSOC)
	Interim Prudential Sourcebook or Friendly Societies	IPRU(FSOC)
	Interim Prudential Sourcebook for Insurers	IPRU(INS)
	Interim Prudential Sourcebook for Investment Business	IPRU(INV)
Business Standards	Conduct of Business Sourcebook	COBS
	Banking Conduct of Business Sourcebook	BCOBS
	Insurance: New Conduct of Business Sourcebook	ICOBS
	Mortgages and Home Finance: Conduct of Business Sourcebook	MCOB
	Client Assets	CASS
	Market Conduct	MAR
	Training and Competence	TC
Regulatory Processes	Supervision Manual	SUP
	Decision Procedures and Penalties Manual	DEPP
Redress	Dispute Resolution: Complaints	DISP
	Compensation	COMP
	Complaints against the FSA	COAF

(*Continued*)

---

[12] As of 1 July 2009.

Block	Topic	FSA Abbreviation
Specialist Sourcebooks	Collective Investment Schemes	COLL
	Credit Unions	CRED
	Electronic Money	ELM
	Professional Firms	PROF
	Regulated Covered Bonds	RCB
	Recognised Investment Exchanges and Recognised Clearing Houses	REC
Listing, Prospectus, and Disclosure	Listing Rules	LR
	Prospectus Rules	PR
	Disclosure Rules and Transparency Rules	DTR

12.07 In addition, the FSA has published the following guides, which, although not part of the FSA Handbook, can be found after the blocks of the Handbook:[13]

Guide	Topic	FSA Abbreviation
Handbook Guides	Energy Market Participants Guide	EMPS
	Oil Market Participants Guide	OMPS
	Service Companies	SERV
Regulatory Guides	The Building Societies Regulatory Guide	BSOG
	The Collective Investment Scheme Information Guide	COLLG
	Enforcement Guide	EG
	The Perimeter Guidance Manual	PERG
	The Responsibilities of Providers and Distributors for the Fair Treatment of Customers	RPPD
	The Unfair Contract Terms Regulatory Guide	UNFCOG

2. General rules

12.08 FSMA, s 138, gives the FSA the power to make 'general rules' applying to authorised persons.[14] The majority of the rules in the FSA Handbook, including the high-level principles, are made under this power. It is beyond the scope of this book to cover in any detail the substantial body of rules made by the FSA; most of the specific rules mentioned below are included because the FSMA itself has included particular provisions to enable the FSA to make them.

---

[13] Ibid.
[14] FSMA, s 138(1) and (2).

The application of general rules to European Economic Area (EEA) firms exercising 12.09
passport rights in the UK is limited, because general rules may not restrict the activities
that they may carry on or regulate matters (such as financial resources) which are reserved
to home State regulators under the Single Market Directives.[15]

General rules apply with respect to the carrying on of regulated activities.[16] The FSA 12.10
has used the general rule-making power, for example, to make rules governing the financial resources and systems and controls necessary for authorised firms to manage
effectively prudential risks in carrying on their business.[17] It has also used the power,
for example, to make rules governing authorised firms' day-to-day conduct of business
with their customers.[18]

The FSA also has the power to make rules with respect to non-regulated activities but 12.11
can only create such general rules for the purpose of protecting consumers of regulated
activity services. The definition of 'consumer' is sufficiently wide to include those with
interests derived from the use of services by others (for example, beneficiaries of a life
policy), the interests of beneficiaries of trusts (whether the user of services or the authorised person is the trustee) and counterparties to principal-to-principal transactions.[19]
Nevertheless, it is important to distinguish between the consumer protection purpose
and the FSA's regulatory objectives in FSMA, s 2(4). Furtherance of the regulatory
objectives alone is not a valid purpose, but rather in making rules for the purpose of
protecting consumers, the FSA must ensure they are compatible with the objectives.
There need not be a direct relationship between the authorised persons to whom the
rules apply and the consumers who are protected by the rules, so rules to prevent systemic risk are possible.[20] Furthermore, it is possible to make rules which take into consideration the activities of companies in the same group as an authorised person.[21]

The FSMA was amended to give the FSA the power to make rules for authorised firms 12.12
which are investment firms within the meaning of the Markets in Financial Instruments
Directive (MiFID) with respect to the provision of 'ancillary services'.[22] Ancillary services are those mentioned in MiFID, Annex 1, s B.[23] They include the safekeeping and
administration of financial instruments, granting credit or loans for the purpose of carrying on a transaction in financial instruments, corporate finance advice, foreign
exchange services connected to the provision of services, investment research, underwriting and derivatives business connected to investment or ancillary services.[24]

The FSA's power to make general rules is not limited by the FSA's other powers.[25] For 12.13
example, the fact that Part 5 gives the FSA specific power to issue broad statements of

---

[15] FSMA, s 138(6).
[16] FSMA, s 136(1)(a).
[17] See the materials contained in the 'Prudential Standards Block of the FSA Handbook'.
[18] See COBS, ICOBs, MCOB and BCOBS.
[19] FSMA, s 138(7).
[20] FSMA, s 138(4).
[21] FSMA, s 138(5).
[22] FSMA, s 138(1A). See FSMA (Markets in Financial Instruments) (Modification of Powers) Regulations
2006 (SI 2006/2975).
[23] FSMA, s 138(1C).
[24] See MiFID, Annex 1, s B.
[25] FSMA, s 138(3).

principle for approved persons has not restricted the FSA's power to make, in PRIN, broad statements of principle for firms themselves.

3. Specific rule-making powers

12.14   FSMA, Part 20, contains a number of specific rule-making powers (and a power for the Treasury to supplement certain rules by order) in addition to the general rule-making power. These include:

(a) *Rules relating to client assets and cancellation rights*

12.15   FSMA, s 139 is not of itself a specific rule-making power. Rather, it deals with specific types of rules which the FSA can make, using its general powers in s 138.

12.16   The FSA may make rules dealing with the handling of clients' money to override certain principles of the general law. In particular, rules may create a statutory trust in England, Wales and Northern Ireland or agency arrangement in Scotland designed to protect clients' money from an authorised person's general creditors in the event of its insolvency, which is an important principle of investor protection. Rules may also permit authorised persons to retain interest earned on clients' money held under such a trust or arrangement, for which the firm might otherwise be accountable.[26] In reliance on ss 138 and 139, the FSA has made the CASS.[27] In particular, CASS 7.7 gives effect to the statutory trust provisions in FSMA, s 139.[28] The scope and application of similar provisions (contained in CASS 4.2.3, which is no longer in force) was considered in *Re Global Europe Trader Ltd*.[29] The court held that, for a statutory trust to arise under CASS 4.2.3, the money had to be held in a segregated account and had to be identifiable. However, citing CASS 7.9.8, the court held that a statutory trust would not arise over monies held outside the segregated account (in the firm's own account) where there was a shortfall in the segregated account because of the firm's failure to transfer funds into the segregated account.[30]

12.17   FSMA, s 139 also enables the FSA's rules on cancellation of contracts to override a contract between an authorised person and its customer by granting the customer unilateral 'cooling-off' rights to cancel or withdraw from a contract after it has been entered into and to recover any premium paid.[31] This is inconsistent with various EC Directives which require cooling-off rights to be given, for example, the Third Life Directive.[32] COBS, ICOBS, MCOB and BCOBS contain provision in respect of which the FSA has relied on FSMA, s 139 to make cancellation rules. COBS, for example, deals with matters such as: the right to cancel; exercising the right to cancel; effects of cancellation; and special situations, such as distance contracts.[33]

---

[26] FSMA, s 139(1) to (3).

[27] <http://fsahandbook.info/FSA/html/handbook/CASS>.

[28] CASS 7.7.1.

[29] [2009] EWHC 602 (Ch).

[30] In light of the collapse of Lehman Brothers International in September 2008, the government is considering possible legislative reforms with respect to client assets and money. (See *Developing Effective Resolution Arrangements for Investment Banks*, HM Treasury Publication, May 2009, p 31 *et seq.*)

[31] FSMA, s 139(4).

[32] 92/96/EEC, art 15.

[33] See COBS 15.

(b) *Rules restricting the activities of managers of unit trusts*

FSMA, s 140, enables the FSA to make rules to implement art 5 of the UCITS 12.18
Management Directive.[34] Art 5 prohibits a manager of an authorised unit trust scheme
from carrying on activities other than those covered by the UCITS management passport. The Collective Investment Schemes Module of the FSA Handbook (COLL)[35]
6 deals generally with the powers and duties of schemes, authorised fund managers and
depositaries, including the manager of an authorised unit trust.[36]

(c) *Rules relating to insurance business*

FSMA, s 141, enables the FSA to make rules implementing requirements of Insurance 12.19
Directives to prohibit insurance companies from carrying on business other than
insurance business. This continues the previous restrictions in the Insurance Act 1982.
The Prudential Sourcebook for Insurers (INSPRU) 1.5.13 sets out the restrictions on
the business of insurers and reinsurers.

FSMA, s 142 allows the Treasury to make regulations applying to the unauthorised 12.20
parent undertakings of authorised insurance companies to supplement the FSA's rules
on the identification of the assets of insurance companies. The Treasury has not yet made
these Regulations.

(d) *Price stabilising rules*

Price stabilisation is the term used to describe a practice employed in offers of securities 12.21
whereby a stabilisation manager, usually an investment bank, purchases or agrees to
purchase securities in the secondary market for a limited period after those securities are
offered to the public. Price stabilisation is undertaken to prevent the price of the offered
securities falling below the price at which they were offered. Price stabilisation is permitted during the initial period after issue because it prevents artificial downward distor-
tions in the price of the offered securities. This helps to maintain an orderly market for
the offered securities thereby avoiding price volatility and market disruption and encouraging new issues of securities. Price stabilisation may, however, amount to market
manipulation because it results in artificial support of the price of the offered securities:
the stabilisation manager is not purchasing the offered securities because it believes
that the offered securities are good investments, but because it has agreed with the issuer
of the offered securities to do so. The stabilisation manager's purchases of offered securities create a potentially misleading appearance of trading activity in and an artificial price
for the offered securities, therefore infringing ss 118 (market abuse) and 397 (misleading
statements and practices) of the FSMA. Moreover, it may also infringe the insider dealing prohibition in the Criminal Justice Act 1993.

FSMA, s 144, enables the FSA to make rules relating to stabilising the price of new 12.22
issues of securities (Stabilisation Rules). Compliance with the FSA stabilisation rules and
the Buy-back and Stabilisation Regulation[37] provides a defence, or safe harbour, for both

---

[34] (2001/107/EC).
[35] <http://fsahandbook.info/FSA/html/handbook/COLL>.
[36] COLL 6.6.2 R. See also Chapter 19 below.
[37] Commission Regulation (2273/2003/EC) on exemptions for buy-back programmes and stabilisation of
financial instruments.

authorised and unauthorised persons against market abuse,[38] misleading statements and practices,[39] and insider dealing.[40] Guidance on the extent to which stabilisation activity has the benefit of a safe harbour from an allegation of market abuse is described more fully in MAR 2.[41] MAR 2.3 contains relevant extracts from the Buy-back and Stabilisation Regulation, MAR 2.4 deals with stabilisation when the Buy-back and Stabilisation Regulation do not apply, and the FSA provided market participants informal advice on the ancillary behaviour permitted by the Buy-back and Stabilisation Regulation in Issue 12 of its *Market Watch* newsletter.[42]

12.23   FSMA, s 144(3) enables the FSA to endorse overseas price stabilisation rules (overseas provisions) for the purposes of creating a defence to market manipulation in s 397(3) so that a person may comply with those rather than the FSA's own rules. MAR 2.5 deals with the overseas provisions and identifies rules in the United States, Japan and Hong Kong.

(e) *Financial promotion rules*

12.24   FSMA, s 145, enables the FSA to make rules regulating the communication of financial promotions by authorised persons and their approval of financial promotions of others.[43] These rules may not apply to a financial promotion that falls under an exemption from the restriction on financial promotion. COBS, ICOBS, MCOB, and BCOBS contain provision in respect of which the FSA has relied on FSMA, s 145 to make financial promotion rules. COBS, for example, deals with matters such as the requirement for the content of communications to be clear, fair, and not misleading, for financial promotions to be identifiable as such, and specific requirements for cold calls and other promotions which are not in writing.[44]

(f) *Money laundering rules*

12.25   FSMA, s 146, enables the FSA to make rules in relation to the prevention and detection of money laundering. These rules were previously located in the FSA Money Laundering Sourcebook; however, these rules were revoked in 2006 and replaced with a high-level statement of systems and controls in relation to compliance, financial crime, and money laundering.[45]

(g) *Control of information rules*

12.26   FSMA, s 147, enables the FSA to make rules requiring or permitting an authorised person not to disclose information or use information for the benefit of another person with whom it does business, which the authorised firm would otherwise have to

---

[38] See FSMA, s 118A(5)(b). See Chapter 10.
[39] See FSMA, s 397(4). See Chapter 29.
[40] See Criminal Justice Act 1993, Sch 1 para 5.
[41] <http://fsahandbook.info/FSA/html/handbook/MAR>.
[42] <http://www.fsa.gov.uk/pubs/newsletters/mw_newsletter12.pdf>.
[43] See Chapter 4.
[44] See COBS 4.
[45] SYSC 3.2.6.

disclose or use. In reliance on s 147, the FSA has made 'Chinese walls' rules in SYSC 10.2.2 R. A Chinese wall is:

[A]n arrangement that requires information held by a person in the course of carrying on one part of the business to be withheld from, or not to be used for, persons with or for whom it acts in the course of carrying on another part of its business.[46]

The FSA does not specify what steps a firm should take but, in practice, these would include: physical separation between different parts of the business; restricting physical access from one part of the business to another part of the business; restricting access to computer drives; the use of code names for particular projects which conceal the name of a client and nature of the project; the signing of confidentiality policies; policies on the disposal of documents; procedures for bringing a person from one part of the business 'over the wall' into another part of the business. When a firm establishes and maintains a Chinese wall it may: (a) withhold or not use the information held; and (b) for that purpose, permit persons employed in the first part of its business to withhold the information held from those employed in that other part of the business.[47]

Acting in conformity with the Chinese wall rules will provide a defence against the following: (a) proceedings brought under FSMA, s 397(2) or (3) (misleading statements and practices);[48] (b) market abuse proceedings;[49] (c) against FSA enforcement action, or an action for damages under FSMA, s 150, based on a breach of a relevant requirement to disclose or use the information held 'behind' a Chinese wall.[50] **12.27**

The establishment of effective Chinese walls may, as a matter of fact, provide an individual, within an authorised person, with a defence to insider dealing under the Criminal Justice Act 1993, Part V, where the individual deals in a security without knowing that the authorised person held price sensitive information relating to that security 'behind' a Chinese wall. **12.28**

4. Modification and waiver

FSMA, s 148, gives the FSA the power to waive or modify its rules[51] on either the application or consent of the person subject to those rules. The FSA provides guidance on waivers in SUP 8. **12.29**

Before granting a waiver, the FSA must satisfy itself of a number of matters, essentially that compliance with the rule concerned is unduly burdensome or does not achieve its purpose, and that the waiver will not result in undue risk to persons protected by the rule.[52] **12.30**

---

[46] SYSC 10.2.2 R(1). 'Maintains' includes taking reasonable steps to ensure that the arrangements remain effective and are adequately monitored, and must be interpreted accordingly (SYSC 10.2.2 R(3)).

[47] Ibid. The business of one of the parts of the business must involve the carrying of regulated or ancillary activities or ancillary services.

[48] See FSMA, s 397(4). See Chapter 29.

[49] See FSMA, s 118A(5)(a). See Chapter 10 above and Henderson 'Misuse of Information, Chinese Walls, and Changes to the FSA's Code of Market Conduct' [2005] *JIBLR*, 1.

[50] SYSC 10.2.3G.

[51] With the exception of rules made under FSMA, ss 247 and 248 relating to trust schemes.

[52] FSMA, s 148(4).

In addition to these statutory requirements, the FSA will also take into consideration other factors including whether the waiver would be compatible with European law.[53]

12.31　The effect of the FSA granting a waiver is that the provisions of the rule to which the waiver relates are no longer applicable. However, if the waiver provides that the rule should apply subject to modifications, then contravention of the modified rule can be subject to FSA enforcement action and (where applicable) action by third parties. The FSA may also bring enforcement action in cases where activity is carried on in breach of a condition of a waiver, and that activity is in contravention of the rule to which the waiver subject to the condition applies.[54]

12.32　The FSA is required to publish waivers, unless it is 'inappropriate or unnecessary'.[55] The FSA is, among other things, required to consider commercial interests and whether the rule to which the waiver relates in actionable by third parties in deciding whether to publish.

5. Procedure for making rules

12.33　The detailed procedure for making rules is an important part of the accountability framework for the FSA. The same procedure applies to all provisions with the status of 'rules' made under the FSMA, other than listing rules, which have their own procedures.[56] The procedural requirements are set out below:

(a) The general duties apply to the function of making rules.[57]

(b) The FSA must consult on draft rules, unless the delay would be prejudicial to consumers.[58] It must also specify a time during which representations may be made, must have regard to such representations and must publish a response to them.[59]

(c) The FSA must perform and publish a cost-benefit analysis of proposed rules.[60] There is a clear link between the results of such cost-benefit analysis and the duty that the FSA must have regard to the proportionality of any burden.[61] The requirement for cost-benefit analysis does not apply if the FSA considers that the proposed rules will not result in a significant increase in the overall cost position.[62] Nor does it apply to proposed rules for funding the compensation scheme, the ombudsman scheme, the legal assistance scheme, or the FSA itself, although consultation on the FSA's fees must be accompanied by a budget.[63]

(d) Consultation drafts of rules must be accompanied by explanations of the purpose of the proposed rules and of how they are compatible with the FSA's general duties.[64]

---

[53] SUP 8.3.1AG.
[54] SUP 8.4.1G.
[55] FSMA, s 148(6) to (8) and SUP 8.3.2G.
[56] FSMA, Sch 7, para 4, and Part 6.
[57] FSMA, s 2(3) and 2(4).
[58] FSMA, s 138(7).
[59] FSMA, s 155.
[60] FSMA, s 155(2)(a).
[61] FSMA, s 2(3)(c).
[62] FSMA, s 155(8).
[63] FSMA, s 155(3) and (9).
[64] FSMA, s 155(2)(b) and (c).

(e) The FSA is required to specify in every rule-making instrument the powers under which the rules have been made.[65]

(f) Rules must be made by the FSA's board as the board cannot delegate its legislative functions.[66]

(g) If the rules as made differ significantly from the consultation draft, the FSA is required to publish details of the difference and perform a further cost-benefit analysis.[67]

(h) The FSA must consult with a Practitioner Panel and a Consumer Panel 'on the extent to which its general policies and practices are consistent with its general duties'.[68]

The FSA, as with any other public authority, is subject to judicial review in making   12.34
rules.[69] Further, an FSA rule, as secondary legislation, is liable to be struck down (or simply disapplied) where it is impossible to interpret it so as to be compatible with rights under the European Convention on Human Rights.[70]

6. Evidential provisions

The FSA is empowered to make a particular type of rule called 'evidential provisions'   12.35
which, if contravened, will not lead to enforcement action or other sanctions.[71] An evidential provision must be linked to another rule and must indicate that its contravention can be relied on as tending to establish contravention of the linked rule, or that compliance with the evidential provision can be relied on as tending to establish compliance with the linked rule (or both). This power enables the FSA to elaborate on rules that are framed at a higher level of generality, including the principles for businesses. For example, evidential provisions are used in the Code of Practice for approved persons in tending to establish whether conduct complies with the statements of principle for approved persons.[72]

7. Breach of Rules

(a) *Public law consequences*

Unlike, for example, breach of the general prohibition or financial promotion   12.36
restriction,[73] the breach of an FSA rule will not give rise to any criminal liability.[74] The FSA may, however, rely on its powers in FSMA, Part 14 to take disciplinary measures against an authorised person for breach of an FSA rule.[75] It may also exercise is powers

---

[65] FSMA, s 153(2).

[66] FSMA, Sch 1, paras 1(2) and 5(2).

[67] FSMA, s 155(6).

[68] FSMA, ss 8 to 11.

[69] See 12.03, above.

[70] Human Rights Act 1998, s 3(2)(c).

[71] FSMA, s 149.

[72] FSMA, s 64 and APER.

[73] See Chapters 3 and 4.

[74] FSMA, s 151(1).

[75] See Chapter 16. The FSA may also rely on its powers in FSMA, Part 11 to gather information and investigate breaches of FSA Rules (see Chapter 13).

in FSMA, Part 25 to apply for injunctions or restitution orders with respect to a breach of any FSA rule.[76]

(b) *Private law consequences*

12.37 A breach of an FSA rule does not make any transaction entered into as result of that breach void or unenforceable.[77] However, FSMA, s 150, creates a right of action in damages for a 'private person' who suffers loss as a result of a rule contravention by an authorised person.[78] A 'private person' is:

(a) any individual who is
  (i) not carrying on any regulated activity, or
  (ii) not carrying on any activity which would be a regulated activity but for the overseas persons or information society exclusions in art 72 and art 72A of the FSMA (Regulated Activities) Order 2001; or
(b) a legal entity, such as a company, which is not acting in the course of a business.[79]

Certain types of claim are not restricted to private persons.[80] These include breaches of any rules prohibiting the use of exclusion clauses, restricting the use of inside information, or requiring an authorised person to respond to a claim for compensation within a specified time limit or pay compensation.[81] Corporate trustees and other fiduciaries acting exclusively for private persons can bring a claim in certain circumstances.[82]

12.38 A claimant is not permitted to rely on FSMA, s 150(1) to make a claim for a breach of:

(a) any rule made under Part 6 or
(b) a rule requiring an authorised person to have or maintain financial resources.[83]

A claimant would not, therefore, be able to bring a claim under FSMA, s 150 for a breach of any rule contained the Listing Rules, Prospectus Rules or Disclosure and Transparency Rules or any rule contained in the Prudential Standards Module of the FSA Handbook.[84] In addition, the FSA may remove the right under FSMA, s 150(1) from particular rules.[85] The FSA has, for example, removed this right with respect to claims for breach of the Principles for Businesses.[86]

12.39 Section 150 is useful for any relevant claimant because, in the case of many FSA rules, there is no need to demonstrate that the defendant acted negligently in breaching the rule. However, the claimant will still need to prove that the breach caused the loss for which he is claiming. For example, in cases dealing with allegations of unsuitable recommendations under s 62 of the Financial Services Act 1986, a similar provision to FSMA,

---

[76] See Chapter 27.

[77] FSMA, s 151(2). *Cf* FSMA, s 26 *et seq* which deal with the enforceability of agreements made in the context of regulated and prohibited activities.

[78] Similar rights of action exist in FSMA, ss 20(3), 71 and 202(2).

[79] FSMA (Rights of Action) Regulations, (SI 2001/2256) Regs 3(1) and 6(1). See FSMA, s 150(5).

[80] FSMA, s 150(3); FSMA (Rights of Action) Regulations, (SI 2001/2256) Reg 6(2).

[81] FSMA (Rights of Action) Regulations, (SI 2001/2256) Reg 6(3)(a), (b) and (d).

[82] FSMA (Rights of Action) Regulations, (SI 2001/2256) Reg 6(3)(c).

[83] FSMA, s 150(4).

[84] The claimant could still have claims under the common law and in the case of the Part 6 Rules, under FSMA, s 90 deals with compensation for statements in listing particulars or a prospectus. See Chapter 8.

[85] FSMA, s 150(2).

[86] PRIN 3.4.4R.

s 150, it was held that it was necessary to show that the claimant actually relied on the recommendation.[87]

Section 150 makes it clear that any claim made under it will be subject to the defences 12.40 and other incidents applying to actions for breach of statutory duty.[88] Therefore, any damages claimed under s 150 will need to be of the type which the FSMA was intended to guard against.[89] Given the nature of the FSMA as legislation governing financial services, as the cases cited above in the context of the Financial Services Act indicate, s 150 will cover claims for financial loss. There is no reason why this should not include loss of profit, subject to this being reasonably foreseeable.[90] However, claims for non-financial loss should be more difficult to show.

The FSMA is silent on exclusions of liability under FSMA, s 150 by an authorised 12.41 firm. However, the FSA handbook prohibits an authorised firm from excluding or restricting its liability for the breach of any FSA rule.[91]

Section 150 does not preclude a claimant from bringing a claim under another statute 12.42 such as, for example, the Misrepresentation Act 1967, or in common law. The courts have considered, for example, whether the rules of the Securities and Futures Authority (one of the FSA's predecessor bodies) financial regulatory rules were incorporated into a client contract.[92]

C. GUIDANCE

1. Guidance

Guidance may either be given individually or generally. Although guidance only consists 12.43 of information and advice, the FSA has made it clear that it will not take action against a person for behaviour that it considers to be in line with guidance, with other materials published by the FSA in support of the FSA Handbook, or with FSA-confirmed Industry Guidance.[93] As an exercise of power by the FSA, the legality of the FSA's decision to give guidance should be subject to judicial review.[94]

2. General guidance

FSMA, s 157(1), gives the FSA power to issue and publish guidance on a wide variety 12.44 of matters, including its own rules and the criminal perimeter created under the FSMA. This guidance may consist only of 'information and advice' and cannot therefore impose binding requirements, vary binding requirements, or change the burden of proof.

---

[87] *Morgan Stanley UK Group v Puglisi Consentino* [1998] CLC 481; *Australia & New Zealand Banking Group v Cattan* [2001] All ER (D) 10.

[88] FSMA, s 150(1) and (3).

[89] See *Clerk & Lindell on Torts*, 19th Ed, 9 - 52.

[90] Ibid.

[91] See COBS 2.1.2 R, ICOBS 2.5.1 R and MCOB 2.6.2 R.

[92] See *Brandeis (Brokers) Ltd v Black* [2001] 2 All ER(Comm) 980.

[93] DEPP 6.2.1(4)G.

[94] See Henderson 'Judicial Review and FSMA', n 3 above, 6 citing *R v Securities and Investments Board and another ex parte Independent Financial Advisers Association and another* [1995] 2 BCLC 76.

But even if it does not formally impose or vary requirements, firms and other persons may in practice heed guidance as an expression of the FSA's views on the application of its requirements and FSMA, to avoid possible enforcement action by the FSA. Firms may also be able to rely on the doctrine of 'legitimate expectation' when relying on FSA guidance. Despite this, firms are not bound by FSA guidance and, especially in an environment of principles-based regulation, can adopt alternative actions to fulfil regulatory requirements; however documenting reasons for not adhering to FSA guidance is recommended. Third-party rights cannot be affected by guidance and guidance does not bind the courts.

12.45   Where guidance is given to persons subject to the FSA's rules and is intended to have continuing effect, it will generally fall within the definition of 'general guidance'.[95] General guidance may be issued by the FSA's Board or a committee or sub-committee thereof and for this purpose the FSA Guidance Committee has been established.[96] The issue of guidance under s 157 in relation to rules requires prior consultation. This, however, is less onerous than the consultation procedure required for the issue of rules; the FSA is not required to produce a cost benefit analysis, an explanation of the purpose of the proposed guidance, nor provide an explanation of why the issuing of the guidance is in compliance with the FSA's general duties.[97]

3. Industry guidance

12.46   The FSA can use its resources to support the giving of information and advice by third parties.[98] Industry guidance is defined by the FSA as 'information created, developed, and freely issued by a person or body, other than the FSA, which is intended to provide guidance from the body concerned to the industry about the provisions of [the FSA] Handbook.'[99] The FSA recognises industry guidance which satisfies certain parameters by issuing 'FSA confirmation'. Before the FSA provides confirmation, industry guidance must (i) explain how it relates to a relevant FSA rule and/or principle, (ii) consider consumer interests and views when it directly affects consumers, (iii) be optional and not proclaim to be an exhaustive statement of compliance with the rule and/or principle in question, (iv) not be anti-competitive, (v) detail the intended audience, and (vi) be publicly available. There is no legal requirement to adopt processes such as cost benefit analysis and consultation for 'FSA confirmation'. FSA confirmation means that the FSA will regard firms correctly following confirmed guidance as complying with the relevant rule and/or principle.[100]

4. Individual guidance

12.47   The FSA's power in s 157 to issue guidance includes power to give guidance on an individual basis both to authorised and unauthorised persons. The FSA's approach to

---

[95] FSMA, s 158(5).
[96] Regulatory reform (FSMA) Order 2007 (SI 2007/1973), Article 14 amending FSMA, Sch 1, para 5.
[97] Ibid, Article 13 amending FSMA, s 157.
[98] FSMA, s 157(2).
[99] See <http://www.fsa.gov.uk/pubs/policy/ps07_12.pdf> for the FSA's policy on industry guidance.
[100] DEPP 6.2.1(4)G.

individual guidance is set out in SUP 9. Just like published guidance, individual guidance cannot impose binding requirements, but may provide information and advice, such as the FSA's interpretation of how a rule applies in a firm's particular circumstances or plans. Individual guidance can be given at the request of the firm or on the FSA's own initiative. A firm may make a request either in writing or orally; however, the FSA expects requests relating to complex matter to be set out in writing and will require sufficient information and time prior to issuing individual guidance.[101] The FSA will generally issue individual guidance on its own initiative if it believes that for the firm in question general guidance is not suitable, that the firm's particular circumstances warrant further guidance or more detailed guidance or that a particular course of action is recommended despite general guidance providing for multiple different courses of action. Furthermore, the FSA will issue individual guidance to firms concerning how best that firm can maintain adequate financial resources.[102]

Individual guidance is not published in the same way as general guidance, but may be made generic and published at the FSA's discretion.[103]   12.48

For enforcement purposes, if a firm acts in accordance with current individual written guidance given to him by the FSA in the circumstances contemplated by that guidance, then the FSA will proceed on the basis that the person has acted in accordance with all aspects of the relevant rule.[104]   12.49

D. COMPETITION SCRUTINY

FSMA, Chapter 3 of Part 20, provides for competition scrutiny of the FSA's rules, general guidance, policy statements, codes and practices. Separate provision for competition scrutiny is necessary as s 164 provides a safe harbour for persons acting in a manner consistent with FSA regulations against competition law violations.[105]   12.50

The Office of Fair Trading (OFT) is under a duty to keep the FSA's regulating provisions and practices under review, and to report on any which have a significantly adverse effect on competition.[106] Any report must be sent to the Treasury, the Competition Commission (hereafter referred to as 'the Commission') and the FSA. The OFT is also under an obligation to publish any report made.   12.51

The Commission must then produce a further report on the matter stating whether, in its opinion, the provisions or practices in question have a significantly adverse effect on competition. The Commission can conclude that the provisions and practices in question do not have a significant adverse effect on competition and no further action is required. However, if the Commission concludes that there is such an effect, the Commission must determine whether the effect is justified, taking into account the   12.52

---

[101] SUP 9.2.1G and 9.2.6G.
[102] SUP 9.3.2G.
[103] SUP 9.1.2G.
[104] SUP 9.4.1G.
[105] Including actions constituting agreements preventing, restricting or distorting competition and abuse of a dominant position in the market under the Competition Act 1998, ss 2(1) and 18(1) respectively.
[106] FSMA, ss 160 and 161 as amended by the Enterprise Act 2002.

FSA's functions under the FSMA. It must also state what action, if any, ought to be taken by the FSA in relation to the matter.

12.53   The final arbiter on the matter of competition will be the Treasury, but its ability to overturn the conclusions of the Commission is limited.[107]If the Commission's opinion is that an adverse effect on competition is not justified, the Treasury must direct the FSA to take appropriate action, unless there are exceptional circumstances or action is unnecessary because the FSA has already taken action. The FSMA does not specify what might constitute exceptional circumstances, but the Treasury have stated that this might include, for example, a grave risk to the financial system if the regulating provisions were changed. In addition, the Treasury cannot direct the FSA to take any action that the FSA has no power to take or which would be incompatible with the FSA's functions or obligations under the FSMA. If the Commission's opinion is that the adverse effect on competition is justified, then the Treasury may override that decision and direct the FSA to make changes only in exceptional circumstances.

---

[107] FSMA, s 163.

13

INFORMATION GATHERING AND INVESTIGATIONS

Helen Marshall

A. INTRODUCTION

Part 11 of the Financial Services and Markets Act 2000 (FSMA) contains the Financial **13.01**
Services Authority's (FSA's) specific, formal powers to obtain the information it requires
to pursue its statutory objectives. There are five discrete sets of powers in Part 11, which
may be summarised as follows:

(a) powers to gather information directly from authorised and other regulated persons;
(b) powers to require reports from skilled persons about authorised persons;
(c) powers to carry out general investigations relating to authorised persons and their
appointed representatives;
(d) powers to investigate where circumstances suggest particular breaches; and
(e) powers to investigate to assist overseas regulators.

Part 11 goes into considerable detail about the scope and extent of each power, and **13.02**
the rights of those under investigation at key stages. It also deals with the admissibility

of compelled answers, powers to enter premises and the consequences of failing to co-operate with the FSA in the exercise of the powers. The FSA's approach to exercising its powers is set out in the Enforcement Guide (EG).

B. POWERS TO GATHER INFORMATION

13.03 The first power in Part 11 is one to require information and documents from authorised persons (FSMA, s 165(1)), or from former authorised persons (s 165(8)), where the information and documents are reasonably required in connection with the FSA's statutory functions (s 165(4)). This power may be used in a wide variety of circumstances, not just to look into what may be a firm-specific problem. The FSA has confirmed that it may use the power in support of its supervision and its enforcement functions (EG 3.2).

13.04 The FSA may require a former or present authorised person, by written notice, to provide information or documents (FSMA, s 165(1) and (8)). The notice must be specific as to the information or documents required, or must describe them in specific terms (s 165(10)). The notice must be complied with by the date and at a place that is reasonably specified by the FSA (s 165(2)).

13.05 The FSA may give written authorisation to an FSA officer, including a member of staff or an agent, to exercise similar powers (FSMA, s 165(3)). The officer may require the information or documents without delay (s 165(3)).

13.06 The FSA may ask for the information provided to be provided in some particular form, and to be verified or authenticated in any particular manner, provided that such requests are reasonable (FSMA, s 165(5) and (6)).

13.07 The powers may be used to require information from operators, trustees, or depositaries of certain overseas collective investment schemes, as well as from recognised investment exchanges and clearing houses (FSMA, s 165(7)).

13.08 Information may also be required to be provided by a person 'connected' with authorised firms (FSMA, s 165(7)(a)). 'Connected' is defined for the purpose in s 165(11) as a person who is or has been a member of the authorised person's group, its controller, a member of the same partnership, or a person mentioned in part 1 of Sch 15, FSMA. Broadly speaking, 'connected' is further expanded in Sch 15 to include officers, managers, employees and agents of the authorised person.

C. REPORTS BY SKILLED PERSONS

13.09 The second formal set of powers in Part 11 allows the FSA to require an authorised person to produce a report to the FSA on any matter which could have been the subject of the information-gathering powers in FSMA, s 165 mentioned above (s 166(1) and (2)). A report required under s 166 must therefore also reasonably be required in connection with the discharge of FSA's statutory functions (s 165(4)).

13.10 By FSMA, s 166(2) the requirement can be imposed on an authorised person, any other member of that person's group, or a partnership of which the authorised person is a member (a more limited class of persons than 'connected persons' under s 165). In each case, it does not matter if the person concerned no longer has that status if the person had it at the relevant time, provided that the person is, or was at the relevant time, carrying on a business.

The person making the report must be nominated or approved by the FSA and must be someone appearing to the FSA to have the skills necessary to make a report on the matter concerned (FSMA, s 166(4)). Section 166 reports have commonly been commissioned to be produced by accountants but a skilled person might also be a lawyer, an actuary, or a person with particular relevant experience, given the subject matter of the report. The FSA has indicated that it will seek to avoid conflicts of interests arising in cases where serious compliance failures are suspected by appointing someone other than the firm's auditors or regular advisers to produce the report.   13.11

The cost of producing such a report falls on the firm. The factors influencing the FSA in the use of this power include whether obtaining expert analysis or recommendations for the purposes of seeking remediation action are part of the FSA's objectives in requiring a report (EG 3.5(2)).   13.12

It is the duty of those providing services to the authorised person to co-operate with whoever is appointed to make the report under FSMA, s 166 by giving such assistance as may reasonably be required (s 166(5)). This means, for example, that the company's in-house accountants would be under a duty to co-operate with the skilled person appointed to write the report.   13.13

The FSA may apply to the Court for a mandatory injunction (in Scotland, an order for specific performance) in the event of non-compliance with the requirement to produce a report (FSMA, s 166(6)).   13.14

D. GENERAL INVESTIGATIONS

The FSA or the Secretary of State may initiate a general investigation under FSMA, s 167, if it appears that there is good reason to do so, into the nature, conduct or state of the business of an authorised person or an appointed representative, any particular aspect of that business, or the ownership or control of an authorised person (s 167(1)). The power is to appoint one or more competent persons to carry out the investigation on behalf of the FSA (or Secretary of State, as the case may be) (s 167(1)).   13.15

It does not matter whether the person under investigation is authorised at the time of the investigation. The power extends to former authorised persons and appointed representatives in relation to business carried on when they had that status, and can cover the ownership and control of a former authorised person at any time when he was an authorised person (FSMA, s 167(4)). Nor is the investigation limited to regulated business: the power to investigate the business or any aspect of it is expressly defined to include unregulated activity (s 167(5)).   13.16

If he thinks it necessary for the purposes of the investigation to do so, the person appointed to investigate may extend the investigation by virtue of FSMA, s 167(2). This allows the investigator to investigate the business of a person who is or was a member of the group of which the person under investigation is part; or a member of the same partnership. An investigator who decides to extend the investigation in this way must given written notice to the person whose business will be investigated as a result of the decision.   13.17

13.18   Where there are circumstances suggesting that the contraventions set out in FSMA, s 97 have occurred (Listing Rule breaches) the FSA will normally appoint investigators under that section. Such investigators will have powers as if appointed under s 167(1).[1]

E. PARTICULAR INVESTIGATIONS

13.19   The FSA may, under FSMA, s 168, appoint investigators in a number of circumstances suggesting particular contraventions of various kinds, both criminal and non-criminal. Persons appointed to investigate in these specific circumstances under s 168 have wider powers of investigation than those appointed under s 167.

13.20   The triggers for investigations are contained in FSMA, s 168(1) and (2). The main triggers for these powers include where it appears to the FSA that there are circumstances suggesting that certain criminal offences may have been committed, such as insider dealing, market manipulation, misleading statements, and unauthorised business. Other key triggers include circumstances suggesting that market abuse may have taken place.

13.21   In addition, the FSA may appoint investigators under FSMA, ss 168(4) and (5) in other circumstances, for example where a person is suspected of having committed an offence under prescribed money laundering regulations, where circumstances suggest that an authorised person may have contravened an FSA rule or that a person approved under s 59 may be guilty of misconduct or may not be fit and proper to perform the controlled function for which approval has been given.

13.22   These powers are much wider than the statutory powers available to FSA under the predecessor statutes and Parliament debated whether the threshold for their exercise should be higher. The then Economic Secretary to the Treasury explained at the time that 'reasonable grounds to suspect' would require the FSA to have a degree of certainty that an offence had been committed before an investigation could be launched and the words 'circumstances suggesting' were adopted so as to enable the FSA to exercise its powers in a broader range of circumstances than other wording would allow.

F. INVESTIGATION INTO COLLECTIVE INVESTMENT SCHEMES

13.23   The FSA may appoint investigators under FSMA, s 284 to conduct an investigation into the affairs of a collective investment scheme if it appears that it is in the interests of the participants to do so or the matter is of public concern.[2]

G. INVESTIGATIONS IN SUPPORT OF OVERSEAS REGULATORS

13.24   FSMA, s 169 provides the FSA with an express power to gather information and investigate to assist an overseas regulator. It has the effect that the FSA may use its s 165

---

[1] See Chapter 8.
[2] See Chapter 19.

information-gathering powers and by extension its powers to require a report from skilled persons under s 166. It may appoint investigators 'to investigate any matter'.

An 'overseas regulator' means an authority, whether in the EU or elsewhere, which   13.25
exercises functions corresponding to any function of the FSA under the FSMA, any function of the competent authority for listing, the companies regulatory responsibilities corresponding to those under the Companies Act 1985, and any function of investigating insider dealing whether criminally or otherwise. There is a residual power for the Treasury to make regulations specifying additional companies or financial services functions for this purpose (FSMA, s 195(3) and (4) applied by s 169(13)).

Where there is discretion to assist the overseas regulator, the FSA may take a number   13.26
of factors into account (FSMA, s 169(4)). These include whether such assistance would be reciprocated, whether the matter to be investigated involves a breach of a law with no close parallel in the UK or assertion of a jurisdiction not recognised in the UK, the seriousness of the case and importance to people in the UK, and whether it would otherwise be in the public interest to assist. The FSA may make it a condition of assistance that the overseas regulator contributes to the costs of the investigation (s 169(5)).

In some circumstances, the FSA will be required as a matter of its Community obliga-   13.27
tions under Single Market Directives to investigate, and FSMA, s 169(3) obliges it to consider whether it must do so. If the FSA considers that Community obligations require it to investigate, the factors listed above, which are relevant to discretionary assistance, fall away and no contribution to costs may be sought (s 169(6)).

The FSA may allow a representative of the overseas regulator to attend and take part   13.28
in any interview conducted for the purposes of the investigation (FSMA, s 169(7)). This will be signalled by FSA direction to the person appointed to investigate. Such a direction cannot be given unless the FSA is satisfied that any information obtained by the overseas regulator as a result of the interview will be subject to obligations to keep the information confidential (s 169(8)). These obligations must be equivalent to those imposed on the FSA, which are contained in Part 23 of the FSMA.

No such 'sitting-in' direction can be given unless the FSA has published a statement,   13.29
approved by the Treasury, setting out its policy on the conduct of interviews carried out with overseas regulators sitting in (FSMA, s 169(9) to (12)).

The FSA's policy on the conduct of such interviews is set out in DEPP 7.   13.30

H. INVESTIGATION POWERS: GENERAL PROVISIONS

The investigating authority, whether it is the FSA or Secretary of State, must notify a   13.31
person whom they have decided should be investigated under FSMA, s 167 or s 168 that investigators have been appointed (s 170(2)). The notice must be in writing and must specify the provisions under which the investigator has been appointed and the reason for the appointment (s 170(4)).

The investigating authority (that is, the FSA or the Secretary of State) may appoint   13.32
any competent person to investigate on its behalf. FSMA, s 170(5) provides that the investigator may be a member of staff. The investigator must submit their report to the investigating authority (s 170(6)).

FSMA, s 170(7) makes clear that it is for the investigating authority to control the   13.33
scope, conduct, duration, and reporting of the investigation by the giving of directions.

These directions are generally a private matter between the investigating authority and the investigator, but where there is a change in scope or conduct of the investigation, the position may be different. Where the investigating authority believes that there is a real risk of significant prejudice to the person under investigation if he remains ignorant of the change, he must be given written notice of it (s 170(9)).

13.34 By virtue of FSMA, s 170(3), notices do not need to be given under section 170 if the investigating authority believes that this would be likely to result in an investigation under s 168(1) or (4) being frustrated. Nor do notices need to be given in certain types of case such as insider dealing, market abuse and other investigations under s 168(2), where the investigation at the outset may be into a set of facts rather than persons and, indeed, it may be unclear who, if anyone, is to be suspected of any wrongdoing (s 170(3)(G)).

I. POWERS OF INVESTIGATORS

1. Powers of investigators appointed under section 167

13.35 The general power to investigate under FSMA, s 167, is available in a wide range of circumstances. The detailed powers conferred on such investigators are accordingly limited, since they may be exercised in circumstances of varying seriousness (s 171).

13.36 By virtue of FSMA, s 171(1), the investigator may require people to attend for interview at a specified place and time or to provide such information as the investigator may require. These requirements may be imposed only on those under investigation and those 'connected' with them within the meaning of s 171(4). There is an additional power in s 171(2) which enables the investigator to require *any* person to produce documents. In every instance, the investigator must reasonably consider the question, information or document to be relevant to the purposes of the investigation (s 171(3)).

2. Additional powers of investigators appointed under section 168

13.37 The powers of investigators appointed under FSMA, s 168 are wider than those available to s 167 investigators, reflecting the more specific and inevitably serious circumstances in which they are appointed (ss 172 and 173).

13.38 In addition to the powers available to FSMA, s 167 investigators (s 172(1)), those investigating under s 168(1) or (4) may require any person to attend for interview and otherwise to provide such information as the investigator may require for the purposes of the investigation (s 172(2)). The investigator must be satisfied that the requirement is necessary or expedient for those purposes (s 172(3)). Those investigating on behalf of overseas regulators under s 169 have the same powers as investigators appointed by virtue of s 168(1) (see s 169(2)).

13.39 Those investigating the specific misconduct mentioned in FSMA, s 168(2), which includes insider dealing, market abuse, unregulated business, and unlawful promotion, have yet broader powers of investigation conferred by s 173. Reflecting the fact that such investigations may need to be mounted without any idea who may be responsible, there is no need to identify and notify a person under investigation and no notion of connected person. The powers available to the investigator include the ability to require any person who may be able to give relevant information to attend for interview, and to give such information or particular documents which may be required for the investigation (s 173 (2)). They may also be required to give all and any other assistance which they are reasonably able to give (s 173 (4)).

3. Supplemental powers of investigators

Where a person could be compelled under Part 11 to produce a document, but that document is in the hands of a third party, the requirement may be imposed on the third party (FSMA, s 175(1)).   13.40

Where a document is produced in response to a Part 11 requirement, copies and extracts may be taken, and the person producing it and any 'relevant person' may be required to provide an explanation of it (FSMA, s 175(2)). 'Relevant person' is defined in s 175(7) and includes directors, controllers, certain professional advisers, and employees of a person. Case law would suggest that this provision should not be narrowly construed.[3]   13.41

A person who is required to produce a document but fails to do so may be required to state where, to the best of his or her knowledge and belief, the document might be found (FSMA, s 175(3)).   13.42

These provisions do not affect any rights a third party might have over any documents, for example, a solicitor's lien (FSMA, s 175(6)). A lawyer may be required to furnish the name and address of his or her client (s 175(4)) but, by virtue of s 413, none of the powers in Part 11 may be used to require the disclosure of privileged information defined in that section under the heading of 'protected items'.   13.43

4. Banking confidentiality

Special provisions apply to information or documents in respect of which a person owes a duty of banking confidence (FSMA, s 175(5)). Such material may not be required of a person unless one of four conditions is present. First, the person required to disclose or produce is the person under investigation or is a member of the same group as the person under investigation. Second, the person to whom the confidence is owed is the person under investigation or a member of that person's group. Third, the person to whom the confidence is owed consents. Fourth, there has been specific authorisation by the investigating authority.   13.44

J. ADMISSIBILITY OF STATEMENTS MADE TO INVESTIGATORS

Where a statement has been compelled as a part of a general or specific investigation under FSMA, s 167 or s 168 the statement will be able to be adduced in criminal proceedings against the maker of the statement in limited circumstances only (s 174). This principle was established by the European Court of Human Rights in the case of *Saunders v United Kingdom*.[4] This does not prevent the prosecutor from adducing in   13.45

---

[3] *Attorney General's Reference (No. 2 of 1998)* [1999] 3 WLR 961.
[4] *Saunders v United Kingdom* (1986) 23 EHRR 313.

evidence documents produced by the person making the statement or from adducing compelled statements in evidence against others.

13.46   There are some types of criminal cases where, exceptionally, it may be possible to adduce compelled statements whether or not the maker of the statements puts them in issue. These are proceedings under FSMA, s 177(4) relating to the provision of false or misleading information in purported compliance with a person exercising Part 11 powers; proceedings under s 398 for misleading the Authority; and certain offences under perjury legislation.

13.47   Subject to one exception, the FSMA expressly allows for compelled statements to be used in non-criminal cases, that is, civil cases and cases imposing regulatory sanctions, provided that they meet the ordinary tests for admissibility which apply to such cases. The exception relates to the market abuse regime. Where the proceedings relate to action to be taken under s 123—which enables the FSA to impose a financial penalty or to censure a person for market abuse—any compelled material obtained from that person will not be admissible against him or her.

K. ENTRY OF PREMISES UNDER WARRANT

13.48   FSMA, s 176 provides for the FSA to apply to a justice of the peace, or, in Scotland, a sheriff for a warrant to enter premises where documents or information is held. The application must be supported by information given on oath by or on behalf of the FSA, the Secretary of State or an investigator.

13.49   There are three bases on which a warrant may be issued. The first is that there are reasonable grounds for believing that a person who has been required to produce documents or information under Part 11 has not complied in full and that there are documents or information on the premises concerned which have already been required to be produced.

13.50   The second basis is that there are reasonable grounds for believing that the premises specified in the warrant are premises of an authorised person or an appointed representative, that there are documents or information on the premises which could be required to be produced under Part 11, and that if they were required to be produced, they would not be produced, or they would be removed, tampered with or destroyed.

13.51   The third basis is that there are reasonable grounds for believing that one of the offences which may give rise to an investigation under FSMA, s 168 (power to appoint investigators in particular cases) has been or is being committed, provided that it is one of the offences for which a prison sentence of at least two years could be imposed. (Such offences include 'perimeter offences', such as carrying on unauthorised business; insider dealing, and market manipulation; and 'misleading statements', whether by authorised or unauthorised persons.) There must also be reasonable grounds for believing that there are documents or information on the premises specified in the warrant which could be required to be produced, under Part 11, and that if they were required to be produced they would not be produced, or they would be removed, tampered with or destroyed.

13.52   Warrants issued under FSMA, s 176 authorise a constable to enter the premises concerned, to search and take possession of documents or information of the relevant kind or to take any other steps which may appear to be necessary for preserving them or preventing interference with them. Section 16(2) of the Police and Criminal Evidence Act 1984 enables persons named on the warrant to accompany the constable in the execution of the warrant and will enable FSA investigators to attend during the execution of the warrant.

Copies of documents or information may be taken and anyone at the premises may be required to say where the relevant kind of documents or information may be found and to provide an explanation of any such document or information. The constable may use such force as may be reasonably necessary to gain entry to the premises. 13.53

In England and Wales, provisions of the Police and Criminal Evidence Act 1984 apply to warrants issued under this section. These provide safeguards for the execution of warrants and their wording. Similar provisions apply in Northern Ireland. 13.54

Where a document is seized under a warrant, it may be retained for three months or until the end of any relevant criminal proceedings commenced within the three-month period (FSMA, s 176(8)). 13.55

L. CONSEQUENCES OF FAILURE TO CO-OPERATE

If any person (other than an investigator) fails to comply with a requirement imposed on him by FSMA, Part 11, the fact may be certified in writing to the court (s 177(1)). If the court is satisfied that the defaulter had no reasonable excuse, it may deal with the defaulter as though there were a contempt of court. Where the defaulter is a company, the court may deal with any director or officer as though they were in contempt.[5] 13.56

FSMA, Part 11, does, however, contain three different offences relating to failure to co-operate. 13.57

Firstly, it will be a criminal offence to interfere with documents which are known or suspected to be relevant to an existing investigation or one which is likely to be conducted, whether by falsifying, concealing, destroying or otherwise disposing of them. It will be a defence to show that there was no intention to conceal relevant facts from the investigator (FSMA, s 177(3)). 13.58

Secondly, a person who knowingly or recklessly provides information which is materially false or misleading in purported compliance with a Part 11 requirement commits an offence (FSMA, s 177(4)). 13.59

These first two offences may be tried in the magistrates' court or Crown Court and the maximum sentence is two years' imprisonment and an unlimited fine. 13.60

Thirdly, intentional obstruction of a warrant is a criminal offence (FSMA, s 177(6)), triable only in the magistrates' court and carrying a maximum sentence of three months' imprisonment and a level 5 fine (currently £5,000). 13.61

---

[5] In *FSA v Christopher Westcott* (9 October 2003) the High Court sentenced Mr Westcott to a period of 28 days imprisonment for his failure to co-operate with an FSA investigation, suspended on condition that he co-operated in future.

14

CONTROL OVER AUTHORISED PERSONS

Andrew Henderson

A. INTRODUCTION

Part 12 of the Financial Services and Markets Act 2000 (FSMA) concerns the control of authorised persons. It creates an obligation to notify the Financial Services Authority (FSA) of an intended acquisition of a controlling interest in an authorised person, of an intended increase in that interest or of an intention to reduce such an interest. This Part creates an obligation on the FSA either to approve (with or without conditions) such acquisitions or changes in control, or to issue an objection to an acquisition or change in a controlling interest, and includes criteria according to which the FSA's approval is to be granted or withheld. It also contains provisions relating to controlling interests that have been acquired in breach of these notification or approval requirements, and creates a number of offences relating to such breaches.   14.01

The provisions of Part 12 will be relevant where, for example, a person wishes to acquire a financial services business in the United Kingdom through a share purchase. In the case of this type of purchase, although the only assets transferred are the shares in the target company, the purchaser acquires all assets, liabilities and obligations, therefore taking control of the business of the target company and triggering the requirements of Part 12. This can be contrasted with a purchase of assets, other than shares, which will not trigger the requirements of Part 12 although the requirements of Part 6 (Control of Business Transfers) will be triggered where the assets form all or part of an insurance business.[1]   14.02

---

[1] See Chapter 9.

14.03   In considering control over authorised persons, the provisions of Part 12 should be read in conjunction with the FSA Supervision Manual (SUP) 11 which deals with 'Controllers and Close Links'.[2]

B. EC LEGISLATION: THE ACQUISITIONS DIRECTIVE

14.04   Controls over the owners and controllers of authorised persons are now governed by the Acquisitions Directive (AD).[3] Prior to this, they were governed by Directives including the Banking Directive,[4] the Third Non-life Insurance Directive,[5] the Reinsurance Directive,[6] and the Markets in Financial Instruments Directive.[7]

14.05   The AD aims to improve the process of supervisory approvals for the acquisition of financial services firms by increasing legal certainty, clarity, transparency and consistency of treatment between different financial sectors. The intention of the AD is to align the process for supervisory approvals of acquisitions to ensure consistency between the credit institutions, insurance and securities sectors.[8]

14.06   More specifically, the AD intends to do the following: set out the entire procedure to be applied by supervisory authorities when assessing acquisitions on prudential grounds; introduce a clear and transparent notification and decision-making process for supervisory authorities and firms; set deadlines, within which the supervisory authority must make the assessment and any 'stopping of the clock' for supervisory authorities to ask for further information from the proposed acquirer, that are limited to one occasion and subject to clear conditions; and to clearly lay out the prudential criteria for the assessment and achieve maximum harmonisation of the provisions relating to the supervisory approvals process.[9]

C. NOTICES OF ACQUISITION

14.07   The AD is implemented in FSMA, Part 12.[10] The provisions that give effect to the AD replace those which required a person to notify the FSA of 'a step' which the person proposed to take which would result in his acquiring or increasing control. The FSA deals specifically with obligations on controllers and persons who decide to acquire or increase control over an authorised person (a proposed controller) in SUP 11.3 which should be read in conjunction with ss 178 to 186 of the FSMA.

---

[2] <http://fsahandbook.info/FSA/html/handbook/SUP/11>.
[3] Directive 2007/44/2007.
[4] Directive 2000/12/EC, art 16.
[5] Directive 92/49/EEC, art 15.
[6] Directive 2005/68/EC, arts 19 to 23.
[7] Directive 2004/39/EC, art 10.
[8] See HM Treasury and FSA *Implementation of the Acquisitions Directive: a consultation document*, September 2008, p 11.
[9] Ibid.
[10] See the FSMA (Controllers) Regulations 2009 (2009/534).

1. A pre-approval obligation for acquisitions or increases in control

A proposed controller must give the FSA notice in writing before making the acquisition 14.08
or increasing control.[11] This is required in order for the FSA to assess the acquisition or
increase and give it unconditional or conditional approval or object to the acquisition
or increase.[12] Making an acquisition before the FSA has approved of it is an offence.[13]
The holding of shares or voting power by a person includes any shares or voting power
held by another if both persons are acting in concert.[14] The FSMA sets out the requirements for the relevant notice and the duties of the FSA with respect to acknowledging
receipt of the notice.[15] The FSA has set out special provisions in SUP regarding pre-
notification and approval for fund managers.[16]

2. An associated duty on authorised persons

Although Part 12 only applies to controllers or proposed controllers, the FSA imposes 14.09
notification obligations on authorised persons with respect to changes of control and
prescribes the content and timing of such notifications.[17] This obligation is linked to an
authorised person's duty to take reasonable steps to keep itself informed about the identity of its controllers.[18] It highlights the fact that in the context of a change of control,
the notification obligations of both the acquirer and the target authorised person must
be considered.

3. Acquiring control

A person (A) must notify the FSA of a proposed acquisition of control over an author- 14.10
ised person (B) where he decides to acquire: 10 per cent or more of the shares in B or its
parent undertaking (P); or 10 per cent or more of the voting power in B or P; or shares
or voting power in B or P as a result of which A can exercise significant influence over
the management of B.[19]

4. Increasing control

A person (A) must notify the FSA of a proposed acquisition of control over an author- 14.11
ised person (B) whenever any of the following three things occur: (i) the percentage of
shares which A holds in B or in a parent undertaking (P) increases from less than 20 per
cent to 20 per cent or more, less than 30 per cent to 30 per cent or more, or less than
50 per cent to 50 per cent or more; (ii) the percentage of the voting power which A holds

---

[11] FSMA, s 178(1) and (3). SUP 11.3.7 deals with the forms of notification when acquiring or increasing
control.
[12] See FSMA, s 185(1).
[13] FSMA, s 191F.
[14] FSMA, s 178(2).
[15] See FSMA, ss 179 and 180.
[16] See SUP 11.3.5.
[17] SUP 11.4.2 to SUP 11.4.9. SUP 11.5 deals with the form of notification.
[18] SUP 11.4.10.
[19] FSMA, s 181(1) and (2). This does not require a 10 per cent holding.

in B or in P increases from less than 20 per cent to 20 per cent or more, less than 30 per cent to 30 per cent or more less than 50 per cent to 50 per cent or more; (iii) or A becomes a parent undertaking of B.[20]

5. A pre-notification obligation for reduction in control

14.12 Where a person decides to reduce or ceases to have control over an authorised person, that person must give the FSA notice in writing before making the disposition that will lead to the person reducing or ceasing to have control.[21] However, the FSA's approval is not required.[22]

14.13 With respect to the notification thresholds for a reduction of control, the obligation to notify is symmetrical to the obligation to seek approval for an acquisition of or increase in control. To the extent that a person (A) wishes to reduce his shareholding or voting power in an authorised person (B) or parent undertaking, A must notify the FSA if his intention would result in the shareholding or voting power falling below any of the above thresholds, that is, 50 per cent, 30 per cent, 20 per cent or 10 per cent, or A otherwise ceasing to be a parent undertaking of B.[23]

6. Disregarded holdings

14.14 The FSMA specifies various circumstances in which shares and voting power that a person holds in an authorised person will be disregarded for the purposes of the notification obligations above. These include shares held for the purposes of clearing and settlement within a short settlement cycle and shares held by a custodian, investment firm, credit institution or management company, subject to specific requirements.[24]

7. Exemptions from the duty to notify

14.15 FSMA empowers the Treasury to provide exemptions from the duty to notify.[25] Exercising this power, the Treasury has created a general exemption that applies in respect of certain non-directive firms so that the obligation to notify only arises at the threshold of a 20 per cent holding of shares or voting power.[26] Specific exemptions apply in respect of building societies (at the threshold of 20 per cent of capital) and for friendly societies.[27]

---

[20] FSMA, s 182(1) and (2).
[21] FSMA, s 191D.
[22] SUP 11.3.5G, FSMA, s191E and SUP 11.3.15A deal with the requirements for notices.
[23] FSMA, s 183(1) and (2).
[24] FSMA, s 184.
[25] FSMA, s 192.
[26] FSMA (Controllers) (Exemption) Order 2009 (SI 2009/774), art 4. See SUP 11.3.2A.
[27] FSMA (Controllers) (Exemption) Order, n 26, arts 5 and 6.

D. ASSESSMENT BY THE FSA

The purpose of requiring notification of the controllers of an authorised person is to permit the FSA to vet them. The FSMA provisions that implement the AD continue the approach whereby positive vetting by the FSA is required, rather than the negative vetting that was the surface characteristic of at least one of its predecessor statutes. The FSMA language is cast in terms of the FSA issuing its 'approval' of shareholder controllers, whereas, for example, the Banking Act 1987, ss 21 to 24, referred instead to the FSA (formerly the Bank of England) issuing only a 'non-objection' to a proposed shareholder controller. Since, however, there was a free-standing test of fitness and propriety of controllers (see below), this difference is more apparent than real.

14.16

1. The test for approving or objecting to a proposed acquisition

The FSMA requires the FSA to: consider the suitability of the proposed controller and the financial soundness of the acquisition in order to ensure the sound and prudent management of the authorised person; have regard to the likely influence that the proposed controller will have on the authorised person; and disregard the economic needs of the market.[28]

14.17

The FSA may only object to an acquisition where the information provided by the proposed controller is incomplete or there are reasonable grounds for doing so on the basis of the following:[29] the reputation of the proposed controller; the reputation and experience of any person who will direct the business of the authorised person as a result of the proposed acquisition; the financial soundness of the proposed controller, in particular in relation to the type of business that the authorised person pursues or envisages pursuing; whether the authorised person will be able to comply with its prudential requirements (including the threshold conditions in relation to all of the regulated activities for which it has or will have permission); if the authorised person is to become part of a group as a result of the acquisition, and whether that group has a structure which makes it possible to exercise effective supervision; exchange of information among regulators; the allocation of responsibility among regulators; and whether there are reasonable grounds to suspect that in connection with the proposed acquisition money laundering or terrorist financing[30] is being or has been committed or attempted or the risk of such activity could increase.[31] In making a determination under section 186, the FSA must consult with other relevant competent authorities outside the UK.[32]

14.18

Although s 185(2), *prima facie*, embodies a general test of suitability, in practice it should be subject to the assessment criteria in s 186, which are more narrowly tailored than those that existed prior to the implementation of the AD. The former provisions required the FSA to be satisfied that the proposed controller was a fit and

14.19

---

[28] FSMA, s 185(2).
[29] FSMA, s 185(3).
[30] Within the meaning of Article 1 of Directive 2005/60/EC.
[31] FSMA, s 186.
[32] FSMA, s 188.

proper person to have the relevant degree of control over an authorised person and to be satisfied that the interests of consumers would not be threatened by the control.[33] The primary change to the assessment criteria is that permission can no longer be refused on consumer-interest grounds. Only prudential criteria can be considered although these include the reputation of the proposed acquirer.

14.20   The former provisions linked the test to the FSA's duty in s 41 to ensure that an authorised person will satisfy and continue to satisfy the threshold conditions in FSMA Schedule 6 in relation to all of the regulated activities for which he has or will continue to have permission. The FSMA does not link the assessment criteria to the threshold conditions and the FSA makes it clear in SUP that the only relevant criteria are those set out in s 186 without providing any guidance on the criteria.[34] This is consistent with the purpose of the AD. One of the Commission's stated reasons for introducing the AD was to improve transparency in the supervisory approvals process of acquisition activity by introducing harmonised standards and guarding against potential abuses by Member States. Therefore, the list of criteria against which the suitability and financial soundness of the proposed acquirer will be judged is exhaustive and cannot be added to by the supervisory authorities, such as the FSA.[35]

14.21   A 'Cross Border Mergers and Acquisitions Task Force' of the three Level 3 Lamfalussy committees has been set up to aid common understanding and consistency of application of the five assessment criteria among Member States to which effect is given in s 186. The Task Force was specifically asked to: reach a common understanding of the five assessment criteria in the AD; establish an exhaustive and uniform list specifying the information required for notifications; define appropriate co-operation arrangements; and develop common guidelines for assessing 'fitness and propriety'. The FSA has indicated that it will place the guidelines on its website.[36]

2. The assessment process

14.22   The FSMA requires the FSA, on receiving a notice of acquisition, to approve the acquisition unconditionally, approve the acquisition subject to conditions or object to the acquisition.[37] The FSA may only impose conditions where, if it did not impose those conditions, it would propose to object to the acquisition and may not impose conditions requiring a particular level of holding to be acquired.[38]

14.23   The FSA has a 60 working day 'assessment period' in which to determine whether it will issue its approval or objection to the acquisition of control over an authorised

---

[33] See the former s 186(1).

[34] See SUP 11.7 (Acquisition or increase of control: assessment process and criteria). However, SUP 11.2.4 G indicates that the requirement for the FSA to be notified of changes in control is linked to its function of monitoring the authorised person's continuing satisfaction of the threshold conditions.

[35] See HM Treasury and FSA *Implementation of the Acquisitions Directive: a consultation document* , n 8, p 16 to 17.

[36] Ibid. See also the Guidelines for prudential assessment under the AD.

[37] FSMA, s 185(1).

[38] FSMA, s 187(2) to (4).

person[39] and may consult with any appropriate home state regulator before making a determination.[40]

The FSA may interrupt the assessment period no more than once by making a request   14.24
for further information no later than the 50th working day of the assessment period.[41]

3. Determinations by the FSA

The FSA must issue its determination in the form of a written notice served on the   14.25
potential controller.[42] It may either approve the acquisition of control unconditionally[43]
or by warning notice and decision notice procedure attach conditions to its approval of
control.[44] The acquirer can object to the FSA's decision by referring the matter to the
Financial Services and Markets Tribunal.[45]

The FSA will be treated as having approved an acquisition if, at the expiry of the   14.26
assessment period, it has neither given notice approving or objecting to the acquisition
nor informed the proposed controller that the notice of acquisition is incomplete.[46] The
approval of an acquisition is effective for as long as the FSA may specify.[47]

E. ENFORCEMENT POWERS

The FSMA gives the FSA various powers with respect to controllers.   14.27

The FSA may object to a person's control over an authorised person where: the person   14.28
failed to notify the FSA prior to the acquisition of control; the person breaches a condition imposed under s 187; or there are grounds for objecting to control on the basis of
the assessment criteria under s 186.[48] The FSMA prescribes warning and decision notice
procedures and gives the person in respect of whom the FSA has objected a right of referral to the Tribunal.[49]

The FSMA also gives the FSA the power to serve a 'restriction notice' on an acquirer   14.29
of shares or voting power which can direct, *inter alia*, that the transfer of the shares or,
in the case of unissued shares, any agreement to transfer or transfer of the right to be
issued with them is void except by court order; that no voting rights are to be exercisable
in respect of them; that no further shares are to be issued to their holder; and that, except
in a liquidation, no payments (for example of dividends) are to be made on the shares.[50]

The FSMA also makes provision for orders by a court for the sale of shares or disposi-   14.30
tion of voting power where a person has control over an authorised person by virtue of

---

[39] FSMA, s 189(1).
[40] FSMA, s 188. See FSMA (Consultation with Competent Authorities Regulations) 2001 (2001/2509).
[41] FSMA, ss 189(2) and 190. Ss 190(3) and (4) provide for a suspension period.
[42] FSMA, s 189(3).
[43] FSMA, s 189(4)(a).
[44] FSMA, s 189(4)(b).
[45] FSMA, s 189(8).
[46] FSMA, s 189(7).
[47] FSMA, s 191.
[48] FSMA, s 191A(1) and (2).
[49] FSMA, s 191A(4), (5), (6) and (7).
[50] FSMA, s 191B.

his holding of shares or voting power and the acquisition or continued holding is in contravention of a final notice confirming an FSA objection to control.[51]

F. OFFENCES

14.31   FSMA, Part 12 creates various offences relating to the failure to notify the FSA of an intention to acquire control over an authorised person and the acquisition of control notwithstanding the FSA's objection or in breach of a condition required by the FSA. Failure to notify the FSA either of a proposed acquisition of control or of a proposed disposal or reduction of a controlling interest is an offence.[52] A criminal offence, as opposed to disciplinary sanction, is appropriate here, as the person concerned may well not be regulated by the FSA.

14.32   Acquiring or disposing of control before having received the FSA's approval or warning notice, while still within the 60 working days or extended assessment period granted by the FSMA, is an offence.[53] Similarly, if a person contravenes an interim condition or makes an acquisition after the FSA's approval has ceased he is guilty of an offence.[54] If the person provides information to the FSA which is false or breaches a direction in a restriction notice, he is also guilty of an offence.[55] These offences are punishable by a fine.[56]

14.33   Going ahead with the acquisition of control in spite of the FSA's having issued a notice of objection is the most serious offence under Part 12.[57] A person guilty of this offence may be convicted either summarily or on indictment. On summary conviction the person is liable to a fine not exceeding the statutory maximum, while on indictment the person is liable to imprisonment for a term not exceeding two years or a fine, or both.[58]

---

[51] FSMA, s 191C.
[52] FSMA, s 191F(1).
[53] FSMA, ss 190(3) and (4) and 191F(2).
[54] FSMA, s 191F(3) and (5).
[55] FSMA, s 191F(6) and (7).
[56] FSMA, s 191F(8).
[57] FSMA, s 191F(4).
[58] FSMA, s 191F(9).

15

INCOMING FIRMS: INTERVENTION BY THE FSA

Helen Marshall

A. INTRODUCTION

Part 13 of the Financial Services and Markets Act 2000 (FSMA) provides a self-contained code for the oversight, within the United Kingdom, of firms coming into the UK in reliance on a Community right to do so. Those rights are described in Part 3, Sch 3, and Sch 4 to the FSMA (see Chapter 5). The central concept in Part 13 is that the Financial Services Authority (FSA) has a power of intervention which can be used in relation to incoming firms. The equivalent for UK firms is contained in Part 4, which sets out the power of the FSA to impose requirements upon a Part 4 permission and to vary a Part 4 permission on the FSA's own initiative (see, in particular, FSMA, ss 43 and 45).   **15.01**

Part 13 follows the standard pattern established in the Single Market Directives, which divides regulatory jurisdiction into home State matters, which are prudential in character, and host State ones, where the interests of consumers and so forth are involved.   **15.02**

Following this pattern, Part 13 contains FSMA, s 194, which relates to the FSA's power to intervene on a host State basis, and s 195, which enables the FSA to exercise a power of intervention at the request of or for the purpose of assisting the home State regulator.   **15.03**

The domestic requirements for exercising the power of intervention under the FSMA reflect different considerations such as fairness to the firm, the need to proceed immediately, co-operation with other regulators, and the different procedures for host State intervention set out in the Single Market Directives. The result is quite complex.   **15.04**

B. DOMESTIC GROUNDS FOR INTERVENTION

15.05 FSMA, s 194 provides the criteria of which the FSA must be satisfied before it exercises a power of intervention in respect of an incoming firm. These are that:

(a) there is an actual or likely contravention of a host State requirement under the Act;
(b) the firm has knowingly or recklessly given false or misleading information to the FSA; or
(c) intervention is desirable to protect the interests of actual or potential customers.

15.06 The FSA's procedure for exercising the power of intervention is set out in FSMA, s 197, in terms that are very similar to the equivalent power of intervention against UK firms in Part 4 (FSMA, s 53). Decisions to intervene using the power in s 196 are referable to the Financial Services and Markets Tribunal (see FSMA, s 197(4)(e)).

15.07 Where intervention is pursuant to provisions set out in a Single Market Directive, there is an additional procedure set out in FSMA, s 199 which must be followed. The Single Market Directives currently applicable are (see Sch 3, Part 1, para 1, FSMA):

1. the Recast Credit Institutions Directive;[1]
2. the insurance directives;[2]
3. the reinsurance directive;[3]
4. the markets in financial instruments directive (MiFID);[4]
5. the insurance mediation directive;[5] and
6. the UCITS directive.[6]

15.08 Where intervention is pursuant to the breach of an MiFID requirement by the UK branch of an investment firm passporting into the UK under MiFID, or a credit institution passporting into the UK under the BCD, a separate process for the exercise of the power of intervention by the FSA will apply under s 194A.

C. SCOPE OF THE POWER OF INTERVENTION

15.09 Under FSMA, s 196, the kind of requirement that can be imposed under Part 13 is the same as under Part 4. Effectively, the FSA has to contemplate, notionally, that the incoming passport is a Part 4 permission, and that satisfying the criteria for exercise of the power of intervention has actually triggered the power under Part 4 to vary a Part 4 permission. This is dealt with in Chapter 6, centering on ss 44(1) and 45(2). Removing a regulated activity, or narrowing its description, or varying a requirement imposed under s 43, are the options most likely to be used by the FSA in exercising the power of intervention.

---

[1] EU Directive 2006/48/EC.
[2] EU Directives 73/239/EEC, 88/357/EEC, 92/49/EEC and 2002/83/EC.
[3] EC Directive 2005/68/EC.
[4] EU Directive 2004/39/EC.
[5] EU Directive 2002/92/EC.
[6] EU Directive 85/611/EEC.

D. EXERCISE OF POWERS IN SUPPORT OF OVERSEAS REGULATORS

FSMA, s 195 offers the second avenue for use of powers of intervention. This contemplates exercise at the request of or for the purpose of assisting an overseas regulator (FSMA, s 195(1)). On analysis, this section breaks down into two separate parts.

First, FSMA, s 195(5) clarifies that where a request from an overseas regulator to exercise the power of intervention is received pursuant to a so-called Community obligation, then the FSA must consider whether exercising it is necessary to comply with the Community obligation. Community obligation is undefined in the FSMA, though the analysis is likely to be consistent with other places in the FSMA, especially Part 4, where if the FSA diagnoses a Community obligation, it is then required to act to give effect to this obligation (see FSMA, s 57). The most likely circumstance where an obligation would be found to exist would be in a flagrant case where the home State had itself taken intervention action, or even withdrawn European Economic Area (EEA) authorisation (expressly captured in FSMA, s 195(5)(b)). Here, the general duty to co-operate with other competent authorities (see, in particular, s 354) might well mean that something similar or parallel had to be put in place in the UK.

Where the FSA believes that an MiFID requirement has been breached by an investment firm passporting into the UK under MiFID or a credit institution passporting into the UK under the BCD, and the requirement is one for which the home State has responsibility, a separate process for the exercise of the power of intervention will apply as set out in FSMA, s 195A.

The second situation in which the FSA can exercise its power to intervene in support of an overseas regulator is in circumstances where there is no Community obligation. The criteria for exercise of the power of intervention at the request of or to assist an overseas regulator in these circumstances are set out in FSMA, s 195(6). These correspond, virtually word for word, to the equivalent criteria for exercise of the FSA's own-initiative power at the request of or to assist specific overseas regulators in s 47(4).

Where requests are received in respect of an incoming EEA firm in respect of certain provisions in the first non-life directive, the life assurance consolidation directive, and the reinsurance directive, FSMA, s 198 enables the court on the application of the FSA to grant injunctions, or interdicts, to restrain the firm from disposing or otherwise dealing with any of its assets, and otherwise to enable the FSA to perform its functions under the FSMA.

E. CONSUMER CREDIT

The power of intervention is also available to the FSA in relation to consumer credit, if the Office of Fair Trading (OFT) informs the FSA that an incoming firm's behaviour falls within s 25(2A)(a) to (e) of the Consumer Credit Act 1974 (see below) (FSMA, s 194(3)). The effect of the subsection is to bring to bear on an incoming EEA firm the FSA's powers of intervention in relation to consumer credit aspects of their business.[7]

15.10

15.11

15.12

15.13

15.14

15.15

---

[7] See for instance the Credit Institutions Directive, annex A, para 2 and Council Directive on Investment Services in the Securities Field (1993/22/EEC), annex, Sch C, para 3.

15.16   There is a second set of sanctions, in FSMA, ss 203 and 204, which are in the hands of the OFT itself, in relation to investment firms passporting into the UK under MiFID and credit or financial institutions passporting into the UK under the BCD, whose EEA authorisation covers any Consumer Credit Act business. If the behaviour, or likely behaviour, of these firms falls within s 25(2A)(a) to (e) of the Consumer Credit Act 1974 (see below), the OFT may impose a 'consumer credit prohibition' on the firm (FSMA, s 203(1) and (4)). Instead of imposing a prohibition, the OFT may also choose to impose a restriction on the firm's consumer credit business where it sees fit (FSMA, s 204(2)).

15.17   The criterion for both sets of sanctions is virtually the same, that is, the OFT's conclusion is that the firm has done anything of the kind specified in s 25(2A)(a) to (e) of the Consumer Credit Act 1974. This list is as follows:

(a) committed any offence involving fraud or other dishonesty or violence;
(b) contravened any provision made by or under—
    (i) this Act;
    (ii) Part 16 of the Financial Services and Markets Act 2000 so far as it relates to the consumer credit jurisdiction under that Part;
    (iii) any other enactment regulating the provision of credit to individuals or other transactions with individuals;
(c) contravened any provision in force in an EEA State which corresponds to a provision of the kind mentioned in paragraph (b);
(d) practised discrimination on grounds of sex, colour, race or ethnic or national origins in, or in connection with, the carrying on of any business; or
(e) engaged in business practices appearing to the OFT to be deceitful or oppressive or otherwise unfair or improper (whether unlawful or not).

15.18   Where the OFT's decision is concerned with likely future contraventions, it is limited to use of own powers as defined in FSMA, ss 203 and 204.

16

DISCIPLINARY MEASURES

Helen Marshall

A. INTRODUCTION

Part 14 of the Financial Services and Markets Act 2000 (FSMA) sets out the disciplinary   16.01
tools available to the Financial Services Authority (FSA) to deal with the misconduct of
authorised persons:[1] the power of public censure which is set out in FSMA, s 205, and
the power to impose a financial penalty in respect of any contravention under the FSMA
which is set out in FSMA, s 206.[2]

The Decision Procedure and Penalties Manual chapter of the FSA Handbook (DEPP)   16.02
and the Enforcement Guide (EG) provide additional guidance on these disciplinary
sanctions. In addition, although there is no reference to private warnings in the FSMA,
the EG explains that in certain circumstances, the FSA may decide that it is not appropriate to bring formal disciplinary action. Instead, the FSA may consider it helpful to

---

[1] An 'authorised person' is defined as '(in accordance with section 31 of the Act (Authorised Persons)) one
of the following: (a) a person who has a Part 4 permission to carry on one or more regulated activities; (b) an
incoming EEA firm; (c) an incoming Treaty firm; (d) a UCITS qualifier; (e) an ICVC; (f) the Society of
Lloyd's'.

[2] As amended by SI 2007/126, the Financial Services and Markets Act 2000 (Markets in Financial
Instruments) Regulations 2007.

make an authorised person aware that it came close to being subject to formal disciplinary action by giving the person a private warning.

B. WHICH CONTRAVENTIONS MAY BE DISCIPLINED?

16.03   The FSMA powers of public censure (s 205) and imposition of a financial penalty (s 206) may be invoked in relation to a contravention of a requirement imposed by or under the Act. The most obvious requirements are those contained in the FSA's rules, which include the 11 Principles for Businesses, made under Part 10 of the FSMA. Many other requirements are imposed by or under the FSMA itself, or deemed to be so imposed. In particular, FSMA, s 20 has the effect that where an authorised person carries on a regulated activity in the UK otherwise than in accordance with his permission to do so, he is to be taken to have contravened a requirement imposed on him by the FSA under the FSMA. Specific requirements may include those imposed under FSMA, s 43 in relation to the way the firm carries on its particular activities and those imposed in the context of investigations under Part 11 of the FSMA (see Chapter 13). Where a firm commits an offence under the FSMA, it will breach a requirement imposed by or under the FSMA, and may therefore be disciplined under Part 14 for the breach.

C. THE FSA's APPROACH TO DISCIPLINE

16.04   Discipline is only one of a number of regulatory tools available to the FSA to address a particular issue. In deciding whether or not to take disciplinary action in respect of conduct appearing to the FSA to constitute a breach, the FSA has stated that it 'will seek to exercise its enforcement powers in a matter that is transparent, proportionate, responsive to the issue, and consistent with its publicly stated policies'.[3] The FSA has stated that it will take a risk-based approach to enforcement and prioritise areas which pose the biggest threat to its regulatory objectives.[4]

D. THE FSA's APPROACH TO PUBLIC CENSURE

16.05   As set out above, the FSA has the statutory power under s 205 of the FSMA to publish a public censure. This is a serious sanction; as the breach will be made public this can have an adverse impact on a person's business and reputation. Public censures may also be accompanied by a press release. Public censure can be imposed at the same time as a financial penalty.

16.06   The criteria for determining whether it is appropriate to impose a public censure are set out in DEPP.

16.07   DEPP 6.4.2 G states that the criteria for determining whether it is appropriate to issue a public censure rather than impose a financial penalty are similar to those for

---

[3] See EG 2.2 (2).
[4] The FSA's regulatory objectives are set out in FSMA, s 2 (2) (a)–(d).

determining the amount of any financial penalty to be imposed (see below). However, the particular considerations stated to be relevant when the FSA determines whether to issue a public censure rather than impose a financial penalty include whether or not deterrence may be effectively achieved by issuing a public censure, the seriousness of the breach, whether the person has brought the breach to the attention of the FSA, and the disciplinary record of the person.[5]

E. THE FSA's APPROACH TO FINANCIAL PENALTIES

As set out above, the FSA can issue a public censure without a fine, but in practice, the FSA usually uses its power to issue a public censure whilst simultaneously imposing a fine. **16.08**

DEPP 6.4.2 G[6] sets out a non-exhaustive list of particular factors which may indicate that a financial penalty is more appropriate than merely a public censure (see above). **16.09**

Aside from its public law duty to behave reasonably, the FSA has a general duty under FSMA, s 2 (3)(c) to have regard to the principle that a burden imposed on a person should be proportionate to the benefits. More particularly, FSMA, s 210 (2) requires that the FSA's policy on determining the size of any penalty must include having regard to the seriousness of the breach, the extent to which it was deliberate or reckless and whether or not the person on whom the penalty is to be imposed is an individual. **16.10**

DEPP 6.5 includes guidance on how the FSA will determine the level of any financial penalty it seeks to impose. DEPP 6.5.2 G sets out a non-exhaustive list of factors that the FSA will take into account. These include the nature, seriousness and impact of the breach in question, the extent to which the breach was deliberate or reckless, whether the person on whom the penalty is to be imposed is an individual, the size and financial resources of the person on whom the penalty is to be imposed, conduct following the breach, and the person's disciplinary record. **16.11**

The FSA therefore recognises that as the facts of each case are likely to differ, to a greater or lesser extent, from any other case, a tariff of penalties is not appropriate.[7] In theory, as there is no tariff, potentially fines can be unlimited. However, the FSA will take into account the factors listed above in setting the amount of any fine, as well as the level of fines previously levied against authorised persons for similar breaches of FSMA requirements.[8] **16.12**

---

[5] See DEPP 6.4.2 G (1)–(8) for a full list of factors that the FSA will consider.

[6] See DEPP 6.4.2 G (1)–(8) for a full list of factors that the FSA will consider.

[7] There is one exception, for the imposition of penalties for late submissions of returns (see DEPP 6.6).

[8] CP09/19 was published in July 2009. Under the new proposals, fines will be linked more closely to income, being based on up to 20 per cent of a company's income from the product or business area linked to the breach, and up to 40 per cent of an individual's salary and benefits (including bonuses) from their job relating to the breach in non-market abuse cases. The minimum starting point for individuals in market abuse cases is proposed to be £100,000. The consultation will close on 21 October 2009, and any new policy is likely to apply to breaches committed after February 2010.

F. EARLY SETTLEMENT SCHEME

16.13   Following an internal review—the Enforcement Process Review, which was conducted in 2005—the FSA introduced a formal discount scheme for early settlement of enforcement cases. The scheme allows for the application of a fixed discount to the penalty that the FSA would otherwise seek to impose for the breach in question.

16.14   The FSA's aim in introducing this scheme was to encourage those subject to enforcement action to settle the case early. The FSA's approach is to agree in principle with the person subject to enforcement action an amount of financial penalty commensurate to the breach in question (having regard to the factors set out in DEPP 6.5.2 G, referred to above). This is referred to by the FSA as the 'starting figure'. The starting figure is then reduced by a fixed percentage depending on the stage at which any settlement is reached.[9]

G. DISCIPLINARY PROCEDURE

16.15   Although FSMA, Part 14 purports to deal with disciplinary measures, most of the substantive provisions on the formal disciplinary procedure are to be found in Part 26 of the Act (see Chapter 28).

16.16   The procedure for the exercise of the powers of public censure (FSMA, s 205) and imposition of a financial penalty (FSMA, s 206) involves the issue by the FSA of a warning notice setting out the proposed statement of censure, or the amount of the penalty as the case may be (FSMA, s 207; see also FSMA, s 387 in Chapter 28). Certain material must then be disclosed by the FSA (see FSMA, s 394 in Chapter 28). The firm may make representations at this point and so may certain third parties. FSMA, s 393 deals with third-party rights in this context. If the FSA decides to proceed further, it is then obliged to give a decision notice, setting out the statement or penalty (FSMA, s 207) in accordance with FSMA, s 388. Chapter 28 sets this out in more detail. The firm may accept the outcome at that stage. Alternatively, the matter may be referred to the Financial Services and Markets Tribunal in accordance with the provisions of Part 9 of the Act (see Chapter 11). The Tribunal is a first-instance tribunal with full jurisdiction over all matters of fact and law.

16.17   While the firm is considering whether or not to exercise its right to refer the matter to the Tribunal, the FSA may not publish the statement or seek to recover the penalty (FSMA, s 133(9)). Once the period in which referral can be made has expired, or any decision so referred has been confirmed by the Tribunal (or on appeal), the FSA may publish the statement or seek to recover the penalty as the case may be. There is a requirement to give the person concerned a final notice at that point (FSMA, s 390).

---

[9] If a settlement is reached during Stage 1 of any investigation, a 30 per cent reduction will apply to the starting figure. Stage 1 starts at the beginning of an investigation and lasts until the FSA has been able to make a reasonable assessment of the appropriate penalty and communicated its assessment to the authorised person. If a settlement is reached during Stage 2 of any investigation, then a 20 per cent reduction will apply to the starting figure. Stage 2 starts at the end of Stage 1 and lasts until the expiry of the period for making written representations (or, if sooner, the date on which written representations are sent in response to the warning notice) (as to which see below). If a settlement is reached during Stage 3 of an investigation, then a 10 per cent reduction will apply to the starting figure. Stage 3 lasts from the end of Stage 2 until the FSA issues a decision notice (as to which see below). No reduction is applicable after this stage. See DEPP 6.7 (Discount for early settlement).

After a statement has been published, a copy must be sent to the firm concerned (FSMA, s 209). A copy must also be sent to potentially prejudiced third parties, being persons to whom a copy of the decision notice was given under FSMA, s 393(4).

H. FINANCIAL PENALTIES: WHAT HAPPENS TO THE MONEY?

FSMA, Sch 1, para 16, requires the FSA to operate a scheme for ensuring that the amounts paid to it by way of penalties imposed under the FSMA are applied for the benefit of authorised persons. The FSA operates such a scheme in tandem with its arrangements for raising annual fees from authorised persons. The FSA allocates authorised persons to different bands according to their size and the services and products they offer. Penalties are allocated to the fee band of the authorised person who has paid the fine, which has the effect of reducing the cost of regulation for other firms in that band, by reducing the level of the annual fee.

16.18

I. ARTICLE 6 OF THE EUROPEAN CONVENTION ON HUMAN RIGHTS

Some have suggested that the safeguards outlined here and in related chapters do not go far enough in relation to discipline, on the basis that disciplinary action is criminal for the purposes of art 6 of the European Convention on Human Rights. Such action is certainly not criminal for domestic purposes, but that is not determinative for art 6 purposes. Were discipline to be criminal for art 6 purposes, certain additional safeguards would automatically flow: for example, in the context of a presumption of innocence, there would be a privilege against self-incrimination in the disciplinary proceedings. There would also be an express right to legal assistance for those of insufficient means when the interests of justice so require. The question whether art 6 applies in its civil or criminal guise to disciplinary proceedings was debated at length in the Joint Committee on Financial Services and Markets and mentioned at various points in the Parliamentary process. The government, advised by Sir Sidney Kentridge QC and James Eadie, took the view that the disciplinary regime was not criminal for art 6 purposes and that, unlike the market abuse regime, there was not sufficient doubt about it to warrant introducing criminal safeguards in case the courts took a different view. It is generally accepted that art 6 applies in full to the disciplinary process as a whole in its civil form. As further explained in Chapters 10 and 28, compliance with art 6 is ultimately secured by the availability of referral to an independent tribunal of full jurisdiction, the Financial Services and Markets Tribunal. The Tribunal's decision in the market abuse case against Philippe Jabre[10] clarified the Tribunal's role, in that once a case has been referred to the Tribunal, all aspects of the case are potentially subject to consideration and determination by the Tribunal anew.

16.19

---

[10] FIN 2006/06: Case 035 Philippe Jabre & Financial Services Authority (Decision on Jurisdiction) July 2006. In Mr. Jabre's case theTribunal ruled that the FSA could re-introduce integrity issues which had previously been rejected by the FSA's Regulatory Decisions Committee. Mr Jabre subsequently withdrew his reference, meaning that the FSA's original decision stood.

17

FINANCIAL SERVICES COMPENSATION SCHEME

Alex Kuczynski

A. INTRODUCTION

Part 15 of the Financial Services and Markets Act 2000 (FSMA) requires the Financial   17.01
Services Authority (FSA) to establish a compensation scheme. In addition to a scheme, the FSA is to establish a 'Scheme Manager'. The compensation scheme supports the FSA's statutory objectives of the protection of consumers and market confidence. It recognises that the FSA does not operate a 'zero failure' regime. The role of the compensation scheme for depositors was considered in detail in a series of Consultation Papers published by the tripartite authorities in advance of the Banking Act 2009 ('the Banking Act').

With effect from 1 December 2001, the FSA established the Financial Services   17.02
Compensation Scheme (FSCS), which is, as the Scheme Manager, a 'one-stop shop' for compensation claims against failed authorised firms in respect of regulated activities. As a unitary scheme, it succeeded numerous predecessors providing compensation in different sectors, for example, the Deposit Protection Board for bank deposits, the Policyholders Protection Board for insurance, and the Investors Compensation Scheme for investment firms.[1]

---

[1] Predecessor schemes under the Banking Act 1987, the Policyholders Protection Act 1975, and the Financial Services Act 1986 respectively.

B. THE SCHEME MANAGER

17.03　The FSA must establish a body corporate to act as the Scheme Manager, and the Financial Services Compensation Scheme Limited is a company limited by guarantee.[2] Its chairman and directors are appointed (and may be removed) by the FSA, with the approval of the Treasury in the case of the chairman. The directors are public interest appointments rather than industry or consumer representatives. The terms of appointment must ensure their operational independence—the FSCS is accountable to, but operationally independent of, the FSA.[3] In addition to its largely non-executive board, FSCS employs in the region of 160 staff to handle or oversee its operations.

17.04　The FSCS is required to provide an annual report to the FSA,[4] and the FSA fixes FSCS's management expenses (on an annual basis).[5]

17.05　The FSMA provides the FSCS with certain powers to obtain documents or information for the 'fair determination' of claims, either from the relevant firm,[6] or an appointed insolvency practitioner[7] or the Official Receiver.[8] Failure to comply may be treated as a contempt of court.[9] The scope of the FSCS's rights to receive information, from the FSA and from the firm, was recently extended by the Banking Act.[10]

17.06　The FSMA gives the FSCS statutory immunity from claims for damages, save for acts or omissions in bad faith or unlawful as a result of Section 6(1) of the Human Rights Act 1998.[11] The FSCS is, however, required to establish European Convention on Human Rights-compliant procedures for the handling of claims under its rules, and the FSCS is accountable for its decisions by way of judicial review, for example, by dissatisfied claimants.[12]

C. EUROPEAN DIRECTIVES

17.07　The establishment of the FSCS delivers the United Kingdom's implementation of certain European Directives. For deposit taking, the Deposit Guarantee Schemes Directive (DGSD),[13] as recently amended[14] and, for investment business, the Investors Compensation Directive (ICD)[15] imposed minimum requirements for compensation

---

[2] Section 212.
[3] Section 212(5).
[4] Section 218.
[5] Section 223.
[6] Section 219.
[7] Section 220.
[8] Section 224.
[9] Section 221.
[10] adding Section 218A and amending Section 219.
[11] Section 222.
[12] *R v Financial Services Compensation Scheme Ltd, ex parte Geologistics Ltd* (2003) EWCA Civ 1905.
[13] 1994/19/EC.
[14] 2009/14/EC.
[15] 1997/9/EC.

schemes in Member States. The European Commission is presently considering whether to introduce a directive for insurance guarantee schemes.

D. THE SCHEME

Section 213(1) requires the FSA to 'by rules establish a scheme for compensating persons in cases where relevant persons are unable, or likely to be unable, to satisfy claims against them'. The scheme is contained in a set of rules, made by the FSA, in the Compensation Sourcebook (COMP Sourcebook) of the FSA's Handbook. Compensation is limited to claims against 'relevant persons' (or appointed representatives) for acts or omissions whilst authorised[16] and the claims are 'in connection with regulated activities carried on (whether or not with permission)'.[17] The Compensation Rules (COMP Rules) set out who can claim, and for what.

17.08

Without limitation, the FSMA[18] sets out the type of provisions which the scheme may contain. Mostly, such provisions are provided for in the COMP Rules, notably: 'the circumstances in which a relevant person is to be taken (for the purposes of the scheme) to be unable, or likely to be unable, to satisfy claims',[19] 'for a claim to be entertained only if it is made by a specified kind of claimant',[20] or if it is a 'specified kind of claim',[21] and 'limiting the amount payable on a claim to a specified maximum amount or a maximum amount calculated in a specified manner'.[22] FSA has recently reviewed the compensation limits payable by the FSCS.[23]

17.09

First, for compensation to be payable a firm must be 'in default'—unable, or likely to be unable, to meet protected claims. The firm may be subject to insolvency proceedings or may have ceased trading and be unable to meet claims.[24] What compensation is then available depends on the type of claim.

17.10

The COMP Sourcebook represents a consolidation of the pre-existing regimes for the protection of depositors, policyholders, and investors, and expanded since 1 December 2001 to reflect the FSA's increased scope, in particular for home finance intermediaries[25] and general insurance intermediaries.[26] As a result, claims against failed firms are dealt with under one of five 'sub-schemes' within COMP: protected deposits, protected insurance business, protected investment business, protected non-investment insurance intermediation, and protected home finance business (for example, mortgage advice and arranging).

17.11

---

[16] Section 213(9).
[17] Section 213(3).
[18] Section 214(1).
[19] Section 214(1)(a).
[20] Section 214(1)(f).
[21] Section 214(1)(g).
[22] Section 214(1)(j).
[23] FSA Consultation Paper 08/15: Financial Services Compensation Scheme: Review of Limits (October 2008) and FSA Policy Statement 09/7 (April 2009).
[24] COMP 6.
[25] from 31 October 2004.
[26] from 15 January 2005.

The Rules set out the eligibility of claimants,[27] the scope of protected business,[28] the compensation limits,[29] and the quantification of claims.[30]

1. Protected Deposits

17.12   The FSCS protects deposits made with authorised UK firms, such as banks and building societies. A claim is 'for' a protected deposit. Certain deposits (for example, secured or non-nominative deposits) are not protected. The maximum compensation payable is £50,000 per claimant, per firm. The COMP Rules exclude certain categories of depositor (as permitted by the DGSD), but protection is generally available to individuals and small businesses.

17.13   Following the Banking Act, the payment of compensation, in respect of a bank, may be as part of the bank insolvency procedure, following the appointment of a bank liquidator. Alternatively, the FSCS may fund the transfer of accounts from the failed bank to another institution.

17.14   The Banking Act also provides different options for the protection of depositors besides payout by the FSCS: the Bank of England may set up a 'bridge bank' or transfer a bank or its business, or a bank may be taken into public ownership by HM Treasury. In such cases, the FSCS may be called upon to contribute to the costs of such 'special resolution regime' under regulations made by the Treasury.[31]

2. Protected Contracts of Insurance

17.15   The FSCS protects claims 'under' contracts of insurance. The scope and level of protection differs depending on the type of insurance. For claims in respect of certain compulsory insurances, for example, under the Employer's Liability (Compulsory Insurance) Act 1969 and the Road Traffic Act 1988, compensation is paid in full, without limit, to all policyholders. For other claims, compensation is limited to £2,000 in full plus 90 per cent of the remainder, unlimited, and to 'eligible' policyholders only (ie individuals and small businesses). This limit will reduce to a flat 90 per cent rate from 1 January 2010.

17.16   The test of whether an insurance contract is protected or not depends on when it is issued—generally, the FSCS protects UK and European Economic Area (EEA) risks[32] for contracts issued by UK insurers after commencement but for contracts issued before 1 December 2001, the test is of a 'UK policy' (taken from the Policyholders Protection Act 1975).

17.17   One distinct feature of the FSCS's insurance role is the objective of securing continuity of cover for insurance business, as opposed to a policyholder payout, for example, by a transfer of policies to, or the issue of substitute policies by, another insurer (under ss 216 and 217 of the FSMA in respect of long-term (life) and general business respectively).

---

[27] COMP 4.
[28] COMP 5.
[29] COMP 10.
[30] COMP 12.
[31] The Financial Services and Markets Act 2000 (Contributions to Costs of Special Resolution Regime) Regulations 2009 (SI 2009 No. 807).
[32] COMP 5.4.

3. Protected Investment Business

The FSCS protection is far wider than required by the ICD. It covers claims 'in connection with' investment business, including advice and arranging.[33] For example, the FSCS has paid compensation for the mis-selling of shares, personal pension policies, endowment policies, as well as for the failure of stockbrokers and others to return client money and assets.

The maximum compensation is £48,000 comprising £30,000 in full and 90 per cent of the next £20,000. The limit is due to increase to £50,000 (representing £50,000 of the loss payable in full) from 1 January 2010. Other than for claims for the return of property, the FSCS has the discretion to quantify the level of compensation. As for protected deposits, generally individuals and small businesses are eligible to claim.

17.18

17.19

4. Protected General Insurance Broking (Non-Investment Insurance Mediation)

This sub-scheme was added to the FSCS following implementation by the FSA of the Insurance Mediation Directive (with effect from 15 January 2005). It protects insurance broking (that is, advice and arranging). The same compensation limits and eligibility criteria apply as for protected insurance business.

17.20

5. Protected Home Finance Mediation

With effect from 31 October 2004, the FSCS protected such activities, including mortgage advice and arranging. This date coincided with such activities becoming regulated by th FSA. The same compensation limits and eligibility criteria apply as for protected investment business.

17.21

6. Geographical scope and EEA firms

Pursuant to Section 214(4), the COMP Rules define the geographical scope of the FSCS. Business conducted by authorised firms from the UK is protected and the nationality or residence of the claimant is generally irrelevant. Further, the FSCS may protect certain business carried out by UK firms from EEA branches (which, for deposits and certain investment business, is required by the DGSD and the ICD).

17.22

E. FUNDING

The FSCS is funded by the financial services industry. It imposes levies 'on authorised persons or any class of authorised person for the purpose of meeting its expenses'.[34] At present, the FSCS is funded on a 'pay-as-you-go' basis by annual levies raised on authorised firms. As such, the FSCS is funded by trading firms. The good 'pay for the bad'.

17.23

---

[33] COMP 5.5.
[34] Section 213(3).

The Banking Act allows for a 'contingency fund' (or pre-fund)[35] but such powers have not yet been exercised.

17.24   The levy raising rules are contained in the Fees Manual (FEES). The costs of the FSCS's existence irrespective of levels of claims activity ('base costs') are paid by the entire financial services industry. The costs of handling claims, and the costs of compensation itself, are funded by levies raised on a class basis, by reference to the business giving rise to the claims. For the purposes of the levy, in addition to the deposit class (containing banks, building societies and credit unions), there are a further four classes divided between providers and intermediaries: general insurance, life and pensions, investment, and home finance. Each class and sub-class is subject to an annual cap on its levy. In the event that the FSCS wishes to levy in excess of the annual cap on a particular sub-class, the connected (provider or intermediary) sub-class will contribute up to its limit; if the levy exceeds the combined class total, the remaining classes contribute up to their maximum annual thresholds (with the exception of home finance providers who contribute solely to the compensation in respect of home finance intermediaries).

17.25   The Banking Act added powers to allow the FSCS to borrow from the National Loans Fund.[36] In respect of the recent banking crisis, prior to commencement of the Banking Act, the FSCS borrowed from government funds to meet its full costs of compensation, rather than raise a levy on the industry at that time.

17.26   In order to mitigate the cost of compensation to levy payers, on the payment of claims, the FSCS takes claimants' rights against the insolvent firms and third parties, which rights the FSCS pursues to make recoveries for the benefit of levy payers. The FSMA (as amended by the Banking Act) provides for the FSCS to take rights of recovery.[37] In practice, the FSCS has usually taken assignments of claimants' rights under the FSMA and the COMP Rules.[38] The FSCS is frequently a significant, if not the largest, creditor of failed financial services firms and plays an active role as a creditor, and litigant, in pursuing recoveries from both the firms and third parties.[39]

F. CLAIMS EXPERIENCE

17.27   In its first seven or so years of operation, the FSCS paid compensation in excess of £1bn to consumers, largely in respect of its insurance and investment sub-schemes. For example, compensation was paid to policyholders of Independent Insurance Company Limited for a wide range of general insurance business, and significant levels of compensation were paid to investors for mis-sold personal pensions and endowment policies.

17.28   In late 2008, the FSCS responded to the banking crisis following the failure of five banks.[40] Under a combination of powers under the Banking (Special Provisions) Act 2008 and the FSMA, the FSCS paid actual or 'deemed' compensation in the region of

---

[35] Section 214A.
[36] Section 223B.
[37] Section 215.
[38] COMP 7.
[39] *FSCS v Abbey National Treasury Services plc* (2008) EWCA 1897.
[40] Bradford & Bingley Plc, Heritable Bank Plc, Kaupthing Singer & Friedlander Limited, Landsbanki Islands hf, and London Scottish Bank Plc.

£20 million to fund either the transfers of protected deposits to other institutions or depositor payouts. Further, under the Banking Act, the FSCS expects to contribute to the cost of resolution of Dunfermline Building Society.

The banking crisis, and the response of the relevant authorities in the UK and abroad, had ensured that the FSCS and its work have a higher public profile than ever before.

17.29

18

FINANCIAL OMBUDSMAN SERVICE

Alex Kuczynski

A. INTRODUCTION

Part 16 of the Financial Services and Markets Act 2000 (FSMA) provides for the **18.01** Financial Services Authority (FSA) to establish a 'scheme under which certain disputes may be resolved quickly and with minimum formality by an independent person'.[1] The FSA established the Ombudsman Scheme, known as the Financial Ombudsman Service (FOS). The FOS replaced previous dispute resolution schemes, including the Banking Ombudsman, the Insurance Ombudsman, and the complaints schemes set up by the Self Regulatory Organisations (under the Financial Services Act 1986), such as the Personal Investment Authority (PIA) Ombudsman.

Although there is no European requirement for the establishment of financial services **18.02** ombudsman schemes, the European Commission encourages informal dispute resolution schemes, setting out criteria in its communiqué (dated 30 March 1998). Those principles, which the FOS satisfies, are independence of decision making, transparency of procedure, adversarial process, effectiveness (such as consumer access), 'legality' (that is, no deprivation of legal rights), 'liberty' (that is, binding if accepted by the parties), and rights of representation.

The scheme is free to consumers and only binding when the consumer elects to accept **18.03** the FOS's decision.

The FOS describes itself as neither a consumer champion nor a defender of the indus- **18.04** try, and as 'settling financial disputes, not taking sides'. It is to provide quick, cheap,

---

[1] Section 225(1).

informal, and effective dispute resolution without the risk of adverse costs orders. The rules applicable to the FOS are contained in the Dispute Resolution: Complaints (DISP) Sourcebook, which also sets down the complaints procedures firms must follow when dealing with customers.

B. THE SCHEME OPERATOR

18.05   The Financial Ombudsman Service Limited—known as the Scheme Operator—is a company established by the FSA to carry out the statutory functions of the Scheme Operator under Part 16 of the FSMA[2] and Part 2 of Schedule 17 to the FSMA.

18.06   As required by Schedule 17, the chairman and board members are appointed (and may be removed) by the FSA, with the approval of the Treasury in the case of the chairman. The board members' terms of appointment are to secure their independence from the FSA in the operation of the scheme. The board are public interest appointments, not representative of consumer or industry sectors.

18.07   The board determines the appointment of the Chief Ombudsman (who functions as a chief executive) and a panel of Ombudsmen (with appropriate qualifications and experience), the making of certain rules of FOS (as to procedure, the levying of case fees and the voluntary jurisdiction), and the approval and recommendation to the FSA of an annual budget (which must be approved by the FSA). The FOS and the Chief Ombudsman must make an annual report to FSA.[3]

18.08   The FSMA provides particular powers and protections to the FOS. For example, the FOS may compel production of documents or information from a 'party to a complaint' where it is necessary for 'determination of the complaint'.[4] Failure to comply may be treated as a contempt of court.[5] The FOS has immunity from liability for damages for acts or omissions in the discharge, or purported discharge, of any functions under the FSMA, unless shown to have been in bad faith or in respect of an award of damages under Section 6(1) of the Human Rights Act 1998.[6]

C. JURISDICTION—COMPULSORY AND VOLUNTARY

18.09   The FSA is responsible for making certain rules, contained in the DISP Sourcebook, setting out the compulsory jurisdiction, those eligible to claim, and when a claim may be made,[7] but, with FSA's consent, the FOS makes certain rules as to the process and procedure.[8] Schedule 17 identifies certain areas for the DISP Rules, for example, time limits, evidence, and process.

---

[2] Section 225(2).
[3] Schedule 17.
[4] Section 231.
[5] Section 232.
[6] Schedule 17, para 10.
[7] Section 226: Schedule 17, para 13.
[8] Schedule 17, para 14.

With some limited exceptions, authorised firms are subject to the compulsory juris- 18.10
diction of the FOS, which applies to acts or omissions by an authorised firm carrying
out a regulated activity.[9] A list of relevant regulated activities is at DISP 2, Annex 1. The
FOS's compulsory jurisdiction has been extended not only to include credit unions,
mortgage business, and general insurance broking, as those firms or activities have
become regulated by the FSA, but also to consumer credit by amendment to the FSMA,[10]
which business is regulated under the Consumer Credit Act 1974 by the Office of Fair
Trading. From 1 November 2009, payments services will follow with FSA's regulation.

The voluntary jurisdiction[11] operates by rules made by the FOS, with the FSA's 18.11
approval, described as 'standard terms'.[12] Voluntary jurisdiction covers non-'compulsory'
business dealt with by previous Ombudsmen schemes, or connected to regulated activities of firms but which activities are or could be specified in the compulsory jurisdiction.
It includes firms which are not required to be authorised but who wish to offer a dispute
resolution service (for example, the Post Office and National Savings & Investments).

D. DISPUTE RESOLUTION

Consumers must first communicate the substance of the complaint to the firm giving it 18.12
a 'reasonable opportunity to deal with it'[13]—the FOS responds to 'deadlock' between a
firm and its customer, and the FOS is not the customer's first resort. A firm must handle
complaints under the rules in DISP 1.[14]

The FOS seeks to resolve disputes first by mediation or settlement between the firm 18.13
and the consumer or by an initial view (or 'adjudication') which may be accepted by the
parties. Case handling is delegated by the Ombudsmen for these purposes. Complaints
may be dismissed if the complainant rejects a 'fair and reasonable' offer of settlement. In
the event that the complaint cannot be resolved at a preliminary stage, an Ombudsman
may make a formal determination. In 2008–09, 51 per cent of cases were resolved by
settlement, 41 per cent by adjudication, and 8 per cent by the final decision of an
Ombudsman.[15]

The FOS's determinations are 'by reference to what is, in the opinion of the 18.14
Ombudsman, fair and reasonable in all the circumstances of the case'.[16] The FOS will
have regard not just to the relevant law and regulations but also 'regulator's rules, guidance and standards, codes of practice and, where appropriate, what [the Ombudsman]
considers to have been good industry practice at the relevant time'.[17]

---

[9] Section 226(2)–(4).
[10] Section 226.A.
[11] Section 227.
[12] Schedule 17, Part 4.
[13] Schedule 17, para 13(3).
[14] Treating complaints fairly.
[15] Annual Review 2008–09.
[16] Section 228.
[17] DISP 3.6.4R.

18.15   The Ombudsman's determination must be by written statement[18] and may include an award against the firm for payment of 'fair compensation for loss or damage',[19] not to exceed a monetary limit fixed by the FSA, although a recommendation of a higher amount may be made.[20] At present, the monetary limit is £100,000. Awards include financial loss but also 'fair' payment for poor administration, distress, or inconvenience.[21] Alternatively, a direction to take 'just and appropriate steps' may be made by the FOS, for example, reinstatement of pension benefits.[22]

18.16   If accepted by the complainant,[23] the Ombudsman's decision is binding on the consumer and the firm and is 'final'. Prompt compliance by a firm with an Ombudsman's decision is required. The FOS awards are enforceable[24]—money awards are registered by the FOS and enforced in the County Court. Although a determination by the FOS may be challenged by judicial review,[25] this regime under the FSMA and DISP has been upheld by the Court of Appeal.[26]

18.17   The FOS may not make costs awards in favour of a firm against a complainant,[27] although a costs award may be made against the parties in certain circumstances (for example, for improper conduct or unreasonable delay).[28]

18.18   The FOS's process are designed to comply with the requirements of the Human Rights Act 1998 and in particular Article 6 of the European Convention on Human Rights (the entitlement to a fair and public hearing within a reasonable time by a independent and impartial tribunal established by law in a determination of any civil rights and obligations). Complaints are usually dealt with on paper. In a few cases each year, the FOS will conduct oral hearings, which are informal.

18.19   The DISP Rules set out the complaint handling process. It is inquisitorial rather than adversarial, and flexible (for example, as to the procedure for, and form of, evidence). The FOS is to serve consumers, that is, private individuals, and small businesses and organisations.[29] Businesses, charities, or trusts are subject to a £1 million test applied to group annual turnover, annual income, or net asset value respectively. Further exclusions apply for the recently-added consumer credit jurisdiction. There are time limits for making complaints to the FOS. Generally, complaints must be made within six months of 'deadlock' (that is, the firm's final response) and DISP applies the principles of limitation and time bar.[30] The FOS may also dismiss claims without consideration of the merits in certain circumstances.[31]

---

[18] Section 228(3) and (4).
[19] Section 229(2)(a).
[20] Section 229(5).
[21] Section 229(3); DISP 3.7.
[22] Section 229(2)(b).
[23] Section 228(5).
[24] Section 229(8) and (9): Schedule 17 para 16.
[25] *R v Financial Ombudsman Service Ltd ex parte Norwich & Peterborough Building Society and others* (2002) EWCA 2379; *R (IFG Financial Services Ltd) v Financial Ombudsman Scheme Ltd* (2005) EWCA 1153.
[26] *R (Heather Moor & Edgecomb Limited) v FOS* (2008) EWCA Civ 642.
[27] Section 230(3).
[28] Section 230(4).
[29] DISP 2.7.
[30] DISP 2.8.
[31] DISP 3.3.

The standard terms for complaints dealt with under the voluntary jurisdiction, albeit made by the FOS, closely follow the compulsory jurisdiction rules.[32]   18.20

In dealing with complaints against live firms, the FOS has a role as to the industry more broadly. From its experience of complaints, the FOS may refer matters with 'wider implications' (for consumers or the market) to the FSA for regulatory review. Alternatively, for discrete issues of general importance, the FOS may determine a 'test case' procedure, seeking the guidance of a court judgment which can then be applied to complaints of a similar nature.[33]   18.21

E. FUNDING

Awards made by the FOS are funded by the respondent firm. The FOS's own costs are funded by levy and case fees on authorised firms, and member firms in respect of the voluntary jurisdiction. Annual fees comprise a general levy and case fees, under rules made under FSMA, s 234 and 234A. Levies are raised on 'industry blocks', which correspond to the FSA's periodic fees blocks. At present, a firm only pays a case fee (of £500) for its fourth and each subsequent chargeable case in a year.   18.22

F. THE FOS's EXPERIENCE

The FOS's caseload has grown consistently since 2001. In 2008–9, the FOS received 113,949 new cases and averaged 865 staff. There are about 40 Ombudsmen. Currently, the most common subjects for complaints are payment protection insurance, credit cards, bank charges, personal pensions, and mortgage endowments.   18.23

At the FOS's invitation, Lord Hunt recently carried out a review of the FOS's relationship with consumers, the financial services industry and other stakeholders. In his report,[34] Lord Hunt supported the principles of a 'fair and reasonable' decision, file-based reviews, no appeals, and no charge for complaints, but made 73 specific recommendations on 'transparency' and 'accessibility'. The FOS is taking forward a programme of implementation, including the publication of complaints data relating to specific firms, but within the existing principles as to its role and structure.   18.24

---

[32] DISP 4.

[33] DISP 3.3.5R.

[34] 'Opening up, reaching out, and aiming high—an agenda for accessibility and excellence in the Financial Ombudsman Scheme' (April 2008).

19

COLLECTIVE INVESTMENT SCHEMES

Andrew Henderson

A. INTRODUCTION

(a) *General*

Part 17 of the Financial Services and Markets Act 2000 (FSMA) governs the regulation of investment funds and other arrangements which fall within the definition of a 'collective investment scheme' (CIS). Since most individuals lack sufficient wealth to invest in a broad portfolio of securities, commodities or property, or to invest in very expensive securities, commodities or property, CISs allow any number of people to pool their money and participate collectively in such investments. In addition, since most people lack the professional expertise or the time to manage their investments, CISs also provide a mechanism whereby they can appoint professionals to manage those investments. These advantages of a CIS highlight its two key characteristics: (i) a pooling of assets; and (ii) the owners of the assets not having day-to-day control over how the pooled assets are managed.[1]   19.01

(b) *Different Types of Funds and Their Regulation*

In classifying the types of investment funds, a useful distinction to note is that between public funds, which may be marketed to the general public, and private funds, which may only be marketed to a limited category of persons, for example, professional investors or high net-worth individuals. An example of a public fund is a unit trust which is   19.02

---

[1] These and the other characteristics that determine whether a fund or other arrangement will be a CIS are discussed in paragraphs 19.12 to 19.18 below.

established under a trust deed and invests in a 'basket' of shares which the manager may purchase, hold, or sell on a regular basis to ensure that the basket matches or 'tracks' the value of an index of shares such as the FTSE 100. An example of a private fund is a private equity fund which is established under a limited partnership agreement and invests in the shares of unlisted companies, where the manager may purchase the entire share capital of the company, participate in the management of the company, and sell or 'exit' the company after a number of years.[2]

19.03   For regulatory purposes, a basic distinction (corresponding to the public fund/private fund distinction) may be drawn between a 'regulated CIS' and an 'unregulated CIS'.[3] Authorised unit trusts (AUTs), open-ended investment companies (OEICs), and overseas recognised schemes (ORSs) are regulated CISs; all other CISs are unregulated.[4]

19.04   The description 'unregulated CIS' requires some clarification. In practice, an unregulated CIS is not free from regulation under the FSMA. Anyone who wishes to promote an unregulated CIS must be authorised by the Financial Services Authority (FSA) to avoid breaching the financial promotion restriction in FSMA, s 21.[5] In addition, anyone who wishes to establish, operate, or wind up an unregulated CIS needs to be authorised by the FSA to avoid breaching the General Prohibition[6]—art 51 of the FSMA (Regulated Activities) Order 2001 (RAO),[7] which identifies the establishing, etc, of a CIS as a regulated activity, does not restrict the establishment, operation, or winding up of a CIS to regulated CISs.[8] Finally, anyone who wishes to carry on other regulated activities with respect to an unregulated CIS, such as managing an unregulated CIS,[9] needs to be authorised by the FSA.[10]

19.05   However, whereas the requirements relating to items such as structure and investment restrictions are prescribed for regulated CISs, such as AUTs and OEICs by the FSMA, secondary legislation, and FSA rules, there are no such requirements for unregulated CISs. In this respect, those wanting to establish an unregulated CIS are not subject to FSA regulation, hence it is said that, for example, a private equity fund is unregulated in that items, such as the fund's structure and investment restrictions, are determined by the agreement of the parties who establish the fund rather than by regulation, such as that for AUTs and OEICs discussed below.

19.06   A fund may also fall outside the scope of the regulation of CISs by virtue of being excluded from the definition of a CIS.[11] An example is an investment trust which, despite its name, is actually a company which, instead of operating a business, invests

---

[2] See, generally, Spangler *The Law of Private Investment Funds* (2008).

[3] As discussed below, as a result of exclusions from the definition of a CIS, some public funds may not be regulated CISs.

[4] The distinction is directly relevant to the restrictions which FSMA, s 238(1) places on the promotion of CISs, discussed in paragraphs 19.24 to 19.29 below.

[5] See Chapter 4.

[6] FSMA, s 19. See Chapter 3.

[7] SI 2001/544.

[8] Art 51(1)(a). *Cf* art 51(1)(b) and (c) which refer specifically to AUTs and OEICs.

[9] See RAO, art 37.

[10] See also the proposed European Directive on Alternative Investment Fund Managers, COM(2009)207.

[11] This is discussed in paragraphs 19.16 to 19.18 below.

and manages its assets (including pooled funds contributed by holders of its shares) in property of any description with a view to spreading investment risk. For the purposes of the public/private distinction, it would be a public fund. As is the case with an unregulated CIS, an investment trust is still subject to FSA regulation under FSMA, Part 6[12] and control under the relevant companies laws. Moreover, those managing assets of the Investment Trust would need to be FSA authorised if located in the UK.[13]

(c) *The European Dimension: UCITS*[14]

The UCITS Directive as amended (UD)[15] requires Member States to harmonise their rules regulating the establishment, operation, and management of 'undertakings for collective investment in transferable securities' (UCITS) and to allow such funds to be marketed on a cross-border basis. It was first implemented in 1985 and subsequently amended.[16] It allows funds to invest in money market instruments and certain deposits, derivatives, and units in other UCITS funds as well as in the transferable securities referred to in their name.[17] A further revision of the UD is currently under discussion, but is not expected to take effect until 2011 or later.[18]   19.07

UCITS funds must operate on the principle of risk spreading and are required to redeem units on demand, or to ensure that the units can be sold on a recognised stock exchange, in each case at a price not significantly different from their net asset value.[19] They are subject to restrictions on their investment policies.[20] The dealing prices of units must be regularly published, as must certain documents including a prospectus and an annual and half-yearly report by the managers.[21]   19.08

A scheme can only carry on activities as a UCITS scheme if it has been approved by the financial regulator in its home jurisdiction, which requires regulatory approval of the manager, the depositary or trustee, and the fund's rules.[22] In particular, the manager and depositary/trustee must be independent of each other.[23]   19.09

Schemes which are authorised in accordance with the terms of the UD may, after making a filing to the host state regulator and waiting for two months, be marketed in other member states.[24] Once they have undergone this process, the host member state may not impose any additional authorisation requirements.[25]   19.10

---

[12] See, in particular, Listing Rule (LR) 15. Part 6 is discussed in Chapter 8.

[13] See FSMA, s 19 and RAO, art 37.

[14] See, generally, the FSA CIS Information Guide (COLLG) 2.

[15] Directive on the co-ordination of laws, regulations, and administrative provisions relating to undertakings for collective investment in transferable securities (UCITS)—Directive 85/611/EEC.

[16] By, *inter alia*, Directive 2008/18/EC and the 'UCITS III' Directives: Directive 2001/107 and Directive 2001/108.

[17] Article 19 of the UD.

[18] See the Green Paper on the Enhancement of the EU Framework for Investment Funds (SEC(2005) 947) and the White Paper on Enhancing the Single Market Framework for Investment Funds (COM (2006) 686).

[19] Article 1(2) of the UD.

[20] Articles 19 to 24a of the UD.

[21] Article 19 of the UD.

[22] Article 4 of the UD.

[23] Article 10 of the UD.

[24] Article 6A of the UD.

[25] Article 6 of the UD.

19.11   In the UK, the provisions of the UD are implemented by the FSMA and by the secondary legislation and FSA rules made thereunder. As described below, these deal both with the requirements for UK schemes and with the recognition of UCITS funds constituted in other European Economic Area (EEA) states. Excluded from the definition are closed-ended schemes, schemes, which raise capital without promotion of units to the general public in at least one EEA state and certain other schemes in which the investment and borrowing powers are considered inappropriate. Both AUTs and OEICs can benefit from the UCITS regime.

1. Definition of a CIS[26]

19.12   The definition of CISs in s 235 is very wide and covers any arrangement with respect to property of any description (including money), the purpose or effect of which is to let investors participate in the profits or income arising from that property (whether by becoming owners of that property or otherwise).[27] The term 'arrangement' has been broadly interpreted.[28] It would cover corporate arrangements, such as OEICS and Limited Liability Partnerships (LLPs),[29] trust arrangements, such as AUTs, and contractual arrangements, such as limited partnerships. The term 'property' has also been interpreted widely to include, for example, ostriches.[30]

19.13   Section 235(2) refines this definition by providing that participants in the scheme must not have any 'day-to-day control' over the management of the property, though they may have a right to be consulted or provide directions. In this respect, it is sufficient if *some* of the scheme's members, such as limited partners in a limited partnership,[31] lack day-to-day control.

19.14   Additionally, s 235(3) provides that an arrangement only constitutes a CIS where (i) there is pooling of contributions and of profit/income, and/or (ii) the property is managed as a whole by or on behalf of the operator of the scheme. In *FSA v Fradley and Woodward*,[32] the Court of Appeal held that this requirement was satisfied where the participants' contributions were paid into a single bank account, even though the money was held on trust and each contribution individually identified.

19.15   Section 235(4) provides that, where there are separate pools of property (such as sub-funds of an umbrella fund) between which investors can choose, these pools will only constitute a *single* CIS if the participants are entitled to exchange or switch between sub-funds.

---

[26] See *Financial Services Law* (2nd Ed) 17.07 *et seq.*
[27] See the FSA Perimeter Guidance Manual (PERG) 9 for further guidance. This definition follows that which existed in the Financial Services Act 1986 (FS Act).
[28] See *The Russell-Cooke Trust Co v Prentis* [2002] EWHC 2227 (Ch.D) considering similar provisions in the FS Act.
[29] See the LLP Act 2000.
[30] See *Pinstripe Farming Co Ltd, Re* [1996] 2 BCLC 295 (Ch.D).
[31] See the Limited Partnership Act 1907.
[32] [2005] EWCA Civ 1183.

2. Exclusions

The wide definition of CISs potentially catches arrangements which might not generally   19.16
be thought of as CISs, including many corporate entities.[33] Therefore, the Treasury has
been given the power to exclude certain types of arrangement from the definition of
CISs.[34]

The current exclusions are set out in the FSMA (CIS) Order 2001,[35] and arrange-   19.17
ments not treated as CISs include:

(1) bank deposits placed with an authorised deposit-taking institution;[36]
(2) schemes not operated by way of business—for example private or family
     arrangements;[37]
(3) certain employee share schemes;[38]
(4) joint ventures;[39]
(5) certain arrangements between members of the same group of companies;[40]
(6) the issuing of depositary receipts;[41]
(7) clearing services operated by an authorised person or recognised exchange or clear-
     ing house;[42]
(8) contracts of insurance;[43]
(9) certain pension arrangements;[44] and
(10) bodies corporate—but for this exclusion, almost any body corporate would fall
     within the definition of a CIS. The exclusion applies to all bodies corporate other
     than OEICs and LLPs.[45] Corporate entities, such as investment trusts, fall under
     this exclusion and are not treated as CISs for the purposes of s 235 but, as
     mentioned above, may be subject to the LR, Companies Act and the FSMA,
     insofar as those managing an investment trust's assets are FSA authorised.

The FSA and Treasury are consulting on whether Islamic finance instruments, known   19.18
as *Sukuk*, should also be excluded.[46]

---

[33] In fact, most corporate entities would be considered CISs if they were not expressly excluded under the
FSMA (CIS) Order 2001 (below). See also PERG 9.4.4 G.

[34] FSMA, s 235(5).

[35] SI 2001/1062, as amended.

[36] SI 2001/1062, para 3.

[37] SI 2001/1062, para 4.

[38] SI 2001/1062, para 8.

[39] The existing business exemption applies to certain schemes entered into wholly or mainly for
commercial purposes related to an existing non-investment business: see SI 2001/1062, para 9 (as amended
in 2003).

[40] SI 2001/1062, para 10.

[41] SI 2001/1062, para 15.

[42] SI 2001/1062, para 16.

[43] SI 2001/1062, para 17.

[44] eg individual pension accounts and occupational / personal pension plans: see SI 2001/1062, paras 19
and 20.

[45] SI 2001/1062, para 21.

[46] See *Financial Services Law*, n 31, 19.92 *et seq*.

3. Open-Ended Investment Companies

19.19　An OEIC is a CIS which has been established as a corporate entity and satisfies both the property and investment conditions set out in s 236.[47]

19.20　The property condition requires that the scheme property must be beneficially owned and managed by or on behalf of a body corporate, having as its purpose the spreading of investment risk and giving its members the benefit of the results of the management of the funds.[48]

19.21　The investment condition requires that the pooled funds be invested so that a reasonable investor would expect to: (i) be able to cash in his investment in the scheme within a reasonable period; and (ii) receive in return an amount calculated wholly or mainly by reference to the net asset value of the scheme property.[49]

19.22　OEICs were first introduced in the UK as a result of the implementation of the UD, as the then existing UK company law did not permit open-ended corporate vehicles with the power to freely sell and redeem their own shares because of the capital maintenance rule.[50]

4. Other definitions

19.23　The FSMA provides definitions for unit trust schemes, trustees, depositaries, operators, units, AUTs, authorised OEICs, and recognised schemes.[51]

B. RESTRICTIONS ON PROMOTION

1. Unregulated CISs

19.24　Whilst the general restriction on financial promotions in s 21[52] only applies to unauthorised persons, s 238(1) imposes a similar ban on authorised persons in relation to the marketing of unregulated CISs. Similarly, s 240 prohibits authorised persons from approving financial promotions in relation to CISs (which would allow third parties to communicate them) where s 238 prevents them from marketing such schemes themselves.[53]

19.25　The remainder of s 238 and the CIS Promotion Order[54] made under s 238(6) set out a number of exceptions to the prohibition. The exceptions in the CIS Promotion Order are broadly equivalent to those in the FSMA Financial Promotion Order (FPO),[55] and thereby ensure that an authorised person is able to promote an unregulated CIS at least as widely as an unauthorised person relying on s 21 and the FPO could. In practice, this

---

[47] FSMA, s 236(1).
[48] FSMA, s 236(2). See also PERG 9.5.
[49] FSMA, s 236(3). See also PERG 9.6 to 9.9.
[50] See *Trevor v Whitworth* (1887) 12 App Cas 409, HL.
[51] FSMA, s 237.
[52] See Chapter 4.
[53] FSMA, s 240(1).
[54] FSMA (Promotion of CIS) Order 2001, SI 2001/1060. FSMA, ss 238(1) and 238(2).
[55] SI 2005/1529.

means that unregulated CISs can only be marketed to investment professionals, certified high net worth individuals, high net worth companies, and similar sophisticated investors, irrespective of whether the person doing the marketing is FSA authorised.[56]

2. Regulated CISs

The restrictions described in paragraphs 19.24 and 19.25 above do not apply to regulated CISs (that is, AUTs, authorised OEICs, and ORSs),[57] and authorised persons can freely market these to the general public. This gives effect, in practice, to the basic distinction between unregulated and regulated CISs highlighted in paragraphs 19.03 to 19.06 above.   19.26

3. Other exclusions from the restrictions

The restrictions do not apply to a communication originating outside the UK unless it is 'capable of having an effect' in the UK[58] or where there is no promotion to the general public.[59]   19.27

Section 239(1) enables the Treasury to create an additional exemption for single property schemes,[60] but no such regulations have yet been made.   19.28

4. Claims for damages

Authorised persons breaching s 238 or s 240 may be liable under s 150[61] to any private person who suffers a loss as a result.[62]   19.29

C. AUTHORISED UNIT TRUST SCHEMES

Sections 242 to 261 govern AUTs, that is, any CIS constituted by way of trust, the first basic type of regulated CIS. They include detailed provisions concerning the authorisation and 'passporting' of such schemes, applicable scheme rules and prospectus requirements, changes to existing schemes, and the ending of authorisation and intervention.   19.30

1. Scheme authorisation

An application to the FSA for an order declaring a unit trust scheme to be authorised must be made jointly by the manager and trustee (or proposed manager and trustee) of   19.31

---

[56] See the discussion of these and other exemptions in chapter 4 which will be directly relevant to the CIS Promotion Order. The main difference between the CIS Promotion Order and the FPO relates to the exemption for one off financial promotions in art 15 of the CIS Promotion Order: see PERG 9.20.

[57] FSMA, s 238(4), and FSMA, s 238(7) in respect of designated territory schemes. See also COLL 9.

[58] FSMA, s 238(3).

[59] FSMA, s 238(5) and (10). See also COBS 4.12.

[60] Exchange-listed schemes investing only in specific buildings or a group of adjacent or contiguous buildings managed as a single enterprise: FSMA, s 239(3).

[61] See Chapter 12.

[62] FSMA, s 241.

the scheme.[63] The manager and trustee must be bodies corporate incorporated in the UK or EEA entities having a place of business in the UK,[64] have FSA permission to manage or to act as a trustee,[65] and must be independent of each other.[66]

19.32   The FSA may make an authorisation order if (i) the scheme complies with the requirements set out in s 243 and COLL, and (ii) a copy of the trust deed and a solicitor's certificate confirming compliance with these requirements have been provided.[67] In particular, the name of the scheme must not be undesirable or misleading,[68] participants in the scheme must be entitled to have their units redeemed at a price close to net asset value,[69] and the scheme's purposes must be reasonably capable of being successfully carried into effect.[70]

19.33   The FSA must determine applications within six months of receiving the completed application,[71] and the warning and decision notice procedures—including a right of referral to the Financial Services and Markets Tribunal (Tribunal)—apply.[72]

19.34   A manager or trustee wishing to 'passport' a scheme for marketing in other EEA states under the UD can also apply for a certificate of EEA compliance.[73] This can be done at any time after establishing the scheme.[74]

2. Trust scheme rules

19.35   Section 247 allows the FSA to make 'trust scheme rules'[75] dealing with matters such as the constitution, management and operation of AUTs,[76] the issue and redemption of units,[77] and the contents of trust deeds.[78] These rules are mandatory and apply irrespective of the terms of the trust deed.[79]

3. Scheme particulars rules

19.36   Section 248 allows the FSA to make rules about the form and content of AUT prospectuses[80] and to impose publication and updating requirements.[81]

---

[63] FSMA, s 242(1).
[64] FSMA, s 243(5).
[65] FSMA, s 243(7).
[66] FSMA, ss 242(2) and 243(4).
[67] FSMA, s 243(1).
[68] FSMA, s 243(8). See also COLL 6.9.
[69] FSMA, s 243(10).
[70] FSMA, s 243(9).
[71] FSMA, s 244(1).
[72] FSMA, s 245(2).
[73] FSMA, s 246(1).
[74] FSMA, s 246(2).
[75] See COLL 3,5, and 6.
[76] FSMA, s 247(1)(d).
[77] FSMA, s 247(2).
[78] FSMA, s 247(3).
[79] FSMA, s 247(4).
[80] FSMA, s 248(2).
[81] FSMA, s 248(1), (3) and (4). See COLL 4.

Where the scheme particulars contain an untrue or misleading statement or omit information required to be included under the rules and a 'qualifying person' suffers loss as a result, the fund manager must compensate them for that loss.[82]   19.37

Any auditor of an AUT or authorised OEIC that breaches the terms of the trust scheme rules may be disqualified from acting as such.[83] The warning and decision notice procedure set out in s 345 applies.[84]   19.38

4. Modification and waiver of rules

The FSA may, on the application of a relevant person, modify or waive the trust scheme rules and/or the scheme particulars rules in respect of a particular person or scheme.[85] The s 148 provisions for modification/waiver of rules apply with certain amendments.[86]   19.39

5. Changes to existing schemes/changes of manager or trustee

The manager of an AUT must inform the FSA of any proposal to change the scheme or to replace the trustee,[87] and the trustee must notify the FSA of any proposal to replace the manager.[88] Changes can take effect only once (i) the FSA has approved the proposal in writing, or (ii) the FSA has failed to object within one month.[89] The FSA will not approve a replacement manager or trustee unless they satisfy the relevant conditions concerning independence, incorporation, authorisation and permission referred to above.[90]   19.40

6. Exclusion clauses

Section 253 invalidates any provision of a trust deed which seeks to exempt the manager or trustee of an AUT from liability for any failure to exercise due care and diligence in the discharge of their functions.   19.41

7. Ending of authorisation

Section 254 gives the FSA the power to revoke the authorisation of an AUT on its own initiative in the circumstances set out in s 254(1), which include one or more of the requirements for making an authorisation order being no longer satisfied.   19.42

If the FSA proposes to issue a compulsory revoking order, warning notice and decision notice procedures (including a right of referral to the Tribunal) apply.[91]   19.43

---

[82] FSMA, s 248(5) and (6). See also COLL 4.2.4.
[83] FSMA, s 249(1).
[84] FSMA, s 249(2).
[85] FSMA, s 250(1) to (3).
[86] FSMA, s 250(4) and (5). See Chapter 12.
[87] FSMA, s 251(1). Additional requirements apply where there is a proposed change to the trust deed: s 251(2).
[88] FSMA, s 251(3).
[89] FSMA, s 251(4). If the FSA intends to object, warning notice and decision notice procedures apply and there is a right of referral to the Tribunal: s 252.
[90] FSMA, s 251(5).
[91] FSMA, s 255.

19.44   Section 256 enables the manager or trustee of an AUT to ask the FSA to revoke the scheme's authorisation.

8. Powers of intervention

19.45   As an alternative to revoking the authorisation of an AUT, the FSA can require the manager of the scheme to cease issuing and/or redeeming units, or require the manager and trustee to wind up the scheme.[92]

19.46   Whenever the FSA can give a direction under s 257, it may also apply to the court for an order removing and replacing the manager and/or trustee or, if there is no suitable replacement, appointing an authorised person to wind up the scheme.[93]

19.47   Separate procedures apply to the giving and varying of directions on the FSA's own initiative,[94] refusing requests to revoke or vary,[95] and granting requests to revoke or vary.[96]

19.48   If the FSA proposes to refuse to vary or revoke an existing direction on application, warning notice and decision notice procedures (including a right of referral to the Tribunal) apply.[97]

D. OPEN-ENDED INVESTMENT COMPANIES

19.49   Section 262 deals with the second basic type of regulated CIS—the OEIC. An OEIC is a CIS established as a body corporate under reg 3 of the OEIC Regulations[98] or its predecessor.[99] The rules applicable to OEICs are set out in the OEIC Regulations, which also give effect to and develop the requirements set out in the UD.

1. Scheme authorisation

19.50   The FSA may make an authorisation order if the scheme will comply with the requirements set out in reg 15,[100] including the requirement that the OEIC and its instrument of incorporation comply with the OEIC Regulations and FSA rules and that the scheme property of the OEIC is entrusted for safekeeping to a depositary.[101]

---

[92] FSMA, s 257.
[93] FSMA, s 258.
[94] FSMA, s 259.
[95] FSMA, s 260.
[96] FSMA, s 261.
[97] FSMA, s 260(2).
[98] Open-Ended Investment Companies Regulations 2001 (SI 2001/1228) (as amended), made by HM Treasury pursuant to FSMA, s. 262. Note that these regulations only apply in Great Britain. Northern Irish OEICs would be governed by regulations made under the Open-Ended Investment Companies Act (Northern Ireland) 2002.
[99] Open-Ended Investment Companies (Investment Companies with Variable Capital) Regulations 1996 (SI 1996/2827). These regulations referred to OEICs as 'investment companies with variable capital' (or 'ICVCs'), and this terminology is still used in the FSA's rules to refer to OEICs.
[100] OEIC Regulations, reg 14(1).
[101] OEIC Regulations, reg 5.

If the FSA refuses an application, it must give the applicant a decision notice and the 19.51
applicant may appeal the decision to the Tribunal.[102]

An OEIC interested in marketing units in other EEA states under a 'passport' under 19.52
the UD can also apply for a certificate of EEA compliance.[103]

2. Trust scheme rules and scheme particulars rules

Regulation 6 of the OEIC Regulations provides that the FSA's rule-making powers in 19.53
relation to trust scheme rules and scheme particulars rules for AUTs in sections 247 and
248 apply to OEICs.

3. Changes to existing OEIC

An OEIC must inform the FSA in writing of any proposal to change its instrument of 19.54
incorporation, prospectus, directors or depositary, or to restructure, merge, or wind up
the OEIC.[104]

If the FSA intends to refuse a proposed change, warning notice and decision notice 19.55
procedures (including a right of referral to the Tribunal) apply.[105]

4. Ending of authorisation

The FSA may revoke the authorisation of an OEIC on its own initiative in circum- 19.56
stances similar to those for revocation of the authorisation of an AUT and with the same
procedures being applicable.[106]

5. Powers of intervention

As an alternative to revoking the authorisation of an OEIC, the FSA can require the 19.57
OEIC to cease issuing and/or redeeming shares, require the OEIC to be wound up or
make related directions.[107]

Whenever the FSA can give a direction in relation to its powers of revocation, it may 19.58
also apply to the court for an order removing and replacing the depositary and/or any
director of the OEIC or, if there is no suitable replacement, appointing an authorised
person to wind up the OEIC.[108]

6. Exclusion clauses

Regulation 62 of the OEIC Regulations invalidates any provision contained in the 19.59
instrument of incorporation of the OEIC or otherwise which seeks to exempt an officer,

---

[102] OEIC Regulations, reg 16.
[103] OEIC Regulations, reg 17.
[104] OEIC Regulations, reg 21.
[105] OEIC Regulations, reg 22.
[106] OEIC Regulations, regs 23 and 24.
[107] OEIC Regulations, reg 25(2).
[108] OEIC Regulations, reg 26(4).

auditor or depositary of an OEIC from liability for any failure to exercise due care and diligence in the discharge of their functions.

7. Modification and waiver of rules

19.60   The modification and waiver rules described in Chapter 5 apply to OEICS.[109]

E. OVERSEAS RECOGNISED SCHEMES

19.61   Sections 264 to 283 deal with the final basic type of regulated CIS by allowing the FSA to 'recognise' ORSs, that is, schemes constituted in other EEA states,[110] designated territory schemes,[111] and other individually recognised overseas schemes.[112] Once recognised by the FSA, such schemes are treated as 'recognised schemes',[113] and may be marketed in the UK by FSA authorised persons.[114]

1. Schemes constituted in other EEA states (UCITS schemes)

19.62   Section 264 enables the operator of a UCITS scheme constituted in another EEA state to 'passport' its scheme into the UK by notifying the FSA of its intention to market the scheme there.[115] The notification must contain or be accompanied by (i) the scheme's rules or instrument of incorporation, (ii) a full and simplified prospectus, and (iii) recent financial reports (if applicable).[116] The notice must also be accompanied by a certificate of UCITS compliance from the regulator in the scheme's home jurisdiction (the home state regulator) and contain an address for service in the UK.[117]

19.63   If the FSA fails to inform the operator and the home regulator within two months of receiving the notice (the notice period required under the UD) that the marketing materials may not comply with relevant UK law, the scheme automatically becomes a 'recognised scheme'.[118] If the FSA intends to object, its response must set out the reasons for objecting and specify a reasonable period (at least 28 days) within which representations may be made.[119] Section 265 gives the operator the right to make representations and the warning notice and decision notice procedures (including a right of referral to the Tribunal) apply.

---

[109] OEIC Regulations, reg 7(1) and (2). Where the rules implement European UCITS legislation (such as Directives 85/611/EEC and 2001/108/EC), no waiver or modification can be granted that would result in non-compliance with the minimum requirements laid down in the relevant Directive.

[110] FSMA, s 264.

[111] FSMA, s 270.

[112] FSMA, s 272.

[113] FSMA, s 237(3). See also COLL 9.

[114] FSMA, s 238(1) and (4)(c).

[115] FSMA (CISs constituted in Other EEA States) Regulations 2001 (as amended) (SI 2001/2383), reg 3.

[116] FSMA, s 264(1)(a) and (3)(c) and SI 2001/2383, reg 4.

[117] FSMA, s 264(3)(a) and (b). See also COLL 9.

[118] FSMA, s 264(2). Note that, at that point, the scheme and its operator and depositary (if any) become FSA authorised persons, even though they may not be carrying out regulated activity in the UK: FSMA, Sch 5, para 1.

[119] FSMA, s 264(3).

In the case of recognised UCITS schemes, most of the FSA's 'host state' regulations **19.64** (apart from rules on financial promotion and on facilities to be provided in the UK) fall away in deference to the control exercised by the fund's home state regulator.[120]

FSMA, s 276 gives the FSA the power to suspend the promotion of a recognised **19.65** UCITS scheme where the operator has marketed it in breach of UK financial promotion rules. This enables the FSA to stop promotion of the scheme, even though it cannot suspend the scheme's recognition. S 268 sets out the procedures for suspending the promotion of a scheme and s 269 sets out the procedure for varying or revoking the suspension of a scheme.

2. Designated territory schemes

The FSA may also recognise schemes from non-EEA states where the country in which **19.66** the scheme is managed and authorised and the type of scheme have been designated by the Treasury.[121] The operator of such a scheme must notify the FSA of its desire for recognition.[122] If the FSA fails to object within two months of the date of application, the scheme automatically becomes recognised.[123] S 271 sets out the procedure where the FSA decides to object.

Before designating a country, the FSMA requires the Treasury to obtain a report from **19.67** the FSA on the country in question and be satisfied that the regulation of CISs and the investor protection afforded thereunder is at least equivalent to that provided under the FSMA and that there are adequate arrangements for co-operation between the FSA and the foreign regulator.[124]

3. Individually recognised overseas schemes

Section 272 enables the FSA to recognise overseas schemes on an individual basis where **19.68** they do not qualify for recognition under ss 264 or 270 but comply with the requirements set out in s 272. In practice, individual recognition is not routinely granted. S 272 sets out various requirements which include adequate protection of participants, adequate constitution and management and adequate allocation of powers and duties between operator and trustee or depositary.[125] The other requirements are similar to those for UK AUTs—see paragraphs 19.31 to 19.34 above.

FSMA, ss 274 to 276 deals with the procedures relevant to individually recognised **19.69** schemes and s 277 deals with the situation where an operator of a recognised scheme wishes to alter the scheme.

---

[120] FSMA, s 266(1). There is an exception for EEA fund management companies under s 266(1A). See also Article 6 of the UD.

[121] FSMA, s 270(1)(a) and (b). See also the FSMA (CIS) (Designated Countries and Territories) Order 2003 (SI 2003/1181) et al. Current designated territories include Bermuda, Guernsey, Jersey and the Isle of Man.

[122] FSMA, s 270(1)(c).

[123] FSMA, s 270(1)(d).

[124] FSMA, s 270(2) and (5). The Treasury is not bound by the FSA's report.

[125] FSMA, s 272(4). Note that the requirement is for 'adequate' protection, unlike the s 270(2) requirement for 'equivalent' protection.

4. Rules applying to designated territory schemes and individually recognised overseas schemes

19.70　Section 278 allows the FSA to require the operators of non-UCITS schemes to publish prospectuses in line with FSA rules.

19.71　　FSMA, ss 279 and 281 give the FSA the power to revoke or suspend the recognition granted to non-UCITS schemes, thereby preventing their marketing in the UK.[126] Ss 280 and 282 set out the applicable procedures.

5. Facilities and information in the UK

19.72　S 283 allows the FSA to require operators of recognised schemes (including UCITS schemes) to maintain 'facilities' in the UK, including sources of information and the ability to redeem units, and to require individual scheme operators to include certain information in financial promotions referring to their scheme.

F. INVESTIGATIONS

19.73　Section 284 gives the FSA special investigative powers in relation to CISs. These are in addition to (and partially overlap with) its general powers of investigation in relation to authorised and approved persons.[127]

19.74　　The FSA or the Secretary of State may appoint a competent person to investigate any type of CIS other than an OEIC[128] (including AUTs and recognised schemes) and their respective operators, trustees and depositaries if it considers that doing so is in the interests of the participants (actual or potential) or otherwise a matter of public concern.[129]

19.75　　The person appointed may also investigate any other scheme that has the same manager, trustee, operator or depositary as the scheme under investigation and the manager, operator or trustee of such other scheme.[130] The investigator may require any person to produce relevant documents in his possession or under his control, to attend before the investigator or otherwise to provide assistance.[131] Various aspects of the provisions of Part 11 concerning investigations are applied to s 284 investigations.[132]

---

[126] FSMA, s 238(1) and (4)(c).

[127] See Chapter 14 of the FSA Enforcement Guide.

[128] Similar powers in respect of an OEIC are contained in reg 30 of the OEIC Regulations, made under s 262(2)(k). The distinction reflects the fact that investigation of companies is generally regarded as a matter for the Secretary of State, not the FSA.

[129] FSMA, s 284(1).

[130] FSMA, s 284(2). In this context, OEICs are included, so as to allow the investigator to form a complete picture of the facts.

[131] FSMA, s 284(3).

[132] See FSMA, s 284(4) to (11).

20

RECOGNISED INVESTMENT EXCHANGES AND CLEARING HOUSES

Emma Vick

A. INTRODUCTION

The recognition regime for Recognised Investment Exchanges (RIEs) and Recognised   20.01
Clearing Houses (RCHs) was introduced in the Financial Services Act 1986, Sch 4. The
regime was designed for effective supervision of exchanges and clearing houses in order
to secure high standards within the markets.

The provisions were substantially re-enacted in Part 18 of the Financial Services and   20.02
Markets Act 2000 (FSMA). The major changes at that time were to confer on the FSA
a power to issue directions and also to confer on recognised bodies (which are the RIEs
and RCHs) the same immunity that the FSA has from civil action by members,
and others, in respect of anything done in the performance of their regulatory functions.

The Treasury's power to bring exchange disciplinary proceedings into the statutory review procedure (s 300) was also potentially a major change.

20.03 The recognition requirements for RIEs and RCHs contain various conditions that must be satisfied by applicant exchanges and clearing houses and which must also be satisfied by recognised bodies on a continuing basis. These conditions include being fit and proper, having sufficient financial resources and as well being able and willing to promote and maintain high standards of integrity and fair dealing in the carrying on of regulated activities. Recognised bodies must also cooperate in the sharing of information with other agencies. Compliance with these conditions is supervised by the FSA.

20.04 Recognised bodies have an exemption under s 285(2) of the Act, permitting them to carry on certain activities which would otherwise require authorisation by the FSA under Part 4 of the Act.

20.05 In this chapter, the origins and nature of operation of each of the RIEs and RCHs are outlined in turn. The recognition regime set up under the Act and the recognition rules are then examined in further detail together with the impact which the Investment Exchanges and Clearing Houses Act 2006 and the Markets in Financial Instruments Directive (MiFID) have had on the recognition regime.

B. THE INVESTMENT EXCHANGES

20.06 There are currently six RIEs in relation to which a recognition order is in force under the FSMA. These are:

- EDX London Ltd
- ICE Futures Europe
- LIFFE Administration and Management
- London Metal Exchange Limited (The) (LME)
- London Stock Exchange plc, and
- PLUS Markets plc.

20.07 Since the first edition of this book, Coredeal and Tradepoint Stock Exchange have ceased to operate as RIEs. Tradepoint became virt-x and a new RIE named virt-x Exchange Limited was formed in 2001; it was renamed SWX Europe Limited in 2008 and derecognised in 2009. NYMEX Europe Limited was recognised in 2005 and wound up in a Members' Voluntary Liquidation in February 2009.

20.08 The origins and functions of the current RIEs are outlined below.

1. EDX London Ltd[1]

20.09 EDX London was created in 2003 by the London Stock Exchange and NASDAQ OMX to bring cash equity and derivatives markets closer together using a common order book to make trading easier and more cost effective. It was built on the foundations of OM London Exchange which had been operating since 1989.

---

[1] See <http://www.londonstockexchange.com/edx/aboutus/history/history.htm>.

EDX became a wholly owned subsidiary of the London Stock Exchange in December 2008.   20.10

2. ICE Futures Europe[2]

When the first edition of this book was published, The International Petroleum Exchange (IPE) was an RIE providing a futures exchange for crude oil and gas contracts through open outcry trading. In June 2001, the IPE was acquired by ICE and is now ICE Futures Europe®, Europe's leading regulated energy futures exchange. It now accounts for approximately half of the world's crude oil and refined futures traded each day. In April 2005, ICE Futures Europe became the first fully electronic energy exchange.   20.11

3. LIFFE Administration and Management[3]

LIFFE, the London International Financial Futures and Options Exchange, was set up in September 1982 to offer trading in financial futures and options on interest rates in the world's major currencies as a means of managing foreign exchange and interest rate risks following the removal of UK foreign exchange controls in 1979.   20.12

In 1992, LIFFE began additionally to offer options on UK equities and on the FTSE 100 and FTSE 250 Indices; this followed LIFFE's merger with the London Traded Options Market (LTOM). Contracts in soft commodities and agricultural products were then added following the merger with the London Commodity Exchange (LCE) in 1996.   20.13

In January 2002, LIFFE was acquired by the Euronext group, which was established in March 2000 and has brought together the exchanges in Amsterdam, Brussels, Lisbon, and Paris. The derivatives businesses of Euronext and LIFFE were operated as Euronext.liffe.   20.14

The name was changed to NYSE Liffe following another major milestone when the NYSE Group and Euronext combined in 2007.   20.15

4. The London Metal Exchange Limited (LME)[4]

Established in 1877 as the London Metal Exchange Company, the LME offers futures and options contracts for aluminium, copper, nickel, tin, zinc, and lead plus two regional aluminium alloy contracts. In 2005 the LME launched the world's first futures contracts for plastics, for polypropylene and linear low-density polyethylene, with the introduction of regional plastics contracts in 2007. In addition, LMEminis—smaller-sized contracts for copper, aluminium, and zinc, plus an index contract—were added in December 2006.   20.16

---

[2] See <http://www.theice.com>.
[3] See <http://www.euroenext .com>.
[4] See <http://lme.co.uk>.

5. London Stock Exchange plc[5]

20.17   The exchange originated in the old coffee houses in the City of London and nearby in the eighteenth century, as entrepreneurs required increasingly large sums for investment in overseas trading expeditions and long shipping voyages. The Muscovy Company was the world's first joint stock company and was set up in London in 1553.

20.18   A number of specialist brokers began to act as intermediaries between the merchants and investors and, in 1760, a group of 150 brokers formed a club at Jonathan's Coffee House to buy and sell shares, after apparently being removed from the Royal Exchange for bad behaviour. The name of the club was changed to the Stock Exchange in 1773. The original deed of settlement of the Stock Exchange was entered into in 1802 and revised in 1875. It was replaced with a new memorandum and articles of association in 1986 when the Exchange became a private limited company after the Big Bang on 27 October 1986.

20.19   With the Big Bang, ownership in member firms was opened to non-Exchange members, minimum commissions were abolished and the earlier distinction between brokers and jobbers was abandoned with all firms becoming dual capacity broker-dealers. Open outcry was replaced by screen trading with the Stock Exchange Automated Quotation system (SEAQ) providing a quote-driven system with dealing generally conducted by telephone. The launch of SETS on 20 October 1997 then created an automated matching service for electronic orders.

20.20   In anticipation of possible future expansion and technical developments, the London Stock Exchange entered into a strategic alliance with the Frankfurt Deutsche Börse in July 1998. In May of the following year, the London Stock Exchange and Deutsche Börse were among eight leading European stock exchanges which signed a Memorandum of Understanding in Madrid to signal ongoing commitment to work jointly towards harmonising the markets for blue-chip securities and establishing a pan-European equity market. The long-term objectives of this European Alliance were to create a single electronic trading platform for blue chip securities, with common rules and regulations.

20.21   It was announced in May 2000 that the London Stock Exchange and Deutsche Börse would merge to create iX-international exchanges, but this plan was abandoned in September 2000.

20.22   Also in 2000, as part of the Exchange's strategy of implementing a more commercial basis of operations and moving away from mutual ownership, the Listing Authority function was transferred from the London Stock Exchange to the UK Listing Authority which was formed by the FSA. Shares in the London Stock Exchange plc itself (now the London Stock Exchange Group plc) were listed on the Exchange's Main Market in July 2001.

20.23   The London Stock Exchange has been pursued by a number of potential suitors in recent years. In 2004, the Exchange was in separate talks with both Deutsche Börse and Euronext. In 2005, it rejected a takeover offer from Macquarie Bank. An approach was made shortly afterwards by NASDAQ; this was revised in December 2006 and then abandoned in September 2007.

---

[5] See <http://www.londonstockexchange.com>.

The London Stock Exchange held an Extraordinary General Meeting in August 2007   20.24
which approved proposals for a merger with Borsa Italiana. AIM Italia—part of Borsa
Italiana—was ready for launch by the end of 2008 to complement the Exchange's
Alternative Investment Market (AIM) for new and growing companies launched in
1995. The merger with Borsa Italiana also helped the Exchange to offer post-trade
services such as netting, clearing and settlement on an efficient and competitive basis, as
well as a comprehensive range of European bond trading services through MTS.

In mid-2009, the London Stock Exchange launched Baikal, a service which will   20.25
aggregate visible (lit) and non-displayed (dark) liquidity across Europe in order to facilitate
trading in larger sizes with minimal market impact. The initial launch of Smart Order
Routing (SOR) capability will be followed later in 2009 by order book functionality and
other functionality. Baikal is an investment firm authorised by the FSA.

6. PLUS Markets plc[6]

PLUS Markets plc (PLUS) is the most recent RIE and was recognised on 19 July 2007.   20.26
It is an exchange for small and mid-cap stock securities, seeking to create the deepest
pool of small- and mid-cap liquidity in Europe.

The origin of PLUS was the Ofex market started in 1995 by market-maker JP Jenkins   20.27
Limited, with the aim of providing an off-exchange market in unlisted and unquoted
companies following the closure of the Stock Exchange's Unlisted Securities Market.

Ofex Holdings plc was floated on the London Stock Exchange's AIM in April 2003.   20.28
It changed its name to PLUS Markets Group plc in November 2004.

PLUS's quote-driven electronic trading platform offers an execution venue for trading   20.29
securities listed elsewhere in London and Europe (its 'PLUS-traded' segment.), as well as
its own PLUS listing/quotation markets, combining independent price formation with
trade reporting.

In addition, the 'PLUS-listed' market offers issuers admitted to the FSA's Official List   20.30
an alternative to listing on the London Stock Exchange's Main Market.

C. THE CLEARING HOUSES TODAY

There are currently four Recognised Clearing Houses: 20.31

- Euroclear UK & Ireland Limited
- European Central Counterparty Ltd
- ICE Clear Europe Limited, and
- LCH.Clearnet Limited.

The origins and functions of the RCHs are outlined below.   20.32

---

[6] <www.plusmarketsgroup.com>.

1. Euroclear UK & Ireland Limited[7] (EUI—formerly CREST)

20.33 CREST was a system set up by the Bank of England in June 1993 after the London Stock Exchange abandoned the TAURUS project in March 1993. The TAURUS project was intended to introduce electronic settlement to replace the Exchange's TALISMAN system (built in 1979) but, despite early progress, TAURUS was abandoned as a consequence of increased costs and delays.

20.34 CRESTCo started operations in 1996 in UK corporate securities. It became responsible for the settlement of government gilts and money market instruments in May 1999 when responsibility for the Central Gilts Office (CGO) and the Central Moneymarkets Office (CMO) was transferred to CRESTCo from the Bank of England.

20.35 CRESTCo joined the Euroclear group in September 2002 and changed its name to Euroclear UK & Ireland.

20.36 Euroclear UK & Ireland provides real-time settlement by Delivery versus Payment (DVP) in central bank money for all English and Irish payments. Standard settlement in the UK is three days after the trade date (T+3) but trade date settlement can be made if required.

20.37 Euroclear UK & Ireland also offers settlement in a wide range of international securities including equities, Eurobonds, and covered warrants. It has direct links to US and European settlement systems to allow settlement in 20 international markets. Central counterparty services and optional settlement netting are available in three electronic markets.

2. European Central Counterparty Limited (EuroCCP)[8]

20.38 European Central Counterparty Limited (EuroCCP) started operations in 2008. It is the European subsidiary of The Depository Trust & Clearing Corporation (DTCC).

20.39 Set up in response to the securities industry changes brought about by initiatives such as MiFID and the European Code of Conduct for Clearing and Settlement, EuroCCP provides central counterparty services for equity trades to Turquoise, SmartPool, NYSE Arca Europe, and Pipeline Financial Group Limited.

3. ICE Clear Europe Limited[9]

20.40 ICE Clear Europe Ltd, which was recognised as an RCH on 12 May 2008, provides clearing services for all ICE Futures Europe contracts and all cleared OTC contracts transacted in ICE's global OTC markets, guaranteeing contract performance by acting as an independent central counterparty to every futures and options contract traded on ICE.

---

[7] See <http://euroclear.com>.
[8] See <http://www.euroccp.co.uk>.
[9] See <http://theice.com/clear>.

4. LCH.Clearnet Limited[10]

The London Clearing House (LCH) was originally established as the London Produce   20.41
Clearing House Ltd in 1888 and was renamed the International Commodities Clearing
House Ltd in 1973 and the London Clearing House Ltd in 1991. LCH was acquired in
October 1996 by LIFFE, the IPE and LME from a syndicate of UK banks.

LCH now clears trades for LIFFE, ICE, the LME and, since February 2001, for the   20.42
London Stock Exchange.

In March 2003, LCH and SIX x-clear Ltd (x-clear—the Swiss central counterparty)   20.43
launched the first pan-European central counterparty (CCP) for the former virt-x
market. The interoperable structure supported both LCH and x-clear as interlinked
central counterparties, offering virt-x members a choice of service.

The LCH.Clearnet Group was formed in 2003 through the merger of the London   20.44
Clearing House and Clearnet SA. LCH.Clearnet now clears a broad range of asset classes
including securities, exchange traded derivatives, energy, freight, interbank interest rate
swaps and euro and sterling denominated bonds and repos.

In December 2008, the London Stock Exchange's central counterparty model was   20.45
expanded to offer competitive clearing with SIS x-clear operating alongside LCH.
Clearnet.

D. THE RECOGNITION REGIME

The regulated activity which is generally relevant to the activities of an RIE is 'Arranging   20.46
deals in investments'[11] which is as follows:

3. Making, or offering or agreeing to make-

   (a) arrangements with a view to another person buying, selling, subscribing for or underwriting
       a particular investment;
   (b) arrangements with a view to a person who participates in the arrangements buying, selling,
       subscribing for or underwriting investments.

Since exchanges and clearing houses are necessarily expert in the operation of their   20.47
markets and have strong incentives in ensuring that they function in a safe and proper
manner, it was considered in the public interest to allow them a wide degree of flexibility
in the determination and application of their own market rules. On recognition, such
bodies are exempt from the need for authorisation under the FSMA although they are
subject to the supervision and oversight of the FSA.

FSMA, s 285(2) states that: 20.48

A recognised investment exchange is exempt from the general prohibition as respects any regulated
activity-

   (a) which is carried on as a part of the exchange's business as an investment exchange; or
   (b) which is carried on for the purposes of, or in connection with, the provision of clearing
       services by the exchange.

---

[10] See <http://lchclearnet.com>.
[11] FSMA, Schedule 2, Part 1.

20.49   Similarly, an RCH is exempt from the general prohibition in respect of any regulated activity it carries on for the purposes of, or in connection with, the provision of clearing services by the clearing house (FSMA 285(3)).

20.50   The following are key differentiators between authorisation and the exempt regime for recognised bodies:

- Recognised bodies have statutory immunity from legal action in carrying out regulatory functions;
- Separate competition law rules are included in Chapters 2 and 3 of Part 18 of the FSMA. These replicate the competition provisions contained in other Parts of the Act and create a parallel regime for RIEs and RCHs; and
- Recognised bodies have protection under the Companies Act 1989 for actions taken in following the default, as described in section H below (Default Rules).

20.51   The main features of the FSA 1986 recognition and exemption regime for investment exchanges and clearing houses were re-enacted in Part 18 of the FSMA. The new Act also gave the FSA power to issue directions to RIEs and RCHs (after consulting the body concerned) to take steps to comply with the recognition requirements.

E. APPLICATIONS FOR RECOGNITION AS AN RIE OR RCH

20.52   Any body corporate or unincorporated association may apply to the FSA for an order declaring it to be a recognised investment exchange or clearing house under FSMA, ss 287(1) and 288(1). Applications must be accompanied by copies of the applicant's rules, a copy of any guidance issued, and required particulars and such other information as may reasonably be requested (ss 287(2) and 288(2)).

20.53   The required particulars include the proposed clearing arrangements to be entered into by an exchange applicant or clearing services to be provided by a clearing applicant (ss 287(3) and 288(3)). The FSA may also require the applicant to provide such further information as it reasonably considers necessary to determine the application (s 289(1)).

20.54   A recognition order is made under s 290(1) where an application has been successful.

F. OVERSEAS INVESTMENT EXCHANGES AND CLEARING HOUSES

20.55   The FSMA also provides for the recognition of investment exchanges and clearing houses which are based outside the UK, which must satisfy the requirements of FSMA 292(3). Eleven Recognised Overseas Investment Exchanges (ROIEs) are currently recognised by the FSA. These are:

- Cantor Financial Futures Exchange (CFEE)
- Chicago Board of Trade (CBOT)
- Chicago Mercantile Exchange (CME)
- Eurex
- ICE Futures US, Inc
- National Association of Securities Dealers Automated Quotations (NASDAQ)
- New York Mercantile Exchange Inc. (NYMEX Inc)

- NQLX LLC
- Swiss Stock Exchange (SIX Swiss Exchange clear)
- Sydney Futures Exchange Limited, and
- US Futures Exchange LLC.

The FSA has also recognised a number of Recognised Overseas Clearing Houses   20.56
(ROCHs). These are:

- Chicago Mercantile Exchange (CME)
- Eurex Clearing AG
- European Multilateral Clearing Facility NV
- ICE Clear US, Inc, and
- SIX x-clear.

An overseas investment exchange or clearing house may apply for recognition under   20.57
FSMA, s 292(1). The applicant must provide an address for service in the United
Kingdom. In such cases, the FSA may (but is not required to) make a recognition order
under s 292(2) where the applicant is subject in its home territory to requirements that
afford investor protection equivalent to the recognition requirements and there are adequate default procedures. The FSA must also consider whether the overseas applicant
and the home supervisory authorities are able and willing to cooperate in the sharing of
information and otherwise (s 292(3)(c) and (d)).

As ROIEs and ROCHs are already subject to extensive controls in their home territo-   20.58
ries, they are not subject to the full requirements imposed on domestic applicants.

An overseas investment exchange or clearing house must, by s 295, provide an annual   20.59
report which must state whether any events have occurred which are likely to affect the
continuing validity of its recognition or have any effect on competition (s 295(1) and (2)).
A copy of the report must be sent to the Treasury and the Office of Fair Trading (s 295(4)).

G. THE RECOGNITION REQUIREMENTS

RIEs and RCHs must comply with principle-based conditions which are set out in the   20.60
Recognition Requirements for Investment Exchanges and Clearing Houses.[12]

The recognition requirements formerly in FSA 1986 were made more flexible under the   20.61
FSMA by allowing the Treasury to set out and amend the relevant criteria by regulations.

In relation to defaulting members, the additional requirements for recognition made   20.62
in the Companies Act 1989, Sch 21, in relation to market contracts (as defined in s 155)
continued in effect. These prevent liquidators from attempting to unwind contracts
made through exchanges or clearing houses.

In considering whether an applicant for recognition or recognised body satisfies the   20.63
recognition requirements, the FSA may take into account all relevant circumstances
including the constitution of the person concerned and its regulatory provisions and
practices within the meaning of s 302(1) of the Act.

The requirements may be satisfied by making outsourcing arrangements for func-   20.64
tions, although the recognised body's responsibility is not affected.

---

[12] Regulations 2001 (SI 2001/995).

20.65   The recognition requirements in respect of investment exchanges are set out in Part 1 of the schedule to the Financial Services and Markets Act 2000 (Recognition Requirements for Investment Exchanges and Clearing Houses) Regulation 2001 [SI 2001/995]. In summary:

Table 20.1

Requirement type	Summary of requirement	Comment
Financial resources	An exchange must have financial resources sufficient for the proper performance of its functions as an RIE	The FSA may take all circumstances into account, including connection with any person and any activity carried on by the exchange, whether or not it is an exempt activity
Suitability	An exchange must have financial resources sufficient for the proper performance of its functions as an RIE	The FSA may take all circumstances into account, including an exchange's connection with any person
Systems and controls	An exchange must ensure that the systems and controls used in the performance of its functions are adequate, and appropriate for the scale and nature of its business	This applies in particular to systems and controls concerning transmission of information; assessment and management of risks; effecting and monitoring of transactions; discharge of obligations; and, where relevant, safeguarding and administration of assets belonging to users
Safeguards for investors	The exchange must ensure that business conducted by means of its facilities is conducted in an orderly manner and so as to afford proper protection to investors	This includes making access to the exchange's facilities subject to criteria to protect the orderly functioning of the market and the interests of investors; making arrangements for information to be made available to persons dealing in investments on the exchange; having arrangements for the timely discharge of the rights and liabilities of parties to transactions effected on the exchange; recording transactions effected on the exchange or to be cleared using its facilities; adopting measures to reduce the extent to which the exchange's facilities can be used for market abuse or financial crime, including measures to facilitate their detection and monitor their incidence; and, where relevant, having arrangements for the safeguarding and administration of assets belonging to users

Table 20.1

Table 20.1 *continued*

Requirement type	Summary of requirement	Comment
Disclosure by issuers of securities	The rules of the exchange must enable the exchange to discontinue the admission of securities to trading; to suspend trading in relevant securities; to publish that an issuer has failed to comply with a disclosure obligation; and to make public itself any information which an issuer has failed to publish	
Promotion and maintenance of standards	The exchange must be able and willing to promote and maintain high standards of integrity and fair dealing in the carrying on of regulated activities by persons in the course of using its facilities. The exchange must be able and willing to cooperate, by sharing information or otherwise, with the FSA or other relevant regulatory bodies	This includes bodies with responsibility in the UK for supervision or regulation of any regulated activity or an overseas regulator within s 195 of the Act
Rules and consultation	The exchange must have appropriate procedures for making rules, keeping them under review and amending them	This must include procedures for consulting with users
Discipline	The exchange must have arrangements for monitoring and enforcing compliance with its rules and for investigating complaints made to the exchange about the conduct of users of its facilities	The arrangements must provide for independent resolution of appeals against disciplinary decisions of the exchange. Any financial penalties imposed by an exchange must be applied by the exchange in one of three specified ways
Complaints	The exchange must have arrangements for investigating and resolving complaints in connection with its regulatory functions	There must be arrangements for an independent review of a complaint if requested. The reviewer may recommend that the exchange makes a compensatory payment to a complainant and/or remedies the matter complained about
Default rules in respect of market contracts	The exchange must have default rules to enable it to take action in respect of a defaulting member's unsettled market contracts	The default rules must provide for certain rights and liabilities of the defaulter to be discharged. The recognition requirements stipulate the content which is required in the default rules

20.66   The requirements for recognition as a clearing house are set out in Part 3 of the Regulations and are almost identical to those for exchanges apart from changes that relate to the different business conducted.

20.67   Special default requirements apply in respect of market contracts under s 155(2) or (3) of the Companies Act 1989. These are set out in Parts 2 (exchanges) and 4 (clearing houses) of the schedule and are described in the following section (H. Default Rules).

20.68   Changes to the Recognition Requirements were made to implement MiFID.[13] These are described in section N (MiFID) below.

H. DEFAULT RULES

20.69   Recognised bodies' default rules must allow for appropriate action to be taken in respect of unsettled market contracts where a member is unable to meet its obligations in respect of one or more contracts. The default rules must enable action to be taken in respect of all unsettled market contracts other than those entered into by an RCH for the purposes of or in connection with the provision of clearing services to an RIE. The effect is to ensure that all rights and liabilities between the parties to an unsettled market contract are discharged and to enable net payments to be made in all relevant cases.

I. THE RIE AND RCH SOURCEBOOK

20.70   The RIE and RCH Sourcebook is the REC section of the FSA's Handbook. The Sourcebook contains the FSA's interpretation of the recognition requirements set out by the Treasury, together with the notification rules for RIEs and RCHs and information on the approach which the FSA takes to the supervision of RIEs and RCHs.

J. COMPLAINTS AGAINST A RECOGNISED BODY

20.71   The FSA must ensure that adequate arrangements are set up for the consideration of relevant complaints against a recognised body (s 299(1)). This relates only to matters which are relevant to whether the body's recognition should be maintained (s 299(2)). The functions of the Financial Services and Markets Tribunal may be extended by Treasury order to include review of disciplinary proceedings held by recognised investment exchanges or clearing houses either generally or one by one (s 300(1)). Such an order may be issued where the Treasury considers it necessary to ensure that disciplinary decisions are consistent with Tribunal decisions taken under Part 9 of the Act or are in accordance with the European Human Rights Convention (s 300(2)). At the time of writing this chapter, there has been no such extension to the function of the Tribunal.

---

[13] Markets in Financial Instruments Directive: Directive 2004/39/EC of the European Parliament and of the Council.

K. COMPETITION SCRUTINY

A separate competition scrutiny regime was set up for recognised bodies under Chapters 2   20.72
and 3 of Part 18 of the FSMA. This is concerned with ensuring that the rules and practices of recognised bodies do not have any significant anticompetitive effects or amount to an abuse of a dominant position. Investigations may be conducted by the Office of Fair Trading and, following a report from the Competition Commission, directions may be given by the Treasury. The general domestic competition law is disapplied by the FSMA, ss 311 and 312. FSMA reviews to date have related to the recognition of exchanges and clearing houses, both domestic and overseas.

1. Practices and regulatory provisions

The competition rules generally apply to practices and regulatory provisions. Practices   20.73
are those of the exchange or clearing house acting as such (s 302(1)). Regulatory provisions include the rules, guidance or required clearing arrangements of the recognised body (s 302(1)).

A regulatory provision or practice will be considered under s 302(2) to have a signifi-   20.74
cantly adverse effect on competition if it has, or is intended or likely to have, that effect or if its effect requires or encourages behaviour which has or is intended or likely to have that effect. Regulatory provisions or practices which require or encourage exploitation of the strength of a market position are to be assumed to have an adverse effect on competition (s 302(3)).

2. Role of the Office of Fair Trading

FSMA 303(1) requires the FSA to send to the Treasury and the Office of Fair Trading   20.75
(OFT) a copy of any regulatory provisions with which it is provided in connection with an application for recognition as well as any information which it considers will assist the OFT in discharging its functions in connection with an application (s 303(2)). The OFT must then issue a report as to whether any particular regulatory provision or combination of regulatory provisions has a significantly adverse effect on competition (s 303(3)). Practices, accordingly, do not feature in their own right at this stage. Reasons must be given for any finding (s 303(4)) and the report copied to the FSA, the Competition Commission and the Treasury (s 303(5)).

3. Continuing reports

The OFT must keep under continuing review the regulatory provisions and practices of   20.76
all recognised bodies (s 304(1)). A report must be made if there is any significantly adverse effect on competition (s 304(2)) and may be made where there is not (s 304(3)). The same requirements as to justification and copying apply where there is an adverse effect (s 304(4) and (5)).

4. Investigations

20.77 The OFT is given substantial powers to investigate initial or continuing competition issues (s 305). It may by notice require any person to produce any specified or described document in the person's custody or control or provide any information at a specified time and place (s 305(2) and (3)). If the person refuses or fails to comply, the OFT may certify that in writing to the High Court or Court of Session in Scotland (s 305(5) and (7)). The court may then hold the defaulter in contempt after hearing any witness or statement produced in defence (s 305(6)). This will apply to any relevant information other than legally privileged communications and others where the defaulter has a reasonable excuse.

5. Competition Commission

20.78 The Competition Commission is required to investigate any matter set out in a report issued by the OFT which is sent to it for consideration (s 306(1)). This may arise when the OFT concludes that there is an adverse effect on competition, whether on an application for recognition or thereafter (s 306(2)). The OFT can also ask the Commission to consider one of its reports even if it finds no significant adverse effect itself (s 306(3)). A separate report must be produced by the Commission unless no useful purpose would be served following a change in circumstances (s 306(4)). The report must confirm whether the regulatory provisions or practices have a significant adverse effect (s 306(6)). The provisions set out in Sch 14 concerning the role of the Commission will generally apply (s 306(11)). Importantly, however, the test is not a pure economic test of competitive effects, since, under s 306(7), (8) and (9), the Commission needs to consider whether the adverse effect is justified and, in this context, the conclusions should, insofar as is reasonably possible, be consistent with the obligations imposed on the recognised body concerned under the Act. They must also be explained to facilitate understanding (s 306(10)). Copies of the report produced must be sent to the Treasury, the FSA and the OFT (s 306(12)).

20.79 An application for a recognition order for an investment exchange or clearing house must be approved by the Treasury (FSMA 2000, s 290(2)). Under s 307(1) and (2), unless the Treasury consider that there are exceptional circumstances, approval must be given if:

(a) the OFT makes a report under s 303 but does not ask the Competition Commission to consider it under s 306; and
(b) the Competition Commission concludes:
   (i) that the applicant's regulatory provisions do not have a significantly adverse effect on competition; or
   (ii) that if those provisions do have that effect, the effect is justified.

20.80 On the other hand, under s 307(3) and (4), the Treasury must refuse approval, unless it considers that there are exceptional circumstances, if the Competition Commission has concluded that the applicant's regulatory provisions have a significantly adverse effect on competition and that effect is not justified. These provisions are intended to keep ministerial involvement in competition decision-making to the minimum.

6. Treasury directions

The Treasury may issue a remedial direction to the FSA following an adverse report from   20.81
the Competition Commission (s 308(5) and (6)). If the conclusion is that the adverse
effect on competition is not justified, the Treasury must give a remedial direction to the
FSA (s 308(2)) unless effective corrective action has already been taken, or there are
exceptional circumstances that would make it inappropriate to do so (s 308(3)). The
remedial direction may require the FSA to withdraw the body's recognition or instruct
the body by a further direction to undertake such action as may be specified (s 308(8)).
The Treasury must issue (and publish) a statement explaining their action in each case
(s 309).

Any body in respect of which a request for approval by the Treasury for recognition is   20.82
to be refused or other corrective action directed and any party affected must be given the
opportunity to make representations before any action is taken (s 310(2)). The representations may relate to either the Director General of Fair Trading's report or that of the
Competition Commission, or the proposed action to be taken in response (s 310(1)).

L. THE FSA's RULE-MAKING POWERS

The FSA was given new powers of supervision by FSMA, s 293. The FSA may issue rules   20.83
requiring notice of specific events or such other information as it may reasonably require
to be provided by any recognised body (s 293(1) and (2)). Written notice must be provided where a domestic recognised body alters or revokes any of its rules or guidance or
makes new rules or guidance (s 293(5)). Changes to clearing arrangements must also be
notified by such bodies (s 293(6) and (7)). These supervision rules may be modified or
disapplied in particular cases (s 294).

M. INVESTMENT EXCHANGES AND CLEARING HOUSES ACT 2006

The Investment Exchanges and Clearing Houses Act 2006 (IEACH) was introduced to   20.84
counter concerns that recognised bodies might introduce regulatory burdens which
could threaten the UK's proportionate and principles-based approach to the regulation
of markets. The concerns were based largely around the potential influence which
non-UK owners of RIEs or RCHs might wish to exert on their operations in the UK.
The Act was believed important in giving market participants a degree of certainty that
the UK approach to regulation would continue in the UK.

Through IEACH, the FSA was granted new powers to review rules and other regula-   20.85
tory provisions made by RIEs and RCHs and to prevent those bodies from making
regulatory provisions which are excessive. Provisions are regarded as excessive if they are
disproportionate to the end to be achieved, or if they are not justified as pursuing a
reasonable regulatory objective. A regulatory provision is stated as meaning any rule,
guidance, arrangements, policy or practice.

20.86   Exercising its rule-making powers under the FSMA, the FSA has clarified[14] that the duty to notify does not apply in a number of instances such as where the regulatory provision is required under Community law or an enactment or rule of law in the UK, or to consequential operating procedures. The following are also excluded: the specification of the standard terms of any derivative; an emergency provision to have effect for no longer than three months; and a provision which does not impose burdens. Finally, the duty to notify does not apply to any other regulatory provision which does not materially:

- increase disclosure, reporting or corporate governance requirements imposed on any person;
- limit the financial instruments which may be listed or admitted to trading;
- limit access to the RIE's facilities; or
- add to the circumstances in which any person may be liable to sanctions or have liability in damages.

20.87   Under s 300B(1) of the FSMA, a UK recognised body that proposes to make any 'regulatory provision' must give written notice of the proposal to the FSA without delay. The recognised body must provide details of the proposed provision, how it fits in with existing related requirements, what regulatory objective it is aimed to pursue, who will be impacted by the regulatory provision (and how), who will benefit from it, how it will be implemented and what consultation is envisaged prior to implementation.

20.88   On submission of a notification, the FSA must decide whether to allow a proposal or to 'call it in' for further consideration—often within 30 days. If the FSA decides to call in a proposal, it must publish a notice giving details of the proposal and setting a period (which the FSA may extend) during which representations may be made on whether the proposal should be disallowed. The FSA must notify the recognised body of its decision within 30 days after the period ends for representations.

N. MiFID

20.89   The MiFID[15] came into force on 1 November 2007 and replaced the Investment Services Directive 1993. MiFID is part of the EU's Financial Services Action Plan (FSAP) to integrate Europe's capital markets to bring down the cost of capital and facilitate enhanced growth and employment.

20.90   MiFID applies to shares which are admitted to trading on an EU regulated market. At the time of writing, there are 6,824 such shares.

20.91   In implementing MiFID, the Treasury considered a number of options and decided to incorporate the Directive's provisions into the existing regime for RIEs. This had three main benefits: it was consistent with the UK's obligation to implement MiFID; it introduced the minimum change necessary consistent with the obligation to implement it

---

[14] In the Recognised Investment Exchanges and Recognised Clearing Houses (Notification Obligations) (Amendment) Instrument 2007 (FSA 2007/72).
[15] Directive 2004/39/EC of the European Parliament and of the Council.

and, thirdly, it enabled exchanges running commodity derivatives markets to operate in other EEA countries on the basis of their authorisation in the UK.

One of the aims of MiFID was to promote competition and a level playing field 20.92 between Europe's trading venues. The Directive set standards for regulated markets and introduced a new category of trading venue: a multilateral trading facility (MTF) is a system which brings together multiple third-party buying and selling interests in financial instruments in accordance with non-discretionary rules. An MTF can be operated by an investment firm or by a market operator. A market operator manages or operates a regulated market and, in the UK, must be an RIE.

MiFID also introduced a new category of execution venue, a Systematic Internaliser, 20.93 which has a quoting obligation in a subset shares admitted to trading on a regulated market. The shares in that subset fulfil specified size criteria and are termed 'liquid'. At the time of writing, there are 13 Systematic Internalisers in the EU. Eight of these are authorised by the UK's FSA.

In promoting competition, MiFID abolished exchanges' ability to have concentration 20.94 rules requiring members to use their facilities. In addition, MiFID required exchanges and clearing houses to give access on equal terms to entities anywhere in the EEA.

MiFID prescribed pre-trade and post-trade transparency requirements for equity 20.95 markets, and set more extensive transaction reporting requirements. The post-trade publication deadline became as close to real time as possible and in any case within three minutes of the transaction unless deferred publication is applicable. MiFID also brought in a standard framework for deferred publication, based on the average daily turnover in bands of securities.

MiFID also restricted the power of exchanges to suspend or remove financial instru- 20.96 ments from trading. The FSA now has the power to require such suspension or removal but it must give notice of, and publish, these decisions.[16] These changes form new Part 18A of the Act.

A number of changes to the FSMA were brought about in Regulations in 2007.[17] 20.97 New section 290(1A) requires the FSA to be satisfied that exchanges applying to become an RIE comply with directly applicable Community legislation made under MiFID. New s 290(1B) and (1C) sets time limits within which the FSA must determine applications for recognition as an investment exchange (but not as an overseas investment exchange).

New section 293A enables the FSA to obtain information about exchanges' compli- 20.98 ance with MiFID and s 296 was amended to give the FSA power to require an exchange to grant it access to the exchange's premises for the purposes of inspecting the premises and documents. In addition, the FSA now has the power to require an exchange temporarily to cease carrying on a regulated activity. Further grounds on which the FSA can remove an exchange's recognition were added into s 297.

New Chapter 1A of Part 18 requires persons acquiring or increasing control (as 20.99 defined in s 301B) to notify the FSA in advance, gives the FSA power in certain cases to refuse to approve an acquisition or increase in control or to object to existing control, makes provision in relation to improperly acquired shares and creates offences in relation

---

[16] Regulation 2006 (SI 2006/3386).
[17] Regulation 2007 (SI 2007/126).

to breaches of the control requirements (transposing Article 38.3 of the Directive). In accordance with the REC Sourcebook, an RIE must itself notify the FSA immediately on becoming aware of a transfer of ownership of the UK RIE which gives rise to a change in the persons who are in a position to exercise significant influence over the management of the UK RIE, whether directly or indirectly.

20.100   New Chapter 3A of Part 18 concerns the 'passport' rights of market operators (as defined in MiFID) to provide services in another EEA State. New s 312A of the Act transposes the rights for EEA market operators under the Directive to make arrangements in the UK for access to their facilities.

20.101   At the time of writing, the CESR database[18] contains 92 Regulated Markets and 162 MTFs. The FSA is the competent authority for six Regulated Markets (which are the RIEs) and 68 MTFs. The MTFs in the UK include several which are making significant competitive advances. Of these the most prominent are Chi-X, Turquoise and BATS Europe. As competition increases, there is fragmentation of liquidity with potentially damaging effects on price formation. Smart order routing capabilities are being rolled out (by, for example, the London Stock Exchange's Baikal) to counter these effects.

O. REVOCATION OF A RECOGNITION ORDER

20.102   A recognition order may be revoked, under s 297, where a recognised body requests or consents to it, or where a recognised body fails to satisfy the recognition requirements or any other obligation imposed under the Act. The FSA must give written notice of its intention to revoke a recognition order to the body concerned (ss 290(5) and 298(1)(a)). The FSA must also take such other steps as it considers reasonably practicable to bring the notice to the attention of members and publish the notice in such manner as it considers appropriate (ss 290(5) and 298(1)(b) and (c)). The notice must give reasons for the proposed decision and draw attention to the right of the body, any member of the body or any other person who is likely to be affected by the proposed order to make representations (ss 290(5) and 298(2) and (3)). Representations must generally be made within two months of the date on which the notice is served (ss 290(5) and 298(4)).

20.103   Instead of revoking recognition, the FSA may, under s 296, direct the body to take specified steps (including making alterations to its rules or suspending or discontinuing such of its operations as may be specified) where it has failed, or is likely to fail, to satisfy the recognition requirements or any other obligation imposed by the FSA or under the Act (s 296(1) and (2)). Such directions are enforceable by injunction in England and Wales or an order for specific performance in Scotland (s 296(3)). The same notification and rights to make representations apply to the giving of directions (s 298(1)) as to refusals of applications and revocation decisions.

---

[18] See <http://www.mifiddatabase.cesr.eu>.

21

LLOYD'S OF LONDON

David Simpson

A. INTRODUCTION

The regulation of Lloyd's of London under the FSMA is, in some ways, reminiscent of   21.01
the system of self-regulating organisations under the predecessor legislation. The Act
focuses upon the Society of Lloyd's (the society of underwriters established as a body
corporate under the Lloyd's Act 1987) and the Council of Lloyd's, which was constituted by section 3 of the Lloyd's Act 1982 as the primary regulatory architecture governing the activities of participants in the Lloyd's market in accordance with the Lloyd's Acts
and the Lloyd's Byelaws. Whilst the FSMA primarily confers on the FSA a watching
brief over the work of the Council, the Act also permits the Financial Services Authority
(FSA) to exercise direct and indirect control over the Society, its members and other
participants to the extent it deems necessary.

Part 19 of the FSMA sets out the extent to which the Society of Lloyd's is subject to   21.02
the general provisions of the Act and the manner in which the FSA may direct the
Council of Lloyd's to exercise its rule-making powers under the Lloyd's Acts.

Section 314(1) and (2) require the FSA to keep itself informed about the affairs of   21.03
Lloyd's and its activities and to review on a continuing basis whether it should exercise
its powers to issue directions under the Act. Lloyd's is accordingly not brought within
the scope of full regulatory control by the FSA but allowed to continue to operate on a
largely autonomous basis. This is, however, subject to the external oversight and direction of the FSA.

The Society of Lloyd's is made an authorised person by s 315(1). Lloyd's is given per-   21.04
mission by s 315(2) to carry on its basic market activity (arranging deals in contracts of
insurance written at Lloyd's), its secondary market activity (arranging deals in participation in syndicates) and other connected activities (s 315(2)). The FSA retains the power
under s 45 to vary the Society's permission on its own initiative. The effect of these

requirements is generally to bring the Society within the control of the FSA and to restrict its activities to traditional Lloyd's market operations.

21.05   Lloyd's members are not required as such to be authorised persons under the FSMA, even though they carry on regulated activities relating to contracts of insurance written at Lloyd's (referred to as 'insurance market activities'). Section 316(1) gives the FSA the power to change that by applying the General Prohibition to Lloyd's members. It has chosen not to apply the General Prohibition, implicitly recognising that Lloyd's members are essentially providers of capital who exercise little if any control over the insurance business that is done in their name. However, section 316(1) also enables the FSA to apply specified 'core provisions' of the Act to Lloyd's members, and the FSA has issued a number of 'insurance market directions' under section 316 applying core provisions to Lloyd's members (see below). Thus members of Lloyd's are subject to specific provisions of the FSMA, even though they are not required to be authorised persons.

21.06   Directions under s 316 are issued only where the FSA so decides, and that decision is guided by three key criteria in s 316(4). These are the interests of policyholders or potential policyholders, where there has been a failure by the Society to implement any relevant European Economic Area (EEA) provision, and the need to ensure the effective exercise of the FSA's functions in relation to Lloyd's (s 316(4)). Directions must be in writing (s 316(5)), and specify each core provision, class of person and kind of activity covered (s 316(7)).

21.07   Rather than issue an insurance market direction, the FSA may act through the Council by imposing an obligation on the Council directly or on the Society, or both, under s 318(1). A section 318 direction may apply to the exercise of powers generally by the body concerned or a specific power (s 318(2)). Exercising powers through the Council does not prevent specific obligations being imposed directly on market participants. This mechanism allows the FSA a certain degree of discretion in regulating the market either through its direct or indirect involvement.

21.08   The FSA must publish a draft direction under either s 316 or s 318 in advance, including a cost-benefit analysis and notice of entitlement to make representations unless any delay would be prejudicial to consumers (s 319(1) and (2)). Any representations made must then be considered (s 319(3)). An account of the representations and the FSA's response must also be published (s 319(4)). A significant change in the final direction must be explained and justified on a cost benefit basis (s 319(5)). These directions accordingly have something of a legislative, rather than an executive or disciplinary, character.

21.09   To deal with the issue of continuing liability following a member leaving Lloyd's, s 320(1) provides that former underwriting members may carry out each contract they have underwritten whether they continue to be authorised or not for the purposes of the Act. The FSA may impose on a former underwriting member any requirements considered to be appropriate for the purpose of protecting policyholders against the risk of not being paid (s 320(3)). To date, the FSA has not exercised this power. The FSA may also make rules imposing any such requirements as it considers appropriate (s 322(1)). Safeguards have been included in connection with the issuance and content of requirements under s 320, including the provision of reasons and the right to make representations (s 321(1) to (12)). The imposition of any requirement and refusal to vary or revoke it may, in particular, be referred to the Financial Services and Markets Tribunal (s 321(11)).

B. POWERS EXERCISED BY THE FSA

By an insurance market direction at Rule 1.5.5D(1) of its Compensation Sourcebook   21.10
(COMP), the FSA has used its power under s 316 to render members of Lloyd's subject
to Part 15 of the FSMA 2000 (Financial Services Compensation Scheme (FSCS)) and to
Part 10 (Rules and Guidance) for the purposes of applying the rules in COMP to them.
The rules in COMP make provision for the payment of compensation to eligible claim-
ants by the FSCS, but only to the extent that the Central Fund maintained by the
Society itself is unlikely to be able to meet those claims. The FSCS is entitled to raise a
levy on the Society to fund this protection.

Rule 2.1.7D of the FSA's Dispute Resolution Sourcebook (DISP) contains a further   21.11
insurance market direction subjecting members to Part 16 of the FSMA (The
Ombudsman Scheme). This direction states that each member of Lloyd's is individually
subject to the rules in DISP. These rules essentially require the Society itself to maintain
a first level of complaints procedure and require members to ensure that their own
arrangements are compatible with those procedures. Only once that level of redress is
exhausted, a complainant is able to take his complaint to the FOS.

A further insurance market direction at Rule 1.5.5D of the FSA's General Prudential   21.12
Sourcebook (GENPRU) makes members subject to just one rule of GENPRU
(GENPRU 1.5.7R), again through the device of imposing Part 10 upon them insofar as
that part has been used to pass the relevant prudential rule. The relevant rule applies—in
a way not seen anywhere else in the FSA Handbook—to all the members of Lloyd's
taken together, and requires them:

at all material times to maintain overall financial resources, including capital and liquidity
resources, that are adequate, both as to amount and quality, to ensure that there is no significant
risk that liabilities under or in respect of contracts of insurance written at Lloyd's will not be met
as they fall due.

Finally, the FSA has also exercised the power to give directions to the Society in   21.13
INSPRU 8.3 in respect of the maintenance of the Central Fund.[1] This direction requires
that in exercising its powers to make payments from the Central Fund or to provide
other forms of financial assistance therefrom, the Society takes no account of the amount
of compensation potentially available to policyholders from the FSCS.

C. OTHER LLOYD'S PARTICIPANTS REGULATED UNDER THE FSMA

The Regulated Activities Order 2001[2] specifies a number of regulated activities relating   21.14
to Lloyds. These are advising on syndicate participation at Lloyd's (Article 56), managing the underwriting capacity of a Lloyd's syndicate as a managing agent at Lloyd's
(Article 57) and arranging deals in contracts of insurance written at Lloyd's (Article 58).

---

[1] INSPRU 8.3.3D, 8.3.4D, 8.3.7D.
[2] SI2001/544.

The Order also designates two 'specified investments' relating to Lloyd's, namely 'underwriting capacity of a Lloyd's syndicate' (Article 86(1)) and 'membership of a Lloyd's syndicate' (article 86(2)). By virtue of these designations the following participants in the Lloyd's market require authorisation under the FSMA:

(a) *managing agents*—a managing agent is defined in Article 3 of the RAO as 'a person who is permitted by the Council of Lloyd's in the conduct of his business as an underwriting agent to perform for a member of Lloyd's one or more of the following functions—(a) underwriting contracts of insurance at Lloyd's; (b) reinsuring such contracts in whole or in part; (c) paying claims on such contracts';

(b) *members' advisers*—whose role is to advise on syndicate participation at Lloyd's;

(c) *members' agents*—who both advise on syndicate participation and act as underwriting agents; and

(d) *underwriting agents*—defined in the FSA Glossary as a firm permitted by the Council of Lloyd's to act as an underwriting agent at Lloyd's.

21.15   The application of the relevant handbook provisions to Lloyd's participants is set out in section of the Insurance: Conduct of Business Sourcebook (ICOBS) and section 18.6 of the Conduct of Business Sourcebook (COBS).

22

PROVISION OF FINANCIAL SERVICES BY MEMBERS OF THE PROFESSIONS

Andrew Henderson

A. INTRODUCTION

Part 20 of the Financial Services and Markets Act 2000 (FSMA) provides a safe harbour **22.01** for members of the professions in their provision of certain financial services, despite the general prohibition contained in s 19. Provision of such services on an 'incidental basis' under Part 20 of the FSMA amounts to carrying on 'exempt regulated activities'.

Professional bodies designated by the Treasury as 'Designated Professional Bodies' **22.02** (DPBs) in the FSMA (Designated Professional Bodies) Order 2001 (SI 2001/1226) (the Treasury Order) have to supervise and regulate their members in carrying on exempt regulated activities, and the Financial Services Authority (FSA) has to keep itself informed as to how they do this.

The FSA may also make directions concerning the safe harbour in relation to particular **22.03** classes of person or different descriptions of regulated activity. Furthermore, the FSA has the power to take the exemption away from a specific person if it believes the person not to be fit and proper.

B. EXEMPTION FROM THE GENERAL PROHIBITION

Section 327 deals with the general test to be applied for permitting professional firms to **22.04** carry on specific regulated activities without authorisation. Technically, the general prohibition in s 19 against carrying on a regulated activity unless authorised to do so does not apply if all the conditions in s 327 are satisfied. These six conditions are:

(1) the firm or person concerned must be, or be controlled by, a member of a profession;

(2) it must be carrying on the regulated activity in a manner which is incidental to the provision of professional services;[1]

(3) it must not be remunerated by commission (any pecuniary reward or other advantage 'from a person other than his client') unless he accounts to the client for the receipt;[2]

(4) it must not carry on, or hold itself out as carrying on, regulated activities other than those which arise out of, or are complementary to, the provision of its professional services;[3]

(5) the regulated activity being carried out must not be one which is excluded from the Treasury Order;[4] and

(6) the regulated activities must be the only regulated activities which the person carries on (apart from any being carried on by it in a separate lawful way, that is as an exempt person).

22.05   The general purpose, therefore, is to enable professional firms carrying on professional business to stray lawfully into the area of regulated activities without being authorised by the FSA, as long as the straying is done on an incidental basis, and as long as any commission received is accounted for to the client. The FSA has provided further guidance in the Professional Firms Sourcebook;[5] 'incidental' financial activity should constitute a major part of the practice of the firm. Factors which the FSA have indicated as relevant to this include the relative proportion of services provided, whether and to what extent the regulated activities are held out as separate services and the impression given, that is, in the firm's advertising or promotion, of how the firm provides them.[6]

22.06   The test of incidentality is enforceable in two separate ways. First, if there is a breach of s 327, the general prohibition in s 19 will apply, and it is therefore possible for the FSA to take any steps normally available to it in relation to the enforcement perimeter set by the FSMA. As explained elsewhere in this guide, these include prosecution, injunction and restitution.[7] Secondly, the test is reinforced by s 332, which requires DPBs to make with the FSA's approval 'restricted activity rules' as to secure that the regulated activities arise out of or are complementary to the provision of the professional service.[8] Thus the FSMA requires that the weight of professional discipline is also available in a case of breach of this 'incidental' (or 'arising out of or complementary') requirement.

---

[1] FSMA, s 327(4).

[2] FSMA, s 327(3).

[3] FSMA, s 327(5) and s 332(4).

[4] FSMA, s 327(6).

[5] <http://fsahandbook.info/FSA/htms/handbook/PROF>.

[6] PROF 2.1.14G.

[7] FSMA, ss 401, 380 and 382 respectively.

[8] PROF 2.1.11G. The rules approved by the FSA are in addition to the conditions in FSMA, s 327 and do not act to override any of the provisions contained in that section.

A professional firm covered by Part 20 is also legally able to make solicited and unso- 22.07
licited financial promotions to a person who has already engaged that firm's professional
services,[9] but only in relation to exempt regulated activities, and only if the exempt regulated activities are incidental to the provision of the professional service.[10]

C. PROFESSIONAL DESIGNATED BODIES

Under s 326 the Treasury may recognise DPBs for the purposes of Part 20. It has desig- 22.08
nated ten to date.[11] The Treasury may only recognise a professional body as a DPB if the
professional body satisfies the 'basic condition'; namely, the professional body has rules
applicable to the carrying on by members of the profession in relation to which it is
established of regulated activities which, if the body were to be designated, would be
exempt regulated activities.[12] The FSMA has no qualitative test about the substance,
vigour, and extent of the rules required by the 'basic condition'.

A candidate professional body must also satisfy one or more additional qualifying 22.09
conditions. These are that it has statutory powers to regulate the profession, a statute
restricts some functions to members of the profession, the body is recognised for other
statutory purposes or the equivalent in another European Economic Area (EEA) state of
any of these.[13]

Under s 325, the FSA must keep itself informed about how DPBs supervise and regu- 22.10
late exempted activities, and how members carry on those activities. DPBs must cooperate by sharing information with the FSA.[14]

D. THE ROLE OF THE FSA

If the FSA has concerns about a particular DPB or about a particular firm supervised 22.11
and regulated by a DPB, the FSA may, under Part 20, disapply the exemption contained
in s 327(1) so that it does not apply to a professional body in whole or in part, or
alternatively does not apply to a particular description of regulated activity.[15]

---

[9] Financial Promotions Order, Article 55.
[10] PERG 8.15.2G.
[11] The Law Society, the Law Society of Scotland, the Law Society of Northern Ireland, the Institute of
Chartered Accountants of England and Wales, the Institute of Chartered Accountants of Scotland, Institute
of Chartered Accountants of Ireland, the Association of Chartered Certificated Accountants, the Institute of
Actuaries, the Council for Licenced Conveyancers and the Royal Institution of Chartered Surveyors.
[12] FSMA 2000, s 326(4).
[13] FSMA 2000, s 326(6): within the UK the statutes recognising a professional body may be Scottish or
Northern Irish Legislation.
[14] PROF 1.1.6G(3) in relation to information and PROF 3.1.2G for a description of the types of information to be shared (complaints and redress arrangements, complaints volumes and their analysis, disciplinary
action, supervisory activity, activities carried on by exempt professional firms, names and addresses of exempt
professional firms carrying on medication activity).
[15] FSMA 2000, s 328.

22.12   To disapply the exemption, the FSA has to be satisfied that during so would protect the interests of clients.[16] Pursuant to s 328(7), the FSA. Should consider:

(1) whether the DPB effectively secures compliance with the rules about the incidental (or 'arising out of or complementary to') nature of the financial activity;
(2) the effectiveness of complaints-handling for the exempted activities concerned;
(3) the effectiveness of arrangements for redress to clients claiming to have suffered loss misconduct in the exempted activities area;
(4) the DPB's co-operation with the FSA.

22.13   To date the FSA has made no directions under s 328.

22.14   The FSA may take action against a particular firm if the person concerned is not a fit and proper person to carry on regulated activities in accordance with s 327, that is, the person should be subjected to full authorisation, or should not be conducting regulated activities at all.

22.15   The procedure for the general withdrawal or restriction of the Part 20 regime[17] is similar to the FSA's rule-making procedure.[18] Decisions about a particular professional body must involve a cost-benefit analysis, and must permit representations. The consultative procedure may be set aside if procedural delays would prejudice the interests of consumers.

22.16   Under the FSMA, the FSA must deliver a warning notice when it FSA proposes to make an order and a decision notice once it has determined the order. If the FSA's concerns relate to a particular individual, it will consider making an order stopping the individual concerned from engaging in exempt regulated activities as opposed to issuing a disapplication order for the firm.[19] Where the FSA's concern is with the firm more generally, the FSA will consider the disciplinary or other action taken by the supervising DPB, the significance of the total risk the firm presents to its clients and the extent the firm has complied with FSA/DPB rules.[20] The FSA, in determining whether to exercise its power will liaise closely with the relevant DPB.[21] There are consequential rights to have the matter determined by the Financial Services and Markets Tribunal.[22]

E. DISCLOSURE OF EXEMPT STATUS

22.17   A person may not describe or hold himself out to be a person to which the general prohibition does not apply, that is, an exempt person.[23] An exempt person must make clear disclosure to its clients that it is not authorised under the FSMA and that clients are not afforded FSA protections for clients of authorised persons.[24] An exempt

---

[16] FSMA 2000, s 328(6).
[17] FSMA 2000, s 330.
[18] See Chapter 12: FSA Rules and Guidance.
[19] EG 16.5.
[20] EG 16.8.
[21] EG 16.9.
[22] FSMA 2000, s 331.
[23] FSMA 2000, s 333.
[24] PROF 4.1.2R.

professional firm should make a statement that it is an exempt professional firm and therefore not an authorised person, detail the nature of the regulated activities being undertaken and the fact they are limited in scope, identify its supervising DPB and a statement that the DPB is responsible for regulating the activities being conducted, and include the nature of the complaints mechanisms available to the client.[25]

F. AUTHORISED PROFESSIONAL FIRMS

A professional firm wishing to provide non-incidental or 'mainstream' financial activities is not exempt under s 327 and must obtain FSA authorisation and comply with FSA rules and guidance. To avoid conferring an unfair competitive advantage on unauthorised members, the FSA will regulate 'non-mainstream regulated activities' that is, particular regulated activities undertaken by an authorised firm which would be exempt if s 327 conditions were met, at an equivalent level to the same activities undertaken as an exempt professional firm.

22.18

---

[25] PROF 4.1.4G(2).

23

MUTUAL SOCIETIES

Paul Kennedy

A. INTRODUCTION

Part 21 of the Financial Services and Markets Act 2000 (FSMA) deals with the disman-   23.01
tling of the former regulatory and other public institutions concerned with the oversight
of the mutual sector. The mutual sector today consists of those building societies that
have not reconstituted themselves as banks, friendly societies, industrial and provident
societies, and credit unions. Across the UK, they have a combined membership of over
30 million savers and total assets of over £400bn, and building societies alone account
for roughly 20 per cent of the UK mortgages and savings markets. For each of these
groups within the mutual sector there is a body of special legislation, and that legislation
remains generally in force, apart from the provisions about the relevant regulator and the
regulation of financial services. This is because the FSA assumed responsibility for the
regulation of mutual societies' provision of financial services in 2001, for which they
require authorisation or exemption under the FSMA in the usual way. Part 21 confers
power on the Treasury to transfer any remaining oversight functions by statutory
instrument.

B. THE MUTUAL SOCIETIES ORDER

In implementation of Part 23, the Financial Services and Markets Act 2000 (Mutual   23.02
Societies) Order 2001[1] (the Order) was made. It created a small regulatory regime for
oversight of mutuals by the FSA which is akin to, but not wholly integrated into, the
FSMA itself.

Under the Order, certain functions of a legislative nature were transferred to the   23.03
Treasury. That apart, however, all the remaining oversight functions, which deal with

---

[1] SI 2001/2617.

matters such as registration and incorporation of mutual societies, including conversions and mergers, were transferred to the FSA at N2 (1 December 2001).

23.04   The Order also enabled the FSA to exercise certain functions ahead of N2, and made consequential amendments, repeals, and transitional provisions and savings to the relevant mutuals legislation, including, principally:

(a) The Friendly and Industrial and Provident Societies Act 1968, c55;
(b) The Friendly Societies Act 1974, c46;
(c) The Industrial and Provident Societies Act 1975, c41;
(d) The Industrial and Provident Societies Act 1978, c34;
(e) The Credit Unions Act 1979, c34;
(f) The Building Societies Act 1986, c53;
(g) The Friendly Societies Act 1992, c40.

23.05   Whilst most of the detail of the Order is of historical interest only, Schedule 2 continues to determine the status of the oversight functions transferred to the FSA. By paragraphs 2 and 8, these functions are treated for most purposes as conferred under the FSMA, so that, for example, they are covered by the FSA's complaints scheme and the jurisdiction of the High Court and the Court of Session, and the FSA has a qualified exemption from liability in damages.

23.06   Paragraphs 4–7 and 9–17 provide that these functions, and related functions such as giving guidance and raising fees, are not subject to the FSA's general duties under section 2 of the FSMA. There is therefore no duty for the FSA to have regard to the regulatory objectives under the FSMA in exercising its general legislative and policy-making functions, and there is no provision for scrutiny of its compliance with the regulatory objectives. In practice, the FSA's expenditure and fees in relation to its oversight of mutual societies are accounted for separately from its regulatory functions.

23.07   Paragraph 3 provides that the FSA is not required to maintain arrangements for monitoring and enforcing mutual societies' obligations under mutuals legislation, but if it does so it may delegate them. The powers of monitoring and enforcement which the FSA now has for exercising oversight of this sector are conferred under the relevant mutuals legislation rather than under the FSMA.

24

AUDITORS AND ACTUARIES

Andrew Henderson

A. INTRODUCTION

Under the UK system of supervision, the FSA utilises external auditors that discharge a number of core functions, in particular the independent verification of financial statements and the confirmation of systems integrity. Auditors prudentially inspect firms alongside general accounting audits, and provide information to the FSA for its supervision of financial institutions. Such information must be reliable for the FSA and therefore must meet standards of independence, objectivity, and integrity. Actuaries similarly assess the liabilities of insurance companies.   24.01

Many financial services firms' annual accounts and reports must be audited under the Companies Acts 1985 and 2006. Under Part 22 of the Financial Services and Markets Act 2000 (FSMA), the FSA may extend similar requirements to other authorised persons, such as partnerships and sole traders. The FSA has issued these rules its Supervision Manual (SUP) 3 and similar rules for actuaries in SUP 4.[1]   24.02

B. APPOINTMENT

The FSA has issued rules to provide for the appointment of an auditor or actuary by a financial institution.[2] Such institutions must appoint an auditor—or, for insurance   24.03

---

[1] <http://fsahandbook.info/FSA/html/handbook/SUP>.
[2] FSMA s 340(1) SUP 3.3 and SUP 4.3.

firms, an actuary—and make notification to the FSA.[3] If a vacancy in the office of an auditor or actuary arises, the firm must notify the FSA without delay and appoint new auditors or actuaries. The FSA may make an appointment if no other appointment has been made or notified.[4] The FSA has also specified the minimum qualifications and experience for auditors and actuaries.[5]

24.04　Under s 340(3), an auditor or actuary may perform other duties as required. They therefore must co-operate with the FSA, maintain independence, and be free of any conflict of interest.[6] These duties uphold the standards of independence, objectivity, and integrity required of auditors and actuaries.

24.05　The FSA has also outlined the duties of auditors of authorised persons which hold client money or custody assets. The auditor must submit a client assets report to the FSA which states whether, in the auditor's opinion, such authorised persons have complied with and maintained adequate systems and controls for its compliance with the FSA custody, collateral, and client money rules.[7] If the auditor thinks the rules have been breached, or is unsure, then the report must specify which requirements have been breached and how, or the reasons the auditor is unsure.[8]

24.06　Under s 340(5), auditors and actuaries must comply with such duties and may exercise such powers as are conferred on them to discharge such duties.

C. INFORMATION

24.07　An authorised person must co-operate with its auditors or actuaries in the discharge of their duties.[9] Any auditor or actuary appointed under or as a result of the FSMA has the right of access, at all times, to the authorised person's books and accounts and is entitled to any such information and explanations necessary from the authorised person's officers.[10] Any person knowingly or recklessly giving an auditor or actuary information which is false or misleading in any material particular may be liable to prosecution.[11] Sections 341 and 346 make provisions which are equivalent to those made for company auditors by the Companies Act 1985, s 389A (where still applicable) and otherwise s 499 and 500 of the Companies Act 2006.

D. DISCLOSURE AND IMMUNITY

24.08　An auditor of a regulated person is subject to a duty of confidentiality. However, the FSMA exempts, in certain circumstances, auditors and actuaries of authorised persons

---

[3] SUP 3.3.2R and SUP 4.3.1R.
[4] SUP 3.3.7R and SUP 4.3.3R.
[5] SUP 3.4.2R and SUP 4.3.9R.
[6] SUP 3.8.2R, SUP 3.8.5R, SUP 3.8.6R, SUP 4.5.1R and SUP 4.5.3R.
[7] SUP 3.10.4R and 3.10.5R.
[8] SUP 3.10.9R and 3.10.10R.
[9] SUP 3.6.1R and SUP 3.6.2G.
[10] FSMA, s 341 and SUP 3.6.3G.
[11] FSMA, s 346.

from liability for breach of this duty. If an auditor or actuary discloses confidential information in good faith to the FSA, and if the disclosure was made in the reasonable belief that it was relevant to any function of the FSA, then the disclosure will not draw liability.[12]

The exemption from liability applies to both current and previous auditors and relates to both disclosure of information acquired, as well as the auditor's or actuary's opinion on such information. It applies whether or not the FSA has requested the information or opinion; including cases of whistle blowing.[13]   24.09

The Treasury may make regulations prescribing when auditors and actuaries of autho-   24.10
rised persons must communicate information and opinions to the FSA which override the duty of confidentiality and are statutorily obligatory.

There are equivalent provisions for disclosure of information by the present or former   24.11
auditor or actuary of a person who 'has close links' with an authorised person.[14] This effectively provides exemption of liability for disclosure of information to the FSA by a current or previous auditor of any parent, subsidiary or sister company of the authorised person.

E. NOTIFICATION ON LEAVING OFFICE

If an auditor or actuary of an authorised person is removed from office, resigns, or is not   24.12
re-appointed, he or she must notify the FSA without delay.[15] Any matter relating to the vacation of office which the auditor or actuary thinks ought to be drawn to the FSA's attention must also be notified. If there is no such matter, the FSA must be notified to that effect.[16]

F. DISQUALIFICATION

The FSA may disqualify an auditor or actuary of an authorised person from acting both   24.13
as an auditor or actuary of authorised persons generally, or of a particular class of autho-rised persons.[17]

The FSA must warn a person if it is considering disqualifying him or her and serve   24.14
notice once the decision to disqualify has been taken. The FSA also has the power to remove any disqualification it has imposed. The decision to disqualify is referable to the Financial Services and Markets Tribunal by the person disqualified.[18]

The FSA deals with the disqualification of auditors and actuaries in Chapter 15 of its   24.15
Enforcement Guide.[19]

---

[12] FSMA, s 342(3).
[13] FSMA, s 342(3)(a) and (b).
[14] FSMA, s 343.
[15] SUP 3.8.11R.
[16] SUP 3.8.12R.
[17] FSMA, s 345(1).
[18] FSMA, s 345.
[19] <http://fsahandbook.info/FSA/extra/5149.pdf>.

25

PUBLIC RECORD, DISCLOSURE OF INFORMATION AND CO-OPERATION

Helen Marshall

A. INTRODUCTION

Part 23 of the Financial Services and Markets Act 2000 (FSMA) imposes three sets of obligations on the FSA in relation to its handling of information. First, it creates an obligation to create a record of certain information which must be available for public inspection. Second, confidential information is prohibited from disclosure except as prescribed. Third, the FSMA places the FSA under an obligation to co-operate with other authorities in the fight against financial crime.   25.01

The information disclosure regime under the FSMA, together with related regulations made by the Treasury pursuant to the FSMA, is a significant consideration in the daily work of the FSA. The Court of Appeal has clearly defined the policy purpose of the information disclosure regime as being both to ensure respect for the private life of the person who is subject to the information and to encourage the timely disclosure to the regulator of information likely to assist in the process of regulation.[1]   25.02

There is inevitably a tension between the increased demands for transparency and accountability now being made on all public bodies including the FSA, along with the requirement to provide confidentiality for the reasons described above. This part of the FSMA provides the FSA with a framework within which to balance these competing pressures.   25.03

---

[1] See *Real Estate Opportunities Ltd v Aberdeen Asset Managers Jersey Ltd and others* [2007] EWCA Civ 197.

25.04   Decisions to disclose information will often also involve consideration of other areas such as data protection, defamation, rehabilitation of offenders, common law confidentiality, public interest immunity, and freedom of information laws.

B. THE PUBLIC RECORD TO BE MAINTAINED BY THE FSA

25.05   The FSA is required by FSMA, s 347 to maintain a record of every person who appears to the FSA to be an authorised person, together with information about others. These include authorised collective investment schemes, recognised investment exchanges and clearing houses (RIEs and RCHs), approved persons, appointed representatives, and individuals prohibited from being employed in the industry.[2]

25.06   Section 347(2) specifies what the record must contain and confers a duty on the FSA to include any information which it considers appropriate. The mandatory elements include information about the services which each authorised person holds himself out as able to provide, together with an address for service.

25.07   In the case of individuals in respect of whom a prohibition order has been made under FSMA, s 56, the FSA must include at least the name of each individual and details of the effect of the order (FSMA, s 397(2)(a)). This provision represented a significant departure from the corresponding provisions in the FSMA's preceding legislation, the Financial Services Act 1986 (FSA 1986). Under that Act, the FSA had only limited powers to make known the names of those disqualified by it from working in the industry. The High Court of Justiciary in Scotland has found that publication of a prohibited person's name in accordance with FSMA, s 347 is not incompatible with the presumption of innocence and the right to a fair trial under the European Convention on Human Rights.[3]

25.08   In the case of an approved person, the FSA will be obliged to publish his or her name, the name of the relevant authorised person for whom the approved person performs controlled functions, and the name of any contractor through whom the functions are performed (FSMA, s 347(2)(g)).

25.09   Entries referring to people or firms who no longer have the relevant status do not have to be deleted, but where it appears to the FSA that an entry is out of date for this reason, it must make a note on the record explaining why it takes that view (FSMA, s 347(3) and (4)).

25.10   The FSA must make the record available for inspection in legible form (FSMA, s 347(5)(a)). It must also provide certified copy entries on request, for which it may charge a fee (FSMA, s 347(5)(b)). It may go further and publish the record or any part of it (FSMA, s 347(6)(a)). The section also expressly allows the FSA to exploit the information commercially (FSMA, s 347(6)(b)).

---

[2] See The FSA Register at <http://www.fsa.gov.uk/register/home.do>.
[3] See *Raymond Coia v Her Majesty's Advocate* (2009 SCCR1).

C. RESTRICTIONS ON DISCLOSURE OF CONFIDENTIAL INFORMATION

The core obligation in FSMA, s 348, is a duty on the FSA and certain other persons not   25.11
to disclose confidential information without the consent of the person who provided it
and, if different, the person to whom it relates. The prohibition is lifted when disclosure
is made through what are often called 'gateways'. These are statutory permissions to
disclose information which depend on the purpose of disclosure and sometimes the
identity of the recipient as well.

This prohibition gives effect to Article 54 of the Markets in Financial Instruments   25.12
Directive (2004/39/EC) and Article 44 of the Recast Credit Institutions Directive
(2006/48/EC), which require that member states provide a professional secrecy regime.

1. What is 'confidential information'?

The words 'confidential information' are explained in FSMA, s 348(2) to (4). There is   25.13
no need for information to be inherently confidential in the common law or equitable
sense for it to be confidential for the purpose of FSMA, s 348.[4] Confidential information
must be information which relates to 'the business or other affairs of any person'. It is
clear from the formulation that not all information about a person is covered. In *Melton
Medes Ltd v Securities and Investments Board* [1995] Ch 137, Lightman J made clear that
similar words in FSA 1986, s 179, required a relationship to the business and affairs of
the individual or company which was not indirect or incidental.

Information is only caught by FSMA, s 348, if it was received by the primary recipient   25.14
for the purposes of, or in the discharge of, any functions of the FSA (including the FSA
as Listing Authority) or of the Secretary of State under or by virtue of the FSMA.
Information received by the FSA in other circumstances, for example, acting solely in its
private capacity, or sent to it by mistake and really intended for a different authority,
would not be caught. However, information received in the course of discharging statutory functions will be caught even if the information was volunteered rather than
obtained in response to a requirement imposed under FSMA, s 348(3)(a).

Similarly, the FSMA makes plain that information received for more than one purpose   25.15
is still capable of being confidential (s 348(3)(b)).

By FSMA, s 348(4)(a), information is not confidential if it has already been made   25.16
available to the public without breaching FSMA, s 348. Hence information will not, for
example, be confidential if it has been disclosed by the FSA in connection with criminal
investigations or proceedings. Furthermore, a person will not be regarded as having
obtained information from the FSA for the purpose of s 348 of the FSMA if he had that
information before it was given to him by the FSA or if he knew that information
already, or, in the case of a body corporate, knowledge of that information was attributed
to it under the general rules as to attribution. [5]

---

[4] See *The Financial Services Authority v The Information Commissioner* [2009] EWHC 1548 (Admin).
[5] See *Real Estate Opportunities Ltd v Aberdeen Asset Managers Jersey Ltd and others* [2009] Z All ER 791.

25.17   Information will not be confidential if it is not possible to ascertain from it information relating to any particular person because it takes the form of a summary or collection of information (FSMA, s 348(4)(b)). The FSA may rely on this provision to use confidential information to compile and publish aggregated statistics about different industry sectors or products, for example.

2. What is a 'primary recipient'?

25.18   The duty not to disclose confidential information applies to 'primary recipients', a term defined in FSMA, s 348(5) by reference to the official function of the recipient rather than being the first person to whom the information was passed. Primary recipients include the FSA (including in its capacity as the Listing Authority), the Secretary of State, and any of their staff. It also includes a skilled person appointed to make a report under FSMA, s 166 as well as auditors or experts instructed by the FSA or the Secretary of State. Experts include, for this purpose, investigators appointed under FSMA, s 97 by the FSA acting as Listing Authority, any person appointed by the FSA or Secretary of State to investigate under Part 11 of the FSMA, and any person to whom monitoring responsibilities are delegated under Sch 1, para 6.

25.19   The duty not to disclose extends from the primary recipient to any person obtaining the information directly or indirectly from a primary recipient (FSMA, s 348(1)).

3. Exceptions from the prohibition from disclosure: 'gateways'

25.20   The FSMA does not prevent disclosure of confidential information for the purpose of facilitating the carrying out of a public function, where there is a 'gateway', that is, where disclosure is permitted under s 349 and the Financial Services and Markets Act 2000 (Disclosure of Confidential Information) Regulations 2001 (as amended) (SI 2001/2188) (the FSMA Disclosure Regulations).

25.21   Gateways provided for by the FSMA Disclosure Regulations include: (i) disclosures made by the FSA, Secretary of State or the Treasury (or their respective staffs) for the purpose of discharging a public function (see Article 3); (ii) disclosures made by a primary recipient for the purpose of any criminal investigation or proceedings in the UK or elsewhere (including for the purpose of initiating or bringing to an end such investigation or proceedings, or of facilitating a determination whether it or they should be initiated or terminated), or for the purpose of any proceedings under Parts 2, 3 or 4 of the Proceeds of Crime Act 2000 (see Article 4); (iii) disclosures made by a primary recipient for the purpose of initiating or terminating civil proceedings, under the FSMA, its preceding legislation, proceedings before the Tribunal and any other civil proceedings to which the FSA is, or is proposed to be, a party, or facilitating a determination of whether such proceedings should be initiated or terminated (see Article 5).

25.22   Article 7 of the FSMA Disclosure Regulations provide that where confidential information is disclosed under the regulations to a person other than the FSA, Secretary of State, the Treasury, or Bank of England and the disclosure is made subject to restrictions, the person to whom the disclosure is made may not use the information in breach of any such restrictions, without the consent of the person who disclosed it to him.

25.23   Part 3 of the FSMA Disclosure Regulations gives effect to co-operation requirements imposed on member states by certain of the EU's directives relating to a single market in financial services. Accordingly, Part 3 and Schedule 1 of the FSMA Disclosure Regulations provide a gateway for specified persons to disclose information in prescribed circumstances as required by those directives.

4. Disclosure of information by the Inland Revenue

The obligations of confidence which apply to the Inland Revenue (now HM Revenue and Customs) have meant that, historically, its ability to be of any assistance to the FSA in specific cases in the past has been relatively limited. FSMA, s 350 enlarged the potential for assistance by providing for disclosure of information to the FSA or the Secretary of State, despite the fact that the Finance Act 1989, s 182, would otherwise make disclosure a criminal offence.   25.24

However, there are limits to the discretion, which mean that disclosure may only be made by or under the authority of the Commissioners for Revenue and Customs (FSMA, s 350(2)) and, by FSMA, s 350(1), the disclosure must be made for the purpose of assisting an investigation (or with a view to the appointment of investigators) under FSMA, s 168. That section deals with investigations triggered by serious specific concerns rather than general investigations.   25.25

Such information may only be used by the FSA or the Secretary of State for a narrow range of quite serious purposes beyond the investigation (or decision to investigate) itself (FSMA, s 350(4)). Those purposes include criminal proceedings brought under the FSMA or under the Criminal Justice Act 1993 (insider dealing), or to take other action under the FSMA against a person as a result of the investigation. Onward disclosure of 'Revenue information' is generally restricted to the same sort of criminal or regulatory proceedings, unless the disclosure is made by or under the authority of the Commissioners (FSMA, s 350(5)).   25.26

5. Competition information

The FSMA gives the Office of Fair Trading and the Competition Commission powers of competition scrutiny. FSMA, s 351 protects from disclosure non-public information relating to the affairs of particular individuals or bodies obtained in the course of such competition scrutiny, whether undertaken under FSMA, s 95 (scrutiny of the FSA as Listing Authority), Part 10, Chapter 3 (scrutiny of the FSA's rules and practices), or Part 18, Chapter 2 (scrutiny of RIEs and RCHs).   25.27

6. Consequences of breaching the prohibition

The wrongful disclosure of regulatory information in breach of the prohibition in ss 348 and 350 will be a criminal offence, by virtue of FSMA, s 352. It may result in a prison sentence of up to two years and an unlimited fine. There is a defence if the accused can show that he did not know and had no reason to suspect that the information was confidential or that it had been disclosed by HM Revenue and Customs to the FSA or the Secretary of State in accordance with FSMA, s 350. It is also a defence to show that the accused has taken all reasonable precautions and exercised all due diligence to avoid committing the offence.   25.28

25.29   The disclosure of confidential information in breach of the prohibition will be unlikely in itself to give rise to civil liability.[6]

7. Removal of other restrictions on disclosure

25.30   The Treasury has, under the power granted under FSMA, s 353, made regulations permitting particular authorities to disclose information for the purpose of discharging prescribed functions in the legislative framework and permitting the disclosure of information by prescribed persons (including the FSA's investigations and skilled persons appointed pursuant to FSMA, s 166) to the FSA to assist it in carrying out its functions (see the Financial Services and Markets Act 2000 (Disclosure of Information by Prescribed Persons) Regulations 2001 (as amended) (SI2001/1857)). These regulations enable the confidentiality obligations to which those authorities prescribed persons would otherwise be subject to be overridden, provided that the disclosure is made in good faith, and the person disclosing the information reasonably believes that the information is relevant to the discharge of a public function by the FSA.

D. DUTY OF THE FSA TO CO-OPERATE WITH OTHER AUTHORITIES

25.31   The FSA is under a duty to do whatever it considers appropriate to co-operate with authorities who have similar functions, whether in the UK or overseas (FSMA, s 354(1)(a)). It must also take such steps as it considers appropriate to co-operate with the Panel on Takeovers and Mergers, an authority designated as a supervisory authority for the purposes of Article 4.1 of the Takeovers Directive; or any other person or body that exercises functions of a public nature, under legislation in any country or territory outside the UK, that appear to the FSA to be similar to the functions of the Panel on Takeovers and Mergers (FSMA, s 354(A)). It is obliged to do whatever it considers appropriate to co-operate with other authorities in the UK and overseas who have functions in relation to the prevention or detection of financial crime, whether or not they have functions similar to the FSA's (FSMA, s 354(1)(b)). Financial crime here has the same meaning as in FSMA, s 6, extending to all offences of fraud and dishonesty, market-related offences and those relating to the handling of proceeds of crime.

25.32   The duty to co-operate with other authorities does not in any way override the confidentiality obligations imposed by other sections of this Part: FSMA, s 354(2) makes clear that co-operation may include the sharing of information which the FSA is not prevented from disclosing.

---

[6] See *Melton Medes Ltd v Securities and Investments Board* [1995] Ch 173, in which Lightman J came to that view in relation to the similar prohibition contained in FSA 1986 s 179.

26

INSOLVENCY

Helen Marshall

A. INTRODUCTION

The Financial Services and Markets Act 2000 (FSMA), Part 24, confers a range of powers 26.01 on the Financial Services Authority (FSA) to deal with situations where customers are at risk because a financial services business has become insolvent. In theory, consumers often have their own rights to take action against the business in these circumstances, but may lack the knowledge or financial resources to do so.

There are, for example, provisions entitling the FSA to petition for winding up even 26.02 when it is not itself a creditor, together with a right to be notified of and heard in insolvency proceedings initiated by others. The provisions of the FSMA in this respect operate by slight modification of the general law of insolvency, as contained in the Insolvency Act 1986, the Insolvency (Northern Ireland) Order 1989 (SI 1989/2405) and the Bankruptcy (Scotland) Act 1985.

It should be noted that the Banking Act 2009 contains provisions relating to insolvent 26.03 and failing banks (including pre-insolvency options), and confers certain powers on the FSA. Those provisions are outside the scope of the FSMA and accordingly of this chapter.

This chapter follows the Part 24 framework, explaining the FSA's rights and powers in 26.04 relation to voluntary arrangements, administration orders, receiverships, voluntary and compulsory winding up, and bankruptcy. It also notes the Act's provisions in relation to debt avoidance, as well as supplemental provision concerning insurers.

B. VOLUNTARY ARRANGEMENTS

26.05   A company in financial difficulties may seek to enter into an arrangement with its creditors for the repayment of their debts, as an alternative to going into liquidation. Where an authorised person which is a company or insolvent partnership has entered into a voluntary arrangement under Part 1 of the Insolvency Act 1986, s 356 of the FSMA gives the FSA the right to apply to the court under s 6 and s 7 of the 1986 Act. Section 6 enables the FSA to challenge the arrangement on the ground that it is in some way unfairly prejudicial or there has been some material irregularity in its establishment, and s 7 allows it to challenge the actions of the supervisor of the voluntary arrangement. FSMA, s 356(3) also permits the FSA to be heard at any hearing of an application by another person under s 6 or s 7.

26.06   Similar provision is made by FSMA, s 357, to enable the FSA to challenge a voluntary arrangement made by an authorised person who is an individual. The FSA also has a right to be heard on an application to the court by an individual who is an authorised person for an interim order imposing a moratorium pending establishment of a voluntary arrangement. At present, it is not possible for a company to obtain a moratorium while seeking to establish a voluntary arrangement, except by going into administration.

26.07   Sections 356 and 357 also apply to the equivalent procedures in Northern Ireland. The position in Scotland in relation to individuals is rather different. Section 358 provides for the FSA to have rights in that jurisdiction in respect of a voluntary trust deed (the alternative to an individual voluntary arrangement under Scottish law) where the debtor is an authorised person. Voluntary trust deeds provide for a person who cannot pay his debts to give his assets to a trustee, who may then arrange a settlement with creditors as an alternative to sequestration (which is the Scottish equivalent of bankruptcy). When the trustee realises that the debtor is an authorised person, he must let the FSA know by sending a copy of the trust deed together with the copy documents sent to creditors. From that point on, the FSA will have the same rights to be given notice of creditor meetings as the creditors themselves. Section 358(5) gives the FSA the right to send a representative to those meetings but does not give the representative a right to vote at them. The FSA has the same rights as creditors who were not given notice of (or who have objected to) the trust deed to petition for the sequestration of a debtor who is an authorised person (s 358(3)).

C. ADMINISTRATION ORDERS

26.08   An administration order enables a company or partnership to remain in business under the supervision of an administrator, as an alternative to winding up. FSMA, s 359 enables the FSA to petition the court under Schedule B1 to the Insolvency Act 1986 (or Schedule B1 to the Insolvency (Northern Ireland) Order 1989) for an administration order in relation to a company or insolvent partnership which is, or has been, an authorised person or an appointed representative. The FSA may also petition for such an order in relation to a company or insolvent partnership which is or has been carrying on regulated activities in breach of the general prohibition under s 19. The court may only make an administration order if it is satisfied that the entity concerned is unable to pay its debts, or is likely to become so. By virtue of FSMA, s 359(3) and (4), the entity will be treated as unable to pay its debts if it has failed to pay any sum due under an agreement where the making or performance of the agreement is (or is part of) its regulated activity or, if it is an authorised deposit taker, if it has failed to make a payment due in respect of a deposit. Finally, an authorised reclaim fund which is in default in paying a claim due under the Dormant Bank & Building Society Accounts Act 2008, will also be treated as being unable to pay its debts.

It is not presently possible for an insurance company to go into administration (Schedule B1 to the Insolvency Act 1986 (s 9(2)). However, FSMA, s 360 enables the Treasury to make an order modifying the law in this respect. 26.09

By virtue of s 361, any administrator is under a duty to report to the FSA without delay where it appears to him that the company or partnership is or has been carrying on unauthorised regulated activity in breach of the general prohibition in s 19. 26.10

The FSA has a range of rights under s 362 to participate in administration proceedings as though it were a creditor. For example, s 362(2) confers rights to be heard at a hearing for the appointment of an administrator to a person who is or was an authorised person or appointed representative or who has been carrying on regulated activities in breach of the general prohibition. The FSA is also entitled to receive notices and documents to creditors (s 362)(3)). Finally, s 362 (A) prevents the appointment of an administrator to such a company by the company itself or its directors without FSA consent. 26.11

D. RECEIVERSHIPS

Where a receiver has been appointed in relation to a company which is or has been an authorised person or appointed representative, or which has been carrying on regulated activities in breach of the general prohibition, the FSA is given by FSMA, s 363 the same statutory rights as unsecured creditors. 26.12

The FSA may be heard at hearings for directions, at the receiver's application, about how the receiver should perform his functions. The FSA is entitled to apply to the court if the receiver defaults on his obligations to file documents, make returns and give notices and to account and make payments to the liquidator when a company goes into liquidation. 26.13

Under FSMA, s 364, a receiver appointed in relation to a company is obliged to inform the FSA without delay if it appears to him that the company is or has been carrying on regulated activities in breach of the general prohibition. 26.14

E. VOLUNTARY WINDING UP

The FSA is given certain rights in relation to authorised companies which are being wound up voluntarily (FSMA, s 365). 26.15

26.16   The rights include rights to receive notices or other documents to creditors, and the right to be heard at any court hearing. The FSA is entitled to send a representative to attend and speak at creditors' meetings. The FSA also has the right to ask the court to decide any questions arising out of the winding up or to request the court to exercise such powers as the court might exercise if it were winding up the company itself.

26.17   A liquidator in a voluntary liquidation of any company must inform the FSA if it appears that the company is, or has been, carrying on a regulated activity in contravention of the general prohibition (ss 19 and 370).

26.18   The fact that a company is in voluntary liquidation does not prevent the FSA from petitioning to have the company wound up by the court (s 365(6)).

26.19   By s 366, a long-term insurer may not be wound up voluntarily without the consent of the FSA. Unless the copy of the winding-up resolution sent to the registrar of companies is accompanied by an FSA certificate of consent, the resolution has no effect. This enables the FSA to secure appropriate arrangements in respect of long-term policyholders before consent is given.

26.20   FSMA, s 366 makes it a criminal offence for a director of such an insurer not to notify the FSA promptly on becoming aware of a notice of intention to propose a voluntary winding up. The procedure in the Companies Act 2006, s 288, for written resolutions of a private company, cannot be used for a resolution for voluntary winding up of a long-term insurer (FSMA, s 366(4)). This means that a general meeting must be held to approve such a resolution, which will have to be a special resolution unless the company is unable to pay its debts, and s 366(4), prevents the members waiving the need for 21 days' notice of a special resolution.

F. WINDING UP BY THE COURT

26.21   Section 367 of the FSMA contains an important extension to the FSA's previous powers under the Financial Services Act 1986. Under s 72 of that Act, the FSA had been able to petition for the winding up of authorised firms and appointed representatives. Under s 367 of the FSMA, the FSA may still petition for the winding up of any company or partnership which is or has been an authorised person or appointed representative. In addition, the FSA may petition for the winding up of any unauthorised company or partnership which is or has been carrying on a regulated activity in contravention of the general prohibition. The FSA's powers also extend to Northern Ireland as well as to the rest of the United Kingdom.

26.22   The grounds on which the court may grant the petition are either that the body is unable to pay its debts (as defined in the Insolvency Act 1986), or that the court is of the opinion that it is just and equitable that it should be wound up. A body is deemed unable to pay its debts if it has failed to pay a sum due under an agreement where the making or performance of that agreement is or is part of a regulated activity.

G. WINDING UP PETITIONS FOR EEA AND TREATY FIRMS

26.23   Where a firm is authorised to do regulated business in the UK by virtue of an authorisation granted in another European Economic Area (EEA) State, decisions to remove its authorisation are for the home State regulator. FSMA, s 368 therefore provides that the FSA may not present a petition to wind up such a firm except at the request of the home State regulator.

1. Duties to inform the FSA in insurance cases

A person applying for the appointment of a provisional liquidator or petitioning for the winding up of an authorised person who is permitted to effect or carry out insurance contracts or is an authorised reclaim fund must serve a copy of the application or petition on the FSA (FSMA, s 369 and s 369A).   26.24

2. Liquidator's duty to report

A liquidator of a company must notify the FSA if it appears that the company is or has been carrying on a regulated activity in breach of the general prohibition (FSMA, ss 19 and 370).   26.25

3. The FSA's participation in a compulsory winding up

Where a person other than the FSA asks the court to wind up a firm which is or has been authorised or an appointed representative or is or has been breaching the general prohibition, the FSA is granted by FSMA, s 371, certain rights of the kind granted in relation to other insolvency procedures. For example, the FSA has the right to be heard at the hearing of the petition and any subsequent hearing. Along with the creditors, the FSA has the right to receive information or proposals sent by the liquidator, to attend and speak at creditors' meetings and to ask the court to intervene or order a scheme to settle debts to be put to a creditors' vote.   26.26

H. BANKRUPTCY

Section 372 confers on the FSA the power to petition for the bankruptcy of an individual (in Scotland, the sequestration of his estate). The individual may be a formerly or currently authorised person, or a person who is or was carrying on business in breach of the general prohibition (s 372(7)). The only grounds on which such a petition may be presented by the FSA are that the individual appears to be unable to pay a regulated activity debt or appears to have no reasonable prospect of being able to pay such a debt (s 372(2)).   26.27

The first of these grounds may be established by showing that the individual has not paid a sum due under an agreement the making or performance of which was, or was part of, a regulated activity (s 372(3) and (8)). The second may be established if the FSA has served a demand requiring the individual to produce satisfactory evidence of a reasonable prospect that he will be able to pay a relevant debt as it falls due (s 372(4)). The FSA must show that at least three weeks have gone by without the demand being complied with or set aside in accordance with insolvency rules.   26.28

Section 373 requires an insolvency practitioner to report to the FSA evidence of unauthorised business which it appears that a bankrupt has at any time carried on.   26.29

Section 374 makes provision for the FSA to participate in and receive information about bankruptcy proceedings brought by another against an individual who is or has been carrying on financial services business, as though the FSA were a creditor.

I. PROVISIONS AGAINST DEBT AVOIDANCE

26.30 Under FSMA, s 375, the FSA may apply to the court for an order under s 423 of the Insolvency Act 1986 (Transactions defrauding creditors), even though the FSA is not itself a victim of the transaction. The application is to be treated as made on behalf of every person who was a victim of the transaction.

26.31 Section 423 of the Insolvency Act 1986 provides that the transaction must be at an undervalue (for example, it provides for property to be given away or sold at much less than its true value). Before making an order under this provision, the court must also be satisfied that its purpose was to put assets beyond the reach of creditors or otherwise to prejudice their interests.

26.32 The FSA will have to show that at the time the transaction was entered into, the debtor was carrying on a regulated activity. The FSA will also have to show that a victim of the transaction is (or was) party to an agreement with the debtor, the making or performance of which was (or was part of) a regulated activity carried on by the debtor.

26.33 Under the Insolvency Act 1986, s 423, the court may make such order as it thinks fit to restore the position to what it would have been if the transaction had not been entered into and to protect the interests of persons who are victims of the transaction.

26.34 There are equivalent provisions in Northern Ireland, but not in Scotland.

J. SUPPLEMENTAL PROVISIONS IN INSURANCE CASES

26.35 When insurance companies are in financial difficulties, special considerations arise for their regulators. Consumers do not necessarily want their money back: what they generally need is for the insurance cover to continue. The need can be particularly acute in relation to long-term insurance, where the policyholder may not now be able to arrange alternative cover. FSMA, s 376 to s 379 therefore makes special provision for such companies. In particular, it provides that the liquidator must carry out any existing long-term insurance contracts with a view to a transfer of the insurer's business as a going concern, unless the court otherwise orders. This is a close parallel to provisions made for the Financial Services Compensation Scheme by ss 216 and 217.

27

INJUNCTIONS AND RESTITUTION

Helen Marshall

A. INTRODUCTION

The provisions of Part 25 of the Financial Services and Markets Act 2000 (FSMA) 27.01
empower the High Court, at the request of the FSA, to grant injunctions requiring any
person who may have contravened a relevant requirement or who has been knowingly
concerned in such a contravention to take steps to remedy the contravention and to
order such persons to make restitution. The FSA may additionally, without recourse to
the Court, order persons authorised by it to make restitution. The FSA has very rarely
exercised its powers under Part 25 of the FSMA.

B. CONTRAVENTION OF RELEVANT REQUIREMENTS

1. Definition of 'relevant requirement'

FSMA, s 380(6), defines the concept of a relevant requirement as a requirement imposed 27.02
by or under the FSMA, or by any directly applicable Community regulation made under
the Markets in Financial Instruments Directive or a requirement imposed by or under
other Acts whose contravention amounts to an offence which may be prosecuted by the
FSA or the Secretary of State by virtue of the FSMA. Breach of a relevant requirement
therefore includes a breach of an FSA principle or other rule, a breach of the provisions
of s 397 (misleading statements and practices) and a breach of the prescribed money
laundering regulations or of the insider dealing provisions of the Criminal Justice
Act 1993. It would also cover the classic 'perimeter' breaches: carrying on regulated
activities in breach of the general prohibition, or unlawful financial promotion. (A similar result is achieved for Scotland even though the FSA and the Secretary of State do not
prosecute there.)

2. Injunction or interdict

27.03   Section 380 contains powers for the High Court to grant the FSA an injunction (in Scotland, an interdict by the Court of Session) where it is satisfied that there is a reasonable likelihood that any person will contravene a relevant requirement. It may also grant an injunction where it is satisfied that any person has already contravened a relevant requirement and there is a reasonable likelihood that the contravention will continue or be repeated.

27.04   Where it appears that there are steps which could be taken to remedy a contravention or to mitigate its effect, the court is given powers to make an order requiring the contravener and any other person who appears to have been knowingly concerned in the contravention to take such steps as the court may direct to remedy it (s 380(2) and (5)).

27.05   In considering what amounts to 'knowing concern' for this purpose, the case law on similar words in the FSMA predecessor Act, the Financial Services Act 1986, has been applied.[1] It would clearly cover a person who knew of the breach and received the unlawful proceeds of it.[2] It would also cover a case where a defendant knew the facts upon which the contravention depended even if he did not realise that there was any breach.[3]

27.06   The other type of order which may be made under s 380 is an order restraining someone who the court is satisfied may be a contravener, or a person knowingly concerned in a contravention, from disposing or otherwise dealing with any of his assets.

27.07   The Secretary of State is also able to bring proceedings under FSMA, s 380, where breach of the relevant requirement is an offence for which the Secretary of State has power to prosecute under the FSMA.

3. Restitution orders

27.08   The FSA or the Secretary of State may apply to the High Court (in Scotland, the Court of Session) under FSMA, s 382, for a restitution order. This may be granted if the court is satisfied that a person has breached a relevant requirement or been knowingly concerned in the contravention and either that he has accrued profits as a result, or one or more persons have suffered loss or been otherwise adversely affected.

27.09   The court has a broad discretion as to the amount which may be awarded. This is such sum as appears to it to be just, having regard to the profits which have accrued to the wrongdoer and/or the losses or adverse effects suffered by the victims.

27.10   The FSA is bound to pay any amount received pursuant to such an order as the court may direct. The payments will be made to qualifying persons within the meaning of s 382(8), being persons to whom the defendant's profits are attributable or those who have suffered losses or adverse effects. There is no requirement for the victim to have entered into a transaction with the contravener.

27.11   FSMA, s 382(4) gives the court power to order the defendant to supply it with accounts or other information to enable it: (a) to establish what are the relevant profits; (b) to establish what losses and adverse effects have been suffered, by whom and to what

---

[1] *Financial Services Authority v Martin and another* [2005] EWCA Civ 1422, [2006] BCLC 193.
[2] *Securities and Investments Board v Pantell SA* [1990] Ch 426.
[3] *Securities and Investments Board v Scandex Capital Management A/S* [1998] 1 WLR 712.

extent; and (c) to determine how any amounts are to be paid out by the FSA. The court may require any such information or accounts to be verified in such manner as it may direct (s 382(5)).

Victims of breaches of relevant requirements may have their own rights to bring proceedings (for example, rights in contract or tort) and nothing in s 382 affects those rights (s 382(7)). Indeed, the FSA has indicated that it is likely to regard the existence of such rights as one of the factors it takes into consideration in deciding whether it should itself seek restitution under the Act.   27.12

The Court of Appeal has found that the court has jurisdiction to make both injunctive and restitutionary orders in the same case, since the two types of order were not mutually exclusive, and therefore the steps required to be taken to remedy a contravention could include making restitution to investors.[4]   27.13

C. MARKET ABUSE

1. Injunctions

More specific provision is made for contraventions in respect of market abuse cases in FSMA, ss 381 and 383. The power in FSMA, ss 381 is framed in very similar terms to that in s 380. Market abuse here has the meaning given to it in s 118. Under ss 381 and 383 the ability to apply for the injunction is reserved to the FSA (rather than being shared with the Secretary of State as is the case under ss 380 and 382, even though, under s 168, the Secretary of State has concurrent power to investigate apparent market abuse).   27.14

The FSA (mindful of its duty, pursuant to FSMA, s 354 to take such steps as it considers appropriate to cooperate with, amongst others, the Panel on Takeovers and Mergers) has entered into Operating Guidelines with the Panel in which it has agreed not to exercise its injunctive powers during a takeover bid prior to the conclusion of the procedures available under the Takeover Code other than at the request of the Panel or in exceptional circumstances (such as where the suspected misconduct threatens or threatened the stability of the financial system).   27.15

2. Restitution orders

The court's power in s 383 to order restitution in cases of market abuse is very similar to its power in s 382 to order restitution for breach of relevant requirements. As in s 382, the ability to apply is reserved to the FSA, rather than being shared with the Secretary of State. However, there are important distinctions between restitution orders in market abuse cases and restitution orders in respect of breach of relevant requirements.   27.16

First, in market abuse restitution cases, third parties can be caught but not on the basis of 'knowing concern'. The test is different. A third party may only be the subject of a restitution order if the court is satisfied that the third party has, by act or omission,   27.17

---

[4] *Financial Services Authority v Martin and another* [2005] EWCA Civ 1422, [2006] BCLC 193.

required or encouraged another person to commit what would be market abuse if the third party himself or herself had done it (s 383(1)(b)).

27.18   Second, the court may not make a restitution order if it is satisfied that the defendant believed on reasonable grounds that his or her behaviour did not amount to market abuse or to requiring or encouraging market abuse as described in s 383(1). Nor may the court make an order if is satisfied that the defendant took all reasonable precautions and exercised all due diligence to avoid behaving in a way which could give rise to such an order. This reflects the limits placed on the FSA's ability to impose a penalty for market abuse by s 123(2) in Part 8.

27.19   The question what is appropriate restitution in a case of market abuse is a very complex one. The FSA has indicated that it is unlikely to use this power in order to seek restitution for every market participant who happened to be active in the market at the time of the abuse (so-called 'contemporaneous traders'). Such actions *are* brought in some other jurisdictions. However, they are capable of involving a very substantial number of market participants each of whom might be alleged to be owed a very small sum, whereas the cost of the litigation may well be significant.

D. RESTITUTION REQUIRED BY THE FSA

27.20   FSMA, s 384, gives the FSA the power to order restitution on much the same basis as the court under s 382 or s 383 for breaches of relevant requirements and market abuse. The FSA's power is, however, more limited in scope than the court's power, in that it may only be used, so far as concerns relevant requirements, against authorised persons who have themselves breached the requirements or been knowingly concerned in the breaches of others. The power of restitution in respect of market abuse appears to be coextensive with that given to the courts.

27.21   Any money which is required to be paid is not paid via the FSA, but directly to the persons who the FSA believes are entitled to restitution (s 384 (5)).

27.22   The procedure which the FSA must use in these cases is the warning notice procedure (described more fully in Chapter 28). Important features of the statutory procedure at the warning notice stage include the right to make representations and to have access to the evidence on which the FSA relies and other material which undermines its case. Where the FSA decides nevertheless to proceed, it must issue a decision notice. In contested cases, there is a right to refer the decision to the Financial Services and Markets Tribunal. Where this occurs, the decision cannot take effect, nor may it be publicised, while the matter is under review.

28

NOTICES

Helen Marshall

A. INTRODUCTION

The administrative procedure followed by the Financial Services Authority (FSA) in reaching key decisions in respect of firms and individuals is prescribed in general terms largely by Part 26 of the Financial Services and Markets Act 2000 (FSMA). These decisions may be of an enforcement or supervisory nature. 28.01

There is a relatively sophisticated procedure for disciplinary and market abuse decisions, which involves giving access to evidence and certain rights to affected third parties (with some exceptions relating to applications to the FSA). There is a simpler procedure commencing with a supervisory notice for other decisions. Both procedures envisage referrals to the Financial Services and Markets Tribunal in contested cases. 28.02

B. STATUTORY NOTICES

Section 395 of the FSMA states that the FSA is required to determine and publish the procedure that it will follow in relation to the giving of statutory notices. The Decision 28.03

Procedure and Penalties Manual (DEPP) provides guidance on the FSA's decision-making procedure for giving such statutory notices.[1]

28.04　　The decision about whether to give a statutory notice will be taken by the FSA's 'decision-maker', which will either be the Regulatory Decisions Committee (RDC) or FSA staff under executive procedures.[2]

28.05　　Section 395 (2) of the FSMA states that the procedure the FSA follows in relation to giving statutory notices must be:

designed to secure, among other things, that the decision which gives rise to the obligation to give any such notice is taken by a person not directly involved in establishing the evidence on which that decision is based.

28.06　　The FSA's guidance on how decision making is allocated is set out more fully in DEPP 2. DEPP 2 Annex 1 G identifies the provisions of the FSMA that give rise to the need for the giving of warning and decision notices, and whether the decision maker is the RDC or FSA staff. The RDC will be the decision maker in cases involving the cancellation of a permission, withdrawal of approved person status, and imposition of a financial penalty or public censure.

C. WARNING NOTICES

28.07　　Warning notices are the first notices given by the FSA in the exercise of a number of its formal 'enforcement' powers. For example, the warning notice procedure applies to cases where the FSA decides to discipline authorised firms and approved persons or to impose a penalty for market abuse.

28.08　　FSMA, s 387 provides that a warning notice must state the action which the FSA intends to take and specify a reasonable period of at least 28 days, within which the recipient may make representations to the FSA. The warning notice must be in writing, giving reasons for the proposed action. Where the access to evidence provisions in FSMA, s 394 apply, the notice must say so, explain what that means in terms of access to material on which the FSA has relied in making its decision, and state whether there is additional, secondary material to which the recipient must be allowed access.

28.09　　Where a warning notice has been given, the FSA may extend the period specified in the notice for a response. This is likely to occur in complex cases where discussions with a view to a possible settlement are in progress. Within a reasonable time, the FSA must decide whether to go on to issue a decision notice.

D. DECISION NOTICES

28.10　　Where the FSA continues to believe that action of the kind envisaged in the warning notice is necessary, despite representations, it must proceed to issue a decision notice (FSMA, s 387(4)). Like warning notices, decision notices must be in writing, giving

---

[1] See DEPP 6.2 (Deciding whether to take action).
[2] See DEPP Chapter 2 (Statutory notices and the allocation of decision making).

reasons for the FSA's action (FSMA, s 388(1)(a) and (b)). A decision notice must state whether the access to evidence provisions in FSMA, s 394 apply and if so what that means and whether any secondary material exists to which the recipient must be given access (FSMA, s 388(1)(c) and (d)). A decision notice must also give an indication of any rights to refer the decision to the Financial Services and Markets Tribunal, and the procedure for doing so (FSMA, s 388(1)(e)).

It is quite possible that a decision notice will indicate that the FSA intends to take   28.11
action which is different from that stated in the warning notice which preceded it. For example, if the FSA intended to impose a penalty, it might decide, having considered representations, that the matter is less serious than it originally thought, and that a public censure would be sufficient. The FSMA expressly provides for the FSA to change the proposed outcome to reflect this. However, FSMA, s 388(2) precludes the FSA from proceeding directly to a decision notice under one Part of the Act where the warning notice was issued under another Part. Thus, for example, it would not be possible to issue a decision notice about a penalty for market abuse under Part 8 when the warning notice related to a proposed penalty for breach of rules applying to authorised persons and was given under Part 14. Different procedures and different rights apply to action taken under different Parts of the Act. FSMA, s 388(2) ensures that those concerned have all the rights to which they are intended to be entitled under the Act and that the FSA cannot dilute those rights by taking the first steps in the process under a different Part.

The first or only decision notice may be given without the consent of the person to   28.12
whom the warning notice was given. A recipient of a decision notice who does not agree with the action proposed in it may refer the matter to the Financial Services and Markets Tribunal. If, after the issue of a decision notice, the FSA changes its mind about the action to be taken, and the recipient of the notice agrees, the FSA may issue a further decision notice stating the action the FSA now intends to take (FSMA, s 388(3) and (4)). These provisions are intended to cover cases where settlement discussions come to fruition only after the first decision notice has been issued. Even in these cases of apparent settlement, any right to refer the matter to the Financial Services and Markets Tribunal is retained, thereby providing a kind of cooling-off period for the subject of the notice (FSMA, s 388(5)).

E. NOTICES OF DISCONTINUANCE

Of course there will be cases where the FSA, having given a warning notice or decision   28.13
notice, decides not to take the action stated. This may arise, for example, where it becomes apparent in the light of representations that the matter is much less serious than it first appeared and does not warrant disciplinary action after all. In these cases, the FSA must give a notice of discontinuance to the recipient of the original notice, identifying the proceedings which are being discontinued (FSMA, s 389). The only exception is where the decision to discontinue amounts to a decision to grant an application (for example, for authorisation) where, of course, the person concerned will be alerted to the outcome in any event (FSMA, s 389(2)).

F. FINAL NOTICES

28.14   The decision-making process may take some time, especially in complex cases. In order that the recipient of the notices is entirely clear that the matter is coming to a close, FSMA, s 390, makes provision for the giving of final notices. These will have to be given when the recipient of a decision notice does not refer the matter to the Financial Services and Markets Tribunal. They are also required to be given when the Financial Services and Markets Tribunal or Court of Appeal (or Court of Session) has made a decision following the referral of an FSA decision notice. They must be issued by the FSA when it moves to implement the Financial Services and Markets Tribunal or Court decision.

28.15   FSMA, s 390 prescribes the content of the final notice, which varies according to whether it relates to a penalty, public censure, or other action. The effect of the section is to require the FSA to make plain what is now going to happen and when. For example, a final notice about a public censure must set out the terms of the statement the FSA is going to make, and give details of the manner in which, and the date on which, the statement will be published (FSMA, s 390(3)). To the extent that the notice states that the recipient must make a payment, it must require that to happen in not less than 14 days (FSMA, s 390(8)).

28.16   If a financial penalty remains unpaid after the due date, the FSA may recover it as a debt due to it, that is, without proving the underlying facts which gave rise to the decision to impose the penalty (FSMA, s 390(9)).

28.17   Where the payment to be made is by way of restitution, and the person concerned fails to make the payment in time, the FSA may apply to the court for an injunction ordering the payment to be made (or, in Scotland, an order under the Court of Session Act 1988, s 45) (FSMA, s 390(10)).

G. PUBLICATION

28.18   FSMA, s 391, provides a careful balance between the competing interests relating to sensitive regulatory information about enforcement action. On the one hand, a firm or individual who is the subject of a warning notice and decision notice will generally wish to keep that matter private. On the other, the public interest in securing the transparency and accountability of the regulatory process is also significant. Generally speaking, FSMA, s 391 addresses this conflict by prohibiting the publication of proceedings until they are completed, but obliging the FSA to publish appropriate information at that point.

28.19   FSMA, s 391(1) prevents publication of warning notices and decision notices or any details about them.

28.20   Where the FSA issues a notice of discontinuance, it may publish such information as it considers appropriate about the discontinued proceedings, but it must alert the recipient of the notice to this possibility in the notice itself and obtain the recipient's consent (FSMA, s 391(2)).

28.21   When a supervisory notice takes effect (that is, when it is no longer open to any further review under the Act), the FSA is obliged to publish such information about it as it considers appropriate (FSMA, s 391(5)). The FSA is similarly obliged to publish such information as it considers appropriate about final notices (FSMA, s 391(4)).

Two general provisions apply to any publication under FSMA, s 391. First, publica- 28.22 tion may be in any manner which the FSA considers appropriate (FSMA, s 391(7)). Second, the FSA is precluded from publishing information under the section if it would, in the FSA's opinion, be unfair to the person with respect to whom the action was taken or prejudicial to the interests of consumers (FSMA, s 391(6)). In practice, the FSA often publishes final notices on its website.

H. THIRD-PARTY RIGHTS

The FSA's disciplinary or supervisory action may, on occasion, be aimed at one person 28.23 but may be triggered at least in part by the actions of another. For example, the FSA may take action against a firm for failing properly to supervise a particular member of staff. In these circumstances, the third party may find himself identified in an FSA notice in a way which is prejudicial to him. On ordinary public law principles, he might expect the FSA to notify him and give him an opportunity to respond.[3]

FSMA, s 393 and FSMA, s 394 give certain third parties in this position a number of 28.24 rights. The rights only arise in relation to warning notices and decision notices given under the provisions of the Act listed in FSMA, s 392.

If any of the reasons set out in a warning notice relate to a matter which identifies a 28.25 third party, and the FSA believes the matter is prejudicial to him, he is entitled to be given a copy of the notice by the FSA (unless he is being given his own separate warning notice) (FSMA, s 393(1) and (2)). A similar provision applies to decision notices (FSMA, s 393(4) and (6)). Copy notices need not be given where the FSA believes this would be impracticable (FSMA, s 393(7)).

A third party who is given a copy warning notice must be given a period of at least 28.26 28 days during which he may make representations to the FSA (FSMA, s 393(3)).

Where a third party receives a copy decision notice with which he takes issue, he may 28.27 refer it to the Financial Services and Markets Tribunal, in so far as it is based on a reason which identifies him and is believed by the FSA to be prejudicial to him (FSMA, s 393(9)(a)). He may also refer to the Financial Services and Markets Tribunal any opinion expressed by the FSA about him (FSMA, s 393(9)(b)). The copy notice must be accompanied by an indication of these rights and how to exercise them (FSMA, s 393(10)). A third party given a copy of a notice can refer it to the Financial Services and Markets Tribunal only if the person who was given the original notice has a right to refer the matter to the Financial Services and Markets Tribunal (FSMA, s 393(8)).

If the third party does not receive a copy decision notice but alleges that he should 28.28 have done, there is provision in FSMA, s 393(11) for him to refer the alleged failure to the Financial Services and Markets Tribunal but only in conjunction with an appeal against the decision or opinion contained in the notice. This right can be exercised only if the person who was given the original notice has a right to refer the matter to the Financial Services and Markets Tribunal (FSMA, s 393(8)).

---

[3] See, for example, *R v LAUTRO, ex parte Ross* [1993] QB 17.

28.29   The access to evidence provisions in FSMA, s 394 apply to the third party receiving the copy notice as they apply to the person to whom the original notice was given but are limited to material relating to the matter which identifies the third party (FSMA, s 393(12)). The copy notice must be accompanied by a description of how FSMA, s 394 applies to the third party (FSMA, s 393(13)).

28.30   There is provision in FSMA, s 393 for third parties to be kept up to date with the progress of the matter. For example, FSMA, s 393(5) provides that a third party who receives a copy warning notice is entitled to a copy of any subsequent decision notice, even if that decision notice does not relate to a matter which identifies him. FSMA, s 393(14) provides that a third party who receives a copy warning notice or decision notice must be sent a copy of any notice of discontinuance applying to the proceedings to which the earlier notice related.

I. ACCESS TO FSA MATERIAL

28.31   FSMA, s 394 makes arrangements for providing those in receipt of notices and copy notices with access to relevant material in the FSA's possession. Following amendments in the House of Lords[4], these provisions are broadly similar to those found in the Criminal Procedure and Investigations Act 1996, even though the procedures to which they relate are civil procedures (including restitution procedures akin to High Court claims). The provisions on access to FSA material apply to persons receiving warning notices and decision notices of the kind specified in FSMA, s 392, and those receiving copies of such notices pursuant to FSMA, s 393.

28.32   A person receiving such a notice must be given access to the material on which the FSA relied in taking the decision to give the notice. It must also give the person access to secondary material which the FSA believes might undermine that decision. Secondary material is defined in FSMA, s 394(6) as material that was not relied on but which was either considered by the FSA in reaching the decision or which was obtained by it in connection with the matter to which the notice relates.

28.33   There are a number of exceptions to the obligation to give access to material. The first relates to what is called 'excluded material': see FSMA, s 394(7). This is material which has been intercepted under warrant or which indicates that such a warrant has been issued or executed, or which is a protected item. FSMA, s 413 contains a definition of what amounts to a protected item. In broad terms, this is material covered by legal professional privilege, whether that be the FSA's privilege or another's. Where the material is withheld because it is a protected item, written notice must be given that such an item exists and is being withheld.

28.34   The second exception is where material relates to another case and was taken into account by the FSA only for comparative purposes.

28.35   The FSA is not obliged to disclose material at this stage if it believes access would not be in the public interest. Nor is it required to give access if it believes that access would not be fair, weighing in the balance the likely significance of the material to the case in question and the potential prejudice to the commercial interests of a third party if the

---

[4] The House of Lords is superseded by the Supreme Court as of 1 October 2009.

material were to be disclosed. In these cases, the FSA must give written notice of its refusal and the reasons for it.

J. SUPERVISORY NOTICES

Part 26 of the FSMA deals in passing with supervisory notices. The term 'supervisory notice' is defined in FSMA, s 395(13). Broadly speaking, supervisory notices are notices concerned with regulatory issues which may need to be referred to the Financial Services and Markets Tribunal, but where the more formal structure of warning notice and decision notice is not required. The cases concerned are: 28.36

(a) exercise by the FSA of its own-initiative power to vary, or propose a variation of, a Part 4 permission;

(b) discontinuance or suspension (actual or proposed) of the listing of securities by the FSA as listing authority;

(c) decisions about intervention in relation to inwardly passporting firms, though not in cases where the Directives provide for a different procedure;

(d) decisions about intervention in relation to collective investment schemes;

(e) decisions about former underwriting members at Lloyd's.

Of these, (a) is likely to be the one most often encountered in practice. Each of the relevant provisions sets out the procedure to be followed: see for example, FSMA, s 53 for the procedure to be followed where the FSA exercises its own-initiative variation of permission power.   28.37

29

CRIMINAL OFFENCES AND THEIR PROSECUTION

Helen Marshall

A. INTRODUCTION

The focus of the Financial Services and Markets Act 2000 (FSMA) is to establish a system of regulation applying (over and above the general law) to a restricted class of persons seeking to enjoy the special privileges of authorisation or approval. However, it also provides for a number of criminal offences of wider application. Part 27 includes the more serious of these offences and sets out who may prosecute them (including the offence of market manipulation, described in more detail below). It provides that the Financial Services Authority (FSA) itself may (except in Scotland) prosecute all the offences contained in the Act.

29.01

B. PROSECUTION OF OFFENCES

1. What may the FSA prosecute?

FSMA, s 401 gives the FSA power to prosecute offences contained in the Act or in subordinate legislation made under the Act. The offences created by the Act itself relate to:

29.02

(a) carrying on or purporting to carry on a regulated activity without authorisation or exemption (s 23);
(b) making false claims to be authorised or exempt (s 24);
(c) communicating an invitation or inducement to engage in investment activity in breach of the restrictions on financial promotion (s 25);
(d) dealing in assets held on trust in a manner not authorised by the FSA, where assets have been transferred to the trustee pursuant to an FSA requirement (s 48(9));

(e) performing or agreeing to perform functions in breach of a prohibition order (s 56(4)). These are orders made by the FSA in relation to individuals who appear not to be fit and proper to perform functions in relation to an authorised person's regulated business;

(f) offering transferable securities to the public, or requesting admission of transferable securities to a regulated market, where a prospectus has not been made available to the public (s 85);

(g) breaching Treasury regulations enacted to maintain the effectiveness of the 'asset identification rules' (s 142(5));

(h) failing to comply with certain requirements under Part 11 of the Act (Information Gathering and Investigations). This includes giving false information to investigators appointed by the FSA or the Secretary of State (s 177);

(i) failing to comply with certain requirements for increasing or decreasing 'control' of an authorised person, and other related offences (s 191F);

(j) carrying on or purporting to carry on business in contravention of a consumer credit restriction or prohibition (ss 203 and 204);

(k) failing to comply with certain requirements in respect of applications to increase or decrease 'control' of a recognised investment exchange, and other related offences (s 301L);

(l) making false claims to be a person to whom the general prohibition does not apply as a result of Part 20, that is, a member of a professional body who qualifies for the exemption outlined in s 327 (s 333);

(m) providing false or misleading information to an auditor or actuary (s 346);

(n) disclosing confidential information in contravention of the statutory restrictions (s 352);

(o) failing, as a director of an insurance company carrying on long-term insurance business, to notify the FSA of a general meeting to propose the company's voluntary winding up (s 366);

(p) misleading by statements and practices, contrary to s 397;

(q) misleading the FSA, contrary to s 398;

(r) failing to comply with certain requirements prior to exercising passporting rights (Sch 3, para 21);

(s) failing to notify the FSA of an exercise of Treaty rights or providing false or misleading information in connection with such a notification (Sch 4, para 6); and

(t) refusing or failing to attend or give evidence at a Tribunal hearing or tampering with, suppressing, concealing, or destroying documents which may be relevant to it (Sch 13, para 11).

29.03 Section 402 gives the FSA power to prosecute two additional types of offence: insider dealing contrary to Part 5 of the Criminal Justice Act 1993, and breaches of prescribed money laundering regulations. In March 2009, the FSA successfully prosecuted two individuals for insider dealing under section 52 of the Criminal Justice Act 1993.[1]

29.04 The FSA may also prosecute some offences under the Building Societies Act 1986, the Friendly Societies Acts 1974 and 1992, the Credit Unions Act 1979, the Industrial and

---

[1] *R v (1) McQuoid (2) Melbourne* [2009] Southwark Crown Court unreported.

Provident Societies Act 1965, and the Friendly and Industrial and Provident Societies Act 1968 (see FSA Enforcement Guide (EG) 12.4C).

The FSMA does not preclude the FSA from prosecuting offences which any other   29.05
private person may prosecute, such as theft and obtaining property by deception. In practice, it is not likely that the FSA will routinely prosecute such offences. However, the FSA has indicated that it will prosecute criminal offences for which it is not the statutory prosecutor, but where the offences form part of the same criminality as the offences it is prosecuting under the Act (see EG 12.1).

In all cases, the FSA power is to prosecute offences in England, Wales and Northern   29.06
Ireland. In Scotland, prosecution remains the responsibility of the Lord Advocate and the Procurator Fiscal.

2. Who else may prosecute?

Others are also given express statutory power to prosecute: the Secretary of State and the   29.07
Director of Public Prosecutions (DPP) may prosecute in England and Wales, as may the DPP for Northern Ireland in Northern Ireland (s 401(2) and (3)). Both DPPs may give consent to any other person to prosecute; but without such consent, no private prosecution may be brought. The Office of Fair Trading may prosecute the offence of contravening a consumer credit prohibition except in Scotland (see s 401(4)). By virtue of s 1 of the Criminal Justice Act 1987, the Serious Fraud Office may also prosecute any offence arising out of serious and complex fraud.

3. FSA decisions to prosecute

The FSA has indicated that, although it is not a Crown prosecutor, it will follow the   29.08
Code for Crown Prosecutors in deciding whether or not to prosecute. This means that decisions whether to prosecute will rest on the answer to two questions: first, is the evidence sufficient to provide a realistic prospect of conviction against the defendant on each charge, and second, having regard to all the circumstances, is criminal prosecution in the public interest?

For matters involving a potential breach of the Money Laundering Regulations, the   29.09
FSA will consider whether the person has followed the Joint Money Laundering Steering Group guidance for the UK financial sector when deciding whether to pursue a prosecution (EG 12.2).

In exercising its power to institute proceedings for an offence, the FSA is also required   29.10
to comply with any conditions or restrictions imposed in writing by the Treasury (ss 401(5) and 402(2)). At the time of writing, no such documents have been made public by the Treasury and the FSA procedure for commencing a prosecution is set out in EG 12.

4. FSA decisions not to prosecute: cautioning policy

In some cases, the FSA may decide to issue a formal caution rather than prosecute. In   29.11
these cases, it will follow the Home Office guidance on cautioning, which requires a number of conditions to be met. In particular, there must be evidence sufficient to give

a realistic prospect of conviction and it must be in the public interest to use a caution to dispose of the matter. In addition, the offender must admit the offence, understand the significance of the caution, and give his or her informed consent to its issue.

29.12   The FSA's policy is not to publish cautions, though it will keep a record of the caution. A copy of the caution will also be available to parties with access to the Police National Computer (EG 12.6).

5. Liaison with other prosecuting authorities

29.13   Where a case indicates possible criminality, it may be that there are a number of agencies apart from the FSA with a potential interest in the case. The FSA has agreed guidelines with other agencies that may have a mutual interest in investigating a case, to ensure efficiency, effectiveness, and best practice in liaison and co-operation. These guidelines are set out in EG Annex 2.

C. SPECIFIC OFFENCES

29.14   Some of the most important offences created by the FSMA are contained in Part 27.

29.15   The offence in s 397(1) and (2), applies to a person who makes a materially false or misleading or deceptive statement, knowingly or recklessly, or who dishonestly conceals material facts. This is an offence if, in summary, the act or omission is for the purpose of inducing any other person to enter into or refrain from entering into a relevant agreement or to exercise rights conferred by such an agreement. 'Relevant agreement' is defined in s 397(9) to mean, in effect, agreement of types defined in the Financial Services and Markets Act 2000 (Misleading Statements and Practices) Order 2001.[2]

29.16   It is notable that this offence may be committed by any person, whether or not they are authorised. Dishonesty is not, however, an essential ingredient of the offence (except where the charge is one of concealing material facts). A successful criminal conviction was secured by the FSA under s 397(1)(c) of the FSMA in 2005 against a company for making a profit forecast to the market which was dependent on three contracts which did not exist at the time of the forecast.[3]

29.17   Section 397(3) defines the important offence generally known as market manipulation. This makes it a criminal act to engage in any course of conduct which creates a false or misleading impression as to the market or price or value of relevant investments if that is done for the purpose of creating that impression and inducing another person to buy, sell, subscribe for, or underwrite those investments or to refrain from doing so. It is also an offence if the ultimate objective is to induce a person to exercise or refrain from exercising rights conferred by those investments. 'Relevant investments' are defined in the Financial Services and Markets Act 2000 (Misleading Statements and Practices) Order 2001.[4]

---

[2] SI 2001/3645.
[3] *R v Rigby, Bailey and Rowley*, 2005 unreported.
[4] SI 2001/3645.

It is suggested that, whilst it is necessary for the prosecution to show that the impression was consciously created for a particular purpose, it is not necessary to show that the person who created the impression believed that it would be false or misleading. This is borne out by s 397(5), which makes it a defence for a defendant to prove—on the balance of probabilities—that he reasonably believed that he would not create a false or misleading impression. This defence would be unnecessary if the burden were on the prosecution to show that he knew that the impression created would be false or misleading. 29.18

There are some circumstances where it may be necessary or desirable to make misleading statements or create a false or misleading impression about the price, value or market in investments. To this end, the FSMA provides a defence against the two offences in s 397, where the defendant can prove, on the balance of probabilities, that the conduct in question was carried out in conformity with the FSA/European Commission rules on price stabilising or control of information rules (s 397 (4) and (5) FSMA). 29.19

The FSA's price stabilisation rules are found in Chapter 2 of the FSA Code of Market Conduct. The price stabilisation rules allow firms, under certain circumstances, to purchase or offer to purchase relevant securities for a predetermined period of time, exclusively to support the market price of the relevant securities due to a selling pressure in the securities. The rules only apply to price stabilisation undertaken in the context of a significant distribution of relevant securities. For the purposes of the price stabilisation defence in s 397(5)(b), it is also necessary for the defendant to show that the purpose of the conduct was to stabilise the price of the investments. 29.20

Rule 10.2.2 of the FSA Senior Management, Systems and Controls sourcebook (SYSC), made under s 147 of the FSMA contains the control of information rules. These rules permit proper control of information between different parts of authorised firms through the use of communication barriers (commonly known as Chinese walls) to ensure that inside information available in one part of the firm is not given to another part of the firm which might enable it to take inappropriate advantage of the information. 29.21

1. Territorial scope of offences under section 397

Section 397(6) makes express provision for the application of s 397 to conduct outside, or having an effect outside the United Kingdom. More specifically, misleading statements may be criminal if they are made in or from the United Kingdom, even if they are made for the purpose of inducing persons located abroad. They may also be criminal if they are made in or from a place outside the United Kingdom if they are directed at inducing persons in the United Kingdom, or the agreement is, or would be, entered into here. 29.22

The offence of market manipulation is not committed unless it is committed in the United Kingdom or the false or misleading impression, whilst caused by activity outside the United Kingdom, is in fact created here. 29.23

2. Sentencing

The offences in s 397 are serious offences which are triable either as a summary offence in the magistrates' court or on indictment in the Crown Court. In the magistrates' courts, a maximum sentence of six months' imprisonment may be imposed, together 29.24

with a fine not exceeding the statutory maximum (currently £5,000). In the Crown Court, the maximum sentence is seven years' imprisonment together with an unlimited fine.

3. Misleading the FSA

29.25 FMSA, s 398, makes it an offence knowingly or recklessly to give false or misleading information to the FSA in purported compliance with any requirement imposed by or under the Act, including requirements imposed by FSA rules.

29.26   This is an indictable but not an imprisonable offence: in the Crown Court, only a fine (albeit an unlimited one) may be imposed.

29.27   There are other offences in the Act of misleading the FSA—misleading an investigator under s 177, for example—which carry higher sentences (in the case of s 177, up to two years' imprisonment). Section 398 makes clear that it is a sweep-up provision: the offence which it creates applies only to behaviour which is not an offence by virtue of some other provision of the Act.

4. Misleading the Office of Fair Trading

29.28 The effect of the FSMA, s 399 is to extend the Competition Act 1998, s 44 and make it an offence under that Act to mislead or give false information to the Office of Fair Trading when it is exercising its functions under the FSMA.

5. Offences related to investigations by the Competition Commission

29.29 Schedule 14 (2A)(5) of the FMSA extends provisions relating to offences in the Enterprise Act 2002 to investigations by the Competition Commission under the FSMA.

6. Applications to officers of bodies corporate, members of a partnership, and unincorporated associations

29.30 Where an offence is committed by a company, officers (including controllers) will also be guilty of an offence if they are shown to have consented or connived in the offence, or if it can be shown to be attributable to negligence on their part (s 400(1) and (2)). Similar provisions extend criminal liability to partners within a partnership, and those purporting to be partners (s 400(3) and (4)). Section 400(6) extends liability to officers and members of governing bodies of unincorporated associations. The Treasury may make an order providing for liability to extend to officers of companies and unincorporated associations formed outside the UK (s 400(7)).

30

MISCELLANEOUS, INTERPRETATION, AND SUPPLEMENTAL

Paul Kennedy

A. INTRODUCTION

This chapter deals with Parts 28, 29 and 30 of the Financial Services and Markets Act 2000 (FSMA). Much of the material in these three final parts is technical and of no specific significance in itself, though practitioners will frequently need to consult Part 29 at least, with its 11 sections containing definitions of different kinds. There is, however, some material of interest in Part 28 (miscellaneous), particularly in relation to reviews of compliance failure and in the international arena.   **30.01**

B. REVIEWS OF COMPLIANCE FAILURES

Section 404 of the FSMA deals with schemes for reviewing past business. It came into the Bill for the FSMA at a relatively late stage (report stage in the House of Lords). It is designed to ensure that, if there ever were another widespread compliance failure, the regulatory system could tackle the problem, and put in place machinery to provide redress to those who had suffered from the compliance failure.   **30.02**

The precedents to date have been, principally, the pension opt-out and transfer problems of the 1990s and, to a much lesser extent, the subsequent review of possible mis-selling of Free-Standing Additional Voluntary Contributions (FSAVCs). Putting right this widespread malaise became a priority for the regulators in the period from   **30.03**

1993 onwards. Although the initiative was led by the Securities and Investments Board (SIB), using its function of oversight of the regulatory system under the Financial Services Act 1986, and the relatively restricted powers relating to that, the real compulsive force of the review was delivered by the Self-Regulating Organisations (SROs) and, in particular, the Personal Investment Authority.

30.04   FSMA, s 404 recognises that, in this respect, the old regime had the benefit that the SROs (by the membership contract) had power to do something which could not have securely been delivered under the previous legislation on its own. New machinery is therefore enabled, by a Treasury 'switch-on' order under the section requiring the affirmative approval of each House of Parliament. In that way, the FSA can be authorised to establish and operate a scheme for enquiring into the specified failure, for establishing the liability of authorised persons to make redress, and for determining the amount of that redress. Indeed, the Treasury used its power to make transitional provision under ss 426–7 of the FSMA to establish the existing review of pensions mis-selling as a 'deemed scheme' under s 404.[1]

30.05   The Treasury's power to trigger the machinery is bounded by conditions. In particular, an order authorising the FSA to create a scheme can be made only if the FSA has reported to the Treasury about the alleged failure and asked the Treasury to make the order (s 404(4)(a)). The FSA has to put forward details of the proposed scheme, and the Treasury has to be satisfied that:

(a) there has been a widespread failure on the part of authorised persons to comply with its rules (s.404(1)(a));

(b) 'private persons' have suffered or will suffer loss for which authorised persons will be liable (s404(1)(b)); and

(c) the proposed scheme is 'an appropriate way of dealing with the failure' (s 404(4)(b) and (c)).

30.06   The meat of the provision is in s 404(6). Once the scheme has been made, then failure by an authorised person to comply with the scheme is treated as a failure to comply with rules. So, all the sanctions available for breach of the FSA's rules are available to back the scheme up with the force of compulsion. Subsection (6) is, however, subject to any provision made by the scheme order concerned: so the section appears to contemplate that the Treasury may wish to pick and choose between the various remedies for failure to comply. However, the usual rights of action for breach of rules (under s 150) were applied to breaches of the 'deemed scheme'.

30.07   The meaning of 'private person' is to be prescribed by Treasury regulations (s 404(9)). However, the term has so far only been prescribed for other purposes. It is not clear at this stage whether the Treasury would have to prescribe a separate meaning under s 404 before being satisfied that private persons have suffered loss, or whether it could rely on the meaning already prescribed under s 150.

30.08   Perhaps surprisingly, there have been no schemes authorised under s 404 itself, even though a number of cases of widespread mis-selling have been considered under the 'wider implications' process established by the FSA and the Financial Ombudsman

---

[1] The Financial Services and Markets Act 2000 (Transitional Provisions)(Reviews of Pensions Business) Order 2001 SI 2001/2512.

Service (FOS) (see Chapter 18). In the case of mortgage endowments, for example, the FSA oversaw a concerted programme to ensure that individuals who might have suffered loss were given an opportunity to complain and seek redress, using individual enforcement powers where necessary. However, the section 404 power remains available if similar measures prove inadequate, albeit with a high threshold.[2]

C. THIRD COUNTRIES: COMMUNITY MEASURES

Sections 405 to 407 of the FSMA provide the machinery to enable the United Kingdom to continue to comply with the requirements of the three leading Single Market Directives in the context of effective market access by firms in the Community into third countries. **30.09**

The three Directives concerned[3] set up machinery enabling the Commission or the Council to take measures against countries outside the European Economic Area (EEA) if they do not allow Community financial services firms effective market access. **30.10**

Most of the machinery in the relevant articles of the Directives is of a diplomatic and political character. But, in order to give credence to the Commission or Council's negotiating position, the Directives enable the Community authorities to require the competent authorities of the member States to limit or suspend decisions about authorisation of, and about approval of controlling arrangements in relation to, bodies corporate originating in their own States. Section 405 accordingly gives the Treasury the power to direct the FSA to refuse or defer decisions on applications for Part 4 permission by UK incorporated bodies. Similarly, the Treasury may direct the FSA to object to proposals for acquisition of control of such bodies. **30.11**

The refusal of permission and the objection to control are made automatic, without reference to the Financial Services and Markets Tribunal; and any requirement on the FSA's part to defer a decision results in a suspension of all relevant time limits (s 407). Section 408 makes further provision, following such a Commission decision, in relation to European Free Trade Association (EFTA) firms, which are subsidiaries of a parent governed by the law of the relevant third country: the effect is to deny the EFTA firm the passport it might otherwise have been entitled to. An EFTA firm currently means a firm based in Norway, Iceland, or Lichtenstein. **30.12**

Interestingly, s 405 limits the Treasury's power of direction to applications by UK companies, and to matters affecting control of UK companies. The latter seems to fit the design of the Directives, which are aimed at the third State and control of community **30.13**

---

[2] In *Reforming Financial Services* (July 2009), the Treasury has proposed measures to lower the threshold under s 404, such as relaxing the requirements for Treasury approval and for the FSA to demonstrate a breach of its rules, as well as consideration of the 'wider implications' process between the FSA and the FOS, and independent arrangements for collective action such as consumer advocates. Many consumer protection measures, including those required to implement single market directives, are increasingly being implemented through non-FSMA instruments rather than FSA rules; and the proposed reforms might also make it easier to ensure that relevant case law and FOS determinations are implemented on a wider basis.

[3] The Markets in Financial Instruments Directive (2004/39/EC), the First Non-life Insurance Directive (73/239/EEC), and the Life Assurance Consolidation Directive (2002/83/EC), The FSA's obligations under the Banking Consolidation Directive 2006/48/EC are implemented in the Capital Requirements Regulations 2006 SI 2006/3221.

companies passing to companies from that State. In relation to authorisation, however, the limitation to UK companies seems curious, as the Directives have no such limitation and appear to contemplate that application for authorisation by branches emanating from the third State should be refused or deferred. However, in this case, no doubt the more general power of direction in s 410 could be used (see below).

D. INTERNATIONAL OBLIGATIONS

30.14 Section 410 of the FSMA is also of some interest internationally. It contains a list of persons who may loosely be described as regulators for the purposes of the FSMA. These are the FSA (including its new capacity as Listing Authority), recognised investment exchanges and recognised clearing houses (RIEs and RCHs) (though not overseas ones), persons providing settlement arrangements of the kind that can be netted in an insolvency (as to which see s 301) and the FOS functioning under Part 16.

30.15   If any of these bodies appears to the Treasury to be proposing to take action which would be incompatible with Community obligations or other international obligations, the Treasury can direct that the action be not taken. Equally, if positive steps are required to be taken by such a person to implement such obligations, the Treasury may require those steps to be taken. The power of the Treasury to intervene in the regulatory system established under the FSMA is highly restricted, but this is one of two cases where it exists (leaving aside ss 405 to 408), the other one being in the context of competition override.

E. GAMING

30.16 Section 412 removes any threat of nullity or unenforceability as a gaming contract of any contract covered by the FSMA. In the past there was some doubt as to whether, in particular, some derivatives contracts might be void or unenforceable as gaming contracts. That ancient public policy for control of antisocial bargains became inappropriate with the regulation of, in particular, investment business under the Financial Services Act 1986, though it took some litigation to establish the true width of the original 1986 provision.[4] Under FSMA, s 412, any contract relating to activities to be specified by the Treasury where either or each party is acting by way of business is saved from the risk of nullity or unenforceability on the ground that it is a gaming or wagering contract.

F. INTERPRETATION

30.17 Part 29 of the FSMA deals with definitions. The bulk of these are in s 417, which is followed by sections dealing with specific issues such as the corporation law definitions of parent, subsidiary, group, controller, etc.

---

[4] See *City Index Ltd v Leslie* [1992] 1 QB 98.

G. SUPPLEMENTAL PROVISIONS

Part 30 (supplemental) of the FSMA contains the closing provisions including important   **30.18**
enabling powers for consequential amendments, transitionals, and repeals. The passage
of the Bill was relatively contentious, protracted, and complex; and only very limited
transitionals and repeals were included in Schedules 2022. Instead the Treasury has
power, in ss 426 and 427, to deal with all the consequential carpentry by subordinate
legislation subject to the negative resolution procedure (s 429(8)). The resulting secondary legislation is of historical interest only, although similar provision (for example, for
grandfathering or interim authorisation of existing practitioners) may be needed whenever the scope of FSA regulation is expanded, whether in reliance on these powers,
powers under Sch 2, para 25 of the FSMA, the European Communities Act 1972, or
other primary legislation.

Section 430 deals with extent, and applies the whole of the FSMA, except the provi-   **30.19**
sions about open-ended investment companies, to Northern Ireland. The FSMA applies
to Scotland without express mention. Financial services remain a matter within the
jurisdiction of the Westminster Parliament, and is not devolved under the Scotland
Act 1998 to the Scottish Parliament or Executive.

APPENDIX

Financial Services and Markets Act 2000

2000 CHAPTER 8

An Act to make provision about the regulation of financial services and markets; to provide for the transfer of certain statutory functions relating to building societies, friendly societies, industrial and provident societies and certain other mutual societies; and for connected purposes.

[14th June 2000]

BE IT ENACTED by the Queen's most Excellent Majesty, by and with the advice and consent of the Lords Spiritual and Temporal, and Commons, in this present Parliament assembled, and by the authority of the same, as follows:—

PART I
THE REGULATOR

1 The Financial Services Authority

(1) The body corporate known as the Financial Services Authority ('the Authority') is to have the functions conferred on it by or under this Act.

(2) The Authority must comply with the requirements as to its constitution set out in Schedule 1.

(3) Schedule 1 also makes provision about the status of the Authority and the exercise of certain of its functions.

[(4) Section 249 of the Banking Act 2009 provides for references to functions of the Authority (whether generally or under this Act) to include references to functions conferred on the Authority by that Act (subject to any order under that section).][1]

The Authority's general duties

2 The Authority's general duties

(1) In discharging its general functions the Authority must, so far as is reasonably possible, act in a way—

(a) which is compatible with the regulatory objectives; and

(b) which the Authority considers most appropriate for the purpose of meeting those objectives.

---

[1] Inserted by the Banking Act 2009, s 249(4); came into force (for the purpose of conferring or relating to any power to make subordinate legislation or codes of practice) 17 February 2009; came into force (for remaining purposes) 21 February 2009.

(2) The regulatory objectives are—
    (a) market confidence;
    (b) public awareness;
    (c) the protection of consumers; and
    (d) the reduction of financial crime.

(3) In discharging its general functions the Authority must have regard to—
    (a) the need to use its resources in the most efficient and economic way;
    (b) the responsibilities of those who manage the affairs of authorised persons;
    (c) the principle that a burden or restriction which is imposed on a person, or on the carrying on of an activity, should be proportionate to the benefits, considered in general terms, which are expected to result from the imposition of that burden or restriction;
    (d) the desirability of facilitating innovation in connection with regulated activities;
    (e) the international character of financial services and markets and the desirability of maintaining the competitive position of the United Kingdom;
    (f) the need to minimise the adverse effects on competition that may arise from anything done in the discharge of those functions;
    (g) the desirability of facilitating competition between those who are subject to any form of regulation by the Authority.

(4) The Authority's general functions are—
    (a) its function of making rules under this Act (considered as a whole);
    (b) its function of preparing and issuing codes under this Act (considered as a whole);
    (c) its functions in relation to the giving of general guidance (considered as a whole); and
    (d) its function of determining the general policy and principles by reference to which it performs particular functions.

(5) "General guidance" has the meaning given in section 158(5).

The regulatory objectives

3 Market confidence

(1) The market confidence objective is: maintaining confidence in the financial system.

(2) "The financial system" means the financial system operating in the United Kingdom and includes—
    (a) financial markets and exchanges;
    (b) regulated activities; and
    (c) other activities connected with financial markets and exchanges.

4 Public awareness

(1) The public awareness objective is: promoting public understanding of the financial system.

(2) It includes, in particular—
    (a) promoting awareness of the benefits and risks associated with different kinds of investment or other financial dealing; and
    (b) the provision of appropriate information and advice.

(3) "The financial system" has the same meaning as in section 3.

5 The protection of consumers

(1) The protection of consumers objective is: securing the appropriate degree of protection for consumers.

(2) In considering what degree of protection may be appropriate, the Authority must have regard to—
    (a) the differing degrees of risk involved in different kinds of investment or other transaction;

    (b) the differing degrees of experience and expertise that different consumers may have in relation to different kinds of regulated activity;

    (c) the needs that consumers may have for advice and accurate information; and

    (d) the general principle that consumers should take responsibility for their decisions.

(3) "Consumers" means persons—

    (a) who are consumers for the purposes of section 138; or

    (b) who, in relation to regulated activities carried on otherwise than by authorised persons, would be consumers for those purposes if the activities were carried on by authorised persons.

6 The reduction of financial crime

(1) The reduction of financial crime objective is: reducing the extent to which it is possible for a business carried on—

    (a) by a regulated person, or

    (b) in contravention of the general prohibition,

to be used for a purpose connected with financial crime.

(2) In considering that objective the Authority must, in particular, have regard to the desirability of—

    (a) regulated persons being aware of the risk of their businesses being used in connection with the commission of financial crime;

    (b) regulated persons taking appropriate measures (in relation to their administration and employment practices, the conduct of transactions by them and otherwise) to prevent financial crime, facilitate its detection and monitor its incidence;

    (c) regulated persons devoting adequate resources to the matters mentioned in paragraph (b).

(3) "Financial crime" includes any offence involving—

    (a) fraud or dishonesty;

    (b) misconduct in, or misuse of information relating to, a financial market; or

    (c) handling the proceeds of crime.

(4) "Offence" includes an act or omission which would be an offence if it had taken place in the United Kingdom.

(5) "Regulated person" means an authorised person, a recognised investment exchange or a recognised clearing house.

Corporate governance

7 Duty of Authority to follow principles of good governance

In managing its affairs, the Authority must have regard to such generally accepted principles of good corporate governance as it is reasonable to regard as applicable to it.

Arrangements for consulting practitioners and consumers

8 The Authority's general duty to consult

The Authority must make and maintain effective arrangements for consulting practitioners and consumers on the extent to which its general policies and practices are consistent with its general duties under section 2.

9 The Practitioner Panel

(1) Arrangements under section 8 must include the establishment and maintenance of a panel of persons (to be known as "the Practitioner Panel") to represent the interests of practitioners.

(2) The Authority must appoint one of the members of the Practitioner Panel to be its chairman.

(3) The Treasury's approval is required for the appointment or dismissal of the chairman.

(4) The Authority must have regard to any representations made to it by the Practitioner Panel.

(5) The Authority must appoint to the Practitioner Panel such—
- (a) individuals who are authorised persons,
- (b) persons representing authorised persons,
- (c) persons representing recognised investment exchanges, and
- (d) persons representing recognised clearing houses,

as it considers appropriate.

10 The Consumer Panel

(1) Arrangements under section 8 must include the establishment and maintenance of a panel of persons (to be known as "the Consumer Panel") to represent the interests of consumers.

(2) The Authority must appoint one of the members of the Consumer Panel to be its chairman.

(3) The Treasury's approval is required for the appointment or dismissal of the chairman.

(4) The Authority must have regard to any representations made to it by the Consumer Panel.

(5) The Authority must appoint to the Consumer Panel such consumers, or persons representing the interests of consumers, as it considers appropriate.

[(5A) The Secretary of State may direct the Authority to appoint as a member of the Consumer Panel a person specified by the Secretary of State who—
- (a) is a non-executive member of the National Consumer Council, and
- (b) is nominated for the purposes of this subsection by the National Consumer Council after consultation with the Authority.

(5B) Only one person may, at any time, be a member of the Consumer Panel appointed in accordance with a direction under subsection (5A); but that does not prevent the Authority appointing as a member of the Consumer Panel any person who is also a member of the National Consumer Council.

(5C) A person appointed in accordance with a direction under subsection (5A) ceases to be a member of the Panel on ceasing to be a non-executive member of the National Consumer Council.][2]

(6) The Authority must secure that the membership of the Consumer Panel is such as to give a fair degree of representation to those who are using, or are or may be contemplating using, services otherwise than in connection with businesses carried on by them.

(7) "Consumers" means persons, other than authorised persons—
- (a) who are consumers for the purposes of section 138; or
- (b) who, in relation to regulated activities carried on otherwise than by authorised persons, would be consumers for those purposes if the activities were carried on by authorised persons.

11 Duty to consider representations by the Panels

(1) This section applies to a representation made, in accordance with arrangements made under section 8, by the Practitioner Panel or by the Consumer Panel.

(2) The Authority must consider the representation.

(3) If the Authority disagrees with a view expressed, or proposal made, in the representation, it must give the Panel a statement in writing of its reasons for disagreeing.

---

[2] Inserted by the Consumers, Estate Agents and Redress Act 2007, s 39; came into force 21 December 2007.

Reviews

12 Reviews

(1) The Treasury may appoint an independent person to conduct a review of the economy, efficiency and effectiveness with which the Authority has used its resources in discharging its functions.

(2) A review may be limited by the Treasury to such functions of the Authority (however described) as the Treasury may specify in appointing the person to conduct it.

(3) A review is not to be concerned with the merits of the Authority's general policy or principles in pursuing regulatory objectives or in exercising functions under Part VI.

(4) On completion of a review, the person conducting it must make a written report to the Treasury—
   (a) setting out the result of the review; and
   (b) making such recommendations (if any) as he considers appropriate.

(5) A copy of the report must be—
   (a) laid before each House of Parliament; and
   (b) published in such manner as the Treasury consider appropriate.

(6) Any expenses reasonably incurred in the conduct of a review are to be met by the Treasury out of money provided by Parliament.

(7) "Independent" means appearing to the Treasury to be independent of the Authority.

13 Right to obtain documents and information

(1) A person conducting a review under section 12—
   (a) has a right of access at any reasonable time to all such documents as he may reasonably require for purposes of the review; and
   (b) may require any person holding or accountable for any such document to provide such information and explanation as are reasonably necessary for that purpose.

(2) Subsection (1) applies only to documents in the custody or under the control of the Authority.

(3) An obligation imposed on a person as a result of the exercise of powers conferred by subsection (1) is enforceable by injunction or, in Scotland, by an order for specific performance under section 45 of the Court of Session Act 1988.

Inquiries

14 Cases in which the Treasury may arrange independent inquiries

(1) This section applies in two cases.

(2) The first is where it appears to the Treasury that—
   (a) events have occurred in relation to—
      (i) a collective investment scheme, or
      (ii) a person who is, or was at the time of the events, carrying on a regulated activity (whether or not as an authorised person),
      which posed or could have posed a grave risk to the financial system or caused or risked causing significant damage to the interests of consumers; and
   (b) those events might not have occurred, or the risk or damage might have been reduced, but for a serious failure in—
      (i) the system established by this Act[, or by any previous statutory provision,][3] for the regulation of such schemes or of such persons and their activities; or
      (ii) the operation of that system.

---

[3] Inserted by the Inquiries Act 2005, s 46(1), (2); came into force 7 June 2005.

(3) The second is where it appears to the Treasury that—

    (a) events have occurred in relation to listed securities or an issuer of listed securities which caused or could have caused significant damage to holders of listed securities; and

    (b) those events might not have occurred but for a serious failure [in—

        (i) the regulatory system established by Part 6 or by any previous statutory provision concerned with the official listing of securities; or

        (ii) the operation of that system].[4]

(4) If the Treasury consider that it is in the public interest that there should be an independent inquiry into the events and the circumstances surrounding them, they may arrange for an inquiry to be held under section 15.

(5) "Consumers" means persons—

    (a) who are consumers for the purposes of section 138; or

    (b) who, in relation to regulated activities carried on otherwise than by authorised persons, would be consumers for those purposes if the activities were carried on by authorised persons.

[(5A) "Event" does not include any event occurring before 1st December 2001 (but no such limitation applies to the reference in subsection (4) to surrounding circumstances).][5]

(6) "The financial system" has the same meaning as in section 3.

(7) "Listed securities" means anything which has been admitted to the official list under Part VI.

15 Power to appoint person to hold an inquiry

(1) If the Treasury decide to arrange for an inquiry to be held under this section, they may appoint such person as they consider appropriate to hold the inquiry.

(2) The Treasury may, by a direction to the appointed person, control—

    (a) the scope of the inquiry;

    (b) the period during which the inquiry is to be held;

    (c) the conduct of the inquiry; and

    (d) the making of reports.

(3) A direction may, in particular—

    (a) confine the inquiry to particular matters;

    (b) extend the inquiry to additional matters;

    (c) require the appointed person to discontinue the inquiry or to take only such steps as are specified in the direction;

    (d) require the appointed person to make such interim reports as are so specified.

16 Powers of appointed person and procedure

(1) The person appointed to hold an inquiry under section 15 may—

    (a) obtain such information from such persons and in such manner as he thinks fit;

    (b) make such inquiries as he thinks fit; and

    (c) determine the procedure to be followed in connection with the inquiry.

(2) The appointed person may require any person who, in his opinion, is able to provide any information, or produce any document, which is relevant to the inquiry to provide any such information or produce any such document.

(3) For the purposes of an inquiry, the appointed person has the same powers as the court in respect of the attendance and examination of witnesses (including the examination of witnesses abroad) and in respect of the production of documents.

(4) "Court" means—

    (a) the High Court; or

    (b) in Scotland, the Court of Session.

---

[4] Substituted by the Inquiries Act 2005, s 46(1), (3); came into force 7 June 2005.

[5] Inserted by the Inquiries Act 2005, s 46(1), (4); came into force 7 June 2005.

17 Conclusion of inquiry

(1) On completion of an inquiry under section 15, the person holding the inquiry must make a written report to the Treasury—
  (a) setting out the result of the inquiry; and
  (b) making such recommendations (if any) as he considers appropriate.

(2) The Treasury may publish the whole, or any part, of the report and may do so in such manner as they consider appropriate.

(3) Subsection (4) applies if the Treasury propose to publish a report but consider that it contains material—
  (a) which relates to the affairs of a particular person whose interests would, in the opinion of the Treasury, be seriously prejudiced by publication of the material; or
  (b) the disclosure of which would be incompatible with an international obligation of the United Kingdom.

(4) The Treasury must ensure that the material is removed before publication.

(5) The Treasury must lay before each House of Parliament a copy of any report or part of a report published under subsection (2).

(6) Any expenses reasonably incurred in holding an inquiry are to be met by the Treasury out of money provided by Parliament.

18 Obstruction and contempt

(1) If a person ("A")—
  (a) fails to comply with a requirement imposed on him by a person holding an inquiry under section 15, or
  (b) otherwise obstructs such an inquiry,
  the person holding the inquiry may certify the matter to the High Court (or, in Scotland, the Court of Session).

(2) The court may enquire into the matter.

(3) If, after hearing—
  (a) any witnesses who may be produced against or on behalf of A, and
  (b) any statement made by or on behalf of A,
  the court is satisfied that A would have been in contempt of court if the inquiry had been proceedings before the court, it may deal with him as if he were in contempt.

PART II
REGULATED AND PROHIBITED ACTIVITIES

The general prohibition

19 The general prohibition

(1) No person may carry on a regulated activity in the United Kingdom, or purport to do so, unless he is—
  (a) an authorised person; or
  (b) an exempt person.

(2) The prohibition is referred to in this Act as the general prohibition.

Requirement for permission

20 Authorised persons acting without permission

(1) If an authorised person carries on a regulated activity in the United Kingdom, or purports to do so, otherwise than in accordance with permission—
  (a) given to him by the Authority under Part IV, or

(b) resulting from any other provision of this Act,

he is to be taken to have contravened a requirement imposed on him by the Authority under this Act.

(2) The contravention does not—

(a) make a person guilty of an offence;

(b) make any transaction void or unenforceable; or

(c) (subject to subsection (3)) give rise to any right of action for breach of statutory duty.

(3) In prescribed cases the contravention is actionable at the suit of a person who suffers loss as a result of the contravention, subject to the defences and other incidents applying to actions for breach of statutory duty.

Financial promotion

21 Restrictions on financial promotion

(1) A person ("A") must not, in the course of business, communicate an invitation or inducement to engage in investment activity.

(2) But subsection (1) does not apply if—

(a) A is an authorised person; or

(b) the content of the communication is approved for the purposes of this section by an authorised person.

(3) In the case of a communication originating outside the United Kingdom, subsection (1) applies only if the communication is capable of having an effect in the United Kingdom.

(4) The Treasury may by order specify circumstances in which a person is to be regarded for the purposes of subsection (1) as—

(a) acting in the course of business;

(b) not acting in the course of business.

(5) The Treasury may by order specify circumstances (which may include compliance with financial promotion rules) in which subsection (1) does not apply.

(6) An order under subsection (5) may, in particular, provide that subsection (1) does not apply in relation to communications—

(a) of a specified description;

(b) originating in a specified country or territory outside the United Kingdom;

(c) originating in a country or territory which falls within a specified description of country or territory outside the United Kingdom; or

(d) originating outside the United Kingdom.

(7) The Treasury may by order repeal subsection (3).

(8) "Engaging in investment activity" means—

(a) entering or offering to enter into an agreement the making or performance of which by either party constitutes a controlled activity; or

(b) exercising any rights conferred by a controlled investment to acquire, dispose of, underwrite or convert a controlled investment.

(9) An activity is a controlled activity if—

(a) it is an activity of a specified kind or one which falls within a specified class of activity; and

(b) it relates to an investment of a specified kind, or to one which falls within a specified class of investment.

(10) An investment is a controlled investment if it is an investment of a specified kind or one which falls within a specified class of investment.

(11) Schedule 2 (except paragraph 26) applies for the purposes of subsections (9) and (10) with references to section 22 being read as references to each of those subsections.

(12) Nothing in Schedule 2, as applied by subsection (11), limits the powers conferred by subsection (9) or (10).

(13) "Communicate" includes causing a communication to be made.

(14) "Investment" includes any asset, right or interest.

(15) "Specified" means specified in an order made by the Treasury.

Regulated activities

22 The classes of activity and categories of investment

(1) An activity is a regulated activity for the purposes of this Act if it is an activity of a specified kind which is carried on by way of business and—

    (a) relates to an investment of a specified kind; or

    (b) in the case of an activity of a kind which is also specified for the purposes of this paragraph, is carried on in relation to property of any kind.

(2) Schedule 2 makes provision supplementing this section.

(3) Nothing in Schedule 2 limits the powers conferred by subsection (1).

(4) "Investment" includes any asset, right or interest.

(5) "Specified" means specified in an order made by the Treasury.

Offences

23 Contravention of the general prohibition

(1) A person who contravenes the general prohibition is guilty of an offence and liable—

    (a) on summary conviction, to imprisonment for a term not exceeding six months or a fine not exceeding the statutory maximum, or both;

    (b) on conviction on indictment, to imprisonment for a term not exceeding two years or a fine, or both.

(2) In this Act "an authorisation offence" means an offence under this section.

(3) In proceedings for an authorisation offence it is a defence for the accused to show that he took all reasonable precautions and exercised all due diligence to avoid committing the offence.

24 False claims to be authorised or exempt

(1) A person who is neither an authorised person nor, in relation to the regulated activity in question, an exempt person is guilty of an offence if he—

    (a) describes himself (in whatever terms) as an authorised person;

    (b) describes himself (in whatever terms) as an exempt person in relation to the regulated activity; or

    (c) behaves, or otherwise holds himself out, in a manner which indicates (or which is reasonably likely to be understood as indicating) that he is—

        (i) an authorised person; or

        (ii) an exempt person in relation to the regulated activity.

(2) In proceedings for an offence under this section it is a defence for the accused to show that he took all reasonable precautions and exercised all due diligence to avoid committing the offence.

(3) A person guilty of an offence under this section is liable on summary conviction to imprisonment for a term not exceeding six months or a fine not exceeding level 5 on the standard scale, or both.

(4) But where the conduct constituting the offence involved or included the public display of any material, the maximum fine for the offence is level 5 on the standard scale multiplied by the number of days for which the display continued.

25 Contravention of section 21

(1) A person who contravenes section 21(1) is guilty of an offence and liable—

    (a) on summary conviction, to imprisonment for a term not exceeding six months or a fine not exceeding the statutory maximum, or both;

(b) on conviction on indictment, to imprisonment for a term not exceeding two years or a fine, or both.

(2) In proceedings for an offence under this section it is a defence for the accused to show—

(a) that he believed on reasonable grounds that the content of the communication was prepared, or approved for the purposes of section 21, by an authorised person; or

(b) that he took all reasonable precautions and exercised all due diligence to avoid committing the offence.

Enforceability of agreements

26 Agreements made by unauthorised persons

(1) An agreement made by a person in the course of carrying on a regulated activity in contravention of the general prohibition is unenforceable against the other party.

(2) The other party is entitled to recover—

(a) any money or other property paid or transferred by him under the agreement; and

(b) compensation for any loss sustained by him as a result of having parted with it.

(3) "Agreement" means an agreement—

(a) made after this section comes into force; and

(b) the making or performance of which constitutes, or is part of, the regulated activity in question.

(4) This section does not apply if the regulated activity is accepting deposits.

27 Agreements made through unauthorised persons

(1) An agreement made by an authorised person ("the provider")—

(a) in the course of carrying on a regulated activity (not in contravention of the general prohibition), but

(b) in consequence of something said or done by another person ("the third party") in the course of a regulated activity carried on by the third party in contravention of the general prohibition,

is unenforceable against the other party.

(2) The other party is entitled to recover—

(a) any money or other property paid or transferred by him under the agreement; and

(b) compensation for any loss sustained by him as a result of having parted with it.

(3) "Agreement" means an agreement—

(a) made after this section comes into force; and

(b) the making or performance of which constitutes, or is part of, the regulated activity in question carried on by the provider.

(4) This section does not apply if the regulated activity is accepting deposits.

28 Agreements made unenforceable by section 26 or 27

(1) This section applies to an agreement which is unenforceable because of section 26 or 27.

(2) The amount of compensation recoverable as a result of that section is—

(a) the amount agreed by the parties; or

(b) on the application of either party, the amount determined by the court.

(3) If the court is satisfied that it is just and equitable in the circumstances of the case, it may allow—

(a) the agreement to be enforced; or

(b) money and property paid or transferred under the agreement to be retained.

(4) In considering whether to allow the agreement to be enforced or (as the case may be) the money or property paid or transferred under the agreement to be retained the court must—

(a) if the case arises as a result of section 26, have regard to the issue mentioned in subsection (5); or

(b) if the case arises as a result of section 27, have regard to the issue mentioned in subsection (6).

(5) The issue is whether the person carrying on the regulated activity concerned reasonably believed that he was not contravening the general prohibition by making the agreement.

(6) The issue is whether the provider knew that the third party was (in carrying on the regulated activity) contravening the general prohibition.

(7) If the person against whom the agreement is unenforceable—

(a) elects not to perform the agreement, or

(b) as a result of this section, recovers money paid or other property transferred by him under the agreement,

he must repay any money and return any other property received by him under the agreement.

(8) If property transferred under the agreement has passed to a third party, a reference in section 26 or 27 or this section to that property is to be read as a reference to its value at the time of its transfer under the agreement.

(9) The commission of an authorisation offence does not make the agreement concerned illegal or invalid to any greater extent than is provided by section 26 or 27.

29 Accepting deposits in breach of general prohibition

(1) This section applies to an agreement between a person ("the depositor") and another person ("the deposit-taker") made in the course of the carrying on by the deposit-taker of accepting deposits in contravention of the general prohibition.

(2) If the depositor is not entitled under the agreement to recover without delay any money deposited by him, he may apply to the court for an order directing the deposit-taker to return the money to him.

(3) The court need not make such an order if it is satisfied that it would not be just and equitable for the money deposited to be returned, having regard to the issue mentioned in subsection (4).

(4) The issue is whether the deposit-taker reasonably believed that he was not contravening the general prohibition by making the agreement.

(5) "Agreement" means an agreement—

(a) made after this section comes into force; and

(b) the making or performance of which constitutes, or is part of, accepting deposits.

30 Enforceability of agreements resulting from unlawful communications

(1) In this section—

"unlawful communication" means a communication in relation to which there has been a contravention of section 21(1);

"controlled agreement" means an agreement the making or performance of which by either party constitutes a controlled activity for the purposes of that section; and

"controlled investment" has the same meaning as in section 21.

(2) If in consequence of an unlawful communication a person enters as a customer into a controlled agreement, it is unenforceable against him and he is entitled to recover—

(a) any money or other property paid or transferred by him under the agreement; and

(b) compensation for any loss sustained by him as a result of having parted with it.

(3) If in consequence of an unlawful communication a person exercises any rights conferred by a controlled investment, no obligation to which he is subject as a result of exercising them is enforceable against him and he is entitled to recover—

(a) any money or other property paid or transferred by him under the obligation; and

(b) compensation for any loss sustained by him as a result of having parted with it.

(4) But the court may allow—

(a) the agreement or obligation to be enforced, or

(b) money or property paid or transferred under the agreement or obligation to be retained, if it is satisfied that it is just and equitable in the circumstances of the case.

(5) In considering whether to allow the agreement or obligation to be enforced or (as the case may be) the money or property paid or transferred under the agreement to be retained the court must have regard to the issues mentioned in subsections (6) and (7).

(6) If the applicant made the unlawful communication, the issue is whether he reasonably believed that he was not making such a communication.

(7) If the applicant did not make the unlawful communication, the issue is whether he knew that the agreement was entered into in consequence of such a communication.

(8) "Applicant" means the person seeking to enforce the agreement or obligation or retain the money or property paid or transferred.

(9) Any reference to making a communication includes causing a communication to be made.

(10) The amount of compensation recoverable as a result of subsection (2) or (3) is—
    (a) the amount agreed between the parties; or
    (b) on the application of either party, the amount determined by the court.

(11) If a person elects not to perform an agreement or an obligation which (by virtue of subsection (2) or (3)) is unenforceable against him, he must repay any money and return any other property received by him under the agreement.

(12) If (by virtue of subsection (2) or (3)) a person recovers money paid or property transferred by him under an agreement or obligation, he must repay any money and return any other property received by him as a result of exercising the rights in question.

(13) If any property required to be returned under this section has passed to a third party, references to that property are to be read as references to its value at the time of its receipt by the person required to return it.

PART III
AUTHORISATION AND EXEMPTION

Authorisation

31 Authorised persons

(1) The following persons are authorised for the purposes of this Act—
    (a) a person who has a Part IV permission to carry on one or more regulated activities;
    (b) an EEA firm qualifying for authorisation under Schedule 3;
    (c) a Treaty firm qualifying for authorisation under Schedule 4;
    (d) a person who is otherwise authorised by a provision of, or made under, this Act.

(2) In this Act "authorised person" means a person who is authorised for the purposes of this Act.

32 Partnerships and unincorporated associations

(1) If a firm is authorised—
    (a) it is authorised to carry on the regulated activities concerned in the name of the firm; and
    (b) its authorisation is not affected by any change in its membership.

(2) If an authorised firm is dissolved, its authorisation continues to have effect in relation to any [individual or][6] firm which succeeds to the business of the dissolved firm.

---

[6] Inserted by SI 2007/1973, arts 2, 3(a); came into force 12 July 2007.

[(3) For the purposes of this section, an individual or firm is to be regarded as succeeding to the business of a dissolved firm only if succession is to the whole or substantially the whole of the business of the former firm.][7]

(4) "Firm" means—

(a) a partnership; or

(b) an unincorporated association of persons.

(5) "Partnership" does not include a partnership which is constituted under the law of any place outside the United Kingdom and is a body corporate.

Ending of authorization

33 Withdrawal of authorisation by the Authority

(1) This section applies if—

(a) an authorised person's Part IV permission is cancelled; and

(b) as a result, there is no regulated activity for which he has permission.

(2) The Authority must give a direction withdrawing that person's status as an authorised person.

34 EEA firms

(1) An EEA firm ceases to qualify for authorisation under Part II of Schedule 3 if it ceases to be an EEA firm as a result of—

(a) having its EEA authorisation withdrawn; or

(b) ceasing to have an EEA right in circumstances in which EEA authorisation is not required.

(2) At the request of an EEA firm, the Authority may give a direction cancelling its authorisation under Part II of Schedule 3.

(3) If an EEA firm has a Part IV permission, it does not cease to be an authorised person merely because it ceases to qualify for authorisation under Part II of Schedule 3.

35 Treaty firms

(1) A Treaty firm ceases to qualify for authorisation under Schedule 4 if its home State authorisation is withdrawn.

(2) At the request of a Treaty firm, the Authority may give a direction cancelling its Schedule 4 authorisation.

(3) If a Treaty firm has a Part IV permission, it does not cease to be an authorised person merely because it ceases to qualify for authorisation under Schedule 4.

36 Persons authorised as a result of paragraph 1(1) of Schedule 5

(1) At the request of a person authorised as a result of paragraph 1(1) of Schedule 5, the Authority may give a direction cancelling his authorisation as such a person.

(2) If a person authorised as a result of paragraph 1(1) of Schedule 5 has a Part IV permission, he does not cease to be an authorised person merely because he ceases to be a person so authorised.

---

[7] Substituted by SI 2007/1973, arts 2, 3(b); came into force 12 July 2007.

Exercise of EEA rights by UK firms

37 Exercise of EEA rights by UK firms

Part III of Schedule 3 makes provision in relation to the exercise outside the United Kingdom of EEA rights by UK firms.

Exemption

38 Exemption orders

(1) The Treasury may by order ("an exemption order") provide for—
  (a) specified persons, or
  (b) persons falling within a specified class,
  to be exempt from the general prohibition.
(2) But a person cannot be an exempt person as a result of an exemption order if he has a Part IV permission.
(3) An exemption order may provide for an exemption to have effect—
  (a) in respect of all regulated activities;
  (b) in respect of one or more specified regulated activities;
  (c) only in specified circumstances;
  (d) only in relation to specified functions;
  (e) subject to conditions.
(4) "Specified" means specified by the exemption order.

39 Exemption of appointed representatives

(1) If a person (other than an authorised person)—
  (a) is a party to a contract with an authorised person ("his principal") which—
    (i) permits or requires him to carry on business of a prescribed description, and
    (ii) complies with such requirements as may be prescribed, and
  (b) is someone for whose activities in carrying on the whole or part of that business his principal has accepted responsibility in writing,
  he is exempt from the general prohibition in relation to any regulated activity comprised in the carrying on of that business for which his principal has accepted responsibility.
[(1A) But a person is not exempt as a result of subsection (1)—
  (a) if his principal is an investment firm or a credit institution, and
  (b) so far as the business for which his principal has accepted responsibility is investment services business,
  unless he is entered on the applicable register.
(1B) The "applicable register" is—
  (a) in the case of a person established in an EEA State (other than the United Kingdom) which permits investment firms authorised by the competent authority of that State to appoint tied agents, the register of tied agents maintained in that State pursuant to Article 23 of the markets in financial instruments directive;
  (b) in the case of a person established in an EEA State which does not permit investment firms authorised as mentioned in paragraph (a) to appoint tied agents—
    (i) if his principal has his relevant office in the United Kingdom, the record maintained by the Authority by virtue of section 347(1)(ha), and
    (ii) if his principal is established in an EEA State (other than the United Kingdom) which permits investment firms authorised by the competent authority of the State to appoint tied agents, the register of tied agents maintained by that State pursuant to Article 23 of the markets in financial instruments directive; and

(c) in any other case, the record maintained by the Authority by virtue of section 347(1)(ha).][8]

(2) A person who is exempt as a result of subsection (1) is referred to in this Act as an appointed representative.

(3) The principal of an appointed representative is responsible, to the same extent as if he had expressly permitted it, for anything done or omitted by the representative in carrying on the business for which he has accepted responsibility.

(4) In determining whether an authorised person has complied with a provision contained in or made under this Act, [or with a provision contained in any directly applicable Community regulation made under the markets in financial instruments directive,][9] anything which a relevant person has done or omitted as respects business for which the authorised person has accepted responsibility is to be treated as having been done or omitted by the authorised person.

(5) "Relevant person" means a person who at the material time is or was an appointed representative by virtue of being a party to a contract with the authorised person.

(6) Nothing in subsection (4) is to cause the knowledge or intentions of an appointed representative to be attributed to his principal for the purpose of determining whether the principal has committed an offence, unless in all the circumstances it is reasonable for them to be attributed to him.

[(7) A person carries on "investment services business" if—
  (a) the business includes providing services or carrying on activities of the kind mentioned in Article 4.1.25 of the markets in financial instruments directive, and
  (b) as a result of providing such services or carrying on such activities he is a tied agent or would be if he were established in an EEA State.

(8) In this section—
  "competent authority" has the meaning given in Article 4.1.22 of the markets in financial instruments directive;
  "credit institution" means—
  (a) a credit institution authorised under the banking consolidation directive, or
  (b) an institution which would satisfy the requirements for authorisation as a credit institution under that directive if it had its relevant office in an EEA State;
  "relevant office" means—
  (a) in relation to a body corporate, its registered office or, if it has no registered office, its head office, and
  (b) in relation to a person other than a body corporate, the person's head office.][10]

[39A Certain tied agents operating outside United Kingdom][11]

[(1) This section applies to an authorised person whose relevant office is in the United Kingdom if—
  (a) he is a party to a contract with a person (other than an authorised person) who is established—
    (i) in the United Kingdom, or
    (ii) in an EEA State which does not permit investment firms authorised by the competent authority of the State to appoint tied agents; and
  (b) the contract is a relevant contract.

---

[8] Inserted by SI 2007/126, reg 3(5), Sch 5, paras 1, 2(a); came into force (for certain purposes) 1 April 2007; came into force (for remaining purposes) 1 November 2007.
 [9] Inserted by SI 2007/126, reg 3(5), Sch 5, paras 1, 2(b); came into force (for certain purposes) 1 April 2007; came into force (for remaining purposes) 1 November 2007.
 [10] Inserted by SI 2007/126, reg 3(5), Sch 5, paras 1, 2(c); came into force (for certain purposes) 1 April 2007; came into force (for remaining purposes) 1 November 2007.
 [11] Inserted by SI 2007/126, reg 3(5), Sch 5, paras 1, 3; came into force (for certain purposes) 1 April 2007; came into force (for remaining purposes) 1 November 2007.

(2) A contract is a "relevant contract" if it satisfies conditions A to C

(3) Condition A is that the contract permits or requires the person mentioned in subsection (1) (a) (the "agent") to carry on investment services business.

(4) Condition B is that either—

    (a) it is a condition of the contract that such business may only be carried on by the agent in an EEA State other than the United Kingdom; or

    (b) in a case not falling within paragraph (a), the Authority is satisfied that no such business is, or is likely to be, carried on by the agent in the United Kingdom.

(5) Condition C is that the business is of a description that, if carried on in the United Kingdom, would be prescribed for the purposes of section 39(1)(a)(i).

(6) An authorised person to whom this section applies who—

    (a) enters into or continues to perform a relevant contract with an agent which does not comply with the applicable requirements,

    (b) enters into or continues to perform a relevant contract without accepting or having accepted responsibility in writing for the agent's activities in carrying on investment services business,

    (c) enters into a relevant contract with an agent who is not entered on the record maintained by the Authority by virtue of section 347(1)(ha), or

    (d) continues to perform a relevant contract with an agent when he knows or ought to know that the agent is not entered on that record,

is to be taken for the purposes of this Act to have contravened a requirement imposed on him by or under this Act.

(7) The "applicable requirements" are the requirements prescribed for the purposes of subsection (1)(a)(ii) of section 39 which have effect in the case of a person to whom subsection (1A) of that section applies.

(8) A person carries on "investment services business" if—

    (a) his business includes providing services or carrying on activities of the kind mentioned in Article 4.1.25 of the markets in financial instruments directive, and

    (b) as a result of providing such services or carrying on such activities he is a tied agent.

(9) In this section—

    "competent authority" has the meaning given in Article 4.1.22 of the markets in financial instruments directive;

    "relevant office" means—

    (a) in relation to a body corporate, its registered office or, if it has no registered office, its head office, and

    (b) in relation to a person other than a body corporate, the person's head office.]

PART IV
PERMISSION TO CARRY ON REGULATED ACTIVITIES

Application for permission

40 Application for permission

(1) An application for permission to carry on one or more regulated activities may be made to the Authority by—

    (a) an individual;

    (b) a body corporate;

    (c) a partnership; or

    (d) an unincorporated association.

(2) An authorised person may not apply for permission under this section if he has a permission—

    (a) given to him by the Authority under this Part, or

    (b) having effect as if so given,

which is in force.

(3) An EEA firm may not apply for permission under this section to carry on a regulated activity which it is, or would be, entitled to carry on in exercise of an EEA right, whether through a United Kingdom branch or by providing services in the United Kingdom.

(4) A permission given by the Authority under this Part or having effect as if so given is referred to in this Act as "a Part IV permission".

41 The threshold conditions

(1) "The threshold conditions", in relation to a regulated activity, means the conditions set out in Schedule 6.

(2) In giving or varying permission, or imposing or varying any requirement, under this Part the Authority must ensure that the person concerned will satisfy, and continue to satisfy, the threshold conditions in relation to all of the regulated activities for which he has or will have permission.

(3) But the duty imposed by subsection (2) does not prevent the Authority, having due regard to that duty, from taking such steps as it considers are necessary, in relation to a particular authorised person, in order to secure its regulatory objective of the protection of consumers.

Permission

42 Giving permission

(1) "The applicant" means an applicant for permission under section 40.

(2) The Authority may give permission for the applicant to carry on the regulated activity or activities to which his application relates or such of them as may be specified in the permission.

(3) If the applicant—

    (a) in relation to a particular regulated activity, is exempt from the general prohibition as a result of section 39(1) or an order made under section 38(1), but

    (b) has applied for permission in relation to another regulated activity,

the application is to be treated as relating to all the regulated activities which, if permission is given, he will carry on.

(4) If the applicant—

    (a) in relation to a particular regulated activity, is exempt from the general prohibition as a result of section 285(2) or (3), but

    (b) has applied for permission in relation to another regulated activity,

the application is to be treated as relating only to that other regulated activity.

(5) If the applicant—

    (a) is a person to whom, in relation to a particular regulated activity, the general prohibition does not apply as a result of Part XIX, but

    (b) has applied for permission in relation to another regulated activity,

the application is to be treated as relating only to that other regulated activity.

(6) If it gives permission, the Authority must specify the permitted regulated activity or activities, described in such manner as the Authority considers appropriate.

(7) The Authority may—

    (a) incorporate in the description of a regulated activity such limitations (for example, as to circumstances in which the activity may, or may not, be carried on) as it considers appropriate;

    (b) specify a narrower or wider description of regulated activity than that to which the application relates;

(c) give permission for the carrying on of a regulated activity which is not included among those to which the application relates.

43 Imposition of requirements

(1) A Part IV permission may include such requirements as the Authority considers appropriate.

(2) A requirement may, in particular, be imposed—
   (a) so as to require the person concerned to take specified action; or
   (b) so as to require him to refrain from taking specified action.

(3) A requirement may extend to activities which are not regulated activities.

(4) A requirement may be imposed by reference to the person's relationship with—
   (a) his group; or
   (b) other members of his group.

(5) A requirement expires at the end of such period as the Authority may specify in the permission.

(6) But subsection (5) does not affect the Authority's powers under section 44 or 45.

Variation and cancellation of Part IV permission

44 Variation etc at request of authorised person

(1) The Authority may, on the application of an authorised person with a Part IV permission, vary the permission by—
   (a) adding a regulated activity to those for which it gives permission;
   (b) removing a regulated activity from those for which it gives permission;
   (c) varying the description of a regulated activity for which it gives permission;
   (d) cancelling a requirement imposed under section 43; or
   (e) varying such a requirement.

(2) The Authority may, on the application of an authorised person with a Part IV permission, cancel the permission.

(3) The Authority may refuse an application under this section if it appears to it—
   (a) that the interests of consumers, or potential consumers, would be adversely affected if the application were to be granted; and
   (b) that it is desirable in the interests of consumers, or potential consumers, for the application to be refused.

(4) If, as a result of a variation of a Part IV permission under this section, there are no longer any regulated activities for which the authorised person concerned has permission, the Authority must, once it is satisfied that it is no longer necessary to keep the permission in force, cancel it.

(5) The Authority's power to vary a Part IV permission under this section extends to including any provision in the permission as varied that could be included if a fresh permission were being given in response to an application under section 40.

45 Variation etc on the Authority's own initiative

(1) The Authority may exercise its power under this section in relation to an authorised person if it appears to it that—
   (a) he is failing, or is likely to fail, to satisfy the threshold conditions;
   (b) he has failed, during a period of at least 12 months, to carry on a regulated activity for which he has a Part IV permission; or
   (c) it is desirable to exercise that power in order to protect the interests of consumers or potential consumers [(whether of the services of the authorised person or of the services of other authorised persons)].[12]

---

[12] Inserted by the Banking Act 2009, s 248; came into force (for the purpose of conferring or relating to any power to make subordinate legislation or codes of practice) 17 February 2009; came into force (for remaining purposes): 21 February 2009.

(2) The Authority's power under this section is the power to vary a Part IV permission in any of the ways mentioned in section 44(1) or to cancel it.

[(2A) Without prejudice to the generality of subsections (1) and (2), the Authority may, in relation to an authorised person who is an investment firm, exercise its power under this section to cancel the Part IV permission of the firm if it appears to it that—

(a) the firm has failed, during a period of at least six months, to carry on a regulated activity which is an investment service or activity for which it has a Part IV permission;

(b) the firm obtained the Part IV permission by making a false statement or by other irregular means;

(c) the firm no longer satisfies the requirements for authorisation pursuant to Chapter I of Title II of the markets in financial instruments directive, or pursuant to or contained in any Community legislation made under that Chapter, in relation to a regulated activity which is an investment service or activity for which it has a Part IV permission; or

(d) the firm has seriously and systematically infringed the operating conditions pursuant to Chapter II of Title II of the markets in financial instruments directive, or pursuant to or contained in any Community legislation made under that Chapter, in relation to a regulated activity which is an investment service or activity for which it has a Part IV permission.

(2B) For the purposes of subsection (2A) a regulated activity is an investment service or activity if it falls within the definition of "investment services and activities" in section 417(1).][13]

(3) If, as a result of a variation of a Part IV permission under this section, there are no longer any regulated activities for which the authorised person concerned has permission, the Authority must, once it is satisfied that it is no longer necessary to keep the permission in force, cancel it.

(4) The Authority's power to vary a Part IV permission under this section extends to including any provision in the permission as varied that could be included if a fresh permission were being given in response to an application under section 40.

(5) The Authority's power under this section is referred to in this Part as its own-initiative power.

46 Variation of permission on acquisition of control

(1) This section applies if it appears to the Authority that—

(a) a person has acquired control over a UK authorised person who has a Part IV permission; but

(b) there are no grounds for exercising its own-initiative power.

(2) If it appears to the Authority that the likely effect of the acquisition of control on the authorised person, or on any of its activities, is uncertain the Authority may vary the authorised person's permission by—

(a) imposing a requirement of a kind that could be imposed under section 43 on giving permission; or

(b) varying a requirement included in the authorised person's permission under that section.

(3) Any reference to a person having acquired control is to be read in accordance with Part XII.

47 Exercise of power in support of overseas regulator

(1) The Authority's own-initiative power may be exercised in respect of an authorised person at the request of, or for the purpose of assisting, a regulator who is—

(a) outside the United Kingdom; and

(b) of a prescribed kind.

---

[13] Inserted by SI 2007/126, reg 3(5), Sch 5, paras 1, 4; came into force (for certain purposes) 1 April 2007; came into force (for remaining purposes) 1 November 2007.

(2) Subsection (1) applies whether or not the Authority has powers which are exercisable in relation to the authorised person by virtue of any provision of Part XIII.

(3) If a request to the Authority for the exercise of its own-initiative power has been made by a regulator who is—

   (a) outside the United Kingdom,

   (b) of a prescribed kind, and

   (c) acting in pursuance of provisions of a prescribed kind,

   the Authority must, in deciding whether or not to exercise that power in response to the request, consider whether it is necessary to do so in order to comply with a Community obligation.

(4) In deciding in any case in which the Authority does not consider that the exercise of its own-initiative power is necessary in order to comply with a Community obligation, it may take into account in particular—

   (a) whether in the country or territory of the regulator concerned, corresponding assistance would be given to a United Kingdom regulatory authority;

   (b) whether the case concerns the breach of a law, or other requirement, which has no close parallel in the United Kingdom or involves the assertion of a jurisdiction not recognised by the United Kingdom;

   (c) the seriousness of the case and its importance to persons in the United Kingdom;

   (d) whether it is otherwise appropriate in the public interest to give the assistance sought.

(5) The Authority may decide not to exercise its own-initiative power, in response to a request, unless the regulator concerned undertakes to make such contribution towards the cost of its exercise as the Authority considers appropriate.

(6) Subsection (5) does not apply if the Authority decides that it is necessary for it to exercise its own-initiative power in order to comply with a Community obligation.

(7) In subsections (4) and (5) "request" means a request of a kind mentioned in subsection (1).

48 Prohibitions and restrictions

(1) This section applies if the Authority—

   (a) on giving a person a Part IV permission, imposes an assets requirement on him; or

   (b) varies an authorised person's Part IV permission so as to alter an assets requirement imposed on him or impose such a requirement on him.

(2) A person on whom an assets requirement is imposed is referred to in this section as "A".

(3) "Assets requirement" means a requirement under section 43—

   (a) prohibiting the disposal of, or other dealing with, any of A's assets (whether in the United Kingdom or elsewhere) or restricting such disposals or dealings; or

   (b) that all or any of A's assets, or all or any assets belonging to consumers but held by A or to his order, must be transferred to and held by a trustee approved by the Authority.

(4) If the Authority—

   (a) imposes a requirement of the kind mentioned in subsection (3)(a), and

   (b) gives notice of the requirement to any institution with whom A keeps an account,

   the notice has the effects mentioned in subsection (5).

(5) Those effects are that—

   (a) the institution does not act in breach of any contract with A if, having been instructed by A (or on his behalf) to transfer any sum or otherwise make any payment out of A's account, it refuses to do so in the reasonably held belief that complying with the instruction would be incompatible with the requirement; and

   (b) if the institution complies with such an instruction, it is liable to pay to the Authority an amount equal to the amount transferred from, or otherwise paid out of, A's account in contravention of the requirement.

(6) If the Authority imposes a requirement of the kind mentioned in subsection (3)(b), no assets held by a person as trustee in accordance with the requirement may, while the requirement is in force, be released or dealt with except with the consent of the Authority.

(7) If, while a requirement of the kind mentioned in subsection (3)(b) is in force, A creates a charge over any assets of his held in accordance with the requirement, the charge is (to the extent that it confers security over the assets) void against the liquidator and any of A's creditors.

(8) Assets held by a person as trustee ("T") are to be taken to be held by T in accordance with a requirement mentioned in subsection (3)(b) only if—

    (a) A has given T written notice that those assets are to be held by T in accordance with the requirement; or

    (b) they are assets into which assets to which paragraph (a) applies have been transposed by T on the instructions of A.

(9) A person who contravenes subsection (6) is guilty of an offence and liable on summary conviction to a fine not exceeding level 5 on the standard scale.

(10) "Charge" includes a mortgage (or in Scotland a security over property).

(11) Subsections (6) and (8) do not affect any equitable interest or remedy in favour of a person who is a beneficiary of a trust as a result of a requirement of the kind mentioned in subsection (3)(b).

Connected persons

49 Persons connected with an applicant

(1) In considering—

    (a) an application for a Part IV permission, or

    (b) whether to vary or cancel a Part IV permission,

the Authority may have regard to any person appearing to it to be, or likely to be, in a relationship with the applicant or person given permission which is relevant.

(2) Before—

    (a) giving permission in response to an application made by a person who is connected with an EEA firm [(other than an EEA firm falling within paragraph 5(e) of Schedule 3 (insurance and reinsurance intermediaries))],[14] or

    [(b) varying any permission given by the Authority to such a person, where the effect of the variation is to grant permission for the purposes of a single market directive other than the one for the purposes of which the existing permission was granted,][15]

the Authority must consult the firm's home state regulator.

[(2A) But subsection (2) does not apply to the extent that the permission relates to—

    (a) an insurance mediation activity (within the meaning given by paragraph 2(5) of Schedule 6); or

    (b) a regulated activity involving a regulated mortgage contract[, a regulated home reversion plan or a regulated home purchase plan].[16]][17]

---

[14] Inserted by SI 2003/1476, art 20(1), (2); came into force (in relation to contracts of long-term care insurance) 31 October 2004; came into force (for remaining purposes) 14 January 2005.

[15] Substituted by SI 2007/1973, arts 2, 4; came into force 12 July 2007.

[16] Inserted by SI 2006/2383, art 28; came into force (for certain purposes) 6 November 2006; came into force (for remaining purposes) 6 April 2007.

[17] Inserted by SI 2001/544, art 97 (as inserted by SI 2004/1610, art 3); came into force (in relation to contracts of long-term care insurance) 31 October 2004; came into force (for remaining purposes) 14 January 2005.

(3) A person ("A") is connected with an EEA firm if—

    (a) A is a subsidiary undertaking of the firm; or

    (b) A is a subsidiary undertaking of a parent undertaking of the firm.

Additional permissions

50 Authority's duty to consider other permissions etc

(1) "Additional Part IV permission" means a Part IV permission which is in force in relation to an EEA firm, a Treaty firm or a person authorised as a result of paragraph 1(1) of Schedule 5.

(2) If the Authority is considering whether, and if so how, to exercise its own-initiative power under this Part in relation to an additional Part IV permission, it must take into account—

    (a) the home State authorisation of the authorised person concerned;

    (b) any relevant directive; and

    (c) relevant provisions of the Treaty.

Procedure

51 Applications under this Part

(1) An application for a Part IV permission must—

    (a) contain a statement of the regulated activity or regulated activities which the applicant proposes to carry on and for which he wishes to have permission; and

    (b) give the address of a place in the United Kingdom for service on the applicant of any notice or other document which is required or authorised to be served on him under this Act.

(2) An application for the variation of a Part IV permission must contain a statement—

    (a) of the desired variation; and

    (b) of the regulated activity or regulated activities which the applicant proposes to carry on if his permission is varied.

(3) Any application under this Part must—

    (a) be made in such manner as the Authority may direct; and

    (b) contain, or be accompanied by, such other information as the Authority may reasonably require.

(4) At any time after receiving an application and before determining it, the Authority may require the applicant to provide it with such further information as it reasonably considers necessary to enable it to determine the application.

(5) Different directions may be given, and different requirements imposed, in relation to different applications or categories of application.

(6) The Authority may require an applicant to provide information which he is required to provide under this section in such form, or to verify it in such a way, as the Authority may direct.

52 Determination of applications

(1) An application under this Part must be determined by the Authority before the end of the period of six months beginning with the date on which it received the completed application.

(2) The Authority may determine an incomplete application if it considers it appropriate to do so; and it must in any event determine such an application within twelve months beginning with the date on which it received the application.

(3) The applicant may withdraw his application, by giving the Authority written notice, at any time before the Authority determines it.

(4) If the Authority grants an application for, or for variation of, a Part IV permission, it must give the applicant written notice.

(5) The notice must state the date from which the permission, or the variation, has effect.

(6) If the Authority proposes—

    (a) to give a Part IV permission but to exercise its power under section 42(7)(a) or (b) or 43(1), or

    (b) to vary a Part IV permission on the application of an authorised person but to exercise its power under any of those provisions (as a result of section 44(5)),

    it must give the applicant a warning notice.

(7) If the Authority proposes to refuse an application made under this Part, it must (unless subsection (8) applies) give the applicant a warning notice.

(8) This subsection applies if it appears to the Authority that—

    (a) the applicant is an EEA firm; and

    (b) the application is made with a view to carrying on a regulated activity in a manner in which the applicant is, or would be, entitled to carry on that activity in the exercise of an EEA right whether through a United Kingdom branch or by providing services in the United Kingdom.

(9) If the Authority decides—

    (a) to give a Part IV permission but to exercise its power under section 42(7)(a) or (b) or 43(1),

    (b) to vary a Part IV permission on the application of an authorised person but to exercise its power under any of those provisions (as a result of section 44(5)), or

    (c) to refuse an application under this Part,

    it must give the applicant a decision notice.

53 Exercise of own-initiative power: procedure

(1) This section applies to an exercise of the Authority's own-initiative power to vary an authorised person's Part IV permission.

(2) A variation takes effect—

    (a) immediately, if the notice given under subsection (4) states that that is the case;

    (b) on such date as may be specified in the notice; or

    (c) if no date is specified in the notice, when the matter to which the notice relates is no longer open to review.

(3) A variation may be expressed to take effect immediately (or on a specified date) only if the Authority, having regard to the ground on which it is exercising its own-initiative power, reasonably considers that it is necessary for the variation to take effect immediately (or on that date).

(4) If the Authority proposes to vary the Part IV permission, or varies it with immediate effect, it must give the authorised person written notice.

(5) The notice must—

    (a) give details of the variation;

    (b) state the Authority's reasons for the variation and for its determination as to when the variation takes effect;

    (c) inform the authorised person that he may make representations to the Authority within such period as may be specified in the notice (whether or not he has referred the matter to the Tribunal);

    (d) inform him of when the variation takes effect; and

    (e) inform him of his right to refer the matter to the Tribunal.

(6) The Authority may extend the period allowed under the notice for making representations.

(7) If, having considered any representations made by the authorised person, the Authority decides—

    (a) to vary the permission in the way proposed, or

    (b) if the permission has been varied, not to rescind the variation,

    it must give him written notice.

(8) If, having considered any representations made by the authorised person, the Authority decides—
- (a) not to vary the permission in the way proposed,
- (b) to vary the permission in a different way, or
- (c) to rescind a variation which has effect,
  it must give him written notice.

(9) A notice given under subsection (7) must inform the authorised person of his right to refer the matter to the Tribunal.

(10) A notice under subsection (8)(b) must comply with subsection (5).

(11) If a notice informs a person of his right to refer a matter to the Tribunal, it must give an indication of the procedure on such a reference.

(12) For the purposes of subsection (2)(c), whether a matter is open to review is to be determined in accordance with section 391(8).

54 Cancellation of Part IV permission: procedure

(1) If the Authority proposes to cancel an authorised person's Part IV permission otherwise than at his request, it must give him a warning notice.

(2) If the Authority decides to cancel an authorised person's Part IV permission otherwise than at his request, it must give him a decision notice.

References to the Tribunal

55 Right to refer matters to the Tribunal

(1) An applicant who is aggrieved by the determination of an application made under this Part may refer the matter to the Tribunal.

(2) An authorised person who is aggrieved by the exercise of the Authority's own-initiative power may refer the matter to the Tribunal.

PART V

PERFORMANCE OF REGULATED ACTIVITIES

Prohibition orders

56 Prohibition orders

(1) Subsection (2) applies if it appears to the Authority that an individual is not a fit and proper person to perform functions in relation to a regulated activity carried on by an authorised person.

(2) The Authority may make an order ("a prohibition order") prohibiting the individual from performing a specified function, any function falling within a specified description or any function.

(3) A prohibition order may relate to—
- (a) a specified regulated activity, any regulated activity falling within a specified description or all regulated activities;
- (b) authorised persons generally or any person within a specified class of authorised person.

(4) An individual who performs or agrees to perform a function in breach of a prohibition order is guilty of an offence and liable on summary conviction to a fine not exceeding level 5 on the standard scale.

(5) In proceedings for an offence under subsection (4) it is a defence for the accused to show that he took all reasonable precautions and exercised all due diligence to avoid committing the offence.

(6) An authorised person must take reasonable care to ensure that no function of his, in relation to the carrying on of a regulated activity, is performed by a person who is prohibited from performing that function by a prohibition order.

(7) The Authority may, on the application of the individual named in a prohibition order, vary or revoke it.

(8) This section applies to the performance of functions in relation to a regulated activity carried on by—

(a) a person who is an exempt person in relation to that activity, and

(b) a person to whom, as a result of Part XX, the general prohibition does not apply in relation to that activity,

as it applies to the performance of functions in relation to a regulated activity carried on by an authorised person.

(9) "Specified" means specified in the prohibition order.

57 Prohibition orders: procedure and right to refer to Tribunal

(1) If the Authority proposes to make a prohibition order it must give the individual concerned a warning notice.

(2) The warning notice must set out the terms of the prohibition.

(3) If the Authority decides to make a prohibition order it must give the individual concerned a decision notice.

(4) The decision notice must—

(a) name the individual to whom the prohibition order applies;

(b) set out the terms of the order; and

(c) be given to the individual named in the order.

(5) A person against whom a decision to make a prohibition order is made may refer the matter to the Tribunal.

58 Applications relating to prohibitions: procedure and right to refer to Tribunal

(1) This section applies to an application for the variation or revocation of a prohibition order.

(2) If the Authority decides to grant the application, it must give the applicant written notice of its decision.

(3) If the Authority proposes to refuse the application, it must give the applicant a warning notice.

(4) If the Authority decides to refuse the application, it must give the applicant a decision notice.

(5) If the Authority gives the applicant a decision notice, he may refer the matter to the Tribunal.

Approval

59 Approval for particular arrangements

(1) An authorised person ("A") must take reasonable care to ensure that no person performs a controlled function under an arrangement entered into by A in relation to the carrying on by A of a regulated activity, unless the Authority approves the performance by that person of the controlled function to which the arrangement relates.

(2) An authorised person ("A") must take reasonable care to ensure that no person performs a controlled function under an arrangement entered into by a contractor of A in relation to the carrying on by A of a regulated activity, unless the Authority approves the performance by that person of the controlled function to which the arrangement relates.

(3) "Controlled function" means a function of a description specified in rules.

(4) The Authority may specify a description of function under subsection (3) only if, in relation to the carrying on of a regulated activity by an authorised person, it is satisfied that the first, second or third condition is met.

(5) The first condition is that the function is likely to enable the person responsible for its performance to exercise a significant influence on the conduct of the authorised person's affairs, so far as relating to the regulated activity.

(6) The second condition is that the function will involve the person performing it in dealing with customers of the authorised person in a manner substantially connected with the carrying on of the regulated activity.

(7) The third condition is that the function will involve the person performing it in dealing with property of customers of the authorised person in a manner substantially connected with the carrying on of the regulated activity.

(8) Neither subsection (1) nor subsection (2) applies to an arrangement which allows a person to perform a function if the question of whether he is a fit and proper person to perform the function is reserved under any of the single market directives to an authority in a country or territory outside the United Kingdom.

(9) In determining whether the first condition is met, the Authority may take into account the likely consequences of a failure to discharge that function properly.

(10) "Arrangement"—
  (a) means any kind of arrangement for the performance of a function of A which is entered into by A or any contractor of his with another person; and
  (b) includes, in particular, that other person's appointment to an office, his becoming a partner or his employment (whether under a contract of service or otherwise).

(11) "Customer", in relation to an authorised person, means a person who is using, or who is or may be contemplating using, any of the services provided by the authorised person.

60 Applications for approval

(1) An application for the Authority's approval under section 59 may be made by the authorised person concerned.

(2) The application must—
  (a) be made in such manner as the Authority may direct; and
  (b) contain, or be accompanied by, such information as the Authority may reasonably require.

(3) At any time after receiving the application and before determining it, the Authority may require the applicant to provide it with such further information as it reasonably considers necessary to enable it to determine the application.

(4) The Authority may require an applicant to present information which he is required to give under this section in such form, or to verify it in such a way, as the Authority may direct.

(5) Different directions may be given, and different requirements imposed, in relation to different applications or categories of application.

(6) "The authorised person concerned" includes a person who has applied for permission under Part IV and will be the authorised person concerned if permission is given.

61 Determination of applications

(1) The Authority may grant an application made under section 60 only if it is satisfied that the person in respect of whom the application is made ("the candidate") is a fit and proper person to perform the function to which the application relates.

(2) In deciding that question, the Authority may have regard (among other things) to whether the candidate, or any person who may perform a function on his behalf—
  (a) has obtained a qualification,
  (b) has undergone, or is undergoing, training, or
  (c) possesses a level of competence,

required by general rules in relation to persons performing functions of the kind to which the application relates.

(3) The Authority must, before the end of the period of three months beginning with the date on which it receives an application made under section 60 ("the period for consideration"), determine whether—

    (a) to grant the application; or

    (b) to give a warning notice under section 62(2).

(4) If the Authority imposes a requirement under section 60(3), the period for consideration stops running on the day on which the requirement is imposed but starts running again—

    (a) on the day on which the required information is received by the Authority; or

    (b) if the information is not provided on a single day, on the last of the days on which it is received by the Authority.

(5) A person who makes an application under section 60 may withdraw his application by giving written notice to the Authority at any time before the Authority determines it, but only with the consent of—

    (a) the candidate; and

    (b) the person by whom the candidate is to be retained to perform the function concerned, if not the applicant.

62 Applications for approval: procedure and right to refer to Tribunal

(1) If the Authority decides to grant an application made under section 60 ("an application"), it must give written notice of its decision to each of the interested parties.

(2) If the Authority proposes to refuse an application, it must give a warning notice to each of the interested parties.

(3) If the Authority decides to refuse an application, it must give a decision notice to each of the interested parties.

(4) If the Authority decides to refuse an application, each of the interested parties may refer the matter to the Tribunal.

(5) "The interested parties", in relation to an application, are—

    (a) the applicant;

    (b) the person in respect of whom the application is made ("A"); and

    (c) the person by whom A's services are to be retained, if not the applicant.

63 Withdrawal of approval

(1) The Authority may withdraw an approval given under section 59 if it considers that the person in respect of whom it was given is not a fit and proper person to perform the function to which the approval relates.

(2) When considering whether to withdraw its approval, the Authority may take into account any matter which it could take into account if it were considering an application made under section 60 in respect of the performance of the function to which the approval relates.

(3) If the Authority proposes to withdraw its approval, it must give each of the interested parties a warning notice.

(4) If the Authority decides to withdraw its approval, it must give each of the interested parties a decision notice.

(5) If the Authority decides to withdraw its approval, each of the interested parties may refer the matter to the Tribunal.

(6) "The interested parties", in relation to an approval, are—

    (a) the person on whose application it was given ("A");

    (b) the person in respect of whom it was given ("B"); and

    (c) the person by whom B's services are retained, if not A.

Conduct

64 Conduct: statements and codes

(1) The Authority may issue statements of principle with respect to the conduct expected of approved persons.

(2) If the Authority issues a statement of principle under subsection (1), it must also issue a code of practice for the purpose of helping to determine whether or not a person's conduct complies with the statement of principle.

(3) A code issued under subsection (2) may specify—

    (a) descriptions of conduct which, in the opinion of the Authority, comply with a statement of principle;

    (b) descriptions of conduct which, in the opinion of the Authority, do not comply with a statement of principle;

    (c) factors which, in the opinion of the Authority, are to be taken into account in determining whether or not a person's conduct complies with a statement of principle.

(4) The Authority may at any time alter or replace a statement or code issued under this section.

(5) If a statement or code is altered or replaced, the altered or replacement statement or code must be issued by the Authority.

(6) A statement or code issued under this section must be published by the Authority in the way appearing to the Authority to be best calculated to bring it to the attention of the public.

(7) A code published under this section and in force at the time when any particular conduct takes place may be relied on so far as it tends to establish whether or not that conduct complies with a statement of principle.

(8) Failure to comply with a statement of principle under this section does not of itself give rise to any right of action by persons affected or affect the validity of any transaction.

(9) A person is not to be taken to have failed to comply with a statement of principle if he shows that, at the time of the alleged failure, it or its associated code of practice had not been published.

(10) The Authority must, without delay, give the Treasury a copy of any statement or code which it publishes under this section.

(11) The power under this section to issue statements of principle and codes of practice—

    (a) includes power to make different provision in relation to persons, cases or circumstances of different descriptions; and

    (b) is to be treated for the purposes of section 2(4)(a) as part of the Authority's rule-making functions.

(12) The Authority may charge a reasonable fee for providing a person with a copy of a statement or code published under this section.

(13) "Approved person" means a person in relation to whom the Authority has given its approval under section 59.

65 Statements and codes: procedure

(1) Before issuing a statement or code under section 64, the Authority must publish a draft of it in the way appearing to the Authority to be best calculated to bring it to the attention of the public.

(2) The draft must be accompanied by—

    (a) a cost benefit analysis; and

    (b) notice that representations about the proposal may be made to the Authority within a specified time.

(3) Before issuing the proposed statement or code, the Authority must have regard to any representations made to it in accordance with subsection (2)(b).

(4) If the Authority issues the proposed statement or code it must publish an account, in general terms, of—

    (a) the representations made to it in accordance with subsection (2)(b); and

    (b) its response to them.

(5) If the statement or code differs from the draft published under subsection (1) in a way which is, in the opinion of the Authority, significant—

    (a) the Authority must (in addition to complying with subsection (4)) publish details of the difference; and

    (b) those details must be accompanied by a cost benefit analysis.

(6) Neither subsection (2)(a) nor subsection (5)(b) applies if the Authority considers—

    (a) that, making the appropriate comparison, there will be no increase in costs; or

    (b) that, making that comparison, there will be an increase in costs but the increase will be of minimal significance.

(7) Subsections (1) to (6) do not apply if the Authority considers that the delay involved in complying with them would prejudice the interests of consumers.

(8) A statement or code must state that it is issued under section 64.

(9) The Authority may charge a reasonable fee for providing a copy of a draft published under subsection (1).

(10) This section also applies to a proposal to alter or replace a statement or code.

(11) "Cost benefit analysis" means an estimate of the costs together with an analysis of the benefits that will arise—

    (a) if the proposed statement or code is issued; or

    (b) if subsection (5)(b) applies, from the statement or code that has been issued.

(12) "The appropriate comparison" means—

    (a) in relation to subsection (2)(a), a comparison between the overall position if the statement or code is issued and the overall position if it is not issued;

    (b) in relation to subsection (5)(b), a comparison between the overall position after the issuing of the statement or code and the overall position before it was issued.

66 Disciplinary powers

(1) The Authority may take action against a person under this section if—

    (a) it appears to the Authority that he is guilty of misconduct; and

    (b) the Authority is satisfied that it is appropriate in all the circumstances to take action against him.

(2) A person is guilty of misconduct if, while an approved person—

    (a) he has failed to comply with a statement of principle issued under section 64; or

    (b) he has been knowingly concerned in a contravention by the relevant authorised person of a requirement imposed on that authorised person by or under this Act [or by any directly applicable Community regulation made under the markets in financial instruments directive].[18]

(3) If the Authority is entitled to take action under this section against a person, it may—

    (a) impose a penalty on him of such amount as it considers appropriate; or

    (b) publish a statement of his misconduct.

(4) The Authority may not take action under this section after the end of the period of two years beginning with the first day on which the Authority knew of the misconduct, unless proceedings in respect of it against the person concerned were begun before the end of that period.

---

[18] Inserted by SI 2007/126, reg 3(5), Sch 5, paras 1, 5; came into force (for certain purposes) 1 April 2007; came into force (for remaining purposes) 1 November 2007.

(5) For the purposes of subsection (4)—
   (a) the Authority is to be treated as knowing of misconduct if it has information from which the misconduct can reasonably be inferred; and
   (b) proceedings against a person in respect of misconduct are to be treated as begun when a warning notice is given to him under section 67(1).

(6) "Approved person" has the same meaning as in section 64.

(7) "Relevant authorised person", in relation to an approved person, means the person on whose application approval under section 59 was given.

67 Disciplinary measures: procedure and right to refer to Tribunal

(1) If the Authority proposes to take action against a person under section 66, it must give him a warning notice.

(2) A warning notice about a proposal to impose a penalty must state the amount of the penalty.

(3) A warning notice about a proposal to publish a statement must set out the terms of the statement.

(4) If the Authority decides to take action against a person under section 66, it must give him a decision notice.

(5) A decision notice about the imposition of a penalty must state the amount of the penalty.

(6) A decision notice about the publication of a statement must set out the terms of the statement.

(7) If the Authority decides to take action against a person under section 66, he may refer the matter to the Tribunal.

68 Publication

After a statement under section 66 is published, the Authority must send a copy of it to the person concerned and to any person to whom a copy of the decision notice was given.

69 Statement of policy

(1) The Authority must prepare and issue a statement of its policy with respect to—
   (a) the imposition of penalties under section 66; and
   (b) the amount of penalties under that section.

(2) The Authority's policy in determining what the amount of a penalty should be must include having regard to—
   (a) the seriousness of the misconduct in question in relation to the nature of the principle or requirement concerned;
   (b) the extent to which that misconduct was deliberate or reckless; and
   (c) whether the person on whom the penalty is to be imposed is an individual.

(3) The Authority may at any time alter or replace a statement issued under this section.

(4) If a statement issued under this section is altered or replaced, the Authority must issue the altered or replacement statement.

(5) The Authority must, without delay, give the Treasury a copy of any statement which it publishes under this section.

(6) A statement issued under this section must be published by the Authority in the way appearing to the Authority to be best calculated to bring it to the attention of the public.

(7) The Authority may charge a reasonable fee for providing a person with a copy of the statement.

(8) In exercising, or deciding whether to exercise, its power under section 66 in the case of any particular misconduct, the Authority must have regard to any statement of policy published under this section and in force at the time when the misconduct in question occurred.

70 Statements of policy: procedure

(1) Before issuing a statement under section 69, the Authority must publish a draft of the proposed statement in the way appearing to the Authority to be best calculated to bring it to the attention of the public.

(2) The draft must be accompanied by notice that representations about the proposal may be made to the Authority within a specified time.

(3) Before issuing the proposed statement, the Authority must have regard to any representations made to it in accordance with subsection (2).

(4) If the Authority issues the proposed statement it must publish an account, in general terms, of—

(a) the representations made to it in accordance with subsection (2); and

(b) its response to them.

(5) If the statement differs from the draft published under subsection (1) in a way which is, in the opinion of the Authority, significant, the Authority must (in addition to complying with subsection (4)) publish details of the difference.

(6) The Authority may charge a reasonable fee for providing a person with a copy of a draft published under subsection (1).

(7) This section also applies to a proposal to alter or replace a statement.

Breach of statutory duty

71 Actions for damages

(1) A contravention of section 56(6) or 59(1) or (2) is actionable at the suit of a private person who suffers loss as a result of the contravention, subject to the defences and other incidents applying to actions for breach of statutory duty.

(2) In prescribed cases, a contravention of that kind which would be actionable at the suit of a private person is actionable at the suit of a person who is not a private person, subject to the defences and other incidents applying to actions for breach of statutory duty.

(3) "Private person" has such meaning as may be prescribed.

PART VI
OFFICIAL LISTING

The competent authority

72 The competent authority

(1) On the coming into force of this section, the functions conferred on the competent authority by this Part are to be exercised by the Authority.

(2) Schedule 7 modifies this Act in its application to the Authority when it acts as the competent authority.

(3) But provision is made by Schedule 8 allowing some or all of those functions to be transferred by the Treasury so as to be exercisable by another person.

73 General duty of the competent authority

(1) In discharging its general functions the competent authority must have regard to—

(a) the need to use its resources in the most efficient and economic way;

(b) the principle that a burden or restriction which is imposed on a person should be proportionate to the benefits, considered in general terms, which are expected to arise from the imposition of that burden or restriction;

[(c) the desirability of facilitating innovation in respect of listed securities and in respect of financial instruments which have otherwise been admitted to trading on a regulated market or for which a request for admission to trading on such a market has been made;][19]

---

[19] Substituted by SI 2005/381, reg 4, Sch 1, para 1(1), (2); came into force 1 July 2005.

(d) the international character of capital markets and the desirability of maintaining the competitive position of the United Kingdom;

(e) the need to minimise the adverse effects on competition of anything done in the discharge of those functions;

[(f) the desirability of facilitating competition in relation to listed securities and in relation to financial instruments which have otherwise been admitted to trading on a regulated market or for which a request for admission to trading on such a market has been made].[20]

[(1A) To the extent that those general functions are functions under or relating to transparency rules, subsection (1)(c) and (f) have effect as if the references to a regulated market were references to a market.][21]

(2) The competent authority's general functions are—

(a) its function of making rules under this Part (considered as a whole);

(b) its functions in relation to the giving of general guidance in relation to this Part (considered as a whole);

(c) its function of determining the general policy and principles by reference to which it performs particular functions under this Part.

[73A Part 6 Rules][22]

[(1) The competent authority may make rules ("Part 6 rules") for the purposes of this Part.

(2) Provisions of Part 6 rules expressed to relate to the official list are referred to in this Part as "listing rules".

(3) Provisions of Part 6 rules expressed to relate to disclosure of information in respect of financial instruments which have been admitted to trading on a regulated market or for which a request for admission to trading on such a market has been made, are referred to in this Part as "disclosure rules".

[(4) Provisions of Part 6 rules expressed to relate to transferable securities are referred to in this Part as "prospectus rules".

(5) In relation to prospectus rules, the purposes of this Part include the purposes of the prospectus directive.][23]

[(6) Transparency rules and corporate governance rules are not listing rules, disclosure rules or prospectus rules, but are Part 6 rules.][24]]

The official list

74 The official list

(1) The competent authority must maintain the official list.

(2) The competent authority may admit to the official list such securities and other things as it considers appropriate.

(3) But—

(a) nothing may be admitted to the official list except in accordance with this Part; and

(b) the Treasury may by order provide that anything which falls within a description or category specified in the order may not be admitted to the official list.

(4) . . .[25]

---

[20] Substituted by SI 2005/381, reg 4, Sch 1, para 1(1), (3); came into force 1 July 2005.

[21] Inserted by the Companies Act 2006, s 1272, Sch 15, Pt 1, paras 1, 2; came into force 8 November 2006.

[22] Inserted by SI 2005/381, reg 4, Sch 1, para 2; came into force 17 March 2005.

[23] Inserted by SI 2005/1433, reg 2(1), Sch 1, para 1; came into force 1 July 2005.

[24] Inserted by the Companies Act 2006, s 1272, Sch 15, Pt 1, paras 1, 3; came into force 8 November 2006.

[25] Repealed by SI 2005/381, reg 4, Sch 1, para 3; came into force 17 March 2005.

(5) In the following provisions of this Part—

...[26]

"listing" means being included in the official list in accordance with this Part.

Listing

75 Applications for listing

(1) Admission to the official list may be granted only on an application made to the competent authority in such manner as may be required by listing rules.

(2) No application for listing may be entertained by the competent authority unless it is made by, or with the consent of, the issuer of the securities concerned.

(3) No application for listing may be entertained by the competent authority in respect of securities which are to be issued by a body of a prescribed kind.

(4) The competent authority may not grant an application for listing unless it is satisfied that—
(a) the requirements of listing rules (so far as they apply to the application), and
(b) any other requirements imposed by the authority in relation to the application,
are complied with.

(5) An application for listing may be refused if, for a reason relating to the issuer, the competent authority considers that granting it would be detrimental to the interests of investors.

(6) An application for listing securities which are already officially listed in another EEA State may be refused if the issuer has failed to comply with any obligations to which he is subject as a result of that listing.

76 Decision on application

(1) The competent authority must notify the applicant of its decision on an application for listing—
(a) before the end of the period of six months beginning with the date on which the application is received; or
(b) if within that period the authority has required the applicant to provide further information in connection with the application, before the end of the period of six months beginning with the date on which that information is provided.

(2) If the competent authority fails to comply with subsection (1), it is to be taken to have decided to refuse the application.

(3) If the competent authority decides to grant an application for listing, it must give the applicant written notice.

(4) If the competent authority proposes to refuse an application for listing, it must give the applicant a warning notice.

(5) If the competent authority decides to refuse an application for listing, it must give the applicant a decision notice.

(6) If the competent authority decides to refuse an application for listing, the applicant may refer the matter to the Tribunal.

(7) If securities are admitted to the official list, their admission may not be called in question on the ground that any requirement or condition for their admission has not been complied with.

77 Discontinuance and suspension of listing

(1) The competent authority may, in accordance with listing rules, discontinue the listing of any securities if satisfied that there are special circumstances which preclude normal regular dealings in them.

---

[26] Definition "security" (omitted) repealed by SI 2005/1433, reg 2(1), Sch 1, para 2; came into force 1 July 2005.

(2) The competent authority may, in accordance with listing rules, suspend the listing of any securities.

[(2A) The competent authority may discontinue under subsection (1) or suspend under subsection (2) the listing of any securities on its own initiative or on the application of the issuer of those securities.][27]

(3) If securities are suspended under subsection (2) they are to be treated, for the purposes of sections 96 and 99, as still being listed.

(4) This section applies to securities whenever they were admitted to the official list.

(5) If the competent authority discontinues or suspends the listing of any securities, [on its own initiative,][28] the issuer may refer the matter to the Tribunal.

78 Discontinuance or suspension: procedure

(1) A discontinuance or suspension [by the competent authority on its own initiative][29] takes effect—

    (a) immediately, if the notice under subsection (2) states that that is the case;

    (b) in any other case, on such date as may be specified in that notice.

(2) If [on its own initiative][30] the competent authority—

    (a) proposes to discontinue or suspend the listing of securities, or

    (b) discontinues or suspends the listing of securities with immediate effect,

it must give the issuer of the securities written notice.

(3) The notice must—

    (a) give details of the discontinuance or suspension;

    (b) state the competent authority's reasons for the discontinuance or suspension and for choosing the date on which it took effect or takes effect;

    (c) inform the issuer of the securities that he may make representations to the competent authority within such period as may be specified in the notice (whether or not he has referred the matter to the Tribunal);

    (d) inform him of the date on which the discontinuance or suspension took effect or will take effect; and

    (e) inform him of his right to refer the matter to the Tribunal.

(4) The competent authority may extend the period within which representations may be made to it.

(5) If, having considered any representations made by the issuer of the securities, the competent authority decides—

    (a) to discontinue or suspend the listing of the securities, or

    (b) if the discontinuance or suspension has taken effect, not to cancel it,

the competent authority must give the issuer of the securities written notice.

(6) A notice given under subsection (5) must inform the issuer of the securities of his right to refer the matter to the Tribunal.

(7) If a notice informs a person of his right to refer a matter to the Tribunal, it must give an indication of the procedure on such a reference.

(8) If the competent authority decides—

    (a) not to discontinue or suspend the listing of the securities, or

    (b) if the discontinuance or suspension has taken effect, to cancel it,

the competent authority must give the issuer of the securities written notice.

---

[27] Inserted by SI 2007/1973, arts 2, 5(a); came into force 12 July 2007.
[28] Inserted by SI 2007/1973, arts 2, 5(b); came into force 12 July 2007.
[29] Inserted by SI 2007/1973, arts 2, 6(a); came into force 12 July 2007.
[30] Inserted by SI 2007/1973, arts 2, 6(b); came into force: 12 July 2007.

(9) The effect of cancelling a discontinuance is that the securities concerned are to be readmitted, without more, to the official list.

(10) If the competent authority has suspended the listing of securities [on its own initiative]³¹ and proposes to refuse an application by the issuer of the securities for the cancellation of the suspension, it must give him a warning notice.

(11) The competent authority must, having considered any representations made in response to the warning notice—

(a) if it decides to refuse the application, give the issuer of the securities a decision notice;

(b) if it grants the application, give him written notice of its decision.

(12) If the competent authority decides to refuse an application for the cancellation of the suspension of listed securities, the applicant may refer the matter to the Tribunal.

(13) "Discontinuance" means a discontinuance of listing under section 77(1).

(14) "Suspension" means a suspension of listing under section 77(2).

[78A Discontinuance or suspension at the request of the issuer: procedure]³²

[(1) A discontinuance or suspension by the competent authority on the application of the issuer of the securities takes effect—

(a) immediately, if the notice under subsection (2) states that this is the case;

(b) in any other case, on such date as may be specified in that notice.

(2) If the competent authority discontinues or suspends the listing of securities on the application of the issuer of the securities it must give him written notice.

(3) The notice must—

(a) give details of the discontinuance or suspension;

(b) inform the issuer of the securities of the date on which the discontinuance or suspension took effect or will take effect; and

(c) inform the issuer of his right to apply for the cancellation of the suspension.

(4) If the competent authority proposes to refuse an application by the issuer of the securities for the discontinuance or suspension of the listing of the securities, it must give him a warning notice.

(5) The competent authority must, having considered any representations made in response to the warning notice, if it decides to refuse the application, give the issuer of the securities a decision notice.

(6) If the competent authority decides to refuse an application by the issuer of the securities for the discontinuance or suspension of the listing of the securities, the issuer may refer the matter to the Tribunal.

(7) If the competent authority has suspended the listing of securities on the application of the issuer of the securities and proposes to refuse an application by the issuer for the cancellation of the suspension, it must give him a warning notice.

(8) The competent authority must, having considered any representations made in response to the warning notice—

(a) if it decides to refuse the application for the cancellation of the suspension, give the issuer of the securities a decision notice;

(b) if it grants the application, give him written notice of its decision.

(9) If the competent authority decides to refuse an application for the cancellation of the suspension of listed securities, the applicant may refer the matter to the Tribunal.

(10) "Discontinuance" means a discontinuance of listing under section 77(1).

(11) "Suspension" means a suspension of listing under section 77(2).]

---

³¹ Inserted by SI 2007/1973, arts 2, 6(c); came into force: 12 July 2007.
³² Inserted by SI 2007/1973, arts 2, 7; came into force: 12 July 2007.

Listing particulars

79 Listing particulars and other documents

(1) Listing rules may provide that securities . . .[33] of a kind specified in the rules may not be admitted to the official list unless—

  (a) listing particulars have been submitted to, and approved by, the competent authority and published; or

  (b) in such cases as may be specified by listing rules, such document (other than listing particulars or a prospectus of a kind required by listing rules) as may be so specified has been published.

(2) "Listing particulars" means a document in such form and containing such information as may be specified in listing rules.

(3) For the purposes of this Part, the persons responsible for listing particulars are to be determined in accordance with regulations made by the Treasury.

[(3A) Listing rules made under subsection (1) may not specify securities of a kind for which an approved prospectus is required as a result of section 85.][34]

(4) Nothing in this section affects the competent authority's general power to make listing rules.

80 General duty of disclosure in listing particulars

(1) Listing particulars submitted to the competent authority under section 79 must contain all such information as investors and their professional advisers would reasonably require, and reasonably expect to find there, for the purpose of making an informed assessment of—

  (a) the assets and liabilities, financial position, profits and losses, and prospects of the issuer of the securities; and

  (b) the rights attaching to the securities.

(2) That information is required in addition to any information required by—

  (a) listing rules, or

  (b) the competent authority,

as a condition of the admission of the securities to the official list.

(3) Subsection (1) applies only to information—

  (a) within the knowledge of any person responsible for the listing particulars; or

  (b) which it would be reasonable for him to obtain by making enquiries.

(4) In determining what information subsection (1) requires to be included in listing particulars, regard must be had (in particular) to—

  (a) the nature of the securities and their issuer;

  (b) the nature of the persons likely to consider acquiring them;

  (c) the fact that certain matters may reasonably be expected to be within the knowledge of professional advisers of a kind which persons likely to acquire the securities may reasonably be expected to consult; and

  (d) any information available to investors or their professional advisers as a result of requirements imposed on the issuer of the securities by a recognised investment exchange, by listing rules or by or under any other enactment.

---

[33] Words (omitted) repealed by SI 2005/1433, reg 2(1), Sch 1, para 3(1), (2); came into force: 1 July 2005.

[34] Inserted by SI 2005/1433, reg 2(1), Sch 1, para 3(1), (3); came into force: 1 July 2005.

81 Supplementary listing particulars

(1) If at any time after the preparation of listing particulars which have been submitted to the competent authority under section 79 and before the commencement of dealings in the securities concerned following their admission to the official list—

    (a) there is a significant change affecting any matter contained in those particulars the inclusion of which was required by—

        (i) section 80,

        (ii) listing rules, or

        (iii) the competent authority, or

    (b) a significant new matter arises, the inclusion of information in respect of which would have been so required if it had arisen when the particulars were prepared, the issuer must, in accordance with listing rules, submit supplementary listing particulars of the change or new matter to the competent authority, for its approval and, if they are approved, publish them.

(2) "Significant" means significant for the purpose of making an informed assessment of the kind mentioned in section 80(1).

(3) If the issuer of the securities is not aware of the change or new matter in question, he is not under a duty to comply with subsection (1) unless he is notified of the change or new matter by a person responsible for the listing particulars.

(4) But it is the duty of any person responsible for those particulars who is aware of such a change or new matter to give notice of it to the issuer.

(5) Subsection (1) applies also as respects matters contained in any supplementary listing particulars previously published under this section in respect of the securities in question.

82 Exemptions from disclosure

(1) The competent authority may authorise the omission from listing particulars of any information, the inclusion of which would otherwise be required by section 80 or 81, on the ground—

    (a) that its disclosure would be contrary to the public interest;

    (b) that its disclosure would be seriously detrimental to the issuer; or

    (c) in the case of securities of a kind specified in listing rules, that its disclosure is unnecessary for persons of the kind who may be expected normally to buy or deal in securities of that kind.

(2) But—

    (a) no authority may be granted under subsection (1)(b) in respect of essential information; and

    (b) no authority granted under subsection (1)(b) extends to any such information.

(3) The Secretary of State or the Treasury may issue a certificate to the effect that the disclosure of any information (including information that would otherwise have to be included in listing particulars for which they are themselves responsible) would be contrary to the public interest.

(4) The competent authority is entitled to act on any such certificate in exercising its powers under subsection (1)(a).

(5) This section does not affect any powers of the competent authority under listing rules made as a result of section 101(2).

(6) "Essential information" means information which a person considering acquiring securities of the kind in question would be likely to need in order not to be misled about any facts which it is essential for him to know in order to make an informed assessment.

(7) "Listing particulars" includes supplementary listing particulars.

83 . . .

. . .[35]

---

[35] Repealed by SI 2005/1433, reg 2(1), Sch 1, para 4; came into force 1 July 2005.

[Transferable securities: public offers and admission to trading][36]

[84 Matters which may be dealt with by prospectus rules][37]

[(1) Prospectus rules may make provision as to—

   (a) the required form and content of a prospectus (including a summary);
   (b) the cases in which a summary need not be included in a prospectus;
   (c) the languages which may be used in a prospectus (including a summary);
   (d) the determination of the persons responsible for a prospectus;
   (e) the manner in which applications to the competent authority for the approval of a prospectus are to be made.

(2) Prospectus rules may also make provision as to—

   (a) the period of validity of a prospectus;
   (b) the disclosure of the maximum price or of the criteria or conditions according to which the final offer price is to be determined, if that information is not contained in a prospectus;
   (c) the disclosure of the amount of the transferable securities which are to be offered to the public or of the criteria or conditions according to which that amount is to be determined, if that information is not contained in a prospectus;
   (d) the required form and content of other summary documents (including the languages which may be used in such a document);
   (e) the ways in which a prospectus that has been approved by the competent authority may be made available to the public;
   (f) the disclosure, publication or other communication of such information as the competent authority may reasonably stipulate;
   (g) the principles to be observed in relation to advertisements in connection with an offer of transferable securities to the public or admission of transferable securities to trading on a regulated market and the enforcement of those principles;
   (h) the suspension of trading in transferable securities where continued trading would be detrimental to the interests of investors;
   (i) elections under section 87 or under Article 2.1(m)(iii) of the prospectus directive as applied for the purposes of this Part by section 102C

(3) Prospectus rules may also make provision as to—

   (a) access to the register of investors maintained under section 87R; and
   (b) the supply of information from that register.

(4) Prospectus rules may make provision for the purpose of dealing with matters arising out of or related to any provision of the prospectus directive.

(5) In relation to cases where the home State in relation to an issuer of transferable securities is an EEA State other than the United Kingdom, prospectus rules may make provision for the recognition of elections made in relation to such securities under the law of that State in accordance with Article 1.3 or 2.1(m)(iii) of the prospectus directive.

(6) In relation to a document relating to transferable securities issued by an issuer incorporated in a non-EEA State and drawn up in accordance with the law of that State, prospectus rules may make provision as to the approval of that document as a prospectus.

(7) Nothing in this section affects the competent authority's general power to make prospectus rules.]

---

[36] Substituted by SI 2005/1433, reg 2(1), Sch 1, para 5; came into force 1 July 2005.

[37] Substituted, together with ss 85–87, 87A–87R, for ss 84–87 as originally enacted, by SI 2005/1433, reg 2(1), Sch 1, para 5; came into force 1 July 2005.

[85 Prohibition of dealing etc in transferable securities without approved prospectus][38]

[(1) It is unlawful for transferable securities to which this subsection applies to be offered to the public in the United Kingdom unless an approved prospectus has been made available to the public before the offer is made.

(2) It is unlawful to request the admission of transferable securities to which this subsection applies to trading on a regulated market situated or operating in the United Kingdom unless an approved prospectus has been made available to the public before the request is made.

(3) A person who contravenes subsection (1) or (2) is guilty of an offence and liable—

(a) on summary conviction, to imprisonment for a term not exceeding 3 months or a fine not exceeding the statutory maximum or both;

(b) on conviction on indictment, to imprisonment for a term not exceeding 2 years or a fine or both.

(4) A contravention of subsection (1) or (2) is actionable, at the suit of a person who suffers loss as a result of the contravention, subject to the defences and other incidents applying to actions for breach of statutory duty.

(5) Subsection (1) applies to all transferable securities other than—

(a) those listed in Schedule 11A;

(b) such other transferable securities as may be specified in prospectus rules.

(6) Subsection (2) applies to all transferable securities other than—

(a) those listed in Part 1 of Schedule 11A;

(b) such other transferable securities as may be specified in prospectus rules.

(7) "Approved prospectus" means, in relation to transferable securities to which this section applies, a prospectus approved by the competent authority of the home State in relation to the issuer of the securities.]

[86 Exempt offers to the public][39]

[(1) A person does not contravene section 85(1) if—

(a) the offer is made to or directed at qualified investors only;

(b) the offer is made to or directed at fewer than 100 persons, other than qualified investors, per EEA State;

(c) the minimum consideration which may be paid by any person for transferable securities acquired by him pursuant to the offer is at least 50,000 euros (or an equivalent amount);

(d) the transferable securities being offered are denominated in amounts of at least 50,000 euros (or equivalent amounts); or

(e) the total consideration for the transferable securities being offered cannot exceed 100,000 euros (or an equivalent amount).

(2) Where—

(a) a person who is not a qualified investor ("the client") has engaged a qualified investor falling within Article 2.1(e)(i) of the prospectus directive to act as his agent, and

(b) the terms on which the qualified investor is engaged enable him to make decisions concerning the acceptance of offers of transferable securities on the client's behalf without reference to the client,

an offer made to or directed at the qualified investor is not to be regarded for the purposes of subsection (1) as also having been made to or directed at the client.

---

[38] Substituted, together with ss 84, 86, 87, 87A–87R, for ss 84–87 as originally enacted, by SI 2005/1433, reg 2(1), Sch 1, para 5; came into force 1 July 2005.

[39] Substituted, together with ss 84, 85, 87, 87A–87R, for ss 84–87 as originally enacted, by SI 2005/1433, reg 2(1), Sch 1, para 5; came into force 1 July 2005.

(3) For the purposes of subsection (1)(b), the making of an offer of transferable securities to—
   (a) trustees of a trust,
   (b) members of a partnership in their capacity as such, or
   (c) two or more persons jointly,
   is to be treated as the making of an offer to a single person.
(4) In determining whether subsection (1)(e) is satisfied in relation to an offer ("offer A"), offer A is to be taken together with any other offer of transferable securities of the same class made by the same person which—
   (a) was open at any time within the period of 12 months ending with the date on which offer A is first made; and
   (b) had previously satisfied subsection (1)(e).
(5) For the purposes of this section, an amount (in relation to an amount denominated in euros) is an "equivalent amount" if it is an amount of equal value denominated wholly or partly in another currency or unit of account.
(6) The equivalent is to be calculated at the latest practicable date before (but in any event not more than 3 working days before) the date on which the offer is first made.
(7) "Qualified investor" means—
   (a) an entity falling within Article 2.1(e)(i), (ii) or (iii) of the prospectus directive;
   (b) an investor registered on the register maintained by the competent authority under section 87R;
   (c) an investor authorised by an EEA State other than the United Kingdom to be considered as a qualified investor for the purposes of the prospectus directive.]

[87 Election to have prospectus][40]

[(1) A person who proposes—
   (a) to issue transferable securities to which this section applies,
   (b) to offer to the public transferable securities to which this section applies, or
   (c) to request the admission to a regulated market of transferable securities to which this section applies,
   may elect, in accordance with prospectus rules, to have a prospectus in relation to the securities.
(2) If a person makes such an election, the provisions of this Part and of prospectus rules apply in relation to those transferable securities as if, in relation to an offer of the securities to the public or the admission of the securities to trading on a regulated market, they were transferable securities for which an approved prospectus would be required as a result of section 85.
(3) Listing rules made under section 79 do not apply to securities which are the subject of an election.
(4) The transferable securities to which this section applies are those which fall within any of the following paragraphs of Schedule 11A—
   (a) paragraph 2,
   (b) paragraph 4,
   (c) paragraph 8, or
   (d) paragraph 9,
   where the United Kingdom is the home State in relation to the issuer of the securities.]

---

[40] Substituted, together with ss 84–86, 87A–87R, for ss 84–87 as originally enacted, by SI 2005/1433, reg 2(1), Sch 1, para 5; came into force 1 July 2005.

[Approval of prospectus][41]

[87A Criteria for approval of prospectus by competent authority][42]

[(1) The competent authority may not approve a prospectus unless it is satisfied that—
   (a) the United Kingdom is the home State in relation to the issuer of the transferable securities to which it relates,
   (b) the prospectus contains the necessary information, and
   (c) all of the other requirements imposed by or in accordance with this Part or the prospectus directive have been complied with (so far as those requirements apply to a prospectus for the transferable securities in question).

(2) The necessary information is the information necessary to enable investors to make an informed assessment of—
   (a) the assets and liabilities, financial position, profits and losses, and prospects of the issuer of the transferable securities and of any guarantor; and
   (b) the rights attaching to the transferable securities.

(3) The necessary information must be presented in a form which is comprehensible and easy to analyse.

(4) The necessary information must be prepared having regard to the particular nature of the transferable securities and their issuer.

(5) The prospectus must include a summary (unless the transferable securities in question are ones in relation to which prospectus rules provide that a summary is not required).

(6) The summary must, briefly and in non-technical language, convey the essential characteristics of, and risks associated with, the issuer, any guarantor and the transferable securities to which the prospectus relates.

(7) Where the prospectus for which approval is sought does not include the final offer price or the amount of transferable securities to be offered to the public, the applicant must inform the competent authority in writing of that information as soon as that element is finalised.

(8) "Prospectus" (except in subsection (5)) includes a supplementary prospectus.]

[87B Exemptions from disclosure][43]

[(1) The competent authority may authorise the omission from a prospectus of any information, the inclusion of which would otherwise be required, on the ground—
   (a) that its disclosure would be contrary to the public interest;
   (b) that its disclosure would be seriously detrimental to the issuer, provided that the omission would be unlikely to mislead the public with regard to any facts or circumstances which are essential for an informed assessment of the kind mentioned in section 87A(2); or
   (c) that the information is only of minor importance for a specific offer to the public or admission to trading on a regulated market and unlikely to influence an informed assessment of the kind mentioned in section 87A(2).

(2) The Secretary of State or the Treasury may issue a certificate to the effect that the disclosure of any information would be contrary to the public interest.

(3) The competent authority is entitled to act on any such certificate in exercising its powers under subsection (1)(a).

---

[41] Substituted, together with ss 84–87, 87B–87R, for ss 84–87 as originally enacted, by SI 2005/1433, reg 2(1), Sch 1, para 5; came into force 1 July 2005.
[42] Substituted, together with ss 84–87, 87B–87R, for ss 84–87 as originally enacted, by SI 2005/1433, reg 2(1), Sch 1, para 5; came into force 1 July 2005.
[43] Substituted, together with ss 84–87, 87A, 87C–87R, for ss 84–87 as originally enacted, by SI 2005/1433, reg 2(1), Sch 1, para 5; came into force 1 July 2005.

(4) This section does not affect any powers of the competent authority under prospectus rules.

(5) "Prospectus" includes a supplementary prospectus.]

[87C Consideration of application for approval][44]

[(1) The competent authority must notify the applicant of its decision on an application for approval of a prospectus before the end of the period for consideration.

(2) The period for consideration—
- (a) begins with the first working day after the date on which the application is received; but
- (b) if the competent authority gives a notice under subsection (4), is to be treated as beginning with the first working day after the date on which the notice is complied with.

(3) The period for consideration is—
- (a) except in the case of a new issuer, 10 working days; or
- (b) in that case, 20 working days.

(4) The competent authority may by notice in writing require a person who has applied for approval of a prospectus to provide—
- (a) specified documents or documents of a specified description, or
- (b) specified information or information of a specified description.

(5) No notice under subsection (4) may be given after the end of the period, beginning with the first working day after the date on which the application is received, of—
- (a) except in the case of a new issuer, 10 working days; or
- (b) in that case, 20 working days.

(6) Subsection (4) applies only to information and documents reasonably required in connection with the exercise by the competent authority of its functions in relation to the application.

(7) The competent authority may require any information provided under this section to be provided in such form as it may reasonably require.

(8) The competent authority may require—
- (a) any information provided, whether in a document or otherwise, to be verified in such manner, or
- (b) any document produced to be authenticated in such manner,

as it may reasonably require.

(9) The competent authority must notify the applicant of its decision on an application for approval of a supplementary prospectus before the end of the period of 7 working days beginning with the date on which the application is received; and subsections (4) and (6) to (8) apply to such an application as they apply to an application for approval of a prospectus.

(10) The competent authority's failure to comply with subsection (1) or (9) does not constitute approval of the application in question.

(11) "New issuer" means an issuer of transferable securities which—
- (a) does not have transferable securities admitted to trading on any regulated market; and
- (b) has not previously offered transferable securities to the public.]

[87D Procedure for decision on application for approval][45]

[(1) If the competent authority approves a prospectus, it must give the applicant written notice.

(2) If the competent authority proposes to refuse to approve a prospectus, it must give the applicant written notice.

---

[44] Substituted, together with ss 84–87, 87A, 87B, 87D–87R, for ss 84–87 as originally enacted, by SI 2005/1433, reg 2(1), Sch 1, para 5; came into force 1 July 2005.

[45] Substituted, together with ss 84–87, 87A–87C, 87E–87R, for ss 84–87 as originally enacted, by SI 2005/1433, reg 2(1), Sch 1, para 5; came into force 1 July 2005.

(3) The notice must state the competent authority's reasons for the proposed refusal.

(4) If the competent authority decides to refuse to approve a prospectus, it must give the applicant written notice.

(5) The notice must—

    (a) give the competent authority's reasons for refusing the application; and

    (b) inform the applicant of his right to refer the matter to the Tribunal.

(6) If the competent authority refuses to approve a prospectus, the applicant may refer the matter to the Tribunal.

(7) In this section "prospectus" includes a supplementary prospectus.]

[Transfer of application for approval of a prospectus]⁴⁶

[87E Transfer by competent authority of application for approval]⁴⁷

[(1) The competent authority may transfer an application for the approval of a prospectus or a supplementary prospectus to the competent authority of another EEA State ("the transferee authority").

(2) Before doing so, the competent authority must obtain the agreement of the transferee authority.

(3) The competent authority must inform the applicant of the transfer within 3 working days beginning with the first working day after the date of the transfer.

(4) On making a transfer under subsection (1), the competent authority ceases to have functions under this Part in relation to the application transferred.]

[87F Transfer to competent authority of application for approval]⁴⁸

[(1) Where the competent authority agrees to the transfer to it of an application for the approval of a prospectus made to the competent authority of another EEA State—

    (a) the United Kingdom is to be treated for the purposes of this Part as the home State in relation to the issuer of the transferable securities to which the prospectus relates, and

    (b) this Part applies to the application as if it had been made to the competent authority but with the modification in subsection (2).

(2) Section 87C applies as if the date of the transfer were the date on which the application was received by the competent authority.]

*[Supplementary prospectus]*⁴⁹

[87G Supplementary prospectus]⁵⁰

[(1) Subsection (2) applies if, during the relevant period, there arises or is noted a significant new factor, material mistake or inaccuracy relating to the information included in a prospectus approved by the competent authority.

(2) The person on whose application the prospectus was approved must, in accordance with prospectus rules, submit a supplementary prospectus containing details of the new factor, mistake or inaccuracy to the competent authority for its approval.

---

⁴⁶ Substituted, together with ss 84–87, 87A–87D, 87F–87R, for ss 84–87 as originally enacted, by SI 2005/1433, reg 2(1), Sch 1, para 5; came into force 1 July 2005.

⁴⁷ Substituted, together with ss 84–87, 87A–87D, 87F–87R, for ss 84–87 as originally enacted, by SI 2005/1433, reg 2(1), Sch 1, para 5; came into force 1 July 2005.

⁴⁸ Substituted, together with ss 84–87, 87A–87E, 87G–87R, for ss 84–87 as originally enacted, by SI 2005/1433, reg 2(1), Sch 1, para 5; came into force 1 July 2005.

⁴⁹ Substituted, together with ss 84–87, 87A–87F, 87H–87R, for ss 84–87 as originally enacted, by SI 2005/1433, reg 2(1), Sch 1, para 5; came into force 1 July 2005.

⁵⁰ Substituted, together with ss 84–87, 87A–87F, 87H–87R, for ss 84–87 as originally enacted, by SI 2005/1433, reg 2(1), Sch 1, para 5; came into force 1 July 2005.

(3) The relevant period begins when the prospectus is approved and ends—

    (a) with the closure of the offer of the transferable securities to which the prospectus relates; or

    (b) when trading in those securities on a regulated market begins.

(4) "Significant" means significant for the purposes of making an informed assessment of the kind mentioned in section 87A(2).

(5) Any person responsible for the prospectus who is aware of any new factor, mistake or inaccuracy which may require the submission of a supplementary prospectus in accordance with subsection (2) must give notice of it to—

    (a) the issuer of the transferable securities to which the prospectus relates, and

    (b) the person on whose application the prospectus was approved.

(6) A supplementary prospectus must provide sufficient information to correct any mistake or inaccuracy which gave rise to the need for it.

(7) Subsection (1) applies also to information contained in any supplementary prospectus published under this section.]

[Passporting][51]

[87H Prospectus approved in another EEA State][52]

[(1) A prospectus approved by the competent authority of an EEA State other than the United Kingdom is not an approved prospectus for the purposes of section 85 unless that authority has provided the competent authority with—

    (a) a certificate of approval;

    (b) a copy of the prospectus as approved; and

    (c) if requested by the competent authority, a translation of the summary of the prospectus.

(2) A document is not a certificate of approval unless it states that the prospectus—

    (a) has been drawn up in accordance with the prospectus directive; and

    (b) has been approved, in accordance with that directive, by the competent authority providing the certificate.

(3) A document is not a certificate of approval unless it states whether (and, if so, why) the competent authority providing it authorised, in accordance with the prospectus directive, the omission from the prospectus of information which would otherwise have been required to be included.

(4) "Prospectus" includes a supplementary prospectus.]

[87I Provision of information to host Member State][53]

[(1) The competent authority must, if requested to do so, supply the competent authority of a specified EEA State with—

    (a) a certificate of approval;

    (b) a copy of the specified prospectus (as approved by the competent authority); and

    (c) a translation of the summary of the specified prospectus (if the request states that one has been requested by the other competent authority).

(2) Only the following may make a request under this section—

    (a) the issuer of the transferable securities to which the specified prospectus relates;

---

[51] Substituted, together with ss 84–87, 87A–87G, 87I–87R, for ss 84–87 as originally enacted, by SI 2005/1433, reg 2(1), Sch 1, para 5; came into force 1 July 2005.

[52] Substituted, together with ss 84–87, 87A–87G, 87I–87R, for ss 84–87 as originally enacted, by SI 2005/1433, reg 2(1), Sch 1, para 5; came into force: 1 July 2005.

[53] Substituted, together with ss 84–87, 87A–87H, 87J–87R, for ss 84–87 as originally enacted, by SI 2005/1433, reg 2(1), Sch 1, para 5; came into force 1 July 2005.

(b) a person who wishes to offer the transferable securities to which the specified prospectus relates to the public in an EEA State other than (or as well as) the United Kingdom;

(c) a person requesting the admission of the transferable securities to which the specified prospectus relates to a regulated market situated or operating in an EEA State other than (or as well as) the United Kingdom.

(3) A certificate of approval must state that the prospectus—

    (a) has been drawn up in accordance with this Part and the prospectus directive; and

    (b) has been approved, in accordance with those provisions, by the competent authority.

(4) A certificate of approval must state whether (and, if so, why) the competent authority authorised, in accordance with section 87B, the omission from the prospectus of information which would otherwise have been required to be included.

(5) The competent authority must comply with a request under this section—

    (a) if the prospectus has been approved before the request is made, within 3 working days beginning with the date of the request; or

    (b) if the request is submitted with an application for the approval of the prospectus, on the first working day after the date on which it approves the prospectus.

(6) "Prospectus" includes a supplementary prospectus.

(7) "Specified" means specified in a request made for the purposes of this section.]

[Transferable securities: powers of competent authority][54]

[87J Requirements imposed as condition of approval][55]

[(1) As a condition of approving a prospectus, the competent authority may by notice in writing—

    (a) require the inclusion in the prospectus of such supplementary information necessary for investor protection as the competent authority may specify;

    (b) require a person controlling, or controlled by, the applicant to provide specified information or documents;

    (c) require an auditor or manager of the applicant to provide specified information or documents;

    (d) require a financial intermediary commissioned to assist either in carrying out the offer to the public of the transferable securities to which the prospectus relates or in requesting their admission to trading on a regulated market, to provide specified information or documents.

(2) "Specified" means specified in the notice.

(3) "Prospectus" includes a supplementary prospectus.]

[87K Power to suspend or prohibit offer to the public][56]

[(1) This section applies where a person ("the offeror") has made an offer of transferable securities to the public in the United Kingdom ("the offer").

(2) If the competent authority has reasonable grounds for suspecting that an applicable provision has been infringed, it may—

    (a) require the offeror to suspend the offer for a period not exceeding 10 working days;

    (b) require a person not to advertise the offer, or to take such steps as the authority may specify to suspend any existing advertisement of the offer, for a period not exceeding 10 working days.

---

[54] Substituted, together with ss 84–87, 87A–87I, 87K–87R, for ss 84–87 as originally enacted, by SI 2005/1433, reg 2(1), Sch 1, para 5; came into force 1 July 2005.

[55] Substituted, together with ss 84–87, 87A–87I, 87K–87R, for ss 84–87 as originally enacted, by SI 2005/1433, reg 2(1), Sch 1, para 5; came into force 1 July 2005.

[56] Substituted, together with ss 84–87, 87A–87J, 87L–87R, for ss 84–87 as originally enacted, by SI 2005/1433, reg 2(1), Sch 1, para 5; came into force 1 July 2005.

(3) If the competent authority has reasonable grounds for suspecting that it is likely that an applicable provision will be infringed, it may require the offeror to withdraw the offer.

(4) If the competent authority finds that an applicable provision has been infringed, it may require the offeror to withdraw the offer.

(5) "An applicable provision" means—

    (a) a provision of this Part,

    (b) a provision contained in prospectus rules,

    (c) any other provision made in accordance with the prospectus directive,

applicable in relation to the offer.]

[87L Power to suspend or prohibit admission to trading on a regulated market]⁵⁷

[(1) This section applies where a person has requested the admission of transferable securities to trading on a regulated market situated or operating in the United Kingdom.

(2) If the competent authority has reasonable grounds for suspecting that an applicable provision has been infringed and the securities have not yet been admitted to trading on the regulated market in question, it may—

    (a) require the person requesting admission to suspend the request for a period not exceeding 10 working days;

    (b) require a person not to advertise the securities to which it relates, or to take such steps as the authority may specify to suspend any existing advertisement in connection with those securities, for a period not exceeding 10 working days.

(3) If the competent authority has reasonable grounds for suspecting that an applicable provision has been infringed and the securities have been admitted to trading on the regulated market in question, it may—

    (a) require the market operator to suspend trading in the securities for a period not exceeding 10 working days;

    (b) require a person not to advertise the securities, or to take such steps as the authority may specify to suspend any existing advertisement in connection with those securities, for a period not exceeding 10 working days.

(4) If the competent authority finds that an applicable provision has been infringed, it may require the market operator to prohibit trading in the securities on the regulated market in question.

(5) "An applicable provision" means—

    (a) a provision of this Part,

    (b) a provision contained in prospectus rules,

    (c) any other provision made in accordance with the prospectus directive,

applicable in relation to the admission of the transferable securities to trading on the regulated market in question.]

[87M Public censure of issuer]⁵⁸

[(1) If the competent authority finds that—

    (a) an issuer of transferable securities,

    (b) a person offering transferable securities to the public, or

    (c) a person requesting the admission of transferable securities to trading on a regulated market,

---

⁵⁷ Substituted, together with ss 84–87, 87A–87K, 87M–87R, for ss 84–87 as originally enacted, by SI 2005/1433, reg 2(1), Sch 1, para 5; came into force 1 July 2005.

⁵⁸ Substituted, together with ss 84–87, 87A–87L, 87N–87R, for ss 84–87 as originally enacted, by SI 2005/1433, reg 2(1), Sch 1, para 5; came into force 1 July 2005.

is failing or has failed to comply with his obligations under an applicable provision, it may publish a statement to that effect.

(2) If the competent authority proposes to publish a statement, it must give the person a warning notice setting out the terms of the proposed statement.

(3) If, after considering any representations made in response to the warning notice, the competent authority decides to make the proposed statement, it must give the person a decision notice setting out the terms of the statement.

(4) "An applicable provision" means—

(a) a provision of this Part,

(b) a provision contained in prospectus rules,

(c) any other provision made in accordance with the prospectus directive,

applicable to a prospectus in relation to the transferable securities in question.

(5) "Prospectus" includes a supplementary prospectus.]

[87N Right to refer matters to the Tribunal][59]

[(1) A person to whom a decision notice is given under section 87M may refer the matter to the Tribunal.

(2) A person to whom a notice is given under section 87O may refer the matter to the Tribunal.]

[87O Procedure under sections 87K and 87L][60]

[(1) A requirement under section 87K or 87L takes effect—

(a) immediately, if the notice under subsection (2) states that that is the case;

(b) in any other case, on such date as may be specified in that notice.

(2) If the competent authority—

(a) proposes to exercise the powers in section 87K or 87L in relation to a person, or

(b) exercises any of those powers in relation to a person with immediate effect,

it must give that person written notice.

(3) The notice must—

(a) give details of the competent authority's action or proposed action;

(b) state the competent authority's reasons for taking the action in question and choosing the date on which it took effect or takes effect;

(c) inform the recipient that he may make representations to the competent authority within such period as may be specified by the notice (whether or not he has referred the matter to the Tribunal);

(d) inform him of the date on which the action took effect or takes effect; and

(e) inform him of his right to refer the matter to the Tribunal.

(4) The competent authority may extend the period within which representations may be made to it.

(5) If, having considered any representations made to it, the competent authority decides to maintain, vary or revoke its earlier decision, it must give written notice to that effect to the person mentioned in subsection (2).

(6) A notice given under subsection (5) must inform that person, where relevant, of his right to refer the matter to the Tribunal.

(7) If a notice informs a person of his right to refer a matter to the Tribunal, it must give an indication of the procedure on such a reference.

---

[59] Substituted, together with ss 84–87, 87A–87M, 87O–87R, for ss 84–87 as originally enacted, by SI 2005/1433, reg 2(1), Sch 1, para 5; came into force 1 July 2005.

[60] Substituted, together with ss 84–87, 87A–87N, 87P–87R, for ss 84–87 as originally enacted, by SI 2005/1433, reg 2(1), Sch 1, para 5; came into force 1 July 2005.

(8) If a notice under this section relates to the exercise of the power conferred by section 87L(3), the notice must also be given to the person at whose request the transferable securities were admitted to trading on the regulated market.]

[87P Exercise of powers at request of competent authority of another EEA State][61]

[(1) This section applies if—
- (a) the competent authority of an EEA State other than the United Kingdom has approved a prospectus,
- (b) the transferable securities to which the prospectus relates have been offered to the public in the United Kingdom or their admission to trading on a regulated market has been requested, and
- (c) that competent authority makes a request that the competent authority assist it in the performance of its functions under the law of that State in connection with the prospectus directive.

(2) For the purpose of complying with the request mentioned in subsection (1)(c), the powers conferred by sections 87K and 87L may be exercised as if the prospectus were one which had been approved by the competent authority.

(3) Section 87N does not apply to an exercise of those powers as a result of this section.

(4) Section 87O does apply to such an exercise of those powers but with the omission of subsections (3)(e), (6) and (7).]

[Rights of investors][62]

[87Q Right of investor to withdraw][63]

[(1) Where a person agrees to buy or subscribe for transferable securities in circumstances where the final offer price or the amount of transferable securities to be offered to the public is not included in the prospectus, he may withdraw his acceptance before the end of the withdrawal period.

(2) The withdrawal period—
- (a) begins with the investor's acceptance; and
- (b) ends at the end of the second working day after the date on which the competent authority is informed of the information in accordance with section 87A(7).

(3) Subsection (1) does not apply if the prospectus contains—
- (a) in the case of the amount of transferable securities to be offered to the public, the criteria or conditions (or both) according to which that element will be determined, or
- (b) in the case of price, the criteria or conditions (or both) according to which that element will be determined or the maximum price.

(4) Where a supplementary prospectus has been published and, prior to the publication, a person agreed to buy or subscribe for transferable securities to which it relates, he may withdraw his acceptance before the end of the period of 2 working days beginning with the first working day after the date on which the supplementary prospectus was published.]

---

[61] Substituted, together with ss 84–87, 87A–87O, 87Q, 87R, for ss 84–87 as originally enacted, by SI 2005/1433, reg 2(1), Sch 1, para 5; came into force 1 July 2005.

[62] Substituted, together with ss 84–87, 87A–87P, 87R, for ss 84–87 as originally enacted, by SI 2005/1433, reg 2(1), Sch 1, para 5; came into force 1 July 2005.

[63] Substituted, together with ss 84–87, 87A–87P, 87R, for ss 84–87 as originally enacted, by SI 2005/1433, reg 2(1), Sch 1, para 5; came into force 1 July 2005.

[Registered investors][64]

[87R Register of investors][65]

[(1) The competent authority must establish and maintain, in accordance with this section and prospectus rules, a register of investors for the purposes of section 86.

(2) An individual may not be entered in the register unless—

(a) he is resident in the United Kingdom; and

(b) he meets at least two of the criteria mentioned in Article 2.2 of the prospectus directive.

(3) A company may not be entered in the register unless—

(a) it falls within the meaning of "small and medium-sized enterprises" in Article 2.1 of the prospectus directive; and

(b) its registered office is in the United Kingdom.

(4) A person who does not fall within subsection (2) or (3) may not be entered in the register.]

Sponsors

88 Sponsors

(1) Listing rules may require a person to make arrangements with a sponsor for the performance by the sponsor of such services in relation to him as may be specified in the rules.

(2) "Sponsor" means a person approved by the competent authority for the purposes of the rules.

(3) Listing rules made by virtue of subsection (1) may—

(a) provide for the competent authority to maintain a list of sponsors;

(b) specify services which must be performed by a sponsor;

(c) impose requirements on a sponsor in relation to the provision of services or specified services;

(d) specify the circumstances in which a person is qualified for being approved as a sponsor.

(4) If the competent authority proposes—

(a) to refuse a person's application for approval as a sponsor, or

(b) to cancel a person's approval as a sponsor [otherwise than at his request],[66]

it must give him a warning notice.

(5) If, after considering any representations made in response to the warning notice, the competent authority decides—

(a) to grant the application for approval, or

(b) not to cancel the approval,

it must give the person concerned, and any person to whom a copy of the warning notice was given, written notice of its decision.

(6) If, after considering any representations made in response to the warning notice, the competent authority decides—

(a) to refuse to grant the application for approval, or

(b) to cancel the approval,

it must give the person concerned a decision notice.

(7) A person to whom a decision notice is given under this section may refer the matter to the Tribunal.

---

[64] Substituted, together with ss 84–87, 87A–87Q for ss 84–87 as originally enacted, by SI 2005/1433, reg 2(1), Sch 1, para 5; came into force 1 July 2005.

[65] Substituted, together with ss 84–87, 87A–87Q for ss 84–87 as originally enacted, by SI 2005/1433, reg 2(1), Sch 1, para 5; came into force 1 July 2005.

[66] Inserted by SI 2007/1973, arts 2, 9; came into force 12 July 2007.

89 Public censure of sponsor

(1) Listing rules may make provision for the competent authority, if it considers that a sponsor has contravened a requirement imposed on him by rules made as a result of section 88(3)(c), to publish a statement to that effect.

(2) If the competent authority proposes to publish a statement it must give the sponsor a warning notice setting out the terms of the proposed statement.

(3) If, after considering any representations made in response to the warning notice, the competent authority decides to make the proposed statement, it must give the sponsor a decision notice setting out the terms of the statement.

(4) A sponsor to whom a decision notice is given under this section may refer the matter to the Tribunal.

[Transparency obligations][67]

[89A Transparency rules][68]

[(1) The competent authority may make rules for the purposes of the transparency obligations directive.

(2) The rules may include provision for dealing with any matters arising out of or related to any provision of the transparency obligations directive.

(3) The competent authority may also make rules—
   (a) for the purpose of ensuring that voteholder information in respect of voting shares traded on a UK market other than a regulated market is made public or notified to the competent authority;
   (b) providing for persons who hold comparable instruments (see section 89F(1)(c)) in respect of voting shares to be treated, in the circumstances specified in the rules, as holding some or all of the voting rights in respect of those shares.

(4) Rules under this section may, in particular, make provision—
   (a) specifying how the proportion of—
      (i) the total voting rights in respect of shares in an issuer, or
      (ii) the total voting rights in respect of a particular class of shares in an issuer,
      held by a person is to be determined;
   (b) specifying the circumstances in which, for the purposes of any determination of the voting rights held by a person ("P") in respect of voting shares in an issuer, any voting rights held, or treated by virtue of subsection (3)(b) as held, by another person in respect of voting shares in the issuer are to be regarded as held by P;
   (c) specifying the nature of the information which must be included in any notification;
   (d) about the form of any notification;
   (e) requiring any notification to be given within a specified period;
   (f) specifying the manner in which any information is to be made public and the period within which it must be made public;
   (g) specifying circumstances in which any of the requirements imposed by rules under this section does not apply.

(5) Rules under this section are referred to in this Part as "transparency rules".

(6) Nothing in sections 89B to 89G affects the generality of the power to make rules under this section.]

---

[67] Inserted by the Companies Act 2006, s 1266(1); for effect see sub-s (2) thereof; came into force 8 November 2006.

[68] Inserted by the Companies Act 2006, s 1266(1); for effect see sub-s (2) thereof; came into force 8 November 2006.

[89B Provision of voteholder information][69]

[(1) Transparency rules may make provision for voteholder information in respect of voting shares to be notified, in circumstances specified in the rules—

(a) to the issuer, or

(b) to the public,

or to both.

(2) Transparency rules may make provision for voteholder information notified to the issuer to be notified at the same time to the competent authority.

(3) In this Part "voteholder information" in respect of voting shares means information relating to the proportion of voting rights held by a person in respect of the shares.

(4) Transparency rules may require notification of voteholder information relating to a person—

(a) initially, not later than such date as may be specified in the rules for the purposes of the first indent of Article 30.2 of the transparency obligations directive, and

(b) subsequently, in accordance with the following provisions.

(5) Transparency rules under subsection (4)(b) may require notification of voteholder information relating to a person only where there is a notifiable change in the proportion of—

(a) the total voting rights in respect of shares in the issuer, or

(b) the total voting rights in respect of a particular class of share in the issuer,

held by the person.

(6) For this purpose there is a "notifiable change" in the proportion of voting rights held by a person when the proportion changes—

(a) from being a proportion less than a designated proportion to a proportion equal to or greater than that designated proportion,

(b) from being a proportion equal to a designated proportion to a proportion greater or less than that designated proportion, or

(c) from being a proportion greater than a designated proportion to a proportion equal to or less than that designated proportion.

(7) In subsection (6) "designated" means designated by the rules.]

[89C Provision of information by issuers of transferable securities][70]

[(1) Transparency rules may make provision requiring the issuer of transferable securities, in circumstances specified in the rules—

(a) to make public information to which this section applies, or

(b) to notify to the competent authority information to which this section applies,

or to do both.

(2) In the case of every issuer, this section applies to—

(a) information required by Article 4 of the transparency obligations directive;

(b) information relating to the rights attached to the transferable securities, including information about the terms and conditions of those securities which could indirectly affect those rights; and

(c) information about new loan issues and about any guarantee or security in connection with any such issue.

(3) In the case of an issuer of debt securities, this section also applies to information required by Article 5 of the transparency obligations directive.

---

[69] Inserted by the Companies Act 2006, s 1266(1); for effect see sub-s (2) thereof; came into force 8 November 2006.

[70] Inserted by the Companies Act 2006, s 1266(1); for effect see sub-s (2) thereof came into force 8 November 2006.

(4) In the case of an issuer of shares, this section also applies to—
  (a) information required by Article 5 of the transparency obligations directive;
  (b) information required by Article 6 of that directive;
  (c) voteholder information—
      (i) notified to the issuer, or
      (ii) relating to the proportion of voting rights held by the issuer in respect of shares in the issuer;
  (d) information relating to the issuer's capital; and
  (e) information relating to the total number of voting rights in respect of shares or shares of a particular class.]

[89D Notification of voting rights held by issuer][71]

[(1) Transparency rules may require notification of voteholder information relating to the proportion of voting rights held by an issuer in respect of voting shares in the issuer—
  (a) initially, not later than such date as may be specified in the rules for the purposes of the second indent of Article 30.2 of the transparency obligations directive, and
  (b) subsequently, in accordance with the following provisions.
(2) Transparency rules under subsection (1)(b) may require notification of voteholder information relating to the proportion of voting rights held by an issuer in respect of voting shares in the issuer only where there is a notifiable change in the proportion of—
  (a) the total voting rights in respect of shares in the issuer, or
  (b) the total voting rights in respect of a particular class of share in the issuer,
held by the issuer.
(3) For this purpose there is a "notifiable change" in the proportion of voting rights held by a person when the proportion changes—
  (a) from being a proportion less than a designated proportion to a proportion equal to or greater than that designated proportion,
  (b) from being a proportion equal to a designated proportion to a proportion greater or less than that designated proportion, or
  (c) from being a proportion greater than a designated proportion to a proportion equal to or less than that designated proportion.
(4) In subsection (3) "designated" means designated by the rules.]

[89E Notification of proposed amendment of issuer's constitution][72]

[Transparency rules may make provision requiring an issuer of transferable securities that are admitted to trading on a regulated market to notify a proposed amendment to its constitution—
  (a) to the competent authority, and
  (b) to the market on which the issuer's securities are admitted,
at times and in circumstances specified in the rules.]

[89F Transparency rules: interpretation etc][73]

[(1) For the purposes of sections 89A to 89G—
  (a) the voting rights in respect of any voting shares are the voting rights attached to those shares,

---

[71] Inserted by the Companies Act 2006, s 1266(1); for effect see sub-s (2) thereof; came into force 8 November 2006.
[72] Inserted by the Companies Act 2006, s 1266(1); for effect see sub-s (2) thereof; came into force 8 November 2006.
[73] Inserted by the Companies Act 2006, s 1266(1); for effect see sub-s (2) thereof; came into force 8 November 2006.

    (b) a person is to be regarded as holding the voting rights in respect of the shares—

        (i) if, by virtue of those shares, he is a shareholder within the meaning of Article 2.1(e) of the transparency obligations directive;

        (ii) if, and to the extent that, he is entitled to acquire, dispose of or exercise those voting rights in one or more of the cases mentioned in Article 10(a) to (h) of the transparency obligations directive;

        (iii) if he holds, directly or indirectly, a financial instrument which results in an entitlement to acquire the shares and is an Article 13 instrument, and

    (c) a person holds a "comparable instrument" in respect of voting shares if he holds, directly or indirectly, a financial instrument in relation to the shares which has similar economic effects to an Article 13 instrument (whether or not the financial instrument results in an entitlement to acquire the shares).

(2) Transparency rules under section 89A(3)(b) may make different provision for different descriptions of comparable instrument.

(3) For the purposes of sections 89A to 89G two or more persons may, at the same time, each be regarded as holding the same voting rights.

(4) In those sections—

    "Article 13 instrument" means a financial instrument of a type determined by the European Commission under Article 13.2 of the transparency obligations directive;

    ["financial instrument" has the meaning given in Article 4.1(17) of Directive 2004/39/EC on markets in financial instruments;][74]

    "UK market" means a market that is situated or operating in the United Kingdom;

    "voting shares" means shares of an issuer to which voting rights are attached.]

[89G Transparency rules: other supplementary provisions][75]

[(1) Transparency rules may impose the same obligations on a person who has applied for the admission of transferable securities to trading on a regulated market without the issuer's consent as they impose on an issuer of transferable securities.

(2) Transparency rules that require a person to make information public may include provision authorising the competent authority to make the information public in the event that the person fails to do so.

(3) The competent authority may make public any information notified to the authority in accordance with transparency rules.

(4) Transparency rules may make provision by reference to any provision of any rules made by the Panel on Takeovers and Mergers under Part 28 of the Companies Act 2006.

(5) Sections 89A to 89F and this section are without prejudice to any other power conferred by this Part to make Part 6 rules.]

[Power of competent authority to call for information][76]

[89H Competent authority's power to call for information][77]

[(1) The competent authority may by notice in writing given to a person to whom this section applies require him—

    (a) to provide specified information or information of a specified description, or

    (b) to produce specified documents or documents of a specified description.

---

[74] Inserted by SI 2008/3053, art 2; came into force: 31 January 2009.

[75] Inserted by the Companies Act 2006, s 1266(1); for effect see sub-s (2) thereof; came into force 8 November 2006.

[76] Inserted by the Companies Act 2006, s 1267; came into force 8 November 2006.

[77] Inserted by the Companies Act 2006, s 1267; came into force 8 November 2006.

(2) This section applies to—
  (a) an issuer in respect of whom transparency rules have effect;
  (b) a voteholder;
  (c) an auditor of—
    (i) an issuer to whom this section applies, or
    (ii) a voteholder;
  (d) a person who controls a voteholder;
  (e) a person controlled by a voteholder;
  (f) a director or other similar officer of an issuer to whom this section applies;
  (g) a director or other similar officer of a voteholder or, where the affairs of a voteholder are managed by its members, a member of the voteholder.

(3) This section applies only to information and documents reasonably required in connection with the exercise by the competent authority of functions conferred on it by or under sections 89A to 89G (transparency rules).

(4) Information or documents required under this section must be provided or produced—
  (a) before the end of such reasonable period as may be specified, and
  (b) at such place as may be specified.

(5) If a person claims a lien on a document, its production under this section does not affect the lien.]

[89I Requirements in connection with call for information][78]

[(1) The competent authority may require any information provided under section 89H to be provided in such form as it may reasonably require.

(2) The competent authority may require—
  (a) any information provided, whether in a document or otherwise, to be verified in such manner as it may reasonably require;
  (b) any document produced to be authenticated in such manner as it may reasonably require.

(3) If a document is produced in response to a requirement imposed under section 89H, the competent authority may—
  (a) take copies of or extracts from the document; or
  (b) require the person producing the document, or any relevant person, to provide an explanation of the document.

(4) In subsection (3)(b) "relevant person", in relation to a person who is required to produce a document, means a person who—
  (a) has been or is a director or controller of that person;
  (b) has been or is an auditor of that person;
  (c) has been or is an actuary, accountant or lawyer appointed or instructed by that person; or
  (d) has been or is an employee of that person.

(5) If a person who is required under section 89H to produce a document fails to do so, the competent authority may require him to state, to the best of his knowledge and belief, where the document is.]

[89J Power to call for information: supplementary provisions][79]

[(1) The competent authority may require an issuer to make public any information provided to the authority under section 89H.

---

[78] Inserted by the Companies Act 2006, s 1267; came into force 8 November 2006.
[79] Inserted by the Companies Act 2006, s 1267; came into force 8 November 2006.

(2) If the issuer fails to comply with a requirement under subsection (1), the competent authority may, after seeking representations from the issuer, make the information public.

(3) In sections 89H and 89I (power of competent authority to call for information)—

"control" and "controlled" have the meaning given by subsection (4) below;

"specified" means specified in the notice;

"voteholder" means a person who—

(a) holds voting rights in respect of any voting shares for the purposes of sections 89A to 89G (transparency rules), or

(b) is treated as holding such rights by virtue of rules under section 89A(3)(b).

(4) For the purposes of those sections a person ("A") controls another person ("B") if—

(a) A holds a majority of the voting rights in B,

(b) A is a member of B and has the right to appoint or remove a majority of the members of the board of directors (or, if there is no such board, the equivalent management body) of B,

(c) A is a member of B and controls alone, pursuant to an agreement with other shareholders or members, a majority of the voting rights in B, or

(d) A has the right to exercise, or actually exercises, dominant influence or control over B.

(5) For the purposes of subsection (4)(b)—

(a) any rights of a person controlled by A, and

(b) any rights of a person acting on behalf of A or a person controlled by A,

are treated as held by A.]

[Powers exercisable in case of infringement of transparency obligation][80]

[89K Public censure of issuer][81]

[(1) If the competent authority finds that an issuer of securities admitted to trading on a regulated market is failing or has failed to comply with an applicable transparency obligation, it may publish a statement to that effect.

(2) If the competent authority proposes to publish a statement, it must give the issuer a warning notice setting out the terms of the proposed statement.

(3) If, after considering any representations made in response to the warning notice, the competent authority decides to make the proposed statement, it must give the issuer a decision notice setting out the terms of the statement.

(4) A notice under this section must inform the issuer of his right to refer the matter to the Tribunal (see section 89N) and give an indication of the procedure on such a reference.

(5) In this section "transparency obligation" means an obligation under—

(a) a provision of transparency rules, or

(b) any other provision made in accordance with the transparency obligations directive.

(6) In relation to an issuer whose home State is a member State other than the United Kingdom, any reference to an applicable transparency obligation must be read subject to section 100A(2).]

[89L Power to suspend or prohibit trading of securities][82]

[(1) This section applies to securities admitted to trading on a regulated market.

(2) If the competent authority has reasonable grounds for suspecting that an applicable transparency obligation has been infringed by an issuer, it may—

(a) suspend trading in the securities for a period not exceeding 10 days,

---

[80] Inserted by the Companies Act 2006, s 1268; came into force 8 November 2006.
[81] Inserted by the Companies Act 2006, s 1268; came into force 8 November 2006.
[82] Inserted by the Companies Act 2006, s 1268; came into force 8 November 2006.

335

  (b) prohibit trading in the securities, or

  (c) make a request to the operator of the market on which the issuer's securities are traded—

   (i) to suspend trading in the securities for a period not exceeding 10 days, or

   (ii) to prohibit trading in the securities.

(3) If the competent authority has reasonable grounds for suspecting that a provision required by the transparency obligations directive has been infringed by a voteholder of an issuer, it may—

  (a) prohibit trading in the securities, or

  (b) make a request to the operator of the market on which the issuer's securities are traded to prohibit trading in the securities.

(4) If the competent authority finds that an applicable transparency obligation has been infringed, it may require the market operator to prohibit trading in the securities.

(5) In this section "transparency obligation" means an obligation under—

  (a) a provision contained in transparency rules, or

  (b) any other provision made in accordance with the transparency obligations directive.

(6) In relation to an issuer whose home State is a member State other than the United Kingdom, any reference to an applicable transparency obligation must be read subject to section 100A(2).]

[89M Procedure under section 89L][83]

[(1) A requirement under section 89L takes effect—

  (a) immediately, if the notice under subsection (2) states that that is the case;

  (b) in any other case, on such date as may be specified in the notice.

(2) If the competent authority—

  (a) proposes to exercise the powers in section 89L in relation to a person, or

  (b) exercises any of those powers in relation to a person with immediate effect,

it must give that person written notice.

(3) The notice must—

  (a) give details of the competent authority's action or proposed action;

  (b) state the competent authority's reasons for taking the action in question and choosing the date on which it took effect or takes effect;

  (c) inform the recipient that he may make representations to the competent authority within such period as may be specified by the notice (whether or not he had referred the matter to the Tribunal);

  (d) inform him of the date on which the action took effect or takes effect;

  (e) inform him of his right to refer the matter to the Tribunal (see section 89N) and give an indication of the procedure on such a reference.

(4) The competent authority may extend the period within which representations may be made to it.

(5) If, having considered any representations made to it, the competent authority decides to maintain, vary or revoke its earlier decision, it must give written notice to that effect to the person mentioned in subsection (2).]

[89N Right to refer matters to the Tribunal][84]

[A person—

  (a) to whom a decision notice is given under section 89K (public censure), or

  (b) to whom a notice is given under section 89M (procedure in connection with suspension or prohibition of trading),

may refer the matter to the Tribunal.]

---

[83] Inserted by the Companies Act 2006, s 1268; came into force 8 November 2006.

[84] Inserted by the Companies Act 2006, s 1268; came into force 8 November 2006.

[Corporate governance][85]

[89O Corporate governance rules][86]

[(1) The competent authority may make rules ("corporate governance rules")—

   (a) for the purpose of implementing, enabling the implementation of or dealing with matters arising out of or related to, any Community obligation relating to the corporate governance of issuers who have requested or approved admission of their securities to trading on a regulated market;

   (b) about corporate governance in relation to such issuers for the purpose of implementing, or dealing with matters arising out of or related to, any Community obligation.

(2) "Corporate governance", in relation to an issuer, includes—

   (a) the nature, constitution or functions of the organs of the issuer;

   (b) the manner in which organs of the issuer conduct themselves;

   (c) the requirements imposed on organs of the issuer;

   (d) the relationship between the different organs of the issuer;

   (e) the relationship between the organs of the issuer and the members of the issuer or holders of the issuer's securities.

(3) The burdens and restrictions imposed by rules under this section on foreign-traded issuers must not be greater than the burdens and restrictions imposed on UK-traded issuers by—

   (a) rules under this section, and

   (b) listing rules.

(4) For this purpose—

"foreign-traded issuer" means an issuer who has requested or approved admission of the issuer's securities to trading on a regulated market situated or operating outside the United Kingdom;

"UK-traded issuer" means an issuer who has requested or approved admission of the issuer's securities to trading on a regulated market situated or operating in the United Kingdom.

(5) This section is without prejudice to any other power conferred by this Part to make Part 6 rules.]

[Compensation for false or misleading statements etc][87]

[90 Compensation for statements in listing particulars or prospectus][88]

(1) Any person responsible for listing particulars is liable to pay compensation to a person who has—

   (a) acquired securities to which the particulars apply; and

   (b) suffered loss in respect of them as a result of—

     (i) any untrue or misleading statement in the particulars; or

     (ii) the omission from the particulars of any matter required to be included by section 80 or 81.

(2) Subsection (1) is subject to exemptions provided by Schedule 10.

(3) If listing particulars are required to include information about the absence of a particular matter, the omission from the particulars of that information is to be treated as a statement in the listing particulars that there is no such matter.

---

[85] Inserted by the Companies Act 2006, s 1269; came into force 8 November 2006.

[86] Inserted by the Companies Act 2006, s 1269; came into force 8 November 2006.

[87] Substituted by the Companies Act 2006, s 1272, Sch 15, Pt 1, paras 1, 4; came into force 8 November 2006.

[88] Substituted by the Companies Act 2006, s 1272, Sch 15, Pt 1, paras 1, 5; came into force 8 November 2006.

(4) Any person who fails to comply with section 81 is liable to pay compensation to any person who has—

(a) acquired securities of the kind in question; and

(b) suffered loss in respect of them as a result of the failure.

(5) Subsection (4) is subject to exemptions provided by Schedule 10.

(6) This section does not affect any liability which may be incurred apart from this section.

(7) References in this section to the acquisition by a person of securities include references to his contracting to acquire them or any interest in them.

(8) No person shall, by reason of being a promoter of a company or otherwise, incur any liability for failing to disclose information which he would not be required to disclose in listing particulars in respect of a company's securities—

(a) if he were responsible for those particulars; or

(b) if he is responsible for them, which he is entitled to omit by virtue of section 82.

(9) The reference in subsection (8) to a person incurring liability includes a reference to any other person being entitled as against that person to be granted any civil remedy or to rescind or repudiate an agreement.

(10) "Listing particulars", in subsection (1) and Schedule 10, includes supplementary listing particulars.

[(11) This section applies in relation to a prospectus as it applies to listing particulars, with the following modifications—

(a) references in this section or in Schedule 10 to listing particulars, supplementary listing particulars or sections 80, 81 or 82 are to be read, respectively, as references to a prospectus, supplementary prospectus and sections 87A, 87G and 87B;

(b) references in Schedule 10 to admission to the official list are to be read as references to admission to trading on a regulated market;

(c) in relation to a prospectus, "securities" means "transferable securities".

(12) A person is not to be subject to civil liability solely on the basis of a summary in a prospectus unless the summary is misleading, inaccurate or inconsistent when read with the rest of the prospectus; and, in this subsection, a summary includes any translation of it.][89]

[90A Compensation for statements in certain publications][90]

[(1) The publications to which this section applies are—

(a) any reports and statements published in response to a requirement imposed by a provision implementing Article 4, 5 or 6 of the transparency obligations directive, and

(b) any preliminary statement made in advance of a report or statement to be published in response to a requirement imposed by a provision implementing Article 4 of that directive, to the extent that it contains information that it is intended—

(i) will appear in the report or statement, and

(ii) will be presented in the report or statement in substantially the same form as that in which it is presented in the preliminary statement.

(2) The securities to which this section applies are—

(a) securities that are traded on a regulated market situated or operating in the United Kingdom, and

(b) securities that—

(i) are traded on a regulated market situated or operating outside the United Kingdom, and

(ii) are issued by an issuer for which the United Kingdom is the home Member State within the meaning of Article 2.1(i) of the transparency obligations directive.

---

[89] Inserted by SI 2005/1433, reg 2(1), Sch 1, para 6(1), (2); came into force 1 July 2005.

[90] Inserted by the Companies Act 2006, s 1270; came into force 8 November 2006.

(3) The issuer of securities to which this section applies is liable to pay compensation to a person who has—
  (a) acquired such securities issued by it, and
  (b) suffered loss in respect of them as a result of—
    (i) any untrue or misleading statement in a publication to which this section applies, or
    (ii) the omission from any such publication of any matter required to be included in it.

(4) The issuer is so liable only if a person discharging managerial responsibilities within the issuer in relation to the publication—
  (a) knew the statement to be untrue or misleading or was reckless as to whether it was untrue or misleading, or
  (b) knew the omission to be dishonest concealment of a material fact.

(5) A loss is not regarded as suffered as a result of the statement or omission in the publication unless the person suffering it acquired the relevant securities—
  (a) in reliance on the information in the publication, and
  (b) at a time when, and in circumstances in which, it was reasonable for him to rely on that information.

(6) Except as mentioned in subsection (8)—
  (a) the issuer is not subject to any other liability than that provided for by this section in respect of loss suffered as a result of reliance by any person on—
    (i) an untrue or misleading statement in a publication to which this section applies, or
    (ii) the omission from any such publication of any matter required to be included in it, and
  (b) a person other than the issuer is not subject to any liability, other than to the issuer, in respect of any such loss.

(7) Any reference in subsection (6) to a person being subject to a liability includes a reference to another person being entitled as against him to be granted any civil remedy or to rescind or repudiate an agreement.

(8) This section does not affect—
  (a) the powers conferred by section 382 and 384 (powers of the court to make a restitution order and of the Authority to require restitution);
  (b) liability for a civil penalty;
  (c) liability for a criminal offence.

(9) For the purposes of this section—
  (a) the following are persons "discharging managerial responsibilities" in relation to a publication—
    (i) any director of the issuer (or person occupying the position of director, by whatever name called),
    (ii) in the case of an issuer whose affairs are managed by its members, any member of the issuer,
    (iii) in the case of an issuer that has no persons within sub- paragraph (i) or (ii), any senior executive of the issuer having responsibilities in relation to the publication;
  (b) references to the acquisition by a person of securities include his contracting to acquire them or any interest in them.]

[90B Power to make further provision about liability for published information][91]

[(1) The Treasury may by regulations make provision about the liability of issuers of securities traded on a regulated market, and other persons, in respect of information published to holders of securities, to the market or to the public generally.

(2) Regulations under this section may amend any primary or subordinate legislation, including any provision of, or made under, this Act.]

---

[91] Inserted by the Companies Act 2006, s 1270; came into force 8 November 2006.

Penalties

91 [Penalties for breach of Part 6 rules][92]

[[(1) If the competent authority considers that—

    (a) an issuer of listed securities, or

    (b) an applicant for listing,

has contravened any provision of listing rules, it may impose on him a penalty of such amount as it considers appropriate.

(1ZA) If the competent authority considers that—

    (a) an issuer who has requested or approved the admission of a financial instrument to trading on a regulated market,

    (b) a person discharging managerial responsibilities within such an issuer, or

    (c) a person connected with such a person discharging managerial responsibilities,

has contravened any provision of disclosure rules, it may impose on him a penalty of such amount as it considers appropriate.][93]

[(1A) If the competent authority considers that—

    (a) an issuer of transferable securities,

    (b) a person offering transferable securities to the public or requesting their admission to trading on a regulated market,

    (c) an applicant for the approval of a prospectus in relation to transferable securities,

    (d) a person on whom a requirement has been imposed under section 87K or 87L, or

    (e) any other person to whom a provision of the prospectus directive applies,

has contravened a provision of this Part or of prospectus rules, or a provision otherwise made in accordance with the prospectus directive or a requirement imposed on him under such a provision, it may impose on him a penalty of such amount as it considers appropriate.][94]

[(1B) If the competent authority considers—

    (a) that a person has contravened—

        (i) a provision of transparency rules or a provision otherwise made in accordance with the transparency obligations directive, or

        (ii) a provision of corporate governance rules, or

    (b) that a person on whom a requirement has been imposed under section 89L (power to suspend or prohibit trading of securities in case of infringement of applicable transparency obligation), has contravened that requirement,

it may impose on the person a penalty of such amount as it considers appropriate.][95]

(2) If, in the case of a contravention [by a person][96] referred to in subsection [(1), (1ZA)(a), (1A) or (1B)][97] [("P")],[98] the competent authority considers that [another person][99] who was at the material time a director of [P][100] was knowingly concerned in the contravention, it may impose upon him a penalty of such amount as it considers appropriate.][101]

---

[92] Substituted by SI 2005/1433, reg 2(1), Sch 1, para 7(1), (4); came into force 1 July 2005.

[93] Substituted by the Companies Act 2006, s 1272, Sch 15, Pt 1, paras 1, 6(1), (2); came into force 8 November 2006.

[94] Inserted by SI 2005/1433, reg 2(1), Sch 1, para 7(1), (2); came into force 1 July 2005.

[95] Inserted by the Companies Act 2006, s 1272, Sch 15, Pt 1, paras 1, 6(1), (3); came into force 8 November 2006.

[96] Substituted by SI 2005/1433, reg 2(1), Sch 1, para 7(1), (3)(a); came into force 1 July 2005.

[97] Substituted by the Companies Act 2006, s 1272, Sch 15, Pt 1, para 6(1), (4); came into force 8 November 2006.

[98] Substituted by SI 2005/1433, reg 2(1), Sch 1, para 7(1), (3)(b); came into force 1 July 2005.

[99] Substituted by SI 2005/1433, reg 2(1), Sch 1, para 7(1), (3)(c); came into force 1 July 2005.

[100] Substituted by SI 2005/1433, reg 2(1), Sch 1, para 7(1), (3)(d); came into force 1 July 2005.

[101] Substituted by SI 2005/381, reg 4, Sch 1, para 4; came into force 1 July 2005.

(3) If the competent authority is entitled to impose a penalty on a person under this section in respect of a particular matter it may, instead of imposing a penalty on him in respect of that matter, publish a statement censuring him.

(4) Nothing in this section prevents the competent authority from taking any other steps which it has power to take under this Part.

(5) A penalty under this section is payable to the competent authority.

(6) The competent authority may not take action against a person under this section after the end of the period of two years beginning with the first day on which it knew of the contravention unless proceedings against that person, in respect of the contravention, were begun before the end of that period.

(7) For the purposes of subsection (6)—

    (a) the competent authority is to be treated as knowing of a contravention if it has information from which the contravention can reasonably be inferred; and

    (b) proceedings against a person in respect of a contravention are to be treated as begun when a warning notice is given to him under section 92.

92 Procedure

(1) If the competent authority proposes to take action against a person under section 91, it must give him a warning notice.

(2) A warning notice about a proposal to impose a penalty must state the amount of the proposed penalty.

(3) A warning notice about a proposal to publish a statement must set out the terms of the proposed statement.

(4) If the competent authority decides to take action against a person under section 91, it must give him a decision notice.

(5) A decision notice about the imposition of a penalty must state the amount of the penalty.

(6) A decision notice about the publication of a statement must set out the terms of the statement.

(7) If the competent authority decides to take action against a person under section 91, he may refer the matter to the Tribunal.

93 Statement of policy

(1) The competent authority must prepare and issue a statement ("its policy statement") of its policy with respect to—

    (a) the imposition of penalties under section 91; and

    (b) the amount of penalties under that section.

(2) The competent authority's policy in determining what the amount of a penalty should be must include having regard to—

    (a) the seriousness of the contravention in question in relation to the nature of the requirement contravened;

    (b) the extent to which that contravention was deliberate or reckless; and

    (c) whether the person on whom the penalty is to be imposed is an individual.

(3) The competent authority may at any time alter or replace its policy statement.

(4) If its policy statement is altered or replaced, the competent authority must issue the altered or replacement statement.

(5) In exercising, or deciding whether to exercise, its power under section 91 in the case of any particular contravention, the competent authority must have regard to any policy statement published under this section and in force at the time when the contravention in question occurred.

(6) The competent authority must publish a statement issued under this section in the way appearing to the competent authority to be best calculated to bring it to the attention of the public.

(7) The competent authority may charge a reasonable fee for providing a person with a copy of the statement.

(8) The competent authority must, without delay, give the Treasury a copy of any policy statement which it publishes under this section.

94 Statements of policy: procedure

(1) Before issuing a statement under section 93, the competent authority must publish a draft of the proposed statement in the way appearing to the competent authority to be best calculated to bring it to the attention of the public.

(2) The draft must be accompanied by notice that representations about the proposal may be made to the competent authority within a specified time.

(3) Before issuing the proposed statement, the competent authority must have regard to any representations made to it in accordance with subsection (2).

(4) If the competent authority issues the proposed statement it must publish an account, in general terms, of—
  (a) the representations made to it in accordance with subsection (2); and
  (b) its response to them.

(5) If the statement differs from the draft published under subsection (1) in a way which is, in the opinion of the competent authority, significant, the competent authority must (in addition to complying with subsection (4)) publish details of the difference.

(6) The competent authority may charge a reasonable fee for providing a person with a copy of a draft published under subsection (1).

(7) This section also applies to a proposal to alter or replace a statement.

Competition

95 Competition scrutiny

(1) The Treasury may by order provide for—
  (a) regulating provisions, and
  (b) the practices of the competent authority in exercising its functions under this Part ("practices"),
to be kept under review.

(2) Provision made as a result of subsection (1) must require the person responsible for keeping regulating provisions and practices under review to consider—
  (a) whether any regulating provision or practice has a significantly adverse effect on competition; or
  (b) whether two or more regulating provisions or practices taken together have, or a particular combination of regulating provisions and practices has, such an effect.

(3) An order under this section may include provision corresponding to that made by any provision of Chapter III of Part X.

(4) Subsection (3) is not to be read as in any way restricting the power conferred by subsection (1).

(5) Subsections (6) to (8) apply for the purposes of provision made by or under this section.

(6) Regulating provisions or practices have a significantly adverse effect on competition if—
  (a) they have, or are intended or likely to have, that effect; or
  (b) the effect that they have, or are intended or likely to have, is to require or encourage behaviour which has, or is intended or likely to have, a significantly adverse effect on competition.

(7) If regulating provisions or practices have, or are intended or likely to have, the effect of requiring or encouraging exploitation of the strength of a market position they are to be taken to have, or be intended or be likely to have, an adverse effect on competition.

(8) In determining whether any of the regulating provisions or practices have, or are intended or likely to have, a particular effect, it may be assumed that the persons to whom the provisions concerned are addressed will act in accordance with them.

(9) "Regulating provisions" means—

  (a) [Part 6 rules],[102]

  (b) general guidance given by the competent authority in connection with its functions under this Part.

MISCELLANEOUS

96 Obligations of issuers of listed securities

(1) Listing rules may—

  (a) specify requirements to be complied with by issuers of listed securities; and

  (b) make provision with respect to the action that may be taken by the competent authority in the event of non-compliance.

(2) If the rules require an issuer to publish information, they may include provision authorising the competent authority to publish it in the event of his failure to do so.

(3) This section applies whenever the listed securities were admitted to the official list.

[96A Disclosure of information requirements][103]

[(1) Disclosure rules must include provision specifying the disclosure of information requirements to be complied with by—

  (a) issuers who have requested or approved admission of their financial instruments to trading on a regulated market in the United Kingdom;

  (b) persons acting on behalf of or for the account of such issuers;

  (c) persons discharging managerial responsibilities within an issuer—

    (i) who is registered in the United Kingdom and who has requested or approved admission of its shares to trading on a regulated market; or

    (ii) who is not registered in the United Kingdom or any other EEA State but who has requested or approved admission of its shares to trading on a regulated market and who is required to file annual information in relation to the shares in the United Kingdom in accordance with Article 10 of the prospectus directive;

  (d) persons connected to such persons discharging managerial responsibilities.

(2) The rules must in particular—

  (a) require an issuer to publish specified inside information;

  (b) require an issuer to publish any significant change concerning information it has already published in accordance with paragraph (a);

  (c) allow an issuer to delay the publication of inside information in specified circumstances;

  (d) require an issuer (or a person acting on his behalf or for his account) who discloses inside information to a third party to publish that information without delay in specified circumstances;

  (e) require an issuer (or person acting on his behalf or for his account) to draw up a list of those persons working for him who have access to inside information relating directly or indirectly to that issuer; and

---

[102] Substituted by SI 2005/381, reg 4, Sch 1, para 5; came into force 1 July 2005.

[103] Inserted by SI 2005/381, reg 4, Sch 1, para 6; came into force 17 March 2005.

(f) require persons discharging managerial responsibilities within an issuer falling within sub-section (1)(c)(i) or (ii), and persons connected to such persons discharging managerial responsibilities, to disclose transactions conducted on their own account in shares of the issuer, or derivatives or any other financial instrument relating to those shares.

(3) Disclosure rules may make provision with respect to the action that may be taken by the competent authority in respect of non-compliance.]

[96B Disclosure rules: persons responsible for compliance][104] [105]

[(1) [For the purposes of the provisions of this Part relating to disclosure rules],[106] a "person discharging managerial responsibilities within an issuer" means—

(a) a director of an issuer falling within section 96A(1)(c)(i) or (ii); or

(b) a senior executive of such an issuer who—

    (i) has regular access to inside information relating, directly or indirectly, to the issuer, and

    (ii) has power to make managerial decisions affecting the future development and business prospects of the issuer.

(2) A person "connected" with a person discharging managerial responsibilities within an issuer means—

(a) a "connected person" within the meaning in section 346 of the Companies Act 1985 (reading that section as if any reference to a director of a company were a reference to a person discharging managerial responsibilities within an issuer);

(b) a relative of a person discharging managerial responsibilities within an issuer, who, on the date of the transaction in question, has shared the same household as that person for at least 12 months;

(c) a body corporate in which—

    (i) a person discharging managerial responsibilities within an issuer, or

    (ii) any person connected with him by virtue of subsection (a) or (b),

is a director or a senior executive who has the power to make management decisions affecting the future development and business prospects of that body corporate.]

[96C Suspension of trading][107]

[(1) The competent authority may, in accordance with disclosure rules, suspend trading in a financial instrument.

(2) If the competent authority does so, the issuer of that financial instrument may refer the matter to the Tribunal.

(3) The provisions relating to suspension of listing of securities in section 78 apply to the suspension of trading in a financial instrument and the references to listing and securities are to be read as references to trading and financial instruments respectively for the purposes of this section.]

97 Appointment by competent authority of persons to carry out investigations

(1) Subsection (2) applies if it appears to the competent authority that there are circumstances suggesting that—

[(a) there may have been a contravention of—

    (i) a provision of this Part or of Part 6 rules, or

    (ii) a provision otherwise made in accordance with the prospectus directive or the transparency obligations directive;

---

[104] Inserted by SI 2005/381, reg 4, Sch 1, para 6; came into force 17 March 2005.

[105] Section heading substituted by the Companies Act 2006, s 1272, Sch 15, Pt 1, paras 1, 7(a); came into force 8 November 2006.

[106] Substituted by the Companies Act 2006, s 1272, Sch 15, Pt 1, paras 1, 7(b); came into force 8 November 2006.

[107] Inserted by SI 2005/381, reg 4, Sch 1, para 6; came into force 17 March 2005.

(b) a person who was at the material time a director of a person mentioned in section 91(1), (1ZA)(a), (1A) or (1B) has been knowingly concerned in a contravention by that person of—
  (i) a provision of this Part or of Part 6 rules, or
  (ii) a provision otherwise made in accordance with the prospectus directive or the transparency obligations directive;][108]
(c) . . .[109]
(d) there may have been a contravention of section 83, 85[, 87G][110] or 98.

(2) The competent authority may appoint one or more competent persons to conduct an investigation on its behalf.

(3) Part XI applies to an investigation under subsection (2) as if—
  (a) the investigator were appointed under section 167(1);
  (b) references to the investigating authority in relation to him were to the competent authority;
  (c) references to the offences mentioned in section 168 were to those mentioned in subsection (1)(d);
  (d) references to an authorised person were references to the person under investigation.

98 . . .

. . .[111]

99 Fees

(1) Listing rules may require the payment of fees to the competent authority in respect of—
  (a) applications for listing;
  (b) the continued inclusion of securities in the official list;
  (c) applications under section 88 for approval as a sponsor; and
  (d) continued inclusion of sponsors in the list of sponsors.

[(1A) Disclosure rules may require the payment of fees to the competent authority in respect of the continued admission of financial instruments to trading on a regulated market.][112]

[(1B) Prospectus rules may require the payment of fees to the competent authority in respect of—
  (a) applications for approval of a prospectus or a supplementary prospectus;
  (b) applications for inclusion in the register of investors;
  (c) the continued inclusion of investors in that register;
  (d) access to that register.][113]

[(1C) Transparency rules may require the payment of fees to the competent authority in respect of the continued admission of financial instruments to trading on a regulated market.][114]

(2) In exercising its powers under subsection (1), the competent authority may set such fees as it considers will (taking account of the income it expects as the competent authority) enable it—
  (a) to meet expenses incurred in carrying out its functions under this Part or for any incidental purpose;
  (b) to maintain adequate reserves; and

---

[108] Substituted by the Companies Act 2006, s 1272, Sch 15, Pt 1, paras 1, 8; came into force 8 November 2006.

[109] Repealed by SI 2005/381, reg 4, Sch 1, para 7(c); came into force 1 July 2005.

[110] Inserted by SI 2005/1433, reg 2(1), Sch 1, para 8(c); came into force 1 July 2005.

[111] Repealed by SI 2005/1433, reg 2(1), Sch 1, para 9; came into force 1 July 2005.

[112] Inserted by SI 2005/381, reg 4, Sch 1, para 8; came into force 1 July 2005.

[113] Inserted by SI 2005/1433, reg 2(1), Sch 1, para 10; came into force 1 July 2005.

[114] Inserted by the Companies Act 2006, s 1272, Sch 15, Pt 1, paras 1, 9; came into force 8 November 2006.

    (c) in the case of the Authority, to repay the principal of, and pay any interest on, any money which it has borrowed and which has been used for the purpose of meeting expenses incurred in relation to—

        (i) its assumption of functions from the London Stock Exchange Limited in relation to the official list; and

        (ii) its assumption of functions under this Part.

(3) In fixing the amount of any fee which is to be payable to the competent authority, no account is to be taken of any sums which it receives, or expects to receive, by way of penalties imposed by it under this Part.

(4) Subsection (2)(c) applies whether expenses were incurred before or after the coming into force of this Part.

(5) Any fee which is owed to the competent authority under any provision made by or under this Part may be recovered as a debt due to it.

100 Penalties

(1) In determining its policy with respect to the amount of penalties to be imposed by it under this Part, the competent authority must take no account of the expenses which it incurs, or expects to incur, in discharging its functions under this Part.

(2) The competent authority must prepare and operate a scheme for ensuring that the amounts paid to it by way of penalties imposed under this Part are applied for the benefit of issuers of securities admitted to the official list[, and issuers who have requested or approved the admission of financial instruments to trading on a regulated market].[115]

(3) The scheme may, in particular, make different provision with respect to different classes of issuer.

(4) Up to date details of the scheme must be set out in a document ("the scheme details").

(5) The scheme details must be published by the competent authority in the way appearing to it to be best calculated to bring them to the attention of the public.

(6) Before making the scheme, the competent authority must publish a draft of the proposed scheme in the way appearing to it to be best calculated to bring it to the attention of the public.

(7) The draft must be accompanied by notice that representations about the proposals may be made to the competent authority within a specified time.

(8) Before making the scheme, the competent authority must have regard to any representations made to it under subsection (7).

(9) If the competent authority makes the proposed scheme, it must publish an account, in general terms, of—

    (a) the representations made to it in accordance with subsection (7); and

    (b) its response to them.

(10) If the scheme differs from the draft published under subsection (6) in a way which is, in the opinion of the competent authority, significant the competent authority must (in addition to complying with subsection (9)) publish details of the difference.

(11) The competent authority must, without delay, give the Treasury a copy of any scheme details published by it.

(12) The competent authority may charge a reasonable fee for providing a person with a copy of—

    (a) a draft published under subsection (6);

    (b) scheme details.

(13) Subsections (6) to (10) and (12) apply also to a proposal to alter or replace the scheme.

---

[115] Inserted by SI 2005/381, reg 4, Sch 1, para 9; came into force 1 July 2005.

[100A Exercise of powers where UK is host member state][116]

[(1) This section applies to the exercise by the competent authority of any power under this Part exercisable in case of infringement of—

(a) a provision of prospectus rules or any other provision made in accordance with the prospectus directive, or

(b) a provision of transparency rules or any other provision made in accordance with the transparency obligations directive,

in relation to an issuer whose home State is a member State other than the United Kingdom.

(2) The competent authority may act in such a case only in respect of the infringement of a provision required by the relevant directive.

Any reference to an applicable provision or applicable transparency obligation shall be read accordingly.

(3) If the authority finds that there has been such an infringement, it must give a notice to that effect to the competent authority of the person's home State requesting it—

(a) to take all appropriate measures for the purpose of ensuring that the person remedies the situation that has given rise to the notice, and

(b) to inform the authority of the measures it proposes to take or has taken or the reasons for not taking such measures.

(4) The authority may not act further unless satisfied—

(a) that the competent authority of the person's home State has failed or refused to take measures for the purpose mentioned in subsection (3)(a), or

(b) that the measures taken by that authority have proved inadequate for that purpose.

This does not affect exercise of the powers under section 87K(2), 87L(2) or (3) or 89L(2) or (3) (powers to protect market).

(5) If the authority is so satisfied, it must, after informing the competent authority of the person's home State, take all appropriate measures to protect investors.

(6) In such a case the authority must inform the Commission of the measures at the earliest opportunity.]

101 [Part 6 rules]:[117] general provisions

(1) [Part 6 rules][118] may make different provision for different cases.

(2) [Part 6 rules][119] may authorise the competent authority to dispense with or modify the application of the rules in particular cases and by reference to any circumstances.

(3) [Part 6 rules][120] must be made by an instrument in writing.

(4) Immediately after an instrument containing [Part 6 rules][121] is made, it must be printed and made available to the public with or without payment.

(5) A person is not to be taken to have contravened [any Part 6 rule][122] if he shows that at the time of the alleged contravention the instrument containing the rule had not been made available as required by subsection (4).

---

[116] Inserted by the Companies Act 2006, s 1271; came into force 8 November 2006.

[117] Substituted by virtue of SI 2005/381, reg 4, Sch 1, para 10(a); came into force 1 July 2005.

[118] Substituted by SI 2005/381, reg 4, Sch 1, para 10(a); came into force 1 July 2005.

[119] Substituted by SI 2005/381, reg 4, Sch 1, para 10(a); came into force 1 July 2005.

[120] Substituted by SI 2005/381, reg 4, Sch 1, para 10(a); came into force 1 July 2005.

[121] Substituted by SI 2005/381, reg 4, Sch 1, para 10(a); came into force 1 July 2005.

[122] Substituted by SI 2005/381, reg 4, Sch 1, para 10(b); came into force 1 July 2005.

(6) The production of a printed copy of an instrument purporting to be made by the competent authority on which is endorsed a certificate signed by an officer of the authority authorised by it for that purpose and stating—

(a) that the instrument was made by the authority,

(b) that the copy is a true copy of the instrument, and

(c) that on a specified date the instrument was made available to the public as required by subsection (4),

is evidence (or in Scotland sufficient evidence) of the facts stated in the certificate.

(7) A certificate purporting to be signed as mentioned in subsection (6) is to be treated as having been properly signed unless the contrary is shown.

(8) A person who wishes in any legal proceedings to rely on a rule-making instrument may require the Authority to endorse a copy of the instrument with a certificate of the kind mentioned in subsection (6).

102 Exemption from liability in damages

(1) Neither the competent authority nor any person who is, or is acting as, a member, officer or member of staff of the competent authority is to be liable in damages for anything done or omitted in the discharge, or purported discharge, of the authority's functions.

(2) Subsection (1) does not apply—

(a) if the act or omission is shown to have been in bad faith; or

(b) so as to prevent an award of damages made in respect of an act or omission on the ground that the act or omission was unlawful as a result of section 6(1) of the Human Rights Act 1998.

[Interpretative provisions][123]

[102A Meaning of "securities" etc][124]

[(1) This section applies for the purposes of this Part.

(2) "Securities" means (except in section 74(2) and the expression "transferable securities") anything which has been, or may be, admitted to the official list.

(3) "Transferable securities" means anything which is a transferable security for the purposes of [Directive 2004/39/EC of the European Parliament and of the Council on markets in financial instruments],[125] other than money-market instruments for the purposes of that directive which have a maturity of less than 12 months.

[(3A) "Debt securities" has the meaning given in Article 2.1(b) of the transparency obligations directive.][126]

(4) "Financial instrument" has [(except in section 89F)][127] the meaning given in Article 1.3 of Directive 2003/6/EC of the European Parliament and of the Council of 28 January 2003 on insider dealing and market manipulation [(as modified by Article 69 of Directive 2004/39/EC on markets in financial instruments)].[128]

---

[123] Substituted, together with ss 102A–102C, 103, for s 103 as originally enacted, by SI 2005/1433, reg 2(1), Sch 1, para 11; came into force 1 July 2005.

[124] Substituted, together with ss 102B, 102C, 103, for s 103 as originally enacted, by SI 2005/1433, reg 2(1), Sch 1, para 11; came into force 1 July 2005.

[125] Substituted by the Companies Act 2006, s 1272, Sch 15, Pt 1, paras 1, 10(1), (3); came into force 8 November 2006.

[126] Inserted by the Companies Act 2006, s 1272, Sch 15, Pt 1, paras 1, 10(1), (2); came in force 8 November 2006.

[127] Inserted by SI 2008/3053, art 3(1), (2)(a); came into force 31 January 2009.

[128] Inserted by SI 2008/3053, art 3(1), (2)(b); came into force 31 January 2009.

(5) "Non-equity transferable securities" means all transferable securities that are not equity securities; and for this purpose "equity securities" has the meaning given in Article 2.1(b) of the prospectus directive.

(6) "Issuer"—

    (a) in relation to an offer of transferable securities to the public or admission of transferable securities to trading on a regulated market for which an approved prospectus is required as a result of section 85, means a legal person who issues or proposes to issue the transferable securities in question,

    [(aa) in relation to transparency rules, means a legal person whose securities are admitted to trading on a regulated market or whose voting shares are admitted to trading on a UK market other than a regulated market, and in the case of depository receipts representing securities, the issuer is the issuer of the securities represented;][129]

    (b) in relation to anything else which is or may be admitted to the official list, has such meaning as may be prescribed by the Treasury, and

    (c) in any other case, means a person who issues financial instruments.]

[102B Meaning of "offer of transferable securities to the public" etc][130]

[(1) For the purposes of this Part there is an offer of transferable securities to the public if there is a communication to any person which presents sufficient information on—

    (a) the transferable securities to be offered, and

    (b) the terms on which they are offered,

to enable an investor to decide to buy or subscribe for the securities in question.

(2) For the purposes of this Part, to the extent that an offer of transferable securities is made to a person in the United Kingdom it is an offer of transferable securities to the public in the United Kingdom.

(3) The communication may be made—

    (a) in any form;

    (b) by any means.

(4) Subsection (1) includes the placing of securities through a financial intermediary.

(5) Subsection (1) does not include a communication in connection with trading on—

    (a) a regulated market;

    (b) a multilateral trading facility; or

    (c) a market prescribed by an order under section 130A(3).

(6) "Multilateral trading facility" means a multilateral system, operated by an investment firm . . .[131] or a market operator, which brings together multiple third-party buying and selling interests in financial instruments in accordance with non-discretionary rules so as to result in a contract.]

[102C Meaning of "home State" in relation to transferable securities][132]

[In this Part, in relation to an issuer of transferable securities, the "home-State" is the EEA State which is the "home Member State" for the purposes of the prospectus directive (which is to be determined in accordance with Article 2.1(m) of that directive).]

---

[129] Inserted by the Companies Act 2006, s 1272, Sch 15, Pt 1, paras 1, 10(1), (4); came into force 8 November 2006.

[130] Substituted, together with ss 102A, 102C, 103, for s 103 as originally enacted, by SI 2005/1433, reg 2(1), Sch 1, para 11; came into force 1 July 2005.

[131] Repealed by SI 2007/126, reg 3(5), Sch 5, paras 1, 6; came into force (for certain purposes) 1 April 2007; came into force (for remaining purposes) 1 November 2007.

[132] Substituted, together with ss 102A, 102B, 103, for s 103 as originally enacted, by SI 2005/1433, reg 2(1), Sch 1, para 11; came into force 1 July 2005.

[103 Interpretation of this Part][133]

[(1) In this Part, save where the context otherwise requires—

"disclosure rules" has the meaning given in section 73A;

"inside information" has the meaning given in section 118C;

"listed securities" means anything which has been admitted to the official list;

"listing" has the meaning given in section 74(5);

"listing particulars" has the meaning given in section 79(2);

"listing rules" has the meaning given in section 73A;

"market operator" means a person who manages or operates the business of a regulated market;

"offer of transferable securities to the public" has the meaning given in section 102B;

"the official list" means the list maintained by the competent authority as that list has effect for the time being;

"Part 6 rules" has the meaning given in section 73A;

"the prospectus directive" means Directive 2003/71/EC of the European Parliament and of the Council of 4 November 2003 on the prospectus to be published when securities are offered to the public or admitted to trading;

"prospectus rules" has the meaning given in section 73A;

"regulated market" has the meaning given in [Article 4.1(14) of Directive 2004/39/EC of the European Parliament and of the Council on markets in financial instruments];[134]

"supplementary prospectus" has the meaning given in section 87G;

["the transparency obligations directive" means Directive 2004/ 109/EC of the European Parliament and of the Council relating to the harmonisation of transparency requirements in relation to information about issuers whose securities are admitted to trading on a regulated market;][135]

["transparency rules" has the meaning given by section 89A(5);

"voteholder information" has the meaning given by section 89B(3);][136]

"working day" means any day other that a Saturday, a Sunday, Christmas Day, Good Friday or a day which is a bank holiday under the Banking and Financial Dealings Act 1971 (c 80) in any part of the United Kingdom.

(2) In relation to any function conferred on the competent authority by this Part, any reference in this Part to the competent authority is to be read as a reference to the person by whom that function is for the time being exercisable.

(3) If, as a result of an order under Schedule 8, different functions conferred on the competent authority by this Part are exercisable by different persons, the powers conferred by section 91 are exercisable by such person as may be determined in accordance with the provisions of the order.]

---

133 Substituted, together with ss 102A, 102B, 102C, for this section as originally enacted, by SI 2005/1433, reg 2(1), Sch 1, para 11; came into force 1 July 2005.

134 Substituted by the Companies Act 2006, s 1272, Sch 15, Pt 1, paras 1, 11(1), (2); came into force 1 October 2008.

135 Inserted by the Companies Act 2006, s 1265; came into force 8 November 2006.

136 Inserted by the Companies Act 2006, s 1272, Sch 15, Pt 1, paras 1, 11(1), (3); came into force 8 November 2006.

PART VII
CONTROL OF BUSINESS TRANSFERS

104 Control of business transfers

No insurance business transfer scheme or banking business transfer scheme is to have effect unless an order has been made in relation to it under section 111(1).

105 Insurance business transfer schemes

(1) A scheme is an insurance business transfer scheme if it—
- (a) satisfies one of the conditions set out in subsection (2);
- (b) results in the business transferred being carried on from an establishment of the transferee in an EEA State; and
- (c) is not an excluded scheme.

(2) The conditions are that—
- (a) the whole or part of the business carried on in one or more member States by a UK authorised person who has permission to effect or carry out contracts of insurance ("the authorised person concerned") is to be transferred to another body ("the transferee");
- (b) the whole or part of the business, so far as it consists of reinsurance, carried on in the United Kingdom through an establishment there by an EEA firm [falling within paragraph 5(d) of Schedule 3 and qualifying for authorisation under that Schedule]¹³⁷ ("the authorised person concerned") is to be transferred to another body ("the transferee");
- (c) the whole or part of the business carried on in the United Kingdom by an authorised person who is neither a UK authorised person nor an EEA firm but who has permission to effect or carry out contracts of insurance ("the authorised person concerned") is to be transferred to another body ("the transferee").

(3) A scheme is an excluded scheme for the purposes of this section if it falls within any of the following cases:

CASE 1

Where the authorised person concerned is a friendly society.

CASE 2

Where—
- (a) the authorised person concerned is a UK authorised person;
- [(aa) the authorised person concerned is not a reinsurance undertaking (within the meaning of Article 2.1(c) of the reinsurance directive);]¹³⁸
- (b) the business to be transferred under the scheme is business which consists of the effecting or carrying out of contracts of reinsurance in one or more EEA States other than the United Kingdom; and
- (c) the scheme has been approved by a court in an EEA State other than the United Kingdom or by the host state regulator.

CASE 3

Where—
- (a) the authorised person concerned is a UK authorised person;

---

¹³⁷ Substituted by SI 2007/3253, reg 2(1), Sch 1, paras 1, 2(1)(a); came into force 10 December 2007.
¹³⁸ Inserted by SI 2007/3253, reg 2(1), Sch 1, paras 1, 2(1)(b); came into force 10 December 2007.

    (b) the business to be transferred under the scheme is carried on in one or more countries or territories (none of which is an EEA State) and does not include policies of insurance . . .[139] against risks arising in an EEA State; and

    (c) the scheme has been approved by a court in a country or territory other than an EEA State or by the authority responsible for the supervision of that business in a country or territory in which it is carried on.

CASE 4

Where[—

    (a) the business to be transferred under the scheme is the whole of the business of the authorised person concerned,][140]

    (b) all the policyholders are controllers of the firm or of firms within the same group as the firm which is the transferee, and

    [(c)][141] all of the policyholders who will be affected by the transfer have consented to it.

[CASE 5

Where—

    (a) the business of the authorised person concerned consists solely of the effecting or carrying out of contracts of reinsurance;

    (b) the business to be transferred is the whole or part of that business;

    (c) the scheme does not fall within Case 4;

    (d) all of the policyholders who will be affected by the transfer have consented to it; and

    (e) a certificate has been obtained under paragraph 2 of Schedule 12 in relation to the proposed transfer.][142]

(4) The parties to a scheme which falls within Case 2, [3, 4 or 5][143] may apply to the court for an order sanctioning the scheme as if it were an insurance business transfer scheme.

[(5) If the scheme involves a compromise or arrangement falling within Part 27 of the Companies Act 2006 (mergers and divisions of public companies), the provisions of that Part (and Part 26 of that Act) apply accordingly but this does not affect the operation of this Part in relation to the scheme.][144]

(8) "UK authorised person" means a body which is an authorised person and which—

    (a) is incorporated in the United Kingdom; or

    (b) is an unincorporated association formed under the law of any part of the United Kingdom.

(9) "Establishment" means, in relation to a person, his head office or a branch of his.

106 Banking business transfer schemes

(1) A scheme is a banking business transfer scheme if it—

    (a) satisfies one of the conditions set out in subsection (2);

    (b) is one under which the whole or part of the business to be transferred includes the accepting of deposits; and

    (c) is not an excluded scheme.

---

[139] Repealed by SI 2007/3253, reg 2(1), Sch 1, paras 1, 2(1)(c); came into force 10 December 2007.

[140] Substituted by SI 2007/3253, reg 2(1), Sch 1, paras 1, 2(1)(d)(i); came into force 10 December 2007.

[141] Numbered as such by SI 2007/3253, reg 2(1), Sch 1, paras 1, 2(1)(d)(ii); came into force 10 December 2007.

[142] Inserted by SI 2007/3253, reg 2(1), Sch 1, paras 1, 2(1)(e); came into force 10 December 2007.

[143] Substituted by SI 2007/3253, reg 2(1), Sch 1, paras 1, 2(1)(f); came into force 10 December 2007.

[144] Substituted, for sub-ss (5)–(7) as originally enacted, by SI 2008/948, arts 3(1)(b), 6, Sch 1, Pt 2, para 211(1); came into force 6 April 2008.

(2) The conditions are that—
- (a) the whole or part of the business carried on by a UK authorised person who has permission to accept deposits ("the authorised person concerned") is to be transferred to another body ("the transferee");
- (b) the whole or part of the business carried on in the United Kingdom by an authorised person who is not a UK authorised person but who has permission to accept deposits ("the authorised person concerned") is to be transferred to another body which will carry it on in the United Kingdom ("the transferee").

(3) A scheme is an excluded scheme for the purposes of this section if—
- (a) the authorised person concerned is a building society or a credit union; or
- [(b) the scheme is a compromise or arrangement to which Part 27 of the Companies Act 2006 (mergers and divisions of public companies) applies].[145]

(4) For the purposes of subsection (2)(a) it is immaterial whether or not the business to be transferred is carried on in the United Kingdom.

(5) "UK authorised person" has the same meaning as in section 105.

(6) "Building society" has the meaning given in the Building Societies Act 1986.

(7) "Credit union" means a credit union within the meaning of—
- (a) the Credit Unions Act 1979;
- (b) the Credit Unions (Northern Ireland) Order 1985.

[106A Reclaim fund business transfer scheme][146]

[(1) A scheme is a reclaim fund business transfer scheme if, under the scheme, the whole or part of the business carried on by a reclaim fund is to be transferred to one or more other reclaim funds.

(2) "Reclaim fund" has the meaning given by section 5(1) of the Dormant Bank and Building Society Accounts Act 2008.]

107 Application for order sanctioning transfer scheme

(1) An application may be made to the court for an order sanctioning an insurance business transfer scheme[, a banking business transfer scheme or a reclaim fund business transfer scheme].[147]

(2) An application may be made by—
- (a) the authorised person concerned;
- (b) the transferee; or
- (c) both.

(3) The application must be made—
- (a) if the authorised person concerned and the transferee are registered or have their head offices in the same jurisdiction, to the court in that jurisdiction;
- (b) if the authorised person concerned and the transferee are registered or have their head offices in different jurisdictions, to the court in either jurisdiction;
- (c) if the transferee is not registered in the United Kingdom and does not have his head office there, to the court which has jurisdiction in relation to the authorised person concerned.

(4) "Court" means—
- (a) the High Court; or
- (b) in Scotland, the Court of Session.

---

[145] Substituted by SI 2008/948, arts 3(1)(b), 6, Sch 1, Pt 2, para 211(2); came into force 6 April 2008.

[146] Inserted by the Dormant Bank and Building Society Accounts Act 2008, s 15, Sch 2, para 2; came into force 12 March 2009.

[147] Substituted by the Dormant Bank and Building Society Accounts Act 2008, s 15, Sch 2, para 3; came into force 12 March 2009.

108 Requirements on applicants

(1) The Treasury may by regulations impose requirements on applicants under section 107.

(2) The court may not determine an application under that section if the applicant has failed to comply with a prescribed requirement.

(3) The regulations may, in particular, include provision—

(a) as to the persons to whom, and periods within which, notice of an application must be given;

(b) enabling the court to waive a requirement of the regulations in prescribed circumstances.

109 Scheme reports

(1) An application under section 107 in respect of an insurance business transfer scheme must be accompanied by a report on the terms of the scheme ("a scheme report").

(2) A scheme report may be made only by a person—

(a) appearing to the Authority to have the skills necessary to enable him to make a proper report; and

(b) nominated or approved for the purpose by the Authority.

(3) A scheme report must be made in a form approved by the Authority.

110 Right to participate in proceedings

On an application under section 107, the following are also entitled to be heard—

(a) the Authority, and

(b) any person (including an employee of the authorised person concerned or of the transferee) who alleges that he would be adversely affected by the carrying out of the scheme.

111 Sanction of the court for business transfer schemes

(1) This section sets out the conditions which must be satisfied before the court may make an order under this section sanctioning an insurance business transfer scheme[, a banking business transfer scheme or a reclaim fund business transfer scheme].[148]

(2) The court must be satisfied that—

(a) [in the case of an insurance business transfer scheme or a banking business transfer scheme,][149] the appropriate certificates have been obtained (as to which see Parts I and II of Schedule 12);

[(aa) in the case of a reclaim fund business transfer scheme, the appropriate certificate has been obtained (as to which see Part 2A of that Schedule);][150]

(b) the transferee has the authorisation required (if any) to enable the business, or part, which is to be transferred to be carried on in the place to which it is to be transferred (or will have it before the scheme takes effect).

(3) The court must consider that, in all the circumstances of the case, it is appropriate to sanction the scheme.

112 Effect of order sanctioning business transfer scheme

(1) If the court makes an order under section 111(1), it may by that or any subsequent order make such provision (if any) as it thinks fit—

(a) for the transfer to the transferee of the whole or any part of the undertaking concerned and of any property or liabilities of the authorised person concerned;

---

[148] Substituted by the Dormant Bank and Building Society Accounts Act 2008, s 15, Sch 2, para 4(1), (2); came into force 12 March 2009.

[149] Inserted by the Dormant Bank and Building Society Accounts Act 2008, s 15, Sch 2, para 4(1), (3)(a); came into force 12 March 2009.

[150] Inserted by the Dormant Bank and Building Society Accounts Act 2008, s 15, Sch 2, para 4(1), (3)(b); came into force 12 March 2009.

(b) for the allotment or appropriation by the transferee of any shares, debentures, policies or other similar interests in the transferee which under the scheme are to be allotted or appropriated to or for any other person;

(c) for the continuation by (or against) the transferee of any pending legal proceedings by (or against) the authorised person concerned;

(d) with respect to such incidental, consequential and supplementary matters as are, in its opinion, necessary to secure that the scheme is fully and effectively carried out.

(2) An order under subsection (1)(a) may—

(a) transfer property or liabilities whether or not the authorised person concerned otherwise has the capacity to effect the transfer in question;

(b) make provision in relation to property which was held by the authorised person concerned as trustee;

(c) make provision as to future or contingent rights or liabilities of the authorised person concerned, including provision as to the construction of instruments (including wills) under which such rights or liabilities may arise;

(d) make provision as to the consequences of the transfer in relation to any [occupational pension scheme (within the meaning of section 150(5) of the Finance Act 2004)][151] operated by or on behalf of the authorised person concerned.

[(2A) Subsection (2)(a) is to be taken to include power to make provision in an order—

(a) for the transfer of property or liabilities which would not otherwise be capable of being transferred or assigned;

(b) for a transfer of property or liabilities to take effect as if there were—

(i) no such requirement to obtain a person's consent or concurrence, and

(ii) no such contravention, liability or interference with any interest or right,

as there would otherwise be (in the case of a transfer apart from this section) by reason of any provision falling within subsection (2B).

(2B) A provision falls within this subsection to the extent that it has effect (whether under an enactment or agreement or otherwise) in relation to the terms on which the authorised person concerned is entitled to the property or subject to the liabilities in question.

(2C) Nothing in subsection (2A) or (2B) is to be read as limiting the scope of subsection (1).][152]

(3) If an order under subsection (1) makes provision for the transfer of property or liabilities—

(a) the property is transferred to and vests in, and

(b) the liabilities are transferred to and become liabilities of,

the transferee as a result of the order.

(4) But if any property or liability included in the order is governed by the law of any country or territory outside the United Kingdom, the order may require the authorised person concerned, if the transferee so requires, to take all necessary steps for securing that the transfer to the transferee of the property or liability is fully effective under the law of that country or territory.

(5) Property transferred as the result of an order under subsection (1) may, if the court so directs, vest in the transferee free from any charge which is (as a result of the scheme) to cease to have effect.

(6) An order under subsection (1) which makes provision for the transfer of property is to be treated as an instrument of transfer for the purposes of [section 770(1) of the Companies Act 2006][153] and any other enactment requiring the delivery of an instrument of transfer for the registration of property.

---

[151] Substituted by SI 2006/745, art 17; came into force 6 April 2006.
[152] Inserted by SI 2008/1468, reg 2(1); came into force 30 June 2008.
[153] Substituted by SI 2008/948, arts 3(1)(b), 6, Sch 1, Pt 2, para 211(3)(a); came into force 6 April 2008.

(7) . . .[154]

(8) If the court makes an order under section 111(1) in relation to an insurance business transfer scheme, it may by that or any subsequent order make such provision (if any) as it thinks fit—

  (a) for dealing with the interests of any person who, within such time and in such manner as the court may direct, objects to the scheme;

  (b) for the dissolution, without winding up, of the authorised person concerned;

  (c) for the reduction, on such terms and subject to such conditions (if any) as it thinks fit, of the benefits payable under—

    (i) any description of policy, or

    (ii) policies generally,

    entered into by the authorised person concerned and transferred as a result of the scheme.

(9) If, in the case of an insurance business transfer scheme, the authorised person concerned is not an EEA firm, it is immaterial for the purposes of subsection (1)(a), (c) or (d) or subsection (2), [(2A),][155] (3) or (4) that the law applicable to any of the contracts of insurance included in the transfer is the law of an EEA State other than the United Kingdom.

(10) The transferee must, if an insurance or banking business transfer scheme is sanctioned by the court, deposit two office copies of the order made under subsection (1) with the Authority within 10 days of the making of the order.

(11) But the Authority may extend that period.

(12) "Property" includes property, rights and powers of any description.

(13) "Liabilities" includes duties.

(14) "Shares" and "debentures" have the same meaning as in [the Companies Acts (see sections 540 and 738 of the Companies Act 2006)].[156]

(15) "Charge" includes a mortgage (or, in Scotland, a security over property).

[112A Rights to terminate etc][157]

[(1) Subsection (2) applies where (apart from that subsection) a person would be entitled, in consequence of anything done or likely to be done by or under this Part in connection with an insurance business transfer scheme or a banking business transfer scheme—

  (a) to terminate, modify, acquire or claim an interest or right; or

  (b) to treat an interest or right as terminated or modified.

(2) The entitlement—

  (a) is not enforceable in relation to that interest or right until after an order has been made under section 112(1) in relation to the scheme; and

  (b) is then enforceable in relation to that interest or right only insofar as the order contains provision to that effect.

(3) Nothing in subsection (1) or (2) is to be read as limiting the scope of section 112(1).]

113 Appointment of actuary in relation to reduction of benefits

(1) This section applies if an order has been made under section 111(1).

---

154 Repealed by SI 2008/948, art 3(1)(b), (2), Sch 1, Pt 2, para 211(3)(b), Sch 2; came into force 6 April 2008.

155 Inserted by SI 2008/1468, reg 2(2); came into force 30 June 2008.

156 Substituted, for paras (a), (b) as originally enacted, by SI 2008/948, arts 3(1)(b), 6, Sch 1, Pt 2, para 211(3)(c); came into force 6 April 2008.

157 Inserted by SI 2008/1468, reg 2(3); came into force 30 June 2008.

(2) The court making the order may, on the application of the Authority, appoint an independent actuary—

    (a) to investigate the business transferred under the scheme; and

    (b) to report to the Authority on any reduction in the benefits payable under policies entered into by the authorised person concerned that, in the opinion of the actuary, ought to be made.

114 Rights of certain policyholders

(1) This section applies in relation to an insurance business transfer scheme if—

    (a) the authorised person concerned is an authorised person other than an EEA firm qualifying for authorisation under Schedule 3;

    (b) the court has made an order under section 111 in relation to the scheme; and

    (c) an EEA State other than the United Kingdom is, as regards any policy included in the transfer which evidences a contract of insurance [(other than a contract of reinsurance)],[158] the State of the commitment or the EEA State in which the risk is situated ("the EEA State concerned").

(2) The court must direct that notice of the making of the order, or the execution of any instrument, giving effect to the transfer must be published by the transferee in the EEA State concerned.

(3) A notice under subsection (2) must specify such period as the court may direct as the period during which the policyholder may exercise any right which he has to cancel the policy.

(4) The order or instrument mentioned in subsection (2) does not bind the policyholder if—

    (a) the notice required under that subsection is not published; or

    (b) the policyholder cancels the policy during the period specified in the notice given under that subsection.

(5) The law of the EEA State concerned governs—

    (a) whether the policyholder has a right to cancel the policy; and

    (b) the conditions, if any, subject to which any such right may be exercised.

(6) Paragraph 6 of Schedule 12 applies for the purposes of this section as it applies for the purposes of that Schedule.

[114A Notice of transfer of reinsurance contracts][159]

[(1) This section applies in relation to an insurance business transfer scheme if—

    (a) the authorised person concerned is an authorised person other than an EEA firm qualifying for authorisation under Schedule 3;

    (b) the court has made an order under section 111 in relation to the scheme; and

    (c) an EEA State other than the United Kingdom is, as regards any policy included in the transfer which evidences a contract of reinsurance, the State in which the establishment of the policyholder to which the policy relates is situated at the date when the contract was entered into ("the EEA State concerned").

(2) The court may direct that notice of the making of the order, or the execution of any instrument, giving effect to the transfer must be published by the transferee in the EEA State concerned.]

---

[158] Inserted by SI 2007/3253, reg 2(1), Sch 1, paras 1, 2(2); came into force 10 December 2007.

[159] Inserted by SI 2007/3253, reg 2(1), Sch 1, paras 1, 2(3); came into force 10 December 2007.

Business transfers outside the United Kingdom

115 Certificates for purposes of insurance business transfers overseas

Part III of Schedule 12 makes provision about certificates which the Authority may issue in relation to insurance business transfers taking place outside the United Kingdom.

116 Effect of insurance business transfers authorised in other EEA States

(1) This section applies if, as a result of an authorised transfer, an EEA firm falling within paragraph 5(d) [or (da)][160] of Schedule 3 transfers to another body all its rights and obligations under any UK policies.

[(2) This section also applies if, as a result of an authorised transfer, any of the following transfers to another body all its rights and obligations under any UK policies—

  (a) an undertaking authorised in an EEA State other than the United Kingdom under Article 51 of the life assurance consolidation directive;

  (b) an undertaking authorised in an EEA State other than the United Kingdom under Article 23 of the first non-life insurance directive;

  (c) an undertaking, whose head office is not within the EEA, authorised under the law of an EEA State other than the United Kingdom to carry out reinsurance activities in its territory (as mentioned in Article 49 of the reinsurance directive).][161]

(3) If appropriate notice of the execution of an instrument giving effect to the transfer is published, the instrument has the effect in law—

  (a) of transferring to the transferee all the transferor's rights and obligations under the UK policies to which the instrument applies, and

  (b) if the instrument so provides, of securing the continuation by or against the transferee of any legal proceedings by or against the transferor which relate to those rights and obligations.

(4) No agreement or consent is required before subsection (3) has the effects mentioned.

(5) "Authorised transfer" means—

  (a) in subsection (1), a transfer authorised in the home State of the EEA firm in accordance with—

    [(i) Article 14 of the life assurance consolidation directive; . . .[162]][163]

    (ii) Article 12 of the third non-life directive; [or][164]

    [(iii) Article 18 of the reinsurance directive; and][165]

  (b) in subsection (2), a transfer authorised in an EEA State other than the United Kingdom in accordance with—

    [(i) Article 53 of the life assurance consolidation directive; . . .[166]][167]

    (ii) Article 28a of the first non-life directive[; or

    (iii) the provisions in the law of that EEA State which provide for the authorisation of transfers of all or part of a portfolio of contracts of an undertaking authorised to carry out reinsurance activities in its territory (as mentioned in Article 49 of the reinsurance directive)].[168]

---

[160] Inserted by SI 2007/3253, reg 2(1), Sch 1, paras 1, 2(4)(a); came into force 10 December 2007.
[161] Substituted by SI 2007/3253, reg 2(1), Sch 1, paras 1, 2(4)(b); came into force 10 December 2007.
[162] Repealed by SI 2007/3253, reg 2(1), Sch 1, paras 1, 2(4)(c)(i); came into force 10 December 2007.
[163] Substituted by SI 2004/3379, reg 6(1), (2)(b); came into force 11 January 2005.
[164] Substituted by SI 2007/3253, reg 2(1), Sch 1, paras 1, 2(4)(c)(ii); came into force 10 December 2007.
[165] Inserted by SI 2007/3253, reg 2(1), Sch 1, paras 1, 2(4)(c)(iii); came into force 10 December 2007.
[166] Repealed by SI 2007/3253, reg 2(1), Sch 1, paras 1, 2(4)(c)(iv); came into force 10 December 2007.
[167] Substituted by SI 2004/3379, reg 6(1), (2)(c); came into force 11 January 2005.
[168] Inserted by SI 2007/3253, reg 2(1), Sch 1, paras 1, 2(4)(c)(v); came into force 10 December 2007.

[(6) "UK policy" means—
  (a) in the case of an authorised transfer within the meaning of paragraph (a)(i) or (ii) or (b)(i) or (ii) of subsection (5), a policy evidencing a contract of insurance (other than a contract of reinsurance) to which the applicable law is the law of a part of the United Kingdom;
  (b) in the case of an authorised transfer within the meaning of paragraph (a)(iii) or (b)(iii) of that subsection, a policy evidencing a contract of reinsurance to which the applicable law is the law of a part of the United Kingdom.][169]

(7) "Appropriate notice" means—
  (a) if the UK policy evidences a contract of insurance in relation to which an EEA State other than the United Kingdom is the State of the commitment, notice given in accordance with the law of that State;
  (b) if the UK policy evidences a contract of insurance where the risk is situated in an EEA State other than the United Kingdom, notice given in accordance with the law of that EEA State;
  (c) in any other case, notice given in accordance with the applicable law.

(8) Paragraph 6 of Schedule 12 applies for the purposes of this section as it applies for the purposes of that Schedule.

Modifications

117 Power to modify this Part

The Treasury may by regulations—
  (a) provide for prescribed provisions of this Part to have effect in relation to prescribed cases with such modifications as may be prescribed;
  (b) make such amendments to any provision of this Part as they consider appropriate for the more effective operation of that or any other provision of this Part.

PART VIII
PENALTIES FOR MARKET ABUSE

Market abuse

[118 Market abuse][170]

[(1) For the purposes of this Act, market abuse is behaviour (whether by one person alone or by two or more persons jointly or in concert) which—
  (a) occurs in relation to—
     (i) qualifying investments admitted to trading on a prescribed market,
     (ii) qualifying investments in respect of which a request for admission to trading on such a market has been made, or
     (iii) in the case of subsection (2) or (3) behaviour, investments which are related investments in relation to such qualifying investments, and
  (b) falls within any one or more of the types of behaviour set out in subsections (2) to (8).

(2) The first type of behaviour is where an insider deals, or attempts to deal, in a qualifying investment or related investment on the basis of inside information relating to the investment in question.

---

[169] Substituted by SI 2007/3253, reg 2(1), Sch 1, paras 1, 2(4)(d); came into force 10 December 2007.
[170] Substituted, together with ss 118A–118C, for this section as originally enacted, by SI 2005/381, reg 5, Sch 2, para 1; came into force 1 July 2005.

(3) The second is where an insider discloses inside information to another person otherwise than in the proper course of the exercise of his employment, profession or duties.

(4) The third is where the behaviour (not falling within subsection (2) or (3))—

    (a) is based on information which is not generally available to those using the market but which, if available to a regular user of the market, would be, or would be likely to be, regarded by him as relevant when deciding the terms on which transactions in qualifying investments should be effected, and

    (b) is likely to be regarded by a regular user of the market as a failure on the part of the person concerned to observe the standard of behaviour reasonably expected of a person in his position in relation to the market.

(5) The fourth is where the behaviour consists of effecting transactions or orders to trade (otherwise than for legitimate reasons and in conformity with accepted market practices on the relevant market) which—

    (a) give, or are likely to give, a false or misleading impression as to the supply of, or demand for, or as to the price of, one or more qualifying investments, or

    (b) secure the price of one or more such investments at an abnormal or artificial level.

(6) The fifth is where the behaviour consists of effecting transactions or orders to trade which employ fictitious devices or any other form of deception or contrivance.

(7) The sixth is where the behaviour consists of the dissemination of information by any means which gives, or is likely to give, a false or misleading impression as to a qualifying investment by a person who knew or could reasonably be expected to have known that the information was false or misleading.

(8) The seventh is where the behaviour (not falling within subsection (5), (6) or (7))—

    (a) is likely to give a regular user of the market a false or misleading impression as to the supply of, demand for or price or value of, qualifying investments, or

    (b) would be, or would be likely to be, regarded by a regular user of the market as behaviour that would distort, or would be likely to distort, the market in such an investment,

and the behaviour is likely to be regarded by a regular user of the market as a failure on the part of the person concerned to observe the standard of behaviour reasonably expected of a person in his position in relation to the market.

(9) Subsections (4) and (8) and the definition of "regular user" in section 130A(3) cease to have effect on [31 December 2009][171] and subsection (1)(b) is then to be read as no longer referring to those subsections.]

[118A Supplementary provision about certain behaviour][172]

[(1) Behaviour is to be taken into account for the purposes of this Part only if it occurs—

    (a) in the United Kingdom, or

    (b) in relation to—

        (i) qualifying investments which are admitted to trading on a prescribed market situated in, or operating in, the United Kingdom,

        (ii) qualifying investments for which a request for admission to trading on such a prescribed market has been made, or

        (iii) in the case of section 118(2) and (3), investments which are related investments in relation to such qualifying investments.

---

[171] Substituted by SI 2008/1439, reg 3(1), (2); came into force 30 June 2008.

[172] Substituted, together with ss 118, 118B, 118C, for s 118 as originally enacted, by SI 2005/381, reg 5, Sch 2, para 1; came into force 1 July 2005.

(2) For the purposes of subsection (1), as it applies in relation to section 118(4) and (8), a prescribed market accessible electronically in the United Kingdom is to be treated as operating in the United Kingdom.

(3) For the purposes of section 118(4) and (8), the behaviour that is to be regarded as occurring in relation to qualifying investments includes behaviour which—

    (a) occurs in relation to anything that is the subject matter, or whose price or value is expressed by reference to the price or value of the qualifying investments, or

    (b) occurs in relation to investments (whether or not they are qualifying investments) whose subject matter is the qualifying investments.

(4) For the purposes of section 118(7), the dissemination of information by a person acting in the capacity of a journalist is to be assessed taking into account the codes governing his profession unless he derives, directly or indirectly, any advantage or profits from the dissemination of the information.

(5) Behaviour does not amount to market abuse for the purposes of this Act if—

    (a) it conforms with a rule which includes a provision to the effect that behaviour conforming with the rule does not amount to market abuse,

    (b) it conforms with the relevant provisions of Commission Regulation (EC) No 2273/2003 of 22 December 2003 implementing Directive 2003/6/EC of the European Parliament and of the Council as regards exemptions for buy-back programmes and stabilisation of financial instruments, or

    (c) it is done by a person acting on behalf of a public authority in pursuit of monetary policies or policies with respect to exchange rates or the management of public debt or foreign exchange reserves.

(6) Subsections (2) and (3) cease to have effect on [31 December 2009].[173]]

[118B Insiders][174]

[For the purposes of this Part an insider is any person who has inside information—

    (a) as a result of his membership of an administrative, management or supervisory body of an issuer of qualifying investments,

    (b) as a result of his holding in the capital of an issuer of qualifying investments,

    (c) as a result of having access to the information through the exercise of his employment, profession or duties,

    (d) as a result of his criminal activities, or

    (e) which he has obtained by other means and which he knows, or could reasonably be expected to know, is inside information.]

[118C Inside information][175]

[(1) This section defines "inside information" for the purposes of this Part.

(2) In relation to qualifying investments, or related investments, which are not commodity derivatives, inside information is information of a precise nature which—

    (a) is not generally available,

    (b) relates, directly or indirectly, to one or more issuers of the qualifying investments or to one or more of the qualifying investments, and

    (c) would, if generally available, be likely to have a significant effect on the price of the qualifying investments or on the price of related investments.

---

[173] Substituted by SI 2008/1439, reg 3(1), (3); came into force 30 June 2008.

[174] Substituted, together with ss 118, 118A, 118C, for s 118 as originally enacted, by SI 2005/381, reg 5, Sch 2, para 1; came into force 1 July 2005.

[175] Substituted, together with ss 118, 118A, 118B, for s 118 as originally enacted, by SI 2005/381, reg 5, Sch 2, para 1; came into force 1 July 2005.

(3) In relation to qualifying investments or related investments which are commodity derivatives, inside information is information of a precise nature which—

(a) is not generally available,

(b) relates, directly or indirectly, to one or more such derivatives, and

(c) users of markets on which the derivatives are traded would expect to receive in accordance with any accepted market practices on those markets.

(4) In relation to a person charged with the execution of orders concerning any qualifying investments or related investments, inside information includes information conveyed by a client and related to the client's pending orders which—

(a) is of a precise nature,

(b) is not generally available,

(c) relates, directly or indirectly, to one or more issuers of qualifying investments or to one or more qualifying investments, and

(d) would, if generally available, be likely to have a significant effect on the price of those qualifying investments or the price of related investments.

(5) Information is precise if it—

(a) indicates circumstances that exist or may reasonably be expected to come into existence or an event that has occurred or may reasonably be expected to occur, and

(b) is specific enough to enable a conclusion to be drawn as to the possible effect of those circumstances or that event on the price of qualifying investments or related investments.

(6) Information would be likely to have a significant effect on price if and only if it is information of a kind which a reasonable investor would be likely to use as part of the basis of his investment decisions.

(7) For the purposes of subsection (3)(c), users of markets on which investments in commodity derivatives are traded are to be treated as expecting to receive information relating directly or indirectly to one or more such derivatives in accordance with any accepted market practices, which is—

(a) routinely made available to the users of those markets, or

(b) required to be disclosed in accordance with any statutory provision, market rules, or contracts or customs on the relevant underlying commodity market or commodity derivatives market.

(8) Information which can be obtained by research or analysis conducted by, or on behalf of, users of a market is to be regarded, for the purposes of this Part, as being generally available to them.]

The code

119 The code

(1) The Authority must prepare and issue a code containing such provisions as the Authority considers will give appropriate guidance to those determining whether or not behaviour amounts to market abuse.

(2) The code may among other things specify—

(a) descriptions of behaviour that, in the opinion of the Authority, amount to market abuse;

(b) descriptions of behaviour that, in the opinion of the Authority, do not amount to market abuse;

(c) factors that, in the opinion of the Authority, are to be taken into account in determining whether or not behaviour amounts to market abuse;

[(d) descriptions of behaviour that are accepted market practices in relation to one or more specified markets;

(e) descriptions of behaviour that are not accepted market practices in relation to one or more specified markets].[176]

---

[176] Inserted by SI 2005/381, reg 5, Sch 2, para 2(1), (2); came into force 1 July 2005.

[(2A) In determining, for the purposes of subsections (2)(d) and (2)(e) or otherwise, what are and what are not accepted market practices, the Authority must have regard to the factors and procedures laid down in Articles 2 and 3 respectively of Commission Directive 2004/72/EC of 29 April 2004 implementing Directive 2003/6/EC of the European Parliament and of the Council.][177]

(3) The code may make different provision in relation to persons, cases or circumstances of different descriptions.

(4) The Authority may at any time alter or replace the code.

(5) If the code is altered or replaced, the altered or replacement code must be issued by the Authority.

(6) A code issued under this section must be published by the Authority in the way appearing to the Authority to be best calculated to bring it to the attention of the public.

(7) The Authority must, without delay, give the Treasury a copy of any code published under this section.

(8) The Authority may charge a reasonable fee for providing a person with a copy of the code.

120 Provisions included in the Authority's code by reference to the City Code

(1) The Authority may include in a code issued by it under section 119 ("the Authority's code") provision to the effect that in its opinion behaviour conforming with the City Code—
   (a) does not amount to market abuse;
   (b) does not amount to market abuse in specified circumstances; or
   (c) does not amount to market abuse if engaged in by a specified description of person.

(2) But the Treasury's approval is required before any such provision may be included in the Authority's code.

(3) If the Authority's code includes provision of a kind authorised by subsection (1), the Authority must keep itself informed of the way in which the Panel on Takeovers and Mergers interprets and administers the relevant provisions of the City Code.

(4) "City Code" means the City Code on Takeovers and Mergers issued by the Panel as it has effect at the time when the behaviour occurs.

(5) "Specified" means specified in the Authority's code.

121 Codes: procedure

(1) Before issuing a code under section 119, the Authority must publish a draft of the proposed code in the way appearing to the Authority to be best calculated to bring it to the attention of the public.

(2) The draft must be accompanied by—
   (a) a cost benefit analysis; and
   (b) notice that representations about the proposal may be made to the Authority within a specified time.

(3) Before issuing the proposed code, the Authority must have regard to any representations made to it in accordance with subsection (2)(b).

(4) If the Authority issues the proposed code it must publish an account, in general terms, of—
   (a) the representations made to it in accordance with subsection (2)(b); and
   (b) its response to them.

(5) If the code differs from the draft published under subsection (1) in a way which is, in the opinion of the Authority, significant—
   (a) the Authority must (in addition to complying with subsection (4)) publish details of the difference; and
   (b) those details must be accompanied by a cost benefit analysis.

---

[177] Inserted by SI 2005/381, reg 5, Sch 2, para 2(1), (3); came into force 1 July 2005.

(6) Subsections (1) to (5) do not apply if the Authority considers that there is an urgent need to publish the code.

(7) Neither subsection (2)(a) nor subsection (5)(b) applies if the Authority considers—

    (a) that, making the appropriate comparison, there will be no increase in costs; or

    (b) that, making that comparison, there will be an increase in costs but the increase will be of minimal significance.

(8) The Authority may charge a reasonable fee for providing a person with a copy of a draft published under subsection (1).

(9) This section also applies to a proposal to alter or replace a code.

(10) "Cost benefit analysis" means an estimate of the costs together with an analysis of the benefits that will arise—

    (a) if the proposed code is issued; or

    (b) if subsection (5)(b) applies, from the code that has been issued.

(11) "The appropriate comparison" means—

    (a) in relation to subsection (2)(a), a comparison between the overall position if the code is issued and the overall position if it is not issued;

    (b) in relation to subsection (5)(b), a comparison between the overall position after the issuing of the code and the overall position before it was issued.

122 Effect of the code

(1) If a person behaves in a way which is described (in the code in force under section 119 at the time of the behaviour) as behaviour that, in the Authority's opinion, does not amount to market abuse that behaviour of his is to be taken, for the purposes of this Act, as not amounting to market abuse.

(2) Otherwise, the code in force under section 119 at the time when particular behaviour occurs may be relied on so far as it indicates whether or not that behaviour should be taken to amount to market abuse.

Power to impose penalties

123 Power to impose penalties in cases of market abuse

(1) If the Authority is satisfied that a person ("A")—

    (a) is or has engaged in market abuse, or

    (b) by taking or refraining from taking any action has required or encouraged another person or persons to engage in behaviour which, if engaged in by A, would amount to market abuse,

it may impose on him a penalty of such amount as it considers appropriate.

(2) But the Authority may not impose a penalty on a person if, having considered any representations made to it in response to a warning notice, there are reasonable grounds for it to be satisfied that—

    (a) he believed, on reasonable grounds, that his behaviour did not fall within paragraph (a) or (b) of subsection (1), or

    (b) he took all reasonable precautions and exercised all due diligence to avoid behaving in a way which fell within paragraph (a) or (b) of that subsection.

(3) If the Authority is entitled to impose a penalty on a person under this section it may, instead of imposing a penalty on him, publish a statement to the effect that he has engaged in market abuse.

Statement of policy

124 Statement of policy

(1) The Authority must prepare and issue a statement of its policy with respect to—

    (a) the imposition of penalties under section 123; and

    (b) the amount of penalties under that section.

(2) The Authority's policy in determining what the amount of a penalty should be must include having regard to—

    (a) whether the behaviour in respect of which the penalty is to be imposed had an adverse effect on the market in question and, if it did, how serious that effect was;

    (b) the extent to which that behaviour was deliberate or reckless; and

    (c) whether the person on whom the penalty is to be imposed is an individual.

(3) A statement issued under this section must include an indication of the circumstances in which the Authority is to be expected to regard a person as—

    (a) having a reasonable belief that his behaviour did not amount to market abuse; or

    (b) having taken reasonable precautions and exercised due diligence to avoid engaging in market abuse.

(4) The Authority may at any time alter or replace a statement issued under this section.

(5) If a statement issued under this section is altered or replaced, the Authority must issue the altered or replacement statement.

(6) In exercising, or deciding whether to exercise, its power under section 123 in the case of any particular behaviour, the Authority must have regard to any statement published under this section and in force at the time when the behaviour concerned occurred.

(7) A statement issued under this section must be published by the Authority in the way appearing to the Authority to be best calculated to bring it to the attention of the public.

(8) The Authority may charge a reasonable fee for providing a person with a copy of a statement published under this section.

(9) The Authority must, without delay, give the Treasury a copy of any statement which it publishes under this section.

125 Statement of policy: procedure

(1) Before issuing a statement of policy under section 124, the Authority must publish a draft of the proposed statement in the way appearing to the Authority to be best calculated to bring it to the attention of the public.

(2) The draft must be accompanied by notice that representations about the proposal may be made to the Authority within a specified time.

(3) Before issuing the proposed statement, the Authority must have regard to any representations made to it in accordance with subsection (2).

(4) If the Authority issues the proposed statement it must publish an account, in general terms, of—

    (a) the representations made to it in accordance with subsection (2); and

    (b) its response to them.

(5) If the statement differs from the draft published under subsection (1) in a way which is, in the opinion of the Authority, significant, the Authority must (in addition to complying with subsection (4)) publish details of the difference.

(6) The Authority may charge a reasonable fee for providing a person with a copy of a draft published under subsection (1).

(7) This section also applies to a proposal to alter or replace a statement.

Procedure

126 Warning notices

(1) If the Authority proposes to take action against a person under section 123, it must give him a warning notice.

(2) A warning notice about a proposal to impose a penalty must state the amount of the proposed penalty.

(3) A warning notice about a proposal to publish a statement must set out the terms of the proposed statement.

127 Decision notices and right to refer to Tribunal

(1) If the Authority decides to take action against a person under section 123, it must give him a decision notice.

(2) A decision notice about the imposition of a penalty must state the amount of the penalty.

(3) A decision notice about the publication of a statement must set out the terms of the statement.

(4) If the Authority decides to take action against a person under section 123, that person may refer the matter to the Tribunal.

Miscellaneous

128 Suspension of investigations

(1) If the Authority considers it desirable or expedient because of the exercise or possible exercise of a power relating to market abuse, it may direct a recognised investment exchange or recognised clearing house—

    (a) to terminate, suspend or limit the scope of any inquiry which the exchange or clearing house is conducting under its rules; or

    (b) not to conduct an inquiry which the exchange or clearing house proposes to conduct under its rules.

(2) A direction under this section—

    (a) must be given to the exchange or clearing house concerned by notice in writing; and

    (b) is enforceable, on the application of the Authority, by injunction or, in Scotland, by an order under section 45 of the Court of Session Act 1988.

(3) The Authority's powers relating to market abuse are its powers—

    (a) to impose penalties under section 123; or

    (b) to appoint a person to conduct an investigation under section 168 in a case falling within subsection (2)(d) of that section.

129 Power of court to impose penalty in cases of market abuse

(1) The Authority may on an application to the court under section 381 or 383 request the court to consider whether the circumstances are such that a penalty should be imposed on the person to whom the application relates.

(2) The court may, if it considers it appropriate, make an order requiring the person concerned to pay to the Authority a penalty of such amount as it considers appropriate.

130 Guidance

(1) The Treasury may from time to time issue written guidance for the purpose of helping relevant authorities to determine the action to be taken in cases where behaviour occurs which is behaviour—

    (a) with respect to which the power in section 123 appears to be exercisable; and

    (b) which appears to involve the commission of an offence under section 397 of this Act or Part V of the Criminal Justice Act 1993 (insider dealing).

(2) The Treasury must obtain the consent of the Attorney General and the Secretary of State before issuing any guidance under this section.

(3) In this section "relevant authorities"—

    (a) in relation to England and Wales, means the Secretary of State, the Authority, the Director of the Serious Fraud Office and the Director of Public Prosecutions;

    (b) in relation to Northern Ireland, means the Secretary of State, the Authority, the Director of the Serious Fraud Office and the Director of Public Prosecutions for Northern Ireland.

(4) Subsections (1) to (3) do not apply to Scotland.

(5) In relation to Scotland, the Lord Advocate may from time to time, after consultation with the Treasury, issue written guidance for the purpose of helping the Authority to determine the action to be taken in cases where behaviour mentioned in subsection (1) occurs.

[130A Interpretation and supplementary provision][178]

[(1) The Treasury may by order specify (whether by name or description)—

    (a) the markets which are prescribed markets for the purposes of specified provisions of this Part, and

    (b) the investments that are qualifying investments in relation to the prescribed markets.

(2) An order may prescribe different investments or descriptions of investment in relation to different markets or descriptions of market.

(3) In this Part—

    "accepted market practices" means practices that are reasonably expected in the financial market or markets in question and are accepted by the Authority or, in the case of a market situated in another EEA State, the competent authority of that EEA State within the meaning of Directive 2003/6/EC of the European Parliament and of the Council of 28 January 2003 on insider dealing and market manipulation (market abuse),

    "behaviour" includes action or inaction,

    "dealing", in relation to an investment, means acquiring or disposing of the investment whether as principal or agent or directly or indirectly, and includes agreeing to acquire or dispose of the investment, and entering into and bringing to an end a contract creating it,

    "investment" is to be read with section 22 and Schedule 2,

    "regular user", in relation to a particular market, means a reasonable person who regularly deals on that market in investments of the kind in question,

    "related investment", in relation to a qualifying investment, means an investment whose price or value depends on the price or value of the qualifying investment.

(4) Any reference in this Act to a person engaged in market abuse is to a person engaged in market abuse either alone or with one or more other persons.]

131 Effect on transactions

The imposition of a penalty under this Part does not make any transaction void or unenforceable.

[131A Protected Disclosures][179]

[(1) A disclosure which satisfies the following three conditions is not to be taken to breach any restriction on the disclosure of information (however imposed).

(2) The first condition is that the information or other matter—

    (a) causes the person making the disclosure (the discloser) to know or suspect, or

    (b) gives him reasonable grounds for knowing or suspecting, that another person has engaged in market abuse.

(3) The second condition is that the information or other matter disclosed came to the discloser in the course of his trade, profession, business or employment.

(4) The third condition is that the disclosure is made to the Authority or to a nominated officer as soon as is practicable after the information or other matter comes to the discloser.

(5) A disclosure to a nominated officer is a disclosure which is made to a person nominated by the discloser's employer to receive disclosures under this section, and is made in the course of the discloser's employment and in accordance with the procedure established by the employer for the purpose.

(6) For the purposes of this section, references to a person's employer include any body, association or organisation (including a voluntary organisation) in connection with whose activities the person exercises a function (whether or not for gain or reward) and references to employment must be construed accordingly.]

---

[178] Inserted by SI 2005/381, reg 5, Sch 2, para 3; came into force 1 July 2005.
[179] Inserted by SI 2005/381, reg 5, Sch 2, para 4; came into force 1 July 2005.

PART IX
HEARINGS AND APPEALS

132 The Financial Services and Markets Tribunal

(1) For the purposes of this Act, there is to be a tribunal known as the Financial Services and Markets Tribunal (but referred to in this Act as "the Tribunal").

(2) The Tribunal is to have the functions conferred on it by or under this Act.

(3) The Lord Chancellor may by rules make such provision as appears to him to be necessary or expedient in respect of the conduct of proceedings before the Tribunal.

(4) Schedule 13 is to have effect as respects the Tribunal and its proceedings (but does not limit the Lord Chancellor's powers under this section).

133 Proceedings: general provision

(1) A reference to the Tribunal under this Act must be made before the end of—
   (a) the period of 28 days beginning with the date on which the decision notice or supervisory notice in question is given; or
   (b) such other period as may be specified in rules made under section 132.

(2) Subject to rules made under section 132, the Tribunal may allow a reference to be made after the end of that period.

(3) On a reference the Tribunal may consider any evidence relating to the subject-matter of the reference, whether or not it was available to the Authority at the material time.

(4) On a reference the Tribunal must determine what (if any) is the appropriate action for the Authority to take in relation to the matter referred to it.

(5) On determining a reference, the Tribunal must remit the matter to the Authority with such directions (if any) as the Tribunal considers appropriate for giving effect to its determination.

(6) In determining a reference made as a result of a decision notice, the Tribunal may not direct the Authority to take action which the Authority would not, as a result of section 388(2), have had power to take when giving the decision notice.

(7) In determining a reference made as a result of a supervisory notice, the Tribunal may not direct the Authority to take action which would have otherwise required the giving of a decision notice.

(8) The Tribunal may, on determining a reference, make recommendations as to the Authority's regulating provisions or its procedures.

(9) The Authority must not take the action specified in a decision notice—
   (a) during the period within which the matter to which the decision notice relates may be referred to the Tribunal; and
   (b) if the matter is so referred, until the reference, and any appeal against the Tribunal's determination, has been finally disposed of.

(10) The Authority must act in accordance with the determination of, and any direction given by, the Tribunal.

(11) An order of the Tribunal may be enforced—
   (a) as if it were an order of a county court; or
   (b) in Scotland, as if it were an order of the Court of Session.

(12) "Supervisory notice" has the same meaning as in section 395.

Legal assistance before the Tribunal

134 Legal assistance scheme

(1) The Lord Chancellor may by regulations establish a scheme governing the provision of legal assistance in connection with proceedings before the Tribunal.

(2) If the Lord Chancellor establishes a scheme under subsection (1), it must provide that a person is eligible for assistance only if—

(a) he falls within subsection (3); and

(b) he fulfils such other criteria (if any) as may be prescribed as a result of section 135(1)(d).

(3) A person falls within this subsection if he is an individual who has referred a matter to the Tribunal under section 127(4).

(4) In this Part of this Act "the legal assistance scheme" means any scheme in force under subsection (1).

135 Provisions of the legal assistance scheme

(1) The legal assistance scheme may, in particular, make provision as to—

(a) the kinds of legal assistance that may be provided;

(b) the persons by whom legal assistance may be provided;

(c) the manner in which applications for legal assistance are to be made;

(d) the criteria on which eligibility for legal assistance is to be determined;

(e) the persons or bodies by whom applications are to be determined;

(f) appeals against refusals of applications;

(g) the revocation or variation of decisions;

(h) its administration and the enforcement of its provisions.

(2) Legal assistance under the legal assistance scheme may be provided subject to conditions or restrictions, including conditions as to the making of contributions by the person to whom it is provided.

136 Funding of the legal assistance scheme

(1) The Authority must pay to the Lord Chancellor such sums at such times as he may, from time to time, determine in respect of the anticipated or actual cost of legal assistance provided in connection with proceedings before the Tribunal under the legal assistance scheme.

(2) In order to enable it to pay any sum which it is obliged to pay under subsection (1), the Authority must make rules requiring the payment to it by authorised persons or any class of authorised person of specified amounts or amounts calculated in a specified way.

(3) Sums received by the Lord Chancellor under subsection (1) must be paid into the Consolidated Fund.

(4) The Lord Chancellor must, out of money provided by Parliament fund the cost of legal assistance provided in connection with proceedings before the Tribunal under the legal assistance scheme.

(5) Subsection (6) applies if, as respects a period determined by the Lord Chancellor, the amount paid to him under subsection (1) as respects that period exceeds the amount he has expended in that period under subsection (4).

(6) The Lord Chancellor must—

(a) repay, out of money provided by Parliament, the excess to the Authority; or

(b) take the excess into account on the next occasion on which he makes a determination under subsection (1).

(7) The Authority must make provision for any sum repaid to it under subsection (6)(a)—

(a) to be distributed among—

(i) the authorised persons on whom a levy was imposed in the period in question as a result of rules made under subsection (2); or

(ii) such of those persons as it may determine;

(b) to be applied in order to reduce any amounts which those persons, or such of them as it may determine, are or will be liable to pay to the Authority, whether under rules made under subsection (2) or otherwise; or

(c) to be partly so distributed and partly so applied.

(8) If the Authority considers that it is not practicable to deal with any part of a sum repaid to it under subsection (6)(a) in accordance with provision made by it as a result of subsection (7), it may, with the consent the Lord Chancellor, apply or dispose of that part of that sum in such manner as it considers appropriate.

(9) "Specified" means specified in the rules.

Appeals

137 Appeal on a point of law

(1) A party to a reference to the Tribunal may with permission appeal—
   (a) to the Court of Appeal, or
   (b) in Scotland, to the Court of Session,
   on a point of law arising from a decision of the Tribunal disposing of the reference.

(2) "Permission" means permission given by the Tribunal or by the Court of Appeal or (in Scotland) the Court of Session.

(3) If, on an appeal under subsection (1), the court considers that the decision of the Tribunal was wrong in law, it may—
   (a) remit the matter to the Tribunal for rehearing and determination by it; or
   (b) itself make a determination.

(4) An appeal may not be brought from a decision of the Court of Appeal under subsection (3) except with the leave of—
   (a) the Court of Appeal; or
   (b) *the House of Lords*
   [(b) *the Supreme Court*].[180]

(5) An appeal lies, with the leave of the Court of Session or the *House of Lords* [*Supreme Court*][181], from any decision of the Court of Session under this section, and such leave may be given on such terms as to costs, expenses or otherwise as the Court of Session or the *House of Lords* [*Supreme Court*][182] may determine.

(6) Rules made under section 132 may make provision for regulating or prescribing any matters incidental to or consequential on an appeal under this section.

PART X
RULES AND GUIDANCE

CHAPTER I
RULE-MAKING POWERS

138 General rule-making power

(1) The Authority may make such rules applying to authorised persons—
   (a) with respect to the carrying on by them of regulated activities, or

---

[180] Substituted by the Constitutional Reform Act 2005, s 40(4), Sch 9, Pt 1, para 70(a); date in force to be appointed, see the Constitutional Reform Act 2005, s 148(1).

[181] Words in italics repealed and words in square brackets substituted by the Constitutional Reform Act 2005, s 40(4), Sch 9, Pt 1, para 70(b); date in force to be appointed: see the Constitutional Reform Act 2005, s 148(1).

[182] Words in italics repealed and words in square brackets substituted by the Constitutional Reform Act 2005, s 40(4), Sch 9, Pt 1, para 70(b); date in force to be appointed: see the Constitutional Reform Act 2005, s 148(1).

(b) with respect to the carrying on by them of activities which are not regulated activities,

as appear to it to be necessary or expedient for the purpose of protecting the interests of consumers.

[(1A) The Authority may also make such rules applying to authorised persons who are investment firms or credit institutions, with respect to the provision by them of a relevant ancillary service, as appear to the Authority to be necessary or expedient for the purpose of protecting the interests of consumers.

(1B) "Credit institution" means—

(a) a credit institution authorised under the banking consolidation directive, or

(b) an institution which would satisfy the requirements for authorisation as a credit institution under that directive if it had its registered office (or if it does not have a registered office, its head office) in an EEA State.

(1C) "Relevant ancillary service" means any service of a kind mentioned in Section B of Annex I to the markets in financial instruments directive the provision of which does not involve the carrying on of a regulated activity.][183]

(2) Rules made under this section are referred to in this Act as the Authority's general rules.

(3) The Authority's power to make general rules is not limited by any other power which it has to make regulating provisions.

(4) The Authority's general rules may make provision applying to authorised persons even though there is no relationship between the authorised persons to whom the rules will apply and the persons whose interests will be protected by the rules.

(5) General rules may contain requirements which take into account, in the case of an authorised person who is a member of a group, any activity of another member of the group.

(6) General rules may not—

(a) make provision prohibiting an EEA firm from carrying on, or holding itself out as carrying on, any activity which it has permission conferred by Part II of Schedule 3 to carry on in the United Kingdom;

(b) make provision, as respects an EEA firm, about any matter responsibility for which is, under any of the single market directives, reserved to the firm's home state regulator.

(7) "Consumers" means persons—

(a) who use, have used, or are or may be contemplating using, any of the services provided by—

(i) authorised persons in carrying on regulated activities; . . .[184]

[(ia) authorised persons who are investment firms or credit institutions in providing a relevant ancillary service; or][185]

(ii) persons acting as appointed representatives;

(b) who have rights or interests which are derived from, or are otherwise attributable to, the use of any such services by other persons; or

(c) who have rights or interests which may be adversely affected by the use of any such services by persons acting on their behalf or in a fiduciary capacity in relation to them.

(8) If an authorised person is carrying on a regulated activity in his capacity as a trustee, the persons who are, have been or may be beneficiaries of the trust are to be treated as persons who use, have used or are or may be contemplating using services provided by the authorised person in his carrying on of that activity.

(9) For the purposes of subsection (7) a person who deals with an authorised person in the course of the authorised person's carrying on of a regulated activity is to be treated as using services provided by the authorised person in carrying on those activities.

---

[183] Inserted by SI 2006/2975, regs 2, 3(a); came into force 6 December 2006.

[184] Repealed by SI 2006/2975, regs 2, 3(b)(i); came into force 6 December 2006.

[185] Inserted by SI 2006/2975, regs 2, 3(b)(ii); came into force 6 December 2006.

139 Miscellaneous ancillary matters

(1) Rules relating to the handling of money held by an authorised person in specified circumstances ("clients' money") may—

    (a) make provision which results in that clients' money being held on trust in accordance with the rules;

    (b) treat two or more accounts as a single account for specified purposes (which may include the distribution of money held in the accounts);

    (c) authorise the retention by the authorised person of interest accruing on the clients' money; and

    (d) make provision as to the distribution of such interest which is not to be retained by him.

(2) An institution with which an account is kept in pursuance of rules relating to the handling of clients' money does not incur any liability as constructive trustee if money is wrongfully paid from the account, unless the institution permits the payment—

    (a) with knowledge that it is wrongful; or

    (b) having deliberately failed to make enquiries in circumstances in which a reasonable and honest person would have done so.

(3) In the application of subsection (1) to Scotland, the reference to money being held on trust is to be read as a reference to its being held as agent for the person who is entitled to call for it to be paid over to him or to be paid on his direction or to have it otherwise credited to him.

(4) Rules may—

    (a) confer rights on persons to rescind agreements with, or withdraw offers to, authorised persons within a specified period; and

    (b) make provision, in respect of authorised persons and persons exercising those rights, for the restitution of property and the making or recovery of payments where those rights are exercised.

(5) "Rules" means general rules.

(6) "Specified" means specified in the rules.

140 Restriction on managers of [certain collective investment schemes][186]

[(1) The Authority may make rules prohibiting an authorised person who has permission to act as—

    (a) the manager of an authorised unit trust scheme, or

    (b) the management company of an authorised UCITS open-ended investment company, from carrying on a specified activity.][187]

(2) Such rules may specify an activity which is not a regulated activity.

[(3) In this section—

    (a) "authorised UCITS open-ended investment company" means an authorised open-ended investment company to which the UCITS directive applies; and

    (b) "management company" has the meaning given by Article 1a.2 of the UCITS directive.][188]

141 Insurance business rules

(1) The Authority may make rules prohibiting an authorised person who has permission to effect or carry out contracts of insurance from carrying on a specified activity.

(2) Such rules may specify an activity which is not a regulated activity.

---

[186] Substituted by SI 2003/2066, reg 5(a); came into force 13 February 2004.
[187] Substituted by SI 2003/2066, reg 5(b); came into force 13 February 2004.
[188] Inserted by SI 2003/2066, reg 5(c); came into force 13 February 2004.

(3) The Authority may make rules in relation to contracts entered into by an authorised person in the course of carrying on business which consists of the effecting or carrying out of contracts of long-term insurance.

(4) Such rules may, in particular—

(a) restrict the descriptions of property or indices of the value of property by reference to which the benefits under such contracts may be determined;

(b) make provision, in the interests of the protection of policyholders, for the substitution of one description of property, or index of value, by reference to which the benefits under a contract are to be determined for another such description of property or index.

(5) Rules made under this section are referred to in this Act as insurance business rules.

142 Insurance business: regulations supplementing Authority's rules

(1) The Treasury may make regulations for the purpose of preventing a person who is not an authorised person but who—

(a) is a parent undertaking of an authorised person who has permission to effect or carry out contracts of insurance, and

(b) falls within a prescribed class,

from doing anything to lessen the effectiveness of asset identification rules.

(2) "Asset identification rules" means rules made by the Authority which require an authorised person who has permission to effect or carry out contracts of insurance to identify assets which belong to him and which are maintained in respect of a particular aspect of his business.

(3) The regulations may, in particular, include provision—

(a) prohibiting the payment of dividends;

(b) prohibiting the creation of charges;

(c) making charges created in contravention of the regulations void.

(4) The Treasury may by regulations provide that, in prescribed circumstances, charges created in contravention of asset identification rules are void.

(5) A person who contravenes regulations under subsection (1) is guilty of an offence and liable on summary conviction to a fine not exceeding level 5 on the standard scale.

(6) "Charges" includes mortgages (or in Scotland securities over property).

143 . . .

. . .[189]

Specific rules

144 Price stabilising rules

(1) The Authority may make rules ("price stabilising rules") as to—

(a) the circumstances and manner in which,

(b) the conditions subject to which, and

(c) the time when or the period during which,

action may be taken for the purpose of stabilising the price of investments of specified kinds.

(2) Price stabilising rules—

(a) are to be made so as to apply only to authorised persons;

(b) may make different provision in relation to different kinds of investment.

(3) The Authority may make rules which, for the purposes of section 397(5)(b), treat a person who acts or engages in conduct—

(a) for the purpose of stabilising the price of investments, and

---

[189] Repealed by the Companies Act 2006, ss 964(1), (2), 1295, Sch 16; came into force 6 April 2007.

   (b) in conformity with such provisions corresponding to price stabilising rules and made by a body or authority outside the United Kingdom as may be specified in the rules under this subsection,

as acting, or engaging in that conduct, for that purpose and in conformity with price stabilising rules.

(4) The Treasury may by order impose limitations on the power to make rules under this section.

(5) Such an order may, in particular—

   (a) specify the kinds of investment in relation to which price stabilising rules may make provision;

   (b) specify the kinds of investment in relation to which rules made under subsection (3) may make provision;

   (c) provide for price stabilising rules to make provision for action to be taken for the purpose of stabilising the price of investments only in such circumstances as the order may specify;

   (d) provide for price stabilising rules to make provision for action to be taken for that purpose only at such times or during such periods as the order may specify.

(6) If provisions specified in rules made under subsection (3) are altered, the rules continue to apply to those provisions as altered, but only if before the alteration the Authority has notified the body or authority concerned (and has not withdrawn its notification) that it is satisfied with its consultation procedures.

[(7) "Consultation procedures" means procedures designed to provide an opportunity for persons likely to be affected by alterations to those provisions to make representations about proposed alterations to any of those provisions.][190]

145 Financial promotion rules

(1) The Authority may make rules applying to authorised persons about the communication by them, or their approval of the communication by others, of invitations or inducements—

   (a) to engage in investment activity; or

   (b) to participate in a collective investment scheme.

(2) Rules under this section may, in particular, make provision about the form and content of communications.

(3) Subsection (1) applies only to communications which—

   (a) if made by a person other than an authorised person, without the approval of an authorised person, would contravene section 21(1);

   (b) may be made by an authorised person without contravening section 238(1).

[(3A) But subsection (3) does not prevent the Authority from making rules under subsection (1) in relation to a communication that would not contravene section 21(1) if made by a person other than an authorised person, without the approval of an authorised person, if the conditions set out in subsection (3B) are satisfied.

(3B) Those conditions are—

   (a) that the communication would not contravene subsection (1) of section 21 because it is a communication to which that subsection does not apply as a result of an order under subsection (5) of that section;

   (b) that the Authority considers that any of the requirements of—

     (i) paragraphs 1 to 8 of Article 19 of the markets in financial instruments directive; or

     (ii) any implementing measure made under paragraph 10 of that Article,

   apply to the communication; and

---

[190] Substituted by the Companies Act 2006, s 964(1), (3); came into force 6 April 2007.

(c) that the Authority considers that the rules are necessary to secure that the communication satisfies such of the requirements mentioned in paragraph (b) as the Authority considers apply to the communication.][191]

(4) "Engage in investment activity" has the same meaning as in section 21.

(5) The Treasury may by order impose limitations on the power to make rules under this section.

146 Money laundering rules

The Authority may make rules in relation to the prevention and detection of money laundering in connection with the carrying on of regulated activities by authorised persons.

147 Control of information rules

(1) The Authority may make rules ("control of information rules") about the disclosure and use of information held by an authorised person ("A").

(2) Control of information rules may—

(a) require the withholding of information which A would otherwise have to disclose to a person ("B") for or with whom A does business in the course of carrying on any regulated or other activity;

(b) specify circumstances in which A may withhold information which he would otherwise have to disclose to B;

(c) require A not to use for the benefit of B information A holds which A would otherwise have to use in that way;

(d) specify circumstances in which A may decide not to use for the benefit of B information A holds which A would otherwise have to use in that way.

Modification or waiver

148 Modification or waiver of rules

(1) . . .[192]

[(2) The Authority may, on the application or with the consent of a person who is subject to rules made by the Authority, direct that all or any of those rules (other than rules made under section 247 (trust scheme rules) or section 248 (scheme particulars rules))—

(a) are not to apply to that person; or

(b) are to apply to him with such modifications as may be specified in the direction.][193]

(3) An application must be made in such manner as the Authority may direct.

(4) The Authority may not give a direction unless it is satisfied that—

(a) compliance by the . . .[194] person with the rules, or with the rules as unmodified, would be unduly burdensome or would not achieve the purpose for which the rules were made; and

(b) the direction would not result in undue risk to persons whose interests the rules are intended to protect.

(5) A direction may be given subject to conditions.

(6) Unless it is satisfied that it is inappropriate or unnecessary to do so, a direction must be published by the Authority in such a way as it thinks most suitable for bringing the direction to the attention of—

(a) those likely to be affected by it; and

(b) others who may be likely to make an application for a similar direction.

---

[191] Inserted by SI 2006/2975, regs 2, 4; came into force 6 December 2006.
[192] Repealed by SI 2007/1973, arts 2, 10(a); came into force 12 July 2007.
[193] Substituted by SI 2007/1973, arts 2, 10(b); came into force 12 July 2007.
[194] Repealed by SI 2007/1973, arts 2, 10(c); came into force 12 July 2007.

(7) In deciding whether it is satisfied as mentioned in subsection (6), the Authority must—

    (a) take into account whether the direction relates to a rule contravention of which is actionable in accordance with section 150;

    (b) consider whether its publication would prejudice, to an unreasonable degree, the commercial interests of the . . .[195] person concerned or any other member of his immediate group; and

    (c) consider whether its publication would be contrary to an international obligation of the United Kingdom.

(8) For the purposes of paragraphs (b) and (c) of subsection (7), the Authority must consider whether it would be possible to publish the direction without either of the consequences mentioned in those paragraphs by publishing it without disclosing the identity of the . . .[196] person concerned.

(9) The Authority may—

    (a) revoke a direction; or

    (b) vary it on the application, or with the consent, of the . . .[197] person to whom it relates.

(10) "Direction" means a direction under subsection (2).

(11) "Immediate group", in relation to [a person][198] ("A"), means—

    (a) A;

    (b) a parent undertaking of A;

    (c) a subsidiary undertaking of A;

    (d) a subsidiary undertaking of a parent undertaking of A;

    (e) a parent undertaking of a subsidiary undertaking of A.

Contravention of rules

149 Evidential provisions

(1) If a particular rule so provides, contravention of the rule does not give rise to any of the consequences provided for by other provisions of this Act.

(2) A rule which so provides must also provide—

    (a) that contravention may be relied on as tending to establish contravention of such other rule as may be specified; or

    (b) that compliance may be relied on as tending to establish compliance with such other rule as may be specified.

(3) A rule may include the provision mentioned in subsection (1) only if the Authority considers that it is appropriate for it also to include the provision required by subsection (2).

150 Actions for damages

(1) A contravention by an authorised person of a rule is actionable at the suit of a private person who suffers loss as a result of the contravention, subject to the defences and other incidents applying to actions for breach of statutory duty.

(2) If rules so provide, subsection (1) does not apply to contravention of a specified provision of those rules.

(3) In prescribed cases, a contravention of a rule which would be actionable at the suit of a private person is actionable at the suit of a person who is not a private person, subject to the defences and other incidents applying to actions for breach of statutory duty.

---

[195] Repealed by SI 2007/1973, arts 2, 10(c); came into force 12 July 2007.
[196] Repealed by SI 2007/1973, arts 2, 10(c); came into force 12 July 2007.
[197] Repealed by SI 2007/1973, arts 2, 10(c); came into force 12 July 2007.
[198] Substituted by SI 2007/1973, arts 2, 10(d); came into force 12 July 2007.

(4) In subsections (1) and (3) "rule" does not include—
    (a) [Part 6 rules];[199] or
    (b) a rule requiring an authorised person to have or maintain financial resources.
(5) "Private person" has such meaning as may be prescribed.

151 Limits on effect of contravening rules

(1) A person is not guilty of an offence by reason of a contravention of a rule made by the Authority.
(2) No such contravention makes any transaction void or unenforceable.

Procedural provisions

152 Notification of rules to the Treasury

(1) If the Authority makes any rules, it must give a copy to the Treasury without delay.
(2) If the Authority alters or revokes any rules, it must give written notice to the Treasury without delay.
(3) Notice of an alteration must include details of the alteration.

153 Rule-making instruments

(1) Any power conferred on the Authority to make rules is exercisable in writing.
(2) An instrument by which rules are made by the Authority ("a rule-making instrument") must specify the provision under which the rules are made.
(3) To the extent to which a rule-making instrument does not comply with subsection (2), it is void.
(4) A rule-making instrument must be published by the Authority in the way appearing to the Authority to be best calculated to bring it to the attention of the public.
(5) The Authority may charge a reasonable fee for providing a person with a copy of a rule-making instrument.
(6) A person is not to be taken to have contravened any rule made by the Authority if he shows that at the time of the alleged contravention the rule-making instrument concerned had not been made available in accordance with this section.

154 Verification of rules

(1) The production of a printed copy of a rule-making instrument purporting to be made by the Authority—
    (a) on which is endorsed a certificate signed by a member of the Authority's staff authorised by it for that purpose, and
    (b) which contains the required statements,
is evidence (or in Scotland sufficient evidence) of the facts stated in the certificate.
(2) The required statements are—
    (a) that the instrument was made by the Authority;
    (b) that the copy is a true copy of the instrument; and
    (c) that on a specified date the instrument was made available to the public in accordance with section 153(4).
(3) A certificate purporting to be signed as mentioned in subsection (1) is to be taken to have been properly signed unless the contrary is shown.

---

[199] Substituted by SI 2005/381, reg 6; came into force 1 July 2005.

(4) A person who wishes in any legal proceedings to rely on a rule-making instrument may require the Authority to endorse a copy of the instrument with a certificate of the kind mentioned in subsection (1).

155 Consultation

(1) If the Authority proposes to make any rules, it must publish a draft of the proposed rules in the way appearing to it to be best calculated to bring them to the attention of the public.

(2) The draft must be accompanied by—
   (a) a cost benefit analysis;
   (b) an explanation of the purpose of the proposed rules;
   (c) an explanation of the Authority's reasons for believing that making the proposed rules is compatible with its general duties under section 2; and
   (d) notice that representations about the proposals may be made to the Authority within a specified time.

(3) In the case of a proposal to make rules under a provision mentioned in subsection (9), the draft must also be accompanied by details of the expected expenditure by reference to which the proposal is made.

(4) Before making the proposed rules, the Authority must have regard to any representations made to it in accordance with subsection (2)(d).

(5) If the Authority makes the proposed rules, it must publish an account, in general terms, of—
   (a) the representations made to it in accordance with subsection (2)(d); and
   (b) its response to them.

(6) If the rules differ from the draft published under subsection (1) in a way which is, in the opinion of the Authority, significant—
   (a) the Authority must (in addition to complying with subsection (5)) publish details of the difference; and
   (b) those details must be accompanied by a cost benefit analysis.

(7) Subsections (1) to (6) do not apply if the Authority considers that the delay involved in complying with them would be prejudicial to the interests of consumers.

(8) Neither subsection (2)(a) nor subsection (6)(b) applies if the Authority considers—
   (a) that, making the appropriate comparison, there will be no increase in costs; or
   (b) that, making that comparison, there will be an increase in costs but the increase will be of minimal significance.

(9) Neither subsection (2)(a) nor subsection (6)(b) requires a cost benefit analysis to be carried out in relation to rules made under—
   (a) section 136(2);
   (b) subsection (1) of section 213 as a result of subsection (4) of that section;
   (c) section 234;
   (d) paragraph 17 of Schedule 1.

(10) "Cost benefit analysis" means an estimate of the costs together with an analysis of the benefits that will arise—
   (a) if the proposed rules are made; or
   (b) if subsection (6) applies, from the rules that have been made.

(11) "The appropriate comparison" means—
   (a) in relation to subsection (2)(a), a comparison between the overall position if the rules are made and the overall position if they are not made;
   (b) in relation to subsection (6)(b), a comparison between the overall position after the making of the rules and the overall position before they were made.

(12) The Authority may charge a reasonable fee for providing a person with a copy of a draft published under subsection (1).

156 General supplementary powers

(1) Rules made by the Authority may make different provision for different cases and may, in particular, make different provision in respect of different descriptions of authorised person, activity or investment.

(2) Rules made by the Authority may contain such incidental, supplemental, consequential and transitional provision as the Authority considers appropriate.

CHAPTER II
GUIDANCE

157 Guidance

(1) The Authority may give guidance consisting of such information and advice as it considers appropriate—
   (a) with respect to the operation of this Act and of any rules made under it;
   (b) with respect to any matters relating to functions of the Authority;
   (c) for the purpose of meeting the regulatory objectives;
   (d) with respect to any other matters about which it appears to the Authority to be desirable to give information or advice.

(2) The Authority may give financial or other assistance to persons giving information or advice of a kind which the Authority could give under this section.

(3) If the Authority proposes to give guidance to regulated persons generally, or to a class of regulated person, in relation to rules to which those persons are subject, [subsections (1), (2)(d) and (4) of section 155 apply to the proposed guidance as they apply to proposed rules, unless the Authority considers that the delay in complying with them would be prejudicial to the interests of consumers].[200]

(4) The Authority may—
   (a) publish its guidance;
   (b) offer copies of its published guidance for sale at a reasonable price; and
   (c) if it gives guidance in response to a request made by any person, make a reasonable charge for that guidance.

(5) In this Chapter [(except in section 158A)][201], references to guidance given by the Authority include references to any recommendation made by the Authority to persons generally, to regulated persons generally or to any class of regulated person.

(6) "Regulated person" means any—
   (a) authorised person;
   (b) person who is otherwise subject to rules made by the Authority.

158 Notification of guidance to the Treasury

(1) On giving any general guidance, the Authority must give the Treasury a copy of the guidance without delay.

(2) If the Authority alters any of its general guidance, it must give written notice to the Treasury without delay.

(3) The notice must include details of the alteration.

(4) If the Authority revokes any of its general guidance, it must give written notice to the Treasury without delay.

---

[200] Substituted by SI 2007/1973, arts 2, 13; came into force 12 July 2007.
[201] Inserted by SI 2006/2975, regs 2, 5; came into force 6 December 2006.

(5) "General guidance" means guidance given by the Authority under section 157 which is—

    (a) given to persons generally, to regulated persons generally or to a class of regulated person;

    (b) intended to have continuing effect; and

    (c) given in writing or other legible form.

(6) "Regulated person" has the same meaning as in section 157.

[158A Guidance on outsourcing by investment firms and credit institutions][202]

[(1) Without prejudice to the generality of section 157, the Authority must give guidance in the terms required by Article 15(3) of Commission Directive 2006/73/EC of 10 August 2006 (requirement to publish statement of policy on outsourcing of investment services by investment firms and credit institutions).

(2) Subsections (1), (2)(b) and (d), (4), (5), (6)(a) and (7) of section 155 apply to guidance which the Authority is required to give under this section as they apply to proposed rules.

(3) The Authority must publish its guidance under this section.

(4) The Authority may offer copies of the published guidance for sale at a reasonable price.

(5) Subsections (1) to (4) of section 158 apply to guidance under this section as they apply to general guidance (as defined by section 158(5)).]

CHAPTER III
COMPETITION SCRUTINY

159 Interpretation

(1) In this Chapter—

    ["OFT" means the Office of Fair Trading;][203]

    "practices", in relation to the Authority, means practices adopted by the Authority in the exercise of functions under this Act;

    "regulating provisions" means any—

    (a) rules;

    (b) general guidance (as defined by section 158(5)) [or guidance under section 158A][204];

    (c) statement issued by the Authority under section 64;

    (d) code issued by the Authority under section 64 or 119.

(2) For the purposes of this Chapter, regulating provisions or practices have a significantly adverse effect on competition if—

    (a) they have, or are intended or likely to have, that effect; or

    (b) the effect that they have, or are intended or likely to have, is to require or encourage behaviour which has, or is intended or likely to have, a significantly adverse effect on competition.

(3) If regulating provisions or practices have, or are intended or likely to have, the effect of requiring or encouraging exploitation of the strength of a market position they are to be taken, for the purposes of this Chapter, to have an adverse effect on competition.

(4) In determining under this Chapter whether any of the regulating provisions have, or are likely to have, a particular effect, it may be assumed that the persons to whom the provisions concerned are addressed will act in accordance with them.

---

[202] Inserted by SI 2006/2975, regs 2, 6; came into force 6 December 2006.

[203] Substituted, for definition "Director" as originally enacted, by the Enterprise Act 2002, s 278(1), Sch 25, para 40(1), (2); came into force 1 April 2003.

[204] Inserted by SI 2006/2975, regs 2, 7; came into force 6 December 2006.

160 Reports by [OFT][205]

(1) The [OFT][206] must keep the regulating provisions and the Authority's practices under review.

(2) If at any time the [OFT][207] considers that—

(a) a regulating provision or practice has a significantly adverse effect on competition, or

(b) two or more regulating provisions or practices taken together, or a particular combination of regulating provisions and practices, have such an effect,

[the OFT][208] must make a report to that effect.

(3) If at any time the [OFT][209] considers that—

(a) a regulating provision or practice does not have a significantly adverse effect on competition, or

(b) two or more regulating provisions or practices taken together, or a particular combination of regulating provisions and practices, do not have any such effect,

[the OFT][210] may make a report to that effect.

(4) A report under subsection (2) must include details of the adverse effect on competition.

(5) If the [OFT][211] makes a report under subsection (2) [the OFT][212] must—

(a) send a copy of it to the Treasury, the Competition Commission and the Authority; and

(b) publish it in the way appearing to [it][213] to be best calculated to bring it to the attention of the public.

(6) If the [OFT][214] makes a report under subsection (3)—

(a) [the OFT][215] must send a copy of it to the Treasury, the Competition Commission and the Authority; and

(b) [the OFT][216] may publish it.

(7) Before publishing a report under this section the [OFT][217] must, so far as practicable, exclude any matter which relates to the private affairs of a particular individual the publication of which, in the opinion of the [OFT][218], would or might seriously and prejudicially affect his interests.

(8) Before publishing such a report the [OFT][219] must, so far as practicable, exclude any matter which relates to the affairs of a particular body the publication of which, in the opinion of the [OFT][220], would or might seriously and prejudicially affect its interests.

(9) Subsections (7) and (8) do not apply in relation to copies of a report which the [OFT][221] is required to send under subsection (5)(a) or (6)(a).

---

[205] Substituted by the Enterprise Act 2002, s 278(1), Sch 25, para 40(1), (3)(b); came into force 1 April 2003.
[206] Substituted by the Enterprise Act 2002, s 278(1), Sch 25, para 40(1), (3)(a); came into force 1 April 2003.
[207] Substituted by the Enterprise Act 2002, s 278(1), Sch 25, para 40(1), (3)(a); came into force 1 April 2003.
[208] Substituted by the Enterprise Act 2002, s 278(1), Sch 25, para 40(1), (3)(a); came into force 1 April 2003.
[209] Substituted by the Enterprise Act 2002, s 278(1), Sch 25, para 40(1), (3)(a); came into force 1 April 2003.
[210] Substituted by the Enterprise Act 2002, s 278(1), Sch 25, para 40(1), (3)(a); came into force 1 April 2003.
[211] Substituted by the Enterprise Act 2002, s 278(1), Sch 25, para 40(1), (3)(a); came into force 1 April 2003.
[212] Substituted by the Enterprise Act 2002, s 278(1), Sch 25, para 40(1), (3)(a); came into force 1 April 2003.
[213] Substituted by the Enterprise Act 2002, s 278(1), Sch 25, para 40(1), (3)(a); came into force 1 April 2003.
[214] Substituted by the Enterprise Act 2002, s 278(1), Sch 25, para 40(1), (3)(a); came into force 1 April 2003.
[215] Substituted by the Enterprise Act 2002, s 278(1), Sch 25, para 40(1), (3)(a); came into force 1 April 2003.
[216] Substituted by the Enterprise Act 2002, s 278(1), Sch 25, para 40(1), (3)(a); came into force 1 April 2003.
[217] Substituted by the Enterprise Act 2002, s 278(1), Sch 25, para 40(1), (3)(a); came into force 1 April 2003.
[218] Substituted by the Enterprise Act 2002, s 278(1), Sch 25, para 40(1), (3)(a); came into force 1 April 2003.
[219] Substituted by the Enterprise Act 2002, s 278(1), Sch 25, para 40(1), (3)(a); came into force 1 April 2003.
[220] Substituted by the Enterprise Act 2002, s 278(1), Sch 25, para 40(1), (3)(a); came into force 1 April 2003.
[221] Substituted by the Enterprise Act 2002, s 278(1), Sch 25, para 40(1), (3)(a); came into force 1 April 2003.

(10) For the purposes of the law of defamation, absolute privilege attaches to any report of the [OFT][222] under this section.

161 Power of [OFT][223] to request information

(1) For the purpose of investigating any matter with a view to its consideration under section 160, the [OFT][224] may exercise the powers conferred on [it][225] by this section.

(2) The [OFT][226] may by notice in writing require any person to produce to [it][227] or to a person appointed by [it][228] for the purpose, at a time and place specified in the notice, any document which—

    (a) is specified or described in the notice; and

    (b) is a document in that person's custody or under his control.

(3) The [OFT][229] may by notice in writing—

    (a) require any person carrying on any business to provide [it][230] with such information as may be specified or described in the notice; and

    (b) specify the time within which, and the manner and form in which, any such information is to be provided.

(4) A requirement may be imposed under subsection (2) or (3)(a) only in respect of documents or information which relate to any matter relevant to the investigation.

(5) If a person ("the defaulter") refuses, or otherwise fails, to comply with a notice under this section, the [OFT][231] may certify that fact in writing to the court and the court may enquire into the case.

(6) If, after hearing any witness who may be produced against or on behalf of the defaulter and any statement which may be offered in defence, the court is satisfied that the defaulter did not have a reasonable excuse for refusing or otherwise failing to comply with the notice, the court may deal with the defaulter as if he were in contempt.

(7) "Court" means—

    (a) the High Court; or

    (b) in relation to Scotland, the Court of Session.

162 Consideration by Competition Commission

(1) If the [OFT][232]—

    (a) makes a report under section 160(2), or

    (b) asks the Commission to consider a report that [the OFT][233] has made under section 160(3),

the Commission must investigate the matter.

(2) The Commission must then make its own report on the matter unless it considers that, as a result of a change of circumstances, no useful purpose would be served by a report.

(3) If the Commission decides in accordance with subsection (2) not to make a report, it must make a statement setting out the change of circumstances which resulted in that decision.

---

[222] Substituted by the Enterprise Act 2002, s 278(1), Sch 25, para 40(1), (3)(a); came into force 1 April 2003.
[223] Substituted by the Enterprise Act 2002, s 278(1), Sch 25, para 40(1), (4); came into force 1 April 2003.
[224] Substituted by the Enterprise Act 2002, s 278(1), Sch 25, para 40(1), (4); came into force 1 April 2003.
[225] Substituted by the Enterprise Act 2002, s 278(1), Sch 25, para 40(1), (4); came into force 1 April 2003.
[226] Substituted by the Enterprise Act 2002, s 278(1), Sch 25, para 40(1), (4); came into force 1 April 2003.
[227] Substituted by the Enterprise Act 2002, s 278(1), Sch 25, para 40(1), (4); came into force 1 April 2003.
[228] Substituted by the Enterprise Act 2002, s 278(1), Sch 25, para 40(1), (4); came into force 1 April 2003.
[229] Substituted by the Enterprise Act 2002, s 278(1), Sch 25, para 40(1), (4); came into force 1 April 2003.
[230] Substituted by the Enterprise Act 2002, s 278(1), Sch 25, para 40(1), (4); came into force 1 April 2003.
[231] Substituted by the Enterprise Act 2002, s 278(1), Sch 25, para 40(1), (4); came into force 1 April 2003.
[232] Substituted by the Enterprise Act 2002, s 278(1), Sch 25, para 40(1), (5); came into force 1 April 2003.
[233] Substituted by the Enterprise Act 2002, s 278(1), Sch 25, para 40(1), (5); came into force 1 April 2003.

(4) A report made under this section must state the Commission's conclusion as to whether—
  (a) the regulating provision or practice which is the subject of the report has a significantly adverse effect on competition; or
  (b) the regulating provisions or practices, or combination of regulating provisions and practices, which are the subject of the report have such an effect.
(5) A report under this section stating the Commission's conclusion that there is a significantly adverse effect on competition must also—
  (a) state whether the Commission considers that that effect is justified; and
  (b) if it states that the Commission considers that it is not justified, state its conclusion as to what action, if any, ought to be taken by the Authority.
(6) Subsection (7) applies whenever the Commission is considering, for the purposes of this section, whether a particular adverse effect on competition is justified.
(7) The Commission must ensure, so far as that is reasonably possible, that the conclusion it reaches is compatible with the functions conferred, and obligations imposed, on the Authority by or under this Act.
(8) A report under this section must contain such an account of the Commission's reasons for its conclusions as is expedient, in the opinion of the Commission, for facilitating proper understanding of them.
(9) Schedule 14 supplements this section.
(10) If the Commission makes a report under this section it must send a copy to the Treasury, the Authority and the [OFT].[234]

163 Role of the Treasury

(1) This section applies if the Competition Commission makes a report under section 162(2) which states its conclusion that there is a significantly adverse effect on competition.
(2) If the Commission's conclusion, as stated in the report, is that the adverse effect on competition is not justified, the Treasury must give a direction to the Authority requiring it to take such action as may be specified in the direction.
(3) But subsection (2) does not apply if the Treasury consider—
  (a) that, as a result of action taken by the Authority in response to the Commission's report, it is unnecessary for them to give a direction; or
  (b) that the exceptional circumstances of the case make it inappropriate or unnecessary for them to do so.
(4) In considering the action to be specified in a direction under subsection (2), the Treasury must have regard to any conclusion of the Commission included in the report because of section 162(5)(b).
(5) Subsection (6) applies if—
  (a) the Commission's conclusion, as stated in its report, is that the adverse effect on competition is justified; but
  (b) the Treasury consider that the exceptional circumstances of the case require them to act.
(6) The Treasury may give a direction to the Authority requiring it to take such action—
  (a) as they consider to be necessary in the light of the exceptional circumstances of the case; and
  (b) as may be specified in the direction.
(7) The Authority may not be required as a result of this section to take any action—
  (a) that it would not have power to take in the absence of a direction under this section; or
  (b) that would otherwise be incompatible with any of the functions conferred, or obligations imposed, on it by or under this Act.

---

[234] Substituted by the Enterprise Act 2002, s 278(1), Sch 25, para 40(1), (5); came into force 1 April 2003.

(8) Subsection (9) applies if the Treasury are considering—
  (a) whether subsection (2) applies and, if so, what action is to be specified in a direction under that subsection; or
  (b) whether to give a direction under subsection (6).

(9) The Treasury must—
  (a) do what they consider appropriate to allow the Authority, and any other person appearing to the Treasury to be affected, an opportunity to make representations; and
  (b) have regard to any such representations.

(10) If, in reliance on subsection (3)(a) or (b), the Treasury decline to act under subsection (2), they must make a statement to that effect, giving their reasons.

(11) If the Treasury give a direction under this section they must make a statement giving—
  (a) details of the direction; and
  (b) if the direction is given under subsection (6), their reasons for giving it.

(12) The Treasury must—
  (a) publish any statement made under this section in the way appearing to them best calculated to bring it to the attention of the public; and
  (b) lay a copy of it before Parliament.

164 The Competition Act 1998

(1) The Chapter I prohibition does not apply to an agreement the parties to which consist of or include—
  (a) an authorised person, or
  (b) a person who is otherwise subject to the Authority's regulating provisions,
to the extent to which the agreement consists of provisions the inclusion of which in the agreement is encouraged by any of the Authority's regulating provisions.

(2) The Chapter I prohibition does not apply to the practices of an authorised person or a person who is otherwise subject to the regulating provisions to the extent to which the practices are encouraged by any of the Authority's regulating provisions.

(3) The Chapter II prohibition does not apply to conduct of—
  (a) an authorised person, or
  (b) a person who is otherwise subject to the Authority's regulating provisions,
to the extent to which the conduct is encouraged by any of the Authority's regulating provisions.

(4) "The Chapter I prohibition" means the prohibition imposed by section 2(1) of the Competition Act 1998.

(5) "The Chapter II prohibition" means the prohibition imposed by section 18(1) of that Act.

PART XI
INFORMATION GATHERING AND INVESTIGATIONS

Powers to gather information

165 Authority's power to require information

(1) The Authority may, by notice in writing given to an authorised person, require him—
  (a) to provide specified information or information of a specified description; or
  (b) to produce specified documents or documents of a specified description.

(2) The information or documents must be provided or produced—
  (a) before the end of such reasonable period as may be specified; and
  (b) at such place as may be specified.

(3) An officer who has written authorisation from the Authority to do so may require an authorised person without delay—

    (a) to provide the officer with specified information or information of a specified description; or

    (b) to produce to him specified documents or documents of a specified description.

(4) This section applies only to information and documents reasonably required in connection with the exercise by the Authority of functions conferred on it by or under this Act.

(5) The Authority may require any information provided under this section to be provided in such form as it may reasonably require.

(6) The Authority may require—

    (a) any information provided, whether in a document or otherwise, to be verified in such manner, or

    (b) any document produced to be authenticated in such manner,

as it may reasonably require.

(7) The powers conferred by subsections (1) and (3) may also be exercised to impose requirements on—

    (a) a person who is connected with an authorised person;

    (b) an operator, trustee or depositary of a scheme recognised under section 270 or 272 who is not an authorised person;

    (c) a recognised investment exchange or recognised clearing house.

(8) "Authorised person" includes a person who was at any time an authorised person but who has ceased to be an authorised person.

(9) "Officer" means an officer of the Authority and includes a member of the Authority's staff or an agent of the Authority.

(10) "Specified" means—

    (a) in subsections (1) and (2), specified in the notice; and

    (b) in subsection (3), specified in the authorisation.

(11) For the purposes of this section, a person is connected with an authorised person ("A") if he is or has at any relevant time been—

    (a) a member of A's group;

    (b) a controller of A;

    (c) any other member of a partnership of which A is a member; or

    (d) in relation to A, a person mentioned in Part I of Schedule 15.

166 Reports by skilled persons

(1) The Authority may, by notice in writing given to a person to whom subsection (2) applies, require him to provide the Authority with a report on any matter about which the Authority has required or could require the provision of information or production of documents under section 165.

(2) This subsection applies to—

    (a) an authorised person ("A"),

    (b) any other member of A's group,

    (c) a partnership of which A is a member, or

    (d) a person who has at any relevant time been a person falling within paragraph (a), (b) or (c),

who is, or was at the relevant time, carrying on a business.

(3) The Authority may require the report to be in such form as may be specified in the notice.

(4) The person appointed to make a report required by subsection (1) must be a person—

    (a) nominated or approved by the Authority; and

    (b) appearing to the Authority to have the skills necessary to make a report on the matter concerned.

(5) It is the duty of any person who is providing (or who at any time has provided) services to a person to whom subsection (2) applies in relation to a matter on which a report is required under subsection (1) to give a person appointed to provide such a report all such assistance as the appointed person may reasonably require.

(6) The obligation imposed by subsection (5) is enforceable, on the application of the Authority, by an injunction or, in Scotland, by an order for specific performance under section 45 of the Court of Session Act 1988.

Appointment of investigators

167 Appointment of persons to carry out general investigations

(1) If it appears to the Authority or the Secretary of State ("the investigating authority") that there is good reason for doing so, the investigating authority may appoint one or more competent persons to conduct an investigation on its behalf into—
  (a) the nature, conduct or state of the business of [a recognised investment exchange or]235 an authorised person or of an appointed representative;
  (b) a particular aspect of that business; or
  (c) the ownership or control of [a recognised investment exchange or]236 an authorised person.

(2) If a person appointed under subsection (1) thinks it necessary for the purposes of his investigation, he may also investigate the business of a person who is or has at any relevant time been—
  (a) a member of the group of which the person under investigation ("A") is part; or
  (b) a partnership of which A is a member.

(3) If a person appointed under subsection (1) decides to investigate the business of any person under subsection (2) he must give that person written notice of his decision.

(4) The power conferred by this section may be exercised in relation to a former authorised person (or appointed representative) but only in relation to—
  (a) business carried on at any time when he was an authorised person (or appointed representative); or
  (b) the ownership or control of a former authorised person at any time when he was an authorised person.

(5) "Business" includes any part of a business even if it does not consist of carrying on regulated activities.

[(6) References in subsection (1) to a recognised investment exchange do not include references to an overseas investment exchange (as defined by section 313(1)).]237

168 Appointment of persons to carry out investigations in particular cases

(1) Subsection (3) applies if it appears to an investigating authority that there are circumstances suggesting that—
  (a) a person may have contravened any regulation made under section 142; or
  (b) a person may be guilty of an offence under section 177, 191, 346 or 398(1) or under Schedule 4.

---

235 Inserted by SI 2007/126, reg 3(5), Sch 5, paras 1, 7(a)(i); came into force (for certain purposes) 1 April 2007; came into force (for remaining purposes) 1 November 2007.
236 Inserted by SI 2007/126, reg 3(5), Sch 5, paras 1, 7(a)(ii); came into force (for certain purposes) 1 April 2007; came into force (for remaining purposes) 1 November 2007.
237 Inserted by SI 2007/126, reg 3(5), Sch 5, paras 1, 7(b); came into force (for certain purposes) 1 April 2007; came into force (for remaining purposes) 1 November 2007.

(2) Subsection (3) also applies if it appears to an investigating authority that there are circumstances suggesting that—

    (a) an offence under section 24(1) or 397 or under Part V of the Criminal Justice Act 1993 may have been committed;

    (b) there may have been a breach of the general prohibition;

    (c) there may have been a contravention of section 21 or 238; or

    (d) market abuse may have taken place.

(3) The investigating authority may appoint one or more competent persons to conduct an investigation on its behalf.

(4) Subsection (5) applies if it appears to the Authority that there are circumstances suggesting that—

    (a) a person may have contravened section 20;

    (b) a person may be guilty of an offence under prescribed regulations relating to money laundering;

    [(ba) a person may be guilty of an offence under Schedule 7 to the Counter-Terrorism Act 2008 (terrorist financing or money laundering);][238]

    (c) an authorised person may have contravened a rule made by the Authority;

    (d) an individual may not be a fit and proper person to perform functions in relation to a regulated activity carried on by an authorised or exempt person;

    (e) an individual may have performed or agreed to perform a function in breach of a prohibition order;

    (f) an authorised or exempt person may have failed to comply with section 56(6);

    (g) an authorised person may have failed to comply with section 59(1) or (2);

    (h) a person in relation to whom the Authority has given its approval under section 59 may not be a fit and proper person to perform the function to which that approval relates; . . .[239]

    (i) a person may be guilty of misconduct for the purposes of section 66[; or

    (j) a person may have contravened any provision made by or under this Act for the purpose of implementing the markets in financial instruments directive or by any directly applicable Community regulation made under that directive][240].

(5) The Authority may appoint one or more competent persons to conduct an investigation on its behalf.

(6) "Investigating authority" means the Authority or the Secretary of State.

Assistance to overseas regulators

169 Investigations etc in support of overseas regulator

(1) At the request of an overseas regulator, the Authority may—

    (a) exercise the power conferred by section 165; or

    (b) appoint one or more competent persons to investigate any matter.

(2) An investigator has the same powers as an investigator appointed under section 168(3) (as a result of subsection (1) of that section).

(3) If the request has been made by a competent authority in pursuance of any Community obligation the Authority must, in deciding whether or not to exercise its investigative power, consider whether its exercise is necessary to comply with any such obligation.

---

[238] Inserted by the Counter-Terrorism Act 2008, s 62, Sch 7, Pt 7, para 33(4); came into force 27 November 2008.

[239] Repealed by SI 2007/126, reg 3(5), Sch 5, paras 1, 8(a); came into force (for certain purposes) 1 April 2007; came into force (for remaining purposes) 1 November 2007.

[240] Inserted by SI 2007/126, reg 3(5), Sch 5, paras 1, 8(b); came into force (for certain purposes) 1 April 2007; came into force (for remaining purposes) 1 November 2007.

(4) In deciding whether or not to exercise its investigative power, the Authority may take into account in particular—

(a) whether in the country or territory of the overseas regulator concerned, corresponding assistance would be given to a United Kingdom regulatory authority;

(b) whether the case concerns the breach of a law, or other requirement, which has no close parallel in the United Kingdom or involves the assertion of a jurisdiction not recognised by the United Kingdom;

(c) the seriousness of the case and its importance to persons in the United Kingdom;

(d) whether it is otherwise appropriate in the public interest to give the assistance sought.

(5) The Authority may decide that it will not exercise its investigative power unless the overseas regulator undertakes to make such contribution towards the cost of its exercise as the Authority considers appropriate.

(6) Subsections (4) and (5) do not apply if the Authority considers that the exercise of its investigative power is necessary to comply with a Community obligation.

(7) If the Authority has appointed an investigator in response to a request from an overseas regulator, it may direct the investigator to permit a representative of that regulator to attend, and take part in, any interview conducted for the purposes of the investigation.

(8) A direction under subsection (7) is not to be given unless the Authority is satisfied that any information obtained by an overseas regulator as a result of the interview will be subject to safeguards equivalent to those contained in Part XXIII.

(9) The Authority must prepare a statement of its policy with respect to the conduct of interviews in relation to which a direction under subsection (7) has been given.

(10) The statement requires the approval of the Treasury.

(11) If the Treasury approve the statement, the Authority must publish it.

(12) No direction may be given under subsection (7) before the statement has been published.

(13) "Overseas regulator" has the same meaning as in section 195.

(14) "Investigative power" means one of the powers mentioned in subsection (1).

(15) "Investigator" means a person appointed under subsection (1)(b).

Conduct of investigations

170 Investigations: general

(1) This section applies if an investigating authority appoints one or more competent persons ("investigators") under section 167 or 168(3) or (5) to conduct an investigation on its behalf.

(2) The investigating authority must give written notice of the appointment of an investigator to the person who is the subject of the investigation ("the person under investigation").

(3) Subsections (2) and (9) do not apply if—

(a) the investigator is appointed as a result of section 168(1) or (4) and the investigating authority believes that the notice required by subsection (2) or (9) would be likely to result in the investigation being frustrated; or

(b) the investigator is appointed as a result of subsection (2) of section 168.

(4) A notice under subsection (2) must—

(a) specify the provisions under which, and as a result of which, the investigator was appointed; and

(b) state the reason for his appointment.

(5) Nothing prevents the investigating authority from appointing a person who is a member of its staff as an investigator.

(6) An investigator must make a report of his investigation to the investigating authority.

(7) The investigating authority may, by a direction to an investigator, control—

(a) the scope of the investigation;

(b) the period during which the investigation is to be conducted;

    (c) the conduct of the investigation; and

    (d) the reporting of the investigation.

(8) A direction may, in particular—

    (a) confine the investigation to particular matters;

    (b) extend the investigation to additional matters;

    (c) require the investigator to discontinue the investigation or to take only such steps as are specified in the direction;

    (d) require the investigator to make such interim reports as are so specified.

(9) If there is a change in the scope or conduct of the investigation and, in the opinion of the investigating authority, the person subject to investigation is likely to be significantly prejudiced by not being made aware of it, that person must be given written notice of the change.

(10) "Investigating authority", in relation to an investigator, means—

    (a) the Authority, if the Authority appointed him;

    (b) the Secretary of State, if the Secretary of State appointed him.

171 Powers of persons appointed under section 167

(1) An investigator may require the person who is the subject of the investigation ("the person under investigation") or any person connected with the person under investigation—

    (a) to attend before the investigator at a specified time and place and answer questions; or

    (b) otherwise to provide such information as the investigator may require.

(2) An investigator may also require any person to produce at a specified time and place any specified documents or documents of a specified description.

(3) A requirement under subsection (1) or (2) may be imposed only so far as the investigator concerned reasonably considers the question, provision of information or production of the document to be relevant to the purposes of the investigation.

[(3A) Where the investigation relates to a recognised investment exchange, an investigator has the additional powers conferred by sections 172 and 173 (and for this purpose references in those sections to an investigator are to be read accordingly).][241]

(4) For the purposes of this section and section 172, a person is connected with the person under investigation ("A") if he is or has at any relevant time been—

    (a) a member of A's group;

    (b) a controller of A;

    (c) a partnership of which A is a member; or

    (d) in relation to A, a person mentioned in Part I or II of Schedule 15.

(5) "Investigator" means a person conducting an investigation under section 167.

(6) "Specified" means specified in a notice in writing.

[(7) The reference in subsection (3A) to a recognised investment exchange does not include a reference to an overseas investment exchange (as defined by section 313(1)).][242]

172 Additional power of persons appointed as a result of section 168(1) or (4)

(1) An investigator has the powers conferred by section 171.

(2) An investigator may also require a person who is neither the subject of the investigation ("the person under investigation") nor a person connected with the person under investigation—

    (a) to attend before the investigator at a specified time and place and answer questions; or

    (b) otherwise to provide such information as the investigator may require for the purposes of the investigation.

---

[241] Inserted by SI 2007/126, reg 3(5), Sch 5, paras 1, 9(a); came into force (for certain purposes) 1 April 2007; came into force (for remaining purposes) 1 November 2007.

[242] Inserted by SI 2007/126, reg 3(5), Sch 5, paras 1, 9(b); came into force (for certain purposes) 1 April 2007; came into force (for remaining purposes) 1 November 2007.

(3) A requirement may only be imposed under subsection (2) if the investigator is satisfied that the requirement is necessary or expedient for the purposes of the investigation.

(4) "Investigator" means a person appointed as a result of subsection (1) or (4) of section 168.

(5) "Specified" means specified in a notice in writing.

173 Powers of persons appointed as a result of section 168(2)

(1) Subsections (2) to (4) apply if an investigator considers that any person ("A") is or may be able to give information which is or may be relevant to the investigation.

(2) The investigator may require A—
   (a) to attend before him at a specified time and place and answer questions; or
   (b) otherwise to provide such information as he may require for the purposes of the investigation.

(3) The investigator may also require A to produce at a specified time and place any specified documents or documents of a specified description which appear to the investigator to relate to any matter relevant to the investigation.

(4) The investigator may also otherwise require A to give him all assistance in connection with the investigation which A is reasonably able to give.

(5) "Investigator" means a person appointed under subsection (3) of section 168 (as a result of subsection (2) of that section).

174 Admissibility of statements made to investigators

(1) A statement made to an investigator by a person in compliance with an information require-ment is admissible in evidence in any proceedings, so long as it also complies with any require-ments governing the admissibility of evidence in the circumstances in question.

(2) But in criminal proceedings in which that person is charged with an offence to which this subsection applies or in proceedings in relation to action to be taken against that person under section 123—
   (a) no evidence relating to the statement may be adduced, and
   (b) no question relating to it may be asked,
   by or on behalf of the prosecution or (as the case may be) the Authority, unless evidence relating to it is adduced, or a question relating to it is asked, in the proceedings by or on behalf of that person.

(3) Subsection (2) applies to any offence other than one—
   (a) under section 177(4) or 398;
   (b) under section 5 of the Perjury Act 1911 (false statements made otherwise than on oath);
   (c) under section 44(2) of the Criminal Law (Consolidation)(Scotland) Act 1995 (false state-ments made otherwise than on oath); or
   (d) under Article 10 of the Perjury (Northern Ireland) Order 1979.

(4) "Investigator" means a person appointed under section 167 or 168(3) or (5).

(5) "Information requirement" means a requirement imposed by an investigator under section 171, 172, 173 or 175.

175 Information and documents: supplemental provisions

(1) If the Authority or an investigator has power under this Part to require a person to produce a document but it appears that the document is in the possession of a third person, that power may be exercised in relation to the third person.

(2) If a document is produced in response to a requirement imposed under this Part, the person to whom it is produced may—
   (a) take copies or extracts from the document; or
   (b) require the person producing the document, or any relevant person, to provide an explanation of the document.

(3) If a person who is required under this Part to produce a document fails to do so, the Authority or an investigator may require him to state, to the best of his knowledge and belief, where the document is.

(4) A lawyer may be required under this Part to furnish the name and address of his client.

(5) No person may be required under this Part to disclose information or produce a document in respect of which he owes an obligation of confidence by virtue of carrying on the business of banking unless—

(a) he is the person under investigation or a member of that person's group;

(b) the person to whom the obligation of confidence is owed is the person under investigation or a member of that person's group;

(c) the person to whom the obligation of confidence is owed consents to the disclosure or production; or

(d) the imposing on him of a requirement with respect to such information or document has been specifically authorised by the investigating authority.

(6) If a person claims a lien on a document, its production under this Part does not affect the lien.

(7) "Relevant person", in relation to a person who is required to produce a document, means a person who—

(a) has been or is or is proposed to be a director or controller of that person;

(b) has been or is an auditor of that person;

(c) has been or is an actuary, accountant or lawyer appointed or instructed by that person; or

(d) has been or is an employee of that person.

(8) "Investigator" means a person appointed under section 167 or 168(3) or (5).

176 Entry of premises under warrant

(1) A justice of the peace may issue a warrant under this section if satisfied on information on oath given by or on behalf of the Secretary of State, the Authority or an investigator that there are reasonable grounds for believing that the first, second or third set of conditions is satisfied.

(2) The first set of conditions is—

(a) that a person on whom an information requirement has been imposed has failed (wholly or in part) to comply with it; and

(b) that on the premises specified in the warrant—

(i) there are documents which have been required; or

(ii) there is information which has been required.

(3) The second set of conditions is—

(a) that the premises specified in the warrant are premises of an authorised person or an appointed representative;

(b) that there are on the premises documents or information in relation to which an information requirement could be imposed; and

(c) that if such a requirement were to be imposed—

(i) it would not be complied with; or

(ii) the documents or information to which it related would be removed, tampered with or destroyed.

(4) The third set of conditions is—

(a) that an offence mentioned in section 168 for which the maximum sentence on conviction on indictment is two years or more has been (or is being) committed by any person;

(b) that there are on the premises specified in the warrant documents or information relevant to whether that offence has been (or is being) committed;

(c) that an information requirement could be imposed in relation to those documents or information; and

(d) that if such a requirement were to be imposed—
  (i) it would not be complied with; or
  (ii) the documents or information to which it related would be removed, tampered with or destroyed.

(5) A warrant under this section shall authorise a constable—
  (a) to enter the premises specified in the warrant;
  (b) to search the premises and take possession of any documents or information appearing to be documents or information of a kind in respect of which a warrant under this section was issued ("the relevant kind") or to take, in relation to any such documents or information, any other steps which may appear to be necessary for preserving them or preventing interference with them;
  (c) to take copies of, or extracts from, any documents or information appearing to be of the relevant kind;
  (d) to require any person on the premises to provide an explanation of any document or information appearing to be of the relevant kind or to state where it may be found; and
  (e) to use such force as may be reasonably necessary.

(6) In England and Wales, sections 15(5) to (8) and section 16 of the Police and Criminal Evidence Act 1984 (execution of search warrants and safeguards) apply to warrants issued under this section.

(7) In Northern Ireland, Articles 17(5) to (8) and 18 of the Police and Criminal Evidence (Northern Ireland) Order 1989 apply to warrants issued under this section.

(8) Any document of which possession is taken under this section may be retained—
  (a) for a period of three months; or
  (b) if within that period proceedings to which the document is relevant are commenced against any person for any criminal offence, until the conclusion of those proceedings.

(9) In the application of this section to Scotland—
  (a) for the references to a justice of the peace substitute references to a justice of the peace or a sheriff; and
  (b) for the references to information on oath substitute references to evidence on oath.

(10) "Investigator" means a person appointed under section 167 or 168(3) or (5).

(11) "Information requirement" means a requirement imposed—
  (a) by the Authority under section [87C, 87J,][243] 165 or 175; or
  (b) by an investigator under section 171, 172, 173 or 175.

Offences

177 Offences

(1) If a person other than the investigator ("the defaulter") fails to comply with a requirement imposed on him under this Part the person imposing the requirement may certify that fact in writing to the court.

(2) If the court is satisfied that the defaulter failed without reasonable excuse to comply with the requirement, it may deal with the defaulter (and in the case of a body corporate, any director or officer) as if he were in contempt[; and "officer", in relation to a limited liability partnership, means a member of the limited liability partnership].[244]

---

[243] Inserted by SI 2005/1433, reg 2(1), Sch 1, para 12; came into force 1 July 2005.
[244] Inserted by SI 2001/1090, reg 9(1), Sch 5, para 21; came into force 6 April 2001.

(3) A person who knows or suspects that an investigation is being or is likely to be conducted under this Part is guilty of an offence if—

(a) he falsifies, conceals, destroys or otherwise disposes of a document which he knows or suspects is or would be relevant to such an investigation, or

(b) he causes or permits the falsification, concealment, destruction or disposal of such a document,

unless he shows that he had no intention of concealing facts disclosed by the documents from the investigator.

(4) A person who, in purported compliance with a requirement imposed on him under this Part—

(a) provides information which he knows to be false or misleading in a material particular, or

(b) recklessly provides information which is false or misleading in a material particular,

is guilty of an offence.

(5) A person guilty of an offence under subsection (3) or (4) is liable—

(a) on summary conviction, to imprisonment for a term not exceeding six months or a fine not exceeding the statutory maximum, or both;

(b) on conviction on indictment, to imprisonment for a term not exceeding two years or a fine, or both.

(6) Any person who intentionally obstructs the exercise of any rights conferred by a warrant under section 176 is guilty of an offence and liable on summary conviction to imprisonment for a term not exceeding *three months* [51 weeks][245] or a fine not exceeding level 5 on the standard scale, or both.

(7) "Court" means—

(a) the High Court;

(b) in Scotland, the Court of Session.

PART XII
CONTROL OVER AUTHORISED PERSONS

[Notices of acquisitions of control over UK authorised persons][246]

[178 Obligation to notify the Authority: acquisitions of control][247]

[(1) A person who decides to acquire or increase control over a UK authorised person must give the Authority notice in writing before making the acquisition.

(2) For the purposes of calculations relating to this section, the holding of shares or voting power by a person ("A1") includes any shares or voting power held by another ("A2") if A1 and A2 are acting in concert.

(3) In this Part, a notice given under this section is a "section 178 notice" and a person giving notice is a "section 178 notice-giver".]

. . .[248]

---

[245] Words in italics repealed and words in square brackets substituted by the Criminal Justice Act 2003, s 280(2), (3), Sch 26, para 54(1), (2); date in force, to be appointed: see the Criminal Justice Act 2003, s 336(3).

[246] Substituted by SI 2009/534, reg 3, Sch 1; came into force 21 March 2009.

[247] Substituted, together with ss 179–191, 191A–G, for ss 178–191 as originally enacted, by SI 2009/534, reg 3, Sch 1; came into force 21 March 2009.

[248] Repealed by virtue of SI 2009/534, reg 3, Sch 1; came into force 21 March 2009.

[179 Requirements for section 178 notices][249]

[(1) A section 178 notice must be in such form, include such information and be accompanied by such documents as the Authority may reasonably require.

(2) The Authority must publish a list of its requirements as to the form, information and accompanying documents for a section 178 notice.

(3) The Authority may impose different requirements for different cases and may vary or waive requirements in particular cases.]

[180 Acknowledgment of receipt][250]

[(1) The Authority must acknowledge receipt of a completed section 178 notice in writing before the end of the second working day following receipt.

(2) If the Authority receives an incomplete section 178 notice it must inform the section 178 notice-giver as soon as reasonably practicable.]

[Acquiring control and other changes of holding][251]

[181 Acquiring control][252]

[(1) For the purposes of this Part, a person ("A") acquires control over a UK authorised person ("B") if any of the cases in subsection (2) begin to apply.

(2) The cases are where A holds—

    (a) 10% or more of the shares in B or in a parent undertaking of B ("P");

    (b) 10% or more of the voting power in B or P; or

    (c) shares or voting power in B or P as a result of which A is able to exercise significant influence over the management of B.]

. . .[253]

[182 Increasing control][254]

[(1) For the purposes of this Part, a person ("A") increases control over a UK authorised person ("B") whenever—

    (a) the percentage of shares which A holds in B or in a parent undertaking of B ("P") increases by any of the steps mentioned in subsection (2);

    (b) the percentage of voting power A holds in B or P increases by any of the steps mentioned in subsection (2); or

    (c) A becomes a parent undertaking of B.

(2) The steps are—

    (a) from less than 20% to 20% or more;

    (b) from less than 30% to 30% or more;

    (c) from less than 50% to 50% or more.]

---

[249] Substituted, together with ss 178, 180–191, 191A–G, for ss 178–191 as originally enacted, by SI 2009/534, reg 3, Sch 1; came into force 21 March 2009.

[250] Substituted, together with ss 178, 179, 181–191, 191A–G, for ss 178–191 as originally enacted, by SI 2009/534, reg 3, Sch 1; came into force 21 March 2009.

[251] Inserted by SI 2009/534, reg 3, Sch 1; came into force 21 March 2009.

[252] Substituted, together with ss 178–180, 182–191, 191A–G, for ss 178–191 as originally enacted, by SI 2009/534, reg 3, Sch 1; came into force 21 March 2009.

[253] Repealed by virtue of SI 2009/534, reg 3, Sch 1; came into force 21 March 2009.

[254] Substituted, together with ss 178–181, 183–191, 191A–G, for ss 178–191 as originally enacted, by SI 2009/534, reg 3, Sch 1; came into force 21 March 2009.

[183 Reducing or ceasing to have control][255]

[(1) For the purposes of this Part, a person ("A") reduces control over a UK authorised person ("B") whenever—

(a) the percentage of shares which A holds in B or in a parent undertaking of B ("P") decreases by any of the steps mentioned in subsection (2);

(b) the percentage of voting power which A holds in B or P decreases by any of the steps mentioned in subsection (2); or

(c) A ceases to be a parent undertaking of B.

(2) The steps are—

(a) from 50% or more to less than 50%;

(b) from 30% or more to less than 30%;

(c) from 20% or more to less than 20%.

(3) For the purposes of this Part, a person ("A") ceases to have control over a UK authorised person ("B") if A ceases to be in the position of holding—

(a) 10% or more of the shares in B or in a parent undertaking of B ("P");

(b) 10% or more of the voting power in B or P; or

(c) shares or voting power in B or P as a result of which A is able to exercise significant influence over the management of B.]

[184 Disregarded holdings][256]

[(1) For the purposes of sections 181 to 183, shares and voting power that a person holds in a UK authorised person ("B") or in a parent undertaking of B ("P") are disregarded in the following circumstances.

(2) Shares held only for the purposes of clearing and settling within a short settlement cycle are disregarded.

(3) Shares held by a custodian or its nominee in a custodian capacity are disregarded, provided that the custodian or nominee is only able to exercise voting power represented by the shares in accordance with instructions given in writing.

(4) Shares representing no more than 5% of the total voting power in B or P held by an investment firm are disregarded, provided that it—

(a) holds the shares in the capacity of a market maker (as defined in article 4.1(8) of the markets in financial instruments directive);

(b) is authorised by its home state regulator under the markets in financial instruments directive; and

(c) neither intervenes in the management of B or P nor exerts any influence on B or P to buy the shares or back the share price.

(5) Shares held by a credit institution or investment firm in its trading book are disregarded, provided that—

(a) the shares represent no more than 5% of the total voting power in B or P; and

(b) the credit institution or investment firm ensures that the voting power is not used to intervene in the management of B or P.

(6) Shares held by a credit institution or an investment firm are disregarded, provided that—

(a) the shares are held as a result of performing the investment services and activities of—

(i) underwriting a share issue; or

(ii) placing shares on a firm commitment basis in accordance with Annex I, section A.6 of the markets in financial instruments directive; and

---

[255] Substituted, together with ss 178–182, 184–191, 191A–G, for ss 178–191 as originally enacted, by SI 2009/534, reg 3, Sch 1; came into force 21 March 2009.

[256] Substituted, together with ss 178–183, 185–191, 191A–G, for ss 178–191 as originally enacted, by SI 2009/534, reg 3, Sch 1; came into force 21 March 2009.

    (b) the credit institution or investment firm—
       (i) does not exercise voting power represented by the shares or otherwise intervene in the management of the issuer; and
       (ii) retains the holding for a period of less than one year.

(7) Where a management company (as defined in Article 1a.2 of the UCITS directive) and its parent undertaking both hold shares or voting power, each may disregard holdings of the other, provided that each exercises its voting power independently of the other.

(8) But subsection (7) does not apply if the management company—
    (a) manages holdings for its parent undertaking or an undertaking in respect of which the parent undertaking is a controller;
    (b) has no discretion as to the exercise of the voting power attached to such holdings; and
    (c) may only exercise the voting power in relation to such holdings under direct or indirect instruction from—
       (i) the parent undertaking; or
       (ii) an undertaking in respect of which of the parent undertaking is a controller.

(9) Where an investment firm and its parent undertaking both hold shares or voting power, the parent undertaking may disregard holdings managed by the investment firm on a client by client basis and the investment firm may disregard holdings of the parent undertaking, provided that the investment firm—
    (a) has permission to provide portfolio management;
    (b) exercises its voting power independently from the parent undertaking; and
    (c) may only exercise the voting power under instructions given in writing, or has appropriate mechanisms in place for ensuring that individual portfolio management services are conducted independently of any other services.]

[Assessment procedure][257]

[185 Assessment: general][258]

[(1) Where the Authority receives a section 178 notice, it must—
    (a) determine whether to approve the acquisition to which it relates unconditionally; or
    (b) propose to—
       (i) approve the acquisition subject to conditions (see section 187); or
       (ii) object to the acquisition.

(2) The Authority must—
    (a) consider the suitability of the section 178 notice-giver and the financial soundness of the acquisition in order to ensure the sound and prudent management of the UK authorised person;
    (b) have regard to the likely influence that the section 178 notice-giver will have on the UK authorised person; and
    (c) disregard the economic needs of the market.

(3) The Authority may only object to an acquisition—
    (a) if there are reasonable grounds for doing so on the basis of the matters set out in section 186; or
    (b) if the information provided by the section 178 notice-giver is incomplete.]

---

[257] Inserted by SI 2009/534, reg 3, Sch 1; came into force 21 March 2009.

[258] Substituted, together with ss 178–184, 186–191, 191A–G, for ss 178–191 as originally enacted, by SI 2009/534, reg 3, Sch 1; came into force 21 March 2009.

[186 Assessment criteria]²⁵⁹

[The matters specified in section 185(3)(a) are—

(a) the reputation of the section 178 notice-giver;

(b) the reputation and experience of any person who will direct the business of the UK authorised person as a result of the proposed acquisition;

(c) the financial soundness of the section 178 notice-giver, in particular in relation to the type of business that the UK authorised person pursues or envisages pursuing;

(d) whether the UK authorised person will be able to comply with its prudential requirements (including the threshold conditions in relation to all of the regulated activities for which it has or will have permission);

(e) if the UK authorised person is to become part of a group as a result of the acquisition, whether that group has a structure which makes it possible to—

  (i) exercise effective supervision;

  (ii) exchange information among regulators; and

  (iii) determine the allocation of responsibility among regulators; and

(f) whether there are reasonable grounds to suspect that in connection with the proposed acquisition—

  (i) money laundering or terrorist financing (within the meaning of Article 1 of Directive 2005/60/EC of the European Parliament and of the Council of 26th October 2005 on the prevention of the use of the financial system for the purpose of money laundering and terrorist financing) is being or has been committed or attempted; or

  (ii) the risk of such activity could increase.]

[187 Approval with conditions]²⁶⁰

[(1) The Authority may impose conditions on its approval of an acquisition.

(2) The Authority may only impose conditions where, if it did not impose those conditions, it would propose to object to the acquisition.

(3) The Authority may not impose conditions requiring a particular level of holding to be acquired.

(4) The Authority may vary or cancel the conditions.]

[188 Assessment: consultation with EC competent authorities]²⁶¹

[(1) The Authority must consult any appropriate home state regulator before making a determination under section 185 and, in doing so, must comply with such requirements as to consultation as may be prescribed.

(2) Where the Authority makes a determination under section 185, it must indicate any views or reservations received from any home state regulator it consults in accordance with subsection (1).

(3) The Authority must cooperate with any equivalent consultation by a host state regulator in relation to a UK authorised person.

(4) In order to comply with an obligation under subsection (1) or (3), the Authority must provide the regulator with—

(a) any relevant information that it requests; and

(b) any information that the Authority considers that it needs.]

. . .²⁶²

---

²⁵⁹ Substituted, together with ss 178–185, 187–191, 191A–G, for ss 178–191 as originally enacted, by SI 2009/534, reg 3, Sch 1; came into force 21 March 2009.

²⁶⁰ Substituted, together with ss 178–186, 188–191, 191A–G, for ss 178–191 as originally enacted, by SI 2009/534, reg 3, Sch 1; came into force 21 March 2009.

²⁶¹ Substituted, together with ss 178–187, 189–191, 191A–G, for ss 178–191 as originally enacted, by SI 2009/534, reg 3, Sch 1; came into force 21 March 2009.

²⁶² Repealed by virtue of SI 2009/534, reg 3, Sch 1; came into force 21 March 2009.

[189 Assessment: Procedure]²⁶³

[(1) The Authority must act under section 185 within a period of 60 working days beginning with the day on which the Authority acknowledges receipt of the section 178 notice ("the assessment period").

(2) The assessment period may be interrupted, no more than once, in accordance with section 190.

(3) The Authority must inform the section 178 notice-giver in writing of—

(a) the duration of the assessment period;

(b) its expiry date; and

(c) any change to the expiry date by virtue of section 190.

(4) The Authority must, within two working days of acting under section 185 (and in any event no later than the expiry date of the assessment period)—

(a) notify the section 178 notice-giver that it has determined to approve the acquisition unconditionally; or

(b) give a warning notice stating that it proposes to—

(i) approve the acquisition subject to conditions; or

(ii) object to the acquisition.

(5) Where the Authority gives a warning notice stating that it proposes to approve the acquisition subject to conditions—

(a) it must, in the warning notice, specify those conditions; and

(b) the conditions take effect as interim conditions.

(6) The Authority is treated as having approved the acquisition if, at the expiry of the assessment period, it has neither—

(a) given notice under subsection (4); nor

(b) informed the section 178 notice-giver that the section 178 notice is incomplete.

(7) If the Authority decides to approve an acquisition subject to conditions or to object to an acquisition it must give the section 178 notice-giver a decision notice.

(8) Following receipt of a decision notice under this section, the section 178 notice-giver may refer the Authority's decision to the Tribunal.]

. . .²⁶⁴

[190 Requests for further information]²⁶⁵

[(1) The Authority may, no later than the 50th working day of the assessment period, in writing ask the section 178 notice-giver to provide any further information necessary to complete its assessment.

(2) On the first occasion that the Authority asks for further information, the assessment period is interrupted from the date of the request until the date the Authority receives the requested information ("the interruption period").

(3) But the interruption period may not exceed 20 working days, unless subsection (4) applies.

(4) The interruption period may not exceed 30 working days if the notice-giver—

(a) is situated or regulated outside the European Community; or

(b) is not subject to supervision under—

(i) the UCITS directive;

(ii) the insurance directives;

---

²⁶³ Substituted, together with ss 178–188, 190–191, 191A–G, for ss 178–191 as originally enacted, by SI 2009/534, reg 3, Sch 1; came into force 21 March 2009.

²⁶⁴ Repealed by virtue of SI 2009/534, reg 3, Sch 1; came into force 21 March 2009.

²⁶⁵ Substituted, together with ss 178–189, 191, 191A–G, for ss 178–191 as originally enacted, by SI 2009/534, reg 3, Sch 1; came into force 21 March 2009.

     (iii) the markets in financial instruments directive;

     (iv) the reinsurance directive; or

     (v) the banking consolidation directive.

(5) The Authority may make further requests for information (but a further request does not result in a further interruption of the assessment period).

(6) The Authority must acknowledge in writing receipt of further information before the end of the second working day following receipt.]

. . .[266]

[191 Duration of approval][267]

[(1) Approval of an acquisition (whether granted unconditionally or subject to conditions) is effective for such period as the Authority may specify in writing.

(2) Where the Authority has specified a period under subsection (1), it may extend the period.

(3) Where the Authority has not specified a period, the approval is effective for one year beginning with the date—

    (a) of the notice given under section 189(4)(a) or (b)(i);

    (b) on which the Authority is treated as having given approval under section 189(6); or

    (c) of a decision on a reference to the Tribunal which results in the person receiving approval.]

[Enforcement procedures][268]

[191A Objection by the Authority][269]

[(1) The Authority may object to a person's control over a UK authorised person in any of the circumstances specified in subsection (2).

(2) The circumstances are that the Authority reasonably believes that—

    (a) the person acquired or increased control without giving notice under section 178(1) in circumstances where notice was required;

    (b) the person is in breach of a condition imposed under section 187; or

    (c) there are grounds for objecting to control on the basis of the matters in section 186.

(3) The Authority—

    (a) must take into account whether influence exercised by the person is likely to operate to the detriment of the sound and prudent management of the UK authorised person; and

    (b) may take into account whether the person has co-operated with any information requests made or requirements imposed by the Authority.

(4) If the Authority proposes to object to a person's control over a UK authorised person, it must give that person a warning notice.

(5) The Authority must consult any appropriate home state regulator before giving a warning notice under this section and, in doing so, must comply with such requirements as to consultation as may be prescribed.

(6) If the Authority decides to object to a person's control over a UK authorised person, it must give that person a decision notice.

(7) A person to whom the Authority gives a decision notice under this section may refer the matter to the Tribunal.]

---

[266] Repealed by virtue of SI 2009/534, reg 3, Sch 1; came into force 21 March 2009.

[267] Substituted, together with ss 178–190, 191A–G, for ss 178–191 as originally enacted, by SI 2009/534, reg 3, Sch 1; came into force 21 March 2009.

[268] Inserted by SI 2009/534, reg 3, Sch 1; came into force 21 March 2009.

[269] Substituted, together with ss 178–191, 191B–G, for ss 178–191 as originally enacted, by SI 2009/534, reg 3, Sch 1; came into force 21 March 2009.

[191B Restriction notices][270]

[(1) The Authority may give notice in writing (a "restriction notice") to a person in the following circumstances.

(2) The circumstances are that—
   (a) the person has control over a UK authorised person by virtue of holding shares or voting power; and
   (b) in relation to the shares or voting power, the Authority has given the person a warning notice or a decision notice under section 189 or 191A or a final notice which confirms a decision notice given under section 189 or 191A.

(3) In a restriction notice, the Authority may direct that shares or voting power to which the notice relates are, until further notice, subject to one or more of the following restrictions—
   (a) except by court order, an agreement to transfer or a transfer of any such shares or voting power or, in the case of unissued shares, any agreement to transfer or transfer of the right to be issued with them, is void;
   (b) no voting power is to be exercisable;
   (c) no further shares are to be issued in pursuance of any right of the holder of any such shares or voting power or in pursuance of any offer made to their holder;
   (d) except in a liquidation, no payment is to be made of any sums due from the body corporate on any such shares, whether in respect of capital or otherwise.

(4) A restriction notice takes effect—
   (a) immediately; or
   (b) on such date as may be specified in the notice.

(5) A restriction notice does not extinguish rights which would be enjoyable but for the notice.

(6) A copy of the restriction notice must be served on—
   (a) the UK authorised person in question; and
   (b) in the case of shares or voting power held in a parent undertaking of a UK authorised person, the parent undertaking.

(7) A person to whom the Authority gives a restriction notice may refer the matter to the Tribunal.]

[191C Orders for sale of shares][271]

[(1) The court may, on the application of the Authority, order the sale of shares or the disposition of voting power in the following circumstances.

(2) The circumstances are that—
   (a) a person has control over a UK authorised person by virtue of holding the shares or voting power; and
   (b) the acquisition or continued holding of the shares or voting power by that person is in contravention of a final notice which confirms a decision notice given under section 189 or section 191A.

(3) Where the court orders the sale of shares or disposition of voting power it may—
   (a) if a restriction notice has been given in relation to the shares or voting power, order that the restrictions cease to apply; and
   (b) make any further order.

---

[270] Substituted, together with ss 178–191, 191A, 191C–G, for ss 178–191 as originally enacted, by SI 2009/534, reg 3, Sch 1; came into force 21 March 2009.
[271] Substituted, together with ss 178–191, 191A, 191B, 191D–G, for ss 178–191 as originally enacted, by SI 2009/534, reg 3, Sch 1; came into force 21 March 2009.

(4) Where the court makes an order under this section, it must take into account the level of holding that the person would have been entitled to acquire, or to continue to hold, without contravening the final notice.

(5) If shares are sold or voting power disposed of in pursuance of an order under this section, any proceeds, less the costs of the sale or disposition, must be paid into court for the benefit of the persons beneficially interested in them; and any such person may apply to the court for payment of a whole or part of the proceeds.

(6) The jurisdiction conferred by this section may be exercised by the High Court and the Court of Session.]

[Notice of reductions of control of UK authorised persons][272]

[191D Obligation to notify the Authority: dispositions of control][273]

[(1) A person who decides to reduce or cease to have control over a UK authorised person must give the Authority notice in writing before making the disposition.

(2) For the purposes of calculations relating to this section, the holding of shares or voting power by a person ("A1") includes any shares or voting power held by another ("A2") if A1 and A2 are acting in concert.]

[191E Requirements for notices under section 191D][274]

[(1) A notice under section 191D must be in such form, include such information and be accompanied by such documents as the Authority may reasonably require.

(2) The Authority must publish a list of its requirements as to the form, information and accompanying documents for a notice under section 191D.

(3) The Authority may impose different requirements for different cases and may vary or waive requirements in particular cases.]

[Offences][275]

[191F Offences under this Part][276]

[(1) A person who fails to comply with an obligation to notify the Authority under section 178(1) or 191D(1) is guilty of an offence.

(2) A person who gives notice to the Authority under section 178(1) and makes the acquisition to which the notice relates before the expiry date of the assessment period is guilty of an offence unless the Authority has approved the acquisition or given a warning notice under section 189(4)(b)(i).

(3) A person who contravenes an interim condition in a warning notice given under section 189(4)(b)(i) or a condition in a decision notice given under section 189(7) or a final notice which confirms a decision notice under that section is guilty of an offence.

(4) A person who makes an acquisition in contravention of a warning notice given under section 189(4)(b)(ii) or a decision notice given under section 189(7) or a final notice which confirms a decision notice under that section is guilty of an offence.

---

[272] Inserted by SI 2009/534, reg 3, Sch 1; came into force 21 March 2009.

[273] Substituted, together with ss 178–191, 191A–C, 191E–G, for ss 178–191 as originally enacted, by SI 2009/534, reg 3, Sch 1; came into force 21 March 2009.

[274] Substituted, together with ss 178–191, 191A–D, 191F, 191G, for ss 178–191 as originally enacted, by SI 2009/534, reg 3, Sch 1; came into force 21 March 2009.

[275] Inserted by SI 2009/534, reg 3, Sch 1; came into force 21 March 2009.

[276] Substituted, together with ss 178–191, 191A–E, 191–G, for ss 178–191 as originally enacted, by SI 2009/534, reg 3, Sch 1; came into force 21 March 2009.

(5) A person who makes an acquisition after the Authority's approval for the acquisition has ceased to be effective by virtue of section 191 is guilty of an offence.

(6) A person who provides information to the Authority which is false in a material particular is guilty of an offence.

(7) A person who breaches a direction contained in a restriction notice given under section 191B is guilty of an offence.

(8) A person guilty of an offence under subsection (1) to (3) or (5) to (7) is liable—

    (a) on summary conviction to a fine not exceeding the statutory maximum; or

    (b) on conviction on indictment, to a fine.

(9) A person guilty of an offence under subsection (4) is liable—

    (a) on summary conviction, to a fine not exceeding the statutory maximum; or

    (b) on conviction on indictment, to imprisonment for a term not exceeding two years or a fine, or both.]

[191G Interpretation][277]

[(1) In this Part—

    "acquisition" means the acquisition of control or of an increase in control over a UK authorised person;

    "credit institution" means—

    (a) a credit institution authorised under the banking consolidation directive; or

    (b) an institution which would satisfy the requirements for authorisation as a credit institution under that directive if it had its registered office (or if it does not have a registered office, its head office) in an EEA State;

    "shares" has the same meaning as in section 422;

    "UK authorised person" means an authorised person who—

    (a) is a body incorporated in, or an unincorporated association formed under the law of, any part of the United Kingdom; and

    (b) is not a person authorised as a result of paragraph 1 of Schedule 5; and

    "voting power" has the same meaning as in section 422.

(2) For the purposes of this Part, a "working day" is a day other than—

    (a) a Saturday or a Sunday; or

    (b) a day which is a bank holiday in England and Wales under the Banking and Financial Dealings Act 1971.]

Miscellaneous

192 Power to change definitions of control etc

The Treasury may by order—

    (a) provide for exemptions from the obligations to notify imposed by sections 178 and [191D][278];

    (b) amend section [181][279] by varying, or removing, any of the cases in which a person is treated as [acquiring][280] control over a UK authorised person or by adding a case;

    (c) amend section [182][281] by varying, or removing, any of the cases in which a person is treated as increasing control over a UK authorised person or by adding a case;

---

[277] Substituted, together with ss 178–191, 191A–F, for ss 178–191 as originally enacted, by SI 2009/534, reg 3, Sch 1; came into force 21 March 2009.

[278] Substituted by SI 2009/534, reg 4(a); came into force 21 March 2009.

[279] Substituted by SI 2009/534, reg 4(b)(i); came into force 21 March 2009.

[280] Substituted by SI 2009/534, reg 4(b)(ii); came into force 21 March 2009.

[281] Substituted by SI 2009/534, reg 4(c); came into force 21 March 2009.

(d) amend section [183]²⁸² by varying, or removing, any of the cases in which a person is treated as [reducing or ceasing to have]²⁸³ control over a UK authorised person or by adding a case;

(e) amend section 422 by varying, or removing, any of the cases in which a person is treated as being a controller of a person or by adding a case.

PART XIII
INCOMING FIRMS: INTERVENTION BY AUTHORITY

Interpretation

193 Interpretation of this Part

(1) In this Part—

"additional procedure" means the procedure described in section 199;

"incoming firm" means—

(a) an EEA firm which is exercising, or has exercised, its right to carry on a regulated activity in the United Kingdom in accordance with Schedule 3; or

(b) a Treaty firm which is exercising, or has exercised, its right to carry on a regulated activity in the United Kingdom in accordance with Schedule 4; and

"power of intervention" means the power conferred on the Authority by section 196.

(2) In relation to an incoming firm which is an EEA firm, expressions used in this Part and in Schedule 3 have the same meaning in this Part as they have in that Schedule.

194 General grounds on which power of intervention is exercisable

(1) The Authority may exercise its power of intervention in respect of an incoming firm if it appears to it that—

(a) the firm has contravened, or is likely to contravene, a requirement which is imposed on it by or under this Act (in a case where the Authority is responsible for enforcing compliance in the United Kingdom);

(b) the firm has, in purported compliance with any requirement imposed by or under this Act, knowingly or recklessly given the Authority information which is false or misleading in a material particular; or

(c) it is desirable to exercise the power in order to protect the interests of actual or potential customers.

(2) Subsection (3) applies to an incoming EEA firm falling within sub-paragraph (a) or (b) of paragraph 5 of Schedule 3 which is exercising an EEA right to carry on any Consumer Credit Act business in the United Kingdom.

(3) The Authority may exercise its power of intervention in respect of the firm if [the Office of Fair Trading]²⁸⁴ has informed the Authority that—

(a) the firm,

(b) any of the firm's employees, agents or associates (whether past or present), or

(c) if the firm is a body corporate, a controller of the firm or an associate of such a controller,

has done any of the things specified in paragraphs [(a) to (e) of section 25(2A)]²⁸⁵ of the Consumer Credit Act 1974.

---

²⁸² Substituted by SI 2009/534, reg 4(d)(i); came into force 21 March 2009.

²⁸³ Substituted by SI 2009/534, reg 4(d)(ii); came into force 21 March 2009.

²⁸⁴ Substituted by the Enterprise Act 2002, s 278(1), Sch 25, para 40(1), (6); came into force 1 April 2003.

²⁸⁵ Substituted by the Consumer Credit Act 2006, s 33(7); came into force 6 April 2008.

(4) "Associate", "Consumer Credit Act business" and "controller" have the same meaning as in section 203.

[194A Contravention by relevant EEA firm with UK branch of requirement under markets in financial instruments directive: Authority primarily responsible for securing compliance][286]

[(1) This section applies if—
   (a) a relevant EEA firm has a branch in the United Kingdom; and
   (b) the Authority ascertains that the firm has contravened, or is contravening, a requirement falling within subsection (3) (in a case to which Article 62.2 of the markets in financial instruments directive applies).

(2) "Relevant EEA firm" means an EEA firm falling within paragraph 5(a) or (b) of Schedule 3 which is exercising in the United Kingdom an EEA right deriving from the markets in financial instruments directive.

(3) A requirement falls within this subsection if it is imposed on the firm—
   (a) by any provision of or made under this Act which implements the markets in financial instruments directive; or
   (b) by any directly applicable Community regulation made under that directive.

(4) The Authority must give the firm written notice which—
   (a) requires the firm to put an end to the contravention;
   (b) states that the Authority's power of intervention will become exercisable in relation to the firm if the firm continues the contravention; and
   (c) indicates any requirements that the Authority proposes to impose on the firm in exercise of its power of intervention in the event of the power becoming exercisable.

(5) The Authority may exercise its power of intervention in respect of the firm if—
   (a) a reasonable time has expired since the giving of the notice under subsection (4);
   (b) the firm has failed to put an end to the contravention within that time; and
   (c) the Authority has informed the firm's home state regulator of its intention to exercise its power of intervention in respect of the firm.

(6) Subsection (5) applies whether or not the Authority's power of intervention is also exercisable as a result of section 194.

(7) If the Authority exercises its power of intervention in respect of a relevant EEA firm by virtue of subsection (5), it must at the earliest opportunity inform the firm's home state regulator and the Commission of—
   (a) the fact that the Authority has exercised that power in respect of the firm; and
   (b) any requirements it has imposed on the firm in exercise of the power.]

195 Exercise of power in support of overseas regulator

(1) The Authority may exercise its power of intervention in respect of an incoming firm at the request of, or for the purpose of assisting, an overseas regulator.

(2) Subsection (1) applies whether or not the Authority's power of intervention is also exercisable as a result of section 194.

(3) "An overseas regulator" means an authority in a country or territory outside the United Kingdom—
   (a) which is a home state regulator; or
   (b) which exercises any function of a kind mentioned in subsection (4).

(4) The functions are—
   (a) a function corresponding to any function of the Authority under this Act;

---

[286] Inserted by SI 2007/126, reg 3(1), Sch 1, paras 1, 2; came into force (for certain purposes) 1 April 2007; came into force (for remaining purposes).

(b) a function corresponding to any function exercised by the competent authority under Part VI . . .;[287]

(c) a function corresponding to any function exercised by the Secretary of State under [the Companies Acts (as defined in section 2 of the Companies Act 2006)];[288]

(d) a function in connection with—

    (i) the investigation of conduct of the kind prohibited by Part V of the Criminal Justice Act 1993 (insider dealing); or

    (ii) the enforcement of rules (whether or not having the force of law) relating to such conduct;

(e) a function prescribed by regulations made for the purposes of this subsection which, in the opinion of the Treasury, relates to companies or financial services.

(5) If—

(a) a request to the Authority for the exercise of its power of intervention has been made by a home state regulator in pursuance of a Community obligation, or

(b) a home state regulator has notified the Authority that an EEA firm's EEA authorisation has been withdrawn,

the Authority must, in deciding whether or not to exercise its power of intervention, consider whether exercising it is necessary in order to comply with a Community obligation.

(6) In deciding in any case in which the Authority does not consider that the exercise of its power of intervention is necessary in order to comply with a Community obligation, it may take into account in particular—

(a) whether in the country or territory of the overseas regulator concerned, corresponding assistance would be given to a United Kingdom regulatory authority;

(b) whether the case concerns the breach of a law, or other requirement, which has no close parallel in the United Kingdom or involves the assertion of a jurisdiction not recognised by the United Kingdom;

(c) the seriousness of the case and its importance to persons in the United Kingdom;

(d) whether it is otherwise appropriate in the public interest to give the assistance sought.

(7) The Authority may decide not to exercise its power of intervention, in response to a request, unless the regulator concerned undertakes to make such contribution to the cost of its exercise as the Authority considers appropriate.

(8) Subsection (7) does not apply if the Authority decides that it is necessary for it to exercise its power of intervention in order to comply with a Community obligation.

[195A Contravention by relevant EEA firm of requirement under markets in financial instruments directive: home state regulator primarily responsible for securing compliance][289]

[(1) This section applies if the Authority has clear and demonstrable grounds for believing that a relevant EEA firm has contravened, or is contravening, a requirement falling within subsection (2) (in a case to which Article 62.1 or 62.3 of the markets in financial instruments directive applies).

(2) A requirement falls within this subsection if it is imposed on the firm—

(a) by or under any provision adopted in the firm's home state for the purpose of implementing the markets in financial instruments directive; or

(b) by any directly applicable Community regulation made under that directive.

---

[287] Repealed by SI 2005/1433, reg 2(1), Sch 1, para 13; came in force 1 July 2005.

[288] Substituted by SI 2007/2194, art 10(1), (2), Sch 4, Pt 3, para 92; came into force 1 October 2007.

[289] Inserted by SI 2007/126, reg 3(1), Sch 1, paras 1, 3; came into force (for certain purposes) 1 April 2007; came into force (for remaining purposes) 1 November 2007.

(3) The Authority must notify the firm's home state regulator of the situation mentioned in subsection (1).

(4) The notice under subsection (3) must—

    (a) request that the home state regulator take all appropriate measures for the purpose of ensuring that the firm puts an end to the contravention;

    (b) state that the Authority's power of intervention is likely to become exercisable in relation to the firm if the firm continues the contravention; and

    (c) indicate any requirements that the Authority proposes to impose on the firm in exercise of its power of intervention in the event of the power becoming exercisable.

(5) The Authority may exercise its power of intervention in respect of the firm if—

    (a) a reasonable time has expired since the giving of the notice under subsection (3); and

    (b) conditions A to C are satisfied.

(6) Condition A is that—

    (a) the firm's home state regulator has failed or refused to take measures for the purpose mentioned in subsection (4)(a); or

    (b) any measures taken by the home state regulator have proved inadequate for that purpose.

(7) Condition B is that the firm is acting in a manner which is clearly prejudicial to the interests of investors in the United Kingdom or the orderly functioning of the markets.

(8) Condition C is that the Authority has informed the firm's home state regulator of its intention to exercise its power of intervention in respect of the firm.

(9) Subsection (5) applies whether or not the Authority's power of intervention is also exercisable as a result of section 194 or 195.

(10) If the Authority exercises its power of intervention in respect of a relevant EEA firm by virtue of subsection (5), it must at the earliest opportunity inform the Commission of—

    (a) the fact that the Authority has exercised that power in respect of the firm; and

    (b) any requirements it has imposed on the firm in exercise of the power.

(11) In this section—

    "home state", in relation to a relevant EEA firm, means—

    (a) in the case of a firm which is a body corporate, the EEA State in which the firm has its registered office or, if it has no registered office, its head office; and

    (b) in any other case, the EEA State in which the firm has its head office;

    "relevant EEA firm" has the same meaning as in section 194A.]

196 The power of intervention

If the Authority is entitled to exercise its power of intervention in respect of an incoming firm under this Part, it may impose any requirement in relation to the firm which it could impose if—

    (a) the firm's permission was a Part IV permission; and

    (b) the Authority was entitled to exercise its power under that Part to vary that permission.

Exercise of power of intervention

197 Procedure on exercise of power of intervention

(1) A requirement takes effect—

    (a) immediately, if the notice given under subsection (3) states that that is the case;

    (b) on such date as may be specified in the notice; or

    (c) if no date is specified in the notice, when the matter to which it relates is no longer open to review.

(2) A requirement may be expressed to take effect immediately (or on a specified date) only if the Authority, having regard to the ground on which it is exercising its power of intervention, considers that it is necessary for the requirement to take effect immediately (or on that date).

(3) If the Authority proposes to impose a requirement under section 196 on an incoming firm, or imposes such a requirement with immediate effect, it must give the firm written notice.

(4) The notice must—

(a) give details of the requirement;

(b) inform the firm of when the requirement takes effect;

(c) state the Authority's reasons for imposing the requirement and for its determination as to when the requirement takes effect;

(d) inform the firm that it may make representations to the Authority within such period as may be specified in the notice (whether or not it has referred the matter to the Tribunal); and

(e) inform it of its right to refer the matter to the Tribunal.

(5) The Authority may extend the period allowed under the notice for making representations.

(6) If, having considered any representations made by the firm, the Authority decides—

(a) to impose the requirement proposed, or

(b) if it has been imposed, not to rescind the requirement,

it must give it written notice.

(7) If, having considered any representations made by the firm, the Authority decides—

(a) not to impose the requirement proposed,

(b) to impose a different requirement from that proposed, or

(c) to rescind a requirement which has effect,

it must give it written notice.

(8) A notice given under subsection (6) must inform the firm of its right to refer the matter to the Tribunal.

(9) A notice under subsection (7)(b) must comply with subsection (4).

(10) If a notice informs a person of his right to refer a matter to the Tribunal, it must give an indication of the procedure on such a reference.

198 Power to apply to court for injunction in respect of certain overseas insurance companies

(1) This section applies if the Authority has received a request made in respect of an incoming EEA firm in accordance with—

(a) Article 20.5 of the first non-life insurance directive; . . .[290]

[(b) Article 37.5 of the life assurance consolidation directive][291][; or

(c) Article 42.4 of the reinsurance directive][292].

(2) The court may, on an application made to it by the Authority with respect to the firm, grant an injunction restraining (or in Scotland an interdict prohibiting) the firm disposing of or otherwise dealing with any of its assets.

(3) If the court grants an injunction, it may by subsequent orders make provision for such incidental, consequential and supplementary matters as it considers necessary to enable the Authority to perform any of its functions under this Act.

(4) "The court" means—

(a) the High Court; or

(b) in Scotland, the Court of Session.

---

[290] Repealed by SI 2007/3253, reg 2(1), Sch 1, paras 1, 3(a); came into force 10 December 2007.

[291] Substituted by SI 2004/3379, reg 6(1), (3); came into force 11 January 2005.

[292] Inserted by SI 2007/3253, reg 2(1), Sch 1, paras 1, 3(b); came into force 10 December 2007.

199 Additional procedure for EEA firms in certain cases

(1) This section applies if it appears to the Authority that its power of intervention is exercisable in relation to an EEA firm exercising EEA rights in the United Kingdom ("an incoming EEA firm") in respect of the contravention of a relevant requirement.

(2) A requirement is relevant if—

  (a) it is imposed by the Authority under this Act; and

  [(b) as respects its contravention, the single market directive in question provides that a procedure of the kind set out in the following provisions of this section (so far as they are relevant in the firm's case) is to apply][293].

(3) The Authority must, in writing, require the firm to remedy the situation.

[(3A) If the firm falls within paragraph 5(da) of Schedule 3, the Authority must at the same time as it gives notice to the firm under subsection (3) refer its findings to the firm's home state regulator.

(3B) Subsections (4) to (8) apply to an incoming EEA firm other than a firm falling within paragraph 5(da) of Schedule 3.][294]

(4) If the firm fails to comply with the requirement under subsection (3) within a reasonable time, the Authority must give a notice to that effect to the firm's home state regulator requesting it—

  (a) to take all appropriate measures for the purpose of ensuring that the firm remedies the situation which has given rise to the notice; and

  (b) to inform the Authority of the measures it proposes to take or has taken or the reasons for not taking such measures.

(5) Except as mentioned in subsection (6), the Authority may not exercise its power of intervention [before informing the firm's home state regulator and][295] unless satisfied—

  (a) that the firm's home state regulator has failed or refused to take measures for the purpose mentioned in subsection (4)(a); or

  (b) that the measures taken by the home state regulator have proved inadequate for that purpose.

(6) If the Authority decides that it should exercise its power of intervention in respect of the incoming EEA firm as a matter of urgency in order to protect the interests of consumers, it may exercise that power—

  (a) before complying with subsections (3) and (4); or

  (b) where it has complied with those subsections, before it is satisfied as mentioned in subsection (5).

(7) In such a case the Authority must at the earliest opportunity inform the firm's home state regulator and the Commission.

(8) If—

  (a) the Authority has (by virtue of subsection (6)) exercised its power of intervention before complying with subsections (3) and (4) or before it is satisfied as mentioned in subsection (5), and

  (b) the Commission decides under any of the single market directives [(other than the markets in financial instruments directive)][296] that the Authority must rescind or vary any requirement imposed in the exercise of its power of intervention,

the Authority must in accordance with the decision rescind or vary the requirement.

---

[293] Substituted by SI 2007/3253, reg 2(1), Sch 1, paras 1, 4(a); came into force 10 December 2007.
[294] Inserted by SI 2007/3253, reg 2(1), Sch 1, paras 1, 4(b); came into force 10 December 2007.
[295] Inserted by SI 2007/3253, reg 2(1), Sch 1, paras 1, 4(c); came into force 10 December 2007.
[296] Inserted by SI 2007/126, reg 3(1), Sch 1, paras 1, 4; came into force (for certain purposes) 1 April 2007; came into force (for remaining purposes) 1 November 2007.

[(9) In the case of a firm falling within paragraph 5(da) of Schedule 3, the Authority may not exercise its power of intervention before informing the firm's home state regulator and unless satisfied—

    (a) that the firm's home state regulator has failed or refused to take all appropriate measures for the purpose of ensuring that the firm remedies the situation which gave rise to the notice under subsection (3); or

    (b) that the measures taken by the home state regulator have proved inadequate for that purpose.][297]

Supplemental

200 Rescission and variation of requirements

(1) The Authority may rescind or vary a requirement imposed in exercise of its power of intervention on its own initiative or on the application of the person subject to the requirement.

(2) The power of the Authority on its own initiative to rescind a requirement is exercisable by written notice given by the Authority to the person concerned, which takes effect on the date specified in the notice.

(3) Section 197 applies to the exercise of the power of the Authority on its own initiative to vary a requirement as it applies to the imposition of a requirement.

(4) If the Authority proposes to refuse an application for the variation or rescission of a requirement, it must give the applicant a warning notice.

(5) If the Authority decides to refuse an application for the variation or rescission of a requirement—

    (a) the Authority must give the applicant a decision notice; and

    (b) that person may refer the matter to the Tribunal.

201 Effect of certain requirements on other persons

If the Authority, in exercising its power of intervention, imposes on an incoming firm a requirement of a kind mentioned in subsection (3) of section 48, the requirement has the same effect in relation to the firm as it would have in relation to an authorised person if it had been imposed on the authorised person by the Authority acting under section 45.

202 Contravention of requirement imposed under this Part

(1) Contravention of a requirement imposed by the Authority under this Part does not—

    (a) make a person guilty of an offence;

    (b) make any transaction void or unenforceable; or

    (c) (subject to subsection (2)) give rise to any right of action for breach of statutory duty.

(2) In prescribed cases the contravention is actionable at the suit of a person who suffers loss as a result of the contravention, subject to the defences and other incidents applying to actions for breach of statutory duty.

Powers of [Office of Fair Trading][298]

203 Power to prohibit the carrying on of Consumer Credit Act business

(1) If it appears to [the Office of Fair Trading ("the OFT")][299] that subsection (4) has been, or is likely to be, contravened as respects a consumer credit EEA firm, [it][300] may by written notice given to the firm impose on the firm a consumer credit prohibition.

---

[297] Inserted by SI 2007/3253, reg 2(1), Sch 1, paras 1, 4(d); came into force 10 December 2007.

[298] Substituted by the Enterprise Act 2002, s 278(1), Sch 25, para 40(1), (7); came into force 1 April 2003.

[299] Substituted by the Enterprise Act 2002, s 278(1), Sch 25, para 40(1), (7)(a)(i); came into force 1 April 2003.

[300] Substituted by the Enterprise Act 2002, s 278(1), Sch 25, para 40(1), (7)(a)(ii); came into force 1 April 2003.

(2) If it appears to the [OFT]³⁰¹ that a restriction imposed under section 204 on an EEA consumer credit firm has not been complied with, [it]³⁰² may by written notice given to the firm impose a consumer credit prohibition.

(3) "Consumer credit prohibition" means a prohibition on carrying on, or purporting to carry on, in the United Kingdom any Consumer Credit Act business which consists of or includes carrying on one or more listed activities.

(4) This subsection is contravened as respects a firm if—
    (a) the firm or any of its employees, agents or associates (whether past or present), or
    (b) if the firm is a body corporate, any controller of the firm or an associate of any such controller,
does any of the things specified in paragraphs [(a) to (e) of section 25(2A)]³⁰³ of the Consumer Credit Act 1974.

(5) A consumer credit prohibition may be absolute or may be imposed—
    (a) for such period,
    (b) until the occurrence of such event, or
    (c) until such conditions are complied with,
as may be specified in the notice given under subsection (1) or (2).

(6) Any period, event or condition so specified may be varied by the [OFT]³⁰⁴ on the application of the firm concerned.

(7) A consumer credit prohibition may be withdrawn by written notice served by the [OFT]³⁰⁵ on the firm concerned, and any such notice takes effect on such date as is specified in the notice.

(8) Schedule 16 has effect as respects consumer credit prohibitions and restrictions under section 204.

(9) A firm contravening a prohibition under this section is guilty of an offence and liable—
    (a) on summary conviction, to a fine not exceeding the statutory maximum;
    (b) on conviction on indictment, to a fine.

(10) In this section and section 204—
    "a consumer credit EEA firm" means an EEA firm falling within any of paragraphs (a) to (c) of paragraph 5 of Schedule 3 whose EEA authorisation covers any Consumer Credit Act business;
    "Consumer Credit Act business" means consumer credit business, consumer hire business or ancillary credit business;
    "consumer credit business", "consumer hire business" and "ancillary credit business" have the same meaning as in the Consumer Credit Act 1974;
    "listed activity" means an activity listed in [Annex 1 to the banking consolidation directive]³⁰⁶ or the Annex to the investment services directive;
    "associate" has the same meaning as in section [25(2A)]³⁰⁷ of the Consumer Credit Act 1974;
    "controller" has the meaning given by section 189(1) of that Act.

---

301 Substituted by the Enterprise Act 2002, s 278(1), Sch 25, para 40(1), (7)(b); came into force 1 April 2003.
302 Substituted by the Enterprise Act 2002, s 278(1), Sch 25, para 40(1), (7)(b); came into force 1 April 2003.
303 Substituted by the Consumer Credit Act 2006, s 33(7); came into force 6 April 2008.
304 Substituted by the Enterprise Act 2002, s 278(1), Sch 25, para 40(1), (7)(c); came into force 1 April 2003.
305 Substituted by the Enterprise Act 2002, s 278(1), Sch 25, para 40(1), (7)(c); came into force 1 April 2003.
306 Substituted by SI 2000/2952, reg 8(1), (2); came into force 22 November 2000.
307 Substituted by the Consumer Credit Act 2006, s 33(8); came into force 6 April 2008.

204 Power to restrict the carrying on of Consumer Credit Act business

(1) In this section "restriction" means a direction that a consumer credit EEA firm may not carry on in the United Kingdom, otherwise than in accordance with such condition or conditions as may be specified in the direction, any Consumer Credit Act business which—

    (a) consists of or includes carrying on any listed activity; and

    (b) is specified in the direction.

(2) If it appears to the [OFT][308] that the situation as respects a consumer credit EEA firm is such that the powers conferred by section 203(1) are exercisable, the [OFT][309] may, instead of imposing a prohibition, impose such restriction as appears to [it][310] desirable.

(3) A restriction—

    (a) may be withdrawn, or

    (b) may be varied with the agreement of the firm concerned,

by written notice served by the [OFT][311] on the firm, and any such notice takes effect on such date as is specified in the notice.

(4) A firm contravening a restriction is guilty of an offence and liable—

    (a) on summary conviction, to a fine not exceeding the statutory maximum;

    (b) on conviction on indictment, to a fine.

PART XIV
DISCIPLINARY MEASURES

205 Public censure

If the Authority considers that an authorised person has contravened a requirement imposed on him by or under this Act, [or by any directly applicable Community regulation made under the markets in financial instruments directive,][312] the Authority may publish a statement to that effect.

206 Financial penalties

(1) If the Authority considers that an authorised person has contravened a requirement imposed on him by or under this Act, [or by any directly applicable Community regulation made under the markets in financial instruments directive,][313] it may impose on him a penalty, in respect of the contravention, of such amount as it considers appropriate.

(2) The Authority may not in respect of any contravention both require a person to pay a penalty under this section and withdraw his authorisation under section 33.

(3) A penalty under this section is payable to the Authority.

207 Proposal to take disciplinary measures

(1) If the Authority proposes—

    (a) to publish a statement in respect of an authorised person (under section 205), or

    (b) to impose a penalty on an authorised person (under section 206),

it must give the authorised person a warning notice.

---

[308] Substituted by the Enterprise Act 2002, s 278(1), Sch 25, para 40(1), (8); came into force 1 April 2003.

[309] Substituted by the Enterprise Act 2002, s 278(1), Sch 25, para 40(1), (8); came into force 1 April 2003.

[310] Substituted by the Enterprise Act 2002, s 278(1), Sch 25, para 40(1), (8); came into force 1 April 2003.

[311] Substituted by the Enterprise Act 2002, s 278(1), Sch 25, para 40(1), (8); came into force 1 April 2003.

[312] Inserted by SI 2007/126, reg 3(5), Sch 5, paras 1, 10; came into force (for certain purposes) 1 April 2007; came into force (for remaining purposes) 1 November 2007.

[313] Inserted by SI 2007/126, reg 3(5), Sch 5, paras 1, 11; came into force (for certain purposes) 1 April 2007; came into force (for remaining purposes) 1 November 2007.

(2) A warning notice about a proposal to publish a statement must set out the terms of the statement.

(3) A warning notice about a proposal to impose a penalty, must state the amount of the penalty.

208 Decision notice

(1) If the Authority decides—
    (a) to publish a statement under section 205 (whether or not in the terms proposed), or
    (b) to impose a penalty under section 206 (whether or not of the amount proposed),
    it must without delay give the authorised person concerned a decision notice.

(2) In the case of a statement, the decision notice must set out the terms of the statement.

(3) In the case of a penalty, the decision notice must state the amount of the penalty.

(4) If the Authority decides to—
    (a) publish a statement in respect of an authorised person under section 205, or (b) impose a penalty on an authorised person under section 206,
    the authorised person may refer the matter to the Tribunal.

209 Publication

After a statement under section 205 is published, the Authority must send a copy of it to the authorised person and to any person on whom a copy of the decision notice was given under section 393(4).

210 Statements of policy

(1) The Authority must prepare and issue a statement of its policy with respect to—
    (a) the imposition of penalties under this Part; and
    (b) the amount of penalties under this Part.

(2) The Authority's policy in determining what the amount of a penalty should be must include having regard to—
    (a) the seriousness of the contravention in question in relation to the nature of the require-
    ment contravened;
    (b) the extent to which that contravention was deliberate or reckless; and
    (c) whether the person on whom the penalty is to be imposed is an individual.

(3) The Authority may at any time alter or replace a statement issued under this section.

(4) If a statement issued under this section is altered or replaced, the Authority must issue the altered or replacement statement.

(5) The Authority must, without delay, give the Treasury a copy of any statement which it publishes under this section.

(6) A statement issued under this section must be published by the Authority in the way appearing to the Authority to be best calculated to bring it to the attention of the public.

(7) In exercising, or deciding whether to exercise, its power under section 206 in the case of any particular contravention, the Authority must have regard to any statement published under this section and in force at the time when the contravention in question occurred.

(8) The Authority may charge a reasonable fee for providing a person with a copy of the statement.

211 Statements of policy: procedure

(1) Before issuing a statement under section 210, the Authority must publish a draft of the proposed statement in the way appearing to the Authority to be best calculated to bring it to the attention of the public.

(2) The draft must be accompanied by notice that representations about the proposal may be made to the Authority within a specified time.

(3) Before issuing the proposed statement, the Authority must have regard to any representations made to it in accordance with subsection (2).

(4) If the Authority issues the proposed statement it must publish an account, in general terms, of—

(a) the representations made to it in accordance with subsection (2); and

(b) its response to them.

(5) If the statement differs from the draft published under subsection (1) in a way which is, in the opinion of the Authority, significant, the Authority must (in addition to complying with subsection (4)) publish details of the difference.

(6) The Authority may charge a reasonable fee for providing a person with a copy of a draft published under subsection (1).

(7) This section also applies to a proposal to alter or replace a statement.

PART XV
THE FINANCIAL SERVICES COMPENSATION SCHEME

The scheme manager

212 The scheme manager

(1) The Authority must establish a body corporate ("the scheme manager") to exercise the functions conferred on the scheme manager by or under this Part.

(2) The Authority must take such steps as are necessary to ensure that the scheme manager is, at all times, capable of exercising those functions.

(3) The constitution of the scheme manager must provide for it to have—

(a) a chairman; and

(b) a board (which must include the chairman) whose members are the scheme manager's directors.

(4) The chairman and other members of the board must be persons appointed, and liable to removal from office, by the Authority (acting, in the case of the chairman, with the approval of the Treasury).

(5) But the terms of their appointment (and in particular those governing removal from office) must be such as to secure their independence from the Authority in the operation of the compensation scheme.

(6) The scheme manager is not to be regarded as exercising functions on behalf of the Crown.

(7) The scheme manager's board members, officers and staff are not to be regarded as Crown servants.

The scheme

213 The compensation scheme

(1) The Authority must by rules establish a scheme for compensating persons in cases where relevant persons are unable, or are likely to be unable, to satisfy claims against them.

(2) The rules are to be known as the Financial Services Compensation Scheme (but are referred to in this Act as "the compensation scheme").

(3) The compensation scheme must, in particular, provide for the scheme manager—

(a) to assess and pay compensation, in accordance with the scheme, to claimants in respect of claims made in connection with regulated activities carried on (whether or not with permission) by relevant persons; and

(b) to have power to impose levies on authorised persons, or any class of authorised person, for the purpose of meeting its expenses (including in particular expenses incurred, or expected to be incurred, in paying compensation, borrowing or insuring risks).

(4) The compensation scheme may provide for the scheme manager to have power to impose levies on authorised persons, or any class of authorised person, for the purpose of recovering the cost (whenever incurred) of establishing the scheme.

(5) In making any provision of the scheme by virtue of subsection (3)(b), the Authority must take account of the desirability of ensuring that the amount of the levies imposed on a particular class of authorised person reflects, so far as practicable, the amount of the claims made, or likely to be made, in respect of that class of person.

(6) An amount payable to the scheme manager as a result of any provision of the scheme made by virtue of subsection (3)(b) or (4) may be recovered as a debt due to the scheme manager.

(7) Sections 214 to 217 make further provision about the scheme but are not to be taken as limiting the power conferred on the Authority by subsection (1) [(*except where limitations are expressly stated*)].[314]

(8) In those sections "specified" means specified in the scheme.

(9) In this Part (except in sections 219, 220 or 224) "relevant person" means a person who was—
  (a) an authorised person at the time the act or omission giving rise to the claim against him took place; or
  (b) an appointed representative at that time.

(10) But a person who, at that time—
  (a) qualified for authorisation under Schedule 3, and
  (b) fell within a prescribed category,

is not to be regarded as a relevant person in relation to any activities for which he had permission as a result of any provision of, or made under, that Schedule unless he had elected to participate in the scheme in relation to those activities at that time.

Provisions of the scheme

214 General

(1) The compensation scheme may, in particular, make provision—
  (a) as to the circumstances in which a relevant person is to be taken (for the purposes of the scheme) to be unable, or likely to be unable, to satisfy claims made against him;
  (b) for the establishment of different funds for meeting different kinds of claim;
  (c) for the imposition of different levies in different cases;
  (d) limiting the levy payable by a person in respect of a specified period;
  (e) for repayment of the whole or part of a levy in specified circumstances;
  (f) for a claim to be entertained only if it is made by a specified kind of claimant;
  (g) for a claim to be entertained only if it falls within a specified kind of claim;
  (h) as to the procedure to be followed in making a claim;
  (i) for the making of interim payments before a claim is finally determined;
  (j) limiting the amount payable on a claim to a specified maximum amount or a maximum amount calculated in a specified manner;
  (k) for payment to be made, in specified circumstances, to a person other than the claimant.

[(1A) Rules by virtue of subsection (1)(h) may, in particular, allow the scheme manager to treat persons who are or may be entitled to claim under the scheme as if they had done so.

(1B) A reference in any enactment or instrument to a claim or claimant under this Part includes a reference to a deemed claim or claimant in accordance with subsection (1A).

(1C) Rules by virtue of subsection (1)(j) may, in particular, allow, or be subject to rules which allow, the scheme manager to settle a class of claim by payment of sums fixed without reference

---

[314] Inserted by the Banking Act 2009, ss 169, 170(2); date in force to be appointed.

to, or by modification of, the normal rules for calculation of maximum entitlement for individual claims.][315]

(2) Different provision may be made with respect to different kinds of claim.

(3) The scheme may provide for the determination and regulation of matters relating to the scheme by the scheme manager.

(4) The scheme, or particular provisions of the scheme, may be made so as to apply only in relation to—

(a) activities carried on,

(b) claimants,

(c) matters arising, or

(d) events occurring,

in specified territories, areas or localities.

(5) The scheme may provide for a person who—

(a) qualifies for authorisation under Schedule 3, and

(b) falls within a prescribed category,

to elect to participate in the scheme in relation to some or all of the activities for which he has permission as a result of any provision of, or made under, that Schedule.

(6) The scheme may provide for the scheme manager to have power—

(a) in specified circumstances,

(b) but only if the scheme manager is satisfied that the claimant is entitled to receive a payment in respect of his claim—

   (i) under a scheme which is comparable to the compensation scheme, or

   (ii) as the result of a guarantee given by a government or other authority,

   to make a full payment of compensation to the claimant and recover the whole or part of the amount of that payment from the other scheme or under that guarantee.

[214A Contingency funding][316]

[(1) The Treasury may make regulations ("contingency fund regulations") permitting the scheme manager to impose levies under section 213 for the purpose of maintaining contingency funds from which possible expenses may be paid.

(2) Contingency fund regulations may make provision about the establishment and management of contingency funds; in particular, the regulations may make provision about—

(a) the number and size of funds;

(b) the circumstances and timing of their establishment;

(c) the classes of person from whom contributions to the funds may be levied;

(d) the amount and timing of payments into and out of funds (which may include provision for different levies for different classes of person);

(e) refunds;

(f) the ways in which funds' contents may be invested (including (i) the extent of reliance on section 223A, and (ii) the application of investment income);

(g) the purposes for which funds may be applied, but only so as to determine whether a fund is to be used (i) for the payment of compensation, (ii) for the purposes of co-operating with a bank liquidator in accordance with section 99 of the Banking Act 2009, or (iii) for contributions under section 214B;

---

[315] Inserted by the Banking Act 2009, ss 169, 174(1); came into force (for the purpose of conferring or relating to any power to make subordinate legislation or codes of practice) 17 February 2009; came into force (for remaining purposes) 21 February 2009.

[316] Inserted by the Banking Act 2009, ss 169, 170(1); date in force to be appointed.

(h) procedures to be followed in connection with funds, including the keeping of records and the provision of information.

(3) The compensation scheme may include provision about contingency funds provided that it is not inconsistent with contingency fund regulations.]

[214B Contribution to costs of special resolution regime][317]

[(1) This section applies where—

(a) a stabilisation power under Part 1 of the Banking Act 2009 has been exercised in respect of a bank, building society or credit union (within the meaning of that Part), and

(b) the Treasury think that the bank, building society or credit union was, or but for the exercise of the stabilisation power would have become, unable to satisfy claims against it.

(2) Where this section applies—

(a) the Treasury may require the scheme manager to make payments in connection with the exercise of the stabilisation power, and

(b) payments shall be treated as expenditure under the scheme for all purposes (including levies, contingency funds and borrowing).

(3) The Treasury shall make regulations—

(a) specifying what expenses the scheme manager may be required to incur under subsection (2),

(b) providing for independent verification of the nature and amount of expenses incurred in connection with the exercise of the stabilisation power (which may include provision about appointment and payment of an auditor), and

(c) providing for the method by which amounts to be paid are to be determined.

(4) The regulations must ensure that payments required do not exceed the amount of compensation that would have been payable under the scheme if the stabilisation power had not been exercised and the bank had been unable to satisfy claims against it; and for that purpose the amount of compensation that would have been payable does not include—

(a) amounts that would have been likely, at the time when the stabilisation power was exercised, to be recovered by the scheme from the bank, or

(b) any compensation actually paid to an eligible depositor of the bank.

(5) The regulations must provide for the appointment of an independent valuer (who may be the person appointed as valuer under section 54 of the Banking Act 2009 in respect of the exercise of the stabilisation power) to calculate the amounts referred to in subsection (4)(a); and the regulations—

(a) must provide for the valuer to be appointed by the Treasury or by a person designated by the Treasury,

(b) must include provision enabling the valuer to reconsider a decision,

(c) must provide a right of appeal to a court or tribunal,

(d) must provide for payment of the valuer,

(e) may replicate or apply a provision of section 54 or 55, and

(f) may apply or include any provision that is or could be made under that section.

(6) Payments required to be made by the scheme by virtue of section 61 of the Banking Act 2009 (special resolution regime: compensation) shall be treated for the purposes of subsection (4) as if required to be made under this section.

(7) The regulations may include provision for payments (including payments under those provisions of the Banking Act 2009) to be made—

(a) before verification in accordance with subsection (3)(b), and

---

[317] Inserted by the Banking Act 2009, ss 169, 171(1); came into force (for the purpose of conferring or relating to any power to make subordinate legislation or codes of practice) 17 February 2009; came into force (for remaining purposes) 21 February 2009.

    (b) before the calculation of the limit imposed by subsection (4), by reference to estimates of that limit and subject to any necessary later adjustment.

(8) The regulations may include provision—

    (a) about timing;

    (b) about procedures to be followed;

    (c) for discretionary functions to be exercised by a specified body or by persons of a specified class;

    (d) about the resolution of disputes (which may include provision conferring jurisdiction on a court or tribunal).

(9) The compensation scheme may include provision about payments under and levies in connection with this section, provided that it is not inconsistent with this section or regulations under it.]

[215 Rights of the scheme in insolvency][318]

[(1) The compensation scheme may make provision—

    (a) about the effect of a payment of compensation under the scheme on rights or obligations arising out of matters in connection with which the compensation was paid;

    (b) giving the scheme manager a right of recovery in respect of those rights or obligations.][319]

(2) Such a right of recovery conferred by the scheme does not, in the event of [a person's insolvency][320], exceed such right (if any) as the claimant would have had in that event.

(3) If a person other than the scheme manager [makes an administration application under Schedule B1 to the 1986 Act or [Schedule B1 to][321] the 1989 Order][322] in relation to a company or partnership which is a relevant person, the scheme manager has the same rights as are conferred on the Authority by section 362.

[(3A) In subsection (3) the reference to making an administration application includes a reference to—

    (a) appointing an administrator under paragraph 14 or 22 of Schedule B1 to the 1986 Act [or paragraph 15 or 23 of Schedule B1 to the 1989 Order][323], or

    (b) filing with the court a copy of notice of intention to appoint an administrator under [any][324] of those paragraphs.][325]

---

[318] Substituted by the Banking Act 2009, ss 169, 175(1), (4); came into force (for the purpose of conferring or relating to any power to make subordinate legislation or codes of practice) 17 February 2009; came into force (for remaining purposes) 21 February 2009.

[319] Substituted by the Banking Act 2009, ss 169, 175(1), (2); came into force (for the purpose of conferring or relating to any power to make subordinate legislation or codes of practice) 17 February 2009; came into force (for remaining purposes) 21 February 2009.

[320] Substituted by the Banking Act 2009, ss 169, 175(1), (3); came into force (for the purpose of conferring or relating to any power to make subordinate legislation or codes of practice) 17 February 2009; came into force (for remaining purposes) 21 February 2009.

[321] Substituted by the Insolvency (Northern Ireland) Order 2005, SI 2005/1455, art 3(3), Sch 2, paras 56, 57(1), (2); came into force 27 March 2006.

[322] Substituted by the Enterprise Act 2002, s 248(3), Sch 17, paras 53, 54(1), (2); came into force 15 September 2003.

[323] Inserted by the Insolvency (Northern Ireland) Order 2005, SI 2005/1455, art 3(3), Sch 2, paras 56, 57(1), (3)(a); came into force 27 March 2006.

[324] Substituted by the Insolvency (Northern Ireland) Order 2005, SI 2005/1455, art 3(3), Sch 2, paras 56, 57(1), (3)(b); came into force 27 March 2006.

[325] Inserted by the Enterprise Act 2002, s 248(3), Sch 17, paras 53, 54(1), (3); came into force 15 September 2003.

(4) If a person other than the scheme manager presents a petition for the winding up of a body which is a relevant person, the scheme manager has the same rights as are conferred on the Authority by section 371.

(5) If a person other than the scheme manager presents a bankruptcy petition to the court in relation to an individual who, or an entity which, is a relevant person, the scheme manager has the same rights as are conferred on the Authority by section 374.

(6) Insolvency rules may be made for the purpose of integrating any procedure for which provision is made as a result of subsection (1) into the general procedure on the administration of a company or partnership or on a winding-up, bankruptcy or sequestration.

(7) "Bankruptcy petition" means a petition to the court—
   (a) under section 264 of the 1986 Act or Article 238 of the 1989 Order for a bankruptcy order to be made against an individual;
   (b) under section 5 of the 1985 Act for the sequestration of the estate of an individual; or
   (c) under section 6 of the 1985 Act for the sequestration of the estate belonging to or held for or jointly by the members of an entity mentioned in subsection (1) of that section.

(8) "Insolvency rules" are—
   (a) for England and Wales, rules made under sections 411 and 412 of the 1986 Act;
   (b) for Scotland, rules made by order by the Treasury, after consultation with the Scottish Ministers, for the purposes of this section; and
   (c) for Northern Ireland, rules made under Article 359 of the 1989 Order and section 55 of the Judicature (Northern Ireland) Act 1978.

(9) "The 1985 Act", "the 1986 Act", "the 1989 Order" and "court" have the same meaning as in Part XXIV.

216 Continuity of long-term insurance policies

(1) The compensation scheme may, in particular, include provision requiring the scheme manager to make arrangements for securing continuity of insurance for policyholders, or policyholders of a specified class, of relevant long-term insurers.

(2) "Relevant long-term insurers" means relevant persons who—
   (a) have permission to effect or carry out contracts of long-term insurance; and
   (b) are unable, or likely to be unable, to satisfy claims made against them.

(3) The scheme may provide for the scheme manager to take such measures as appear to him to be appropriate—
   (a) for securing or facilitating the transfer of a relevant long-term insurer's business so far as it consists of the carrying out of contracts of long-term insurance, or of any part of that business, to another authorised person;
   (b) for securing the issue by another authorised person to the policyholders concerned of policies in substitution for their existing policies.

(4) The scheme may also provide for the scheme manager to make payments to the policyholders concerned—
   (a) during any period while he is seeking to make arrangements mentioned in subsection (1);
   (b) if it appears to him that it is not reasonably practicable to make such arrangements.

(5) A provision of the scheme made by virtue of section 213(3)(b) may include power to impose levies for the purpose of meeting expenses of the scheme manager incurred in—
   (a) taking measures as a result of any provision of the scheme made by virtue of subsection (3);
   (b) making payments as a result of any such provision made by virtue of subsection (4).

217 Insurers in financial difficulties

(1) The compensation scheme may, in particular, include provision for the scheme manager to have power to take measures for safeguarding policyholders, or policyholders of a specified class, of relevant insurers.

(2) "Relevant insurers" means relevant persons who—
  (a) have permission to effect or carry out contracts of insurance; and
  (b) are in financial difficulties.

(3) The measures may include such measures as the scheme manager considers appropriate for—
  (a) securing or facilitating the transfer of a relevant insurer's business so far as it consists of the carrying out of contracts of insurance, or of any part of that business, to another authorised person;
  (b) giving assistance to the relevant insurer to enable it to continue to effect or carry out contracts of insurance.

(4) The scheme may provide—
  (a) that if measures of a kind mentioned in subsection (3)(a) are to be taken, they should be on terms appearing to the scheme manager to be appropriate, including terms reducing, or deferring payment of, any of the things to which any of those who are eligible policyholders in relation to the relevant insurer are entitled in their capacity as such;
  (b) that if measures of a kind mentioned in subsection (3)(b) are to be taken, they should be conditional on the reduction of, or the deferment of the payment of, the things to which any of those who are eligible policyholders in relation to the relevant insurer are entitled in their capacity as such;
  (c) for ensuring that measures of a kind mentioned in subsection (3)(b) do not benefit to any material extent persons who were members of a relevant insurer when it began to be in financial difficulties or who had any responsibility for, or who may have profited from, the circumstances giving rise to its financial difficulties, except in specified circumstances;
  (d) for requiring the scheme manager to be satisfied that any measures he proposes to take are likely to cost less than it would cost to pay compensation under the scheme if the relevant insurer became unable, or likely to be unable, to satisfy claims made against him.

(5) The scheme may provide for the Authority to have power—
  (a) to give such assistance to the scheme manager as it considers appropriate for assisting the scheme manager to determine what measures are practicable or desirable in the case of a particular relevant insurer;
  (b) to impose constraints on the taking of measures by the scheme manager in the case of a particular relevant insurer;
  (c) to require the scheme manager to provide it with information about any particular measures which the scheme manager is proposing to take.

(6) The scheme may include provision for the scheme manager to have power—
  (a) to make interim payments in respect of eligible policyholders of a relevant insurer;
  (b) to indemnify any person making payments to eligible policyholders of a relevant insurer.

(7) A provision of the scheme made by virtue of section 213(3)(b) may include power to impose levies for the purpose of meeting expenses of the scheme manager incurred in—
  (a) taking measures as a result of any provision of the scheme made by virtue of subsection (1);
  (b) making payments or giving indemnities as a result of any such provision made by virtue of subsection (6).

(8) "Financial difficulties" and "eligible policyholders" have such meanings as may be specified.

Annual report

218 Annual report

(1) At least once a year, the scheme manager must make a report to the Authority [*and the Treasury*]326 on the discharge of its functions.

---

326 Inserted by the Banking Act 2009, s 170(3)(a); date in force to be appointed: see the Banking Act 2009, s 263(1).

(2) The report must—
- (a) include a statement setting out the value of each of the funds established by the compensation scheme; and
- (b) comply with any requirements specified in rules made by the Authority [*or in contingency fund regulations*].[327]

(3) The scheme manager must publish each report in the way it considers appropriate.

Information and documents

[218A Authority's power to require information][328]

[(1) The Authority may make rules enabling the Authority to require authorised persons to provide information, which may then be made available to the scheme manager by the Authority.

(2) A requirement may be imposed only if the Authority thinks the information is of a kind that may be of use to the scheme manager in connection with functions in respect of the scheme.

(3) A requirement under this section may apply—
- (a) to authorised persons generally or only to specified persons or classes of person;
- (b) to the provision of information at specified periods, in connection with specified events or in other ways.

(4) In addition to requirements under this section, a notice under section 165 may relate to information or documents which the Authority thinks are reasonably required by the scheme manager in connection with the performance of functions in respect of the scheme; and section 165(4) is subject to this subsection.

(5) Rules under subsection (1) shall be prepared, made and treated in the same way as (and may be combined with) the Authority's general rules.]

219 Scheme manager's power to require information

(1) The scheme manager may, by notice in writing [require a person][329]—
- (a) to provide specified information or information of a specified description; or
- (b) to produce specified documents or documents of a specified description.

[(1A) A requirement may be imposed only—
- (a) on a person (P) against whom a claim has been made under the scheme,
- (b) on a person (P) who is unable or likely to be unable to satisfy claims under the scheme against P,
- (c) on a person ("the Third Party") whom the scheme manager thinks was knowingly involved in matters giving rise to a claim against another person (P) under the scheme, or
- (d) on a person ("the Third Party") whom the scheme manager thinks was knowingly involved in matters giving rise to the actual or likely inability of another person (P) to satisfy claims under the scheme.

---

[327] Inserted by the Banking Act 2009, s 170(3)(b); date in force to be appointed: see the Banking Act 2009, s 263(1).

[328] Inserted by the Banking Act 2009, ss 169, 176(1); came into force (for the purpose of conferring or relating to any power to make subordinate legislation or codes of practice) 17 February 2009; came into force (for remaining purposes) 21 February 2009.

[329] Substituted by the Banking Act 2009, ss 169, 176(2), (3); came into force (for the purpose of conferring or relating to any power to make subordinate legislation or codes of practice) 17 February 2009; came into force (for remaining purposes) 21 February 2009.

(1B) For the purposes of subsection (1A)(b) and (d) whether P is unable or likely to be unable to satisfy claims shall be determined in accordance with provision to be made by the scheme (which may, in particular—
   (a) apply or replicate, with or without modifications, a provision of an enactment;
   (b) confer discretion on a specified person).][330]

(2) The information or documents must be provided or produced—
   (a) before the end of such reasonable period as may be specified; and
   (b) in the case of information, in such manner or form as may be specified.

(3) This section applies only to information and documents the provision or production of which the scheme manager considers [to be necessary (or likely to be necessary) for the fair determination of claims which have been or may be made against P].[331]

[(3A) Where a stabilisation power under Part 1 of the Banking Act 2009 has been exercised in respect of a bank, the scheme manager may by notice in writing require the bank or the Bank of England to provide information that the scheme manager requires for the purpose of applying regulations under section 214B(3) above.][332]

(4) If a document is produced in response to a requirement imposed under this section, the scheme manager may—
   (a) take copies or extracts from the document; or
   (b) require the person producing the document to provide an explanation of the document.

(5) If a person who is required under this section to produce a document fails to do so, the scheme manager may require the person to state, to the best of his knowledge and belief, where the document is.

(6) If [P][333] is insolvent, no requirement may be imposed under this section on a person to whom section 220 or 224 applies.

(7) If a person claims a lien on a document, its production under this Part does not affect the lien.

(8) . . .[334]

(9) "Specified" means specified in the notice given under subsection (1).

(10) . . .[335]

220 Scheme manager's power to inspect information held by liquidator etc

(1) For the purpose of assisting the scheme manager to discharge its functions in relation to a claim made in respect of an insolvent relevant person, a person to whom this section applies must permit a person authorised by the scheme manager to inspect relevant documents.

---

[330] Inserted by the Banking Act 2009, ss 169, 176(2), (4); came into force (for the purpose of conferring or relating to any power to make subordinate legislation or codes of practice) 17 February 2009; came into force (for remaining purposes) 21 February 2009.

[331] Substituted by the Banking Act 2009, ss 169, 176(2), (5); came into force (for the purpose of conferring or relating to any power to make subordinate legislation or codes of practice) 17 February 2009; came into force (for remaining purposes) 21 February 2009.

[332] Inserted by the Banking Act 2009, ss 169, 176(2), (6); came into force (for the purpose of conferring or relating to any power to make subordinate legislation or codes of practice) 17 February 2009; came into force (for remaining purposes) 21 February 2009.

[333] Substituted by the Banking Act 2009, ss 169, 176(2), (7); came into force (for the purpose of conferring or relating to any power to make subordinate legislation or codes of practice) 17 February 2009; came into force (for remaining purposes) 21 February 2009.

[334] Repealed by the Banking Act 2009, ss 169, 176(2), (8); came into force (for the purpose of conferring or relating to any power to make subordinate legislation or codes of practice) 17 February 2009; came into force (for remaining purposes) 21 February 2009.

[335] Repealed by the Banking Act 2009, ss 169, 176(2), (9); came into force (for the purpose of conferring or relating to any power to make subordinate legislation or codes of practice) 17 February 2009; came into force (for remaining purposes) 21 February 2009.

(2) A person inspecting a document under this section may take copies of, or extracts from, the document.

(3) This section applies to—

    (a) the administrative receiver, administrator, liquidator[, bank liquidator]336[, building society liquidator]337 or trustee in bankruptcy of an insolvent relevant person;

    (b) the permanent trustee, within the meaning of the Bankruptcy (Scotland) Act 1985, on the estate of an insolvent relevant person.

(4) This section does not apply to a liquidator, administrator or trustee in bankruptcy who is—

    (a) the Official Receiver;

    (b) the Official Receiver for Northern Ireland; or

    (c) the Accountant in Bankruptcy.

(5) "Relevant person" has the same meaning as in section 224.

221 Powers of court where information required

(1) If a person ("the defaulter")—

    (a) fails to comply with a requirement imposed under section 219, or

    (b) fails to permit documents to be inspected under section 220,

the scheme manager may certify that fact in writing to the court and the court may enquire into the case.

(2) If the court is satisfied that the defaulter failed without reasonable excuse to comply with the requirement (or to permit the documents to be inspected), it may deal with the defaulter (and, in the case of a body corporate, any director or officer) as if he were in contempt[; and "officer", in relation to a limited liability partnership, means a member of the limited liability partnership].338

(3) "Court" means—

    (a) the High Court;

    (b) in Scotland, the Court of Session.

Miscellaneous

[221A Delegation of functions]339

[(1) The scheme manager may arrange for any of its functions to be discharged on its behalf by another person (a "scheme agent").

(2) Before entering into arrangements the scheme manager must be satisfied that the scheme agent—

    (a) is competent to discharge the function, and

    (b) has been given sufficient directions to enable the agent to take any decisions required in the course of exercising the function in accordance with policy determined by the scheme manager.

(3) Arrangements may include provision for payments to be made by the scheme manager to the scheme agent (which payments are management expenses of the scheme manager).]

---

336 Inserted by the Banking Act 2009, s 123(3); came into force (for the purpose of conferring or relating to any power to make subordinate legislation or codes of practice) 17 February 2009; came into force (for remaining purposes) 21 February 2009.

337 Inserted by SI 2009/805, art 15; came into force 29 March 2009.

338 Inserted by SI 2001/1090, reg 9(1), Sch 5, para 21; came into force 6 April 2001.

339 Inserted by the Banking Act 2009, ss 169, 179(1); came into force (for the purpose of conferring or relating to any power to make subordinate legislation or codes of practice) 17 February 2009; came into force (for remaining purposes) 21 February 2009.

222 Statutory immunity

(1) Neither the scheme manager nor any person who is, or is acting as, its board member, officer [, scheme agent]340 or member of staff is to be liable in damages for anything done or omitted in the discharge, or purported discharge, of the scheme manager's functions.

(2) Subsection (1) does not apply—

    (a) if the act or omission is shown to have been in bad faith; or

    (b) so as to prevent an award of damages made in respect of an act or omission on the ground that the act or omission was unlawful as a result of section 6(1) of the Human Rights Act 1998.

223 Management expenses

(1) The amount which the scheme manager may recover, from the sums levied under the scheme, as management expenses attributable to a particular period may not exceed such amount as may be fixed by the scheme as the limit applicable to that period.

(2) In calculating the amount of any levy to be imposed by the scheme manager, no amount may be included to reflect management expenses unless the limit mentioned in subsection (1) has been fixed by the scheme.

(3) "Management expenses" means expenses incurred, or expected to be incurred, by the scheme manager in connection with its functions under this Act other than those incurred—

    (a) in paying compensation;

    (b) as a result of any provision of the scheme made by virtue of section 216(3) or (4) or 217(1) or (6)[;

    (c) under section 214B].341

[223A Investing in National Loans Fund]342

[(1) Sums levied for the purpose of maintaining a contingency fund may be paid to the Treasury.

(2) The Treasury may receive sums under subsection (1) and may set terms and conditions of receipts.

(3) Sums received shall be treated as if raised under section 12 of the National Loans Act 1968 (and shall therefore be invested as part of the National Loans Fund).

(4) Interest accruing on the invested sums may be credited to the contingency fund (subject to any terms and conditions set under subsection (2)).

(5) The Treasury shall comply with any request of the scheme manager to arrange for the return of sums for the purpose of making payments out of a contingency fund (subject to any terms and conditions set under subsection (2)).]

[223B Borrowing from National Loans Fund]343

[(1) The scheme manager may request a loan from the National Loans Fund for the purpose of funding expenses incurred or expected to be incurred under the scheme.

---

340 Inserted by the Banking Act 2009, s 179(2); came into force (for the purpose of conferring or relating to any power to make subordinate legislation or codes of practice) 17 February 2009; came into force (for remaining purposes) 21 February 2009.

341 Inserted by the Banking Act 2009, ss 169, 171(2); came into force (for the purpose of conferring or relating to any power to make subordinate legislation or codes of practice) 17 February 2009; came into force (for remaining purposes) 21 February 2009.

342 Inserted by the Banking Act 2009, ss 169, 172; date in force to be appointed.

343 Inserted by the Banking Act 2009, ss 169, 173; came into force (for the purpose of conferring or relating to any power to make subordinate legislation or codes of practice) 17 February 2009; came into force (for remaining purposes) 21 February 2009.

(2) The Treasury may arrange for money to be paid out of the National Loans Fund in pursuance of a request under subsection (1).

(3) The Treasury shall determine—

(a) the rate of interest on a loan, and

(b) other terms and conditions.

(4) The Treasury may make regulations—

(a) about the amounts that may be borrowed under this section;

(b) permitting the scheme manager to impose levies under section 213 for the purpose of meeting expenses in connection with loans under this section (and the regulations may have effect despite any provision of this Act);

(c) about the classes of person on whom those levies may be imposed;

(d) about the amounts and timing of those levies.

(5) The compensation scheme may include provision about borrowing under this section provided that it is not inconsistent with regulations under this section.]

[223C Payments in error]344

[(1) Payments made by the scheme manager in error may be provided for in setting a levy by virtue of section 213, 214A, 214B or 223B.

(2) This section does not apply to payments made in bad faith.]

224 Scheme manager's power to inspect documents held by Official Receiver etc

(1) If, as a result of the insolvency or bankruptcy of a relevant person, any documents have come into the possession of a person to whom this section applies, he must permit any person authorised by the scheme manager to inspect the documents for the purpose of establishing—

(a) the identity of persons to whom the scheme manager may be liable to make a payment in accordance with the compensation scheme; or

(b) the amount of any payment which the scheme manager may be liable to make.

(2) A person inspecting a document under this section may take copies or extracts from the document.

(3) In this section "relevant person" means a person who was—

(a) an authorised person at the time the act or omission which may give rise to the liability mentioned in subsection (1)(a) took place; or

(b) an appointed representative at that time.

(4) But a person who, at that time—

(a) qualified for authorisation under Schedule 3, and

(b) fell within a prescribed category,

is not to be regarded as a relevant person for the purposes of this section in relation to any activities for which he had permission as a result of any provision of, or made under, that Schedule unless he had elected to participate in the scheme in relation to those activities at that time.

(5) This section applies to—

(a) the Official Receiver;

(b) the Official Receiver for Northern Ireland; and

(c) the Accountant in Bankruptcy.

---

344 Inserted by the Banking Act 2009, ss 169, 177; came into force (for the purpose of conferring or relating to any power to make subordinate legislation or codes of practice) 17 February 2009; came into force (for remaining purposes) 21 February 2009.

[224A Functions under the Banking Act 2009][345]

[A reference in this Part to functions of the scheme manager (including a reference to functions conferred by or under this Part) includes a reference to functions conferred by or under the Banking Act 2009.]

PART XVI
THE OMBUDSMAN SCHEME

The scheme

225 The scheme and the scheme operator

(1) This Part provides for a scheme under which certain disputes may be resolved quickly and with minimum formality by an independent person.

(2) The scheme is to be administered by a body corporate ("the scheme operator").

(3) The scheme is to be operated under a name chosen by the scheme operator but is referred to in this Act as "the ombudsman scheme".

(4) Schedule 17 makes provision in connection with the ombudsman scheme and the scheme operator.

226 Compulsory jurisdiction

(1) A complaint which relates to an act or omission of a person ("the respondent") in carrying on an activity to which compulsory jurisdiction rules apply is to be dealt with under the ombudsman scheme if the conditions mentioned in subsection (2) are satisfied.

(2) The conditions are that—
   (a) the complainant is eligible and wishes to have the complaint dealt with under the scheme;
   (b) the respondent was an authorised person[, or a payment service provider within the meaning of the Payment Services Regulations 2009,][346] at the time of the act or omission to which the complaint relates; and
   (c) the act or omission to which the complaint relates occurred at a time when compulsory jurisdiction rules were in force in relation to the activity in question.

(3) "Compulsory jurisdiction rules" means rules—
   (a) made by the Authority for the purposes of this section; and
   (b) specifying the activities to which they apply.

(4) Only activities which are regulated activities, or which could be made regulated activities by an order under section 22, may be specified.

(5) Activities may be specified by reference to specified categories (however described).

(6) A complainant is eligible, in relation to the compulsory jurisdiction of the ombudsman scheme, if he falls within a class of person specified in the rules as eligible.

(7) The rules—
   (a) may include provision for persons other than individuals to be eligible; but
   (b) may not provide for authorised persons to be eligible except in specified circumstances or in relation to complaints of a specified kind.

---

[345] Inserted by the Banking Act 2009, ss 169, 180; came into force (for the purpose of conferring or relating to any power to make subordinate legislation or codes of practice) 17 February 2009; came into force (for remaining purposes) 21 February 2009.

[346] Inserted by SI 2009/209, reg 126, Sch 6, Pt 1, para 1(1)(a); came into force 2 March 2009.

(8) The jurisdiction of the scheme which results from this section is referred to in this Act as the "compulsory jurisdiction".

[226A Consumer credit jurisdiction]347

[(1) A complaint which relates to an act or omission of a person ("the respondent") is to be dealt with under the ombudsman scheme if the conditions mentioned in subsection (2) are satisfied.

(2) The conditions are that—
    (a) the complainant is eligible and wishes to have the complaint dealt with under the scheme;
    (b) the complaint falls within a description specified in consumer credit rules;
    (c) at the time of the act or omission the respondent was the licensee under a standard licence or was authorised to carry on an activity by virtue of section 34A of the Consumer Credit Act 1974;
    (d) the act or omission occurred in the course of a business being carried on by the respondent which was of a type mentioned in subsection (3);
    (e) at the time of the act or omission that type of business was specified in an order made by the Secretary of State; and
    (f) the complaint cannot be dealt with under the compulsory jurisdiction.

(3) The types of business referred to in subsection (2)(d) are—
    (a) a consumer credit business;
    (b) a consumer hire business;
    (c) a business so far as it comprises or relates to credit brokerage;
    (d) a business so far as it comprises or relates to debt-adjusting;
    (e) a business so far as it comprises or relates to debt-counselling;
    (f) a business so far as it comprises or relates to debt-collecting;
    (g) a business so far as it comprises or relates to debt administration;
    (h) a business so far as it comprises or relates to the provision of credit information services;
    (i) a business so far as it comprises or relates to the operation of a credit reference agency.

(4) A complainant is eligible if—
    (a) he is—
        (i) an individual; or
        (ii) a surety in relation to a security provided to the respondent in connection with the business mentioned in subsection (2)(d); and
    (b) he falls within a class of person specified in consumer credit rules.

(5) The approval of the Treasury is required for an order under subsection (2)(e).

(6) The jurisdiction of the scheme which results from this section is referred to in this Act as the "consumer credit jurisdiction".

(7) In this Act "consumer credit rules" means rules made by the scheme operator with the approval of the Authority for the purposes of the consumer credit jurisdiction.

(8) Consumer credit rules under this section may make different provision for different cases.

(9) Expressions used in the Consumer Credit Act 1974 have the same meaning in this section as they have in that Act.]

227 Voluntary jurisdiction

(1) A complaint which relates to an act or omission of a person ("the respondent") in carrying on an activity to which voluntary jurisdiction rules apply is to be dealt with under the ombudsman scheme if the conditions mentioned in subsection (2) are satisfied.

---

347 Inserted by the Consumer Credit Act 2006, s 59(1); came into force 16 June 2006.

(2) The conditions are that—
  (a) the complainant is eligible and wishes to have the complaint dealt with under the scheme;
  (b) at the time of the act or omission to which the complaint relates, the respondent was participating in the scheme;
  (c) at the time when the complaint is referred under the scheme, the respondent has not withdrawn from the scheme in accordance with its provisions;
  (d) the act or omission to which the complaint relates occurred at a time when voluntary jurisdiction rules were in force in relation to the activity in question; and
  (e) the complaint cannot be dealt with under the compulsory jurisdiction [or the consumer credit jurisdiction].[348]

(3) "Voluntary jurisdiction rules" means rules—
  (a) made by the scheme operator for the purposes of this section; and
  (b) specifying the activities to which they apply.

(4) The only activities which may be specified in the rules are activities which are, or could be, specified in compulsory jurisdiction rules.

(5) Activities may be specified by reference to specified categories (however described).

(6) The rules require the Authority's approval.

(7) A complainant is eligible, in relation to the voluntary jurisdiction of the ombudsman scheme, if he falls within a class of person specified in the rules as eligible.

(8) The rules may include provision for persons other than individuals to be eligible.

(9) A person qualifies for participation in the ombudsman scheme if he falls within a class of person specified in the rules in relation to the activity in question.

(10) Provision may be made in the rules for persons other than authorised persons to participate in the ombudsman scheme.

(11) The rules may make different provision in relation to complaints arising from different activities.

(12) The jurisdiction of the scheme which results from this section is referred to in this Act as the "voluntary jurisdiction".

(13) In such circumstances as may be specified in voluntary jurisdiction rules, a complaint—
  (a) which relates to an act or omission occurring at a time before the rules came into force, and
  (b) which could have been dealt with under a scheme which has to any extent been replaced by the voluntary jurisdiction,
  is to be dealt with under the ombudsman scheme even though paragraph (b) or (d) of subsection (2) would otherwise prevent that.

(14) In such circumstances as may be specified in voluntary jurisdiction rules, a complaint is to be dealt with under the ombudsman scheme even though—
  (a) paragraph (b) or (d) of subsection (2) would otherwise prevent that, and
  (b) the complaint is not brought within the scheme as a result of subsection (13),
  but only if the respondent has agreed that complaints of that kind were to be dealt with under the scheme.

---

[348] Inserted by the Consumer Credit Act 2006, s 61(2); came into force 16 June 2006.

Determination of complaints

228 Determination under the compulsory jurisdiction

(1) This section applies only in relation to the compulsory jurisdiction [and to the consumer credit jurisdiction].[349]

(2) A complaint is to be determined by reference to what is, in the opinion of the ombudsman, fair and reasonable in all the circumstances of the case.

(3) When the ombudsman has determined a complaint he must give a written statement of his determination to the respondent and to the complainant.

(4) The statement must—

    (a) give the ombudsman's reasons for his determination;

    (b) be signed by him; and

    (c) require the complainant to notify him in writing, before a date specified in the statement, whether he accepts or rejects the determination.

(5) If the complainant notifies the ombudsman that he accepts the determination, it is binding on the respondent and the complainant and final.

(6) If, by the specified date, the complainant has not notified the ombudsman of his acceptance or rejection of the determination he is to be treated as having rejected it.

(7) The ombudsman must notify the respondent of the outcome.

(8) A copy of the determination on which appears a certificate signed by an ombudsman is evidence (or in Scotland sufficient evidence) that the determination was made under the scheme.

(9) Such a certificate purporting to be signed by an ombudsman is to be taken to have been duly signed unless the contrary is shown.

229 Awards

(1) This section applies only in relation to the compulsory jurisdiction [and to the consumer credit jurisdiction].[350]

(2) If a complaint which has been dealt with under the scheme is determined in favour of the complainant, the determination may include—

    (a) an award against the respondent of such amount as the ombudsman considers fair compensation for loss or damage (of a kind falling within subsection (3)) suffered by the complainant ("a money award");

    (b) a direction that the respondent take such steps in relation to the complainant as the ombudsman considers just and appropriate (whether or not a court could order those steps to be taken).

(3) A money award may compensate for—

    (a) financial loss; or

    (b) any other loss, or any damage, of a specified kind.

(4) The Authority may specify [for the purposes of the compulsory jurisdiction][351] the maximum amount which may be regarded as fair compensation for a particular kind of loss or damage specified under subsection (3)(b).

[(4A) The scheme operator may specify for the purposes of the consumer credit jurisdiction the maximum amount which may be regarded as fair compensation for a particular kind of loss or damage specified under subsection (3)(b).][352]

---

[349] Inserted by the Consumer Credit Act 2006, s 61(3); came into force 16 June 2006.

[350] Inserted by the Consumer Credit Act 2006, s 61(3); came into force 16 June 2006.

[351] Inserted by the Consumer Credit Act 2006, s 61(4); came into force 16 June 2006.

[352] Inserted by the Consumer Credit Act 2006, s 61(5); came into force 16 June 2006.

(5) A money award may not exceed the monetary limit; but the ombudsman may, if he considers that fair compensation requires payment of a larger amount, recommend that the respondent pay the complainant the balance.

(6) The monetary limit is such amount as may be specified.

(7) Different amounts may be specified in relation to different kinds of complaint.

(8) A money award—

    (a) may provide for the amount payable under the award to bear interest at a rate and as from a date specified in the award; and

    (b) is enforceable by the complainant in accordance with Part III of Schedule 17 [or (as the case may be) Part 3A of that Schedule].[353]

(9) Compliance with a direction under subsection (2)(b)—

    (a) is enforceable by an injunction; or

    (b) in Scotland, is enforceable by an order under section 45 of the Court of Session Act 1988.

(10) Only the complainant may bring proceedings for an injunction or proceedings for an order.

[(11) "Specified" means—

    (a) for the purposes of the compulsory jurisdiction, specified in compulsory jurisdiction rules;

    (b) for the purposes of the consumer credit jurisdiction, specified in consumer credit rules.

(12) Consumer credit rules under this section may make different provision for different cases.][354]

230 Costs

(1) The scheme operator may by rules ("costs rules") provide for an ombudsman to have power, on determining a complaint under the compulsory jurisdiction [or the consumer credit jurisdiction],[355] to award costs in accordance with the provisions of the rules.

(2) Costs rules require the approval of the Authority.

(3) Costs rules may not provide for the making of an award against the complainant in respect of the respondent's costs.

(4) But they may provide for the making of an award against the complainant in favour of the scheme operator, for the purpose of providing a contribution to resources deployed in dealing with the complaint, if in the opinion of the ombudsman—

    (a) the complainant's conduct was improper or unreasonable; or

    (b) the complainant was responsible for an unreasonable delay.

(5) Costs rules may authorise an ombudsman making an award in accordance with the rules to order that the amount payable under the award bears interest at a rate and as from a date specified in the order.

(6) An amount due under an award made in favour of the scheme operator is recoverable as a debt due to the scheme operator.

(7) Any other award made against the respondent is to be treated as a money award for the purposes of paragraph 16 of Schedule 17 [or (as the case may be) paragraph 16D of that Schedule].[356]

[353] Inserted by the Consumer Credit Act 2006, s 61(6); came into force 16 June 2006.

[354] Substituted, for sub-s (11) as originally enacted, by the Consumer Credit Act 2006, s 61(7); came into force 16 June 2006.

[355] Inserted by the Consumer Credit Act 2006, s 61(8)(a); came into force 16 June 2006.

[356] Inserted by the Consumer Credit Act 2006, s 61(8)(b); came into force 16 June 2006.

Information

231 Ombudsman's power to require information

(1) An ombudsman may, by notice in writing given to a party to a complaint, require that party—
  (a) to provide specified information or information of a specified description; or
  (b) to produce specified documents or documents of a specified description.
(2) The information or documents must be provided or produced—
  (a) before the end of such reasonable period as may be specified; and
  (b) in the case of information, in such manner or form as may be specified.
(3) This section applies only to information and documents the production of which the ombudsman considers necessary for the determination of the complaint.
(4) If a document is produced in response to a requirement imposed under this section, the ombudsman may—
  (a) take copies or extracts from the document; or
  (b) require the person producing the document to provide an explanation of the document.
(5) If a person who is required under this section to produce a document fails to do so, the ombudsman may require him to state, to the best of his knowledge and belief, where the document is.
(6) If a person claims a lien on a document, its production under this Part does not affect the lien.
(7) "Specified" means specified in the notice given under subsection (1).

232 Powers of court where information required

(1) If a person ("the defaulter") fails to comply with a requirement imposed under section 231, the ombudsman may certify that fact in writing to the court and the court may enquire into the case.
(2) If the court is satisfied that the defaulter failed without reasonable excuse to comply with the requirement, it may deal with the defaulter (and, in the case of a body corporate, any director or officer) as if he were in contempt[; and "officer", in relation to a limited liability partnership, means a member of the limited liability partnership].[357]
(3) "Court" means—
  (a) the High Court;
  (b) in Scotland, the Court of Session.

233 Data protection

In section 31 of the Data Protection Act 1998 (regulatory activity), after subsection (4), insert—

"(4A) Personal data processed for the purpose of discharging any function which is conferred by or under Part XVI of the Financial Services and Markets Act 2000 on the body established by the Financial Services Authority for the purposes of that Part are exempt from the subject information provisions in any case to the extent to which the application of those provisions to the data would be likely to prejudice the proper discharge of the function."

Funding

234 Industry funding

(1) For the purpose of funding—
  (a) the establishment of the ombudsman scheme (whenever any relevant expense is incurred), and

---

[357] Inserted by SI 2001/1090, reg 9(1), Sch 5, para 21; came into force 6 April 2001.

(b) its operation in relation to the compulsory jurisdiction,

the Authority may make rules requiring the payment to it or to the scheme operator, by authorised persons or any class of authorised person [or any payment service provider within the meaning of the Payment Services Regulations 2009][358] of specified amounts (or amounts calculated in a specified way).

(2) "Specified" means specified in the rules.

[234A Funding by consumer credit licensees etc][359]

[(1) For the purpose of funding—

    (a) the establishment of the ombudsman scheme so far as it relates to the consumer credit jurisdiction (whenever any relevant expense is incurred), and

    (b) its operation in relation to the consumer credit jurisdiction,

    the scheme operator may from time to time with the approval of the Authority determine a sum which is to be raised by way of contributions under this section.

(2) A sum determined under subsection (1) may include a component to cover the costs of the collection of contributions to that sum ("collection costs") under this section.

(3) The scheme operator must notify the OFT of every determination under subsection (1).

(4) The OFT must give general notice of every determination so notified.

(5) The OFT may by general notice impose requirements on—

    (a) licensees to whom this section applies, or

    (b) persons who make applications to which this section applies,

    to pay contributions to the OFT for the purpose of raising sums determined under subsection (1).

(6) The amount of the contribution payable by a person under such a requirement—

    (a) shall be the amount specified in or determined under the general notice; and

    (b) shall be paid before the end of the period or at the time so specified or determined.

(7) A general notice under subsection (5) may—

    (a) impose requirements only on descriptions of licensees or applicants specified in the notice;

    (b) provide for exceptions from any requirement imposed on a description of licensees or applicants;

    (c) impose different requirements on different descriptions of licensees or applicants;

    (d) make provision for refunds in specified circumstances.

(8) Contributions received by the OFT must be paid to the scheme operator.

(9) As soon as practicable after the end of—

    (a) each financial year of the scheme operator, or

    (b) if the OFT and the scheme operator agree that this paragraph is to apply instead of paragraph (a) for the time being, each period agreed by them,

    the scheme operator must pay to the OFT an amount representing the extent to which collection costs are covered in accordance with subsection (2) by the total amount of the contributions paid by the OFT to it during the year or (as the case may be) the agreed period.

(10) Amounts received by the OFT from the scheme operator are to be retained by it for the purpose of meeting its costs.

(11) The Secretary of State may by order provide that the functions of the OFT under this section are for the time being to be carried out by the scheme operator.

---

[358] Inserted by SI 2009/209, reg 126, Sch 6, Pt 1, para 1(1)(b); came into force 2 March 2009.
[359] Inserted by the Consumer Credit Act 2006, s 60; came into force 16 June 2006.

(12) An order under subsection (11) may provide that while the order is in force this section shall have effect subject to such modifications as may be set out in the order.

(13) The licensees to whom this section applies are licensees under standard licences which cover to any extent the carrying on of a type of business specified in an order under section 226A(2)(e).

(14) The applications to which this section applies are applications for—
    (a) standard licences covering to any extent the carrying on of a business of such a type;
    (b) the renewal of standard licences on terms covering to any extent the carrying on of a business of such a type.

(15) Expressions used in the Consumer Credit Act 1974 have the same meaning in this section as they have in that Act.]

PART XVII
COLLECTIVE INVESTMENT SCHEMES

CHAPTER I
INTERPRETATION

235 Collective investment schemes

(1) In this Part "collective investment scheme" means any arrangements with respect to property of any description, including money, the purpose or effect of which is to enable persons taking part in the arrangements (whether by becoming owners of the property or any part of it or otherwise) to participate in or receive profits or income arising from the acquisition, holding, management or disposal of the property or sums paid out of such profits or income.

(2) The arrangements must be such that the persons who are to participate ("participants") do not have day-to-day control over the management of the property, whether or not they have the right to be consulted or to give directions.

(3) The arrangements must also have either or both of the following characteristics—
    (a) the contributions of the participants and the profits or income out of which payments are to be made to them are pooled;
    (b) the property is managed as a whole by or on behalf of the operator of the scheme.

(4) If arrangements provide for such pooling as is mentioned in subsection (3)(a) in relation to separate parts of the property, the arrangements are not to be regarded as constituting a single collective investment scheme unless the participants are entitled to exchange rights in one part for rights in another.

(5) The Treasury may by order provide that arrangements do not amount to a collective investment scheme—
    (a) in specified circumstances; or
    (b) if the arrangements fall within a specified category of arrangement.

236 Open-ended investment companies

(1) In this Part "an open-ended investment company" means a collective investment scheme which satisfies both the property condition and the investment condition.

(2) The property condition is that the property belongs beneficially to, and is managed by or on behalf of, a body corporate ("BC") having as its purpose the investment of its funds with the aim of—
    (a) spreading investment risk; and
    (b) giving its members the benefit of the results of the management of those funds by or on behalf of that body.

(3) The investment condition is that, in relation to BC, a reasonable investor would, if he were to participate in the scheme—

(a) expect that he would be able to realize, within a period appearing to him to be reasonable, his investment in the scheme (represented, at any given time, by the value of shares in, or securities of, BC held by him as a participant in the scheme); and

(b) be satisfied that his investment would be realized on a basis calculated wholly or mainly by reference to the value of property in respect of which the scheme makes arrangements.

(4) In determining whether the investment condition is satisfied, no account is to be taken of any actual or potential redemption or repurchase of shares or securities under—

(a) Chapter VII of Part V of the Companies Act 1985;

(b) Chapter VII of Part VI of the Companies (Northern Ireland) Order 1986;

(c) corresponding provisions in force in another EEA State; or

(d) provisions in force in a country or territory other than an EEA state which the Treasury have, by order, designated as corresponding provisions.

(5) The Treasury may by order amend the definition of "an open-ended investment company" for the purposes of this Part.

237 Other definitions

(1) In this Part "unit trust scheme" means a collective investment scheme under which the property is held on trust for the participants.

(2) In this Part—

"trustee", in relation to a unit trust scheme, means the person holding the property in question on trust for the participants;

"depositary", in relation to—

(a) a collective investment scheme which is constituted by a body incorporated by virtue of regulations under section 262, or

(b) any other collective investment scheme which is not a unit trust scheme,

means any person to whom the property subject to the scheme is entrusted for safekeeping;

"the operator", in relation to a unit trust scheme with a separate trustee, means the manager and in relation to an open-ended investment company, means that company;

"units" means the rights or interests (however described) of the participants in a collective investment scheme.

(3) In this Part—

"an authorised unit trust scheme" means a unit trust scheme which is authorised for the purposes of this Act by an authorisation order in force under section 243;

"an authorised open-ended investment company" means a body incorporated by virtue of regulations under section 262 in respect of which an authorisation order is in force under any provision made in such regulations by virtue of subsection (2)(l) of that section;

"a recognised scheme" means a scheme recognised under section 264, 270 or 272.

CHAPTER II
RESTRICTIONS ON PROMOTION

238 Restrictions on promotion

(1) An authorised person must not communicate an invitation or inducement to participate in a collective investment scheme.

(2) But that is subject to the following provisions of this section and to section 239.

(3) Subsection (1) applies in the case of a communication originating outside the United Kingdom only if the communication is capable of having an effect in the United Kingdom.

(4) Subsection (1) does not apply in relation to—

    (a) an authorised unit trust scheme;

    (b) a scheme constituted by an authorised open-ended investment company; or

    (c) a recognised scheme.

(5) Subsection (1) does not apply to anything done in accordance with rules made by the Authority for the purpose of exempting from that subsection the promotion otherwise than to the general public of schemes of specified descriptions.

(6) The Treasury may by order specify circumstances in which subsection (1) does not apply.

(7) An order under subsection (6) may, in particular, provide that subsection (1) does not apply in relation to communications—

    (a) of a specified description;

    (b) originating in a specified country or territory outside the United Kingdom;

    (c) originating in a country or territory which falls within a specified description of country or territory outside the United Kingdom; or

    (d) originating outside the United Kingdom.

(8) The Treasury may by order repeal subsection (3).

(9) "Communicate" includes causing a communication to be made.

(10) "Promotion otherwise than to the general public" includes promotion in a way designed to reduce, so far as possible, the risk of participation by persons for whom participation would be unsuitable.

(11) "Participate", in relation to a collective investment scheme, means become a participant (within the meaning given by section 235(2)) in the scheme.

239 Single property schemes

(1) The Treasury may by regulations make provision for exempting single property schemes from section 238(1).

(2) For the purposes of subsection (1) a single property scheme is a scheme which has the characteristics mentioned in subsection (3) and satisfies such other requirements as are prescribed by the regulations conferring the exemption.

(3) The characteristics are—

    (a) that the property subject to the scheme (apart from cash or other assets held for management purposes) consists of—

        (i) a single building (or a single building with ancillary buildings) managed by or on behalf of the operator of the scheme, or

        (ii) a group of adjacent or contiguous buildings managed by him or on his behalf as a single enterprise,

    with or without ancillary land and with or without furniture, fittings or other contents of the building or buildings in question; and

    (b) that the units of the participants in the scheme are either dealt in on a recognised investment exchange or offered on terms such that any agreement for their acquisition is conditional on their admission to dealings on such an exchange.

(4) If regulations are made under subsection (1), the Authority may make rules imposing duties or liabilities on the operator and (if any) the trustee or depositary of a scheme exempted by the regulations.

(5) The rules may include, to such extent as the Authority thinks appropriate, provision for purposes corresponding to those for which provision can be made under section 248 in relation to authorised unit trust schemes.

240 Restriction on approval of promotion

(1) An authorised person may not approve for the purposes of section 21 the content of a communication relating to a collective investment scheme if he would be prohibited by section 238(1) from effecting the communication himself or from causing it to be communicated.

(2) For the purposes of determining in any case whether there has been a contravention of section 21(1), an approval given in contravention of subsection (1) is to be regarded as not having been given.

241 Actions for damages

If an authorised person contravenes a requirement imposed on him by section 238 or 240, section 150 applies to the contravention as it applies to a contravention mentioned in that section.

CHAPTER III
AUTHORISED UNIT TRUST SCHEMES

Applications for authorization

242 Applications for authorisation of unit trust schemes

(1) Any application for an order declaring a unit trust scheme to be an authorised unit trust scheme must be made to the Authority by the manager and trustee, or proposed manager and trustee, of the scheme.

(2) The manager and trustee (or proposed manager and trustee) must be different persons.

(3) The application—
   (a) must be made in such manner as the Authority may direct; and
   (b) must contain or be accompanied by such information as the Authority may reasonably require for the purpose of determining the application.

(4) At any time after receiving an application and before determining it, the Authority may require the applicants to provide it with such further information as it reasonably considers necessary to enable it to determine the application.

(5) Different directions may be given, and different requirements imposed, in relation to different applications.

(6) The Authority may require applicants to present information which they are required to give under this section in such form, or to verify it in such a way, as the Authority may direct.

243 Authorisation orders

(1) If, on an application under section 242 in respect of a unit trust scheme, the Authority—
   (a) is satisfied that the scheme complies with the requirements set out in this section,
   (b) is satisfied that the scheme complies with the requirements of the trust scheme rules, and
   (c) has been provided with a copy of the trust deed and a certificate signed by a solicitor to the effect that it complies with such of the requirements of this section or those rules as relate to its contents,
the Authority may make an order declaring the scheme to be an authorised unit trust scheme.

(2) If the Authority makes an order under subsection (1), it must give written notice of the order to the applicant.

(3) In this Chapter "authorisation order" means an order under subsection (1).

(4) The manager and the trustee must be persons who are independent of each other.

(5) The manager and the trustee must each—
   (a) be a body corporate incorporated in the United Kingdom or another EEA State, and
   (b) have a place of business in the United Kingdom,
and the affairs of each must be administered in the country in which it is incorporated.

(6) If the manager is incorporated in another EEA State, the scheme must not be one which satisfies the requirements prescribed for the purposes of section 264.

(7) The manager and the trustee must each be an authorised person and the manager must have permission to act as manager and the trustee must have permission to act as trustee.

(8) The name of the scheme must not be undesirable or misleading.

(9) The purposes of the scheme must be reasonably capable of being successfully carried into effect.

(10) The participants must be entitled to have their units redeemed in accordance with the scheme at a price—

(a) related to the net value of the property to which the units relate; and

(b) determined in accordance with the scheme.

(11) But a scheme is to be treated as complying with subsection (10) if it requires the manager to ensure that a participant is able to sell his units on an investment exchange at a price not significantly different from that mentioned in that subsection.

244 Determination of applications

(1) An application under section 242 must be determined by the Authority before the end of the period of six months beginning with the date on which it receives the completed application.

(2) The Authority may determine an incomplete application if it considers it appropriate to do so; and it must in any event determine such an application within twelve months beginning with the date on which it first receives the application.

(3) The applicant may withdraw his application, by giving the Authority written notice, at any time before the Authority determines it.

Applications refused

245 Procedure when refusing an application

(1) If the Authority proposes to refuse an application made under section 242 it must give each of the applicants a warning notice.

(2) If the Authority decides to refuse the application—

(a) it must give each of the applicants a decision notice; and

(b) either applicant may refer the matter to the Tribunal.

Certificates

246 Certificates

(1) If the manager or trustee of a unit trust scheme which complies with the conditions necessary for it to enjoy the rights conferred by any relevant Community instrument so requests, the Authority may issue a certificate to the effect that the scheme complies with those conditions.

(2) Such a certificate may be issued on the making of an authorisation order in respect of the scheme or at any subsequent time.

Rules

247 Trust scheme rules

(1) The Authority may make rules ("trust scheme rules") as to—

(a) the constitution, management and operation of authorised unit trust schemes;

(b) the powers, duties, rights and liabilities of the manager and trustee of any such scheme;

(c) the rights and duties of the participants in any such scheme; and

(d) the winding up of any such scheme.

(2) Trust scheme rules may, in particular, make provision—

(a) as to the issue and redemption of the units under the scheme;

(b) as to the expenses of the scheme and the means of meeting them;

(c) for the appointment, removal, powers and duties of an auditor for the scheme;

(d) for restricting or regulating the investment and borrowing powers exercisable in relation to the scheme;

(e) requiring the keeping of records with respect to the transactions and financial position of the scheme and for the inspection of those records;

(f) requiring the preparation of periodical reports with respect to the scheme and the provision of those reports to the participants and to the Authority; and

(g) with respect to the amendment of the scheme.

(3) Trust scheme rules may make provision as to the contents of the trust deed, including provision requiring any of the matters mentioned in subsection (2) to be dealt with in the deed.

(4) But trust scheme rules are binding on the manager, trustee and participants independently of the contents of the trust deed and, in the case of the participants, have effect as if contained in it.

(5) If—

(a) a modification is made of the statutory provisions in force in Great Britain or Northern Ireland relating to companies,

(b) the modification relates to the rights and duties of persons who hold the beneficial title to any shares in a company without also holding the legal title, and

(c) it appears to the Treasury that, for the purpose of assimilating the law relating to authorised unit trust schemes to the law relating to companies as so modified, it is expedient to modify the rule-making powers conferred on the Authority by this section,

the Treasury may by order make such modifications of those powers as they consider appropriate.

248 Scheme particulars rules

(1) The Authority may make rules ("scheme particulars rules") requiring the manager of an authorised unit trust scheme—

(a) to submit scheme particulars to the Authority; and

(b) to publish scheme particulars or make them available to the public on request.

(2) "Scheme particulars" means particulars in such form, containing such information about the scheme and complying with such requirements, as are specified in scheme particulars rules.

(3) Scheme particulars rules may require the manager of an authorised unit trust scheme to submit, and to publish or make available, revised or further scheme particulars if there is a significant change affecting any matter—

(a) which is contained in scheme particulars previously published or made available; and

(b) whose inclusion in those particulars was required by the rules.

(4) Scheme particulars rules may require the manager of an authorised unit trust scheme to submit, and to publish or make available, revised or further scheme particulars if—

(a) a significant new matter arises; and

(b) the inclusion of information in respect of that matter would have been required in previous particulars if it had arisen when those particulars were prepared.

(5) Scheme particulars rules may provide for the payment, by the person or persons who in accordance with the rules are treated as responsible for any scheme particulars, of compensation to any qualifying person who has suffered loss as a result of—

(a) any untrue or misleading statement in the particulars; or

(b) the omission from them of any matter required by the rules to be included.

(6) "Qualifying person" means a person who—

(a) has become or agreed to become a participant in the scheme; or

(b) although not being a participant, has a beneficial interest in units in the scheme.

(7) Scheme particulars rules do not affect any liability which any person may incur apart from the rules.

249 Disqualification of auditor for breach of trust scheme rules

(1) If it appears to the Authority that an auditor has failed to comply with a duty imposed on him by trust scheme rules, it may disqualify him from being the auditor for any authorised unit trust scheme or authorised open-ended investment company.

(2) Subsections (2) to (5) of section 345 have effect in relation to disqualification under subsection (1) as they have effect in relation to disqualification under subsection (1) of that section.

250 Modification or waiver of rules

(1) In this section "rules" means—
   (a) trust scheme rules; or
   (b) scheme particulars rules.

(2) The Authority may, on the application or with the consent of any person to whom any rules apply, direct that all or any of the rules—
   (a) are not to apply to him as respects a particular scheme; or
   (b) are to apply to him, as respects a particular scheme, with such modifications as may be specified in the direction.

(3) The Authority may, on the application or with the consent of the manager and trustee of a particular scheme acting jointly, direct that all or any of the rules—
   (a) are not to apply to the scheme; or
   (b) are to apply to the scheme with such modifications as may be specified in the direction.

(4) Subsections (3) to (9) and (11) of section 148 have effect in relation to a direction under subsection (2) as they have effect in relation to a direction under section 148(2) but with the following modifications—
   (a) . . .[360]
   (b) any reference to the [person][361] is to be read as a reference to the person mentioned in subsection (2); and
   (c) subsection (7)(b) is to be read, in relation to a participant of the scheme, as if the word "commercial" were omitted.

(5) Subsections (3) to (9) and (11) of section 148 have effect in relation to a direction under subsection (3) as they have effect in relation to a direction under section 148(2) but with the following modifications—
   (a) subsection (4)(a) is to be read as if the words "by the . . .[362] person" were omitted;
   (b) subsections (7)(b) and (11) are to be read as if references to the . . .[363] person were references to each of the manager and the trustee of the scheme;
   (c) subsection (7)(b) is to be read, in relation to a participant of the scheme, as if the word "commercial" were omitted;
   (d) subsection (8) is to be read as if the reference to the . . .[364] person concerned were a reference to the scheme concerned and to its manager and trustee; and
   (e) subsection (9) is to be read as if the reference to the . . .[365] person were a reference to the manager and trustee of the scheme acting jointly.

Alterations

251 Alteration of schemes and changes of manager or trustee

(1) The manager of an authorised unit trust scheme must give written notice to the Authority of any proposal to alter the scheme or to replace its trustee.

---

[360] Repealed by SI 2007/1973, arts 2, 11(a); came into force 12 July 2007.
[361] Substituted by SI 2007/1973, arts 2, 11(b); came into force 12 July 2007.
[362] Repealed by SI 2007/1973, arts 2, 11(c); came into force 12 July 2007.
[363] Repealed by SI 2007/1973, arts 2, 11(c); came into force 12 July 2007.
[364] Repealed by SI 2007/1973, arts 2, 11(c); came into force 12 July 2007.
[365] Repealed by SI 2007/1973, arts 2, 11(c); came into force 12 July 2007.

(2) Any notice given in respect of a proposal to alter the scheme involving a change in the trust deed must be accompanied by a certificate signed by a solicitor to the effect that the change will not affect the compliance of the deed with the trust scheme rules.

(3) The trustee of an authorised unit trust scheme must give written notice to the Authority of any proposal to replace the manager of the scheme.

(4) Effect is not to be given to any proposal of which notice has been given under subsection (1) or (3) unless—

    (a) the Authority, by written notice, has given its approval to the proposal; or

    (b) one month, beginning with the date on which the notice was given, has expired without the manager or trustee having received from the Authority a warning notice under section 252 in respect of the proposal.

(5) The Authority must not approve a proposal to replace the manager or the trustee of an authorised unit trust scheme unless it is satisfied that, if the proposed replacement is made, the scheme will continue to comply with the requirements of section 243(4) to (7).

252 Procedure when refusing approval of change of manager or trustee

(1) If the Authority proposes to refuse approval of a proposal to replace the trustee or manager of an authorised unit trust scheme, it must give a warning notice to the person by whom notice of the proposal was given under section 251(1) or (3).

(2) If the Authority proposes to refuse approval of a proposal to alter an authorised unit trust scheme it must give separate warning notices to the manager and the trustee of the scheme.

(3) To be valid the warning notice must be received by that person before the end of one month beginning with the date on which notice of the proposal was given.

(4) If, having given a warning notice to a person, the Authority decides to refuse approval—

    (a) it must give him a decision notice; and

    (b) he may refer the matter to the Tribunal.

Exclusion clauses

253 Avoidance of exclusion clauses

Any provision of the trust deed of an authorised unit trust scheme is void in so far as it would have the effect of exempting the manager or trustee from liability for any failure to exercise due care and diligence in the discharge of his functions in respect of the scheme.

Ending of authorization

254 Revocation of authorisation order otherwise than by consent

(1) An authorisation order may be revoked by an order made by the Authority if it appears to the Authority that—

    (a) one or more of the requirements for the making of the order are no longer satisfied;

    (b) the manager or trustee of the scheme concerned has contravened a requirement imposed on him by or under this Act;

    (c) the manager or trustee of the scheme has, in purported compliance with any such requirement, knowingly or recklessly given the Authority information which is false or misleading in a material particular;

    (d) no regulated activity is being carried on in relation to the scheme and the period of that inactivity began at least twelve months earlier; or

    (e) none of paragraphs (a) to (d) applies, but it is desirable to revoke the authorisation order in order to protect the interests of participants or potential participants in the scheme.

(2) For the purposes of subsection (1)(e), the Authority may take into account any matter relating to—

    (a) the scheme;

    (b) the manager or trustee;

    (c) any person employed by or associated with the manager or trustee in connection with the scheme;

    (d) any director of the manager or trustee;

    (e) any person exercising influence over the manager or trustee;

    (f) any body corporate in the same group as the manager or trustee;

    (g) any director of any such body corporate;

    (h) any person exercising influence over any such body corporate.

255 Procedure

(1) If the Authority proposes to make an order under section 254 revoking an authorisation order ("a revoking order"), it must give separate warning notices to the manager and the trustee of the scheme.

(2) If the Authority decides to make a revoking order, it must without delay give each of them a decision notice and either of them may refer the matter to the Tribunal.

256 Requests for revocation of authorisation order

(1) An authorisation order may be revoked by an order made by the Authority at the request of the manager or trustee of the scheme concerned.

(2) If the Authority makes an order under subsection (1), it must give written notice of the order to the manager and trustee of the scheme concerned.

(3) The Authority may refuse a request to make an order under this section if it considers that—

    (a) the public interest requires that any matter concerning the scheme should be investigated before a decision is taken as to whether the authorisation order should be revoked; or

    (b) revocation would not be in the interests of the participants or would be incompatible with a Community obligation.

(4) If the Authority proposes to refuse a request under this section, it must give separate warning notices to the manager and the trustee of the scheme.

(5) If the Authority decides to refuse the request, it must without delay give each of them a decision notice and either of them may refer the matter to the Tribunal.

Powers of intervention

257 Directions

(1) The Authority may give a direction under this section if it appears to the Authority that—

    (a) one or more of the requirements for the making of an authorisation order are no longer satisfied;

    (b) the manager or trustee of an authorised unit trust scheme has contravened, or is likely to contravene, a requirement imposed on him by or under this Act;

    (c) the manager or trustee of such a scheme has, in purported compliance with any such requirement, knowingly or recklessly given the Authority information which is false or misleading in a material particular; or

    (d) none of paragraphs (a) to (c) applies, but it is desirable to give a direction in order to protect the interests of participants or potential participants in such a scheme.

(2) A direction under this section may—

    (a) require the manager of the scheme to cease the issue or redemption, or both the issue and redemption, of units under the scheme;

    (b) require the manager and trustee of the scheme to wind it up.

(3) If the authorisation order is revoked, the revocation does not affect any direction under this section which is then in force.

(4) A direction may be given under this section in relation to a scheme in the case of which the authorisation order has been revoked if a direction under this section was already in force at the time of revocation.

(5) If a person contravenes a direction under this section, section 150 applies to the contravention as it applies to a contravention mentioned in that section.

(6) The Authority may, either on its own initiative or on the application of the manager or trustee of the scheme concerned, revoke or vary a direction given under this section if it appears to the Authority—

    (a) in the case of revocation, that it is no longer necessary for the direction to take effect or continue in force;

    (b) in the case of variation, that the direction should take effect or continue in force in a different form.

258 Applications to the court

(1) If the Authority could give a direction under section 257, it may also apply to the court for an order—

    (a) removing the manager or the trustee, or both the manager and the trustee, of the scheme; and

    (b) replacing the person or persons removed with a suitable person or persons nominated by the Authority.

(2) The Authority may nominate a person for the purposes of subsection (1)(b) only if it is satisfied that, if the order was made, the requirements of section 243(4) to (7) would be complied with.

(3) If it appears to the Authority that there is no person it can nominate for the purposes of subsection (1)(b), it may apply to the court for an order—

    (a) removing the manager or the trustee, or both the manager and the trustee, of the scheme; and

    (b) appointing an authorised person to wind up the scheme.

(4) On an application under this section the court may make such order as it thinks fit.

(5) The court may, on the application of the Authority, rescind any such order as is mentioned in subsection (3) and substitute such an order as is mentioned in subsection (1).

(6) The Authority must give written notice of the making of an application under this section to the manager and trustee of the scheme concerned.

(7) The jurisdiction conferred by this section may be exercised by—

    (a) the High Court;

    (b) in Scotland, the Court of Session.

259 Procedure on giving directions under section 257 and varying them on Authority's own initiative

(1) A direction takes effect—

    (a) immediately, if the notice given under subsection (3) states that that is the case;

    (b) on such date as may be specified in the notice; or

    (c) if no date is specified in the notice, when the matter to which it relates is no longer open to review.

(2) A direction may be expressed to take effect immediately (or on a specified date) only if the Authority, having regard to the ground on which it is exercising its power under section 257, considers that it is necessary for the direction to take effect immediately (or on that date).

(3) If the Authority proposes to give a direction under section 257, or gives such a direction with immediate effect, it must give separate written notice to the manager and the trustee of the scheme concerned.

(4) The notice must—
  (a) give details of the direction;
  (b) inform the person to whom it is given of when the direction takes effect;
  (c) state the Authority's reasons for giving the direction and for its determination as to when the direction takes effect;
  (d) inform the person to whom it is given that he may make representations to the Authority within such period as may be specified in it (whether or not he has referred the matter to the Tribunal); and
  (e) inform him of his right to refer the matter to the Tribunal.

(5) If the direction imposes a requirement under section 257(2)(a), the notice must state that the requirement has effect until—
  (a) a specified date; or
  (b) a further direction.

(6) If the direction imposes a requirement under section 257(2)(b), the scheme must be wound up—
  (a) by a date specified in the notice; or
  (b) if no date is specified, as soon as practicable.

(7) The Authority may extend the period allowed under the notice for making representations.

(8) If, having considered any representations made by a person to whom the notice was given, the Authority decides—
  (a) to give the direction in the way proposed, or
  (b) if it has been given, not to revoke the direction,
  it must give separate written notice to the manager and the trustee of the scheme concerned.

(9) If, having considered any representations made by a person to whom the notice was given, the Authority decides—
  (a) not to give the direction in the way proposed,
  (b) to give the direction in a way other than that proposed, or
  (c) to revoke a direction which has effect,
  it must give separate written notice to the manager and the trustee of the scheme concerned.

(10) A notice given under subsection (8) must inform the person to whom it is given of his right to refer the matter to the Tribunal.

(11) A notice under subsection (9)(b) must comply with subsection (4).

(12) If a notice informs a person of his right to refer a matter to the Tribunal, it must give an indication of the procedure on such a reference.

(13) This section applies to the variation of a direction on the Authority's own initiative as it applies to the giving of a direction.

(14) For the purposes of subsection (1)(c), whether a matter is open to review is to be determined in accordance with section 391(8).

260 Procedure: refusal to revoke or vary direction

(1) If on an application under section 257(6) for a direction to be revoked or varied the Authority proposes—
  (a) to vary the direction otherwise than in accordance with the application, or
  (b) to refuse to revoke or vary the direction,
  it must give the applicant a warning notice.

(2) If the Authority decides to refuse to revoke or vary the direction—
  (a) it must give the applicant a decision notice; and
  (b) the applicant may refer the matter to the Tribunal.

261 Procedure: revocation of direction and grant of request for variation

(1) If the Authority decides on its own initiative to revoke a direction under section 257 it must give separate written notices of its decision to the manager and trustee of the scheme.

(2) If on an application under section 257(6) for a direction to be revoked or varied the Authority decides to revoke the direction or vary it in accordance with the application, it must give the applicant written notice of its decision.

(3) A notice under this section must specify the date on which the decision takes effect.

(4) The Authority may publish such information about the revocation or variation, in such way, as it considers appropriate.

CHAPTER IV
OPEN-ENDED INVESTMENT COMPANIES

262 Open-ended investment companies

(1) The Treasury may by regulations make provision for—
   (a) facilitating the carrying on of collective investment by means of open-ended investment companies;
   (b) regulating such companies.

(2) The regulations may, in particular, make provision—
   (a) for the incorporation and registration in Great Britain of bodies corporate;
   (b) for a body incorporated by virtue of the regulations to take such form as may be determined in accordance with the regulations;
   (c) as to the purposes for which such a body may exist, the investments which it may issue and otherwise as to its constitution;
   (d) as to the management and operation of such a body and the management of its property;
   (e) as to the powers, duties, rights and liabilities of such a body and of other persons, including—
      (i) the directors or sole director of such a body;
      (ii) its depositary (if any);
      (iii) its shareholders, and persons who hold the beneficial title to shares in it without holding the legal title;
      (iv) its auditor; and
      (v) any persons who act or purport to act on its behalf;
   (f) as to the merger of one or more such bodies and the division of such a body;
   (g) for the appointment and removal of an auditor for such a body;
   (h) as to the winding up and dissolution of such a body;
   (i) for such a body, or any director or depositary of such a body, to be required to comply with directions given by the Authority;
   (j) enabling the Authority to apply to a court for an order removing and replacing any director or depositary of such a body;
   (k) for the carrying out of investigations by persons appointed by the Authority or the Secretary of State;
   (l) corresponding to any provision made in relation to unit trust schemes by Chapter III of this Part.

(3) Regulations under this section may—
   (a) impose criminal liability;
   (b) confer functions on the Authority;
   (c) in the case of provision made by virtue of subsection (2)(l), authorise the making of rules by the Authority;

    (d) confer jurisdiction on any court or on the Tribunal;

    (e) provide for fees to be charged by the Authority in connection with the carrying out of any of its functions under the regulations (including fees payable on a periodical basis);

    (f) modify, exclude or apply (with or without modifications) any primary or subordinate legislation (including any provision of, or made under, this Act);

    (g) make consequential amendments, repeals and revocations of any such legislation;

    (h) modify or exclude any rule of law.

(4) The provision that may be made by virtue of subsection (3)(f) includes provision extending or adapting any power to make subordinate legislation.

(5) Regulations under this section may, in particular—

    (a) revoke the Open-Ended Investment Companies (Investment Companies with Variable Capital) Regulations 1996; and

    (b) provide for things done under or in accordance with those regulations to be treated as if they had been done under or in accordance with regulations under this section.

263 ...

. . .[366]

CHAPTER V
RECOGNISED OVERSEAS SCHEMES

Schemes constituted in other EEA States

264 Schemes constituted in other EEA States

(1) A collective investment scheme constituted in another EEA State is a recognised scheme if—

    (a) it satisfies such requirements as are prescribed for the purposes of this section; and

    (b) not less than two months before inviting persons in the United Kingdom to become participants in the scheme, the operator of the scheme gives notice to the Authority of his intention to do so, specifying the way in which the invitation is to be made.

(2) But this section does not make the scheme a recognised scheme if within two months of receiving the notice under subsection (1) the Authority notifies—

    (a) the operator of the scheme, and

    (b) the authorities of the State in question who are responsible for the authorisation of collective investment schemes,

that the way in which the invitation is to be made does not comply with the law in force in the United Kingdom.

(3) The notice to be given to the Authority under subsection (1)—

    (a) must be accompanied by a certificate from the authorities mentioned in subsection (2)(b) to the effect that the scheme complies with the conditions necessary for it to enjoy the rights conferred by any relevant Community instrument;

    (b) must contain the address of a place in the United Kingdom for the service on the operator of notices or other documents required or authorised to be served on him under this Act; and

    (c) must contain or be accompanied by such other information and documents as may be prescribed.

---

[366] This section is now spent. See also the Companies Act 2006, s 1295, Sch 16. Effective from: 21 December 2002.

(4) A notice given by the Authority under subsection (2) must—

    (a) give the reasons for which the Authority considers that the law in force in the United Kingdom will not be complied with; and

    (b) specify a reasonable period (which may not be less than 28 days) within which any person to whom it is given may make representations to the Authority.

(5) For the purposes of this section a collective investment scheme is constituted in another EEA State if—

    (a) it is constituted under the law of that State by a contract or under a trust and is managed by a body corporate incorporated under that law; or

    (b) it takes the form of an open-ended investment company incorporated under that law.

(6) The operator of a recognised scheme may give written notice to the Authority that he desires the scheme to be no longer recognised by virtue of this section.

(7) On the giving of notice under subsection (6), the scheme ceases to be a recognised scheme.

265 Representations and references to the Tribunal

(1) This section applies if any representations are made to the Authority, before the period for making representations has ended, by a person to whom a notice was given by the Authority under section 264(2).

(2) The Authority must, within a reasonable period, decide in the light of those representations whether or not to withdraw its notice.

(3) If the Authority withdraws its notice the scheme is a recognised scheme from the date on which the notice is withdrawn.

(4) If the Authority decides not to withdraw its notice, it must give a decision notice to each person to whom the notice under section 264(2) was given.

(5) The operator of the scheme to whom the decision notice is given may refer the matter to the Tribunal.

266 Disapplication of rules

(1) Apart from—

    (a) financial promotion rules, and

    (b) rules under section 283(1),

rules made by the Authority under this Act do not apply to the operator, trustee or depositary of a scheme in relation to the carrying on by him of regulated activities for which he has permission in that capacity.

[(1A) But subsection (1) does not affect the application of rules to an operator of a scheme if the operator is an EEA firm falling within paragraph 5(f) of Schedule 3 who qualifies for authorisation under that Schedule.][367]

(2) "Scheme" means a scheme which is a recognised scheme by virtue of section 264.

267 Power of Authority to suspend promotion of scheme

(1) Subsection (2) applies if it appears to the Authority that the operator of a scheme has communicated an invitation or inducement in relation to the scheme in a manner contrary to financial promotion rules.

(2) The Authority may direct that—

    (a) the exemption from subsection (1) of section 238 provided by subsection (4)(c) of that section is not to apply in relation to the scheme; and

    (b) subsection (5) of that section does not apply with respect to things done in relation to the scheme.

---

[367] Inserted by SI 2003/2066, reg 9; came into force 13 February 2004.

(3) A direction under subsection (2) has effect—
  (a) for a specified period;
  (b) until the occurrence of a specified event; or
  (c) until specified conditions are complied with.

(4) The Authority may, either on its own initiative or on the application of the operator of the scheme concerned, vary a direction given under subsection (2) if it appears to the Authority that the direction should take effect or continue in force in a different form.

(5) The Authority may, either on its own initiative or on the application of the operator of the recognised scheme concerned, revoke a direction given under subsection (2) if it appears to the Authority—
  (a) that the conditions specified in the direction have been complied with; or
  (b) that it is no longer necessary for the direction to take effect or continue in force.

(6) If an event is specified, the direction ceases to have effect (unless revoked earlier) on the occurrence of that event.

(7) For the purposes of this section and sections 268 and 269—
  (a) the scheme's home State is the EEA State in which the scheme is constituted (within the meaning given by section 264);
  (b) the competent authorities in the scheme's home State are the authorities in that State who are responsible for the authorisation of collective investment schemes.

(8) "Scheme" means a scheme which is a recognised scheme by virtue of section 264.

(9) "Specified", in relation to a direction, means specified in it.

268 Procedure on giving directions under section 267 and varying them on Authority's own initiative

(1) A direction under section 267 takes effect—
  (a) immediately, if the notice given under subsection (3)(a) states that that is the case;
  (b) on such date as may be specified in the notice; or
  (c) if no date is specified in the notice, when the matter to which it relates is no longer open to review.

(2) A direction may be expressed to take effect immediately (or on a specified date) only if the Authority, having regard to its reasons for exercising its power under section 267, considers that it is necessary for the direction to take effect immediately (or on that date).

(3) If the Authority proposes to give a direction under section 267, or gives such a direction with immediate effect, it must—
  (a) give the operator of the scheme concerned written notice; and
  (b) inform the competent authorities in the scheme's home State of its proposal or (as the case may be) of the direction.

(4) The notice must—
  (a) give details of the direction;
  (b) inform the operator of when the direction takes effect;
  (c) state the Authority's reasons for giving the direction and for its determination as to when the direction takes effect;
  (d) inform the operator that he may make representations to the Authority within such period as may be specified in it (whether or not he has referred the matter to the Tribunal); and
  (e) inform him of his right to refer the matter to the Tribunal.

(5) The Authority may extend the period allowed under the notice for making representations.

(6) Subsection (7) applies if, having considered any representations made by the operator, the Authority decides—
  (a) to give the direction in the way proposed, or
  (b) if it has been given, not to revoke the direction.

(7) The Authority must—
    (a) give the operator of the scheme concerned written notice; and
    (b) inform the competent authorities in the scheme's home State of the direction.

(8) Subsection (9) applies if, having considered any representations made by a person to whom the notice was given, the Authority decides—
    (a) not to give the direction in the way proposed,
    (b) to give the direction in a way other than that proposed, or
    (c) to revoke a direction which has effect.

(9) The Authority must—
    (a) give the operator of the scheme concerned written notice; and
    (b) inform the competent authorities in the scheme's home State of its decision.

(10) A notice given under subsection (7)(a) must inform the operator of his right to refer the matter to the Tribunal.

(11) A notice under subsection (9)(a) given as a result of subsection (8)(b) must comply with subsection (4).

(12) If a notice informs a person of his right to refer a matter to the Tribunal, it must give an indication of the procedure on such a reference.

(13) This section applies to the variation of a direction on the Authority's own initiative as it applies to the giving of a direction.

(14) For the purposes of subsection (1)(c), whether a matter is open to review is to be determined in accordance with section 391(8).

269 Procedure on application for variation or revocation of direction

(1) If, on an application under subsection (4) or (5) of section 267, the Authority proposes—
    (a) to vary a direction otherwise than in accordance with the application, or
    (b) to refuse the application,
    it must give the operator of the scheme concerned a warning notice.

(2) If, on such an application, the Authority decides—
    (a) to vary a direction otherwise than in accordance with the application, or
    (b) to refuse the application,
    it must give the operator of the scheme concerned a decision notice.

(3) If the application is refused, the operator of the scheme may refer the matter to the Tribunal.

(4) If, on such an application, the Authority decides to grant the application it must give the operator of the scheme concerned written notice.

(5) If the Authority decides on its own initiative to revoke a direction given under section 267 it must give the operator of the scheme concerned written notice.

(6) The Authority must inform the competent authorities in the scheme's home State of any notice given under this section.

Schemes authorised in designated countries or territories

270 Schemes authorised in designated countries or territories

(1) A collective investment scheme which is not a recognised scheme by virtue of section 264 but is managed in, and authorised under the law of, a country or territory outside the United Kingdom is a recognised scheme if—
    (a) that country or territory is designated for the purposes of this section by an order made by the Treasury;
    (b) the scheme is of a class specified by the order;
    (c) the operator of the scheme has given written notice to the Authority that he wishes it to be recognised; and

(d) either—

    (i) the Authority, by written notice, has given its approval to the scheme's being recognised; or

    (ii) two months, beginning with the date on which notice was given under paragraph (c), have expired without the operator receiving a warning notice from the Authority under section 271.

(2) The Treasury may not make an order designating any country or territory for the purposes of this section unless satisfied—

    (a) that the law and practice under which relevant collective investment schemes are authorised and supervised in that country or territory affords to investors in the United Kingdom protection at least equivalent to that provided for them by or under this Part in the case of comparable authorised schemes; and

    (b) that adequate arrangements exist, or will exist, for co-operation between the authorities of the country or territory responsible for the authorisation and supervision of relevant collective investment schemes and the Authority.

(3) "Relevant collective investment schemes" means collective investment schemes of the class or classes to be specified by the order.

(4) "Comparable authorised schemes" means whichever of the following the Treasury consider to be the most appropriate, having regard to the class or classes of scheme to be specified by the order—

    (a) authorised unit trust schemes;

    (b) authorised open-ended investment companies;

    (c) both such unit trust schemes and such companies.

(5) If the Treasury are considering whether to make an order designating a country or territory for the purposes of this section—

    (a) the Treasury must ask the Authority for a report—

        (i) on the law and practice of that country or territory in relation to the authorisation and supervision of relevant collective investment schemes,

        (ii) on any existing or proposed arrangements for co-operation between it and the authorities responsible in that country or territory for the authorisation and supervision of relevant collective investment schemes,

    having regard to the Treasury's need to be satisfied as mentioned in subsection (2);

    (b) the Authority must provide the Treasury with such a report; and

    (c) the Treasury must have regard to it in deciding whether to make the order.

(6) The notice to be given by the operator under subsection (1)(c)—

    (a) must contain the address of a place in the United Kingdom for the service on the operator of notices or other documents required or authorised to be served on him under this Act; and

    (b) must contain or be accompanied by such information and documents as may be specified by the Authority.

271 Procedure

(1) If the Authority proposes to refuse approval of a scheme's being a recognised scheme by virtue of section 270, it must give the operator of the scheme a warning notice.

(2) To be valid the warning notice must be received by the operator before the end of two months beginning with the date on which notice was given under section 270(1)(c).

(3) If, having given a warning notice, the Authority decides to refuse approval—

    (a) it must give the operator of the scheme a decision notice; and

    (b) the operator may refer the matter to the Tribunal.

Individually recognised overseas schemes

272 Individually recognised overseas schemes

(1) The Authority may, on the application of the operator of a collective investment scheme which—

    (a) is managed in a country or territory outside the United Kingdom,

    (b) does not satisfy the requirements prescribed for the purposes of section 264,

    (c) is not managed in a country or territory designated for the purposes of section 270 or, if it is so managed, is of a class not specified by the designation order, and

    (d) appears to the Authority to satisfy the requirements set out in the following provisions of this section,

    make an order declaring the scheme to be a recognised scheme.

(2) Adequate protection must be afforded to participants in the scheme.

(3) The arrangements for the scheme's constitution and management must be adequate.

(4) The powers and duties of the operator and, if the scheme has a trustee or depositary, of the trustee or depositary must be adequate.

(5) In deciding whether the matters mentioned in subsection (3) or (4) are adequate, the Authority must have regard to—

    (a) any rule of law, and

    (b) any matters which are, or could be, the subject of rules,

    applicable in relation to comparable authorised schemes.

(6) "Comparable authorised schemes" means whichever of the following the Authority considers the most appropriate, having regard to the nature of scheme in respect of which the application is made—

    (a) authorised unit trust schemes;

    (b) authorised open-ended investment companies;

    (c) both such unit trust schemes and such companies.

(7) The scheme must take the form of an open-ended investment company or (if it does not take that form) the operator must be a body corporate.

(8) The operator of the scheme must—

    (a) if an authorised person, have permission to act as operator;

    (b) if not an authorised person, be a fit and proper person to act as operator.

(9) The trustee or depositary (if any) of the scheme must—

    (a) if an authorised person, have permission to act as trustee or depositary;

    (b) if not an authorised person, be a fit and proper person to act as trustee or depositary.

(10) The operator and the trustee or depositary (if any) of the scheme must be able and willing to co-operate with the Authority by the sharing of information and in other ways.

(11) The name of the scheme must not be undesirable or misleading.

(12) The purposes of the scheme must be reasonably capable of being successfully carried into effect.

(13) The participants must be entitled to have their units redeemed in accordance with the scheme at a price related to the net value of the property to which the units relate and determined in accordance with the scheme.

(14) But a scheme is to be treated as complying with subsection (13) if it requires the operator to ensure that a participant is able to sell his units on an investment exchange at a price not significantly different from that mentioned in that subsection.

(15) Subsection (13) is not to be read as imposing a requirement that the participants must be entitled to have their units redeemed (or sold as mentioned in subsection (14)) immediately following a demand to that effect.

273 Matters that may be taken into account

For the purposes of subsections (8)(b) and (9)(b) of section 272, the Authority may take into account any matter relating to—

(a) any person who is or will be employed by or associated with the operator, trustee or depositary in connection with the scheme;

(b) any director of the operator, trustee or depositary;

(c) any person exercising influence over the operator, trustee or depositary;

(d) any body corporate in the same group as the operator, trustee or depositary;

(e) any director of any such body corporate;

(f) any person exercising influence over any such body corporate.

274 Applications for recognition of individual schemes

(1) An application under section 272 for an order declaring a scheme to be a recognised scheme must be made to the Authority by the operator of the scheme.

(2) The application—

(a) must be made in such manner as the Authority may direct;

(b) must contain the address of a place in the United Kingdom for the service on the operator of notices or other documents required or authorised to be served on him under this Act;

(c) must contain or be accompanied by such information as the Authority may reasonably require for the purpose of determining the application.

(3) At any time after receiving an application and before determining it, the Authority may require the applicant to provide it with such further information as it reasonably considers necessary to enable it to determine the application.

(4) Different directions may be given, and different requirements imposed, in relation to different applications.

(5) The Authority may require an applicant to present information which he is required to give under this section in such form, or to verify it in such a way, as the Authority may direct.

275 Determination of applications

(1) An application under section 272 must be determined by the Authority before the end of the period of six months beginning with the date on which it receives the completed application.

(2) The Authority may determine an incomplete application if it considers it appropriate to do so; and it must in any event determine such an application within twelve months beginning with the date on which it first receives the application.

(3) If the Authority makes an order under section 272(1), it must give written notice of the order to the applicant.

276 Procedure when refusing an application

(1) If the Authority proposes to refuse an application made under section 272 it must give the applicant a warning notice.

(2) If the Authority decides to refuse the application—

(a) it must give the applicant a decision notice; and

(b) the applicant may refer the matter to the Tribunal.

277 Alteration of schemes and changes of operator, trustee or depositary

(1) The operator of a scheme recognised by virtue of section 272 must give written notice to the Authority of any proposed alteration to the scheme.

(2) Effect is not to be given to any such proposal unless—

(a) the Authority, by written notice, has given its approval to the proposal; or

(b) one month, beginning with the date on which notice was given under subsection (1), has expired without the Authority having given written notice to the operator that it has decided to refuse approval.

(3) At least one month before any replacement of the operator, trustee or depositary of such a scheme, notice of the proposed replacement must be given to the Authority—

    (a) by the operator, trustee or depositary (as the case may be); or

    (b) by the person who is to replace him.

Schemes recognised under sections 270 and 272

278 Rules as to scheme particulars

The Authority may make rules imposing duties or liabilities on the operator of a scheme recognised under section 270 or 272 for purposes corresponding to those for which rules may be made under section 248 in relation to authorised unit trust schemes.

279 Revocation of recognition

The Authority may direct that a scheme is to cease to be recognised by virtue of section 270 or revoke an order under section 272 if it appears to the Authority—

    (a) that the operator, trustee or depositary of the scheme has contravened a requirement imposed on him by or under this Act;

    (b) that the operator, trustee or depositary of the scheme has, in purported compliance with any such requirement, knowingly or recklessly given the Authority information which is false or misleading in a material particular;

    (c) in the case of an order under section 272, that one or more of the requirements for the making of the order are no longer satisfied; or

    (d) that none of paragraphs (a) to (c) applies, but it is undesirable in the interests of the participants or potential participants that the scheme should continue to be recognised.

280 Procedure

(1) If the Authority proposes to give a direction under section 279 or to make an order under that section revoking a recognition order, it must give a warning notice to the operator and (if any) the trustee or depositary of the scheme.

(2) If the Authority decides to give a direction or make an order under that section—

    (a) it must without delay give a decision notice to the operator and (if any) the trustee or depositary of the scheme; and

    (b) the operator or the trustee or depositary may refer the matter to the Tribunal.

281 Directions

(1) In this section a "relevant recognised scheme" means a scheme recognised under section 270 or 272.

(2) If it appears to the Authority that—

    (a) the operator, trustee or depositary of a relevant recognised scheme has contravened, or is likely to contravene, a requirement imposed on him by or under this Act,

    (b) the operator, trustee or depositary of such a scheme has, in purported compliance with any such requirement, knowingly or recklessly given the Authority information which is false or misleading in a material particular,

    (c) one or more of the requirements for the recognition of a scheme under section 272 are no longer satisfied, or

    (d) none of paragraphs (a) to (c) applies, but the exercise of the power conferred by this section is desirable in order to protect the interests of participants or potential participants in a relevant recognised scheme who are in the United Kingdom,

it may direct that the scheme is not to be a recognised scheme for a specified period or until the occurrence of a specified event or until specified conditions are complied with.

282 Procedure on giving directions under section 281 and varying them otherwise than as requested

(1) A direction takes effect—

    (a) immediately, if the notice given under subsection (3) states that that is the case;

    (b) on such date as may be specified in the notice; or

    (c) if no date is specified in the notice, when the matter to which it relates is no longer open to review.

(2) A direction may be expressed to take effect immediately (or on a specified date) only if the Authority, having regard to the ground on which it is exercising its power under section 281, considers that it is necessary for the direction to take effect immediately (or on that date).

(3) If the Authority proposes to give a direction under section 281, or gives such a direction with immediate effect, it must give separate written notice to the operator and (if any) the trustee or depositary of the scheme concerned.

(4) The notice must—

    (a) give details of the direction;

    (b) inform the person to whom it is given of when the direction takes effect;

    (c) state the Authority's reasons for giving the direction and for its determination as to when the direction takes effect;

    (d) inform the person to whom it is given that he may make representations to the Authority within such period as may be specified in it (whether or not he has referred the matter to the Tribunal); and

    (e) inform him of his right to refer the matter to the Tribunal.

(5) The Authority may extend the period allowed under the notice for making representations.

(6) If, having considered any representations made by a person to whom the notice was given, the Authority decides—

    (a) to give the direction in the way proposed, or

    (b) if it has been given, not to revoke the direction,

    it must give separate written notice to the operator and (if any) the trustee or depositary of the scheme concerned.

(7) If, having considered any representations made by a person to whom the notice was given, the Authority decides—

    (a) not to give the direction in the way proposed,

    (b) to give the direction in a way other than that proposed, or

    (c) to revoke a direction which has effect,

    it must give separate written notice to the operator and (if any) the trustee or depositary of the scheme concerned.

(8) A notice given under subsection (6) must inform the person to whom it is given of his right to refer the matter to the Tribunal.

(9) A notice under subsection (7)(b) must comply with subsection (4).

(10) If a notice informs a person of his right to refer a matter to the Tribunal, it must give an indication of the procedure on such a reference.

(11) This section applies to the variation of a direction on the Authority's own initiative as it applies to the giving of a direction.

(12) For the purposes of subsection (1)(c), whether a matter is open to review is to be determined in accordance with section 391(8).

Facilities and information in UK

283 Facilities and information in UK

(1) The Authority may make rules requiring operators of recognised schemes to maintain in the United Kingdom, or in such part or parts of it as may be specified, such facilities as the Authority thinks desirable in the interests of participants and as are specified in rules.

(2) The Authority may by notice in writing require the operator of any recognised scheme to include such explanatory information as is specified in the notice in any communication of his which—

(a) is a communication of an invitation or inducement of a kind mentioned in section 21(1); and

(b) names the scheme.

(3) In the case of a communication originating outside the United Kingdom, subsection (2) only applies if the communication is capable of having an effect in the United Kingdom.

CHAPTER VI
INVESTIGATIONS

284 Power to investigate

(1) An investigating authority may appoint one or more competent persons to investigate on its behalf—

(a) the affairs of, or of the manager or trustee of, any authorised unit trust scheme,

(b) the affairs of, or of the operator, trustee or depositary of, any recognised scheme so far as relating to activities carried on in the United Kingdom, or

(c) the affairs of, or of the operator, trustee or depositary of, any other collective investment scheme except a body incorporated by virtue of regulations under section 262,

if it appears to the investigating authority that it is in the interests of the participants or potential participants to do so or that the matter is of public concern.

(2) A person appointed under subsection (1) to investigate the affairs of, or of the manager, trustee, operator or depositary of, any scheme (scheme "A"), may also, if he thinks it necessary for the purposes of that investigation, investigate—

(a) the affairs of, or of the manager, trustee, operator or depositary of, any other such scheme as is mentioned in subsection (1) whose manager, trustee, operator or depositary is the same person as the manager, trustee, operator or depositary of scheme A;

(b) the affairs of such other schemes and persons (including bodies incorporated by virtue of regulations under section 262 and the directors and depositaries of such bodies) as may be prescribed.

(3) If the person appointed to conduct an investigation under this section ("B") considers that a person ("C") is or may be able to give information which is relevant to the investigation, B may require C—

(a) to produce to B any documents in C's possession or under his control which appear to B to be relevant to the investigation,

(b) to attend before B, and

(c) otherwise to give B all assistance in connection with the investigation which C is reasonably able to give,

and it is C's duty to comply with that requirement.

(4) Subsections (5) to (9) of section 170 apply if an investigating authority appoints a person under this section to conduct an investigation on its behalf as they apply in the case mentioned in subsection (1) of that section.

(5) Section 174 applies to a statement made by a person in compliance with a requirement imposed under this section as it applies to a statement mentioned in that section.

(6) Subsections (2) to (4) and (6) of section 175 and section 177 have effect as if this section were contained in Part XI.

(7) Subsections (1) to (9) of section 176 apply in relation to a person appointed under subsection (1) as if—

(a) references to an investigator were references to a person so appointed;

    (b) references to an information requirement were references to a requirement imposed under section 175 or under subsection (3) by a person so appointed;

    (c) the premises mentioned in subsection (3)(a) were the premises of a person whose affairs are the subject of an investigation under this section or of an appointed representative of such a person.

(8) No person may be required under this section to disclose information or produce a document in respect of which he owes an obligation of confidence by virtue of carrying on the business of banking unless subsection (9) or (10) applies.

(9) This subsection applies if—

    (a) the person to whom the obligation of confidence is owed consents to the disclosure or production; or

    (b) the imposing on the person concerned of a requirement with respect to information or a document of a kind mentioned in subsection (8) has been specifically authorised by the investigating authority.

(10) This subsection applies if the person owing the obligation of confidence or the person to whom it is owed is—

    (a) the manager, trustee, operator or depositary of any collective investment scheme which is under investigation;

    (b) the director of a body incorporated by virtue of regulations under section 262 which is under investigation;

    (c) any other person whose own affairs are under investigation.

(11) "Investigating authority" means the Authority or the Secretary of State.

PART XVIII
RECOGNISED INVESTMENT EXCHANGES AND CLEARING HOUSES

CHAPTER I
EXEMPTION

General

285 Exemption for recognised investment exchanges and clearing houses

(1) In this Act—

    (a) "recognised investment exchange" means an investment exchange in relation to which a recognition order is in force; and

    (b) "recognised clearing house" means a clearing house in relation to which a recognition order is in force.

(2) A recognised investment exchange is exempt from the general prohibition as respects any regulated activity—

    (a) which is carried on as a part of the exchange's business as an investment exchange; or

    (b) which is carried on for the purposes of, or in connection with, the provision of clearing services by the exchange.

(3) A recognised clearing house is exempt from the general prohibition as respects any regulated activity which is carried on for the purposes of, or in connection with, the provision of clearing services by the clearing house.

286 Qualification for recognition

(1) The Treasury may make regulations setting out the requirements—

    (a) which must be satisfied by an investment exchange or clearing house if it is to qualify as a body in respect of which the Authority may make a recognition order under this Part; and

(b) which, if a recognition order is made, it must continue to satisfy if it is to remain a recognised body.

(2) But if regulations contain provision as to the default rules of an investment exchange or clearing house, or as to proceedings taken under such rules by such a body, they require the approval of the Secretary of State.

(3) "Default rules" means rules of an investment exchange or clearing house which provide for the taking of action in the event of a person's appearing to be unable, or likely to become unable, to meet his obligations in respect of one or more market contracts connected with the exchange or clearing house.

(4) "Market contract" means—

(a) a contract to which Part VII of the Companies Act 1989 applies as a result of section 155 of that Act or a contract to which Part V of the Companies (No 2)(Northern Ireland) Order 1990 applies as a result of Article 80 of that Order; and

(b) such other kind of contract as may be prescribed.

[(4A) If regulations under subsection (1) require an investment exchange to make information available to the public in accordance with—

(a) Article 29.1 of the markets in financial instruments directive and the Commission Regulation, or

(b) Article 44.1 of that directive and that Regulation,

the regulations may authorise the Authority to waive the requirement in the circumstances specified in the relevant provisions.

(4B) The "relevant provisions" for the purposes of subsection (4A) are—

(a) in a case falling within paragraph (a) of that subsection, Article 29.2 of the markets in financial instruments directive and the Commission Regulation, and

(b) in a case falling within paragraph (b) of that subsection, Article 44.2 of that directive and that Regulation.

(4C) If regulations under subsection (1) require an investment exchange to make information available to the public in accordance with—

(a) Article 30.1 of the markets in financial instruments directive and the Commission Regulation, or

(b) Article 45.1 of that directive and that Regulation,

the regulations may authorise the Authority to defer the requirement in the circumstances specified, and subject to the requirements contained, in the relevant provisions.

(4D) The "relevant provisions" for the purposes of subsection (4C) are—

(a) in a case falling within paragraph (a) of that subsection, Article 30.2 of the markets in financial instruments directive and the Commission Regulation, and

(b) in a case falling within paragraph (b) of that subsection, Article 45.2 of that directive and that Regulation.

(4E) "The Commission Regulation" means Commission Regulation 1287/2006 of 10 August 2006.][368]

(5) Requirements resulting from this section are referred to in this Part as "recognition requirements".

[(6) In the case of an investment exchange, requirements resulting from this section are in addition to requirements which must be satisfied by the exchange as a result of section 290(1A) before the Authority may make a recognition order declaring the exchange to be a recognised investment exchange.][369]

---

[368] Inserted by SI 2006/2975, regs 2, 8; came into force 6 December 2006.

[369] Inserted by SI 2007/126, reg 3(2), Sch 2, paras 1, 2; came into force (for certain purposes) 1 April 2007; came into force (for remaining purposes) 1 November 2007.

Applications for recognition

287 Application by an investment exchange

(1) Any body corporate or unincorporated association may apply to the Authority for an order declaring it to be a recognised investment exchange for the purposes of this Act.

(2) The application must be made in such manner as the Authority may direct and must be accompanied by—

    (a) a copy of the applicant's rules;

    (b) a copy of any guidance issued by the applicant;

    (c) the required particulars; and

    (d) such other information as the Authority may reasonably require for the purpose of determining the application.

(3) The required particulars are—

    (a) particulars of any arrangements which the applicant has made, or proposes to make, for the provision of clearing services in respect of transactions effected on the exchange;

    (b) if the applicant proposes to provide clearing services in respect of transactions other than those effected on the exchange, particulars of the criteria which the applicant will apply when determining to whom it will provide those services[;

    (c) a programme of operations which includes the types of business the applicant proposes to undertake and the applicant's proposed organisational structure;

    (d) such particulars of the persons who effectively direct the business and operations of the exchange as the Authority may reasonably require;

    (e) such particulars of the ownership of the exchange, and in particular of the identity and scale of interests of the persons who are in a position to exercise significant influence over the management of the exchange, whether directly or indirectly, as the Authority may reasonably require].[370]

[(4) Subsection (3)(c) to (e) does not apply to an application by an overseas applicant.][371]

288 Application by a clearing house

(1) Any body corporate or unincorporated association may apply to the Authority for an order declaring it to be a recognised clearing house for the purposes of this Act.

(2) The application must be made in such manner as the Authority may direct and must be accompanied by—

    (a) a copy of the applicant's rules;

    (b) a copy of any guidance issued by the applicant;

    (c) the required particulars; and

    (d) such other information as the Authority may reasonably require for the purpose of determining the application.

(3) The required particulars are—

    (a) if the applicant makes, or proposes to make, clearing arrangements with a recognised investment exchange, particulars of those arrangements;

    (b) if the applicant proposes to provide clearing services for persons other than recognised investment exchanges, particulars of the criteria which it will apply when determining to whom it will provide those services.

---

[370] Inserted by SI 2007/126, reg 3(2), Sch 2, paras 1, 3(a); came into force (for certain purposes) 1 April 2007; came into force (for remaining purposes) 1 November 2007.

[371] Inserted by SI 2007/126, reg 3(2), Sch 2, paras 1, 3(b); came into force (for certain purposes) 1 April 2007; came into force (for remaining purposes) 1 November 2007.

289 Applications: supplementary

(1) At any time after receiving an application and before determining it, the Authority may require the applicant to provide such further information as it reasonably considers necessary to enable it to determine the application.

(2) Information which the Authority requires in connection with an application must be provided in such form, or verified in such manner, as the Authority may direct.

(3) Different directions may be given, or requirements imposed, by the Authority with respect to different applications.

290 Recognition orders

(1) If it appears to the Authority that the applicant satisfies the recognition requirements applicable in its case, the Authority may make a recognition order declaring the applicant to be—
  (a) a recognised investment exchange, if the application is made under section 287;
  (b) a recognised clearing house, if it is made under section 288.

[(1A) In the case of an application for an order declaring the applicant to be a recognised investment exchange, the reference in subsection (1) to the recognition requirements applicable in its case includes a reference to requirements contained in any directly applicable Community regulation made under the markets in financial instruments directive.

(1B) In the case mentioned in subsection (1A), the application must be determined by the Authority before the end of the period of six months beginning with the date on which it receives the completed application.

(1C) Subsection (1B) does not apply in the case of an application by an overseas applicant.][372]

(2) The Treasury's approval of the making of a recognition order is required under section 307.

(3) In considering an application, the Authority may have regard to any information which it considers is relevant to the application.

(4) A recognition order must specify a date on which it is to take effect.

(5) Section 298 has effect in relation to a decision to refuse to make a recognition order—
  (a) as it has effect in relation to a decision to revoke such an order; and
  (b) as if references to a recognised body were references to the applicant.

(6) Subsection (5) does not apply in a case in which the Treasury have failed to give their approval under section 307.

[290A Refusal of recognition on ground of excessive regulatory provision][373]

[(1) The Authority must not make a recognition order if it appears to the Authority that an existing or proposed regulatory provision of the applicant in connection with—
  (a) the applicant's business as an investment exchange, or
  (b) the provision by the applicant of clearing services,
imposes or will impose an excessive requirement on the persons affected (directly or indirectly) by it.

(2) The reference in section 290(1) (making of recognition order) to satisfying the applicable recognition requirements shall be read accordingly.

(3) Expressions used in subsection (1) above that are defined for the purposes of section 300A (power of Authority to disallow excessive regulatory provision) have the same meaning as in that section.

---

[372] Inserted by SI 2007/126, Sch 2, paras 1, 4; came into force (for certain purposes) 1 April 2007; came into force (for remaining purposes) 1 November 2007.

[373] Inserted by the Investment Exchanges and Clearing Houses Act 2006, s 4; came into force 20 December 2006.

(4) The provisions of section 300A(3) and (4) (determination whether regulatory provision excessive) apply for the purposes of this section as for the purposes of section 300A.

(5) Section 298 has effect in relation to a decision under this section to refuse a recognition order—

(a) as it has effect in relation to a decision to revoke such an order, and

(b) as if references to a recognised body were references to the applicant.

(6) This section does not apply to an application for recognition as an overseas investment exchange or overseas clearing house.]

291 Liability in relation to recognised body's regulatory functions

(1) A recognised body and its officers and staff are not to be liable in damages for anything done or omitted in the discharge of the recognised body's regulatory functions unless it is shown that the act or omission was in bad faith.

(2) But subsection (1) does not prevent an award of damages made in respect of an act or omission on the ground that the act or omission was unlawful as a result of section 6(1) of the Human Rights Act 1998.

(3) "Regulatory functions" means the functions of the recognised body so far as relating to, or to matters arising out of, the obligations to which the body is subject under or by virtue of this Act.

292 Overseas investment exchanges and overseas clearing houses

(1) An application under section 287 or 288 by an overseas applicant must contain the address of a place in the United Kingdom for the service on the applicant of notices or other documents required or authorised to be served on it under this Act.

(2) If it appears to the Authority that an overseas applicant satisfies the requirements of subsection (3) it may make a recognition order declaring the applicant to be—

(a) a recognised investment exchange;

(b) a recognised clearing house.

(3) The requirements are that—

(a) investors are afforded protection equivalent to that which they would be afforded if the body concerned were required to comply with recognition requirements[, other than any such requirements which are expressed in regulations under section 286 not to apply for the purposes of this paragraph];[374]

(b) there are adequate procedures for dealing with a person who is unable, or likely to become unable, to meet his obligations in respect of one or more market contracts connected with the investment exchange or clearing house;

(c) the applicant is able and willing to co-operate with the Authority by the sharing of information and in other ways;

(d) adequate arrangements exist for co-operation between the Authority and those responsible for the supervision of the applicant in the country or territory in which the applicant's head office is situated.

(4) In considering whether it is satisfied as to the requirements mentioned in subsection (3)(a) and (b), the Authority is to have regard to—

(a) the relevant law and practice of the country or territory in which the applicant's head office is situated;

(b) the rules and practices of the applicant.

---

[374] Inserted by SI 2006/2975, regs 2, 9; came into force 6 December 2006.

(5) In relation to an overseas applicant and a body or association declared to be a recognised investment exchange or recognised clearing house by a recognition order made by virtue of subsection (2)—

    (a) the reference in section 313(2) to recognition requirements is to be read as a reference to matters corresponding to the matters in respect of which provision is made in the recognition requirements;

    (b) sections 296(1) and 297(2) have effect as if the requirements mentioned in section 296(1)(a) and section 297(2)(a) were those of subsection (3)(a), (b), and (c) of this section;

    (c) section 297(2) has effect as if the grounds on which a recognition order may be revoked under that provision included the ground that in the opinion of the Authority arrangements of the kind mentioned in subsection (3)(d) no longer exist.

[Publication of information by recognised investment exchange][375]

[292A Publication of information by recognised investment exchange][376]

[(1) A recognised investment exchange must as soon as practicable after a recognition order is made in respect of it publish such particulars of the ownership of the exchange as the Authority may reasonably require.

(2) The particulars published under subsection (1) must include particulars of the identity and scale of interests of the persons who are in a position to exercise significant influence over the management of the exchange, whether directly or indirectly.

(3) If an ownership transfer takes place in relation to a recognised investment exchange, the exchange must as soon as practicable after becoming aware of the transfer publish such particulars relating to the transfer as the Authority may reasonably require.

(4) "Ownership transfer", in relation to an exchange, means a transfer of ownership which gives rise to a change in the persons who are in a position to exercise significant influence over the management of the exchange, whether directly or indirectly.

(5) A recognised investment exchange must publish such particulars of any decision it makes to suspend or remove a financial instrument from trading on a regulated market operated by it as the Authority may reasonably require.

(6) The Authority may determine the manner of publication under subsections (1), (3) and (5) and the timing of publication under subsection (5).

(7) This section does not apply to an overseas investment exchange.]

Supervision

293 Notification requirements

(1) The Authority may make rules requiring a recognised body to give it—

    (a) notice of such events relating to the body as may be specified; and

    (b) such information in respect of those events as may be specified.

(2) The rules may also require a recognised body to give the Authority, at such times or in respect of such periods as may be specified, such information relating to the body as may be specified.

(3) An obligation imposed by the rules extends only to a notice or information which the Authority may reasonably require for the exercise of its functions under this Act.

---

[375] Inserted by SI 2007/126, reg 3(2), Sch 2, paras 1, 5; came into force (for certain purposes) 1 April 2007; came into force (for remaining purposes) 1 November 2007.

[376] Inserted by SI 2007/126, reg 3(2), Sch 2, paras 1, 5; came into force (for certain purposes) 1 April 2007; came into force (for remaining purposes) 1 November 2007.

(4) The rules may require information to be given in a specified form and to be verified in a specified manner.

(5) If a recognised body—

(a) alters or revokes any of its rules or guidance, or

(b) makes new rules or issues new guidance,

it must give written notice to the Authority without delay.

(6) If a recognised investment exchange makes a change—

(a) in the arrangements it makes for the provision of clearing services in respect of transactions effected on the exchange, or

(b) in the criteria which it applies when determining to whom it will provide clearing services,

it must give written notice to the Authority without delay.

(7) If a recognised clearing house makes a change—

(a) in the recognised investment exchanges for whom it provides clearing services, or

(b) in the criteria which it applies when determining to whom (other than recognised investment exchanges) it will provide clearing services,

it must give written notice to the Authority without delay.

(8) Subsections (5) to (7) do not apply to an overseas investment exchange or an overseas clearing house.

(9) "Specified" means specified in the Authority's rules.

[293A Information: compliance of recognised investment exchanges with directly applicable Community regulations][377]

[The Authority may require a recognised investment exchange to give the Authority such information as it reasonably requires in order to satisfy itself that the exchange is complying with any directly applicable Community regulation made under the markets in financial instruments directive.]

294 Modification or waiver of rules

(1) The Authority may, on the application or with the consent of a recognised body, direct that rules made under section 293 or 295—

(a) are not to apply to the body; or

(b) are to apply to the body with such modifications as may be specified in the direction.

(2) An application must be made in such manner as the Authority may direct.

(3) Subsections (4) to (6) apply to a direction given under subsection (1).

(4) The Authority may not give a direction unless it is satisfied that—

(a) compliance by the recognised body with the rules, or with the rules as unmodified, would be unduly burdensome or would not achieve the purpose for which the rules were made; and

(b) the direction would not result in undue risk to persons whose interests the rules are intended to protect.

(5) A direction may be given subject to conditions.

(6) The Authority may—

(a) revoke a direction; or

(b) vary it on the application, or with the consent, of the recognised body to which it relates.

---

[377] Inserted by SI 2007/126, reg 3(2), Sch 2, paras 1, 6; came into force (for certain purposes) 1 April 2007; came into force (for remaining purposes) 1 November 2007.

295 Notification: overseas investment exchanges and overseas clearing houses

(1) At least once a year, every overseas investment exchange and overseas clearing house must provide the Authority with a report.

(2) The report must contain a statement as to whether any events have occurred which are likely—
  (a) to affect the Authority's assessment of whether it is satisfied as to the requirements set out in section 292(3); or
  (b) to have any effect on competition.

(3) The report must also contain such information as may be specified in rules made by the Authority.

(4) The investment exchange or clearing house must provide the Treasury and the [OFT][378] with a copy of the report.

296 Authority's power to give directions

(1) This section applies if it appears to the Authority that a recognised body—
  (a) has failed, or is likely to fail, to satisfy the recognition requirements; or
  (b) has failed to comply with any other obligation imposed on it by or under this Act.

[(1A) This section also applies in the case of a recognised body which is a recognised investment exchange if it appears to the Authority that the body has failed, or is likely to fail, to comply with any obligation imposed on it by any directly applicable Community regulation made under the markets in financial instruments directive.][379]

(2) The Authority may direct the body to take specified steps for the purpose of securing the body's compliance with—
  (a) the recognition requirements; or
  (b) any obligation of the kind in question.

[(2A) In the case of a recognised investment exchange other than an overseas investment exchange, those steps may include—
  (a) the granting to the Authority of access to the premises of the exchange for the purpose of inspecting—
    (i) those premises; or
    (ii) any documents on the premises which appear to the Authority to be relevant for the purpose mentioned in subsection (2);
  (b) the suspension of the carrying on of any regulated activity by the exchange for the period specified in the direction.][380]

(3) A direction under this section is enforceable, on the application of the Authority, by an injunction or, in Scotland, by an order for specific performance under section 45 of the Court of Session Act 1988.

(4) The fact that a rule made by a recognised body has been altered in response to a direction given by the Authority does not prevent it from being subsequently altered or revoked by the recognised body.

297 Revoking recognition

(1) A recognition order may be revoked by an order made by the Authority at the request, or with the consent, of the recognised body concerned.

---

[378] Substituted by the Enterprise Act 2002, s 278(1), Sch 25, para 40(1), (9); came into force 1 April 2003.

[379] Inserted by SI 2007/126, reg 3(2), Sch 2, paras 1, 7(a); came into force (for certain purposes) 1 April 2007; came into force (for remaining purposes) 1 November 2007.

[380] Inserted by SI 2007/126, reg 3(2), Sch 2, paras 1, 7(b); came into force (for certain purposes) 1 April 2007; came into force (for remaining purposes) 1 November 2007.

(2) If it appears to the Authority that a recognised body—

    (a) is failing, or has failed, to satisfy the recognition requirements, or

    (b) is failing, or has failed, to comply with any other obligation imposed on it by or under this Act,

it may make an order revoking the recognition order for that body even though the body does not wish the order to be made.

[(2A) If it appears to the Authority that a recognised body which is a recognised investment exchange—

    (a) has not carried on the business of an investment exchange during the period of twelve months beginning with the day on which the recognition order took effect in relation to it,

    (b) has not carried on the business of an investment exchange at any time during the period of six months ending with the relevant day, or

    (c) has failed, or is likely to fail, to comply with any obligation imposed on it by a directly applicable Community regulation made under the markets in financial instruments directive,

it may make an order revoking the recognition order for that body even though the body does not wish the order to be made.

(2B) The "relevant day", for the purposes of paragraph (b) of subsection (2A), is the day on which the power to make an order under that subsection is exercised.

(2C) Subsection (2A) does not apply to an overseas investment exchange.][381]

(3) An order under this section ("a revocation order") must specify the date on which it is to take effect.

(4) In the case of a revocation order made under subsection (2) [or (2A)],[382] the specified date must not be earlier than the end of the period of three months beginning with the day on which the order is made.

(5) A revocation order may contain such transitional provisions as the Authority thinks necessary or expedient.

298 Directions and revocation: procedure

(1) Before giving a direction under section 296, or making a revocation order under section 297(2) [or (2A)],[383] the Authority must—

    (a) give written notice of its intention to do so to the recognised body concerned;

    (b) take such steps as it considers reasonably practicable to bring the notice to the attention of members (if any) of that body; and

    (c) publish the notice in such manner as it thinks appropriate for bringing it to the attention of other persons who are, in its opinion, likely to be affected.

(2) A notice under subsection (1) must—

    (a) state why the Authority intends to give the direction or make the order; and

    (b) draw attention to the right to make representations conferred by subsection (3).

(3) Before the end of the period for making representations—

    (a) the recognised body,

    (b) any member of that body, and

    (c) any other person who is likely to be affected by the proposed direction or revocation order,

may make representations to the Authority.

---

[381] Inserted by SI 2007/126, reg 3(2), Sch 2, paras 1, 8(a); came into force (for certain purposes) 1 April 2007; came into force (for remaining purposes) 1 November 2007.

[382] Inserted by SI 2007/126, reg 3(2), Sch 2, paras 1, 8(b); came into force (for certain purposes) 1 April 2007; came into force (for remaining purposes) 1 November 2007.

[383] Inserted by SI 2007/126, reg 3(2), Sch 2, paras 1, 9; came into force (for certain purposes) 1 April 2007; came into force (for remaining purposes) 1 November 2007.

(4) The period for making representations is—
  (a) two months beginning—
    (i) with the date on which the notice is served on the recognised body; or
    (ii) if later, with the date on which the notice is published; or
  (b) such longer period as the Authority may allow in the particular case.

(5) In deciding whether to—
  (a) give a direction, or
  (b) make a revocation order,
the Authority must have regard to any representations made in accordance with sub-section (3).

(6) When the Authority has decided whether to give a direction under section 296 or to make the proposed revocation order, it must—
  (a) give the recognised body written notice of its decision; and
  (b) if it has decided to give a direction or make an order, take such steps as it considers reasonably practicable for bringing its decision to the attention of members of the body or of other persons who are, in the Authority's opinion, likely to be affected.

(7) If the Authority considers it essential to do so, it may give a direction under section 296—
  (a) without following the procedure set out in this section; or
  (b) if the Authority has begun to follow that procedure, regardless of whether the period for making representations has expired.

(8) If the Authority has, in relation to a particular matter, followed the procedure set out in sub-sections (1) to (5), it need not follow it again if, in relation to that matter, it decides to take action other than that specified in its notice under subsection (1).

299 Complaints about recognised bodies

(1) The Authority must make arrangements for the investigation of any relevant complaint about a recognised body.

(2) "Relevant complaint" means a complaint which the Authority considers is relevant to the question of whether the body concerned should remain a recognised body.

300 Extension of functions of Tribunal

(1) If the Treasury are satisfied that the condition mentioned in subsection (2) is satisfied, they may by order confer functions on the Tribunal with respect to disciplinary proceedings—
  (a) of one or more investment exchanges in relation to which a recognition order under section 290 is in force or of such investment exchanges generally, or
  (b) of one or more clearing houses in relation to which a recognition order under that section is in force or of such clearing houses generally.

(2) The condition is that it is desirable to exercise the power conferred under subsection (1) with a view to ensuring that—
  (a) decisions taken in disciplinary proceedings with respect to which functions are to be conferred on the Tribunal are consistent with—
    (i) decisions of the Tribunal in cases arising under Part VIII; and
    (ii) decisions taken in other disciplinary proceedings with respect to which the Tribunal has functions as a result of an order under this section; or
  (b) the disciplinary proceedings are in accordance with the Convention rights.

(3) An order under this section may modify or exclude any provision made by or under this Act with respect to proceedings before the Tribunal.

(4) "Disciplinary proceedings" means proceedings under the rules of an investment exchange or clearing house in relation to market abuse by persons subject to the rules.

(5) "The Convention rights" has the meaning given in section 1 of the Human Rights Act 1998.

[Power to disallow excessive regulatory provision][384]

[300A Power of Authority to disallow excessive regulatory provision][385]

[(1) This section applies where a recognised body proposes to make any regulatory provision in connection with its business as an investment exchange or the provision by it of clearing services.

(2) If it appears to the Authority—
- (a) that the proposed provision will impose a requirement on persons affected (directly or indirectly) by it, and
- (b) that the requirement is excessive,

the Authority may direct that the proposed provision must not be made.

(3) A requirement is excessive if—
- (a) it is not required under Community law or any enactment or rule of law in the United Kingdom, and
- (b) either—
  - (i) it is not justified as pursuing a reasonable regulatory objective, or
  - (ii) it is disproportionate to the end to be achieved.

(4) In considering whether a requirement is excessive the Authority must have regard to all the relevant circumstances, including—
- (a) the effect of existing legal and other requirements,
- (b) the global character of financial services and markets and the international mobility of activity,
- (c) the desirability of facilitating innovation, and
- (d) the impact of the proposed provision on market confidence.

(5) In this section "requirement" includes any obligation or burden.

(6) Any provision made in contravention of a direction under this section is of no effect.]

[300B Duty to notify proposal to make regulatory provision][386]

[(1) A recognised body that proposes to make any regulatory provision must give written notice of the proposal to the Authority without delay.

(2) The Authority may by rules under section 293 (notification requirements)—
- (a) specify descriptions of regulatory provision in relation to which, or circumstances in which, the duty in subsection (1) above does not apply, or
- (b) provide that the duty applies only to specified descriptions of regulatory provision or in specified circumstances.

(3) The Authority may also by rules under that section—
- (a) make provision as to the form and contents of the notice required, and
- (b) require the body to provide such information relating to the proposal as may be specified in the rules or as the Authority may reasonably require.]

---

[384] Inserted by the Investment Exchanges and Clearing Houses Act 2006, s 1; came into force 20 December 2006.

[385] Inserted by the Investment Exchanges and Clearing Houses Act 2006, s 1; came into force 20 December 2006.

[386] Inserted by the Investment Exchanges and Clearing Houses Act 2006, s 2; came into force 20 December 2006.

[300C **Restriction on making provision before Authority decides whether to act**][387]

[(1) Where notice of a proposal to make regulatory provision is required to be given to the Authority under section 300B, the provision must not be made—
   (a) before that notice is given, or
   (b) subject to the following provisions of this section, before the end of the initial period.
(2) The initial period is—
   (a) the period of 30 days beginning with the day on which the Authority receives notice of the proposal, or
   (b) if any consultation period announced by the body in relation to the proposal ends after that 30-day period, the end of the consultation period.
(3) If before the end of the initial period the Authority notifies the body that it is calling in the proposal, the provisions of section 300D (consideration by Authority whether to disallow proposed provision) apply as to when the provision may be made.
(4) If—
   (a) before the end of the initial period the Authority notifies the body that it is not calling in the proposal, or
   (b) the initial period ends without the Authority having notified the body that it is calling in the proposal,
   the body may then make the proposed provision.
(5) Any provision made in contravention of this section is of no effect.]

[300D **Consideration by Authority whether to disallow proposed provision**][388]

[(1) This section applies where the Authority notifies a recognised body that it is calling in a proposal to make regulatory provision.
(2) The Authority must publish a notice—
   (a) giving details of the proposed provision,
   (b) stating that it has called in the proposal in order to consider whether to disallow it, and
   (c) specifying a period during which representations with respect to that question may be made to it.
(3) The Authority may extend the period for making representations.
(4) The Authority must notify the body of its decision whether to disallow the provision not later than 30 days after the end of the period for making representations, and must publish the decision and the reasons for it.
(5) The body must not make the provision unless and until—
   (a) the Authority notifies it of its decision not to disallow it, or
   (b) the 30-day period specified in subsection (4) ends without the Authority having notified any decision.
(6) If the Authority notifies the body of its decision to disallow the provision and that decision is questioned in legal proceedings—
   (a) the body must not make the provision until those proceedings, and any proceedings on appeal, are finally determined,
   (b) if the Authority's decision is quashed and the matter is remitted to it for reconsideration, the court may give directions as to the period within which the Authority is to complete its reconsideration, and

---

[387] Inserted by the Investment Exchanges and Clearing Houses Act 2006, s 2; came into force 20 December 2006.
[388] Inserted by the Investment Exchanges and Clearing Houses Act 2006, s 2; came into force 20 December 2006.

(c) the body must not make the provision until—
    (i) the Authority notifies it of its decision on reconsideration not to disallow the provision, or
    (ii) the period specified by the court ends without the Authority having notified any decision.

(7) Any provision made in contravention of subsection (5) or (6) is of no effect.]

[300E Power to disallow excessive regulatory provision: supplementary][389]

[(1) In sections 300A to 300D—
    (a) "regulatory provision" means any rule, guidance, arrangements, policy or practice, and
    (b) references to making provision shall be read accordingly as including, as the case may require, issuing guidance, entering into arrangements or adopting a policy or practice.
(2) For the purposes of those sections a variation of a proposal is treated as a new proposal.
(3) Those sections do not apply to an overseas investment exchange or overseas clearing house.]

Other matters

301 Supervision of certain contracts

(1) The Secretary of State and the Treasury, acting jointly, may by regulations provide for—
    (a) Part VII of the Companies Act 1989 (financial markets and insolvency), and
    (b) Part V of the Companies (No 2)(Northern Ireland) Order 1990,
to apply to relevant contracts as it applies to contracts connected with a recognised body.

(2) "Relevant contracts" means contracts of a prescribed description in relation to which settlement arrangements are provided by a person for the time being included in a list ("the list") maintained by the Authority for the purposes of this section.

(3) Regulations may be made under this section only if the Secretary of State and the Treasury are satisfied, having regard to the extent to which the relevant contracts concerned are contracts of a kind dealt in by persons supervised by the Authority, that it is appropriate for the arrangements mentioned in subsection (2) to be supervised by the Authority.

(4) The approval of the Treasury is required for—
    (a) the conditions set by the Authority for admission to the list; and
    (b) the arrangements for admission to, and removal from, the list.

(5) If the Treasury withdraw an approval given by them under subsection (4), all regulations made under this section and then in force are to be treated as suspended.

(6) But if—
    (a) the Authority changes the conditions or arrangements (or both), and
    (b) the Treasury give a fresh approval under subsection (4),
the suspension of the regulations ends on such date as the Treasury may, in giving the fresh approval, specify.

(7) The Authority must—
    (a) publish the list as for the time being in force; and
    (b) provide a certified copy of it to any person who wishes to refer to it in legal proceedings.

(8) A certified copy of the list is evidence (or in Scotland sufficient evidence) of the contents of the list.

(9) A copy of the list which purports to be certified by or on behalf of the Authority is to be taken to have been duly certified unless the contrary is shown.

---

[389] Inserted by the Investment Exchanges and Clearing Houses Act 2006, s 2; came into force 20 December 2006.

(10) Regulations under this section may, in relation to a person included in the list—

    (a) apply (with such exceptions, additions and modifications as appear to the Secretary of State and the Treasury to be necessary or expedient) such provisions of, or made under, this Act as they consider appropriate;

    (b) provide for the provisions of Part VII of the Companies Act 1989 and Part V of the Companies (No 2)(Northern Ireland) Order 1990 to apply (with such exceptions, additions or modifications as appear to the Secretary of State and the Treasury to be necessary or expedient).

[CHAPTER 1A
CONTROL OVER RECOGNISED INVESTMENT EXCHANGE][390]

[Notices of acquisitions of control over recognised investment exchanges][391]

[301A Obligation to notify the Authority: acquisitions of control][392]

[(1) A person who decides to acquire or increase control over a recognised investment exchange must give the Authority notice in writing before making the acquisition.

(2) A person who acquires or increases control over a recognised investment exchange in circumstances where notice is not required under subsection (1) must give the Authority notice in writing before the end of 14 days beginning with—

    (a) the day the person acquired or increased the control; or

    (b) if later, the day on which the person first became aware that the control had been acquired or increased.

(3) For the purposes of calculations relating to this section, the holding of shares or voting power by a person ("A1") includes any shares or voting power held by another ("A2") if A1 and A2 are acting in concert.

(4) A notice given under this section is a "section 301A notice" and a person giving notice is a "section 301A notice-giver".]

[. . .][393]

[301B Requirements for section 301A notices][394]

[(1) A section 301A notice must be in such form, include such information and be accompanied by such documents as the Authority may reasonably require.

(2) The Authority must publish a list of its requirements as to the form, information and accompanying documents for a section 301A notice.

(3) The Authority may impose different requirements for different cases and may vary or waive requirements in particular cases.]

---

[390] Substituted by SI 2009/534, reg 5, Sch 2; came into force 21 March 2009.

[391] Substituted by SI 2009/534, reg 5, Sch 2; came into force 21 March 2009.

[392] Substituted, together with ss 301B–301M, for ss 301A–301G, by SI 2009/534, reg 5, Sch 2; came into force 21 March 2009.

[393] Inserted by SI 2007/126, reg 3(2), Sch 2, paras 1, 10; came into force (for certain purposes) 1 April 2007; came into force (for remaining purposes) 1 November 2007; repealed by virtue of SI 2009/534, reg 5, Sch 2; came into force 21 March 2009.

[394] Substituted, together with ss 301A, 301C–301M, for ss 301A–301G, by SI 2009/534, reg 5, Sch 2; came into force 21 March 2009.

*[. . .]*395

[301C Acknowledgment of receipt]396

[(1) The Authority must acknowledge receipt of a section 301A notice in writing before the end of the second working day following receipt.

(2) If the Authority receives an incomplete section 301A notice it must inform the section 301A notice-giver as soon as reasonably practicable.]

*[Acquiring and increasing control]*397

[301D Acquiring and increasing control]398

[(1) For the purposes of this Chapter, a person ("A") acquires control over a recognised investment exchange ("B") if any of the cases in subsection (2) begin to apply.

(2) The cases are where A holds—

    (a) 20% or more of the shares in B or in a parent undertaking of B ("P");

    (b) 20% or more of the voting power in B or P; or

    (c) shares or voting power in B or P as a result of which A is able to exercise significant influence over the management of B.

(3) For the purposes of this Chapter, a person ("A") increases control over a recognised investment exchange ("B") whenever—

    (a) the percentage of shares which A holds in B or in a parent undertaking of B ("P") increases from less than 50% to 50% or more;

    (b) the percentage of voting power A holds in B or P increases from less than 50% to 50% or more; or

    (c) A becomes a parent undertaking of B.]

*[. . .]*399

[301E Disregarded holdings]400

[(1) For the purpose of section 301D, shares and voting power that a person holds in a recognised investment exchange ("B") or in a parent undertaking of B ("P") are disregarded in the following circumstances.

(2) Shares held only for the purposes of clearing and settling within a short settlement cycle are disregarded.

(3) Shares held by a custodian or its nominee in a custodian capacity are disregarded, provided that the custodian or nominee is only able to exercise voting power represented by the shares in accordance with instructions given in writing.

---

395 Inserted by SI 2007/126, reg 3(2), Sch 2, paras 1, 10; came into force (for certain purposes) 1 April 2007; came into force (for remaining purposes) 1 November 2007; repealed by virtue of SI 2009/534, reg 5, Sch 2; came into force 21 March 2009.

396 Substituted, together with ss 301A, 301B, 301D–301M, for ss 301A–301G, by SI 2009/534, reg 5, Sch 2; came into force 21 March 2009.

397 Inserted by SI 2009/534, reg 5, Sch 2; came into force 21 March 2009.

398 Substituted, together with ss 301A–C, 301E–301M, for ss 301A–301G, by SI 2009/534, reg 5, Sch 2; came into force 21 March 2009.

399 Inserted by SI 2007/126, reg 3(2), Sch 2, paras 1, 10; came into force (for certain purposes) 1 April 2007; came into force (for remaining purposes) 1 November 2007; repealed by virtue of SI 2009/534, reg 5, Sch 2; came into force 21 March 2009.

400 Substituted, together with ss 301A–D, 301F–301M, for ss 301A–301G, by SI 2009/534, reg 5, Sch 2; came into force 21 March 2009.

(4) Shares representing no more than 5% of the total voting power in B or P held by an investment firm are disregarded, provided that it—

(a) holds the shares in the capacity of a market maker (as defined in article 4.1(8) of the markets in financial instruments directive);

(b) is authorised by its home state regulator under the markets in financial instruments directive; and

(c) neither intervenes in the management of B or P nor exerts any influence on B or P to buy the shares or back the share price.

(5) Shares held by a credit institution or investment firm in its trading book are disregarded, provided that—

(a) the shares represent no more than 5% of the total voting power in B or P; and

(b) the credit institution or investment firm ensures that the voting power is not exercised nor otherwise used to intervene in the management of B or P.

(6) Shares held by a credit institution or an investment firm are disregarded, provided that—

(a) the shares are held as a result of performing the investment services and activities of—

(i) underwriting a share issue; or

(ii) placing shares on a firm commitment basis in accordance with Annex I, section A.6 of the markets in financial instruments directive; and

(b) the credit institution or investment firm—

(i) does not exercise voting power represented by the shares or otherwise intervene in the management of the issuer; and

(ii) retains the holding for a period of less than one year.

(7) Where a management company (as defined in Article 1a.2 of the UCITS directive) and its parent undertaking both hold shares or voting power, each may disregard holdings of the other, provided that each exercises its voting power independently of the other.

(8) But subsection (7) does not apply if the management company—

(a) manages holdings for its parent undertaking or an undertaking in respect of which the parent undertaking is a controller;

(b) has no discretion as to the exercise of the voting power attached to such holdings; and

(c) may only exercise the voting power in relation to such holdings under direct or indirect instruction from—

(i) the parent undertaking; or

(ii) an undertaking in respect of which of the parent undertaking is a controller.

(9) Where an investment firm and its parent undertaking both hold shares or voting power, the parent undertaking may disregard holdings managed by the investment firm on a client by client basis and the investment firm may disregard holdings of the parent undertaking, provided that the investment firm—

(a) has permission to provide portfolio management;

(b) exercises its voting power independently from the parent undertaking; and

(c) may only exercise the voting power under instructions given in writing, or has appropriate mechanisms in place for ensuring that individual portfolio management services are conducted independently of any other services.]

[Assessment procedure][401]

[301F Assessment: general][402]

[(1) Where the Authority receives a section 301A notice, it must—

(a) determine whether to approve the acquisition to which it relates; or

---

[401] Substituted by SI 2009/534, reg 5, Sch 2; came into force 21 March 2009.

[402] Substituted, together with ss 301A–E, 301G–301M, for ss 301A–301G, by SI 2009/534, reg 5, Sch 2; came into force 21 March 2009.

   (b) propose to object to the acquisition.

(2) In making its determination the Authority must—

   (a) consider the suitability of the section 301A notice-giver and the financial soundness of the acquisition in order to ensure the sound and prudent management of the recognised investment exchange in question; and

   (b) have regard to the likely influence that the section 301A notice-giver will have on the recognised investment exchange.

(3) The Authority may only object to an acquisition if it is not satisfied that the approval requirement is met.

(4) The approval requirement is that the acquisition in question by the notice-giver does not pose a threat to the sound and prudent management of any financial market operated by the recognised investment exchange.]

[. . .][403]

[301G Assessment: Procedure][404]

[(1) The Authority must act under section 301F within a period three months from the date the Authority receives the completed section 301A notice ("the assessment period").

(2) The Authority must inform the section 301A notice-giver in writing of—

   (a) the duration of the assessment period; and

   (b) its expiry date.

(3) The Authority must, within two working days of acting under section 301F (and in any event no later than the expiry date of the assessment period)—

   (a) notify the section 301A notice-giver that it has determined to approve the acquisition; or

   (b) in the case of a proposed objection to an acquisition, give a warning notice.

(4) The Authority is treated as having approved the acquisition if, at the expiry of the assessment period, it has neither—

   (a) given notice under subsection (3); nor

   (b) informed the section 301A notice-giver that the notice is incomplete.

(5) If the Authority decides to object to an acquisition it must give the section 301A notice-giver a decision notice.

(6) Following receipt of a decision notice under this section, the section 301A notice-giver may refer the Authority's decision to the Tribunal.]

[301H Duration of approval][405]

[(1) Approval of an acquisition is effective for such period as the Authority may specify in writing.

(2) Where the Authority has specified a period under subsection (1), it may extend the period.

(3) Where the Authority has not specified a period, the approval is effective for one year beginning with the date—

   (a) of the notice given under section 301G(3)(a);

   (b) on which the Authority is treated as having given approval under section 301G(5); or

   (c) of a decision on a reference to the Tribunal which results in the person receiving approval.]

---

[403] Inserted by SI 2007/126, reg 3(2), Sch 2, paras 1, 10; came into force (for certain purposes) 1 April 2007; came into force (for remaining purposes) 1 November 2007; repealed by virtue of SI 2009/534, reg 5, Sch 2; came into force 21 March 2009.

[404] Substituted, together with ss 301A–F, 301H–301M, for ss 301A–301G, by SI 2009/534, reg 5, Sch 2; came into force 21 March 2009.

[405] Substituted, together with ss 301A–G, 301I–301M, for ss 301A–301G, by SI 2009/534, reg 5, Sch 2; came into force 21 March 2009.

[Enforcement procedures][406]

[301I Objections by the Authority][407]

[(1) The Authority may object to a person's control over a recognised investment exchange in any of the circumstances specified in subsection (2).

(2) The circumstances are that the Authority reasonably believes that—
- (a) the person acquired or increased control without giving notice under section 301A in circumstances where notice was required; and
- (b) there are grounds for objecting to control on the basis of the approval requirement in section 301F(4).

(3) If the Authority proposes to object to a person's control over a recognised investment exchange, it must give that person a warning notice.

(4) If the Authority decides to object to a person's control over a UK authorised person, it must give that person a decision notice.

(5) A person to whom the Authority gives a decision notice under this section may refer the matter to the Tribunal.]

[301J Restriction notices][408]

[(1) The Authority may give notice in writing (a "restriction notice") to a person in the following circumstances.

(2) The circumstances are that—
- (a) the person has control over a recognised investment exchange by virtue of holding shares or voting power; and
- (b) in relation to the shares or voting power, the Authority has given the person a warning notice or a decision notice under section 301G or 301I or a final notice which confirms a decision notice given under section 301G or 301I.

(3) In a restriction notice, the Authority may direct that shares or voting power to which the notice relates are, until further notice, subject to one or more of the following restrictions—
- (a) except by court order, an agreement to transfer or a transfer of any such shares or voting power or, in the case of unissued shares, any agreement to transfer or transfer of the right to be issued with them, is void;
- (b) no voting power is to be exercisable;
- (c) no further shares are to be issued in pursuance of any right of the holder of any such shares or voting power or in pursuance of any offer made to their holder;
- (d) except in a liquidation, no payment is to be made of any sums due from the body corporate on any such shares, whether in respect of capital or otherwise.

(4) A restriction notice takes effect—
- (a) immediately; or
- (b) on such date as may be specified in the notice.

(5) A restriction notice does not extinguish rights which would be enjoyable but for the notice.

(6) A copy of the restriction notice must be served on—
- (a) the recognised investment exchange in question; and
- (b) in the case of shares or voting power held in a parent undertaking of a recognised investment exchange, the parent undertaking.

---

[406] Inserted by SI 2009/534, reg 5, Sch 2; came into force 21 March 2009.
[407] Substituted, together with ss 301A–H, 301J–301M, for ss 301A–301G, by SI 2009/534, reg 5, Sch 2; came into force 21 March 2009.
[408] Substituted, together with ss 301A–I, 301K–301M, for ss 301A–301G, by SI 2009/534, reg 5, Sch 2; came into force 21 March 2009.

(7) A person to whom the Authority gives a restriction notice may refer the matter to the Tribunal.]

[301K Orders for sale of shares][409]

[(1) The court may, on the application of the Authority, order the sale of shares or the disposition of voting power in the following circumstances.

(2) The circumstances are that—
- (a) a person has control over a recognised investment exchange by virtue of holding the shares or voting power; and
- (b) the acquisition or continued holding of the shares or voting power by that person is in contravention of a final notice which confirms a decision notice given under section 301G or section 301I.

(3) Where the court orders the sale of shares or disposition of voting power it may—
- (a) if a restriction notice has been given in relation to the shares or voting power, order that the restrictions cease to apply; and
- (b) make any further order.

(4) Where the court makes an order under this section, it must take into account the level of holding that the person would have been entitled to acquire, or to continue to hold, without contravening the final notice.

(5) If shares are sold or voting power disposed of in pursuance of an order under this section, any proceeds, less the costs of the sale or disposition, must be paid into court for the benefit of the persons beneficially interested in them; and any such person may apply to the court for payment of a whole or part of the proceeds.

(6) The jurisdiction conferred by this section may be exercised by the High Court and the Court of Session.]

[Offences][410]

[301L Offences under this Chapter][411]

[(1) A person who fails to comply with an obligation to notify the Authority under section 301A(1) or (2) is guilty of an offence.

(2) A person who gives notice to the Authority under section 301A(1) and makes the acquisition to which the notice relates before the expiry date of the assessment period is guilty of an offence unless the Authority has approved the acquisition.

(3) A person who makes an acquisition in contravention of a warning notice or a decision notice given under section 301G or a final notice which confirms a decision notice under that section is guilty of an offence.

(4) A person who makes an acquisition after the Authority's approval for the acquisition has ceased to be effective by virtue of section 301H is guilty of an offence.

(5) A person who provides information to the Authority which is false in a material particular is guilty of an offence.

(6) A person who breaches a direction contained in a restriction notice given under section 301J is guilty of an offence.

(7) A person guilty of an offence under subsection (1), (2) or (4) to (6) is liable—
- (a) on summary conviction to a fine not exceeding the statutory maximum; or
- (b) on conviction on indictment, to a fine.

---

[409] Substituted, together with ss 301A–J, 301L–301M, for ss 301A–301G, by SI 2009/534, reg 5, Sch 2; came into force 21 March 2009.

[410] Inserted by SI 2009/534, reg 5, Sch 2; came into force 21 March 2009.

[411] Substituted, together with ss 301A–K, 301M, for ss 301A–301G, by SI 2009/534, reg 5, Sch 2; came into force 21 March 2009.

(8) A person guilty of an offence under subsection (3) is liable—
  (a) on summary conviction, to a fine not exceeding the statutory maximum; or
  (b) on conviction on indictment, to imprisonment for a term not exceeding two years or a fine, or both.
(9) It is a defence for a person charged with an offence under subsection (1) in relation to section 301A(2) to show that the person had, at the time of the alleged offence, no knowledge of the act or circumstances by virtue of which the duty to notify the Authority arose.]

[Interpretation][412]

[301M Interpretation][413]

[(1) In this Chapter—
"acquisition" means the acquisition of control or of an increase in control over a recognised investment exchange;
"credit institution" means—
  (a) a credit institution authorised under the banking consolidation directive; or
  (b) an institution which would satisfy the requirements for authorisation as a credit institution under that directive if it had its registered office (or if it does not have a registered office, its head office) in an EEA State; and
"shares" and "voting power" have the same meaning as in section 422.
(2) For the purposes of this Chapter, a "working day" is a day other than—
  (a) a Saturday or a Sunday; or
  (b) a day which is a bank holiday in England and Wales under the Banking and Financial Dealings Act 1971.]

CHAPTER II
COMPETITION SCRUTINY

302 Interpretation

(1) In this Chapter and Chapter III—
"practices" means—
  (a) in relation to a recognised investment exchange, the practices of the exchange in its capacity as such; and
  (b) in relation to a recognised clearing house, the practices of the clearing house in respect of its clearing arrangements;
"regulatory provisions" means—
  (a) the rules of an investment exchange or a clearing house;
  (b) any guidance issued by an investment exchange or clearing house;
  (c) in the case of an investment exchange, the arrangements and criteria mentioned in section [287(3)(a) and (b)][414];
  (d) in the case of a clearing house, the arrangements and criteria mentioned in section 288(3).
(2) For the purposes of this Chapter, regulatory provisions or practices have a significantly adverse effect on competition if—
  (a) they have, or are intended or likely to have, that effect; or

---

[412] Inserted by SI 2009/534, reg 5, Sch 2; came into force 21 March 2009.
[413] Substituted, together with ss 301A–L, for ss 301A–301G, by SI 2009/534, reg 5, Sch 2; came into force 21 March 2009.
[414] Substituted by SI 2007/126, reg 3(2), Sch 2, paras 1, 11; came into force (for certain purposes) 1 April 2007; came into force (for remaining purposes) 1 November 2007.

(b) the effect that they have, or are intended or likely to have, is to require or encourage behaviour which has, or is intended or likely to have, a significantly adverse effect on competition.

(3) If regulatory provisions or practices have, or are intended or likely to have, the effect of requiring or encouraging exploitation of the strength of a market position they are to be taken, for the purposes of this Chapter, to have an adverse effect on competition.

(4) In determining under this Chapter whether any regulatory provisions have, or are intended or likely to have, a particular effect, it may be assumed that persons to whom the provisions concerned are addressed will act in accordance with them.

Role of [Office of Fair Trading][415]

303 Initial report by [OFT][416]

(1) The Authority must send to the Treasury and to the [OFT][417] a copy of any regulatory provisions with which it is provided on an application for recognition under section 287 or 288.

(2) The Authority must send to the [OFT][418] such information in its possession as a result of the application for recognition as it considers will assist [the OFT][419] in discharging [its][420] functions in connection with the application.

(3) The [OFT][421] must issue a report as to whether—

(a) a regulatory provision of which a copy has been sent to [it][422] under subsection (1) has a significantly adverse effect on competition; or

(b) a combination of regulatory provisions so copied to [it][423] have such an effect.

(4) If the [OFT's][424] conclusion is that one or more provisions have a significantly adverse effect on competition, [it][425] must state [its][426] reasons for that conclusion.

(5) When the [OFT][427] issues a report under subsection (3), [the OFT][428] must send a copy of it to the Authority, the Competition Commission and the Treasury.

[(6) In the case of an application for recognition under section 287, the OFT must issue its report under subsection (3) before the end of the period of 12 weeks beginning with the date on which it receives the copy sent to it under subsection (1).

(7) Subsection (6) does not apply if the application is made by an overseas investment exchange.][429]

---

[415] Substituted by the Enterprise Act 2002, s 278(1), Sch 25, para 40(1), (10); came into force 1 April 2003.

[416] Substituted by the Enterprise Act 2002, s 278(1), Sch 25, para 40(1), (10)(f); came into force 1 April 2003.

[417] Substituted by the Enterprise Act 2002, s 278(1), Sch 25, para 40(1), (10)(a); came into force 1 April 2003.

[418] Substituted by the Enterprise Act 2002, s 278(1), Sch 25, para 40(1), (10)(b); came into force 1 April 2003.

[419] Substituted by the Enterprise Act 2002, s 278(1), Sch 25, para 40(1), (10)(b); came into force 1 April 2003.

[420] Substituted by the Enterprise Act 2002, s 278(1), Sch 25, para 40(1), (10)(b); came into force 1 April 2003.

[421] Substituted by the Enterprise Act 2002, s 278(1), Sch 25, para 40(1), (10)(c); came into force 1 April 2003.

[422] Substituted by the Enterprise Act 2002, s 278(1), Sch 25, para 40(1), (10)(c); came into force 1 April 2003.

[423] Substituted by the Enterprise Act 2002, s 278(1), Sch 25, para 40(1), (10)(c); came into force 1 April 2003.

[424] Substituted by the Enterprise Act 2002, s 278(1), Sch 25, para 40(1), (10)(d); came into force 1 April 2003.

[425] Substituted by the Enterprise Act 2002, s 278(1), Sch 25, para 40(1), (10)(d); came into force 1 April 2003.

[426] Substituted by the Enterprise Act 2002, s 278(1), Sch 25, para 40(1), (10)(d); came into force 1 April 2003.

[427] Substituted by the Enterprise Act 2002, s 278(1), Sch 25, para 40(1), (10)(e); came into force 1 April 2003.

[428] Substituted by the Enterprise Act 2002, s 278(1), Sch 25, para 40(1), (10)(e); came into force 1 April 2003.

[429] Inserted by SI 2007/126, reg 3(2), Sch 2, paras 1, 12; came into force (for certain purposes) 1 April 2007; came into force (for remaining purposes) 1 November 2007.

304 Further reports by [OFT][430]

(1) The [OFT][431] must keep under review the regulatory provisions and practices of recognised bodies.

(2) If at any time the [OFT][432] considers that—

    (a) a regulatory provision or practice has a significantly adverse effect on competition, or

    (b) regulatory provisions or practices, or a combination of regulating provisions and practices have such an effect,

    [the OFT][433] must make a report.

(3) If at any time the [OFT][434] considers that—

    (a) a regulatory provision or practice does not have a significantly adverse effect on competition, or

    (b) regulatory provisions or practices, or a combination of regulatory provisions and practices do not have any such effect,

    [the OFT][435] may make a report to that effect.

(4) A report under subsection (2) must contain details of the adverse effect on competition.

(5) If the [OFT][436] makes a report under subsection (2), [the OFT][437] must—

    (a) send a copy of it to the Treasury, to the Competition Commission and to the Authority; and

    (b) publish it in the way appearing to [the OFT][438] to be best calculated to bring it to the attention of the public.

(6) If the [OFT][439] makes a report under subsection (3)—

    (a) [the OFT][440] must send a copy of it to the Treasury, to the Competition Commission and to the Authority; and

    (b) [the OFT][441] may publish it.

(7) Before publishing a report under this section, the [OFT][442] must, so far as practicable, exclude any matter which relates to the private affairs of a particular individual the publication of which, in the opinion of the [OFT][443], would or might seriously and prejudicially affect his interests.

(8) Before publishing such a report, the [OFT][444] must exclude any matter which relates to the affairs of a particular body the publication of which, in the opinion of the [OFT][445], would or might seriously and prejudicially affect its interests.

---

[430] Substituted by the Enterprise Act 2002, s 278(1), Sch 25, para 40(1), (11)(a); came into force 1 April 2003.
[431] Substituted by the Enterprise Act 2002, s 278(1), Sch 25, para 40(1), (11)(a); came into force 1 April 2003.
[432] Substituted by the Enterprise Act 2002, s 278(1), Sch 25, para 40(1), (11)(a); came into force 1 April 2003.
[433] Substituted by the Enterprise Act 2002, s 278(1), Sch 25, para 40(1), (11)(a); came into force 1 April 2003.
[434] Substituted by the Enterprise Act 2002, s 278(1), Sch 25, para 40(1), (11)(a); came into force 1 April 2003.
[435] Substituted by the Enterprise Act 2002, s 278(1), Sch 25, para 40(1), (11)(a); came into force 1 April 2003.
[436] Substituted by the Enterprise Act 2002, s 278(1), Sch 25, para 40(1), (11)(a); came into force 1 April 2003.
[437] Substituted by the Enterprise Act 2002, s 278(1), Sch 25, para 40(1), (11)(a); came into force 1 April 2003.
[438] Substituted by the Enterprise Act 2002, s 278(1), Sch 25, para 40(1), (11)(b); came into force 1 April 2003.
[439] Substituted by the Enterprise Act 2002, s 278(1), Sch 25, para 40(1), (11)(a); came into force 1 April 2003.
[440] Substituted by the Enterprise Act 2002, s 278(1), Sch 25, para 40(1), (11)(a); came into force 1 April 2003.
[441] Substituted by the Enterprise Act 2002, s 278(1), Sch 25, para 40(1), (11)(a); came into force 1 April 2003.
[442] Substituted by the Enterprise Act 2002, s 278(1), Sch 25, para 40(1), (11)(a); came into force 1 April 2003.
[443] Substituted by the Enterprise Act 2002, s 278(1), Sch 25, para 40(1), (11)(a); came into force 1 April 2003.
[444] Substituted by the Enterprise Act 2002, s 278(1), Sch 25, para 40(1), (11)(a); came into force 1 April 2003.
[445] Substituted by the Enterprise Act 2002, s 278(1), Sch 25, para 40(1), (11)(a); came into force 1 April 2003.

(9) Subsections (7) and (8) do not apply to the copy of a report which the [OFT][446] is required to send to the Treasury, the Competition Commission and the Authority under subsection (5)(a) or (6)(a).

(10) For the purposes of the law of defamation, absolute privilege attaches to any report of the [OFT][447] under this section.

305 Investigations by [OFT][448]

(1) For the purpose of investigating any matter with a view to its consideration under section 303 or 304, the [OFT][449] may exercise the powers conferred on [it][450] by this section.

(2) The [OFT][451] may by notice in writing require any person to produce to [it][452] or to a person appointed by [it][453] for the purpose, at a time and place specified in the notice, any document which—
  (a) is specified or described in the notice; and
  (b) is a document in that person's custody or under his control.

(3) The [OFT][454] may by notice in writing—
  (a) require any person carrying on any business to provide [it][455] with such information as may be specified or described in the notice; and
  (b) specify the time within which, and the manner and form in which, any such information is to be provided.

(4) A requirement may be imposed under subsection (2) or (3)(a) only in respect of documents or information which relate to any matter relevant to the investigation.

(5) If a person ("the defaulter") refuses, or otherwise fails, to comply with a notice under this section, the [OFT][456] may certify that fact in writing to the court and the court may enquire into the case.

(6) If, after hearing any witness who may be produced against or on behalf of the defaulter and any statement which may be offered in defence, the court is satisfied that the defaulter did not have a reasonable excuse for refusing or otherwise failing to comply with the notice, the court may deal with the defaulter as if he were in contempt.

(7) In this section, "the court" means—
  (a) the High Court; or
  (b) in Scotland, the Court of Session.

Role of Competition Commission

306 Consideration by Competition Commission

(1) If subsection (2) or (3) applies, the Commission must investigate the matter which is the subject of the [OFT's][457] report.

---

[446] Substituted by the Enterprise Act 2002, s 278(1), Sch 25, para 40(1), (11)(a); came into force 1 April 2003.
[447] Substituted by the Enterprise Act 2002, s 278(1), Sch 25, para 40(1), (11)(a); came into force 1 April 2003.
[448] Substituted by the Enterprise Act 2002, s 278(1), Sch 25, para 40(1), (12); came into force 1 April 2003.
[449] Substituted by the Enterprise Act 2002, s 278(1), Sch 25, para 40(1), (12); came into force 1 April 2003.
[450] Substituted by the Enterprise Act 2002, s 278(1), Sch 25, para 40(1), (12); came into force 1 April 2003.
[451] Substituted by the Enterprise Act 2002, s 278(1), Sch 25, para 40(1), (12); came into force 1 April 2003.
[452] Substituted by the Enterprise Act 2002, s 278(1), Sch 25, para 40(1), (12); came into force 1 April 2003.
[453] Substituted by the Enterprise Act 2002, s 278(1), Sch 25, para 40(1), (12); came into force 1 April 2003.
[454] Substituted by the Enterprise Act 2002, s 278(1), Sch 25, para 40(1), (12); came into force 1 April 2003.
[455] Substituted by the Enterprise Act 2002, s 278(1), Sch 25, para 40(1), (12); came into force 1 April 2003.
[456] Substituted by the Enterprise Act 2002, s 278(1), Sch 25, para 40(1), (12); came into force 1 April 2003.
[457] Substituted by the Enterprise Act 2002, s 278(1), Sch 25, para 40(1), (13); came into force 1 April 2003.

(2) This subsection applies if the [OFT][458] sends to the Competition Commission a report—

    (a) issued by [the OFT][459] under section 303(3) which concludes that one or more regulatory provisions have a significantly adverse effect on competition, or

    (b) made by [the OFT][460] under section 304(2).

(3) This subsection applies if the [OFT][461] asks the Commission to consider a report—

    (a) issued by [the OFT][462] under section 303(3) which concludes that one or more regulatory provisions do not have a significantly adverse effect on competition, or

    (b) made by [the OFT][463] under section 304(3).

(4) The Commission must then make its own report on the matter unless it considers that, as a result of a change of circumstances, no useful purpose would be served by a report.

(5) If the Commission decides in accordance with subsection (4) not to make a report, it must make a statement setting out the change of circumstances which resulted in that decision.

(6) A report made under this section must state the Commission's conclusion as to whether—

    (a) the regulatory provision or practice which is the subject of the report has a significantly adverse effect on competition, or

    (b) the regulatory provisions or practices or combination of regulatory provisions and practices which are the subject of the report have such an effect.

(7) A report under this section stating the Commission's conclusion that there is a significantly adverse effect on competition must also—

    (a) state whether the Commission considers that that effect is justified; and

    (b) if it states that the Commission considers that it is not justified, state its conclusion as to what action, if any, the Treasury ought to direct the Authority to take.

(8) Subsection (9) applies whenever the Commission is considering, for the purposes of this section, whether a particular adverse effect on competition is justified.

(9) The Commission must ensure, so far as that is reasonably possible, that the conclusion it reaches is compatible with the obligations imposed on the recognised body concerned by or under this Act.

(10) A report under this section must contain such an account of the Commission's reasons for its conclusions as is expedient, in the opinion of the Commission, for facilitating proper understanding of them.

(11) The provisions of Schedule 14 (except paragraph 2(b)) apply for the purposes of this section as they apply for the purposes of section 162.

(12) If the Commission makes a report under this section it must send a copy to the Treasury, the Authority and the [OFT][464].

[(13) Subsection (14) applies if—

    (a) the case relates to an application for recognition under section 287, other than an application by an overseas applicant; and

    (b) subsection (2)(a) or (3)(a) of this section applies.

(14) The Commission must—

    (a) make a report under this section, or a statement under subsection (5), before the end of the period of 12 weeks beginning with the date on which it receives a copy of the OFT's report under section 303(3); and

[458] Substituted by the Enterprise Act 2002, s 278(1), Sch 25, para 40(1), (13); came into force 1 April 2003.

[459] Substituted by the Enterprise Act 2002, s 278(1), Sch 25, para 40(1), (13); came into force 1 April 2003.

[460] Substituted by the Enterprise Act 2002, s 278(1), Sch 25, para 40(1), (13); came into force 1 April 2003.

[461] Substituted by the Enterprise Act 2002, s 278(1), Sch 25, para 40(1), (13); came into force 1 April 2003.

[462] Substituted by the Enterprise Act 2002, s 278(1), Sch 25, para 40(1), (13); came into force 1 April 2003.

[463] Substituted by the Enterprise Act 2002, s 278(1), Sch 25, para 40(1), (13); came into force 1 April 2003.

[464] Substituted by the Enterprise Act 2002, s 278(1), Sch 25, para 40(1), (13); came into force 1 April 2003.

(b) if it makes a statement under subsection (5), send a copy to the Authority and the Treasury.]⁴⁶⁵

Role of the Treasury

307 Recognition orders: role of the Treasury

(1) Subsection (2) applies if, on an application for a recognition order—
  (a) the [OFT]⁴⁶⁶ makes a report under section 303 but does not ask the Competition Commission to consider it under section 306;
  (b) the Competition Commission concludes—
    (i) that the applicant's regulatory provisions do not have a significantly adverse effect on competition; or
    (ii) that if those provisions do have that effect, the effect is justified.
(2) The Treasury may refuse to approve the making of the recognition order only if they consider that the exceptional circumstances of the case make it inappropriate for them to give their approval.
(3) Subsection (4) applies if, on an application for a recognition order, the Competition Commission concludes—
  (a) that the applicant's regulatory provisions have a significantly adverse effect on competition; and
  (b) that that effect is not justified.
(4) The Treasury must refuse to approve the making of the recognition order unless they consider that the exceptional circumstances of the case make it inappropriate for them to refuse their approval.
[(5) Subsection (6) applies in the case of an application for recognition under section 287, other than an application by an overseas applicant.
(6) The Treasury must decide whether to approve the application before the end of the period of 10 days beginning with—
  (a) in a case falling within subsection (2)(a) or (3)(a) of section 306, the date on which they receive a copy of the report under that section or, if no such report was made, of the statement under subsection (5) of that section;
  (b) in any other case, the date on which they receive a copy of the report from the OFT under section 303.]⁴⁶⁷

308 Directions by the Treasury

(1) This section applies if the Competition Commission makes a report under section 306(4) (other than a report on an application for a recognition order) which states the Commission's conclusion that there is a significantly adverse effect on competition.
(2) If the Commission's conclusion, as stated in the report, is that the adverse effect on competition is not justified, the Treasury must give a remedial direction to the Authority.
(3) But subsection (2) does not apply if the Treasury consider—
  (a) that, as a result of action taken by the Authority or the recognised body concerned in response to the Commission's report, it is unnecessary for them to give a direction; or

---

⁴⁶⁵ Inserted by SI 2007/126, reg 3(2), Sch 2, paras 1, 13; came into force (for certain purposes) 1 April 2007; came into force (for remaining purposes) 1 November 2007.
⁴⁶⁶ Substituted by the Enterprise Act 2002, s 278(1), Sch 25, para 40(1), (14)(a); came into force 1 April 2003.
⁴⁶⁷ Inserted by SI 2007/126, reg 3(2), Sch 2, paras 1, 14; came into force (for certain purposes) 1 April 2007; came into force (for remaining purposes) 1 November 2007.

(b) that the exceptional circumstances of the case make it inappropriate or unnecessary for them to do so.

(4) In considering the action to be specified in a remedial direction, the Treasury must have regard to any conclusion of the Commission included in the report because of section 306(7)(b).

(5) Subsection (6) applies if—

(a) the Commission's conclusion, as stated in its report, is that the adverse effect on competition is justified; but

(b) the Treasury consider that the exceptional circumstances of the case require them to act.

(6) The Treasury may give a direction to the Authority requiring it to take such action—

(a) as they consider to be necessary in the light of the exceptional circumstances of the case; and

(b) as may be specified in the direction.

(7) If the action specified in a remedial direction is the giving by the Authority of a direction—

(a) the direction to be given must be compatible with the recognition requirements applicable to the recognised body in relation to which it is given; and

(b) subsections (3) and (4) of section 296 apply to it as if it were a direction given under that section.

(8) "Remedial direction" means a direction requiring the Authority—

(a) to revoke the recognition order for the body concerned; or

(b) to give such directions to the body concerned as may be specified in it.

309 Statements by the Treasury

(1) If, in reliance on subsection (3)(a) or (b) of section 308, the Treasury decline to act under subsection (2) of that section, they must make a statement to that effect, giving their reasons.

(2) If the Treasury give a direction under section 308 they must make a statement giving—

(a) details of the direction; and

(b) if the direction is given under subsection (6) of that section, their reasons for giving it.

(3) The Treasury must—

(a) publish any statement made under this section in the way appearing to them best calculated to bring it to the attention of the public; and

(b) lay a copy of it before Parliament.

310 Procedure on exercise of certain powers by the Treasury

(1) Subsection (2) applies if the Treasury are considering—

(a) whether to refuse their approval under section 307;

(b) whether section 308(2) applies; or

(c) whether to give a direction under section 308(6).

(2) The Treasury must—

(a) take such steps as they consider appropriate to allow the exchange or clearing house concerned, and any other person appearing to the Treasury to be affected, an opportunity to make representations—

(i) about any report made by the [OFT][468] under section 303 or 304 or by the Competition Commission under section 306;

(ii) as to whether, and if so how, the Treasury should exercise their powers under section 307 or 308; and

(b) have regard to any such representations.

---

[468] Substituted by the Enterprise Act 2002, s 278(1), Sch 25, para 40(1), (14)(b); came into force 1 April 2003.

CHAPTER III
EXCLUSION FROM THE COMPETITION ACT 1998

311 The Chapter I prohibition

(1) The Chapter I prohibition does not apply to an agreement for the constitution of a recognised body to the extent to which the agreement relates to the regulatory provisions of that body.

(2) If the conditions set out in subsection (3) are satisfied, the Chapter I prohibition does not apply to an agreement for the constitution of—

(a) an investment exchange which is not a recognised investment exchange, or

(b) a clearing house which is not a recognised clearing house,

to the extent to which the agreement relates to the regulatory provisions of that body.

(3) The conditions are that—

(a) the body has applied for a recognition order in accordance with the provisions of this Act; and

(b) the application has not been determined.

(4) The Chapter I prohibition does not apply to a recognised body's regulatory provisions.

(5) The Chapter I prohibition does not apply to a decision made by a recognised body to the extent to which the decision relates to any of that body's regulatory provisions or practices.

(6) The Chapter I prohibition does not apply to practices of a recognised body.

(7) The Chapter I prohibition does not apply to an agreement the parties to which consist of or include—

(a) a recognised body, or

(b) a person who is subject to the rules of a recognised body,

to the extent to which the agreement consists of provisions the inclusion of which is required or encouraged by any of the body's regulatory provisions or practices.

(8) If a recognised body's recognition order is revoked, this section is to have effect as if that body had continued to be recognised until the end of the period of six months beginning with the day on which the revocation took effect.

(9) "The Chapter I prohibition" means the prohibition imposed by section 2(1) of the Competition Act 1998.

(10) Expressions used in this section which are also used in Part I of the Competition Act 1998 are to be interpreted in the same way as for the purposes of that Part of that Act.

312 The Chapter II prohibition

(1) The Chapter II prohibition does not apply to—

(a) practices of a recognised body;

(b) the adoption or enforcement of such a body's regulatory provisions;

(c) any conduct which is engaged in by such a body or by a person who is subject to the rules of such a body to the extent to which it is encouraged or required by the regulatory provisions of the body.

(2) The Chapter II prohibition means the prohibition imposed by section 18(1) of the Competition Act 1998.

[CHAPTER 3A
PASSPORT RIGHTS][469]

[EEA market operators in United Kingdom][470]

[312A Exercise of passport rights by EEA market operator][471]

[(1) An EEA market operator may, in pursuance of the right under the applicable provision, make arrangements in the United Kingdom to facilitate access to, or use of, a specified regulated market or specified multilateral trading facility operated by it if—

(a) the operator has given its home state regulator notice of its intention to make such arrangements; and

(b) the home state regulator has given the Authority notice of the operator's intention.

(2) In making arrangements under subsection (1), the operator is exempt from the general prohibition as respects any regulated activity which is carried on as a part of its business of operating the market or facility in question, or in connection with, or for the purposes of, that business.

(3) "Specified" means specified in the notice referred to in subsection (1)(a).

(4) This section does not apply to an overseas investment exchange.]

[312B Removal of passport rights from EEA market operator][472]

[(1) The Authority may prohibit an EEA market operator from making or, as the case may be, continuing arrangements in the United Kingdom, in pursuance of the applicable provision, to facilitate access to, or use of, a regulated market or multilateral trading facility operated by the operator if—

(a) the Authority has clear and demonstrable grounds for believing that the operator has contravened a relevant requirement, and

(b) the Authority has first complied with subsections (3) to (9).

(2) A requirement is relevant if it is imposed—

(a) by the operator's home state regulator in the implementation of the markets in financial instruments directive or any Community legislation made under that directive;

(b) by provision implementing that directive, or any Community legislation made under it, in the operator's home state; or

(c) by any directly applicable Community regulation made under that directive.

(3) The Authority must notify the operator and its home state regulator of its finding under subsection (1)(a).

(4) The notice to the home state regulator under subsection (3) must—

(a) request that the home state regulator take all appropriate measures for the purpose of ensuring that the operator puts an end to the contravention; and

(b) state that the Authority proposes to exercise the power under subsection (1) if the operator continues the contravention.

---

[469] Inserted by SI 2007/126, reg 3(2), Sch 2, paras 1, 15; came into force (for certain purposes) 1 April 2007; came into force (for remaining purposes) 1 November 2007.

[470] Inserted by SI 2007/126, reg 3(2), Sch 2, paras 1, 15; came into force (for certain purposes) 1 April 2007; came into force (for remaining purposes) 1 November 2007.

[471] Inserted by SI 2007/126, reg 3(2), Sch 2, paras 1, 15; came into force (for certain purposes) 1 April 2007; came into force (for remaining purposes) 1 November 2007.

[472] Inserted by SI 2007/126, reg 3(2), Sch 2, paras 1, 15; came into force (for certain purposes) 1 April 2007; came into force (for remaining purposes) 1 November 2007.

(5) The Authority may not exercise the power under subsection (1) unless satisfied—
  (a) either—
    (i) that the home state regulator has failed or refused to take measures for the purpose mentioned in subsection (4)(a); or
    (ii) that the measures taken by the home state regulator have proved inadequate for that purpose; and
  (b) that the operator is acting in a manner which is clearly prejudicial to the interests of investors in the United Kingdom or the orderly functioning of the financial markets.

(6) If the Authority is satisfied as mentioned in subsection (5), it must give written notice to—
  (a) the operator, and
  (b) the home state regulator,
  of its intention to exercise the power under subsection (1).

(7) A notice under subsection (6) must—
  (a) state why the Authority intends to exercise its power under subsection (1), and
  (b) in the case of the notice to the operator, inform the operator that it may make representations to the Authority before the end of the representation period.

(8) The representation period is—
  (a) the period of two months beginning with the date on which the notice is given to the operator; or
  (b) such longer period as the Authority may allow in a particular case.

(9) If, having considered any representations made by the operator, the Authority decides to exercise the power under subsection (1), it must—
  (a) notify the operator in writing that it will be prohibited from making or, as the case may be, continuing the arrangements mentioned in that subsection from the date specified in the notice; and
  (b) notify the home state regulator of the action to be taken in relation to the operator.

(10) If the Authority exercises the power under subsection (1) it must at the earliest opportunity notify the Commission of the action taken in relation to the operator.

(11) The exemption conferred on an operator by section 312A(2) ceases to apply if the Authority exercises the power under subsection (1) in relation to the operator.

(12) The right to make the arrangements mentioned in subsection (1) may be reinstated in relation to the operator (together with the exemption mentioned in subsection (11)) if the Authority is satisfied that the contravention which led to the Authority exercising the power under subsection (1) has been remedied.]

[Recognised investment exchanges operating in EEA States (other than the United Kingdom)][473]

[312C Exercise of passport rights by recognised investment exchange][474]

[(1) Subject to subsection (4), a recognised investment exchange may, in pursuance of the right under the applicable provision, make arrangements in an EEA State (other than the United Kingdom) to facilitate access to, or use of, a regulated market or multilateral trading facility operated by the exchange ("the relevant arrangements").

(2) The exchange must give the Authority written notice of its intention to make the relevant arrangements which—
  (a) describes the arrangements, and
  (b) identifies the EEA State in which it intends to make them.

---

[473] Inserted by SI 2007/126, reg 3(2), Sch 2, paras 1, 15; came into force (for certain purposes) 1 April 2007; came into force (for remaining purposes) 1 November 2007.
[474] Inserted by SI 2007/126, reg 3(2), Sch 2, paras 1, 15; came into force (for certain purposes) 1 April 2007; came into force (for remaining purposes) 1 November 2007.

(3) The Authority must, within one month of receiving a notice under subsection (2), send a copy of it to the host state regulator.

(4) The exchange may not make the relevant arrangements until the Authority has complied with subsection (3).

(5) Subsection (6) applies if the Authority receives a request for information—

    (a) under the second sub-paragraph of Article 31.6 of the markets in financial instruments directive (in the case of relevant arrangements relating to a multilateral trading facility), or

    (b) under the third sub-paragraph of Article 42.6 of that directive (in the case of relevant arrangements relating to a regulated market),

from the host state regulator.

(6) The Authority must, as soon as reasonably practicable, comply with the request.

(7) "Host state regulator" means the competent authority (within the meaning of Article 4.1.22 of the markets in financial instruments directive) of the EEA State in which the exchange intends to make, or has made, the relevant arrangements.

(8) This section does not apply to an overseas investment exchange.]

[Interpretation][475]

[312D Interpretation of Chapter 3A][476]

[In this Chapter—

"the applicable provision" means—

    (a) in the case of arrangements relating to a multilateral trading facility, Article 31.5 of the markets in financial instruments directive; and

    (b) in the case of arrangements relating to a regulated market, the first sub-paragraph of Article 42.6 of that directive;

"EEA market operator" means a person who is a market operator (within the meaning of Article 4.1.13 of the markets in financial instruments directive) whose home state is an EEA State other than the United Kingdom;

"home state", in relation to an EEA market operator, means the EEA State in which it has its registered office, or if it has no registered office, its head office;

"home state regulator" means the competent authority (within the meaning of Article 4.1.22 of the markets in financial instruments directive) of the EEA State which is the home state in relation to the EEA market operator concerned.]

CHAPTER IV
INTERPRETATION

313 Interpretation of Part XVIII

(1) In this Part—

"application" means an application for a recognition order made under section 287 or 288;

"applicant" means a body corporate or unincorporated association which has applied for a recognition order;

---

[475] Inserted by SI 2007/126, reg 3(2), Sch 2, paras 1, 15; came into force (for certain purposes) 1 April 2007; came into force (for remaining purposes) 1 November 2007.

[476] Inserted by SI 2007/126, reg 3(2), Sch 2, paras 1, 15; came into force (for certain purposes) 1 April 2007; came into force (for remaining purposes) 1 November 2007.

["multilateral trading facility" has the meaning given in Article 4.1.15 of the markets in financial instruments directive;][477]

["OFT" means the Office of Fair Trading;][478]

"overseas applicant" means a body corporate or association which has neither its head office nor its registered office in the United Kingdom and which has applied for a recognition order;

"overseas investment exchange" means a body corporate or association which has neither its head office nor its registered office in the United Kingdom and in relation to which a recognition order is in force;

"overseas clearing house" means a body corporate or association which has neither its head office nor its registered office in the United Kingdom and in relation to which a recognition order is in force;

"recognised body" means a recognised investment exchange or a recognised clearing house;

"recognised clearing house" has the meaning given in section 285;

"recognised investment exchange" has the meaning given in section 285;

"recognition order" means an order made under section 290 or 292;

"recognition requirements" has the meaning given by section 286;

["regulated market" has the meaning given in Article 4.1.14 of the markets in financial instruments directive;][479]

"remedial direction" has the meaning given in section 308(8);

"revocation order" has the meaning given in section 297.

(2) References in this Part to rules of an investment exchange (or a clearing house) are to rules made, or conditions imposed, by the investment exchange (or the clearing house) with respect to—

(a) recognition requirements;

(b) admission of persons to, or their exclusion from the use of, its facilities; or

(c) matters relating to its constitution.

(3) References in this Part to guidance issued by an investment exchange are references to guidance issued, or any recommendation made, in writing or other legible form and intended to have continuing effect, by the investment exchange to—

(a) all or any class of its members or users, or

(b) persons seeking to become members of the investment exchange or to use its facilities, with respect to any of the matters mentioned in subsection (2)(a) to (c).

(4) References in this Part to guidance issued by a clearing house are to guidance issued, or any recommendation made, in writing or other legible form and intended to have continuing effect, by the clearing house to—

(a) all or any class of its members, or

(b) persons using or seeking to use its services, with respect to the provision by it or its members of clearing services.

---

[477] Inserted by SI 2007/126, reg 3(2), Sch 2, paras 1, 16; came into force (for certain purposes) 1 April 2007; came into force (for remaining purposes) 1 November 2007.

[478] Substituted for definition "Director" as originally enacted by the Enterprise Act 2002, s 278(1), Sch 25, para 40(1), (15); came into force 1 April 2003.

[479] Inserted by SI 2007/126, reg 3(2), Sch 2, paras 1, 16; came into force (for certain purposes) 1 April 2007; came into force (for remaining purposes) 1 November 2007.

[PART 18A
SUSPENSION AND REMOVAL OF FINANCIAL INSTRUMENTS FROM
TRADING][480]

[313A Authority's power to require suspension or removal of financial instruments from trading][481]

[(1) The Authority may, for the purpose of protecting—
    (a) the interests of investors, or
    (b) the orderly functioning of the financial markets,
require an institution to suspend or remove a financial instrument from trading.
(2) If the Authority exercises the power conferred by subsection (1), the institution concerned or, if any, the issuer of the financial instrument concerned may refer the matter to the Tribunal.
(3) In this section, "trading" includes trading otherwise than on a regulated market or a multilateral trading facility.]

[313B Suspension or removal of financial instruments from trading: procedure][482]

[(1) A requirement imposed on an institution under section 313A (a "relevant requirement") takes effect—
    (a) immediately, if the notice given under subsection (2) states that this is the case;
    (b) in any other case, on such date as may be specified in the notice.
(2) If the Authority proposes to impose a relevant requirement on an institution, or imposes such a requirement with immediate effect, it must give written notice to—
    (a) the institution, and
    (b) if any, the issuer of the financial instrument in question.
(3) The notice must—
    (a) give details of the relevant requirement;
    (b) state the Authority's reasons for imposing the requirement and choosing the date on which it took effect or takes effect;
    (c) inform the recipient that he may make representations to the Authority within such period as may be specified by the notice (whether or not he has referred the matter to the Tribunal);
    (d) inform him of the date on which the requirement took effect or takes effect; and
    (e) inform him of his right to refer the matter to the Tribunal and give an indication of the procedure on such a reference.
(4) The Authority may extend the period within which representations may be made to it.
(5) If, having considered any representations made to it by the institution or any issuer, the Authority decides—
    (a) to impose the relevant requirement proposed, or
    (b) if it has been imposed, not to revoke it,
it must give the institution and any issuer written notice.
(6) If, having considered any representations made to it by the institution or any issuer, the Authority decides—
    (a) not to impose the relevant requirement proposed, or
    (b) to revoke a requirement which has been imposed,
it must give the institution and any issuer written notice.

---

[480] Inserted by SI 2007/126, reg 3(3), Sch 3; came into force (for certain purposes) 1 April 2007; came into force (for remaining purposes) 1 November 2007.
[481] Inserted by SI 2007/126, reg 3(3), Sch 3; came into force (for certain purposes) 1 April 2007; came into force (for remaining purposes) 1 November 2007.
[482] Inserted by SI 2007/126, reg 3(3), Sch 3; came into force (for certain purposes) 1 April 2007; came into force (for remaining purposes) 1 November 2007.

(7) A notice given under subsection (5) must inform the recipient of his right to refer the matter to the Tribunal.

(8) Subsections (9) and (10) apply if—

    (a) the Authority has imposed a relevant requirement on an institution, and

    (b) the institution or any issuer of the financial instrument in question has applied for the revocation of the requirement.

(9) If the Authority decides to grant the application, it must give the institution and any issuer written notice of its decision.

(10) If the Authority proposes to refuse the application, it must give the institution and any issuer a warning notice.

(11) If, having considered any representations made in response to the warning notice, the Authority decides to refuse the application, it must give the institution and any issuer a decision notice.

(12) If the Authority gives a decision notice under subsection (11), the recipient may refer the matter to the Tribunal.]

[313C Notification in relation to suspension or removal of a financial instrument from trading][483]

[(1) If the Authority exercises the power under section 313A(1) in relation to a financial instrument traded on a regulated market, it must as soon as reasonably practicable—

    (a) publish its decision in such manner as it considers appropriate, and

    (b) inform the competent authorities of all other EEA States of its decision.

(2) If the Authority receives notice from a recognised investment exchange that the exchange has suspended or removed a financial instrument from trading on a regulated market operated by it, the Authority must inform the competent authorities of all other EEA States of the action taken by the exchange.

(3) Subsections (4) and (5) apply if the Authority receives notice from the competent authority of another EEA State that that authority, pursuant to Article 41.2 of the markets in financial instruments directive—

    (a) has required the suspension of a financial instrument from trading, or

    (b) has required the removal of a financial instrument from trading.

(4) In the case of a notice under subsection (3)(a), the Authority—

    (a) must require each recognised investment exchange to suspend the instrument from trading on any regulated market operated by the exchange, and

    (b) must require each institution operating a multilateral trading facility to suspend the instrument from trading on that facility,

unless such a step would be likely to cause significant damage to the interests of investors or the orderly functioning of the financial markets.

(5) In the case of a notice under subsection (3)(b), the Authority—

    (a) must require each recognised investment exchange to remove the instrument from trading on any regulated market operated by the exchange, and

    (b) must require each institution operating a multilateral trading facility to remove the instrument from trading on that facility,

unless such a step would be likely to cause significant damage to the interests of investors or the orderly functioning of the financial markets.

(6) "Competent authority" has the meaning given in Article 4.1.22 of the markets in financial instruments directive.]

---

[483] Inserted by SI 2007/126, reg 3(3), Sch 3; came into force (for certain purposes) 1 April 2007; came into force (for remaining purposes) 1 November 2007.

[313D Interpretation of Part 18A][484]

[In this Part—

"financial instrument" has the meaning given in Article 4.1.17 of the markets in financial instruments directive;

"institution" means—

(a) a recognised investment exchange, other than an overseas investment exchange (within the meaning of Part 18);

(b) an investment firm;

(c) a credit institution authorised under the banking consolidation directive, when carrying on investment services and activities; or

(d) an institution which would satisfy the requirements for authorisation as a credit institution under that directive if it had its registered office (or if it does not have a registered office, its head office) in an EEA State,

but does not include an EEA firm qualifying for authorisation under Schedule 3;

"issuer", in relation to a financial instrument, means the person who issued the instrument;

"multilateral trading facility" has the meaning given in Article 4.1.15 of the markets in financial instruments directive;

"regulated market" has the meaning given in Article 4.1.14 of the markets in financial instruments directive.]

PART XIX
LLOYD'S

General

314 Authority's general duty

(1) The Authority must keep itself informed about—

(a) the way in which the Council supervises and regulates the market at Lloyd's; and

(b) the way in which regulated activities are being carried on in that market.

(2) The Authority must keep under review the desirability of exercising—

(a) any of its powers under this Part;

(b) any powers which it has in relation to the Society as a result of section 315.

The Society

315 The Society: authorisation and permission

(1) The Society is an authorised person.

(2) The Society has permission to carry on a regulated activity of any of the following kinds—

(a) arranging deals in contracts of insurance written at Lloyd's ("the basic market activity");

(b) arranging deals in participation in Lloyd's syndicates ("the secondary market activity"); and

(c) an activity carried on in connection with, or for the purposes of, the basic or secondary market activity.

(3) For the purposes of Part IV, the Society's permission is to be treated as if it had been given on an application for permission under that Part.

---

[484] Inserted by SI 2007/126, reg 3(3), Sch 3; came into force (for certain purposes) 1 April 2007; came into force (for remaining purposes) 1 November 2007.

(4) The power conferred on the Authority by section 45 may be exercised in anticipation of the coming into force of the Society's permission (or at any other time).

(5) The Society is not subject to any requirement of this Act concerning the registered office of a body corporate.

Power to apply Act to Lloyd's underwriting

316 Direction by Authority

(1) The general prohibition or (if the general prohibition is not applied under this section) a core provision applies to the carrying on of an insurance market activity by—

    (a) a member of the Society, or

    (b) the members of the Society taken together,

only if the Authority so directs.

(2) A direction given under subsection (1) which applies a core provision is referred to in this Part as "an insurance market direction".

(3) In subsection (1)—

"core provision" means a provision of this Act mentioned in section 317; and

"insurance market activity" means a regulated activity relating to contracts of insurance written at Lloyd's.

(4) In deciding whether to give a direction under subsection (1), the Authority must have particular regard to—

    (a) the interests of policyholders and potential policyholders;

    (b) any failure by the Society to satisfy an obligation to which it is subject as a result of a provision of the law of another EEA State which—

        (i) gives effect to any of the insurance directives; and

        (ii) is applicable to an activity carried on in that State by a person to whom this section applies;

    (c) the need to ensure the effective exercise of the functions which the Authority has in relation to the Society as a result of section 315.

(5) A direction under subsection (1) must be in writing.

(6) A direction under subsection (1) applying the general prohibition may apply it in relation to different classes of person.

(7) An insurance market direction—

    (a) must specify each core provision, class of person and kind of activity to which it applies;

    (b) may apply different provisions in relation to different classes of person and different kinds of activity.

(8) A direction under subsection (1) has effect from the date specified in it, which may not be earlier than the date on which it is made.

(9) A direction under subsection (1) must be published in the way appearing to the Authority to be best calculated to bring it to the attention of the public.

(10) The Authority may charge a reasonable fee for providing a person with a copy of the direction.

(11) The Authority must, without delay, give the Treasury a copy of any direction which it gives under this section.

317 The core provisions

(1) The core provisions are Parts V, X, XI, XII, XIV, XV, XVI, XXII and XXIV, sections 384 to 386 and Part XXVI.

(2) References in an applied core provision to an authorised person are (where necessary) to be read as references to a person in the class to which the insurance market direction applies.

(3) An insurance market direction may provide that a core provision is to have effect, in relation to persons to whom the provision is applied by the direction, with modifications.

318 Exercise of powers through Council

(1) The Authority may give a direction under this subsection to the Council or to the Society (acting through the Council) or to both.

(2) A direction under subsection (1) is one given to the body concerned—
   (a) in relation to the exercise of its powers generally with a view to achieving, or in support of, a specified objective; or
   (b) in relation to the exercise of a specified power which it has, whether in a specified manner or with a view to achieving, or in support of, a specified objective.

(3) "Specified" means specified in the direction.

(4) A direction under subsection (1) may be given—
   (a) instead of giving a direction under section 316(1); or
   (b) if the Authority considers it necessary or expedient to do so, at the same time as, or following, the giving of such a direction.

(5) A direction may also be given under subsection (1) in respect of underwriting agents as if they were among the persons mentioned in section 316(1).

(6) A direction under this section—
   (a) does not, at any time, prevent the exercise by the Authority of any of its powers;
   (b) must be in writing.

(7) A direction under subsection (1) must be published in the way appearing to the Authority to be best calculated to bring it to the attention of the public.

(8) The Authority may charge a reasonable fee for providing a person with a copy of the direction.

(9) The Authority must, without delay, give the Treasury a copy of any direction which it gives under this section.

319 Consultation

(1) Before giving a direction under section 316 or 318, the Authority must publish a draft of the proposed direction.

(2) The draft must be accompanied by—
   (a) a cost benefit analysis; and
   (b) notice that representations about the proposed direction may be made to the Authority within a specified time.

(3) Before giving the proposed direction, the Authority must have regard to any representations made to it in accordance with subsection (2)(b).

(4) If the Authority gives the proposed direction it must publish an account, in general terms, of—
   (a) the representations made to it in accordance with subsection (2)(b); and
   (b) its response to them.

(5) If the direction differs from the draft published under subsection (1) in a way which is, in the opinion of the Authority, significant—
   (a) the Authority must (in addition to complying with subsection (4)) publish details of the difference; and
   (b) those details must be accompanied by a cost benefit analysis.

(6) Subsections (1) to (5) do not apply if the Authority considers that the delay involved in complying with them would be prejudicial to the interests of consumers.

(7) Neither subsection (2)(a) nor subsection (5)(b) applies if the Authority considers—
   (a) that, making the appropriate comparison, there will be no increase in costs; or
   (b) that, making that comparison, there will be an increase in costs but the increase will be of minimal significance.

(8) The Authority may charge a reasonable fee for providing a person with a copy of a draft published under subsection (1).

(9) When the Authority is required to publish a document under this section it must do so in the way appearing to it to be best calculated to bring it to the attention of the public.

(10) "Cost benefit analysis" means an estimate of the costs together with an analysis of the benefits that will arise—

(a) if the proposed direction is given; or

(b) if subsection (5)(b) applies, from the direction that has been given.

(11) "The appropriate comparison" means—

(a) in relation to subsection (2)(a), a comparison between the overall position if the direction is given and the overall position if it is not given;

(b) in relation to subsection (5)(b), a comparison between the overall position after the giving of the direction and the overall position before it was given.

Former underwriting members

320 Former underwriting members

(1) A former underwriting member may carry out each contract of insurance that he has underwritten at Lloyd's whether or not he is an authorised person.

(2) If he is an authorised person, any Part IV permission that he has does not extend to his activities in carrying out any of those contracts.

(3) The Authority may impose on a former underwriting member such requirements as appear to it to be appropriate for the purpose of protecting policyholders against the risk that he may not be able to meet his liabilities.

(4) A person on whom a requirement is imposed may refer the matter to the Tribunal.

321 Requirements imposed under section 320

(1) A requirement imposed under section 320 takes effect—

(a) immediately, if the notice given under subsection (2) states that that is the case;

(b) in any other case, on such date as may be specified in that notice.

(2) If the Authority proposes to impose a requirement on a former underwriting member ("A") under section 320, or imposes such a requirement on him which takes effect immediately, it must give him written notice.

(3) The notice must—

(a) give details of the requirement;

(b) state the Authority's reasons for imposing it;

(c) inform A that he may make representations to the Authority within such period as may be specified in the notice (whether or not he has referred the matter to the Tribunal);

(d) inform him of the date on which the requirement took effect or will take effect; and

(e) inform him of his right to refer the matter to the Tribunal.

(4) The Authority may extend the period allowed under the notice for making representations.

(5) If, having considered any representations made by A, the Authority decides—

(a) to impose the proposed requirement, or

(b) if it has been imposed, not to revoke it,

it must give him written notice.

(6) If the Authority decides—

(a) not to impose a proposed requirement, or

(b) to revoke a requirement that has been imposed,

it must give A written notice.

(7) If the Authority decides to grant an application by A for the variation or revocation of a requirement, it must give him written notice of its decision.

(8) If the Authority proposes to refuse an application by A for the variation or revocation of a requirement it must give him a warning notice.

(9) If the Authority, having considered any representations made in response to the warning notice, decides to refuse the application, it must give A a decision notice.

(10) A notice given under—

(a) subsection (5), or

(b) subsection (9) in the case of a decision to refuse the application,

must inform A of his right to refer the matter to the Tribunal.

(11) If the Authority decides to refuse an application for a variation or revocation of the requirement, the applicant may refer the matter to the Tribunal.

(12) If a notice informs a person of his right to refer a matter to the Tribunal, it must give an indication of the procedure on such a reference.

322 Rules applicable to former underwriting members

(1) The Authority may make rules imposing such requirements on persons to whom the rules apply as appear to it to be appropriate for protecting policyholders against the risk that those persons may not be able to meet their liabilities.

(2) The rules may apply to—

(a) former underwriting members generally; or

(b) to a class of former underwriting member specified in them.

(3) Section 319 applies to the making of proposed rules under this section as it applies to the giving of a proposed direction under section 316.

(4) Part X (except sections 152 to 154) does not apply to rules made under this section.

Transfers of business done at Lloyd's

323 Transfer schemes

The Treasury may by order provide for the application of any provision of Part VII (with or without modification) in relation to schemes for the transfer of the whole or any part of the business carried on by one or more [underwriting members of the Society or by one or more persons who have ceased to be such a member (whether before, on or after 24th December 1996)][485].

Supplemental

324 Interpretation of this Part

(1) In this Part—

"arranging deals", in relation to the investments to which this Part applies, has the same meaning as in paragraph 3 of Schedule 2;

"former underwriting member" means a person ceasing to be an underwriting member of the Society on, or at any time after, 24 December 1996; and

"participation in Lloyd's syndicates", in relation to the secondary market activity, means the investment described in sub-paragraph (1) of paragraph 21 of Schedule 2.

(2) A term used in this Part which is defined in Lloyd's Act 1982 has the same meaning as in that Act.

---

[485] Substituted by SI 2008/1469, reg 2; came into force 30 June 2008.

PART XX
PROVISION OF FINANCIAL SERVICES BY MEMBERS OF
THE PROFESSIONS

325 Authority's general duty

(1) The Authority must keep itself informed about—
- (a) the way in which designated professional bodies supervise and regulate the carrying on of exempt regulated activities by members of the professions in relation to which they are established;
- (b) the way in which such members are carrying on exempt regulated activities.

(2) In this Part—

"exempt regulated activities" means regulated activities which may, as a result of this Part, be carried on by members of a profession which is supervised and regulated by a designated professional body without breaching the general prohibition; and

"members", in relation to a profession, means persons who are entitled to practise the profession in question and, in practising it, are subject to the rules of the body designated in relation to that profession, whether or not they are members of that body.

(3) The Authority must keep under review the desirability of exercising any of its powers under this Part.

(4) Each designated professional body must co-operate with the Authority, by the sharing of information and in other ways, in order to enable the Authority to perform its functions under this Part.

326 Designation of professional bodies

(1) The Treasury may by order designate bodies for the purposes of this Part.

(2) A body designated under subsection (1) is referred to in this Part as a designated professional body.

(3) The Treasury may designate a body under subsection (1) only if they are satisfied that—
- (a) the basic condition, and
- (b) one or more of the additional conditions,

are met in relation to it.

(4) The basic condition is that the body has rules applicable to the carrying on by members of the profession in relation to which it is established of regulated activities which, if the body were to be designated, would be exempt regulated activities.

(5) The additional conditions are that—
- (a) the body has power under any enactment to regulate the practice of the profession;
- (b) being a member of the profession is a requirement under any enactment for the exercise of particular functions or the holding of a particular office;
- (c) the body has been recognised for the purpose of any enactment other than this Act and the recognition has not been withdrawn;
- (d) the body is established in an EEA State other than the United Kingdom and in that State—
  - (i) the body has power corresponding to that mentioned in paragraph (a);
  - (ii) there is a requirement in relation to the body corresponding to that mentioned in paragraph (b); or
  - (iii) the body is recognised in a manner corresponding to that mentioned in paragraph (c).

(6) "Enactment" includes an Act of the Scottish Parliament, Northern Ireland legislation and subordinate legislation (whether made under an Act, an Act of the Scottish Parliament or Northern Ireland legislation).

(7) "Recognised" means recognised by—
- (a) a Minister of the Crown;
- (b) the Scottish Ministers;

(c) a Northern Ireland Minister;

(d) a Northern Ireland department or its head.

327 Exemption from the general prohibition

(1) The general prohibition does not apply to the carrying on of a regulated activity by a person ("P") if—

  (a) the conditions set out in subsections (2) to (7) are satisfied; and

  (b) there is not in force—

    (i) a direction under section 328, or

    (ii) an order under section 329,

  which prevents this subsection from applying to the carrying on of that activity by him.

(2) P must be—

  (a) a member of a profession; or

  (b) controlled or managed by one or more such members.

(3) P must not receive from a person other than his client any pecuniary reward or other advantage, for which he does not account to his client, arising out of his carrying on of any of the activities.

(4) The manner of the provision by P of any service in the course of carrying on the activities must be incidental to the provision by him of professional services.

(5) P must not carry on, or hold himself out as carrying on, a regulated activity other than—

  (a) one which rules made as a result of section 332(3) allow him to carry on; or

  (b) one in relation to which he is an exempt person.

(6) The activities must not be of a description, or relate to an investment of a description, specified in an order made by the Treasury for the purposes of this subsection.

(7) The activities must be the only regulated activities carried on by P (other than regulated activities in relation to which he is an exempt person).

(8) "Professional services" means services—

  (a) which do not constitute carrying on a regulated activity, and

  (b) the provision of which is supervised and regulated by a designated professional body.

328 Directions in relation to the general prohibition

(1) The Authority may direct that section 327(1) is not to apply to the extent specified in the direction.

(2) A direction under subsection (1)—

  (a) must be in writing;

  (b) may be given in relation to different classes of person or different descriptions of regulated activity.

(3) A direction under subsection (1) must be published in the way appearing to the Authority to be best calculated to bring it to the attention of the public.

(4) The Authority may charge a reasonable fee for providing a person with a copy of the direction.

(5) The Authority must, without delay, give the Treasury a copy of any direction which it gives under this section.

[(6) The Authority may exercise the power conferred by subsection (1) only if it is satisfied either—

  (a) that it is desirable to do so in order to protect the interests of clients; or

  (b) that it is necessary to do so in order to comply with a Community obligation imposed by the insurance mediation directive.][486]

---

[486] Substituted by SI 2003/1473, reg 9(a); came into force 14 January 2005.

(7) In considering whether it is [satisfied of the matter specified in subsection (6)(a)],[487] the Authority must have regard amongst other things to the effectiveness of any arrangements made by any designated professional body—

(a) for securing compliance with rules made under section 332(1);

(b) for dealing with complaints against its members in relation to the carrying on by them of exempt regulated activities;

(c) in order to offer redress to clients who suffer, or claim to have suffered, loss as a result of misconduct by its members in their carrying on of exempt regulated activities;

(d) for co-operating with the Authority under section 325(4).

(8) In this Part "clients" means—

(a) persons who use, have used or are or may be contemplating using, any of the services provided by a member of a profession in the course of carrying on exempt regulated activities;

(b) persons who have rights or interests which are derived from, or otherwise attributable to, the use of any such services by other persons; or

(c) persons who have rights or interests which may be adversely affected by the use of any such services by persons acting on their behalf or in a fiduciary capacity in relation to them.

(9) If a member of a profession is carrying on an exempt regulated activity in his capacity as a trustee, the persons who are, have been or may be beneficiaries of the trust are to be treated as persons who use, have used or are or may be contemplating using services provided by that person in his carrying on of that activity.

329 Orders in relation to the general prohibition

(1) Subsection (2) applies if it appears to the Authority that a person to whom, as a result of section 327(1), the general prohibition does not apply is not a fit and proper person to carry on regulated activities in accordance with that section.

(2) The Authority may make an order disapplying section 327(1) in relation to that person to the extent specified in the order.

(3) The Authority may, on the application of the person named in an order under subsection (1), vary or revoke it.

(4) "Specified" means specified in the order.

(5) If a partnership is named in an order under this section, the order is not affected by any change in its membership.

(6) If a partnership named in an order under this section is dissolved, the order continues to have effect in relation to any partnership which succeeds to the business of the dissolved partnership.

(7) For the purposes of subsection (6), a partnership is to be regarded as succeeding to the business of another partnership only if—

(a) the members of the resulting partnership are substantially the same as those of the former partnership; and

(b) succession is to the whole or substantially the whole of the business of the former partnership.

330 Consultation

(1) Before giving a direction under section 328(1), the Authority must publish a draft of the proposed direction.

(2) The draft must be accompanied by—

(a) a cost benefit analysis; and

(b) notice that representations about the proposed direction may be made to the Authority within a specified time.

---

[487] Substituted by SI 2003/1473, reg 9(b); came into force 14 January 2005.

(3) Before giving the proposed direction, the Authority must have regard to any representations made to it in accordance with subsection (2)(b).

(4) If the Authority gives the proposed direction it must publish an account, in general terms, of—

    (a) the representations made to it in accordance with subsection (2)(b); and

    (b) its response to them.

(5) If the direction differs from the draft published under subsection (1) in a way which is, in the opinion of the Authority, significant—

    (a) the Authority must (in addition to complying with subsection (4)) publish details of the difference; and

    (b) those details must be accompanied by a cost benefit analysis.

(6) Subsections (1) to (5) do not apply if the Authority considers that the delay involved in complying with them would prejudice the interests of consumers.

(7) Neither subsection (2)(a) nor subsection (5)(b) applies if the Authority considers—

    (a) that, making the appropriate comparison, there will be no increase in costs; or

    (b) that, making that comparison, there will be an increase in costs but the increase will be of minimal significance.

(8) The Authority may charge a reasonable fee for providing a person with a copy of a draft published under subsection (1).

(9) When the Authority is required to publish a document under this section it must do so in the way appearing to it to be best calculated to bring it to the attention of the public.

(10) "Cost benefit analysis" means an estimate of the costs together with an analysis of the benefits that will arise—

    (a) if the proposed direction is given; or

    (b) if subsection (5)(b) applies, from the direction that has been given.

(11) "The appropriate comparison" means—

    (a) in relation to subsection (2)(a), a comparison between the overall position if the direction is given and the overall position if it is not given;

    (b) in relation to subsection (5)(b), a comparison between the overall position after the giving of the direction and the overall position before it was given.

331 Procedure on making or varying orders under section 329

(1) If the Authority proposes to make an order under section 329, it must give the person concerned a warning notice.

(2) The warning notice must set out the terms of the proposed order.

(3) If the Authority decides to make an order under section 329, it must give the person concerned a decision notice.

(4) The decision notice must—

    (a) name the person to whom the order applies;

    (b) set out the terms of the order; and

    (c) be given to the person named in the order.

(5) Subsections (6) to (8) apply to an application for the variation or revocation of an order under section 329.

(6) If the Authority decides to grant the application, it must give the applicant written notice of its decision.

(7) If the Authority proposes to refuse the application, it must give the applicant a warning notice.

(8) If the Authority decides to refuse the application, it must give the applicant a decision notice.

(9) A person—

    (a) against whom the Authority have decided to make an order under section 329, or

    (b) whose application for the variation or revocation of such an order the Authority had decided to refuse,

may refer the matter to the Tribunal.

(10) The Authority may not make an order under section 329 unless—
- (a) the period within which the decision to make to the order may be referred to the Tribunal has expired and no such reference has been made; or
- (b) if such a reference has been made, the reference has been determined.

332 Rules in relation to persons to whom the general prohibition does not apply

(1) The Authority may make rules applicable to persons to whom, as a result of section 327(1), the general prohibition does not apply.

(2) The power conferred by subsection (1) is to be exercised for the purpose of ensuring that clients are aware that such persons are not authorised persons.

(3) A designated professional body must make rules—
- (a) applicable to members of the profession in relation to which it is established who are not authorised persons; and
- (b) governing the carrying on by those members of regulated activities (other than regulated activities in relation to which they are exempt persons).

(4) Rules made in compliance with subsection (3) must be designed to secure that, in providing a particular professional service to a particular client, the member carries on only regulated activities which arise out of, or are complementary to, the provision by him of that service to that client.

(5) Rules made by a designated professional body under subsection (3) require the approval of the Authority.

333 False claims to be a person to whom the general prohibition does not apply

(1) A person who—
- (a) describes himself (in whatever terms) as a person to whom the general prohibition does not apply, in relation to a particular regulated activity, as a result of this Part, or
- (b) behaves, or otherwise holds himself out, in a manner which indicates (or which is reasonably likely to be understood as indicating) that he is such a person,

is guilty of an offence if he is not such a person.

(2) In proceedings for an offence under this section it is a defence for the accused to show that he took all reasonable precautions and exercised all due diligence to avoid committing the offence.

(3) A person guilty of an offence under this section is liable on summary conviction to imprisonment for a term not exceeding six months or a fine not exceeding level 5 on the standard scale, or both.

(4) But where the conduct constituting the offence involved or included the public display of any material, the maximum fine for the offence is level 5 on the standard scale multiplied by the number of days for which the display continued.

PART XXI
MUTUAL SOCIETIES

Friendly societies

334 The Friendly Societies Commission

(1) The Treasury may by order provide—
- (a) for any functions of the Friendly Societies Commission to be transferred to the Authority;
- (b) for any functions of the Friendly Societies Commission which have not been, or are not being, transferred to the Authority to be transferred to the Treasury.

(2) If the Treasury consider it appropriate to do so, they may by order provide for the Friendly Societies Commission to cease to exist on a day specified in or determined in accordance with the order.

(3) The enactments relating to friendly societies which are mentioned in Part I of Schedule 18 are amended as set out in that Part.

(4) Part II of Schedule 18—

    (a) removes certain restrictions on the ability of incorporated friendly societies to form subsidiaries and control corporate bodies; and

    (b) makes connected amendments.

335 The Registry of Friendly Societies

(1) The Treasury may by order provide—

    (a) for any functions of the Chief Registrar of Friendly Societies, or of an assistant registrar of friendly societies for the central registration area, to be transferred to the Authority;

    (b) for any of their functions which have not been, or are not being, transferred to the Authority to be transferred to the Treasury.

(2) The Treasury may by order provide—

    (a) for any functions of the central office of the registry of friendly societies to be transferred to the Authority;

    (b) for any functions of that office which have not been, or are not being, transferred to the Authority to be transferred to the Treasury.

(3) The Treasury may by order provide—

    (a) for any functions of the assistant registrar of friendly societies for Scotland to be transferred to the Authority;

    (b) for any functions of the assistant registrar which have not been, or are not being, transferred to the Authority to be transferred to the Treasury.

(4) If the Treasury consider it appropriate to do so, they may by order provide for—

    (a) the office of Chief Registrar of Friendly Societies,

    (b) the office of assistant registrar of friendly societies for the central registration area,

    (c) the central office, or

    (d) the office of assistant registrar of friendly societies for Scotland,

to cease to exist on a day specified in or determined in accordance with the order.

Building societies

336 The Building Societies Commission

(1) The Treasury may by order provide—

    (a) for any functions of the Building Societies Commission to be transferred to the Authority;

    (b) for any functions of the Building Societies Commission which have not been, or are not being, transferred to the Authority to be transferred to the Treasury.

(2) If the Treasury consider it appropriate to do so, they may by order provide for the Building Societies Commission to cease to exist on a day specified in or determined in accordance with the order.

(3) The enactments relating to building societies which are mentioned in Part III of Schedule 18 are amended as set out in that Part.

337 The Building Societies Investor Protection Board

The Treasury may by order provide for the Building Societies Investor Protection Board to cease to exist on a day specified in or determined in accordance with the order.

Industrial and provident societies and credit unions

338 Industrial and provident societies and credit unions

(1) The Treasury may by order provide for the transfer to the Authority of any functions conferred by—

    (a) the Industrial and Provident Societies Act 1965;

    (b) the Industrial and Provident Societies Act 1967;

    (c) the Friendly and Industrial and Provident Societies Act 1968;

    (d) the Industrial and Provident Societies Act 1975;

    (e) the Industrial and Provident Societies Act 1978;

    (f) the Credit Unions Act 1979.

(2) The Treasury may by order provide for the transfer to the Treasury of any functions under those enactments which have not been, or are not being, transferred to the Authority.

(3) The enactments relating to industrial and provident societies which are mentioned in Part IV of Schedule 18 are amended as set out in that Part.

(4) The enactments relating to credit unions which are mentioned in Part V of Schedule 18 are amended as set out in that Part.

Supplemental

339 Supplemental provisions

(1) The additional powers conferred by section 428 on a person making an order under this Act include power for the Treasury, when making an order under section 334, 335, 336 or 338 which transfers functions, to include provision—

    (a) for the transfer of any functions of a member of the body, or servant or agent of the body or person, whose functions are transferred by the order;

    (b) for the transfer of any property, rights or liabilities held, enjoyed or incurred by any person in connection with transferred functions;

    (c) for the carrying on and completion by or under the authority of the person to whom functions are transferred of any proceedings, investigations or other matters commenced, before the order takes effect, by or under the authority of the person from whom the functions are transferred;

    (d) amending any enactment relating to transferred functions in connection with their exercise by, or under the authority of, the person to whom they are transferred;

    (e) for the substitution of the person to whom functions are transferred for the person from whom they are transferred, in any instrument, contract or legal proceedings made or begun before the order takes effect.

(2) The additional powers conferred by section 428 on a person making an order under this Act include power for the Treasury, when making an order under section 334(2), 335(4), 336(2) or 337, to include provision—

    (a) for the transfer of any property, rights or liabilities held, enjoyed or incurred by any person in connection with the office or body which ceases to have effect as a result of the order;

    (b) for the carrying on and completion by or under the authority of such person as may be specified in the order of any proceedings, investigations or other matters commenced, before the order takes effect, by or under the authority of the person whose office, or the body which, ceases to exist as a result of the order;

    (c) amending any enactment which makes provision with respect to that office or body;

    (d) for the substitution of the Authority, the Treasury or such other body as may be specified in the order in any instrument, contract or legal proceedings made or begun before the order takes effect.

(3) On or after the making of an order under any of sections 334 to 338 ("the original order"), the Treasury may by order make any incidental, supplemental, consequential or transitional provision which they had power to include in the original order.

(4) A certificate issued by the Treasury that property vested in a person immediately before an order under this Part takes effect has been transferred as a result of the order is conclusive evidence of the transfer.

(5) Subsections (1) and (2) are not to be read as affecting in any way the powers conferred by section 428.

PART XXII
AUDITORS AND ACTUARIES

Appointment

340 Appointment

(1) Rules may require an authorised person, or an authorised person falling within a specified class—
 (a) to appoint an auditor, or
 (b) to appoint an actuary,
if he is not already under an obligation to do so imposed by another enactment.

(2) Rules may require an authorised person, or an authorised person falling within a specified class—
 (a) to produce periodic financial reports; and
 (b) to have them reported on by an auditor or an actuary.

(3) Rules may impose such other duties on auditors of, or actuaries acting for, authorised persons as may be specified.

(4) Rules under subsection (1) may make provision—
 (a) specifying the manner in which and time within which an auditor or actuary is to be appointed;
 (b) requiring the Authority to be notified of an appointment;
 (c) enabling the Authority to make an appointment if no appointment has been made or notified;
 (d) as to remuneration;
 (e) as to the term of office, removal and resignation of an auditor or actuary.

(5) An auditor or actuary appointed as a result of rules under subsection (1), or on whom duties are imposed by rules under subsection (3)—
 (a) must act in accordance with such provision as may be made by rules; and
 (b) is to have such powers in connection with the discharge of his functions as may be provided by rules.

(6) In subsections (1) to (3) "auditor" or "actuary" means an auditor, or actuary, who satisfies such requirements as to qualifications, experience and other matters (if any) as may be specified.

(7) "Specified" means specified in rules.

Information

341 Access to books etc

(1) An appointed auditor of, or an appointed actuary acting for, an authorised person—
 (a) has a right of access at all times to the authorised person's books, accounts and vouchers; and
 (b) is entitled to require from the authorised person's officers such information and explanations as he reasonably considers necessary for the performance of his duties as auditor or actuary.

(2) "Appointed" means appointed under or as a result of this Act.

342 Information given by auditor or actuary to the Authority

(1) This section applies to a person who is, or has been, an auditor of an authorised person appointed under or as a result of a statutory provision.

(2) This section also applies to a person who is, or has been, an actuary acting for an authorised person and appointed under or as a result of a statutory provision.

(3) An auditor or actuary does not contravene any duty to which he is subject merely because he gives to the Authority—

    (a) information on a matter of which he has, or had, become aware in his capacity as auditor of, or actuary acting for, the authorised person, or

    (b) his opinion on such a matter,

    if he is acting in good faith and he reasonably believes that the information or opinion is relevant to any functions of the Authority.

(4) Subsection (3) applies whether or not the auditor or actuary is responding to a request from the Authority.

(5) The Treasury may make regulations prescribing circumstances in which an auditor or actuary must communicate matters to the Authority as mentioned in subsection (3).

(6) It is the duty of an auditor or actuary to whom any such regulations apply to communicate a matter to the Authority in the circumstances prescribed by the regulations.

(7) The matters to be communicated to the Authority in accordance with the regulations may include matters relating to persons other than the authorised person concerned.

343 Information given by auditor or actuary to the Authority: persons with close links

(1) This section applies to a person who—

    (a) is, or has been, an auditor of an authorised person appointed under or as a result of a statutory provision; and

    (b) is, or has been, an auditor of a person ("CL") who has close links with the authorised person.

(2) This section also applies to a person who—

    (a) is, or has been, an actuary acting for an authorised person and appointed under or as a result of a statutory provision; and

    (b) is, or has been, an actuary acting for a person ("CL") who has close links with the authorised person.

(3) An auditor or actuary does not contravene any duty to which he is subject merely because he gives to the Authority—

    (a) information on a matter concerning the authorised person of which he has, or had, become aware in his capacity as auditor of, or actuary acting for, CL, or

    (b) his opinion on such a matter,

    if he is acting in good faith and he reasonably believes that the information or opinion is relevant to any functions of the Authority.

(4) Subsection (3) applies whether or not the auditor or actuary is responding to a request from the Authority.

(5) The Treasury may make regulations prescribing circumstances in which an auditor or actuary must communicate matters to the Authority as mentioned in subsection (3).

(6) It is the duty of an auditor or actuary to whom any such regulations apply to communicate a matter to the Authority in the circumstances prescribed by the regulations.

(7) The matters to be communicated to the Authority in accordance with the regulations may include matters relating to persons other than the authorised person concerned.

(8) CL has close links with the authorised person concerned ("A") if CL is—
  (a) a parent undertaking of A;
  (b) a subsidiary undertaking of A;
  (c) a parent undertaking of a subsidiary undertaking of A; or
  (d) a subsidiary undertaking of a parent undertaking of A.

(9) "Subsidiary undertaking" includes all the instances mentioned in Article 1(1) and (2) of the Seventh Company Law Directive in which an entity may be a subsidiary of an undertaking.

344 Duty of auditor or actuary resigning etc to give notice

(1) This section applies to an auditor or actuary to whom section 342 applies.
(2) He must without delay notify the Authority if he—
  (a) is removed from office by an authorised person;
  (b) resigns before the expiry of his term of office with such a person; or
  (c) is not re-appointed by such a person.
(3) If he ceases to be an auditor of, or actuary acting for, such a person, he must without delay notify the Authority—
  (a) of any matter connected with his so ceasing which he thinks ought to be drawn to the Authority's attention; or
  (b) that there is no such matter.

Disqualification

345 Disqualification

(1) If it appears to the Authority that an auditor or actuary to whom section 342 applies has failed to comply with a duty imposed on him under this Act, it may disqualify him from being the auditor of, or (as the case may be) from acting as an actuary for, any authorised person or any particular class of authorised person.
(2) If the Authority proposes to disqualify a person under this section it must give him a warning notice.
(3) If it decides to disqualify him it must give him a decision notice.
(4) The Authority may remove any disqualification imposed under this section if satisfied that the disqualified person will in future comply with the duty in question.
(5) A person who has been disqualified under this section may refer the matter to the Tribunal.

Offence

346 Provision of false or misleading information to auditor or actuary

(1) An authorised person who knowingly or recklessly gives an appointed auditor or actuary information which is false or misleading in a material particular is guilty of an offence and liable—
  (a) on summary conviction, to imprisonment for a term not exceeding six months or a fine not exceeding the statutory maximum, or both;
  (b) on conviction on indictment, to imprisonment for a term not exceeding two years or a fine, or both.
(2) Subsection (1) applies equally to an officer, controller or manager of an authorised person.
(3) "Appointed" means appointed under or as a result of this Act.

PART XXIII
PUBLIC RECORD, DISCLOSURE OF INFORMATION AND CO-OPERATION

The public record

347 The record of authorised persons etc

(1) The Authority must maintain a record of every—

    (a) person who appears to the Authority to be an authorised person;

    (b) authorised unit trust scheme;

    (c) authorised open-ended investment company;

    (d) recognised scheme;

    (e) recognised investment exchange;

    (f) recognised clearing house;

    (g) individual to whom a prohibition order relates;

    (h) approved person; . . .[488]

    [(ha) person to whom subsection (2A) applies; and][489]

    (i) person falling within such other class (if any) as the Authority may determine.

(2) The record must include such information as the Authority considers appropriate and at least the following information—

    (a) in the case of a person appearing to the Authority to be an authorised person—

        (i) information as to the services which he holds himself out as able to provide; and

        (ii) any address of which the Authority is aware at which a notice or other document may be served on him;

    (b) in the case of an authorised unit trust scheme, the name and address of the manager and trustee of the scheme;

    (c) in the case of an authorised open-ended investment company, the name and address of—

        (i) the company;

        (ii) if it has only one director, the director; and

        (iii) its depositary (if any);

    (d) in the case of a recognised scheme, the name and address of—

        (i) the operator of the scheme; and

        (ii) any representative of the operator in the United Kingdom;

    (e) in the case of a recognised investment exchange or recognised clearing house, the name and address of the exchange or clearing house;

    (f) in the case of an individual to whom a prohibition order relates—

        (i) his name; and

        (ii) details of the effect of the order;

    (g) in the case of a person who is an approved person—

        (i) his name;

        (ii) the name of the relevant authorised person;

        (iii) if the approved person is performing a controlled function under an arrangement with a contractor of the relevant authorised person, the name of the contractor.

[(2A) This subsection applies to—

    (a) an appointed representative to whom subsection (1A) of section 39 applies for whom the applicable register (as defined by subsection (1B) of that section) is the record maintained by virtue of subsection (1)(ha) above;

    (b) a person mentioned in subsection (1)(a) of section 39A if—

        (i) the contract with an authorised person to which he is party complies with the applicable requirements (as defined by subsection (7) of that section), and

        (ii) the authorised person has accepted responsibility in writing for the person's activities in carrying on investment services business (as defined by subsection (8) of that section); and

    (c) any person not falling within paragraph (a) or (b) in respect of whom the Authority considers that a record must be maintained for the purpose of securing compliance with Article 23.3 of the markets in financial instruments directive (registration of tied agents).][490]

(3) If it appears to the Authority that a person in respect of whom there is an entry in the record as a result of one of the paragraphs of subsection (1) has ceased to be a person to whom that paragraph applies, the Authority may remove the entry from the record.

(4) But if the Authority decides not to remove the entry, it must—

    (a) make a note to that effect in the record; and

    (b) state why it considers that the person has ceased to be a person to whom that paragraph applies.

(5) The Authority must—

    (a) make the record available for inspection by members of the public in a legible form at such times and in such place or places as the Authority may determine; and

    (b) provide a certified copy of the record, or any part of it, to any person who asks for it—

        (i) on payment of the fee (if any) fixed by the Authority; and

        (ii) in a form (either written or electronic) in which it is legible to the person asking for it.

(6) The Authority may—

    (a) publish the record, or any part of it;

    (b) exploit commercially the information contained in the record, or any part of that information.

(7) "Authorised unit trust scheme", "authorised open-ended investment company" and "recognised scheme" have the same meaning as in Part XVII, and associated expressions are to be read accordingly.

(8) "Approved person" means a person in relation to whom the Authority has given its approval under section 59 and "controlled function" and "arrangement" have the same meaning as in that section.

(9) "Relevant authorised person" has the meaning given in section 66.

Disclosure of information

348 Restrictions on disclosure of confidential information by Authority etc

(1) Confidential information must not be disclosed by a primary recipient, or by any person obtaining the information directly or indirectly from a primary recipient, without the consent of—

    (a) the person from whom the primary recipient obtained the information; and

    (b) if different, the person to whom it relates.

(2) In this Part "confidential information" means information which—

    (a) relates to the business or other affairs of any person;

---

[490] Inserted by SI 2007/126, reg 3(5), Sch 5, paras 1, 12(c); came into force (for certain purposes) 1 April 2007; came into force (for remaining purposes) 1 November 2007.

    (b) was received by the primary recipient for the purposes of, or in the discharge of, any functions of the Authority, the competent authority for the purposes of Part VI or the Secretary of State under any provision made by or under this Act; and

    (c) is not prevented from being confidential information by subsection (4).

(3) It is immaterial for the purposes of subsection (2) whether or not the information was received—

    (a) by virtue of a requirement to provide it imposed by or under this Act;

    (b) for other purposes as well as purposes mentioned in that subsection.

(4) Information is not confidential information if—

    (a) it has been made available to the public by virtue of being disclosed in any circumstances in which, or for any purposes for which, disclosure is not precluded by this section; or

    (b) it is in the form of a summary or collection of information so framed that it is not possible to ascertain from it information relating to any particular person.

(5) Each of the following is a primary recipient for the purposes of this Part—

    (a) the Authority;

    (b) any person exercising functions conferred by Part VI on the competent authority;

    (c) the Secretary of State;

    (d) a person appointed to make a report under section 166;

    (e) any person who is or has been employed by a person mentioned in paragraphs (a) to (c);

    (f) any auditor or expert instructed by a person mentioned in those paragraphs.

(6) In subsection (5)(f) "expert" includes—

    (a) a competent person appointed by the competent authority under section 97;

    (b) a competent person appointed by the Authority or the Secretary of State to conduct an investigation under Part XI;

    (c) any body or person appointed under paragraph 6 of Schedule 1 to perform a function on behalf of the Authority.

349 Exceptions from section 348

(1) Section 348 does not prevent a disclosure of confidential information which is—

    (a) made for the purpose of facilitating the carrying out of a public function; and

    (b) permitted by regulations made by the Treasury under this section.

(2) The regulations may, in particular, make provision permitting the disclosure of confidential information or of confidential information of a prescribed kind—

    (a) by prescribed recipients, or recipients of a prescribed description, to any person for the purpose of enabling or assisting the recipient to discharge prescribed public functions;

    (b) by prescribed recipients, or recipients of a prescribed description, to prescribed persons, or persons of prescribed descriptions, for the purpose of enabling or assisting those persons to discharge prescribed public functions;

    (c) by the Authority to the Treasury or the Secretary of State for any purpose;

    (d) by any recipient if the disclosure is with a view to or in connection with prescribed proceedings.

(3) The regulations may also include provision—

    (a) making any permission to disclose confidential information subject to conditions (which may relate to the obtaining of consents or any other matter);

    (b) restricting the uses to which confidential information disclosed under the regulations may be put.

[(3A) Section 348 does not apply to—

    (a) the disclosure by a recipient to which subsection (3B) applies of confidential information disclosed to it by the Authority in reliance on subsection (1);

    (b) the disclosure of such information by a person obtaining it directly or indirectly from a recipient to which subsection (3B) applies.

(3B) This subsection applies to—

    (a) the Panel on Takeovers and Mergers;

    (b) an authority designated as a supervisory authority for the purposes of Article 4.1 of the Takeovers Directive;

    (c) any other person or body that exercises public functions, under legislation in an EEA State other than the United Kingdom, that are similar to the Authority's functions or those of the Panel on Takeovers and Mergers.][491]

(4) In relation to confidential information, each of the following is a "recipient"—

    (a) a primary recipient;

    (b) a person obtaining the information directly or indirectly from a primary recipient.

(5) "Public functions" includes—

    (a) functions conferred by or in accordance with any provision contained in any enactment or subordinate legislation;

    (b) functions conferred by or in accordance with any provision contained in the Community Treaties or any Community instrument;

    (c) similar functions conferred on persons by or under provisions having effect as part of the law of a country or territory outside the United Kingdom;

    (d) functions exercisable in relation to prescribed disciplinary proceedings.

(6) "Enactment" includes—

    (a) an Act of the Scottish Parliament;

    (b) Northern Ireland legislation.

(7) "Subordinate legislation" has the meaning given in the Interpretation Act 1978 and also includes an instrument made under an Act of the Scottish Parliament or under Northern Ireland legislation.

[(8) . . .[492]][493]

350 Disclosure of information by the Inland Revenue

(1) No obligation as to secrecy imposed by statute or otherwise prevents the disclosure of Revenue information to—

    (a) the Authority, or

    (b) the Secretary of State,

if the disclosure is made for the purpose of assisting in the investigation of a matter under section 168 or with a view to the appointment of an investigator under that section.

(2) A disclosure may only be made under subsection (1) by or under the authority of the Commissioners of Inland Revenue.

(3) Section 348 does not apply to Revenue information.

(4) Information obtained as a result of subsection (1) may not be used except—

    (a) for the purpose of deciding whether to appoint an investigator under section 168;

    (b) in the conduct of an investigation under section 168;

    (c) in criminal proceedings brought against a person under this Act or the Criminal Justice Act 1993 as a result of an investigation under section 168;

    (d) for the purpose of taking action under this Act against a person as a result of an investigation under section 168;

    (e) in proceedings before the Tribunal as a result of action taken as mentioned in paragraph (d).

---

[491] Inserted by the Companies Act 2006, s 964(1), (4); came into force 6 April 2007.

[492] Repealed by SI 2007/1093, art 7, Sch 5; came into force 6 April 2007.

[493] Inserted by SI 2006/1183, reg 18(3), (5); came into force 20 May 2006.

(5) Information obtained as a result of subsection (1) may not be disclosed except—
    (a) by or under the authority of the Commissioners of Inland Revenue;
    (b) in proceedings mentioned in subsection (4)(c) or (e) or with a view to their institution.

(6) Subsection (5) does not prevent the disclosure of information obtained as a result of subsection (1) to a person to whom it could have been disclosed under subsection (1).

(7) "Revenue information" means information held by a person which it would be an offence under section 182 of the Finance Act 1989 for him to disclose.

351 Competition information

(1) . . .

(2) . . .

(3) . . .[494]

(4) Section 348 does not apply to competition information.

(5) "Competition information" means information which—
    (a) relates to the affairs of a particular individual or body;
    (b) is not otherwise in the public domain; and
    (c) was obtained under or by virtue of a competition provision.

(6) "Competition provision" means any provision of—
    (a) an order made under section 95;
    (b) Chapter III of Part X; or
    (c) Chapter II of Part XVIII.

(7) . . .[495]

352 Offences

(1) A person who discloses information in contravention of section 348 or 350(5) is guilty of an offence.

(2) A person guilty of an offence under subsection (1) is liable—
    (a) on summary conviction, to imprisonment for a term not exceeding three months or a fine not exceeding the statutory maximum, or both;
    (b) on conviction on indictment, to imprisonment for a term not exceeding two years or a fine, or both.

(3) A person is guilty of an offence if, in contravention of any provision of regulations made under section 349, he uses information which has been disclosed to him in accordance with the regulations.

(4) A person is guilty of an offence if, in contravention of subsection (4) of section 350, he uses information which has been disclosed to him in accordance with that section.

(5) A person guilty of an offence under subsection (3) or (4) is liable on summary conviction to imprisonment for a term not exceeding *three months* [51 weeks][496] or a fine not exceeding level 5 on the standard scale, or both.

(6) In proceedings for an offence under this section it is a defence for the accused to prove—
    (a) that he did not know and had no reason to suspect that the information was confidential information or that it had been disclosed in accordance with section 350;
    (b) that he took all reasonable precautions and exercised all due diligence to avoid committing the offence.

---

[494] Repealed by the Enterprise Act 2002, ss 247(k), 278(2), Sch 26; came into force 20 June 2003.

[495] Repealed by the Enterprise Act 2002, ss 247(k), 278(2), Sch 26; came into force 20 June 2003.

[496] Words "three months" in italics repealed and words in square brackets substituted by the Criminal Justice Act 2003, s 280(2), (3), Sch 26, para 54(1), (3); date in force to be appointed, see the Criminal Justice Act 2003, s 336(3).

353 Removal of other restrictions on disclosure

(1) The Treasury may make regulations permitting the disclosure of any information, or of information of a prescribed kind—

    (a) by prescribed persons for the purpose of assisting or enabling them to discharge prescribed functions under this Act or any rules or regulations made under it;

    (b) by prescribed persons, or persons of a prescribed description, to the Authority for the purpose of assisting or enabling the Authority to discharge prescribed functions;

    [(c) by the scheme operator to the Office of Fair Trading for the purpose of assisting or enabling that Office to discharge prescribed functions under the Consumer Credit Act 1974].[497]

(2) Regulations under this section may not make any provision in relation to the disclosure of confidential information by primary recipients or by any person obtaining confidential information directly or indirectly from a primary recipient.

(3) If a person discloses any information as permitted by regulations under this section the disclosure is not to be taken as a contravention of any duty to which he is subject.

Co-operation

354 Authority's duty to co-operate with others

(1) The Authority must take such steps as it considers appropriate to co-operate with other persons (whether in the United Kingdom or elsewhere) who have functions—

    (a) similar to those of the Authority; or

    (b) in relation to the prevention or detection of financial crime.

[(1A) The Authority must take such steps as it considers appropriate to co- operate with—

    (a) the Panel on Takeovers and Mergers;

    (b) an authority designated as a supervisory authority for the purposes of Article 4.1 of the Takeovers Directive;

    (c) any other person or body that exercises functions of a public nature, under legislation in any country or territory outside the United Kingdom, that appear to the Authority to be similar to those of the Panel on Takeovers and Mergers.][498]

(2) Co-operation may include the sharing of information which the Authority is not prevented from disclosing.

(3) "Financial crime" has the same meaning as in section 6.

PART XXIV
INSOLVENCY

Interpretation

355 Interpretation of this Part

(1) In this Part—

    "the 1985 Act" means the Bankruptcy (Scotland) Act 1985;

"the 1986 Act" means the Insolvency Act 1986;

    "the 1989 Order" means the Insolvency (Northern Ireland) Order 1989;

---

[497] Inserted by the Consumer Credit Act 2006, s 61(9); came into force 16 June 2006.
[498] Inserted by the Companies Act 2006, s 964(1), (5); came into force 6 April 2007.

"body" means a body of persons—

(a) over which the court has jurisdiction under any provision of, or made under, the 1986 Act (or the 1989 Order); but

(b) which is not a building society, a friendly society or an industrial and provident society; and

"court" means—

(a) the court having jurisdiction for the purposes of the 1985 Act or the 1986 Act; or

(b) in Northern Ireland, the High Court.

(2) In this Part "insurer" has such meaning as may be specified in an order made by the Treasury.

Voluntary arrangements

356 Authority's powers to participate in proceedings: company voluntary arrangements

[(1) Where a voluntary arrangement has effect under Part I of the 1986 Act in respect of a company or insolvent partnership which is an authorised person, the Authority may apply to the court under section 6 or 7 of that Act.]⁴⁹⁹

[(2) Where a voluntary arrangement has been approved under Part II of the 1989 Order in respect of a company or insolvent partnership which is an authorised person, the Authority may apply to the court under Article 19 or 20 of that Order.]⁵⁰⁰

(3) If a person other than the Authority makes an application to the court in relation to the company or insolvent partnership under [any]⁵⁰¹ of those provisions, the Authority is entitled to be heard at any hearing relating to the application.

357 Authority's powers to participate in proceedings: individual voluntary arrangements

(1) The Authority is entitled to be heard on an application by an individual who is an authorised person under section 253 of the 1986 Act (or Article 227 of the 1989 Order).

(2) Subsections (3) to (6) apply if such an order is made on the application of such a person.

(3) A person appointed for the purpose by the Authority is entitled to attend any meeting of creditors of the debtor summoned under section 257 of the 1986 Act (or Article 231 of the 1989 Order).

(4) Notice of the result of a meeting so summoned is to be given to the Authority by the chairman of the meeting.

(5) The Authority may apply to the court—

(a) under section 262 of the 1986 Act (or Article 236 of the 1989 Order); or

(b) under section 263 of the 1986 Act (or Article 237 of the 1989 Order).

(6) If a person other than the Authority makes an application to the court under any provision mentioned in subsection (5), the Authority is entitled to be heard at any hearing relating to the application.

358 Authority's powers to participate in proceedings: trust deeds for creditors in Scotland

(1) This section applies where a trust deed has been granted by or on behalf of a debtor who is an authorised person.

(2) The trustee must, as soon as practicable after he becomes aware that the debtor is an authorised person, send to the Authority—

(a) in every case, a copy of the trust deed;

(b) where any other document or information is sent to every creditor known to the trustee in pursuance of paragraph 5(1)(c) of Schedule 5 to the 1985 Act, a copy of such document or information.

---

⁴⁹⁹ Substituted by the Insolvency Act 2000, s 15(3)(a); came into force 1 January 2003.

⁵⁰⁰ Substituted by the Insolvency Act 2000, s 15(3)(b); came into force 1 January 2003.

⁵⁰¹ Substituted by the Insolvency Act 2000, s 15(3)(c); came into force 1 January 2003.

(3) Paragraph 7 of that Schedule applies to the Authority as if it were a qualified creditor who has not been sent a copy of the notice as mentioned in paragraph 5(1)(c) of the Schedule.

(4) The Authority must be given the same notice as the creditors of any meeting of creditors held in relation to the trust deed.

(5) A person appointed for the purpose by the Authority is entitled to attend and participate in (but not to vote at) any such meeting of creditors as if the Authority were a creditor under the deed.

(6) This section does not affect any right the Authority has as a creditor of a debtor who is an authorised person.

(7) Expressions used in this section and in the 1985 Act have the same meaning in this section as in that Act.

Administration orders

[359 Administration order][502]

[(1) The Authority may make an administration application under Schedule B1 to the 1986 Act [or Schedule B1 to the 1989 Order][503] in relation to a company or insolvent partnership which—

(a) is or has been an authorised person,

(b) is or has been an appointed representative, or

(c) is carrying on or has carried on a regulated activity in contravention of the general prohibition.

(2) Subsection (3) applies in relation to an administration application made (or a petition presented) by the Authority by virtue of this section.

(3) Any of the following shall be treated for the purpose of paragraph 11(a) of Schedule B1 to the 1986 Act [or paragraph 12(a) of Schedule B1 to the 1989 Order][504] as unable to pay its debts—

(a) a company or partnership in default on an obligation to pay a sum due and payable under an agreement, . . .[505]

(b) an authorised deposit taker in default on an obligation to pay a sum due and payable in respect of a relevant deposit[, and

(c) an authorised reclaim fund in default on an obligation to pay a sum payable as a result of a claim made by virtue of section 1(2)(b) or 2(2)(b) of the Dormant Bank and Building Society Accounts Act 2008].[506]

(4) In this section—

"agreement" means an agreement the making or performance of which constitutes or is part of a regulated activity carried on by the company or partnership,

"authorised deposit taker" means a person with a Part IV permission to accept deposits (but not a person who has a Part IV permission to accept deposits only for the purpose of carrying on another regulated activity in accordance with that permission),

---

[502] Substituted by the Enterprise Act 2002, s 248(3), Sch 17, paras 53, 55; came into force 15 September 2003.

[503] Substituted by the Insolvency (Northern Ireland) Order 2005, SI 2005/1455, art 3(3), Sch 2, paras 56, 58(1), (2); came into force 27 March 2006.

[504] Substituted by the Insolvency (Northern Ireland) Order 2005, SI 2005/1455, art 3(3), Sch 2, paras 56, 58(1), (3); came into force 27 March 2006.

[505] Repealed by the Dormant Bank and Building Society Accounts Act 2008, s 15, Sch 2, para 6(1), (2); came into force 12 March 2009.

[506] Inserted by the Dormant Bank and Building Society Accounts Act 2008, s 15, Sch 2, para 6(1), (2); came into force 12 March 2009.

["authorised reclaim fund" means a reclaim fund within the meaning given by section 5(1) of the Dormant Bank and Building Society Accounts Act 2008 that is authorised for the purposes of this Act,][507]

"company" means a company—

    (a) in respect of which an administrator may be appointed under Schedule B1 to the 1986 Act, or

    [(b) in respect of which an administrator may be appointed under Schedule B1 to the 1989 Order,][508] and

"relevant deposit" shall, ignoring any restriction on the meaning of deposit arising from the identity of the person making the deposit, be construed in accordance with—

    (a) section 22,

    (b) any relevant order under that section, and

    (c) Schedule 2.

(5) The definition of "authorised deposit taker" in subsection (4) shall be construed in accordance with—

    (a) section 22,

    (b) any relevant order under that section, and

    (c) Schedule 2.]

360 Insurers

(1) The Treasury may by order provide that such provisions of Part II of the 1986 Act (or Part III of the 1989 Order) as may be specified are to apply in relation to insurers with such modifications as may be specified.

(2) An order under this section—

    (a) may provide that such provisions of this Part as may be specified are to apply in relation to the administration of insurers in accordance with the order with such modifications as may be specified; and

    (b) requires the consent of the Secretary of State.

(3) "Specified" means specified in the order.

[361 Administrator's duty to report to Authority][509]

[(1) This section applies where a company or partnership is—

    (a) in administration within the meaning of Schedule B1 to the 1986 Act, or

    [(b) in administration within the meaning of Schedule B1 to the 1989 Order][510].

(2) If the administrator thinks that the company or partnership is carrying on or has carried on a regulated activity in contravention of the general prohibition, he must report to the Authority without delay.

(3) Subsection (2) does not apply where the administration arises out of an administration order made on an application made or petition presented by the Authority.]

---

[507] Inserted by the Dormant Bank and Building Society Accounts Act 2008, s 15, Sch 2, para 6(1), (3); came into force 12 March 2009.

[508] Substituted by the Insolvency (Northern Ireland) Order 2005, SI 2005/1455, art 3(3), Sch 2, paras 56, 58(1), (4); came into force 27 March 2006.

[509] Substituted by the Enterprise Act 2002, s 248(3), Sch 17, paras 53, 56; came into force 15 September 2003.

[510] Substituted by the Insolvency (Northern Ireland) Order 2005, SI 2005/1455, art 3(3), Sch 2, paras 56, 59; came into force 27 March 2006.

362 Authority's powers to participate in proceedings

(1) This section applies if a person other than the Authority [makes an administration application under Schedule B1 to the 1986 Act][511] [or Schedule B1 to the 1989 Order][512] in relation to a company or partnership which—

    (a) is, or has been, an authorised person;

    (b) is, or has been, an appointed representative; or

    (c) is carrying on, or has carried on, a regulated activity in contravention of the general prohibition.

[(1A) This section also applies in relation to—

    (a) the appointment under paragraph 14 or 22 of Schedule B1 to the 1986 Act [or paragraph 15 or 23 of Schedule B1 to the 1989 Order][513] of an administrator of a company of a kind described in subsection (1)(a) to (c), or

    (b) the filing with the court of a copy of notice of intention to appoint an administrator under [any][514] of those paragraphs.][515]

(2) The Authority is entitled to be heard—

    (a) at the hearing of the [administration application . . .[516]];[517] and

    (b) at any other hearing of the court in relation to the company or partnership under Part II of the 1986 Act (or Part III of the 1989 Order).

(3) Any notice or other document required to be sent to a creditor of the company or partnership must also be sent to the Authority.

[(4) The Authority may apply to the court under paragraph 74 of Schedule B1 to the 1986 Act [or paragraph 75 of Schedule B1 to the 1989 Order].[518]

(4A) In respect of an application under subsection (4)—

    (a) paragraph 74(1)(a) and (b) shall have effect as if for the words "harm the interests of the applicant (whether alone or in common with some or all other members or creditors)" there were substituted the words "harm the interests of some or all members or creditors", and

    [(b) paragraph 75(1)(a) and (b) of Schedule B1 to the 1989 Order shall have effect as if for the words "harm the interests of the applicant (whether alone or in common with some or all other members or creditors)" there were substituted the words "harm the interests of some or all members or creditors"][519].][520]

---

[511] Substituted by the Enterprise Act 2002, s 248(3), Sch 17, paras 53, 57(a); came into force 15 September 2003.

[512] Substituted by the Insolvency (Northern Ireland) Order 2005, SI 2005/1455, art 3(3), Sch 2, paras 56, 60(1), (2); came into force 27 March 2006.

[513] Inserted by the Insolvency (Northern Ireland) Order 2005, SI 2005/1455, art 3(3), Sch 2, paras 56, 60(1), (3)(a); came into force 27 March 2006.

[514] Substituted by the Insolvency (Northern Ireland) Order 2005, SI 2005/1455, art 3(3), Sch 2, paras 56, 60(1), (3)(b); came into force 27 March 2006.

[515] Inserted by the Enterprise Act 2002, s 248(3), Sch 17, paras 53, 57(b); came into force 15 September 2003.

[516] Repealed by the Insolvency (Northern Ireland) Order 2005, SI 2005/1455, arts 3(3), 31, Sch 2, paras 56, 60(1), (4), Sch 9; came into force 27 March 2006.

[517] Substituted by the Enterprise Act 2002, s 248(3), Sch 17, paras 53, 57(c); came into force 15 September 2003.

[518] Substituted by the Insolvency (Northern Ireland) Order 2005, SI 2005/1455, art 3(3), Sch 2, paras 56, 60(1), (5); came into force 27 March 2006.

[519] Substituted by the Insolvency (Northern Ireland) Order 2005, SI 2005/1455, art 3(3) Sch 2, paras 56, 60(1), (6); came into force 27 March 2006.

[520] Substituted, for sub-s (4) as originally enacted, by the Enterprise Act 2002, s 248(3), Sch 17, paras 53, 57(d); came into force 15 September 2003.

(5) A person appointed for the purpose by the Authority is entitled—

    (a) to attend any meeting of creditors of the company or partnership summoned under any enactment;

    (b) to attend any meeting of a committee established under [paragraph 57 of Schedule B1 to the 1986 Act][521] [or paragraph 58 of Schedule B1 to the 1989 Order];[522] and

    (c) to make representations as to any matter for decision at such a meeting.

(6) If, during the course of the administration of a company, a compromise or arrangement is proposed between the company and its creditors, or any class of them, the Authority may apply to the court under [section 896 or 899 of the Companies Act 2006].[523]

[362A Administrator appointed by company or directors][524]

[(1) This section applies in relation to a company of a kind described in section 362(1)(a) to (c).

(2) An administrator of the company may not be appointed under paragraph 22 of Schedule B1 to the 1986 Act [or paragraph 23 of Schedule B1 to the 1989 Order][525] without the consent of the Authority.

(3) Consent under subsection (2)—

    (a) must be in writing, and

    (b) must be filed with the court along with the notice of intention to appoint under paragraph 27 of [Schedule B1 to the 1986 Act or paragraph 28 of Schedule B1 to the 1989 Order].[526]

(4) In a case where no notice of intention to appoint is required—

    (a) subsection (3)(b) shall not apply, but

    (b) consent under subsection (2) must accompany the notice of appointment filed under paragraph 29 of [Schedule B1 to the 1986 Act or paragraph 30 of Schedule B1 to the 1989 Order].[527]]

Receivership

363 Authority's powers to participate in proceedings

(1) This section applies if a receiver has been appointed in relation to a company which—

    (a) is, or has been, an authorised person;

    (b) is, or has been, an appointed representative; or

    (c) is carrying on, or has carried on, a regulated activity in contravention of the general prohibition.

(2) The Authority is entitled to be heard on an application made under section 35 or 63 of the 1986 Act (or Article 45 of the 1989 Order).

(3) The Authority is entitled to make an application under section 41(1)(a) or 69(1)(a) of the 1986 Act (or Article 51(1)(a) of the 1989 Order).

---

[521] Substituted by the Enterprise Act 2002, s 248(3), Sch 17, paras 53, 57(e); came into force 15 September 2003.

[522] Substituted by the Insolvency (Northern Ireland) Order 2005, SI 2005/1455, art 3(3), Sch 2, paras 56, 60(1), (7); came into force 27 March 2006.

[523] Substituted by SI 2008/948, arts 3(1)(b), 6, Sch 1, Pt 2, para 211(4); came into force 6 April 2008.

[524] Inserted by the Enterprise Act 2002, s 248(3), Sch 17, paras 53, 58; came into force 15 September 2003.

[525] Inserted by the Insolvency (Northern Ireland) Order 2005, SI 2005/1455, art 3(3), Sch 2, paras 56, 61(1), (2); came into force 27 March 2006.

[526] Substituted by the Insolvency (Northern Ireland) Order 2005, SI 2005/1455, art 3(3), Sch 2, paras 56, 61(1), (3); came into force 27 March 2006.

[527] Substituted by the Insolvency (Northern Ireland) Order 2005, SI 2005/1455, art 3(3), Sch 2, paras 56, 61(1), (4); came into force 27 March 2006.

(4) A report under section 48(1) or 67(1) of the 1986 Act (or Article 58(1) of the 1989 Order) must be sent by the person making it to the Authority.

(5) A person appointed for the purpose by the Authority is entitled—

    (a) to attend any meeting of creditors of the company summoned under any enactment;

    (b) to attend any meeting of a committee established under section 49 or 68 of the 1986 Act (or Article 59 of the 1989 Order); and

    (c) to make representations as to any matter for decision at such a meeting.

364 Receiver's duty to report to Authority

If—

    (a) a receiver has been appointed in relation to a company, and

    (b) it appears to the receiver that the company is carrying on, or has carried on, a regulated activity in contravention of the general prohibition,

the receiver must report the matter to the Authority without delay.

Voluntary winding up

365 Authority's powers to participate in proceedings

(1) This section applies in relation to a company which—

    (a) is being wound up voluntarily;

    (b) is an authorised person; and

    (c) is not an insurer effecting or carrying out contracts of long-term insurance.

(2) The Authority may apply to the court under section 112 of the 1986 Act (or Article 98 of the 1989 Order) in respect of the company.

(3) The Authority is entitled to be heard at any hearing of the court in relation to the voluntary winding up of the company.

(4) Any notice or other document required to be sent to a creditor of the company must also be sent to the Authority.

(5) A person appointed for the purpose by the Authority is entitled—

    (a) to attend any meeting of creditors of the company summoned under any enactment;

    (b) to attend any meeting of a committee established under section 101 of the 1986 Act (or Article 87 of the 1989 Order); and

    (c) to make representations as to any matter for decision at such a meeting.

(6) The voluntary winding up of the company does not bar the right of the Authority to have it wound up by the court.

(7) If, during the course of the winding up of the company, a compromise or arrangement is proposed between the company and its creditors, or any class of them, the Authority may apply to the court under [section 896 or 899 of the Companies Act 2006].[528]

366 Insurers effecting or carrying out long-term contracts or insurance

(1) An insurer effecting or carrying out contracts of long-term insurance may not be wound up voluntarily without the consent of the Authority.

(2) If notice of a general meeting of such an insurer is given, specifying the intention to propose a resolution for voluntary winding up of the insurer, a director of the insurer must notify the Authority as soon as practicable after he becomes aware of it.

(3) A person who fails to comply with subsection (2) is guilty of an offence and liable on summary conviction to a fine not exceeding level 5 on the standard scale.

---

[528] Substituted by SI 2008/948, arts 3(1)(b), 6, Sch 1, Pt 2, para 211(4); came into force 6 April 2008.

[(4) A winding up resolution may not be passed—

    (a) as a written resolution (in accordance with Chapter 2 of Part 13 of the Companies Act 2006), or

    (b) at a meeting called in accordance with section 307(4) to (6) or 337(2) of that Act (agreement of members to calling of meeting at short notice).][529]

(5) A copy of a winding-up resolution forwarded to the registrar of companies in accordance with [section 30 of the Companies Act 2006][530] must be accompanied by a certificate issued by the Authority stating that it consents to the voluntary winding up of the insurer.

(6) If subsection (5) is complied with, the voluntary winding up is to be treated as having commenced at the time the resolution was passed.

(7) If subsection (5) is not complied with, the resolution has no effect.

(8) "Winding-up resolution" means a resolution for voluntary winding up of an insurer effecting or carrying out contracts of long-term insurance.

Winding up by the court

367 Winding-up petitions

(1) The Authority may present a petition to the court for the winding up of a body which—

    (a) is, or has been, an authorised person;

    (b) is, or has been, an appointed representative; or

    (c) is carrying on, or has carried on, a regulated activity in contravention of the general prohibition.

(2) In subsection (1) "body" includes any partnership.

(3) On such a petition, the court may wind up the body if—

    (a) the body is unable to pay its debts within the meaning of section 123 or 221 of the 1986 Act (or Article 103 or 185 of the 1989 Order); or

    (b) the court is of the opinion that it is just and equitable that it should be wound up.

(4) If a body is in default on an obligation to pay a sum due and payable under an agreement, it is to be treated for the purpose of subsection (3)(a) as unable to pay its debts.

(5) "Agreement" means an agreement the making or performance of which constitutes or is part of a regulated activity carried on by the body concerned.

(6) Subsection (7) applies if a petition is presented under subsection (1) for the winding up of a partnership—

    (a) on the ground mentioned in subsection (3)(b); or

    (b) in Scotland, on a ground mentioned in subsection (3)(a) or (b).

(7) The court has jurisdiction, and the 1986 Act (or the 1989 Order) has effect, as if the partnership were an unregistered company as defined by section 220 of that Act (or Article 184 of that Order).

368 Winding-up petitions: EEA and Treaty firms

The Authority may not present a petition to the court under section 367 for the winding up of—

    (a) an EEA firm which qualifies for authorisation under Schedule 3, or

    (b) a Treaty firm which qualifies for authorisation under Schedule 4,

unless it has been asked to do so by the home state regulator of the firm concerned.

---

[529] Substituted by SI 2007/2194, art 10(1), (2), Sch 4, Pt 3, para 93(1), (2); came into force 1 October 2007.

[530] Substituted by SI 2007/2194, art 10(1), (2), Sch 4, Pt 3, para 93(1), (3); came into force 1 October 2007.

369 Insurers: service of petition etc on Authority

(1) If a person other than the Authority presents a petition for the winding up of an authorised person with permission to effect or carry out contracts of insurance, the petitioner must serve a copy of the petition on the Authority.

(2) If a person other than the Authority applies to have a provisional liquidator appointed under section 135 of the 1986 Act (or Article 115 of the 1989 Order) in respect of an authorised person with permission to effect or carry out contracts of insurance, the applicant must serve a copy of the application on the Authority.

[369A Reclaim funds: service of petition etc on Authority][531]

[(1) If a person other than the Authority presents a petition for the winding up of an authorised reclaim fund, the petitioner must serve a copy of the petition on the Authority.

(2) If a person other than the Authority applies to have a provisional liquidator appointed under section 135 of the 1986 Act (or Article 115 of the 1989 Order) in respect of an authorised reclaim fund, the applicant must serve a copy of the application on the Authority.

(3) In this section "authorised reclaim fund" means a reclaim fund within the meaning given by section 5(1) of the Dormant Bank and Building Society Accounts Act 2008 that is authorised for the purposes of this Act.]

370 Liquidator's duty to report to Authority

If—

    (a) a company is being wound up voluntarily or a body is being wound up on a petition presented by a person other than the Authority, and

    (b) it appears to the liquidator that the company or body is carrying on, or has carried on, a regulated activity in contravention of the general prohibition,

the liquidator must report the matter to the Authority without delay.

371 Authority's powers to participate in proceedings

(1) This section applies if a person other than the Authority presents a petition for the winding up of a body which—

    (a) is, or has been, an authorised person;

    (b) is, or has been, an appointed representative; or

    (c) is carrying on, or has carried on, a regulated activity in contravention of the general prohibition.

(2) The Authority is entitled to be heard—

    (a) at the hearing of the petition; and

    (b) at any other hearing of the court in relation to the body under or by virtue of Part IV or V of the 1986 Act (or Part V or VI of the 1989 Order).

(3) Any notice or other document required to be sent to a creditor of the body must also be sent to the Authority.

(4) A person appointed for the purpose by the Authority is entitled—

    (a) to attend any meeting of creditors of the body;

    (b) to attend any meeting of a committee established for the purposes of Part IV or V of the 1986 Act under section 101 of that Act or under section 141 or 142 of that Act;

    (c) to attend any meeting of a committee established for the purposes of Part V or VI of the 1989 Order under Article 87 of that Order or under Article 120 of that Order; and

    (d) to make representations as to any matter for decision at such a meeting.

---

[531] Inserted by the Dormant Bank and Building Society Accounts Act 2008, s 15, Sch 2, para 7; came into force 12 March 2009.

(5) If, during the course of the winding up of a company, a compromise or arrangement is proposed between the company and its creditors, or any class of them, the Authority may apply to the court under [section 896 or 899 of the Companies Act 2006].[532]

Bankruptcy

372 Petitions

(1) The Authority may present a petition to the court—
  (a) under section 264 of the 1986 Act (or Article 238 of the 1989 Order) for a bankruptcy order to be made against an individual; or
  (b) under section 5 of the 1985 Act for the sequestration of the estate of an individual.
(2) But such a petition may be presented only on the ground that—
  (a) the individual appears to be unable to pay a regulated activity debt; or
  (b) the individual appears to have no reasonable prospect of being able to pay a regulated activity debt.
(3) An individual appears to be unable to pay a regulated activity debt if he is in default on an obligation to pay a sum due and payable under an agreement.
(4) An individual appears to have no reasonable prospect of being able to pay a regulated activity debt if—
  (a) the Authority has served on him a demand requiring him to establish to the satisfaction of the Authority that there is a reasonable prospect that he will be able to pay a sum payable under an agreement when it falls due;
  (b) at least three weeks have elapsed since the demand was served; and
  (c) the demand has been neither complied with nor set aside in accordance with rules.
(5) A demand made under subsection (4)(a) is to be treated for the purposes of the 1986 Act (or the 1989 Order) as if it were a statutory demand under section 268 of that Act (or Article 242 of that Order).
(6) For the purposes of a petition presented in accordance with subsection (1)(b)—
  (a) the Authority is to be treated as a qualified creditor; and
  (b) a ground mentioned in subsection (2) constitutes apparent insolvency.
(7) "Individual" means an individual—
  (a) who is, or has been, an authorised person; or
  (b) who is carrying on, or has carried on, a regulated activity in contravention of the general prohibition.
(8) "Agreement" means an agreement the making or performance of which constitutes or is part of a regulated activity carried on by the individual concerned.
(9) "Rules" means—
  (a) in England and Wales, rules made under section 412 of the 1986 Act;
  (b) in Scotland, rules made by order by the Treasury, after consultation with the Scottish Ministers, for the purposes of this section; and
  (c) in Northern Ireland, rules made under Article 359 of the 1989 Order.

373 Insolvency practitioner's duty to report to Authority

(1) If—
  (a) a bankruptcy order or sequestration award is in force in relation to an individual by virtue of a petition presented by a person other than the Authority, and
  (b) it appears to the insolvency practitioner that the individual is carrying on, or has carried on, a regulated activity in contravention of the general prohibition,
  the insolvency practitioner must report the matter to the Authority without delay.

---

[532] Substituted by SI 2008/948, arts 3(1)(b), 6, Sch 1, Pt 2, para 211(4); came into force 6 April 2008.

(2) "Bankruptcy order" means a bankruptcy order under Part IX of the 1986 Act (or Part IX of the 1989 Order).

(3) "Sequestration award" means an award of sequestration under section 12 of the 1985 Act.

(4) "Individual" includes an entity mentioned in section 374(1)(c).

374 Authority's powers to participate in proceedings

(1) This section applies if a person other than the Authority presents a petition to the court—
   (a) under section 264 of the 1986 Act (or Article 238 of the 1989 Order) for a bankruptcy order to be made against an individual;
   (b) under section 5 of the 1985 Act for the sequestration of the estate of an individual; or
   (c) under section 6 of the 1985 Act for the sequestration of the estate belonging to or held for or jointly by the members of an entity mentioned in subsection (1) of that section.

(2) The Authority is entitled to be heard—
   (a) at the hearing of the petition; and
   (b) at any other hearing in relation to the individual or entity under—
      (i) Part IX of the 1986 Act;
      (ii) Part IX of the 1989 Order; or
      (iii) the 1985 Act.

(3) A copy of the report prepared under section 274 of the 1986 Act (or Article 248 of the 1989 Order) must also be sent to the Authority.

(4) A person appointed for the purpose by the Authority is entitled—
   (a) to attend any meeting of creditors of the individual or entity;
   (b) to attend any meeting of a committee established under section 301 of the 1986 Act (or Article 274 of the 1989 Order);
   (c) to attend any meeting of commissioners held under paragraph 17 or 18 of Schedule 6 to the 1985 Act; and
   (d) to make representations as to any matter for decision at such a meeting.

(5) "Individual" means an individual who—
   (a) is, or has been, an authorised person; or
   (b) is carrying on, or has carried on, a regulated activity in contravention of the general prohibition.

(6) "Entity" means an entity which—
   (a) is, or has been, an authorised person; or
   (b) is carrying on, or has carried on, a regulated activity in contravention of the general prohibition.

Provisions against debt avoidance

375 Authority's right to apply for an order

(1) The Authority may apply for an order under section 423 of the 1986 Act (or Article 367 of the 1989 Order) in relation to a debtor if—
   (a) at the time the transaction at an undervalue was entered into, the debtor was carrying on a regulated activity (whether or not in contravention of the general prohibition); and
   (b) a victim of the transaction is or was party to an agreement entered into with the debtor, the making or performance of which constituted or was part of a regulated activity carried on by the debtor.

(2) An application made under this section is to be treated as made on behalf of every victim of the transaction to whom subsection (1)(b) applies.

(3) Expressions which are given a meaning in Part XVI of the 1986 Act (or Article 367, 368 or 369 of the 1989 Order) have the same meaning when used in this section.

376 Continuation of contracts of long-term insurance where insurer in liquidation

(1) This section applies in relation to the winding up of an insurer which effects or carries out contracts of long-term insurance.

(2) Unless the court otherwise orders, the liquidator must carry on the insurer's business so far as it consists of carrying out the insurer's contracts of long-term insurance with a view to its being transferred as a going concern to a person who may lawfully carry out those contracts.

(3) In carrying on the business, the liquidator—

    (a) may agree to the variation of any contracts of insurance in existence when the winding up order is made; but

    (b) must not effect any new contracts of insurance.

(4) If the liquidator is satisfied that the interests of the creditors in respect of liabilities of the insurer attributable to contracts of long-term insurance effected by it require the appointment of a special manager, he may apply to the court.

(5) On such an application, the court may appoint a special manager to act during such time as the court may direct.

(6) The special manager is to have such powers, including any of the powers of a receiver or manager, as the court may direct.

(7) Section 177(5) of the 1986 Act (or Article 151(5) of the 1989 Order) applies to a special manager appointed under subsection (5) as it applies to a special manager appointed under section 177 of the 1986 Act (or Article 151 of the 1989 Order).

(8) If the court thinks fit, it may reduce the value of one or more of the contracts of long-term insurance effected by the insurer.

(9) Any reduction is to be on such terms and subject to such conditions (if any) as the court thinks fit.

(10) The court may, on the application of an official, appoint an independent actuary to investigate the insurer's business so far as it consists of carrying out its contracts of long-term insurance and to report to the official—

    (a) on the desirability or otherwise of that part of the insurer's business being continued; and

    (b) on any reduction in the contracts of long-term insurance effected by the insurer that may be necessary for successful continuation of that part of the insurer's business.

(11) "Official" means—

    (a) the liquidator;

    (b) a special manager appointed under subsection (5); or

    (c) the Authority.

(12) The liquidator may make an application in the name of the insurer and on its behalf under Part VII without obtaining the permission that would otherwise be required by section 167 of, and Schedule 4 to, the 1986 Act (or Article 142 of, and Schedule 2 to, the 1989 Order).

377 Reducing the value of contracts instead of winding up

(1) This section applies in relation to an insurer which has been proved to be unable to pay its debts.

(2) If the court thinks fit, it may reduce the value of one or more of the insurer's contracts instead of making a winding up order.

(3) Any reduction is to be on such terms and subject to such conditions (if any) as the court thinks fit.

378 Treatment of assets on winding up

(1) The Treasury may by regulations provide for the treatment of the assets of an insurer on its winding up.

(2) The regulations may, in particular, provide for—

   (a) assets representing a particular part of the insurer's business to be available only for meeting liabilities attributable to that part of the insurer's business;

   (b) separate general meetings of the creditors to be held in respect of liabilities attributable to a particular part of the insurer's business.

379 Winding-up rules

(1) Winding-up rules may include provision—

   (a) for determining the amount of the liabilities of an insurer to policyholders of any class or description for the purpose of proof in a winding up; and

   (b) generally for carrying into effect the provisions of this Part with respect to the winding up of insurers.

(2) Winding-up rules may, in particular, make provision for all or any of the following matters—

   (a) the identification of assets and liabilities;

   (b) the apportionment, between assets of different classes or descriptions, of—

     (i) the costs, charges and expenses of the winding up; and

     (ii) any debts of the insurer of a specified class or description;

   (c) the determination of the amount of liabilities of a specified description;

   (d) the application of assets for meeting liabilities of a specified description;

   (e) the application of assets representing any excess of a specified description.

(3) "Specified" means specified in winding-up rules.

(4) "Winding-up rules" means rules made under section 411 of the 1986 Act (or Article 359 of the 1989 Order).

(5) Nothing in this section affects the power to make winding-up rules under the 1986 Act or the 1989 Order.

PART XXV
INJUNCTIONS AND RESTITUTION

Injunctions

380 Injunctions

(1) If, on the application of the Authority or the Secretary of State, the court is satisfied—

   (a) that there is a reasonable likelihood that any person will contravene a relevant requirement, or

   (b) that any person has contravened a relevant requirement and that there is a reasonable likelihood that the contravention will continue or be repeated,

the court may make an order restraining (or in Scotland an interdict prohibiting) the contravention.

(2) If on the application of the Authority or the Secretary of State the court is satisfied—

   (a) that any person has contravened a relevant requirement, and

   (b) that there are steps which could be taken for remedying the contravention,

the court may make an order requiring that person, and any other person who appears to have been knowingly concerned in the contravention, to take such steps as the court may direct to remedy it.

(3) If, on the application of the Authority or the Secretary of State, the court is satisfied that any person may have—
    (a) contravened a relevant requirement, or
    (b) been knowingly concerned in the contravention of such a requirement,
it may make an order restraining (or in Scotland an interdict prohibiting) him from disposing of, or otherwise dealing with, any assets of his which it is satisfied he is reasonably likely to dispose of or otherwise deal with.

(4) The jurisdiction conferred by this section is exercisable by the High Court and the Court of Session.

(5) In subsection (2), references to remedying a contravention include references to mitigating its effect.

(6) "Relevant requirement"—
    (a) in relation to an application by the Authority, means a requirement—
        (i) which is imposed by or under this Act [or by any directly applicable Community regulation made under the markets in financial instruments directive];[533] or
        (ii) which is imposed by or under any other Act and whose contravention constitutes an offence which the Authority has power to prosecute under this Act;
    (b) in relation to an application by the Secretary of State, means a requirement which is imposed by or under this Act and whose contravention constitutes an offence which the Secretary of State has power to prosecute under this Act.

(7) In the application of subsection (6) to Scotland—
    (a) in paragraph (a)(ii) for "which the Authority has power to prosecute under this Act" substitute "mentioned in paragraph (a) or (b) of section 402(1)"; and
    (b) in paragraph (b) omit "which the Secretary of State has power to prosecute under this Act".

381 Injunctions in cases of market abuse

(1) If, on the application of the Authority, the court is satisfied—
    (a) that there is a reasonable likelihood that any person will engage in market abuse, or
    (b) that any person is or has engaged in market abuse and that there is a reasonable likelihood that the market abuse will continue or be repeated,
the court may make an order restraining (or in Scotland an interdict prohibiting) the market abuse.

(2) If on the application of the Authority the court is satisfied—
    (a) that any person is or has engaged in market abuse, and
    (b) that there are steps which could be taken for remedying the market abuse,
the court may make an order requiring him to take such steps as the court may direct to remedy it.

(3) Subsection (4) applies if, on the application of the Authority, the court is satisfied that any person—
    (a) may be engaged in market abuse; or
    (b) may have been engaged in market abuse.

(4) The court make an order restraining (or in Scotland an interdict prohibiting) the person concerned from disposing of, or otherwise dealing with, any assets of his which it is satisfied that he is reasonably likely to dispose of, or otherwise deal with.

(5) The jurisdiction conferred by this section is exercisable by the High Court and the Court of Session.

---

[533] Inserted by SI 2007/126, reg 3(5), Sch 5, paras 1, 13; came into force (for certain purposes) 1 April 2007; came into force (for remaining purposes) 1 November 2007.

(6) In subsection (2), references to remedying any market abuse include references to mitigating its effect.

Restitution orders

382 Restitution orders

(1) The court may, on the application of the Authority or the Secretary of State, make an order under subsection (2) if it is satisfied that a person has contravened a relevant requirement, or been knowingly concerned in the contravention of such a requirement, and—

    (a) that profits have accrued to him as a result of the contravention; or

    (b) that one or more persons have suffered loss or been otherwise adversely affected as a result of the contravention.

(2) The court may order the person concerned to pay to the Authority such sum as appears to the court to be just having regard—

    (a) in a case within paragraph (a) of subsection (1), to the profits appearing to the court to have accrued;

    (b) in a case within paragraph (b) of that subsection, to the extent of the loss or other adverse effect;

    (c) in a case within both of those paragraphs, to the profits appearing to the court to have accrued and to the extent of the loss or other adverse effect.

(3) Any amount paid to the Authority in pursuance of an order under subsection (2) must be paid by it to such qualifying person or distributed by it among such qualifying persons as the court may direct.

(4) On an application under subsection (1) the court may require the person concerned to supply it with such accounts or other information as it may require for any one or more of the following purposes—

    (a) establishing whether any and, if so, what profits have accrued to him as mentioned in paragraph (a) of that subsection;

    (b) establishing whether any person or persons have suffered any loss or adverse effect as mentioned in paragraph (b) of that subsection and, if so, the extent of that loss or adverse effect; and

    (c) determining how any amounts are to be paid or distributed under subsection (3).

(5) The court may require any accounts or other information supplied under subsection (4) to be verified in such manner as it may direct.

(6) The jurisdiction conferred by this section is exercisable by the High Court and the Court of Session.

(7) Nothing in this section affects the right of any person other than the Authority or the Secretary of State to bring proceedings in respect of the matters to which this section applies.

(8) "Qualifying person" means a person appearing to the court to be someone—

    (a) to whom the profits mentioned in subsection (1)(a) are attributable; or

    (b) who has suffered the loss or adverse effect mentioned in subsection (1)(b).

(9) "Relevant requirement"—

    (a) in relation to an application by the Authority, means a requirement—

        (i) which is imposed by or under this Act [or by any directly applicable Community regulation made under the markets in financial instruments directive];[534] or

        (ii) which is imposed by or under any other Act and whose contravention constitutes an offence which the Authority has power to prosecute under this Act;

---

[534] Inserted by SI 2007/126, reg 3(5), Sch 5, paras 1, 14; came into force (for certain purposes) 1 April 2007; came into force (for remaining purposes) 1 November 2007.

    (b) in relation to an application by the Secretary of State, means a requirement which is imposed by or under this Act and whose contravention constitutes an offence which the Secretary of State has power to prosecute under this Act.

(10) In the application of subsection (9) to Scotland—

    (a) in paragraph (a)(ii) for "which the Authority has power to prosecute under this Act" substitute "mentioned in paragraph (a) or (b) of section 402(1); and

    (b) in paragraph (b) omit "which the Secretary of State has power to prosecute under this Act".

383 Restitution orders in cases of market abuse

(1) The court may, on the application of the Authority, make an order under subsection (4) if it is satisfied that a person ("the person concerned")—

    (a) has engaged in market abuse, or

    (b) by taking or refraining from taking any action has required or encouraged another person or persons to engage in behaviour which, if engaged in by the person concerned, would amount to market abuse,

and the condition mentioned in subsection (2) is fulfilled.

(2) The condition is—

    (a) that profits have accrued to the person concerned as a result; or

    (b) that one or more persons have suffered loss or been otherwise adversely affected as a result.

(3) But the court may not make an order under subsection (4) if it is satisfied that—

    (a) the person concerned believed, on reasonable grounds, that his behaviour did not fall within paragraph (a) or (b) of subsection (1); or

    (b) he took all reasonable precautions and exercised all due diligence to avoid behaving in a way which fell within paragraph (a) or (b) of subsection (1).

(4) The court may order the person concerned to pay to the Authority such sum as appears to the court to be just having regard—

    (a) in a case within paragraph (a) of subsection (2), to the profits appearing to the court to have accrued;

    (b) in a case within paragraph (b) of that subsection, to the extent of the loss or other adverse effect;

    (c) in a case within both of those paragraphs, to the profits appearing to the court to have accrued and to the extent of the loss or other adverse effect.

(5) Any amount paid to the Authority in pursuance of an order under subsection (4) must be paid by it to such qualifying person or distributed by it among such qualifying persons as the court may direct.

(6) On an application under subsection (1) the court may require the person concerned to supply it with such accounts or other information as it may require for any one or more of the following purposes—

    (a) establishing whether any and, if so, what profits have accrued to him as mentioned in subsection (2)(a);

    (b) establishing whether any person or persons have suffered any loss or adverse effect as mentioned in subsection (2)(b) and, if so, the extent of that loss or adverse effect; and

    (c) determining how any amounts are to be paid or distributed under subsection (5).

(7) The court may require any accounts or other information supplied under subsection (6) to be verified in such manner as it may direct.

(8) The jurisdiction conferred by this section is exercisable by the High Court and the Court of Session.

(9) Nothing in this section affects the right of any person other than the Authority to bring proceedings in respect of the matters to which this section applies.

(10) "Qualifying person" means a person appearing to the court to be someone—
    (a) to whom the profits mentioned in paragraph (a) of subsection (2) are attributable; or
    (b) who has suffered the loss or adverse effect mentioned in paragraph (b) of that subsection.

Restitution required by Authority

384 Power of Authority to require restitution

(1) The Authority may exercise the power in subsection (5) if it is satisfied that an authorised person ("the person concerned") has contravened a relevant requirement, or been knowingly concerned in the contravention of such a requirement, and—
    (a) that profits have accrued to him as a result of the contravention; or
    (b) that one or more persons have suffered loss or been otherwise adversely affected as a result of the contravention.
(2) The Authority may exercise the power in subsection (5) if it is satisfied that a person ("the person concerned")—
    (a) has engaged in market abuse, or
    (b) by taking or refraining from taking any action has required or encouraged another person or persons to engage in behaviour which, if engaged in by the person concerned, would amount to market abuse,
and the condition mentioned in subsection (3) is fulfilled,
(3) The condition is—
    (a) that profits have accrued to the person concerned as a result of the market abuse; or
    (b) that one or more persons have suffered loss or been otherwise adversely affected as a result of the market abuse.
(4) But the Authority may not exercise that power as a result of subsection (2) if, having considered any representations made to it in response to a warning notice, there are reasonable grounds for it to be satisfied that—
    (a) the person concerned believed, on reasonable grounds, that his behaviour did not fall within paragraph (a) or (b) of that subsection; or
    (b) he took all reasonable precautions and exercised all due diligence to avoid behaving in a way which fell within paragraph (a) or (b) of that subsection.
(5) The power referred to in subsections (1) and (2) is a power to require the person concerned, in accordance with such arrangements as the Authority considers appropriate, to pay to the appropriate person or distribute among the appropriate persons such amount as appears to the Authority to be just having regard—
    (a) in a case within paragraph (a) of subsection (1) or (3), to the profits appearing to the Authority to have accrued;
    (b) in a case within paragraph (b) of subsection (1) or (3), to the extent of the loss or other adverse effect;
    (c) in a case within paragraphs (a) and (b) of subsection (1) or (3), to the profits appearing to the Authority to have accrued and to the extent of the loss or other adverse effect.
(6) "Appropriate person" means a person appearing to the Authority to be someone—
    (a) to whom the profits mentioned in paragraph (a) of subsection (1) or (3) are attributable; or
    (b) who has suffered the loss or adverse effect mentioned in paragraph (b) of subsection (1) or (3).
(7) "Relevant requirement" means—
    (a) a requirement imposed by or under this Act [or by any directly applicable Community regulation made under the markets in financial instruments directive];[535] and

---

[535] Inserted by SI 2007/126, reg 3(5), Sch 5, paras 1, 15; came into force (for certain purposes) 1 April 2007; came into force (for remaining purposes) 1 November 2007.

(b) a requirement which is imposed by or under any other Act and whose contravention constitutes an offence in relation to which this Act confers power to prosecute on the Authority.

(8) In the application of subsection (7) to Scotland, in paragraph (b) for "in relation to which this Act confers power to prosecute on the Authority" substitute "mentioned in paragraph (a) or (b) of section 402(1)".

385 Warning notices

(1) If the Authority proposes to exercise the power under section 384(5) in relation to a person, it must give him a warning notice.

(2) A warning notice under this section must specify the amount which the Authority proposes to require the person concerned to pay or distribute as mentioned in section 384(5).

386 Decision notices

(1) If the Authority decides to exercise the power under section 384(5), it must give a decision notice to the person in relation to whom the power is exercised.

(2) The decision notice must—
    (a) state the amount that he is to pay or distribute as mentioned in section 384(5);
    (b) identify the person or persons to whom that amount is to be paid or among whom that amount is to be distributed; and
    (c) state the arrangements in accordance with which the payment or distribution is to be made.

(3) If the Authority decides to exercise the power under section 384(5), the person in relation to whom it is exercised may refer the matter to the Tribunal.

PART XXVI
NOTICES

Warning notices

387 Warning notices

(1) A warning notice must—
    (a) state the action which the Authority proposes to take;
    (b) be in writing;
    (c) give reasons for the proposed action;
    (d) state whether section 394 applies; and
    (e) if that section applies, describe its effect and state whether any secondary material exists to which the person concerned must be allowed access under it.

(2) The warning notice must specify a reasonable period (which may not be less than 28 days) within which the person to whom it is given may make representations to the Authority.

(3) The Authority may extend the period specified in the notice.

(4) The Authority must then decide, within a reasonable period, whether to give the person concerned a decision notice.

Decision notices

388 Decision notices

(1) A decision notice must—
    (a) be in writing;
    (b) give the Authority's reasons for the decision to take the action to which the notice relates;

   (c) state whether section 394 applies;

   (d) if that section applies, describe its effect and state whether any secondary material exists to which the person concerned must be allowed access under it; and

   (e) give an indication of—

      (i) any right to have the matter referred to the Tribunal which is given by this Act; and

     (ii) the procedure on such a reference.

(2) If the decision notice was preceded by a warning notice, the action to which the decision notice relates must be action under the same Part as the action proposed in the warning notice.

(3) The Authority may, before it takes the action to which a decision notice ("the original notice") relates, give the person concerned a further decision notice which relates to different action in respect of the same matter.

(4) The Authority may give a further decision notice as a result of subsection (3) only if the person to whom the original notice was given consents.

(5) If the person to whom a decision notice is given under subsection (3) had the right to refer the matter to which the original decision notice related to the Tribunal, he has that right as respects the decision notice under subsection (3).

Conclusion of proceedings

389 Notices of discontinuance

(1) If the Authority decides not to take—

   (a) the action proposed in a warning notice, or

   (b) the action to which a decision notice relates,

it must give a notice of discontinuance to the person to whom the warning notice or decision notice was given.

(2) But subsection (1) does not apply if the discontinuance of the proceedings concerned results in the granting of an application made by the person to whom the warning or decision notice was given.

(3) A notice of discontinuance must identify the proceedings which are being discontinued.

390 Final notices

(1) If the Authority has given a person a decision notice and the matter was not referred to the Tribunal within the period mentioned in section 133(1), the Authority must, on taking the action to which the decision notice relates, give the person concerned and any person to whom the decision notice was copied a final notice.

(2) If the Authority has given a person a decision notice and the matter was referred to the Tribunal, the Authority must, on taking action in accordance with any directions given by—

   (a) the Tribunal, or

   (b) the court under section 137,

give that person and any person to whom the decision notice was copied a final notice.

(3) A final notice about a statement must—

   (a) set out the terms of the statement;

   (b) give details of the manner in which, and the date on which, the statement will be published.

(4) A final notice about an order must—

   (a) set out the terms of the order;

   (b) state the date from which the order has effect.

(5) A final notice about a penalty must—

   (a) state the amount of the penalty;

   (b) state the manner in which, and the period within which, the penalty is to be paid;

   (c) give details of the way in which the penalty will be recovered if it is not paid by the date stated in the notice.

(6) A final notice about a requirement to make a payment or distribution in accordance with section 384(5) must state—
    (a) the persons to whom,
    (b) the manner in which, and
    (c) the period within which,
    it must be made.

(7) In any other case, the final notice must—
    (a) give details of the action being taken;
    (b) state the date on which the action is to be taken.

(8) The period stated under subsection (5)(b) or (6)(c) may not be less than 14 days beginning with the date on which the final notice is given.

(9) If all or any of the amount of a penalty payable under a final notice is outstanding at the end of the period stated under subsection (5)(b), the Authority may recover the outstanding amount as a debt due to it.

(10) If all or any of a required payment or distribution has not been made at the end of a period stated in a final notice under subsection (6)(c), the obligation to make the payment is enforceable, on the application of the Authority, by injunction or, in Scotland, by an order under section 45 of the Court of Session Act 1988.

Publication

391 Publication

(1) Neither the Authority nor a person to whom a warning notice or decision notice is given or copied may publish the notice or any details concerning it.

(2) A notice of discontinuance must state that, if the person to whom the notice is given consents, the Authority may publish such information as it considers appropriate about the matter to which the discontinued proceedings related.

(3) A copy of a notice of discontinuance must be accompanied by a statement that, if the person to whom the notice is copied consents, the Authority may publish such information as it considers appropriate about the matter to which the discontinued proceedings related, so far as relevant to that person.

(4) The Authority must publish such information about the matter to which a final notice relates as it considers appropriate.

(5) When a supervisory notice takes effect, the Authority must publish such information about the matter to which the notice relates as it considers appropriate.

(6) But the Authority may not publish information under this section if publication of it would, in its opinion, be unfair to the person with respect to whom the action was taken or prejudicial to the interests of consumers.

(7) Information is to be published under this section in such manner as the Authority considers appropriate.

(8) For the purposes of determining when a supervisory notice takes effect, a matter to which the notice relates is open to review if—
    (a) the period during which any person may refer the matter to the Tribunal is still running;
    (b) the matter has been referred to the Tribunal but has not been dealt with;
    (c) the matter has been referred to the Tribunal and dealt with but the period during which an appeal may be brought against the Tribunal's decision is still running; or
    (d) such an appeal has been brought but has not been determined.

(9) "Notice of discontinuance" means a notice given under section 389.

(10) "Supervisory notice" has the same meaning as in section 395.

(11) "Consumers" means persons who are consumers for the purposes of section 138.

Third party rights and access to evidence

392 Application of sections 393 and 394

Sections 393 and 394 apply to—

    (a) a warning notice given in accordance with section 54(1), 57(1), 63(3), 67(1), 88(4)(b), 89(2), 92(1), 126(1), 207(1), 255(1), 280(1), 331(1), 345(2) (whether as a result of subsection (1) of that section or section 249(1))[, 385(1) or 412B(4) or (8)];[536]

    (b) a decision notice given in accordance with section 54(2), 57(3), 63(4), 67(4), 88(6)(b), 89(3), 92(4), 127(1), 208(1), 255(2), 280(2), 331(3), 345(3) (whether as a result of subsection (1) of that section or section 249(1))[, 386(1) or 412B(5) or (9)].[537]

393 Third party rights

(1) If any of the reasons contained in a warning notice to which this section applies relates to a matter which—

    (a) identifies a person ("the third party") other than the person to whom the notice is given, and

    (b) in the opinion of the Authority, is prejudicial to the third party,

    a copy of the notice must be given to the third party.

(2) Subsection (1) does not require a copy to be given to the third party if the Authority—

    (a) has given him a separate warning notice in relation to the same matter; or

    (b) gives him such a notice at the same time as it gives the warning notice which identifies him.

(3) The notice copied to a third party under subsection (1) must specify a reasonable period (which may not be less than 28 days) within which he may make representations to the Authority.

(4) If any of the reasons contained in a decision notice to which this section applies relates to a matter which—

    (a) identifies a person ("the third party") other than the person to whom the decision notice is given, and

    (b) in the opinion of the Authority, is prejudicial to the third party,

    a copy of the notice must be given to the third party.

(5) If the decision notice was preceded by a warning notice, a copy of the decision notice must (unless it has been given under subsection (4)) be given to each person to whom the warning notice was copied.

(6) Subsection (4) does not require a copy to be given to the third party if the Authority—

    (a) has given him a separate decision notice in relation to the same matter; or

    (b) gives him such a notice at the same time as it gives the decision notice which identifies him.

(7) Neither subsection (1) nor subsection (4) requires a copy of a notice to be given to a third party if the Authority considers it impracticable to do so.

(8) Subsections (9) to (11) apply if the person to whom a decision notice is given has a right to refer the matter to the Tribunal.

(9) A person to whom a copy of the notice is given under this section may refer to the Tribunal—

    (a) the decision in question, so far as it is based on a reason of the kind mentioned in subsection (4); or

    (b) any opinion expressed by the Authority in relation to him.

---

[536] Substituted by SI 2007/126, reg 3(5), Sch 5, paras 1, 16(a); came into force (for certain purposes) 1 April 2007; came into force (for remaining purposes) 1 November 2007.

[537] Substituted by SI 2007/126, reg 3(5), Sch 5, paras 1, 16(b); came into force (for certain purposes) 1 April 2007; came into force (for remaining purposes) 1 November 2007.

(10) The copy must be accompanied by an indication of the third party's right to make a reference under subsection (9) and of the procedure on such a reference.

(11) A person who alleges that a copy of the notice should have been given to him, but was not, may refer to the Tribunal the alleged failure and—

    (a) the decision in question, so far as it is based on a reason of the kind mentioned in subsection (4); or

    (b) any opinion expressed by the Authority in relation to him.

(12) Section 394 applies to a third party as it applies to the person to whom the notice to which this section applies was given, in so far as the material which the Authority must disclose under that section relates to the matter which identifies the third party.

(13) A copy of a notice given to a third party under this section must be accompanied by a description of the effect of section 394 as it applies to him.

(14) Any person to whom a warning notice or decision notice was copied under this section must be given a copy of a notice of discontinuance applicable to the proceedings to which the warning notice or decision notice related.

394 Access to Authority material

(1) If the Authority gives a person ("A") a notice to which this section applies, it must—

    (a) allow him access to the material on which it relied in taking the decision which gave rise to the obligation to give the notice;

    (b) allow him access to any secondary material which, in the opinion of the Authority, might undermine that decision.

(2) But the Authority does not have to allow A access to material under subsection (1) if the material is excluded material or it—

    (a) relates to a case involving a person other than A; and

    (b) was taken into account by the Authority in A's case only for purposes of comparison with other cases.

(3) The Authority may refuse A access to particular material which it would otherwise have to allow him access to if, in its opinion, allowing him access to the material—

    (a) would not be in the public interest; or

    (b) would not be fair, having regard to—

        (i) the likely significance of the material to A in relation to the matter in respect of which he has been given a notice to which this section applies; and

        (ii) the potential prejudice to the commercial interests of a person other than A which would be caused by the material's disclosure.

(4) If the Authority does not allow A access to material because it is excluded material consisting of a protected item, it must give A written notice of—

    (a) the existence of the protected item; and

    (b) the Authority's decision not to allow him access to it.

(5) If the Authority refuses under subsection (3) to allow A access to material, it must give him written notice of—

    (a) the refusal; and

    (b) the reasons for it.

(6) "Secondary material" means material, other than material falling within paragraph (a) of subsection (1) which—

    (a) was considered by the Authority in reaching the decision mentioned in that paragraph; or

    (b) was obtained by the Authority in connection with the matter to which the notice to which this section applies relates but which was not considered by it in reaching that decision.

(7) "Excluded material" means material which—

 [(a) is material the disclosure of which for the purposes of or in connection with any legal proceedings is prohibited by section 17 of the Regulation of Investigatory Powers Act 2000; or][538]

 (c) is a protected item (as defined in section 413).

The Authority's procedures

395 The Authority's procedures

(1) The Authority must determine the procedure that it proposes to follow in relation to the giving of—

 (a) supervisory notices; and

 (b) warning notices and decision notices.

(2) That procedure must be designed to secure, among other things, that the decision which gives rise to the obligation to give any such notice is taken by a person not directly involved in establishing the evidence on which that decision is based.

(3) But the procedure may permit a decision which gives rise to an obligation to give a supervisory notice to be taken by a person other than a person mentioned in subsection (2) if—

 (a) the Authority considers that, in the particular case, it is necessary in order to protect the interests of consumers; and

 (b) the person taking the decision is of a level of seniority laid down by the procedure.

(4) A level of seniority laid down by the procedure for the purposes of subsection (3)(b) must be appropriate to the importance of the decision.

(5) The Authority must issue a statement of the procedure.

(6) The statement must be published in the way appearing to the Authority to be best calculated to bring it to the attention of the public.

(7) The Authority may charge a reasonable fee for providing a person with a copy of the statement.

(8) The Authority must, without delay, give the Treasury a copy of any statement which it issues under this section.

(9) When giving a supervisory notice, or a warning notice or decision notice, the Authority must follow its stated procedure.

(10) If the Authority changes the procedure in a material way, it must publish a revised statement.

(11) The Authority's failure in a particular case to follow its procedure as set out in the latest published statement does not affect the validity of a notice given in that case.

(12) But subsection (11) does not prevent the Tribunal from taking into account any such failure in considering a matter referred to it.

(13) "Supervisory notice" means a notice given in accordance with section—

 (a) 53(4), (7) or (8)(b);

 (b) 78(2) or (5);

 [(bza) 78A(2) or (8)(b);][539]

 [(ba) 96C;][540]

 [(bb) 87O(2) or (5);][541]

 [(bc) 191B(1);][542]

---

[538] Substituted for paras (a), (b) as originally enacted, by the Regulation of Investigatory Powers Act 2000, s 82(1), Sch 4, para 11; came into force 2 October 2000.

[539] Inserted by SI 2007/1973, arts 2, 8; came into force 12 July 2007.

[540] Inserted by SI 2005/381, reg 7; came into force 1 July 2005.

[541] Inserted by SI 2005/1433, reg 2(1), Sch 1, para 14; came into force 1 July 2005.

[542] Inserted by SI 2009/534, reg 6(a); came into force 21 March 2009.

(c) 197(3), (6) or (7)(b);

(d) 259(3), (8) or (9)(b);

(e) 268(3), (7)(a) or (9)(a) (as a result of subsection (8)(b));

(f) 282(3), (6) or (7)(b);

[(fa) 301J(1);][543]

(g) 321(2) or (5).

396 Statements under section 395: consultation

(1) Before issuing a statement of procedure under section 395, the Authority must publish a draft of the proposed statement in the way appearing to the Authority to be best calculated to bring it to the attention of the public.

(2) The draft must be accompanied by notice that representations about the proposal may be made to the Authority within a specified time.

(3) Before issuing the proposed statement of procedure, the Authority must have regard to any representations made to it in accordance with subsection (2).

(4) If the Authority issues the proposed statement of procedure it must publish an account, in general terms, of—

(a) the representations made to it in accordance with subsection (2); and

(b) its response to them.

(5) If the statement of procedure differs from the draft published under subsection (1) in a way which is, in the opinion of the Authority, significant, the Authority must (in addition to complying with subsection (4)) publish details of the difference.

(6) The Authority may charge a reasonable fee for providing a person with a copy of a draft published under subsection (1).

(7) This section also applies to a proposal to revise a statement of policy.

PART XXVII
OFFENCES

Miscellaneous offences

397 Misleading statements and practices

(1) This subsection applies to a person who—

(a) makes a statement, promise or forecast which he knows to be misleading, false or deceptive in a material particular;

(b) dishonestly conceals any material facts whether in connection with a statement, promise or forecast made by him or otherwise; or

(c) recklessly makes (dishonestly or otherwise) a statement, promise or forecast which is misleading, false or deceptive in a material particular.

(2) A person to whom subsection (1) applies is guilty of an offence if he makes the statement, promise or forecast or conceals the facts for the purpose of inducing, or is reckless as to whether it may induce, another person (whether or not the person to whom the statement, promise or forecast is made)—

(a) to enter or offer to enter into, or to refrain from entering or offering to enter into, a relevant agreement; or

(b) to exercise, or refrain from exercising, any rights conferred by a relevant investment.

---

[543] Inserted by SI 2009/534, reg 6(b); came into force 21 March 2009.

(3) Any person who does any act or engages in any course of conduct which creates a false or misleading impression as to the market in or the price or value of any relevant investments is guilty of an offence if he does so for the purpose of creating that impression and of thereby inducing another person to acquire, dispose of, subscribe for or underwrite those investments or to refrain from doing so or to exercise, or refrain from exercising, any rights conferred by those investments.

(4) In proceedings for an offence under subsection (2) brought against a person to whom subsection (1) applies as a result of paragraph (a) of that subsection, it is a defence for him to show that the statement, promise or forecast was made in conformity with[—

    (a) price stabilising rules;

    (b) control of information rules; or

    (c) the relevant provisions of Commission Regulation (EC) No 2273/2003 of 22 December 2003 implementing Directive 2003/6/EC of the European Parliament and of the Council as regards exemptions for buy-back programmes and stabilisation of financial instruments].[544]

(5) In proceedings brought against any person for an offence under subsection (3) it is a defence for him to show—

    (a) that he reasonably believed that his act or conduct would not create an impression that was false or misleading as to the matters mentioned in that subsection;

    (b) that he acted or engaged in the conduct—

      (i) for the purpose of stabilising the price of investments; and

      (ii) in conformity with price stabilising rules; . . .[545]

    (c) that he acted or engaged in the conduct in conformity with control of information rules[; or

    (d) that he acted or engaged in the conduct in conformity with the relevant provisions of Commission Regulation (EC) No 2273/2003 of 22 December 2003 implementing Directive 2003/6/EC of the European Parliament and of the Council as regards exemptions for buy-back programmes and stabilisation of financial instruments].[546]

(6) Subsections (1) and (2) do not apply unless—

    (a) the statement, promise or forecast is made in or from, or the facts are concealed in or from, the United Kingdom or arrangements are made in or from the United Kingdom for the statement, promise or forecast to be made or the facts to be concealed;

    (b) the person on whom the inducement is intended to or may have effect is in the United Kingdom; or

    (c) the agreement is or would be entered into or the rights are or would be exercised in the United Kingdom.

(7) Subsection (3) does not apply unless—

    (a) the act is done, or the course of conduct is engaged in, in the United Kingdom; or

    (b) the false or misleading impression is created there.

(8) A person guilty of an offence under this section is liable—

    (a) on summary conviction, to imprisonment for a term not exceeding six months or a fine not exceeding the statutory maximum, or both;

    (b) on conviction on indictment, to imprisonment for a term not exceeding seven years or a fine, or both.

---

[544] Substituted by SI 2005/381, reg 8(1), (2); came into force 17 March 2005.

[545] Repealed by SI 2005/381, reg 8(1), (3); came into force 17 March 2005.

[546] Inserted by SI 2005/381, reg 8(1), (3); came into force 17 March 2005.

(9) "Relevant agreement" means an agreement—
- (a) the entering into or performance of which by either party constitutes an activity of a specified kind or one which falls within a specified class of activity; and
- (b) which relates to a relevant investment.

(10) "Relevant investment" means an investment of a specified kind or one which falls within a prescribed class of investment.

(11) Schedule 2 (except paragraphs 25 and 26) applies for the purposes of subsections (9) and (10) with references to section 22 being read as references to each of those subsections.

(12) Nothing in Schedule 2, as applied by subsection (11), limits the power conferred by subsection (9) or (10).

(13) "Investment" includes any asset, right or interest.

(14) "Specified" means specified in an order made by the Treasury.

398 Misleading the Authority: residual cases

(1) A person who, in purported compliance with any requirement imposed by or under this Act, knowingly or recklessly gives the Authority information which is false or misleading in a material particular is guilty of an offence.

(2) Subsection (1) applies only to a requirement in relation to which no other provision of this Act creates an offence in connection with the giving of information.

(3) A person guilty of an offence under this section is liable—
- (a) on summary conviction, to a fine not exceeding the statutory maximum;
- (b) on conviction on indictment, to a fine.

399 Misleading [the OFT][547]

Section 44 of the Competition Act 1998 (offences connected with the provision of false or misleading information) applies in relation to any function of [the Office of Fair Trading][548] under this Act as if it were a function under Part I of that Act.

Bodies corporate and partnerships

400 Offences by bodies corporate etc

(1) If an offence under this Act committed by a body corporate is shown—
- (a) to have been committed with the consent or connivance of an officer, or
- (b) to be attributable to any neglect on his part,

the officer as well as the body corporate is guilty of the offence and liable to be proceeded against and punished accordingly.

(2) If the affairs of a body corporate are managed by its members, subsection (1) applies in relation to the acts and defaults of a member in connection with his functions of management as if he were a director of the body.

(3) If an offence under this Act committed by a partnership is shown—
- (a) to have been committed with the consent or connivance of a partner, or
- (b) to be attributable to any neglect on his part,

the partner as well as the partnership is guilty of the offence and liable to be proceeded against and punished accordingly.

(4) In subsection (3) "partner" includes a person purporting to act as a partner.

---

[547] Substituted by the Enterprise Act 2002, s 278(1), Sch 25, para 40(1), (16)(b); came into force 1 April 2003.
[548] Substituted by the Enterprise Act 2002, s 278(1), Sch 25, para 40(1), (16)(a); came into force 1 April 2003.

(5) "Officer", in relation to a body corporate, means—

    (a) a director, member of the committee of management, chief executive, manager, secretary or other similar officer of the body, or a person purporting to act in any such capacity; and

    (b) an individual who is a controller of the body.

(6) If an offence under this Act committed by an unincorporated association (other than a partnership) is shown—

    (a) to have been committed with the consent or connivance of an officer of the association or a member of its governing body, or

    (b) to be attributable to any neglect on the part of such an officer or member,

that officer or member as well as the association is guilty of the offence and liable to be proceeded against and punished accordingly.

(7) Regulations may provide for the application of any provision of this section, with such modifications as the Treasury consider appropriate, to a body corporate or unincorporated association formed or recognised under the law of a territory outside the United Kingdom.

Institution of proceedings

401 Proceedings for offences

(1) In this section "offence" means an offence under this Act or subordinate legislation made under this Act.

(2) Proceedings for an offence may be instituted in England and Wales only—

    (a) by the Authority or the Secretary of State; or

    (b) by or with the consent of the Director of Public Prosecutions.

(3) Proceedings for an offence may be instituted in Northern Ireland only—

    (a) by the Authority or the Secretary of State; or

    (b) by or with the consent of the Director of Public Prosecutions for Northern Ireland.

(4) Except in Scotland, proceedings for an offence under section 203 may also be instituted by [the Office of Fair Trading].[549]

(5) In exercising its power to institute proceedings for an offence, the Authority must comply with any conditions or restrictions imposed in writing by the Treasury.

(6) Conditions or restrictions may be imposed under subsection (5) in relation to—

    (a) proceedings generally; or

    (b) such proceedings, or categories of proceedings, as the Treasury may direct.

402 Power of the Authority to institute proceedings for certain other offences

(1) Except in Scotland, the Authority may institute proceedings for an offence under—

    (a) Part V of the Criminal Justice Act 1993 (insider dealing); . . .[550]

    (b) prescribed regulations relating to money laundering;[;][or

    (c) Schedule 7 to the Counter-Terrorism Act 2008 (terrorist financing or money laundering)].[551]

(2) In exercising its power to institute proceedings for any such offence, the Authority must comply with any conditions or restrictions imposed in writing by the Treasury.

(3) Conditions or restrictions may be imposed under subsection (2) in relation to—

    (a) proceedings generally; or

    (b) such proceedings, or categories of proceedings, as the Treasury may direct.

---

[549] Substituted by the Enterprise Act 2002, s 278(1), Sch 25, para 40(1), (17); came into force 1 April 2003.

[550] Repealed by the Counter-Terrorism Act 2008, s 62, Sch 7, Pt 7, para 33(4); came into force 27 November 2008.

[551] Inserted by the Counter-Terrorism Act 2008, s 62, Sch 7, Pt 7, para 33(4); came into force 27 November 2008.

403 Jurisdiction and procedure in respect of offences

(1) A fine imposed on an unincorporated association on its conviction of an offence is to be paid out of the funds of the association.

(2) Proceedings for an offence alleged to have been committed by an unincorporated association must be brought in the name of the association (and not in that of any of its members).

(3) Rules of court relating to the service of documents are to have effect as if the association were a body corporate.

(4) In proceedings for an offence brought against an unincorporated association—

　　(a) section 33 of the Criminal Justice Act 1925 and Schedule 3 to the Magistrates' Courts Act 1980 (procedure) apply as they do in relation to a body corporate;

　　(b) section 70 of the Criminal Procedure (Scotland) Act 1995 (procedure) applies as if the association were a body corporate;

　　(c) section 18 of the Criminal Justice (Northern Ireland) Act 1945 and Schedule 4 to the Magistrates' Courts (Northern Ireland) Order 1981 (procedure) apply as they do in relation to a body corporate.

(5) Summary proceedings for an offence may be taken—

　　(a) against a body corporate or unincorporated association at any place at which it has a place of business;

　　(b) against an individual at any place where he is for the time being.

(6) Subsection (5) does not affect any jurisdiction exercisable apart from this section.

(7) "Offence" means an offence under this Act.

PART XXVIII
MISCELLANEOUS

Schemes for reviewing past business

404　Schemes for reviewing past business

(1) Subsection (2) applies if the Treasury are satisfied that there is evidence suggesting—

　　(a) that there has been a widespread or regular failure on the part of authorised persons to comply with rules relating to a particular kind of activity; and

　　(b) that, as a result, private persons have suffered (or will suffer) loss in respect of which authorised persons are (or will be) liable to make payments ("compensation payments").

(2) The Treasury may by order ("a scheme order") authorise the Authority to establish and operate a scheme for—

　　(a) determining the nature and extent of the failure;

　　(b) establishing the liability of authorised persons to make compensation payments; and

　　(c) determining the amounts payable by way of compensation payments.

(3) An authorised scheme must be made so as to comply with specified requirements.

(4) A scheme order may be made only if—

　　(a) the Authority has given the Treasury a report about the alleged failure and asked them to make a scheme order;

　　(b) the report contains details of the scheme which the Authority propose to make; and

　　(c) the Treasury are satisfied that the proposed scheme is an appropriate way of dealing with the failure.

(5) A scheme order may provide for specified provisions of or made under this Act to apply in relation to any provision of, or determination made under, the resulting authorised scheme subject to such modifications (if any) as may be specified.

(6) For the purposes of this Act, failure on the part of an authorised person to comply with any provision of an authorised scheme is to be treated (subject to any provision made by the scheme order concerned) as a failure on his part to comply with rules.

(7) The Treasury may prescribe circumstances in which loss suffered by a person ("A") acting in a fiduciary or other prescribed capacity is to be treated, for the purposes of an authorised scheme, as suffered by a private person in relation to whom A was acting in that capacity.

(8) This section applies whenever the failure in question occurred.

(9) "Authorised scheme" means a scheme authorised by a scheme order.

(10) "Private person" has such meaning as may be prescribed.

(11) "Specified" means specified in a scheme order.

THIRD COUNTRIES

405 Directions

(1) For the purpose of implementing a third country decision, the Treasury may direct the Authority to—

   (a) refuse an application for permission under Part IV made by a body incorporated in, or formed under the law of, any part of the United Kingdom;

   (b) defer its decision on such an application either indefinitely or for such period as may be specified in the direction;

   (c) give a notice of objection to a person who has served a notice of control to the effect that he proposes to acquire a 50% stake in a UK authorised person; or

   (d) give a notice of objection to a person who has acquired a 50% stake in a UK authorised person without having served the required notice of control.

(2) A direction may also be given in relation to—

   (a) any person falling within a class specified in the direction;

   (b) future applications, notices of control or acquisitions.

(3) The Treasury may revoke a direction at any time.

(4) But revocation does not affect anything done in accordance with the direction before it was revoked.

(5) "Third country decision" means a decision of the Council or the Commission under—

   [(a) Article 15(3) of the markets in financial instruments directive;][552]

   (b) . . .[553]

   (c) Article 29b(4) of the first non-life insurance directive; or

   [(d) Article 59(4) of the life assurance consolidation directive].[554]

406 Interpretation of section 405

(1) For the purposes of section 405, a person ("the acquirer") acquires a 50% stake in a UK authorised person ("A") on first falling within any of the cases set out in subsection (2).

(2) The cases are where the acquirer—

   (a) holds 50% or more of the shares in A;

   (b) holds 50% or more of the shares in a parent undertaking ("P") of A;

   (c) is entitled to exercise, or control the exercise of, 50% or more of the voting power in A; or

   (d) is entitled to exercise, or control the exercise of, 50% or more of the voting power in P.

---

[552] Substituted by SI 2007/126, reg 3(5), Sch 5, paras 1, 17; came into force (for certain purposes) 1 April 2007; came into force (for remaining purposes) 1 November 2007.

[553] Repealed by SI 2006/3221, reg 29(1), Sch 3, para 1; came into force 1 January 2007.

[554] Substituted by SI 2004/3379, reg 6(1), (4); came into force 11 January 2005.

(3) In subsection (2) "the acquirer" means—
- (a) the acquirer;
- (b) any of the acquirer's associates; or
- (c) the acquirer and any of his associates.

(4) "Associate", "shares" and "voting power" have the same meaning as in section 422.

407 Consequences of a direction under section 405

(1) If the Authority refuses an application for permission as a result of a direction under section 405(1)(a)—
- (a) subsections (7) to (9) of section 52 do not apply in relation to the refusal; but
- (b) the Authority must notify the applicant of the refusal and the reasons for it.

(2) If the Authority defers its decision on an application for permission as a result of a direction under section 405(1)(b)—
- (a) the time limit for determining the application mentioned in section 52(1) or (2) stops running on the day of the deferral and starts running again (if at all) on the day the period specified in the direction (if any) ends or the day the direction is revoked; and
- (b) the Authority must notify the applicant of the deferral and the reasons for it.

(3) If the Authority gives a notice of objection to a person as a result of a direction under section 405(1)(c) or (d)—
- (a) sections 189 and 191 have effect as if the notice was a notice of objection within the meaning of Part XII; and
- (b) the Authority must state in the notice the reasons for it.

408 EFTA firms

(1) If a third country decision has been taken, the Treasury may make a determination in relation to an EFTA firm which is a subsidiary undertaking of a parent undertaking which is governed by the law of the country to which the decision relates.

(2) "Determination" means a determination that the firm concerned does not qualify for authorisation under Schedule 3 even if it satisfies the conditions in paragraph 13 or 14 of that Schedule.

(3) A determination may also be made in relation to any firm falling within a class specified in the determination.

(4) The Treasury may withdraw a determination at any time.

(5) But withdrawal does not affect anything done in accordance with the determination before it was withdrawn.

(6) If the Treasury make a determination in respect of a particular firm, or withdraw such a determination, they must give written notice to that firm.

(7) The Treasury must publish notice of any determination (or the withdrawal of any determination)—
- (a) in such a way as they think most suitable for bringing the determination (or withdrawal) to the attention of those likely to be affected by it; and
- (b) on, or as soon as practicable after, the date of the determination (or withdrawal).

(8) "EFTA firm" means a firm, institution or undertaking which—
- (a) is an EEA firm as a result of paragraph 5(a), (b) or (d) of Schedule 3; and
- (b) is incorporated in, or formed under the law of, an EEA State which is not a member State.

(9) "Third country decision" has the same meaning as in section 405.

409 Gibraltar

(1) The Treasury may by order—
- (a) modify Schedule 3 so as to provide for Gibraltar firms of a specified description to qualify for authorisation under that Schedule in specified circumstances;
- (b) modify Schedule 3 so as to make provision in relation to the exercise by UK firms of rights under the law of Gibraltar which correspond to EEA rights;

(c) modify Schedule 4 so as to provide for Gibraltar firms of a specified description to qualify for authorisation under that Schedule in specified circumstances;

(d) modify section 264 so as to make provision in relation to collective investment schemes constituted under the law of Gibraltar;

(e) provide for the Authority to be able to give notice under section 264(2) on grounds relating to the law of Gibraltar;

(f) provide for this Act to apply to a Gibraltar recognised scheme as if the scheme were a scheme recognised under section 264.

(2) The fact that a firm may qualify for authorisation under Schedule 3 as a result of an order under subsection (1) does not prevent it from applying for a Part IV permission.

(3) "Gibraltar firm" means a firm which has its head office in Gibraltar or is otherwise connected with Gibraltar.

(4) "Gibraltar recognised scheme" means a collective investment scheme—

(a) constituted in an EEA State other than the United Kingdom, and

(b) recognised in Gibraltar under provisions which appear to the Treasury to give effect to the provisions of a relevant Community instrument.

(5) "Specified" means specified in the order.

(6) "UK firm" and "EEA right" have the same meaning as in Schedule 3.

International obligations

410 International obligations

(1) If it appears to the Treasury that any action proposed to be taken by a relevant person would be incompatible with Community obligations or any other international obligations of the United Kingdom, they may direct that person not to take that action.

(2) If it appears to the Treasury that any action which a relevant person has power to take is required for the purpose of implementing any such obligations, they may direct that person to take that action.

(3) A direction under this section—

(a) may include such supplemental or incidental requirements as the Treasury consider necessary or expedient; and

(b) is enforceable, on an application made by the Treasury, by injunction or, in Scotland, by an order for specific performance under section 45 of the Court of Session Act 1988.

(4) "Relevant person" means—

(a) the Authority;

(b) any person exercising functions conferred by Part VI on the competent authority;

(c) any recognised investment exchange (other than one which is an overseas investment exchange);

(d) any recognised clearing house (other than one which is an overseas clearing house);

(e) a person included in the list maintained under section 301; or

(f) the scheme operator of the ombudsman scheme.

Tax treatment of levies and repayments

411 Tax treatment of levies and repayments

(1) . . .[555]

[(2) After section 76 of the 1988 Act insert—

"76A Levies and repayments under the Financial Services and Markets Act 2000

---

[555] Repealed by SI 2001/3629, art 109, Schedule; came into force 1 December 2001 (the date on which the Financial Services and Markets Act 2000, ss 411, 432(1), Sch 20 came fully into force).

(1) In computing the amount of the profits to be charged under Case I of Schedule D arising from a trade carried on by an authorised person (other than an investment company)—

    (a to the extent that it would not be deductible apart from this section, any sum expended by the authorised person in paying a levy may be deducted as an allowable expense;

    (b) any payment which is made to the authorised person as a result of a repayment provision is to be treated as a trading receipt.

(2) "Levy" has the meaning given in section 76(7A).

(3) "Repayment provision" means any provision made by virtue of—

    (a) section 136(7) of the Financial Services and Markets Act 2000 ("the Act of 2000");

    (b) section 214(1)(e) of the Act of 2000.

(4) "Authorised person" has the same meaning as in the Act of 2000.

76B Levies and repayments under the Financial Services and Markets Act 2000: investment companies

(1) For the purposes of section 75 any sums paid by an investment company—

    (a) by way of a levy, or

    (b) as a result of an award of costs under costs rules,

shall be treated as part of its expenses of management.

(2) If a payment is made to an investment company as a result of a repayment provision, the company shall be charged to tax under Case VI of Schedule D on the amount of that payment.

(3) "Levy" has the meaning given in section 76(7A).

(4) "Costs rules" means—

    (a) rules made under section 230 of the Financial Services and Markets Act 2000;

    (b) provision relating to costs contained in the standard terms fixed under paragraph 18 of Schedule 17 to that Act.

(5) "Repayment provision" has the meaning given in section 76A(3)."][556]

Gaming contracts

412 Gaming contracts

(1) No contract to which this section applies is void or unenforceable because of—

    (a) . . .[557] Article 170 of the Betting, Gaming, Lotteries and Amusements (Northern Ireland) Order 1985; or

    (b) . . ..[558]

(2) This section applies to a contract if—

    (a) it is entered into by either or each party by way of business;

    (b) the entering into or performance of it by either party constitutes an activity of a specified kind or one which falls within a specified class of activity; and

    (c) it relates to an investment of a specified kind or one which falls within a specified class of investment.

---

[556] To be repealed by the Corporation Tax Act 2009, s 1326, Sch 3, Pt 1; Date in force: this repeal has effect for corporation tax purposes for accounting periods ending on or after 1 April 2009: see the Corporation Tax Act 2009, s 1329(1)(a): Date in force: this repeal has effect for income tax and capital gains tax purposes for the tax year 2009–10 and subsequent tax years: see the Corporation Tax Act 2009, s 1329(1)(b).

[557] Repealed by the Gambling Act 2005, ss 334(1)(e)(i), (2), 356(4), Sch 17; came into force 1 September 2007.

[558] Repealed by the Gambling Act 2005, ss 334(1)(e)(ii), (2), 356(4), Sch 17; came into force 1 September 2007.

(3) Part II of Schedule 2 applies for the purposes of subsection (2)(c), with the references to section 22 being read as references to that subsection.

(4) Nothing in Part II of Schedule 2, as applied by subsection (3), limits the power conferred by subsection (2)(c).

(5) "Investment" includes any asset, right or interest.

(6) "Specified" means specified in an order made by the Treasury.

*[Trade-matching and reporting systems]*559

[412A Approval and monitoring of trade-matching and reporting systems]560

[(1) A relevant system is an approved relevant system if it is approved by the Authority under subsection (2) for the purposes of Article 25.5 of the markets in financial instruments directive; and references in this section and section 412B to an "approved relevant system" are to be read accordingly.

(2) The Authority must approve a relevant system if, on an application by the operator of the system, it is satisfied that the arrangements established by the system for reporting transactions comply with Article 12(1) of Commission Regulation 1287/2006 of 10 August 2006 ("the Regulation").

(3) Section 51(3) and (4) applies to an application under this section as it applies to an application under Part 4.

(4) If, at any time after approving a relevant system under subsection (2), the Authority is not satisfied as mentioned in that subsection, it may suspend or withdraw the approval.

(5) The Authority must keep under review the arrangements established by an approved relevant system for reporting transactions for the purpose of ensuring that the arrangements comply with Article 12(1) of the Regulation; and for the purposes of this subsection the Authority must have regard to information provided to it under subsections (6) and (7).

(6) The operator of an approved relevant system must make reports to the Authority at specified intervals containing specified information relating to—
   (a) the system,
   (b) the reports made by the system in accordance with Article 25 of the markets in financial instruments directive and the Regulation, and
   (c) the transactions to which those reports relate.
   "Specified" means specified by the Authority.

(7) The Authority may by written notice require the operator of an approved relevant system to provide such additional information as may be specified in the notice, by such reasonable time as may be so specified, about any of the matters mentioned in subsection (6).

(8) The recipient of a notice under subsection (7) must provide the information by the time specified in the notice.

(9) In this section and section 412B, "relevant system" means a trade-matching or reporting system of a kind described in Article 12 of the Regulation.]

[412B Procedure for approval and suspension or withdrawal of approval]561

[(1) If the Authority approves a relevant system, it must give the operator of the system written notice specifying the date from which the approval has effect.

---

559 Inserted by SI 2007/126, reg 3(5), Sch 5, paras 1, 18; came into force (for certain purposes) 1 April 2007; came into force (for remaining purposes) 1 November 2007.

560 Inserted by SI 2007/126, reg 3(5), Sch 5, paras 1, 18; came into force (for certain purposes) 1 April 2007; came into force (for remaining purposes) 1 November 2007.

561 Inserted by SI 2007/126, reg 3(5), Sch 5, paras 1, 18; came into force (for certain purposes) 1 April 2007; came into force (for remaining purposes) 1 November 2007.

(2) If the Authority proposes to refuse to approve a relevant system, it must give the operator of the system a warning notice.

(3) If the Authority decides to refuse to approve a relevant system, it must give the operator of the system a decision notice.

(4) If the Authority proposes to suspend or withdraw its approval in relation to an approved relevant system, it must give the operator of the system a warning notice.

(5) If the Authority decides to suspend or withdraw its approval in relation to an approved relevant system, it must give the operator of the system a decision notice specifying the date from which the suspension or withdrawal is to take effect.

(6) Subsections (7) to (9) apply if—
  (a) the Authority has suspended its approval in relation to an approved relevant system, and
  (b) the operator of the system has applied for the suspension to be cancelled.

(7) The Authority must grant the application if it is satisfied as mentioned in section 412A(2); and in such a case the Authority must give written notice to the operator that the suspension is to be cancelled from the date specified in the notice.

(8) If the Authority proposes to refuse the application, it must give the operator a warning notice.

(9) If the Authority decides to refuse the application, it must give the operator a decision notice.

(10) A person who receives a decision notice under subsection (3), (5) or (9) may refer the matter to the Tribunal.]

Limitation on powers to require documents

413 Protected items

(1) A person may not be required under this Act to produce, disclose or permit the inspection of protected items.

(2) "Protected items" means—
  (a) communications between a professional legal adviser and his client or any person representing his client which fall within subsection (3);
  (b) communications between a professional legal adviser, his client or any person representing his client and any other person which fall within subsection (3) (as a result of paragraph (b) of that subsection);
  (c) items which—
    (i) are enclosed with, or referred to in, such communications;
    (ii) fall within subsection (3); and
    (iii) are in the possession of a person entitled to possession of them.

(3) A communication or item falls within this subsection if it is made—
  (a) in connection with the giving of legal advice to the client; or
  (b) in connection with, or in contemplation of, legal proceedings and for the purposes of those proceedings.

(4) A communication or item is not a protected item if it is held with the intention of furthering a criminal purpose.

Service of notices

414 Service of notices

(1) The Treasury may by regulations make provision with respect to the procedure to be followed, or rules to be applied, when a provision of or made under this Act requires a notice, direction or document of any kind to be given or authorises the imposition of a requirement.

(2) The regulations may, in particular, make provision—
  (a) as to the manner in which a document must be given;
  (b) as to the address to which a document must be sent;

(c) requiring, or allowing, a document to be sent electronically;

(d) for treating a document as having been given, or as having been received, on a date or at a time determined in accordance with the regulations;

(e) as to what must, or may, be done if the person to whom a document is required to be given is not an individual;

(f) as to what must, or may, be done if the intended recipient of a document is outside the United Kingdom.

(3) Subsection (1) applies however the obligation to give a document is expressed (and so, in particular, includes a provision which requires a document to be served or sent).

(4) Section 7 of the Interpretation Act 1978 (service of notice by post) has effect in relation to provisions made by or under this Act subject to any provision made by regulations under this section.

Jurisdiction

415 Jurisdiction in civil proceedings

(1) Proceedings arising out of any act or omission (or proposed act or omission) of—
   (a) the Authority,
   (b) the competent authority for the purposes of Part VI,
   (c) the scheme manager, or
   (d) the scheme operator,
   in the discharge or purported discharge of any of its functions under this Act may be brought before the High Court or the Court of Session.

(2) The jurisdiction conferred by subsection (1) is in addition to any other jurisdiction exercisable by those courts.

Removal of certain unnecessary provisions

416 Provisions relating to industrial assurance and certain other enactments

(1) The following enactments are to cease to have effect—
   (a) the Industrial Assurance Act 1923;
   (b) the Industrial Assurance and Friendly Societies Act 1948;
   (c) the Insurance Brokers (Registration) Act 1977.

(2) The Industrial Assurance (Northern Ireland) Order 1979 is revoked.

(3) The following bodies are to cease to exist—
   (a) the Insurance Brokers Registration Council;
   (b) the Policyholders Protection Board;
   (c) the Deposit Protection Board;
   (d) the Board of Banking Supervision.

(4) If the Treasury consider that, as a consequence of any provision of this section, it is appropriate to do so, they may by order make any provision of a kind that they could make under this Act (and in particular any provision of a kind mentioned in section 339) with respect to anything done by or under any provision of Part XXI.

(5) Subsection (4) is not to be read as affecting in any way any other power conferred on the Treasury by this Act.

PART XXIX
INTERPRETATION

417 Definitions

(1) In this Act—
   "appointed representative" has the meaning given in section 39(2);

"auditors and actuaries rules" means rules made under section 340;

"authorisation offence" has the meaning given in section 23(2);

"authorised open-ended investment company" has the meaning given in section 237(3);

"authorised person" has the meaning given in section 31(2);

"the Authority" means the Financial Services Authority;

"body corporate" includes a body corporate constituted under the law of a country or territory outside the United Kingdom;

"chief executive"—

(a) in relation to a body corporate whose principal place of business is within the United Kingdom, means an employee of that body who, alone or jointly with one or more others, is responsible under the immediate authority of the directors, for the conduct of the whole of the business of that body; and

(b) in relation to a body corporate whose principal place of business is outside the United Kingdom, means the person who, alone or jointly with one or more others, is responsible for the conduct of its business within the United Kingdom;

["claim", in relation to the Financial Services Compensation Scheme under Part XV, is to be construed in accordance with section 214(1B);][562]

"collective investment scheme" has the meaning given in section 235;

"the Commission" means the European Commission (except in provisions relating to the Competition Commission);

"the compensation scheme" has the meaning given in section 213(2);

"control of information rules" has the meaning given in section 147(1);

"director", in relation to a body corporate, includes—

(a) a person occupying in relation to it the position of a director (by whatever name called); and

(b) a person in accordance with whose directions or instructions (not being advice given in a professional capacity) the directors of that body are accustomed to act;

"documents" includes information recorded in any form and, in relation to information recorded otherwise than in legible form, references to its production include references to producing a copy of the information in legible form[, or in a form from which it can readily be produced in visible and legible form];[563]

["electronic commerce directive" means Directive 2000/31/EC of the European Parliament and the Council of 8 June 2000 on certain legal aspects of information society services, in particular electronic commerce, in the Internal Market (Directive on electronic commerce);][564]

"exempt person", in relation to a regulated activity, means a person who is exempt from the general prohibition in relation to that activity as a result of an exemption order made under section 38(1) or as a result of section 39(1) or 285(2) or (3);

"financial promotion rules" means rules made under section 145;

"friendly society" means an incorporated or registered friendly society;

"general prohibition" has the meaning given in section 19(2);

"general rules" has the meaning given in section 138(2);

---

[562] Inserted by the Banking Act 2009, ss 169, 174(2); came into force (for the purpose of conferring or relating to any power to make subordinate legislation or codes of practice) 17 February 2009; came into force (for remaining purposes) 21 February 2009.

[563] Inserted by the Criminal Justice and Police Act 2001, s 70, Sch 2, Pt 2, para 16(1), (2)(f); came into force 1 April 2003.

[564] Inserted by SI 2002/1775, reg 13(1), (2)(a); came into force (for the purpose of enabling the Financial Services Authority to make rules) 18 July 2002; came into force (for remaining purposes) 21 August 2002.

"incorporated friendly society" means a society incorporated under the Friendly Societies Act 1992;

"industrial and provident society" means a society registered or deemed to be registered under the Industrial and Provident Societies Act 1965 or the Industrial and Provident Societies Act (Northern Ireland) 1969;

["information society service" means an information society service within the meaning of Article 2(a) of the electronic commerce directive;][565]

["investment services and activities" has the meaning given in Article 4.1.2 of the markets in financial instruments directive, read with—

(a) Chapter VI of Commission Regulation 1287/2006 of 10 August 2006, and

(b) Article 52 of Commission Directive 2006/73/EC of 10 August 2006;][566]

"market abuse" has the meaning given in section 118;

"Minister of the Crown" has the same meaning as in the Ministers of the Crown Act 1975;

"money laundering rules" means rules made under section 146;

"notice of control" [(except in Chapter 1A of Part 18)][567] has the meaning given in section 178(5);

"the ombudsman scheme" has the meaning given in section 225(3);

"open-ended investment company" has the meaning given in section 236;

"Part IV permission" has the meaning given in section 40(4);

"partnership" includes a partnership constituted under the law of a country or territory outside the United Kingdom;

"prescribed" (where not otherwise defined) means prescribed in regulations made by the Treasury;

"price stabilising rules" means rules made under section 144;

"private company" has the meaning given in section 1(3) of the Companies Act 1985 or in Article 12(3) of the Companies (Northern Ireland) Order 1986;

"prohibition order" has the meaning given in section 56(2);

"recognised clearing house" and "recognised investment exchange" have the meaning given in section 285;

"registered friendly society" means a society which is—

(a) a friendly society within the meaning of section 7(1)(a) of the Friendly Societies Act 1974; and

(b) registered within the meaning of that Act;

"regulated activity" has the meaning given in section 22;

"regulating provisions" has the meaning given in section 159(1);

"regulatory objectives" means the objectives mentioned in section 2;

"regulatory provisions" has the meaning given in section 302;

"rule" means a rule made by the Authority under this Act;

"rule-making instrument" has the meaning given in section 153;

"the scheme manager" has the meaning given in section 212(1);

"the scheme operator" has the meaning given in section 225(2);

"scheme particulars rules" has the meaning given in section 248(1);

"Seventh Company Law Directive" means the European Council Seventh Company Law Directive of 13 June 1983 on consolidated accounts (No 83/349/EEC);

---

[565] Inserted by SI 2002/1775, reg 13(1), (2)(b); came into force (for the purpose of enabling the Financial Services Authority to make rules); 18 July 2002; came into force (for remaining purposes) 21 August 2002.

[566] Inserted by SI 2007/126, reg 3(5), Sch 5, paras 1, 19(a); came into force (for certain purposes) 1 April 2007; came into force (for remaining purposes) 1 November 2007.

[567] Inserted by SI 2007/126, reg 3(5), Sch 5, paras 1, 19(b); came into force (for certain purposes) 1 April 2007; came into force (for remaining purposes) 1 November 2007.

["Takeovers Directive" means Directive 2004/25/EC of the European Parliament and of the
   Council;][568]

"threshold conditions", in relation to a regulated activity, has the meaning given in
   section 41;

   "the Treaty" means the treaty establishing the European Community;

   "trust scheme rules" has the meaning given in section 247(1);

   "UK authorised person" has the meaning given in section 178(4); and

   "unit trust scheme" has the meaning given in section 237.

(2) In the application of this Act to Scotland, references to a matter being actionable at the suit
   of a person are to be read as references to the matter being actionable at the instance of that
   person.

(3) For the purposes of any provision of this Act [(other than a provision of Part 6)][569] authorising
   or requiring a person to do anything within a specified number of days no account is to be
   taken of any day which is a public holiday in any part of the United Kingdom.

[(4) For the purposes of this Act—

   (a) an information society service is provided from an EEA State if it is provided from an
       establishment in that State;

   (b) an establishment, in connection with an information society service, is the place at which
       the provider of the service (being a national of an EEA State or a company or firm as
       mentioned in Article 48 of the Treaty) effectively pursues an economic activity for an
       indefinite period;

   (c) the presence or use in a particular place of equipment or other technical means of providing
       an information society service does not, of itself, constitute that place as an establishment
       of the kind mentioned in paragraph (b);

   (d) where it cannot be determined from which of a number of establishments a given infor-
       mation society service is provided, that service is to be regarded as provided from the
       establishment where the provider has the centre of his activities relating to the service.][570]

418 Carrying on regulated activities in the United Kingdom

(1) In the [five][571] cases described in this section, a person who—

   (a) is carrying on a regulated activity, but

   (b) would not otherwise be regarded as carrying it on in the United Kingdom,

   is, for the purposes of this Act, to be regarded as carrying it on in the United Kingdom.

(2) The first case is where—

   (a) his registered office (or if he does not have a registered office his head office) is in the
       United Kingdom;

   (b) he is entitled to exercise rights under a single market directive as a UK firm; and

   (c) he is carrying on in another EEA State a regulated activity to which that directive
       applies.

(3) The second case is where—

   (a) his registered office (or if he does not have a registered office his head office) is in the
       United Kingdom;

---

568 Inserted by the Companies Act 2006, s 964(1), (6); came into force 6 April 2007.

569 Inserted by SI 2005/1433, reg 2(1), Sch 1, para 15; came into force 1 July 2005.

570 Inserted by SI 2002/1775, reg 13(1), (2)(c); came into force (for the purpose of enabling the Financial
Services Authority to make rules) 18 July 2002; came into force (for remaining purposes) 21 August 2002.

571 Substituted by SI 2002/1775, reg 13(1), (3)(a); came into force (for the purpose of enabling the
Financial Services Authority to make rules): 18 July 2002; came into force (for remaining purposes) 21 August
2002.

(b) he is the manager of a scheme which is entitled to enjoy the rights conferred by an instrument which is a relevant Community instrument for the purposes of section 264; and

(c) persons in another EEA State are invited to become participants in the scheme.

(4) The third case is where—

    (a) his registered office (or if he does not have a registered office his head office) is in the United Kingdom;

    (b) the day-to-day management of the carrying on of the regulated activity is the responsibility of—

      (i) his registered office (or head office); or

      (ii) another establishment maintained by him in the United Kingdom.

(5) The fourth case is where—

    (a) his head office is not in the United Kingdom; but

    (b) the activity is carried on from an establishment maintained by him in the United Kingdom.

[(5A) The fifth case is any other case where the activity—

    (a) consists of the provision of an information society service to a person or persons in one or more EEA States; and

    (b) is carried on from an establishment in the United Kingdom.][572]

(6) For the purposes of subsections (2) to [(5A)][573] it is irrelevant where the person with whom the activity is carried on is situated.

419 Carrying on regulated activities by way of business

(1) The Treasury may by order make provision—

    (a) as to the circumstances in which a person who would otherwise not be regarded as carrying on a regulated activity by way of business is to be regarded as doing so;

    (b) as to the circumstances in which a person who would otherwise be regarded as carrying on a regulated activity by way of business is to be regarded as not doing so.

(2) An order under subsection (1) may be made so as to apply—

    (a) generally in relation to all regulated activities;

    (b) in relation to a specified category of regulated activity; or

    (c) in relation to a particular regulated activity.

(3) An order under subsection (1) may be made so as to apply—

    (a) for the purposes of all provisions;

    (b) for a specified group of provisions; or

    (c) for a specified provision.

(4) "Provision" means a provision of, or made under, this Act.

(5) Nothing in this section is to be read as affecting the provisions of section 428(3).

420 Parent and subsidiary undertaking

(1) In this Act, except in relation to an incorporated friendly society, "parent undertaking" and "subsidiary undertaking" have the same meaning as in [the Companies Acts (see section 1162 of, and Schedule 7 to, the Companies Act 2006)].[574]

---

[572] Inserted by SI 2002/1775, reg 13(1), (3)(b); came into force (for the purpose of enabling the Financial Services Authority to make rules) 18 July 2002; came into force (for remaining purposes) 21 August 2002.

[573] Substituted by SI 2002/1775, reg 13(1), (3)(c); came into force (for the purpose of enabling the Financial Services Authority to make rules) 18 July 2002; came into force (for remaining purposes) 21 August 2002.

[574] Substituted by SI 2008/948, arts 3(1)(b), 6, Sch 1, Pt 2, para 212(1); came into force 6 April 2008.

(2) But—

    (a) "parent undertaking" also includes an individual who would be a parent undertaking for the purposes of those provisions if he were taken to be an undertaking (and "subsidiary undertaking" is to be read accordingly);

    (b) "subsidiary undertaking" also includes, in relation to a body incorporated in or formed under the law of an EEA State other than the United Kingdom, an undertaking which is a subsidiary undertaking within the meaning of any rule of law in force in that State for purposes connected with implementation of the Seventh Company Law Directive (and "parent undertaking" is to be read accordingly).

(3) In this Act "subsidiary undertaking", in relation to an incorporated friendly society, means a body corporate of which the society has control within the meaning of section 13(9)(a) or (aa) of the Friendly Societies Act 1992 (and "parent undertaking" is to be read accordingly).

421 Group

(1) In this Act "group", in relation to a person ("A"), means A and any person who is—

    (a) a parent undertaking of A;

    (b) a subsidiary undertaking of A;

    (c) a subsidiary undertaking of a parent undertaking of A;

    (d) a parent undertaking of a subsidiary undertaking of A;

    (e) an undertaking in which A or an undertaking mentioned in paragraph (a), (b), (c) or (d) has a participating interest;

    (f) if A or an undertaking mentioned in paragraph (a) or (d) is a building society, an associated undertaking of the society; or

    (g) if A or an undertaking mentioned in paragraph (a) or (d) is an incorporated friendly society, a body corporate of which the society has joint control (within the meaning of section 13(9)(c) or (cc) of the Friendly Societies Act 1992).

(2) "Participating interest" [has the meaning given in section 421A];[575] but also includes an interest held by an individual which would be a participating interest for the purposes of those provisions if he were taken to be an undertaking.

(3) "Associated undertaking" has the meaning given in section 119(1) of the Building Societies Act 1986.

[421A Meaning of "participating interest"][576]

[(1) In section 421 a "participating interest" means an interest held by an undertaking in the shares of another undertaking which it holds on a long-term basis for the purpose of securing a contribution to its activities by the exercise of control or influence arising from or related to that interest.

(2) A holding of 20% or more of the shares of an undertaking is presumed to be a participating interest unless the contrary is shown.

(3) The reference in subsection (1) to an interest in shares includes—

    (a) an interest which is convertible into an interest in shares, and

    (b) an option to acquire shares or any such interest;

And an interest or option falls within paragraph (a) or (b) notwithstanding that the shares to which it relates are, until the conversion or the exercise of the option, unissued.

(4) For the purposes of this section an interest held on behalf of an undertaking shall be treated as held by it.

---

[575] Substituted by SI 2008/948, arts 3(1)(b), 6, Sch 1, Pt 2, para 212(2); came into force 6 April 2008.
[576] Inserted by SI 2008/948, arts 3(1)(b), 6, Sch 1, Pt 2, para 212(3); came into force 6 April 2008.

(5) In this section "undertaking" has the same meaning as in the Companies Acts (see section 1161(1) of the Companies Act 2006).]

[422 Controller][577]

[(1) In this Act "controller", in relation to an undertaking ("B"), means a person ("A") who falls within any of the cases in subsection (2).

(2) The cases are where A holds—
- (a) 10% or more of the shares in B or in a parent undertaking of B ("P");
- (b) 10% or more of the voting power in B or P; or
- (c) shares or voting power in B or P as a result of which A is able to exercise significant influence over the management of B.

(3) For the purposes of calculations relating to this section, the holding of shares or voting power by a person ("A1") includes any shares or voting power held by another ("A2") if A1 and A2 are acting in concert.

(4) In this section "shares"—
- (a) in relation to an undertaking with a share capital, means allotted shares;
- (b) in relation to an undertaking with capital but no share capital, means rights to share in the capital of the undertaking;
- (c) in relation to an undertaking without capital, means interests—
  - (i) conferring any right to share in the profits, or liability to contribute to the losses, of the undertaking; or
  - (ii) giving rise to an obligation to contribute to the debts or expenses of the undertaking in the event of a winding up.

(5) In this section "voting power"—
- (a) includes, in relation to a person ("H")—
  - (i) voting power held by a third party with whom H has concluded an agreement, which obliges H and the third party to adopt, by concerted exercise of the voting power they hold, a lasting common policy towards the management of the undertaking in question;
  - (ii) voting power held by a third party under an agreement concluded with H providing for the temporary transfer for consideration of the voting power in question;
  - (iii) voting power attaching to shares which are lodged as collateral with H, provided that H controls the voting power and declares an intention to exercise it;
  - (iv) voting power attaching to shares in which H has a life interest;
  - (v) voting power which is held, or may be exercised within the meaning of subparagraphs (i) to (iv), by a subsidiary undertaking of H;
  - (vi) voting power attaching to shares deposited with H which H has discretion to exercise in the absence of specific instructions from the shareholders;
  - (vii) voting power held in the name of a third party on behalf of H;
  - (viii) voting power which H may exercise as a proxy where H has discretion about the exercise of the voting power in the absence of specific instructions from the shareholders; and
- (b) in relation to an undertaking which does not have general meetings at which matters are decided by the exercise of voting rights, means the right under the constitution of the undertaking to direct the overall policy of the undertaking or alter the terms of its constitution.]

---

[577] Substituted, together with s 422A, for s 422 as originally enacted, by SI 2009/534, reg 7, Sch 3; came into force 21 March 2009.

[422A Disregarded holdings][578]

[(1) For the purposes of section 422, shares and voting power that a person holds in an undertaking ("B") or in a parent undertaking of B ("P") are disregarded in the following circumstances.

(2) Shares held only for the purposes of clearing and settling within a short settlement cycle are disregarded.

(3) Shares held by a custodian or its nominee in a custodian capacity are disregarded, provided that the custodian or nominee is only able to exercise voting power attached to the shares in accordance with instructions given in writing.

(4) Shares representing no more than 5% of the total voting power in B or P held by an investment firm are disregarded, provided that it—

    (a) holds the shares in the capacity of a market maker (as defined in article 4.1(8) of the markets in financial instruments directive);

    (b) is authorised by its home state regulator under the markets in financial instruments directive; and

    (c) neither intervenes in the management of B or P nor exerts any influence on B or P to buy the shares or back the share price.

(5) Shares held by a credit institution or investment firm in its trading book are disregarded, provided that—

    (a) the shares represent no more than 5% of the total voting power in B or P; and

    (b) the credit institution or investment firm ensures that the voting power is not used to intervene in the management of B or P.

(6) Shares held by a credit institution or an investment firm are disregarded, provided that—

    (a) the shares are held as a result of performing the investment services and activities of—

        (i) underwriting shares; or

        (ii) placing shares on a firm commitment basis in accordance with Annex I, section A.6 of the markets in financial instruments directive; and

    (b) the credit institution or investment firm—

        (i) does not exercise voting power represented by the shares or otherwise intervene in the management of the issuer; and

        (ii) retains the holding for a period of less than one year.

(7) Where a management company (as defined in Article 1a.2 of the UCITS directive) and its parent undertaking both hold shares or voting power, each may disregard holdings of the other, provided that each exercises its voting power independently of the other.

(8) But subsection (7) does not apply if the management company—

    (a) manages holdings for its parent undertaking or an undertaking in respect of which the parent undertaking is a controller;

    (b) has no discretion to exercise the voting power attached to such holdings; and

    (c) may only exercise the voting power in relation to such holdings under direct or indirect instruction from—

        (i) its parent undertaking; or

        (ii) an undertaking in respect of which of the parent undertaking is a controller.

(9) Where an investment firm and its parent undertaking both hold shares or voting power, the parent undertaking may disregard holdings managed by the investment firm on a client by client basis and the investment firm may disregard holdings of the parent undertaking, provided that the investment firm—

    (a) has permission to provide portfolio management;

---

[578] Substituted, together with s 422, for s 422 as originally enacted, by SI 2009/534, reg 7, Sch 3; came into force 21 March 2009.

   (b) exercises its voting power independently from the parent undertaking; and

   (c) may only exercise the voting power under instructions given in writing, or has appropriate mechanisms in place for ensuring that individual portfolio management services are conducted independently of any other services.

(10) In this section "credit institution" means—

   (a) a credit institution authorised under the banking consolidation directive; or

   (b) an institution which would satisfy the requirements for authorisation as a credit institution under that directive if it had its registered office (or if it does not have a registered office, its head office) in an EEA State.]

423 Manager

(1) In this Act, except in relation to a unit trust scheme or a registered friendly society, "manager" means an employee who—

   (a) under the immediate authority of his employer is responsible, either alone or jointly with one or more other persons, for the conduct of his employer's business; or

   (b) under the immediate authority of his employer or of a person who is a manager by virtue of paragraph (a) exercises managerial functions or is responsible for maintaining accounts or other records of his employer.

(2) If the employer is not an individual, references in subsection (1) to the authority of the employer are references to the authority—

   (a) in the case of a body corporate, of the directors;

   (b) in the case of a partnership, of the partners; and

   (c) in the case of an unincorporated association, of its officers or the members of its governing body.

(3) "Manager", in relation to a body corporate, means a person (other than an employee of the body) who is appointed by the body to manage any part of its business and includes an employee of the body corporate (other than the chief executive) who, under the immediate authority of a director or chief executive of the body corporate, exercises managerial functions or is responsible for maintaining accounts or other records of the body corporate.

424 Insurance

(1) In this Act, references to—

   (a) contracts of insurance,

   (b) reinsurance,

   (c) contracts of long-term insurance,

   (d) contracts of general insurance,

are to be read with section 22 and Schedule 2.

(2) In this Act "policy" and "policyholder", in relation to a contract of insurance, have such meaning as the Treasury may by order specify.

(3) The law applicable to a contract of insurance, the effecting of which constitutes the carrying on of a regulated activity, is to be determined, if it is of a prescribed description, in accordance with regulations made by the Treasury.

[424A Investment firm][579]

[(1) In this Act, "investment firm" has the meaning given in Article 4.1.1 of the markets in financial instruments directive.

(2) Subsection (1) is subject to subsections (3) to (5).

---

[579] Inserted by SI 2006/2975, regs 2, 10; came into force 6 December 2006.

[(3) References in this Act to an "investment firm" include references to a person who would be an investment firm (within the meaning of Article 4.1.1 of the markets in financial instruments directive) if—

(a) in the case of a body corporate, his registered office or, if he has no registered office, his head office, and

(b) in the case of a person other than a body corporate, his head office,

were in an EEA State.][580]

(4) But subsection (3) does not apply if the person in question is one to whom the markets in financial instruments directive would not apply by virtue of Article 2 of that directive.

(5) References in this Act to an "investment firm" do not include references to—

(a) a person to whom the markets in financial instruments directive does not apply by virtue of Article 2 of the directive; or

(b) a person whose home Member State (within the meaning of Article 4.1.20 of the markets in financial instruments directive) is an EEA State and to whom, by reason of the fact that the State has given effect to Article 3 of that directive, that directive does not apply by virtue of that Article.]

425 Expressions relating to authorisation elsewhere in the single market

(1) In this Act—

[(a) "banking consolidation directive", ["life assurance consolidation directive",][581] "EEA authorisation", "EEA firm", "EEA right", "EEA State", . . .[582] "first non-life insurance directive", "insurance directives", ["reinsurance directive",][583] "insurance mediation directive", . . .[584] ["markets in financial instruments directive",][585] "single market directives"[, "tied agent"][586] and "UCITS directive" have the meaning given in Schedule 3; and][587]

(b) "home state regulator", in relation to an EEA firm, has the meaning given in Schedule 3.

(2) In this Act—

(a) "home state authorisation" has the meaning given in Schedule 4;

(b) "Treaty firm" has the meaning given in Schedule 4; and

(c) "home state regulator", in relation to a Treaty firm, has the meaning given in Schedule 4.

PART XXX
SUPPLEMENTAL

426 Consequential and supplementary provision

(1) A Minister of the Crown may by order make such incidental, consequential, transitional or supplemental provision as he considers necessary or expedient for the general purposes, or any particular purpose, of this Act or in consequence of any provision made by or under this Act or for giving full effect to this Act or any such provision.

---

[580] Substituted by SI 2007/126, reg 3(5), Sch 5, paras 1, 21; came into force (for certain purposes) 1 April 2007; came into force (for remaining purposes) 1 November 2007.

[581] Inserted by SI 2004/3379, reg 6(1), (5)(a); came into force 11 January 2005.

[582] Repealed by SI 2004/3379, reg 6(1), (5)(b); came into force 11 January 2005.

[583] Inserted by SI 2007/3253, reg 2(1), Sch 1, paras 1, 5; came into force 10 December 2007.

[584] Repealed by SI 2007/126, reg 3(5), Sch 5, paras 1, 22(a); came into force (for certain purposes) 1 April 2007; came into force (for remaining purposes) 1 November 2007.

[585] Inserted by SI 2006/2975, regs 2, 11; came into force 6 December 2006.

[586] Inserted by SI 2007/126, reg 3(5), Sch 5, paras 1, 22(b); came into force (for certain purposes) 1 April 2007; came into force (for remaining purposes) 1 November 2007.

[587] Substituted by SI 2003/2066, reg 2(1); came into force 13 February 2004.

(2) An order under subsection (1) may, in particular, make provision—

    (a) for enabling any person by whom any powers will become exercisable, on a date set by or under this Act, by virtue of any provision made by or under this Act to take before that date any steps which are necessary as a preliminary to the exercise of those powers;

    (b) for applying (with or without modifications) or amending, repealing or revoking any provision of or made under an Act passed before this Act or in the same Session;

    (c) dissolving any body corporate established by any Act passed, or instrument made, before the passing of this Act;

    (d) for making savings, or additional savings, from the effect of any repeal or revocation made by or under this Act.

(3) Amendments made under this section are additional, and without prejudice, to those made by or under any other provision of this Act.

(4) No other provision of this Act restricts the powers conferred by this section.

427 Transitional provisions

(1) Subsections (2) and (3) apply to an order under section 426 which makes transitional provisions or savings.

(2) The order may, in particular—

    (a) if it makes provision about the authorisation and permission of persons who before commencement were entitled to carry on any activities, also include provision for such persons not to be treated as having any authorisation or permission (whether on an application to the Authority or otherwise);

    (b) make provision enabling the Authority to require persons of such descriptions as it may direct to re-apply for permissions having effect by virtue of the order;

    (c) make provision for the continuation as rules of such provisions (including primary and subordinate legislation) as may be designated in accordance with the order by the Authority, including provision for the modification by the Authority of provisions designated;

    (d) make provision about the effect of requirements imposed, liabilities incurred and any other things done before commencement, including provision for and about investigations, penalties and the taking or continuing of any other action in respect of contraventions;

    (e) make provision for the continuation of disciplinary and other proceedings begun before commencement, including provision about the decisions available to bodies before which such proceedings take place and the effect of their decisions;

    (f) make provision as regards the Authority's obligation to maintain a record under section 347 as respects persons in relation to whom provision is made by the order.

(3) The order may—

    (a) confer functions on the Treasury, the Secretary of State, the Authority, the scheme manager, the scheme operator, members of the panel established under paragraph 4 of Schedule 17, the Competition Commission or [the Office of Fair Trading];[588]

    (b) confer jurisdiction on the Tribunal;

    (c) provide for fees to be charged in connection with the carrying out of functions conferred under the order;

    (d) modify, exclude or apply (with or without modifications) any primary or subordinate legislation (including any provision of, or made under, this Act).

---

[588] Substituted by the Enterprise Act 2002, s 278(1), Sch 25, para 40(1), (18); came into force 1 April 2003.

(4) In subsection (2) "commencement" means the commencement of such provisions of this Act as may be specified by the order.

428 Regulations and orders

(1) Any power to make an order which is conferred on a Minister of the Crown by this Act and any power to make regulations which is conferred by this Act is exercisable by statutory instrument.

(2) The Lord Chancellor's power to make rules under section 132 is exercisable by statutory instrument.

(3) Any statutory instrument made under this Act may—

    (a) contain such incidental, supplemental, consequential and transitional provision as the person making it considers appropriate; and

    (b) make different provision for different cases.

429 Parliamentary control of statutory instruments

(1) No order is to be made under—

    (a) section 144(4), 192(b) or (e), 236(5), 404 or 419, or

    (b) paragraph 1 of Schedule 8,

unless a draft of the order has been laid before Parliament and approved by a resolution of each House.

(2) No regulations are to be made under section [90B[, 214A, 214B][589] or][590] 262 unless a draft of the regulations has been laid before Parliament and approved by a resolution of each House.

(3) An order to which, if it is made, subsection (4) or (5) will apply is not to be made unless a draft of the order has been laid before Parliament and approved by a resolution of each House.

(4) This subsection applies to an order under section 21 if—

    (a) it is the first order to be made, or to contain provisions made, under section 21(4);

    (b) it varies an order made under section 21(4) so as to make section 21(1) apply in circumstances in which it did not previously apply;

    (c) it is the first order to be made, or to contain provision made, under section 21(5);

    (d) it varies a previous order made under section 21(5) so as to make section 21(1) apply in circumstances in which it did not, as a result of that previous order, apply;

    (e) it is the first order to be made, or to contain provisions made, under section 21(9) or (10);

    (f) it adds one or more activities to those that are controlled activities for the purposes of section 21; or

    (g) it adds one or more investments to those which are controlled investments for the purposes of section 21.

(5) This subsection applies to an order under section 38 if—

    (a) it is the first order to be made, or to contain provisions made, under that section; or

    (b) it contains provisions restricting or removing an exemption provided by an earlier order made under that section.

---

[589] Inserted by the Banking Act 2009, ss 169, 178; came in force (for the purpose of conferring or relating to any power to make subordinate legislation or codes of practice) 17 February 2009; came into force (for remaining purposes) 21 February 2009.

[590] Inserted by the Companies Act 2006, s 1272, Sch 15, Pt 1, paras 1, 12; came into force 8 November 2006.

(6) An order containing a provision to which, if the order is made, subsection (7) will apply is not to be made unless a draft of the order has been laid before Parliament and approved by a resolution of each House.

(7) This subsection applies to a provision contained in an order if—

(a) it is the first to be made in the exercise of the power conferred by subsection (1) of section 326 or it removes a body from those for the time being designated under that subsection; or

(b) it is the first to be made in the exercise of the power conferred by subsection (6) of section 327 or it adds a description of regulated activity or investment to those for the time being specified for the purposes of that subsection.

(8) Any other statutory instrument made under this Act, apart from one made under section 431(2) or to which paragraph 26 of Schedule 2 applies, shall be subject to annulment in pursuance of a resolution of either House of Parliament.

430 Extent

(1) This Act, except Chapter IV of Part XVII, extends to Northern Ireland.

(2) Except where Her Majesty by Order in Council provides otherwise, the extent of any amendment or repeal made by or under this Act is the same as the extent of the provision amended or repealed.

(3) Her Majesty may by Order in Council provide for any provision of or made under this Act relating to a matter which is the subject of other legislation which extends to any of the Channel Islands or the Isle of Man to extend there with such modifications (if any) as may be specified in the Order.

431 Commencement

(1) The following provisions come into force on the passing of this Act—

(a) this section;

(b) sections 428, 430 and 433;

(c) paragraphs 1 and 2 of Schedule 21.

(2) The other provisions of this Act come into force on such day as the Treasury may by order appoint; and different days may be appointed for different purposes.

432 Minor and consequential amendments, transitional provisions and repeals

(1) Schedule 20 makes minor and consequential amendments.

(2) Schedule 21 makes transitional provisions.

(3) The enactments set out in Schedule 22 are repealed.

433 Short title

This Act may be cited as the Financial Services and Markets Act 2000.

SCHEDULE 1
THE FINANCIAL SERVICES AUTHORITY

Section 1

PART I
GENERAL

Interpretation

1. - (1) In this Schedule—

"the 1985 Act" means the Companies Act 1985;

"non-executive committee" means the committee maintained under paragraph 3;

"functions", in relation to the Authority, means functions conferred on the Authority by or under any provision of this Act.

(2) For the purposes of this Schedule, the following are the Authority's legislative functions—

(a) making rules;

(b) issuing codes under section 64 or 119;

(c) issuing statements under section 64, 69, 124 or 210;

(d) giving directions under section 316, 318 or 328;

(e) issuing general guidance (as defined by section 158(5)) [or guidance under section 158A].[591]

Constitution

2. - (1) The constitution of the Authority must continue to provide for the Authority to have—

(a) a chairman; and

(b) a governing body.

(2) The governing body must include the chairman.

(3) The chairman and other members of the governing body must be appointed, and be liable to removal from office, by the Treasury.

(4) The validity of any act of the Authority is not affected—

(a) by a vacancy in the office of chairman; or

(b) by a defect in the appointment of a person as a member of the governing body or as chairman.

Non-executive members of the governing body

3. - (1) The Authority must secure—

(a) that the majority of the members of its governing body are non-executive members; and

(b) that a committee of its governing body, consisting solely of the non-executive members, is set up and maintained for the purposes of discharging the functions conferred on the committee by this Schedule.

(2) The members of the non-executive committee are to be appointed by the Authority.

(3) The non-executive committee is to have a chairman appointed by the Treasury from among its members.

Functions of the non-executive committee

4. - (1) In this paragraph "the committee" means the non-executive committee.

(2) The non-executive functions are functions of the Authority but must be discharged by the committee.

(3) The non-executive functions are—

(a) keeping under review the question whether the Authority is, in discharging its functions in accordance with decisions of its governing body, using its resources in the most efficient and economic way;

(b) keeping under review the question whether the Authority's internal financial controls secure the proper conduct of its financial affairs; and

(c) determining the remuneration of—

(i) the chairman of the Authority's governing body; and

(ii) the executive members of that body.

(4) The function mentioned in sub-paragraph (3)(b) and those mentioned in sub-paragraph (3)(c) may be discharged on behalf of the committee by a sub-committee.

---

[591] Inserted by SI 2006/2975, regs 2, 12; came into force 6 December 2006.

(5) Any sub-committee of the committee—
  (a) must have as its chairman the chairman of the committee; but
  (b) may include persons other than members of the committee.
(6) The committee must prepare a report on the discharge of its functions for inclusion in the Authority's annual report to the Treasury under paragraph 10.
(7) The committee's report must relate to the same period as that covered by the Authority's report.

Arrangements for discharging functions

5. - (1) The Authority may make arrangements for any of its functions to be discharged by a committee, sub-committee, officer or member of staff of the Authority.
[(2) But—
  (a) in exercising the legislative functions mentioned in paragraph 1(2)(a) to (d), the Authority must act through its governing body; and
  (b) the legislative function mentioned in paragraph 1(2)(e) may not be discharged by an officer or member of staff of the Authority.][592]
(3) Sub-paragraph (1) does not apply to the non-executive functions.

Monitoring and enforcement

6. - (1) The Authority must maintain arrangements designed to enable it to determine whether persons on whom requirements are imposed by or under this Act[, or by any directly applicable Community regulation made under the markets in financial instruments directive,][593] are complying with them.
(2) Those arrangements may provide for functions to be performed on behalf of the Authority by any body or person who, in its opinion, is competent to perform them.
(3) The Authority must also maintain arrangements for enforcing the provisions of, or made under, this Act [or of any directly applicable Community regulation made under the markets in financial instruments directive].[594]
(4) Sub-paragraph (2) does not affect the Authority's duty under sub-paragraph (1).

Arrangements for the investigation of complaints

7. - (1) The Authority must—
  (a) make arrangements ("the complaints scheme") for the investigation of complaints arising in connection with the exercise of, or failure to exercise, any of its functions (other than its legislative functions); and
  (b) appoint an independent person ("the investigator") to be responsible for the conduct of investigations in accordance with the complaints scheme.
(2) The complaints scheme must be designed so that, as far as reasonably practicable, complaints are investigated quickly.
(3) The Treasury's approval is required for the appointment or dismissal of the investigator.
(4) The terms and conditions on which the investigator is appointed must be such as, in the opinion of the Authority, are reasonably designed to secure—
  (a) that he will be free at all times to act independently of the Authority; and
  (b) that complaints will be investigated under the complaints scheme without favouring the Authority.

---

[592] Substituted by SI 2007/1973, arts 2, 14; came into force 12 July 2007.
[593] Inserted by SI 2007/126, reg 3(5), Sch 5, paras 1, 23(1); came into force (for certain purposes) 1 April 2007; came into force (for remaining purposes) 1 November 2007.
[594] Inserted by SI 2007/126, reg 3(5), Sch 5, paras 1, 23(b); came into force (for certain purposes) 1 April 2007; came into force (for remaining purposes) 1 November 2007.

(5) Before making the complaints scheme, the Authority must publish a draft of the proposed scheme in the way appearing to the Authority best calculated to bring it to the attention of the public.

(6) The draft must be accompanied by notice that representations about it may be made to the Authority within a specified time.

(7) Before making the proposed complaints scheme, the Authority must have regard to any representations made to it in accordance with sub-paragraph (6).

(8) If the Authority makes the proposed complaints scheme, it must publish an account, in general terms, of—

(a) the representations made to it in accordance with sub-paragraph (6); and

(b) its response to them.

(9) If the complaints scheme differs from the draft published under sub-paragraph (5) in a way which is, in the opinion of the Authority, significant the Authority must (in addition to complying with sub-paragraph (8)) publish details of the difference.

(10) The Authority must publish up-to-date details of the complaints scheme including, in particular, details of—

(a) the provision made under paragraph 8(5); and

(b) the powers which the investigator has to investigate a complaint.

(11) Those details must be published in the way appearing to the Authority to be best calculated to bring them to the attention of the public.

(12) The Authority must, without delay, give the Treasury a copy of any details published by it under this paragraph.

(13) The Authority may charge a reasonable fee for providing a person with a copy of—

(a) a draft published under sub-paragraph (5);

(b) details published under sub-paragraph (10).

(14) Sub-paragraphs (5) to (9) and (13)(a) also apply to a proposal to alter or replace the complaints scheme.

Investigation of complaints

8. - (1) The Authority is not obliged to investigate a complaint in accordance with the complaints scheme which it reasonably considers would be more appropriately dealt with in another way (for example, by referring the matter to the Tribunal or by the institution of other legal proceedings).

(2) The complaints scheme must provide—

(a) for reference to the investigator of any complaint which the Authority is investigating; and

(b) for him—

(i) to have the means to conduct a full investigation of the complaint;

(ii) to report on the result of his investigation to the Authority and the complainant; and

(iii) to be able to publish his report (or any part of it) if he considers that it (or the part) ought to be brought to the attention of the public.

(3) If the Authority has decided not to investigate a complaint, it must notify the investigator.

(4) If the investigator considers that a complaint of which he has been notified under sub-paragraph (3) ought to be investigated, he may proceed as if the complaint had been referred to him under the complaints scheme.

(5) The complaints scheme must confer on the investigator the power to recommend, if he thinks it appropriate, that the Authority—

(a) makes a compensatory payment to the complainant,

(b) remedies the matter complained of,

or takes both of those steps.

(6) The complaints scheme must require the Authority, in a case where the investigator—

    (a) has reported that a complaint is well-founded, or

    (b) has criticised the Authority in his report,

to inform the investigator and the complainant of the steps which it proposes to take in response to the report.

(7) The investigator may require the Authority to publish the whole or a specified part of the response.

(8) The investigator may appoint a person to conduct the investigation on his behalf but subject to his direction.

(9) Neither an officer nor an employee of the Authority may be appointed under sub-paragraph (8).

(10) Sub-paragraph (2) is not to be taken as preventing the Authority from making arrangements for the initial investigation of a complaint to be conducted by the Authority.

Records

9. - The Authority must maintain satisfactory arrangements for—

    (a) recording decisions made in the exercise of its functions; and

    (b) the safe-keeping of those records which it considers ought to be preserved.

Annual report

10. - (1) At least once a year the Authority must make a report to the Treasury on—

    (a) the discharge of its functions;

    (b) the extent to which, in its opinion, the regulatory objectives have been met;

    (c) its consideration of the matters mentioned in section 2(3); and

    (d) such other matters as the Treasury may from time to time direct.

(2) The report must be accompanied by—

    (a) the report prepared by the non-executive committee under paragraph 4(6); and

    (b) such other reports or information, prepared by such persons, as the Treasury may from time to time direct.

(3) The Treasury must lay before Parliament a copy of each report received by them under this paragraph.

(4) The Treasury may—

    (a) require the Authority to comply with any provisions of *the 1985 Act* [the Companies Act 2006][595] about accounts and their audit which would not otherwise apply to it; or

    (b) direct that any such provision of that Act is to apply to the Authority with such modifications as are specified in the direction.

(5) Compliance with any requirement imposed under sub-paragraph (4)(a) or (b) is enforceable by injunction or, in Scotland, an order under section 45(b) of the Court of Session Act 1988.

(6) Proceedings under sub-paragraph (5) may be brought only by the Treasury.

Annual public meeting

11. - (1) Not later than three months after making a report under paragraph 10, the Authority must hold a public meeting ("the annual meeting") for the purposes of enabling that report to be considered.

(2) The Authority must organise the annual meeting so as to allow—

    (a) a general discussion of the contents of the report which is being considered; and

---

[595] Words in italics repealed and subsequent words in square brackets substituted by SI 2008/948, arts 3(1) (b), 6, Sch 1, Pt 2, para 213; came into force 6 April 2008.

    (b) a reasonable opportunity for those attending the meeting to put questions to the Authority about the way in which it discharged, or failed to discharge, its functions during the period to which the report relates.

(3) But otherwise the annual meeting is to be organised and conducted in such a way as the Authority considers appropriate.

(4) The Authority must give reasonable notice of its annual meeting.

(5) That notice must—

    (a) give details of the time and place at which the meeting is to be held;

    (b) set out the proposed agenda for the meeting;

    (c) indicate the proposed duration of the meeting;

    (d) give details of the Authority's arrangements for enabling persons to attend; and

    (e) be published by the Authority in the way appearing to it to be most suitable for bringing the notice to the attention of the public.

(6) If the Authority proposes to alter any of the arrangements which have been included in the notice given under sub-paragraph (4) it must—

    (a) give reasonable notice of the alteration; and

    (b) publish that notice in the way appearing to the Authority to be best calculated to bring it to the attention of the public.

Report of annual meeting

12. - Not later than one month after its annual meeting, the Authority must publish a report of the proceedings of the meeting.

PART II
STATUS

13. - In relation to any of its functions—

    (a) the Authority is not to be regarded as acting on behalf of the Crown; and

    (b) its members, officers and staff are not to be regarded as Crown servants.

Exemption from requirement of "limited" in Authority's name

14. - The Authority is to continue to be exempt from the requirements of the 1985 Act relating to the use of "limited" as part of its name.

15. - If the Secretary of State is satisfied that any action taken by the Authority makes it inappropriate for the exemption given by paragraph 14 to continue he may, after consulting the Treasury, give a direction removing it.

PART III
PENALTIES AND FEES

Penalties

16. - (1) In determining its policy with respect to the amounts of penalties to be imposed by it under this Act, the Authority must take no account of the expenses which it incurs, or expects to incur, in discharging its functions.

(2) The Authority must prepare and operate a scheme for ensuring that the amounts paid to the Authority by way of penalties imposed under this Act are applied for the benefit of authorised persons.

(3) The scheme may, in particular, make different provision with respect to different classes of authorised person.

(4) Up to date details of the scheme must be set out in a document ("the scheme details").

(5) The scheme details must be published by the Authority in the way appearing to it to be best calculated to bring them to the attention of the public.

(6) Before making the scheme, the Authority must publish a draft of the proposed scheme in the way appearing to the Authority to be best calculated to bring it to the attention of the public.

(7) The draft must be accompanied by notice that representations about the proposals may be made to the Authority within a specified time.

(8) Before making the scheme, the Authority must have regard to any representations made to it in accordance with sub-paragraph (7).

(9) If the Authority makes the proposed scheme, it must publish an account, in general terms, of—
    (a) the representations made to it in accordance with sub-paragraph (7); and
    (b) its response to them.

(10) If the scheme differs from the draft published under sub-paragraph (6) in a way which is, in the opinion of the Authority, significant the Authority must (in addition to complying with sub-paragraph (9)) publish details of the difference.

(11) The Authority must, without delay, give the Treasury a copy of any scheme details published by it.

(12) The Authority may charge a reasonable fee for providing a person with a copy of—
    (a) a draft published under sub-paragraph (6);
    (b) scheme details.

(13) Sub-paragraphs (6) to (10) and (12)(a) also apply to a proposal to alter or replace the complaints scheme.

Fees

17. - (1) The Authority may make rules providing for the payment to it of such fees, in connection with the discharge of any of its functions under or as a result of this Act, as it considers will (taking account of its expected income from fees and charges provided for by any other provision of this Act) enable it—
    (a) to meet expenses incurred in carrying out its functions or for any incidental purpose;
    (b) to repay the principal of, and pay any interest on, any money which it has borrowed and which has been used for the purpose of meeting expenses incurred in relation to its assumption of functions under this Act or the Bank of England Act 1998; and
    (c) to maintain adequate reserves.

(2) In fixing the amount of any fee which is to be payable to the Authority, no account is to be taken of any sums which the Authority receives, or expects to receive, by way of penalties imposed by it under this Act.

(3) Sub-paragraph (1)(b) applies whether expenses were incurred before or after the coming into force of this Act or the Bank of England Act 1998.

(4) Any fee which is owed to the Authority under any provision made by or under this Act may be recovered as a debt due to the Authority.

Services for which fees may not be charged

18. - The power conferred by paragraph 17 may not be used to require—
    (a) a fee to be paid in respect of the discharge of any of the Authority's functions under paragraphs 13, 14, 19 or 20 of Schedule 3; or
    (b) a fee to be paid by any person whose application for approval under section 59 has been granted.

PART IV
MISCELLANEOUS

Exemption from liability in damages

19. - (1) Neither the Authority nor any person who is, or is acting as, a member, officer or member of staff of the Authority is to be liable in damages for anything done or omitted in the discharge, or purported discharge, of the Authority's functions.

(2) Neither the investigator appointed under paragraph 7 nor a person appointed to conduct an investigation on his behalf under paragraph 8(8) is to be liable in damages for anything done or omitted in the discharge, or purported discharge, of his functions in relation to the investigation of a complaint.

(3) Neither sub-paragraph (1) nor sub-paragraph (2) applies—

(a) if the act or omission is shown to have been in bad faith; or

(b) so as to prevent an award of damages made in respect of an act or omission on the ground that the act or omission was unlawful as a result of section 6(1) of the Human Rights Act 1998.

[19A. - For the purposes of this Act anything done by an accredited financial investigator within the meaning of the Proceeds of Crime Act 2002 who is—

(a) a member of the staff of the Authority, or

(b) a person appointed by the Authority under section 97, 167 or 168 to conduct an investigation,

must be treated as done in the exercise or discharge of a function of the Authority.]596

Disqualification for membership of House of Commons

20. - In Part III of Schedule 1 to the House of Commons Disqualification Act 1975 (disqualifying offices), insert at the appropriate place—

"Member of the governing body of the Financial Services Authority".

Disqualification for membership of Northern Ireland Assembly

21. - In Part III of Schedule 1 to the Northern Ireland Assembly Disqualification Act 1975 (disqualifying offices), insert at the appropriate place—

"Member of the governing body of the Financial Services Authority".

SCHEDULE 2
REGULATED ACTIVITIES   Section 22(2)

[PART I
REGULATED ACTIVITIES: GENERAL]597

General

1. - The matters with respect to which provision may be made under section 22(1) in respect of activities include, in particular, those described in general terms in this Part of this Schedule.

---

596 Inserted by the Proceeds of Crime Act 2002, s 456, Sch 11, paras 1, 38; came into force 24 February 2003.

597 Substituted by the Dormant Bank and Building Society Accounts Act 2008, s 15, Sch 2, para 1(1), (2); came into force 12 March 2009.

Dealing in investments

2. - (1) Buying, selling, subscribing for or underwriting investments or offering or agreeing to do so, either as a principal or as an agent.

(2) In the case of an investment which is a contract of insurance, that includes carrying out the contract.

Arranging deals in investments

3. - Making, or offering or agreeing to make—

    (a) arrangements with a view to another person buying, selling, subscribing for or underwriting a particular investment;

    (b) arrangements with a view to a person who participates in the arrangements buying, selling, subscribing for or underwriting investments.

Deposit taking

4. - Accepting deposits.

Safekeeping and administration of assets

5. - (1) Safeguarding and administering assets belonging to another which consist of or include investments or offering or agreeing to do so.

(2) Arranging for the safeguarding and administration of assets belonging to another, or offering or agreeing to do so.

Managing investments

6. - Managing, or offering or agreeing to manage, assets belonging to another person where—

    (a) the assets consist of or include investments; or

    (b) the arrangements for their management are such that the assets may consist of or include investments at the discretion of the person managing or offering or agreeing to manage them.

Investment advice

7. - Giving or offering or agreeing to give advice to persons on—

    (a) buying, selling, subscribing for or underwriting an investment; or

    (b) exercising any right conferred by an investment to acquire, dispose of, underwrite or convert an investment.

Establishing collective investment schemes

8. - Establishing, operating or winding up a collective investment scheme, including acting as—

    (a) trustee of a unit trust scheme;

    (b) depositary of a collective investment scheme other than a unit trust scheme; or

    (c) sole director of a body incorporated by virtue of regulations under section 262.

Using computer-based systems for giving investment instructions

9. - (1) Sending on behalf of another person instructions relating to an investment by means of a computer-based system which enables investments to be transferred without a written instrument.

(2) Offering or agreeing to send such instructions by such means on behalf of another person.

(3) Causing such instructions to be sent by such means on behalf of another person.

(4) Offering or agreeing to cause such instructions to be sent by such means on behalf of another person.

[PART 1A
REGULATED ACTIVITIES: RECLAIM FUNDS][598]

[Activities of reclaim funds

9A. - (1) The matters with respect to which provision may be made under section 22(1) in respect of activities include, in particular, any of the activities of a reclaim fund.

(2) "Reclaim fund" has the meaning given by section 5(1) of the Dormant Bank and Building Society Accounts Act 2008.][599]

PART II
INVESTMENTS

General

10. - The matters with respect to which provision may be made under section 22(1) in respect of investments include, in particular, those described in general terms in this Part of this Schedule.

Securities

11. - (1) Shares or stock in the share capital of a company.

(2) "Company" includes—
  (a) any body corporate (wherever incorporated), and
  (b) any unincorporated body constituted under the law of a country or territory outside the United Kingdom,

other than an open-ended investment company.

Instruments creating or acknowledging indebtedness

12. - Any of the following—
  (a) debentures;
  (b) debenture stock;
  (c) loan stock;
  (d) bonds;
  (e) certificates of deposit;
  (f) any other instruments creating or acknowledging a present or future indebtedness.

Government and public securities

13. - (1) Loan stock, bonds and other instruments—
  (a) creating or acknowledging indebtedness; and
  (b) issued by or on behalf of a government, local authority or public authority.

(2) "Government, local authority or public authority" means—
  (a) the government of the United Kingdom, of Northern Ireland, or of any country or territory outside the United Kingdom;
  (b) a local authority in the United Kingdom or elsewhere;
  (c) any international organisation the members of which include the United Kingdom or another member State.

---

[598] Inserted by the Dormant Bank and Building Society Accounts Act 2008, s 15, Sch 2, para 1(1), (3); came into force 12 March 2009.

[599] Inserted by the Dormant Bank and Building Society Accounts Act 2008, s 15, Sch 2, para 1(1), (3); came into force 12 March 2009.

Instruments giving entitlement to investments

14. - (1) Warrants or other instruments entitling the holder to subscribe for any investment.

(2) It is immaterial whether the investment is in existence or identifiable.

Certificates representing securities

15. - Certificates or other instruments which confer contractual or property rights—

(a) in respect of any investment held by someone other than the person on whom the rights are conferred by the certificate or other instrument; and

(b) the transfer of which may be effected without requiring the consent of that person.

Units in collective investment schemes

16. - (1) Shares in or securities of an open-ended investment company.

(2) Any right to participate in a collective investment scheme.

Options

17. - Options to acquire or dispose of property.

Futures

18. - Rights under a contract for the sale of a commodity or property of any other description under which delivery is to be made at a future date.

Contracts for differences

19. - Rights under—

(a) a contract for differences; or

(b) any other contract the purpose or pretended purpose of which is to secure a profit or avoid a loss by reference to fluctuations in—

(i) the value or price of property of any description; or

(ii) an index or other factor designated for that purpose in the contract.

Contracts of insurance

20. - Rights under a contract of insurance, including rights under contracts falling within head C of Schedule 2 to the Friendly Societies Act 1992.

Participation in Lloyd's syndicates

21. - (1) The underwriting capacity of a Lloyd's syndicate.

(2) A person's membership (or prospective membership) of a Lloyd's syndicate.

Deposits

22. - Rights under any contract under which a sum of money (whether or not denominated in a currency) is paid on terms under which it will be repaid, with or without interest or a premium, and either on demand or at a time or in circumstances agreed by or on behalf of the person making the payment and the person receiving it.

Loans secured on land

23. - (1) Rights under any contract under which—

(a) one person provides another with credit; and

(b) the obligation of the borrower to repay is secured on land.

(2) "Credit" includes any cash loan or other financial accommodation.

(3) "Cash" includes money in any form.

[Other finance arrangements involving land

23A. - (1) Rights under any arrangement for the provision of finance under which the person providing the finance either—
- (a) acquires a major interest in land from the person to whom the finance is provided, or
- (b) disposes of a major interest in land to that person,

as part of the arrangement.

(2) References in sub-paragraph (1) to a "major interest" in land are to—
- (a) in relation to land in England or Wales—
  - (i) an estate in fee simple absolute, or
  - (ii) a term of years absolute,

  whether subsisting at law or in equity;
- (b) in relation to land in Scotland—
  - (i) the interest of an owner of land, or
  - (ii) the tenant's right over or interest in a property subject to a lease;
- (c) in relation to land in Northern Ireland—
  - (i) any freehold estate, or
  - (ii) any leasehold estate,

  whether subsisting at law or in equity.

(3) It is immaterial for the purposes of sub-paragraph (1) whether either party acquires or (as the case may be) disposes of the interest in land—
- (a) directly, or
- (b) indirectly.][600]

Rights in investments

24. - Any right or interest in anything which is an investment as a result of any other provision made under section 22(1).

PART III
SUPPLEMENTAL PROVISIONS

The order-making power

25. - (1) An order under section 22(1) may—
- (a) provide for exemptions;
- (b) confer powers on the Treasury or the Authority;
- (c) authorise the making of regulations or other instruments by the Treasury for purposes of, or connected with, any relevant provision;
- (d) authorise the making of rules or other instruments by the Authority for purposes of, or connected with, any relevant provision;
- (e) make provision in respect of any information or document which, in the opinion of the Treasury or the Authority, is relevant for purposes of, or connected with, any relevant provision;
- (f) make such consequential, transitional or supplemental provision as the Treasury consider appropriate for purposes of, or connected with, any relevant provision.

(2) Provision made as a result of sub-paragraph (1)(f) may amend any primary or subordinate legislation, including any provision of, or made under, this Act.

---

[600] Inserted by the Regulation of Financial Services (Land Transactions) Act 2005, s 1; came into force 19 February 2006.

(3) "Relevant provision" means any provision—
    (a) of section 22 or this Schedule; or
    (b) made under that section or this Schedule.

Parliamentary control

26. - (1) This paragraph applies to the first order made under section 22(1).

(2) This paragraph also applies to any subsequent order made under section 22(1) which contains a statement by the Treasury that, in their opinion, the effect (or one of the effects) of the proposed order would be that an activity which is not a regulated activity would become a regulated activity.

(3) An order to which this paragraph applies—
    (a) must be laid before Parliament after being made; and
    (b) ceases to have effect at the end of the relevant period unless before the end of that period the order is approved by a resolution of each House of Parliament (but without that affecting anything done under the order or the power to make a new order).

(4) "Relevant period" means a period of twenty-eight days beginning with the day on which the order is made.

(5) In calculating the relevant period no account is to be taken of any time during which Parliament is dissolved or prorogued or during which both Houses are adjourned for more than four days.

Interpretation

27. - (1) In this Schedule—
    "buying" includes acquiring for valuable consideration;
    "offering" includes inviting to treat;
    "property" includes currency of the United Kingdom or any other country or territory; and
    "selling" includes disposing for valuable consideration.

(2) In sub-paragraph (1) "disposing" includes—
    (a) in the case of an investment consisting of rights under a contract—
        (i) surrendering, assigning or converting those rights; or
        (ii) assuming the corresponding liabilities under the contract;
    (b) in the case of an investment consisting of rights under other arrangements, assuming the corresponding liabilities under the contract or arrangements;
    (c) in the case of any other investment, issuing or creating the investment or granting the rights or interests of which it consists.

(3) In this Schedule references to an instrument include references to any record (whether or not in the form of a document).

SCHEDULE 3
EEA PASSPORT RIGHTS   Sections 31(1)(b) and 37

PART I
DEFINED TERMS

The single market directives

1. - "The single market directives" means—
    [(a) the banking consolidation directive;][601]

---

[601] Substituted, for sub-paras (a), (b) as originally enacted, by SI 2000/2952, reg 8(1), (5)(a); came into force 22 November 2000.

(c) the insurance directives; . . .[602]

[(ca) the reinsurance directive;][603]

(d) the [markets in financial instruments directive][604][; . . .][605]

(e) the insurance mediation directive][606][; and

(f) the UCITS directive].[607]

The banking [consolidation directive][608]

[2. - "The banking consolidation directive" means Directive 2006/48/EC of the European Parliament and of the Council of 14 June 2006 relating to the taking up and pursuit of the business of credit institutions.][609]

The insurance directives

3. - (1) "The insurance directives" means the first, second and third non-life insurance directives and the [life assurance consolidation directive].[610]

(2) "First non-life insurance directive" means the Council Directive of 24 July 1973 on the co-ordination of laws, regulations and administrative provisions relating to the taking up and pursuit of the business of direct insurance other than life assurance (No 73/239/EEC).

(3) "Second non-life insurance directive" means the Council Directive of 22 June 1988 on the co-ordination of laws, etc, and laying down provisions to facilitate the effective exercise of freedom to provide services and amending Directive 73/239/EEC (No 88/357/EEC).

(4) "Third non-life insurance directive" means the Council Directive of 18 June 1992 on the co-ordination of laws, etc, and amending Directives 73/239/EEC and 88/357/EEC (No 92/49/EEC).

[(8) "Life assurance consolidation directive" means Directive 2002/83/EC of the European Parliament and of the Council of 5th November 2002 concerning life assurance.][611]

[The reinsurance directive

3A. - "The reinsurance directive" means Directive 2005/68/EC of the European Parliament and of the Council of 16 November 2005 on reinsurance and amending Council Directives 73/239/EEC, 92/49/EEC as well as Directives 98/78/EC and 2002/83/EC.][612]

. . .

4. - . . .[613]

[602] Repealed by SI 2003/1473, reg 2(2)(a)(i); came into force 14 January 2005.

[603] Inserted by SI 2007/3253, reg 2(1), Sch 1, paras 1, 6(a); came into force 10 December 2007.

[604] Substituted by SI 2007/126, reg 3(4), Sch 4, paras 1, 2; came into force (for certain purposes) 1 April 2007; came into force (for remaining purposes) 1 November 2007.

[605] Repealed by SI 2003/2066, reg 2(2)(a)(i); came into force 13 February 2004.

[606] Inserted by SI 2003/1473, reg 2(2)(a)(ii); came into force 14 January 2005.

[607] Inserted by SI 2003/2066, reg 2(2)(a)(ii); came into force 13 February 2004.

[608] Substituted by virtue of SI 2000/2952, reg 8(1), (5)(b); came into force 22 November 2000.

[609] Substituted by SI 2006/3221, reg 29(1), Sch 3, para 2(1), (2); came into force 1 January 2007.

[610] Substituted by SI 2004/3379, reg 6(1), (6)(a)(i); came into force 11 January 2005.

[611] Substituted, for sub-paras (5)–(7) as originally enacted, by SI 2004/3379, reg 6(1), (6)(a)(ii); came into force 11 January 2005.

[612] Inserted by SI 2007/3253, reg 2(1), Sch 1, paras 1, 6(b); came into force 10 December 2007.

[613] Repealed by SI 2007/126, reg 3(4), Sch 4, paras 1, 3; came into force (for certain purposes) 1 April 2007; came into force (for remaining purposes) 1 November 2007.

[The insurance mediation directive
4A. - "The insurance mediation directive" means the European Parliament and Council Directive of 9th December 2002 on insurance mediation (No 2002/92/EC).][614]

[The UCITS directive
4B. - "The UCITS directive" means the Council Directive of 20 December 1985 on the coordination of laws, regulations and administrative provisions relating to undertakings for collective investment in transferable securities (No 85/611/EEC).][615]

[The markets in financial instruments directive
4C. - "The markets in financial instruments directive" means Directive 2004/39/EC of the European Parliament and of the Council of 21 April 2004 on markets in financial instruments.][616]

EEA firm
5. - "EEA firm" means any of the following if it does not have its [relevant office][617] in the United Kingdom—
   (a) an investment firm (as defined in [Article 4.1.1 of the markets in financial instruments directive][618]) which is authorised (within the meaning of [Article 5][619]) by its home state regulator;
   [(b) a credit institution (as defined in Article 4.1 of the banking consolidation directive) which is authorised (within the meaning of Article 4.2) by its home state regulator;
   (c) a financial institution (as defined in Article 4.5 of the banking consolidation directive) which is a subsidiary of the kind mentioned in Article 24 and which fulfils the conditions in that Article;][620]
   (d) an undertaking pursuing the activity of direct insurance (within the meaning of [Article 2 of the life assurance consolidation directive or Article 1 of the first non-life insurance directive][621]) which has received authorisation under [Article 4 of the life assurance consolidation directive or Article 6 of the first non-life insurance directive][622] from its home state regulator[; . . .][623]
   [(da) an undertaking pursuing the activity of reinsurance (within the meaning of Article 2.1(a) of the reinsurance directive) which has received authorisation under (or is deemed to be authorised in accordance with) Article 3 of the reinsurance directive from its home state regulator;][624]
   (e) an insurance intermediary (as defined in Article 2.5 of the insurance mediation directive), or a reinsurance intermediary (as defined in Article 2.6) which is registered with its home state regulator under Article 3][625][; or

---

[614] Inserted by SI 2003/1473, reg 2(2)(b); came into force 14 January 2005.
[615] Inserted by SI 2003/2066, reg 2(2)(b); came into force 13 February 2004.
[616] Inserted by SI 2006/2975, regs 2, 13; came into force 6 December 2006.
[617] Substituted by SI 2003/1473, reg 2(2)(c)(i); came into force 14 January 2005.
[618] Substituted by SI 2007/126, reg 3(4), Sch 4, paras 1, 4(a); came into force (for certain purposes) 1 April 2007; came into force (for remaining purposes) 1 November 2007.
[619] Substituted by SI 2007/126, reg 3(4), Sch 4, paras 1, 4(b); came into force (for certain purposes) 1 April 2007; came into force (for remaining purposes) 1 November 2007.
[620] Substituted by SI 2006/3221, reg 29(1), Sch 3, para 2(1), (3); came into force 1 January 2007.
[621] Substituted by SI 2004/3379, reg 6(1), (6)(b)(i); came into force 11 January 2005.
[622] Substituted by SI 2004/3379, reg 6(1), (6)(b)(ii); came into force 11 January 2005.
[623] Repealed by SI 2003/2066, reg 2(2)(c)(i); came into force 13 February 2004.
[624] Inserted by SI 2007/3253, reg 2(1), Sch 1, paras 1, 6(c); came into force 10 December 2007.
[625] Inserted by SI 2003/1473, reg 2(2)(c)(iii); came into force 14 January 2005.

(f) a management company (as defined in Article 1a.2 of the UCITS directive) which is authorised (within the meaning of Article 5) by its home state regulator].[626]

[5A. - In paragraph 5, "relevant office" means—

(a) in relation to a firm falling within sub-paragraph (e) of that paragraph which has a registered office, its registered office;

(b) in relation to any other firm, its head office.][627]

EEA authorization

[6. - "EEA authorisation" means—

(a) in relation to an EEA firm falling within paragraph 5(e), registration with its home state regulator under Article 3 of the insurance mediation directive;

(b) in relation to any other EEA firm, authorisation granted to an EEA firm by its home state regulator for the purpose of the relevant single market directive.][628]

EEA right

7. - "EEA right" means the entitlement of a person to establish a branch, or provide services, in an EEA State other than that in which he has his [relevant office][629]—

(a) in accordance with the Treaty as applied in the EEA; and

(b) subject to the conditions of the relevant single market directive.

[7A. - In paragraph 7, "relevant office" means—

(a) in relation to a person who has a registered office and whose entitlement is subject to the conditions of the insurance mediation directive, his registered office;

(b) in relation to any other person, his head office.][630]

EEA State

[8. - "EEA State" has the meaning given by Schedule 1 to the Interpretation Act 1978.][631]

Home state regulator

9. - "Home state regulator" means the competent authority (within the meaning of the relevant single market directive) of an EEA State (other than the United Kingdom) in relation to the EEA firm concerned.

UK firm

10. - "UK firm" means a person whose [relevant office][632] is in the UK and who has an EEA right to carry on activity in an EEA State other than the United Kingdom.

[10A. - In paragraph 10, "relevant office" means—

(a) in relation to a firm whose EEA right derives from the insurance mediation directive and which has a registered office, its registered office;

(b) in relation to any other firm, its head office.][633]

---

[626] Inserted by SI 2003/2066, reg 2(2)(c)(ii); came into force 13 February 2004.

[627] Inserted by SI 2003/1473, reg 2(2)(d); came into force 14 January 2005.

[628] Substituted by SI 2003/1473, reg 2(2)(e); came into force 14 January 2005.

[629] Substituted by SI 2003/1473, reg 2(2)(f); came into force 14 January 2005.

[630] Inserted by SI 2003/1473, reg 2(2)(g); came into force 14 January 2005.

[631] Substituted by SI 2007/108, reg 2; came into force 13 February 2007.

[632] Substituted by SI 2003/1473, reg 2(2)(h); came into force 14 January 2005.

[633] Inserted by SI 2003/1473, reg 2(2)(i); came into force 14 January 2005.

[UK investment firm

10B. - "UK investment firm" means a UK firm—
  (a) which is an investment firm, and
  (b) whose EEA right derives from the markets in financial instruments directive.]634

Host state regulator

11. - "Host state regulator" means the competent authority (within the meaning of the relevant single market directive) of an EEA State (other than the United Kingdom) in relation to a UK firm's exercise of EEA rights there.

[Tied agent

11A. - "Tied agent" has the meaning given in Article 4.1.25 of the markets in financial instruments directive.]635

PART II
EXERCISE OF PASSPORT RIGHTS BY EEA FIRMS

Firms qualifying for authorisation

12. - (1) Once an EEA firm which is seeking to establish a branch in the United Kingdom in exercise of an EEA right satisfies the establishment conditions, it qualifies for authorisation.
  (2) Once an EEA firm which is seeking to provide services in the United Kingdom in exercise of an EEA right satisfies the service conditions, it qualifies for authorisation.
  [(3) If an EEA firm falling within paragraph 5(a) is seeking to use a tied agent established in the United Kingdom in connection with the exercise of an EEA right deriving from the markets in financial instruments directive, this Part of this Schedule applies as if the firm were seeking to establish a branch in the United Kingdom.
  (4) But if—
      (a) an EEA firm already qualifies for authorisation by virtue of sub-paragraph (1); and
      (b) the EEA right which it is exercising derives from the markets in financial instruments directive,
    sub-paragraph (3) does not require the firm to satisfy the establishment conditions in respect of its use of the tied agent in question.]636
  [(5) An EEA firm which falls within paragraph 5(da) which establishes a branch in the United Kingdom, or provides services in the United Kingdom, in exercise of an EEA right qualifies for authorisation.
  (6) Sub-paragraphs (1) and (2) do not apply to an EEA firm falling within paragraph 5(da).]637

---

634 Inserted by SI 2007/126, reg 3(4), Sch 4, paras 1, 5; came into force (for certain purposes) 1 April 2007; came into force (for remaining purposes) 1 November 2007.
635 Inserted by SI 2007/126, reg 3(4), Sch 4, paras 1, 6; came into force (for certain purposes) 1 April 2007; came into force (for remaining purposes) 1 November 2007.
636 Inserted by SI 2007/126, reg 3(4), Sch 4, paras 1, 7; came into force (for certain purposes) 1 April 2007; came into force (for remaining purposes) 1 November 2007.
637 Inserted by SI 2007/3253, reg 2(1), Sch 1, paras 1, 6(d); came into force 10 December 2007.

Establishment

13. - (1) [If the firm falls within paragraph 5(a), (b), [(c), (d) or (f)][638],][639] the establishment conditions are that—
- (a) the Authority has received notice ("a consent notice") from the firm's home state regulator that it has given the firm consent to establish a branch in the United Kingdom;
- (b) the consent notice—
  - (i) is given in accordance with the relevant single market directive;
  - (ii) identifies the activities to which consent relates; and
  - (iii) includes such other information as may be prescribed; . . .[640]
- [(ba) in the case of a firm falling within paragraph 5(a), the Authority has given the firm notice for the purposes of this paragraph or two months have elapsed beginning with the date when the home state regulator gave the consent notice; and][641]
- (c) [in the case of a firm falling within paragraph 5(b), (c), (d) or (f),][642] the firm has been informed of the applicable provisions or two months have elapsed beginning with the date when the Authority received the consent notice.

[(1A) If the firm falls within paragraph 5(e), the establishment conditions are that—
- (a) the firm has given its home state regulator notice of its intention to establish a branch in the United Kingdom;
- (b) the Authority has received notice ("a regulator's notice") from the firm's home state regulator that the firm intends to establish a branch in the United Kingdom;
- (c) the firm's home state regulator has informed the firm that the regulator's notice has been sent to the Authority; and
- (d) one month has elapsed beginning with the date on which the firm's home state regulator informed the firm that the regulator's notice has been sent to the Authority.][643]

(2) If the Authority has received a consent notice, it must—
- (a) prepare for the firm's supervision;
- (b) [except if the firm falls within paragraph 5(a),][644] notify the firm of the applicable provisions (if any); and
- (c) if the firm falls within paragraph 5(d), notify its home state regulator of the applicable provisions (if any).

(3) A notice under sub-paragraph (2)(b) or (c) must be given before the end of the period of two months beginning with the day on which the Authority received the consent notice.

(4) For the purposes of this paragraph—
"applicable provisions" means the host state rules with which the firm is required to comply when carrying on a permitted activity through a branch in the United Kingdom;
"host state rules" means rules—
- (a) made in accordance with the relevant single market directive; and
- (b) which are the responsibility of the United Kingdom (both as to implementation and as to supervision of compliance) in accordance with that directive; and

---

[638] Substituted by SI 2003/2066, reg 3(1)(a); came into force 13 February 2004.

[639] Inserted by SI 2003/1473, reg 3(1), (2); came into force 14 January 2005.

[640] Repealed by SI 2007/126, reg 3(4), Sch 4, paras 1, 8(a)(i); came into force (for certain purposes) 1 April 2007; came into force (for remaining purposes) 1 November 2007.

[641] Inserted by SI 2007/126, reg 3(4), Sch 4, paras 1, 8(a)(ii); came into force (for certain purposes) 1 April 2007; came into force (for remaining purposes) 1 November 2007.

[642] Inserted by SI 2007/126, reg 3(4), Sch 4, paras 1, 8(a)(iii); came into force (for certain purposes) 1 April 2007; came into force (for remaining purposes) 1 November 2007.

[643] Inserted by SI 2003/1473, reg 3(1), (3); came into force 14 January 2005.

[644] Inserted by SI 2007/126, reg 3(4), Sch 4, paras 1, 8(b); came into force (for certain purposes) 1 April 2007; came into force (for remaining purposes) 1 November 2007.

"permitted activity" means an activity identified in the consent notice [or regulator's notice, as the case may be].[645]

Services

14. - (1) The service conditions are that—

(a) the firm has given its home state regulator notice of its intention to provide services in the United Kingdom ("a notice of intention");

(b) if the firm falls within [paragraph 5(a), [(d), (e) or (f)][646]],[647] the Authority has received notice ("a regulator's notice") from the firm's home state regulator containing such information as may be prescribed; . . .[648]

[(ba) if the firm falls within paragraph 5(b) and is seeking to provide services in exercise of the right under Article 31.5 of the markets in financial instruments directive, the Authority has received notice ("a regulator's notice") from the firm's home state regulator stating that the firm intends to exercise that right in the United Kingdom;][649]

(c) if the firm falls within [paragraph 5(d) or (e)],[650] its home state regulator has informed it that the regulator's notice has been sent to the Authority[; and

(d) if the firm falls within paragraph 5(e), one month has elapsed beginning with the date on which the firm's home state regulator informed the firm that the regulator's notice has been sent to the Authority].[651]

(2) If the Authority has received a regulator's notice or, where none is required by sub-paragraph (1), has been informed of the firm's intention to provide services in the United Kingdom, it must[, unless the firm falls within paragraph 5(e),][652]—

(a) prepare for the firm's supervision; and

(b) notify the firm of the applicable provisions (if any).

[(2A) Sub-paragraph (2)(b) does not apply in the case of a firm falling within paragraph 5(a).][653]

(3) A notice under sub-paragraph (2)(b) must be given before the end of the period of two months beginning on the day on which the Authority received the regulator's notice, or was informed of the firm's intention.

(4) For the purposes of this paragraph—

"applicable provisions" means the host state rules with which the firm is required to comply when carrying on a permitted activity by providing services in the United Kingdom;

"host state rules" means rules—

(a) made in accordance with the relevant single market directive; and

(b) which are the responsibility of the United Kingdom (both as to implementation and as to supervision of compliance) in accordance with that directive; and

"permitted activity" means an activity identified in—

(a) the regulator's notice; or

(b) where none is required by sub-paragraph (1), the notice of intention.

---

[645] Inserted by SI 2003/1473, reg 3(1), (4); came into force 14 January 2005.

[646] Substituted by SI 2003/2066, reg 3(1)(b); came into force 13 February 2004.

[647] Substituted by SI 2003/1473, reg 4(1), (2)(a); came into force 14 January 2005.

[648] Repealed by SI 2003/1473, reg 4(1), (2)(b); came into force 14 January 2005.

[649] Inserted by SI 2007/126, reg 3(4), Sch 4, paras 1, 9(a); came into force (for certain purposes) 1 April 2007; came into force (for remaining purposes) 1 November 2007.

[650] Substituted by SI 2003/1473, reg 4(1), (2)(c); came into force 14 January 2005.

[651] Inserted by SI 2003/1473, reg 4(1), (3)(d); came into force 14 January 2005.

[652] Inserted by SI 2003/1473, reg 4(1), (3); came into force.

[653] Inserted by SI 2007/126, reg 3(4), Sch 4, paras 1, 9(b); came into force (for certain purposes) 1 April 2007; came into force (for remaining purposes) 1 November 2007.

Grant of permission

15. - (1) On qualifying for authorisation as a result of [paragraph 12(1), (2) or (3)],[654] a firm has, in respect of each permitted activity which is a regulated activity, permission to carry it on through its United Kingdom branch (if it satisfies the establishment conditions) or by providing services in the United Kingdom (if it satisfies the service conditions).

[(1A) Sub-paragraph (1) is to be read subject to paragraph 15A(3).][655]

(2) The permission is to be treated as being on terms equivalent to those appearing from the consent notice, regulator's notice or notice of intention.

(3) Sections [21 and 39(1)][656] of the Consumer Credit Act 1974 (business requiring a licence under that Act) do not apply in relation to the carrying on of a permitted activity which is Consumer Credit Act business by a firm which qualifies for authorisation as a result of paragraph 12, unless [the Office of Fair Trading][657] has exercised the power conferred on [it][658] by section 203 in relation to the firm.

(4) "Consumer Credit Act business" has the same meaning as in section 203.

[(5) A firm which qualifies for authorisation as a result of paragraph 12(5) has, in respect of each permitted activity which is a regulated activity, permission to carry it on through its United Kingdom branch or by providing services in the United Kingdom.

(6) The permission is to be treated as being on terms equivalent to those appearing in the authorisation granted to the firm under Article 3 of the reinsurance directive by its home state regulator ("its home authorisation").

(7) For the purposes of sub-paragraph (5), "permitted activity" means an activity which the firm is permitted to carry on under its home authorisation.][659]

[Power to Restrict Permission of Management Companies

15A. - (1) Sub-paragraph (2) applies if—

(a) a firm falling within paragraph 5(f) qualifies for authorisation as a result of paragraph 12(1) (establishment conditions satisfied); but

(b) the Authority determines that the way in which the firm intends to invite persons in the United Kingdom to become participants in any collective investment scheme which that firm manages does not comply with the law in force in the United Kingdom.

(2) The Authority may give a notice to the firm and the firm's home state regulator of the Authority's determination under sub-paragraph (1)(b).

(3) Paragraph 15(1) does not give a firm to which the Authority has given (and not withdrawn) a notice under sub-paragraph (2) permission to carry on through the firm's United Kingdom branch the regulated activity of dealing in units in the collective investment schemes which the firm manages.

(4) Any notice given under sub-paragraph (2) must be given before the end of the period of two months beginning with the day on which the Authority received the consent notice.

(5) Sections 264(4) and 265(1), (2) and (4) apply to a notice given under sub-paragraph (2) as they apply to a notice given by the Authority under section 264(2).

(6) If a decision notice is given to the firm under section 265(4), by virtue of sub-paragraph (5), the firm may refer the matter to the Tribunal.

---

[654] Substituted by SI 2007/3253, reg 2(1), Sch 1, paras 1, 6(e)(i); came into force 10 December 2007.

[655] Inserted by SI 2003/2066, reg 3(1)(c); came into force 13 February 2004.

[656] Substituted by the Consumer Credit Act 2006, s 33(9); came into force 6 April 2008.

[657] Substituted by the Enterprise Act 2002, s 278(1), Sch 25, para 40(1), (19)(a); came into force 1 April 2003.

[658] Substituted by the Enterprise Act 2002, s 278(1), Sch 25, para 40(1), (19)(a); came into force 1 April 2003.

[659] Inserted by SI 2007/3253, reg 2(1), Sch 1, paras 1, 6(e)(ii); came into force 10 December 2007.

(7) In sub-paragraph (3)—
    (a) "units" has the meaning given by section 237(2); and
    (b) the reference to "dealing in" units in a collective investment scheme must be read with—
        (i) section 22;
        (ii) any relevant order under that section; and
        (iii) Schedule 2.][660]

Effect of carrying on regulated activity when not qualified for authorization

16. - (1) This paragraph applies to an EEA firm which is not qualified for authorisation under paragraph 12.

(2) Section 26 does not apply to an agreement entered into by the firm.

(3) Section 27 does not apply to an agreement in relation to which the firm is a third party for the purposes of that section.

(4) Section 29 does not apply to an agreement in relation to which the firm is the deposit-taker.

Continuing regulation of EEA firms

17. - Regulations may—
    (a) modify any provision of this Act which is an applicable provision (within the meaning of paragraph 13 or 14) in its application to an EEA firm qualifying for authorisation;
    (b) make provision as to any change (or proposed change) of a prescribed kind relating to an EEA firm or to an activity that it carries on in the United Kingdom and as to the procedure to be followed in relation to such cases;
    (c) provide that the Authority may treat an EEA firm's notification that it is to cease to carry on regulated activity in the United Kingdom as a request for cancellation of its qualification for authorisation under this Schedule.

Giving up right to authorization

18. - Regulations may provide that in prescribed circumstances an EEA firm falling within paragraph 5(c) may, on following the prescribed procedure—
    (a) have its qualification for authorisation under this Schedule cancelled; and
    (b) seek to become an authorised person by applying for a Part IV permission.

PART III
EXERCISE OF PASSPORT RIGHTS BY UK FIRMS

Establishment

19. - (1) [Subject to [sub-paragraphs (5ZA) and (5A)][661],][662] a UK firm may not exercise an EEA right to establish a branch unless three conditions are satisfied.

(2) The first is that the firm has given the Authority, in the specified way, notice of its intention to establish a branch ("a notice of intention") which—
    (a) identifies the activities which it seeks to carry on through the branch; and
    (b) includes such other information as may be specified.

---

[660] Inserted by SI 2003/2066, reg 3(1)(d); came into force 13 February 2004.
[661] Substituted by SI 2007/3253, reg 2(1), Sch 1, paras 1, 6(f); came into force 10 December 2007.
[662] Inserted by SI 2003/1473, reg 5(1), (2); came into force 14 January 2005.

(3) [Subject to sub-paragraph (5B), the]663 activities identified in a notice of intention may include activities which are not regulated activities.

(4) The second is that the Authority has given notice in specified terms ("a consent notice") to the host state regulator.

[(5) The third is—

    (a) if the EEA right in question derives from the insurance mediation directive, that one month has elapsed beginning with the date on which the firm received notice, in accordance with sub-paragraph (11), that the Authority has given a consent notice;

    (b) in any other case, that either—

        (i) the host state regulator has notified the firm (or, where the EEA right in question derives from any of the insurance directives, the Authority) of the applicable provisions; or

        (ii) two months have elapsed beginning with the date on which the Authority gave the consent notice.]664

[(5ZA) This paragraph does not apply to a UK firm having an EEA right which is subject to the conditions of the reinsurance directive.]665

[(5A) If—

    (a) the EEA right in question derives from the insurance mediation directive, and

    (b) the EEA State in which the firm intends to establish a branch has not notified the Commission, in accordance with Article 6(2) of that directive, of its wish to be informed of the intention of any UK firm to establish a branch in its territory,

the second and third conditions do not apply (and so the firm may establish the branch to which its notice of intention relates as soon as the first condition is satisfied).]666

[(5B) If the firm is a UK investment firm, a notice of intention may not include ancillary services unless such services are to be provided in connection with the carrying on of one or more investment services and activities.

(5C) In sub-paragraph (5B) "ancillary services" has the meaning given in Article 4.1.3 of the markets in financial instruments directive.]667

(6) If the firm's EEA right derives from [the banking consolidation directive, [the UCITS directive or, in the case of a credit institution authorised under the banking consolidation directive, the markets in financial instruments directive]668]669 and the first condition is satisfied, the Authority must give a consent notice to the host state regulator unless it has reason to doubt the adequacy of the firm's resources or its administrative structure.

(7) If the firm's EEA right derives from any of the insurance directives and the first condition is satisfied, the Authority must give a consent notice unless it has reason—

    (a) to doubt the adequacy of the firm's resources or its administrative structure, or

    (b) to question the reputation, qualifications or experience of the directors or managers of the firm or the person proposed as the branch's authorised agent for the purposes of those directives,

in relation to the business to be conducted through the proposed branch.

---

663 Substituted by SI 2007/126, reg 3(4), Sch 4, paras 1, 10(a); came into force (for certain purposes) 1 April 2007; came into force (for remaining purposes) 1 November 2007.

664 Substituted by SI 2003/1473, reg 5(1), (3); came into force 14 January 2005.

665 Inserted by SI 2007/3253, reg 2(1), Sch 1, paras 1, 6(g); came into force 10 December 2007.

666 Inserted by SI 2003/1473, reg 5(1), (4); came into force 14 January 2005.

667 Inserted by SI 2007/126, reg 3(4), Sch 4, paras 1, 10(b); came into force (for certain purposes) 1 April 2007; came into force (for remaining purposes) 1 November 2007.

668 Substituted by SI 2007/126, reg 3(4), Sch 4, paras 1, 10(c); came into force (for certain purposes) 1 April 2007; came into force (for remaining purposes) 1 November 2007.

669 Substituted by SI 2003/2066, reg 4(1)(a)(i); came into force 13 February 2004.

[(7A) If—
  (a) the firm's EEA right derives from the insurance mediation directive,
  (b) the first condition is satisfied, and
  (c) the second condition applies,
  the Authority must give a consent notice, and must do so within one month beginning with the date on which it received the firm's notice of intention.][670]
[(7B) If the firm is a UK investment firm and the first condition is satisfied, the Authority must give a consent notice to the host state regulator within three months beginning with the date on which it received the firm's notice of intention unless the Authority has reason to doubt the adequacy of the firm's resources or its administrative structure.][671]
 (8) If the Authority proposes to refuse to give a consent notice it must give the firm concerned a warning notice.
 (9) If the firm's EEA right derives from any of the insurance directives and the host state regulator has notified it of the applicable provisions, the Authority must inform the firm of those provisions.
(10) Rules may specify the procedure to be followed by the Authority in exercising its functions under this paragraph.
(11) If the Authority gives a consent notice it must give written notice that it has done so to the firm concerned.
(12) If the Authority decides to refuse to give a consent notice—
  (a) it must, [within the relevant period],[672] give the person who gave that notice a decision notice to that effect; and
  (b) that person may refer the matter to the Tribunal.
[(12A) In sub-paragraph (12), "the relevant period" means—
  (a) if the firm's EEA right derives from the UCITS directive, two months beginning with the date on which the Authority received the notice of intention;
  (b) in any other case, three months beginning with that date.][673]
(13) In this paragraph, "applicable provisions" means the host state rules with which the firm will be required to comply when conducting business through the proposed branch in the EEA State concerned.
(14) In sub-paragraph (13), "host state rules" means rules—
  (a) made in accordance with the relevant single market directive; and
  (b) which are the responsibility of the EEA State concerned (both as to implementation and as to supervision of compliance) in accordance with that directive.
(15) "Specified" means specified in rules.

Services

20. - (1) [Subject to sub-paragraph (4D),][674] a UK firm may not exercise an EEA right to provide services unless the firm has given the Authority, in the specified way, notice of its intention to provide services ("a notice of intention") which—
  (a) identifies the activities which it seeks to carry out by way of provision of services; and
  (b) includes such other information as may be specified.

---

[670] Inserted by SI 2003/1473, reg 5(1), (5); came into force 14 January 2005.
[671] Inserted by SI 2007/126, reg 3(4), Sch 4, paras 1, 10(d); came into force (for certain purposes) 1 April 2007; came into force (for remaining purposes) 1 November 2007.
[672] Substituted by SI 2003/2066, reg 4(1)(a)(ii); came into force 13 February 2004.
[673] Inserted by SI 2003/2066, reg 4(1)(a)(iii); came into force 13 February 2004.
[674] Inserted by SI 2007/3253, reg 2(1), Sch 1, paras 1, 6(h); came into force 10 December 2007.

(2) [Subject to sub-paragraph (2A), the][675] activities identified in a notice of intention may include activities which are not regulated activities.

[(2A) If the firm is a UK investment firm, a notice of intention may not include ancillary services unless such services are to be provided in connection with the carrying on of one or more investment services and activities.

(2B) In sub-paragraph (2A) "ancillary services" has the meaning given in Article 4.1.3 of the markets in financial instruments directive.][676]

(3) If the firm's EEA right derives from [the banking consolidation directive, the [markets in financial instruments directive][677] or the UCITS directive],[678] the Authority must, within one month of receiving a notice of intention, send a copy of it to the host state regulator [with such other information as may be specified].[679]

[(3A) If the firm's EEA right derives from any of the insurance directives, the Authority must, within one month of receiving the notice of intention—

(a) give notice in specified terms ("a consent notice") to the host state regulator; or

(b) give written notice to the firm of—

(i) its refusal to give a consent notice; and

(ii) its reasons for that refusal.][680]

[(3B) If the firm's EEA right derives from the insurance mediation directive and the EEA State in which the firm intends to provide services has notified the Commission, in accordance with Article 6(2) of that directive, of its wish to be informed of the intention of any UK firm to provide services in its territory—

(a) the Authority must, within one month of receiving the notice of intention, send a copy of it to the host state regulator;

(b) the Authority, when it sends the copy in accordance with sub-paragraph (a), must give written notice to the firm concerned that it has done so; and

(c) the firm concerned must not provide the services to which its notice of intention relates until one month, beginning with the date on which it receives the notice under sub-paragraph (b), has elapsed.][681]

(4) When the Authority sends the copy under sub-paragraph (3) [or gives a consent notice],[682] it must give written notice to the firm concerned.

[(4A) If the firm is given notice under sub-paragraph (3A)(b), it may refer the matter to the Tribunal.

(4B) If the firm's EEA right derives from any of the insurance directives [or from the markets in financial instruments directive],[683] it must not provide the services to which its notice of intention relates until it has received written notice under sub-paragraph (4).

---

[675] Substituted by SI 2007/126, reg 3(4), Sch 4, paras 1, 11(a); came into force (for certain purposes) 1 April 2007; came into force (for remaining purposes) 1 November 2007.

[676] Inserted by SI 2007/126, reg 3(4), Sch 4, paras 1, 11(b); came into force (for certain purposes) 1 April 2007; came into force (for remaining purposes) 1 November 2007.

[677] Substituted by SI 2007/126, reg 3(4), Sch 4, paras 1, 11(c); came into force (for certain purposes) 1 April 2007; came into force (for remaining purposes) 1 November 2007.

[678] Substituted by SI 2003/2066, reg 4(1)(b)(i); came into force 13 February 2004.

[679] Inserted by SI 2003/2066, reg 4(1)(b)(ii); came into force 13 February 2004.

[680] Inserted by SI 2001/1376, reg 2(1), (2); came into force 30 April 2001.

[681] Inserted by SI 2003/1473, reg 6(1); came into force 14 January 2005.

[682] Inserted by SI 2001/1376, reg 2(1), (3); came into force 30 April 2001.

[683] Inserted by SI 2007/126, reg 3(4), Sch 4, paras 1, 11(d); came into force (for certain purposes) 1 April 2007; came into force (for remaining purposes) 1 November 2007.

[(4BA) If the firm's EEA right derives from the markets in financial instruments directive, the Authority must comply as soon as reasonably practicable with a request for information under the second sub-paragraph of Article 31.6 of that directive from the host state regulator.]684

(4C) Rules may specify the procedure to be followed by the Authority under this paragraph.]685

[(4D) This paragraph does not apply to a UK firm having an EEA right which is subject to the conditions of the reinsurance directive.]686

(5) . . .687

(6) "Specified" means specified in rules.

[Tied agents

20A. - (1) If a UK investment firm is seeking to use a tied agent established in an EEA State (other than the United Kingdom) in connection with the exercise of an EEA right deriving from the markets in financial instruments directive, this Part of this Schedule applies as if the firm were seeking to establish a branch in that State.

(2) But if—

    (a) a UK investment firm has already established a branch in an EEA State other than the United Kingdom in accordance with paragraph 19; and

    (b) the EEA right which it is exercising derives from the markets in financial instruments directive,

paragraph 19 does not apply in respect of its use of the tied agent in question.]688

Offence relating to exercise of passport rights

21. - (1) If a UK firm which is not an authorised person contravenes the prohibition imposed by—

    (a) sub-paragraph (1) of paragraph 19, or

    (b) [sub-paragraph (1), (3B)(c) or (4B)]689 of paragraph 20,

it is guilty of an offence.

(2) A firm guilty of an offence under sub-paragraph (1) is liable—

    (a) on summary conviction, to a fine not exceeding the statutory maximum; or

    (b) on conviction on indictment, to a fine.

(3) In proceedings for an offence under sub-paragraph (1), it is a defence for the firm to show that it took all reasonable precautions and exercised all due diligence to avoid committing the offence.

Continuing regulation of UK firms

22. - (1) Regulations may make such provision as the Treasury consider appropriate in relation to a UK firm's exercise of EEA rights, and may in particular provide for the application (with or without modification) of any provision of, or made under, this Act in relation to an activity of a UK firm.

(2) Regulations may—

    (a) make provision as to any change (or proposed change) of a prescribed kind relating to a UK firm or to an activity that it carries on and as to the procedure to be followed in relation to such cases;

---

684 Inserted by SI 2007/126, reg 3(4), Sch 4, paras 1, 11(e); came into force (for certain purposes) 1 April 2007; came into force (for remaining purposes) 1 November 2007.

685 Inserted by SI 2001/1376, reg 2(1), (4); came into force 30 April 2001.

686 Inserted by SI 2007/3253, reg 2(1), Sch 1, paras 1, 6(i); came into force 10 December 2007.

687 Repealed by SI 2001/1376, reg 2(1), (5); came into force 30 April 2001.

688 Inserted by SI 2007/126, reg 3(4), Sch 4, paras 1, 12; came into force (for certain purposes) 1 April 2007; came into force (for remaining purposes) 1 November 2007.

689 Substituted by SI 2003/1473, reg 6(2); came into force 14 January 2005.

    (b) make provision with respect to the consequences of the firm's failure to comply with a provision of the regulations.

(3) Where a provision of the kind mentioned in sub-paragraph (2) requires the Authority's consent to a change (or proposed change)—

    (a) consent may be refused only on prescribed grounds; and

    (b) if the Authority decides to refuse consent, the firm concerned may refer the matter to the Tribunal.

23. - (1) [Sub-paragraphs (2) and (2A) apply][690] if a UK firm—

    (a) has a Part IV permission; and

    (b) is exercising an EEA right to carry on any Consumer Credit Act business in an EEA State other than the United Kingdom.

(2) The Authority may exercise its power under section 45 in respect of the firm if [the Office of Fair Trading][691] has informed the Authority that—

    (a) the firm,

    (b) any of the firm's employees, agents or associates (whether past or present), or

    (c) if the firm is a body corporate, a controller of the firm or an associate of such a controller,

has done any of the things specified in paragraphs [(a) to (e) of section 25(2A)][692] of the Consumer Credit Act 1974.

[(2A) The Authority may also exercise its power under section 45 in respect of the firm if the Office of Fair Trading has informed the Authority that it has concerns about any of the following—

    (a) the firm's skills, knowledge and experience in relation to Consumer Credit Act businesses;

    (b) such skills, knowledge and experience of other persons who are participating in any Consumer Credit Act business being carried on by the firm;

    (c) practices and procedures that the firm is implementing in connection with any such business.][693]

(3) "Associate", "Consumer Credit Act business" and "controller" have the same meaning as in section 203.

24. - (1) Sub-paragraph (2) applies if a UK firm—

    (a) is not required to have a Part IV permission in relation to the business which it is carrying on; and

    (b) is exercising the right conferred by [[Article 24][694] of the banking consolidation directive][695] to carry on that business in an EEA State other than the United Kingdom.

(2) If requested to do so by the host state regulator in the EEA State in which the UK firm's business is being carried on, the Authority may impose any requirement in relation to the firm which it could impose if—

    (a) the firm had a Part IV permission in relation to the business which it is carrying on; and

    (b) the Authority was entitled to exercise its power under that Part to vary that permission.

[690] Substituted by the Consumer Credit Act 2006, s 33(10); came into force 6 April 2008.
[691] Substituted by the Enterprise Act 2002, s 278(1), Sch 25, para 40(1), (19)(b); came into force 1 April 2003.
[692] Substituted by the Consumer Credit Act 2006, s 33(11); came into force 6 April 2008.
[693] Inserted by the Consumer Credit Act 2006, s 33(12); came into force 6 April 2008.
[694] Substituted by SI 2006/3221, reg 29(1), Sch 3, para 2(1), (4); came into force 1 January 2007.
[695] Substituted by SI 2000/2952, reg 8(1), (5)(f); came into force 22 November 2000.

[Information to be included in the public record
25. - The Authority must include in the record that it maintains under section 347 in relation to any UK firm whose EEA right derives from the insurance mediation directive information as to each EEA State in which the UK firm, in accordance with such a right—
(a) has established a branch; or
(b) is providing services.]696

SCHEDULE 4
TREATY RIGHTS

Section 31(1)(c)

Definitions
1. - In this Schedule—
"consumers" means persons who are consumers for the purposes of section 138;
"Treaty firm" means a person—
(a) whose head office is situated in an EEA State (its "home state") other than the United Kingdom; and
(b) which is recognised under the law of that State as its national; and
"home state regulator", in relation to a Treaty firm, means the competent authority of the firm's home state for the purpose of its home state authorisation (as to which see paragraph 3(1)(a)).

Firms qualifying for authorization
2. - Once a Treaty firm which is seeking to carry on a regulated activity satisfies the conditions set out in paragraph 3(1), it qualifies for authorisation.

Exercise of Treaty rights
3. - (1) The conditions are that—
(a) the firm has received authorisation ("home state authorisation") under the law of its home state to carry on the regulated activity in question ("the permitted activity");
(b) the relevant provisions of the law of the firm's home state—
(i) afford equivalent protection; or
(ii) satisfy the conditions laid down by a Community instrument for the co-ordination or approximation of laws, regulations or administrative provisions of member States relating to the carrying on of that activity; and
(c) the firm has no EEA right to carry on that activity in the manner in which it is seeking to carry it on.
(2) A firm is not to be regarded as having home state authorisation unless its home state regulator has so informed the Authority in writing.
(3) Provisions afford equivalent protection if, in relation to the firm's carrying on of the permitted activity, they afford consumers protection which is at least equivalent to that afforded by or under this Act in relation to that activity.
(4) A certificate issued by the Treasury that the provisions of the law of a particular EEA State afford equivalent protection in relation to the activities specified in the certificate is conclusive evidence of that fact.

---

696 Inserted by SI 2003/1473, reg 7; came into force 14 January 2005.

Permission

4. - (1) On qualifying for authorisation under this Schedule, a Treaty firm has permission to carry on each permitted activity through its United Kingdom branch or by providing services in the United Kingdom.

(2) The permission is to be treated as being on terms equivalent to those to which the firm's home state authorisation is subject.

(3) If, on qualifying for authorisation under this Schedule, a firm has a Part IV permission which includes permission to carry on a permitted activity, the Authority must give a direction cancelling the permission so far as it relates to that activity.

(4) The Authority need not give a direction under sub-paragraph (3) if it considers that there are good reasons for not doing so.

Notice to Authority

5. - (1) Sub-paragraph (2) applies to a Treaty firm which—

   (a) qualifies for authorisation under this Schedule, but
   (b) is not carrying on in the United Kingdom the regulated activity, or any of the regulated activities, which it has permission to carry on there.

(2) At least seven days before it begins to carry on such a regulated activity, the firm must give the Authority written notice of its intention to do so.

(3) If a Treaty firm to which sub-paragraph (2) applies has given notice under that sub-paragraph, it need not give such a notice if it again becomes a firm to which that sub-paragraph applies.

(4) Subsections (1), (3) and (6) of section 51 apply to a notice under sub-paragraph (2) as they apply to an application for a Part IV permission.

Offences

6. - (1) A person who contravenes paragraph 5(2) is guilty of an offence.

(2) In proceedings against a person for an offence under sub-paragraph (1) it is a defence for him to show that he took all reasonable precautions and exercised all due diligence to avoid committing the offence.

(3) A person is guilty of an offence if in, or in connection with, a notice given by him under paragraph 5(2) he—

   (a) provides information which he knows to be false or misleading in a material particular; or
   (b) recklessly provides information which is false or misleading in a material particular.

(4) A person guilty of an offence under this paragraph is liable—

   (a) on summary conviction, to a fine not exceeding the statutory maximum;
   (b) on conviction on indictment, to a fine.

SCHEDULE 5
PERSONS CONCERNED IN COLLECTIVE INVESTMENT SCHEMES
Section 36

Authorisation

1. - (1) A person who for the time being is an operator, trustee or depositary of a recognised collective investment scheme is an authorised person.

(2) "Recognised" means recognised by virtue of section 264.

(3) An authorised open-ended investment company is an authorised person.

[(4) A body—

   (a) incorporated by virtue of regulations made under section 1 of the Open-Ended Investment Companies Act (Northern Ireland) 2002 in respect of which an authorisation order is in force, and

(b) to which the UCITS directive applies,

is an authorised person.

(5) "Authorisation order" means an order made under (or having effect as made under) any provision of those regulations which is made by virtue of section 1(2)(1) of that Act (provision corresponding to Chapter 3 of Part 17 of the Act).][697]

Permission

2. - (1) A person authorised as a result of paragraph 1(1) has permission to carry on, so far as it is a regulated activity—

(a) any activity, appropriate to the capacity in which he acts in relation to the scheme, of the kind described in paragraph 8 of Schedule 2;

(b) any activity in connection with, or for the purposes of, the scheme.

(2) A person authorised as a result of paragraph 1(3) [or (4)][698] has permission to carry on, so far as it is a regulated activity—

(a) the operation of the scheme;

(b) any activity in connection with, or for the purposes of, the operation of the scheme.

SCHEDULE 6
THRESHOLD CONDITIONS   Section 41

PART I
PART IV PERMISSION

Legal status

1. - (1) If the regulated activity concerned is the effecting or carrying out of contracts of insurance the authorised person must be a body corporate [(other than a limited liability partnership)],[699] a registered friendly society or a member of Lloyd's.

(2) If the person concerned appears to the Authority to be seeking to carry on, or to be carrying on, a regulated activity constituting accepting deposits [or issuing electronic money],[700] it must be—

(a) a body corporate; or

(b) a partnership.

Location of offices

2. - (1) [Subject to [sub-paragraphs (2A) and (3)],[701]][702] if the person concerned is a body corporate constituted under the law of any part of the United Kingdom—

(a) its head office, and

(b) if it has a registered office, that office,

must be in the United Kingdom.

(2) If the person concerned has its head office in the United Kingdom but is not a body corporate, it must carry on business in the United Kingdom.

---

[697] Inserted by SI 2003/2066, reg 10(a); came into force 13 February 2004.

[698] Inserted by SI 2003/2066, reg 10(b); came into force 13 February 2004.

[699] Inserted by SI 2001/2507, art 2; came into force 3 September 2001.

[700] Inserted by SI 2002/682, art 8; came into force 27 April 2002

[701] Substituted by SI 2007/126, reg 3(5), Sch 5, paras 1, 24(a); came into force (for certain purposes) 1 April 2007; came into force (for remaining purposes) 1 November 2007.

[702] Inserted by SI 2003/1476, art 19(a); came into force (in relation to contracts of long-term care insurance): 31 October 2004; came into force (for remaining purposes) 14 January 2005.

[(2A) If—
(a) the regulated activity concerned is any of the investment services and activities, and
(b) the person concerned is a body corporate with no registered office,
sub-paragraph (2B) applies in place of sub-paragraph (1).
(2B) If the person concerned has its head office in the United Kingdom, it must carry on business in the United Kingdom.][703]
[(3) If the regulated activity concerned is an insurance mediation activity, sub-paragraph (1) does not apply.
(4) If the regulated activity concerned is an insurance mediation activity, the person concerned—
(a) if he is a body corporate constituted under the law of any part of the United Kingdom, must have its registered office, or if it has no registered office, its head office, in the United Kingdom;
(b) if he is a natural person, is to be treated for the purposes of sub-paragraph (2), as having his head office in the United Kingdom if his residence is situated there.
(5) "Insurance mediation activity" means any of the following activities—
(a) dealing in rights under a contract of insurance as agent;
(b) arranging deals in rights under a contract of insurance;
(c) assisting in the administration and performance of a contract of insurance;
(d) advising on buying or selling rights under a contract of insurance;
(e) agreeing to do any of the activities specified in sub-paragraph (a) to (d).
(6) Paragraph (5) must be read with—
(a) section 22;
(b) any relevant order under that section; and
(c) Schedule 2.][704]

[Appointment of claims representatives
2A. - (1) If it appears to the Authority that—
(a) the regulated activity that the person concerned is carrying on, or is seeking to carry on, is the effecting or carrying out of contracts of insurance, and
(b) contracts of insurance against damage arising out of or in connection with the use of motor vehicles on land (other than carrier's liability) are being, or will be, effected or carried out by the person concerned,
that person must have a claims representative in each EEA State other than the United Kingdom.
(2) For the purposes of sub-paragraph (1)(b), contracts of reinsurance are to be disregarded.
(3) A claims representative is a person with responsibility for handling and settling claims arising from accidents of the kind mentioned in Article 1(2) of the fourth motor insurance directive.
(4) In this paragraph "fourth motor insurance directive" means Directive 2000/26/EC of the European Parliament and of the Council of 16th May 2000 on the approximation of the laws of the Member States relating to insurance against civil liability in respect of the use of motor vehicles and amending Council Directives 73/239/EEC and 88/357/EEC.][705]

---

[703] Inserted by SI 2007/126, reg 3(5), Sch 5, paras 1, 24(b); came into force (for certain purposes) 1 April 2007; came into force (for remaining purposes) 1 November 2007.
[704] Inserted by SI 2003/1476, art 19(b); came into force (in relation to contracts of long-term care insurance) 31 October 2004; came into force (for remaining purposes) 14 January 2005.
[705] Inserted by SI 2002/2707, art 2; came into force 19 January 2003.

Close links

3. - (1) If the person concerned ("A") has close links with another person ("CL") the Authority must be satisfied—

    (a) that those links are not likely to prevent the Authority's effective supervision of A; and

    (b) if it appears to the Authority that CL is subject to the laws, regulations or administrative provisions of a territory which is not an EEA State ("the foreign provisions"), that neither the foreign provisions, nor any deficiency in their enforcement, would prevent the Authority's effective supervision of A.

(2) A has close links with CL if—

    (a) CL is a parent undertaking of A;

    (b) CL is a subsidiary undertaking of A;

    (c) CL is a parent undertaking of a subsidiary undertaking of A;

    (d) CL is a subsidiary undertaking of a parent undertaking of A;

    (e) CL owns or controls 20% or more of the voting rights or capital of A; or

    (f) A owns or controls 20% or more of the voting rights or capital of CL.

(3) "Subsidiary undertaking" includes all the instances mentioned in Article 1(1) and (2) of the Seventh Company Law Directive in which an entity may be a subsidiary of an undertaking.

Adequate resources

4. - (1) The resources of the person concerned must, in the opinion of the Authority, be adequate in relation to the regulated activities that he seeks to carry on, or carries on.

(2) In reaching that opinion, the Authority may—

    (a) take into account the person's membership of a group and any effect which that membership may have; and

    (b) have regard to—

        (i) the provision he makes and, if he is a member of a group, which other members of the group make in respect of liabilities (including contingent and future liabilities); and

        (ii) the means by which he manages and, if he is a member of a group, which other members of the group manage the incidence of risk in connection with his business.

Suitability

5. - The person concerned must satisfy the Authority that he is a fit and proper person having regard to all the circumstances, including—

    (a) his connection with any person;

    (b) the nature of any regulated activity that he carries on or seeks to carry on; and

    (c) the need to ensure that his affairs are conducted soundly and prudently.

PART II
AUTHORISATION

Authorisation under Schedule 3

6. - In relation to an EEA firm qualifying for authorisation under Schedule 3, the conditions set out in paragraphs 1 and 3 to 5 apply, so far as relevant, to—

    (a) an application for permission under Part IV;

    (b) exercise of the Authority's own-initiative power under section 45 in relation to a Part IV permission.

Authorisation under Schedule 4

7. - In relation to a person who qualifies for authorisation under Schedule 4, the conditions set out in paragraphs 1 and 3 to 5 apply, so far as relevant, to—

(a) an application for an additional permission;

(b) the exercise of the Authority's own-initiative power under section 45 in relation to additional permission.

PART III
ADDITIONAL CONDITIONS

8. - (1) If this paragraph applies to the person concerned, he must, for the purposes of such provisions of this Act as may be specified, satisfy specified additional conditions.

(2) This paragraph applies to a person who—

(a) has his head office outside the EEA; and

(b) appears to the Authority to be seeking to carry on a regulated activity relating to insurance business.

(3) "Specified" means specified in, or in accordance with, an order made by the Treasury.

9. - The Treasury may by order—

(a) vary or remove any of the conditions set out in Parts I and II;

(b) add to those conditions.

SCHEDULE 7
THE AUTHORITY AS COMPETENT
AUTHORITY FOR PART VI   Section 72(2)

General

1. - This Act applies in relation to the Authority when it is exercising functions under Part VI as the competent authority subject to the following modifications.

The Authority's general functions

2. - In section 2—

(a) subsection (4)(a) does not apply to [Part 6 rules];[706]

(b) subsection (4)(c) does not apply to general guidance given in relation to Part VI; and

(c) subsection (4)(d) does not apply to functions under Part VI.

Duty to consult

3. - Section 8 does not apply.

Rules

4. - (1) Sections 149, 153, 154 and 156 do not apply.

(2) Section 155 has effect as if—

(a) the reference in subsection (2)(c) to the general duties of the Authority under section 2 were a reference to its duty under section 73; and

(b) section 99 were included in the provisions referred to in subsection (9).

---

[706] Substituted by SI 2005/381, reg 4, Sch 1, para 12; came into force 1 July 2005.

Statements of policy

5. - (1) Paragraph 5 of Schedule 1 has effect as if the requirement to act through the Authority's governing body applied also to the exercise of its functions of publishing statements under section 93.

(2) Paragraph 1 of Schedule 1 has effect as if section 93 were included in the provisions referred to in sub-paragraph (2)(d).

Penalties

6. - Paragraph 16 of Schedule 1 does not apply in relation to penalties under Part VI (for which separate provision is made by section 100).

Fees

7. - Paragraph 17 of Schedule 1 does not apply in relation to fees payable under Part VI (for which separate provision is made by section 99).

Exemption from liability in damages

8. - Schedule 1 has effect as if—
  (a) sub-paragraph (1) of paragraph 19 were omitted (similar provision being made in relation to the competent authority by section 102); and
  (b) for the words from the beginning to "(a)" in sub-paragraph (3) of that paragraph, there were substituted "Sub-paragraph (2) does not apply".

SCHEDULE 8
TRANSFER OF FUNCTIONS UNDER PART VI   Section 72(3)

The power to transfer

1. - (1) The Treasury may by order provide for any function conferred on the competent authority which is exercisable for the time being by a particular person to be transferred so as to be exercisable by another person.

(2) An order may be made under this paragraph only if—
  (a) the person from whom the relevant functions are to be transferred has agreed in writing that the order should be made;
  (b) the Treasury are satisfied that the manner in which, or efficiency with which, the functions are discharged would be significantly improved if they were transferred to the transferee; or
  (c) the Treasury are satisfied that it is otherwise in the public interest that the order should be made.

Supplemental

2. - (1) An order under this Schedule does not affect anything previously done by any person ("the previous authority") in the exercise of functions which are transferred by the order to another person ("the new authority").

(2) Such an order may, in particular, include provision—
  (a) modifying or excluding any provision of Part VI, IX or XXVI in its application to any such functions;
  (b) for reviews similar to that made, in relation to the Authority, by section 12;
  (c) imposing on the new authority requirements similar to those imposed, in relation to the Authority, by sections 152, 155 and 354;
  (d) as to the giving of guidance by the new authority;
  (e) for the delegation by the new authority of the exercise of functions under Part VI and as to the consequences of delegation;

   (f) for the transfer of any property, rights or liabilities relating to any such functions from the previous authority to the new authority;

   (g) for the carrying on and completion by the new authority of anything in the process of being done by the previous authority when the order takes effect;

   (h) for the substitution of the new authority for the previous authority in any instrument, contract or legal proceedings;

   (i) for the transfer of persons employed by the previous authority to the new authority and as to the terms on which they are to transfer;

   (j) making such amendments to any primary or subordinate legislation (including any provision of, or made under, this Act) as the Treasury consider appropriate in consequence of the transfer of functions effected by the order.

(3) Nothing in this paragraph is to be taken as restricting the powers conferred by section 428.

3. - If the Treasury have made an order under paragraph 1 ("the transfer order") they may, by a separate order made under this paragraph, make any provision of a kind that could have been included in the transfer order.

SCHEDULE 9

. . .

. . .[707]

SCHEDULE 10
COMPENSATION: EXEMPTIONS   Section 90(2) and (5)

Statements believed to be true

1. - (1) In this paragraph "statement" means—

   (a) any untrue or misleading statement in listing particulars; or

   (b) the omission from listing particulars of any matter required to be included by section 80 or 81.

(2) A person does not incur any liability under section 90(1) for loss caused by a statement if he satisfies the court that, at the time when the listing particulars were submitted to the competent authority, he reasonably believed (having made such enquiries, if any, as were reasonable) that—

   (a) the statement was true and not misleading, or

   (b) the matter whose omission caused the loss was properly omitted,

and that one or more of the conditions set out in sub-paragraph (3) are satisfied.

(3) The conditions are that—

   (a) he continued in his belief until the time when the securities in question were acquired;

   (b) they were acquired before it was reasonably practicable to bring a correction to the attention of persons likely to acquire them;

   (c) before the securities were acquired, he had taken all such steps as it was reasonable for him to have taken to secure that a correction was brought to the attention of those persons;

   (d) he continued in his belief until after the commencement of dealings in the securities following their admission to the official list and they were acquired after such a lapse of time that he ought in the circumstances to be reasonably excused.

---

[707] Repealed by SI 2005/1433, reg 2(1), Sch 1, para 16; came into force 1 July 2005.

Statements by experts

2. - (1) In this paragraph "statement" means a statement included in listing particulars which—

(a) purports to be made by, or on the authority of, another person as an expert; and

(b) is stated to be included in the listing particulars with that other person's consent.

(2) A person does not incur any liability under section 90(1) for loss in respect of any securities caused by a statement if he satisfies the court that, at the time when the listing particulars were submitted to the competent authority, he reasonably believed that the other person—

(a) was competent to make or authorise the statement, and

(b) had consented to its inclusion in the form and context in which it was included,

and that one or more of the conditions set out in sub-paragraph (3) are satisfied.

(3) The conditions are that—

(a) he continued in his belief until the time when the securities were acquired;

(b) they were acquired before it was reasonably practicable to bring the fact that the expert was not competent, or had not consented, to the attention of persons likely to acquire the securities in question;

(c) before the securities were acquired he had taken all such steps as it was reasonable for him to have taken to secure that that fact was brought to the attention of those persons;

(d) he continued in his belief until after the commencement of dealings in the securities following their admission to the official list and they were acquired after such a lapse of time that he ought in the circumstances to be reasonably excused.

Corrections of statements

3. - (1) In this paragraph "statement" has the same meaning as in paragraph 1.

(2) A person does not incur liability under section 90(1) for loss caused by a statement if he satisfies the court—

(a) that before the securities in question were acquired, a correction had been published in a manner calculated to bring it to the attention of persons likely to acquire the securities; or

(b) that he took all such steps as it was reasonable for him to take to secure such publication and reasonably believed that it had taken place before the securities were acquired.

(3) Nothing in this paragraph is to be taken as affecting paragraph 1.

Corrections of statements by experts

4. - (1) In this paragraph "statement" has the same meaning as in paragraph 2.

(2) A person does not incur liability under section 90(1) for loss caused by a statement if he satisfies the court—

(a) that before the securities in question were acquired, the fact that the expert was not competent or had not consented had been published in a manner calculated to bring it to the attention of persons likely to acquire the securities; or

(b) that he took all such steps as it was reasonable for him to take to secure such publication and reasonably believed that it had taken place before the securities were acquired.

(3) Nothing in this paragraph is to be taken as affecting paragraph 2.

Official statements

5. - A person does not incur any liability under section 90(1) for loss resulting from—

(a) a statement made by an official person which is included in the listing particulars, or

(b) a statement contained in a public official document which is included in the listing particulars,

if he satisfies the court that the statement is accurately and fairly reproduced.

False or misleading information known about

6. - A person does not incur any liability under section 90(1) or (4) if he satisfies the court that the person suffering the loss acquired the securities in question with knowledge—

(a) that the statement was false or misleading,

(b) of the omitted matter, or

(c) of the change or new matter,

as the case may be.

Belief that supplementary listing particulars not called for

7. - A person does not incur any liability under section 90(4) if he satisfies the court that he reasonably believed that the change or new matter in question was not such as to call for supplementary listing particulars.

Meaning of "expert"

8. - "Expert" includes any engineer, valuer, accountant or other person whose profession, qualifications or experience give authority to a statement made by him.

SCHEDULE 11
. . .[708]

. . .[709]

. . .[710]

[SCHEDULE 11A
TRANSFERABLE SECURITIES][711]   [Section 85(5)(a)][712]

[PART 1][713]

[1. - Units (within the meaning in section 237(2)) in an open-ended collective investment scheme.

2. - Non-equity transferable securities issued by

(a) the government of an EEA State;

(b) a local or regional authority of an EEA State;

(c) a public international body of which an EEA State is a member;

(d) the European Central Bank;

(e) the central bank of an EEA State.

3. - Shares in the share capital of the central bank of an EEA State.

4. - Transferable securities unconditionally and irrevocably guaranteed by the government, or a local or regional authority, of an EEA State.

5. - (1) Non-equity transferable securities, issued in a continuous or repeated manner by a credit institution, which satisfy the conditions in sub-paragraph (2).

(2) The conditions are that the transferable securities—

(a) are not subordinated, convertible or exchangeable;

---

[708] Repealed by SI 2005/1433, reg 2(1), Sch 1, para 16; came into force 1 July 2005.

[709] Repealed by SI 2005/1433, reg 2(1), Sch 1, para 16; came into force 1 July 2005.

[710] Repealed by SI 2005/1433, reg 2(1), Sch 1, para 16; came into force 1 July 2005.

[711] Inserted by SI 2005/1433, reg 2(2), Sch 2; came into force 1 July 2005.

[712] Inserted by SI 2005/1433, reg 2(2), Sch 2; came into force 1 July 2005.

[713] Inserted by SI 2005/1433, reg 2(2), Sch 2; came into force 1 July 2005.

(b) do not give a right to subscribe to or acquire other types of securities and are not linked to a derivative instrument;

(c) materialise reception of repayable deposits; and

(d) are covered by a deposit guarantee under directive 94/19/EC of the European Parliament and of the Council on deposit-guarantee schemes.

6. - Non-fungible shares of capital—

(a) the main purpose of which is to provide the holder with a right to occupy any immoveable property, and

(b) which cannot be sold without that right being given up.][714]

[PART 2][715]

[7. - (1) Transferable securities issued by a body specified in sub-paragraph (2) if, and only if, the proceeds of the offer of the transferable securities to the public will be used solely for the purposes of the issuer's objectives.

(2) The bodies are

(a) a charity within the meaning of—

(i) section 96(1) of the Charities Act 1993 (c 10), or

(ii) section 35 of the Charities Act (Northern Ireland) 1964 (c 33 (NI));

[(b) a body entered in the Scottish Charity Register;][716]

(c) a housing association within the meaning of—

(i) section 5(1) of the Housing Act 1985 (c 68),

(ii) section 1 of the Housing Associations Act 1985 (c 69), or

(iii) Article 3 of the Housing (Northern Ireland) Order 1992 (SI 1992/1725 (NI 15));

(d) an industrial and provident society registered in accordance with—

(i) section 1(2)(b) of the Industrial and Provident Societies Act 1965 (c 12), or

(ii) section 1(2)(b) of the Industrial and Provident Societies Act (Northern Ireland) 1969 (c 24 (NI));

(e) a non-profit making association or body recognised by an EEA State with objectives similar to those of a body falling within any of sub-paragraphs (a) to (d).

8. - (1) Non-equity transferable securities, issued in a continuous or repeated manner by a credit institution, which satisfy the conditions in sub-paragraph (2).

(2) The conditions are—

(a) that the total consideration of the offer is less than 50,000,000 euros (or an equivalent amount); and

(b) those mentioned in paragraph 5(2)(a) and (b).

(3) In determining whether sub-paragraph (2)(a) is satisfied in relation to an offer ("offer A"), offer A is to be taken together with any other offer of transferable securities of the same class made by the same person which—

(a) was open at any time within the period of 12 months ending with the date on which offer A is first made; and

(b) had previously satisfied sub-paragraph (2)(a).

(4) For the purposes of this paragraph, an amount (in relation to an amount denominated in euros) is an "equivalent amount" if it is an amount of equal value denominated wholly or partly in another currency or unit of account.

---

[714] Inserted by SI 2005/1433, reg 2(2), Sch 2; came into force 1 July 2005.
[715] Inserted by SI 2005/1433, reg 2(2), Sch 2; came into force 1 July 2005.
[716] Substituted by SI 2006/242, art 5, Schedule, Pt 1, para 7; came into force 1 April 2006.

(5) The equivalent is to be calculated at the latest practicable date before (but in any event not more than 3 working days before) the date on which the offer is first made.

(6) "Credit institution" means a credit institution as defined in [Article 4(1)(a)][717] of the banking consolidation directive.

9. - (1) Transferable securities included in an offer where the total consideration of the offer is less than 2,500,000 euros (or an equivalent amount).

(2) Sub-paragraphs (3) to (5) of paragraph 8 apply for the purposes of this paragraph but with the references in sub-paragraph (3) to "sub-paragraph (2)(a)" being read as references to "paragraph 9(1)".][718]

SCHEDULE 12
TRANSFER SCHEMES:
CERTIFICATES   Sections 111(2) and 115

PART I
INSURANCE BUSINESS TRANSFER SCHEMES

1. - (1) For the purposes of section 111(2) the appropriate certificates, in relation to an insurance business transfer scheme, are—

(a) a certificate under paragraph 2;

(b) if sub-paragraph (2) applies, a certificate under paragraph 3;

(c) if sub-paragraph (3) applies, a certificate under paragraph 4;

(d) if sub-paragraph (4) applies, a certificate under paragraph 5;

[(e) if sub-paragraph (5) applies, the certificates under paragraph 5A].[719]

(2) This sub-paragraph applies if—

(a) the authorised person concerned is a UK authorised person which has received authorisation under [Article 4 of the life assurance consolidation directive or Article 6][720] of the first non-life insurance directive from the Authority; and

(b) the establishment from which the business is to be transferred under the proposed insurance business transfer scheme is in an EEA State other than the United Kingdom.

(3) This sub-paragraph applies if—

(a) the authorised person concerned has received authorisation under [Article 4 [or Article 51][721] of the life assurance consolidation directive][722] from the Authority;

(b) the proposed transfer relates to business which consists of the effecting or carrying out of contracts of long-term insurance; and

(c) as regards any policy which is included in the proposed transfer and which evidences a contract of insurance (other than reinsurance), an EEA State other than the United Kingdom is the State of the commitment.

(4) This sub-paragraph applies if—

(a) the authorised person concerned has received authorisation under Article 6 [or Article 23][723] of the first non-life insurance directive from the Authority;

---

[717] Substituted by SI 2006/3221, reg 29(1), Sch 3, para 3; came into force 1 January 2007.

[718] Inserted by SI 2005/1433, reg 2(2), Sch 2; came into force 1 July 2005.

[719] Inserted by SI 2007/3253, reg 2(1), Sch 1, paras 1, 2(5)(a); came into force 10 December 2007.

[720] Substituted by SI 2004/3379, reg 6(1), (7)(a)(i); came into force 11 January 2005.

[721] Inserted by SI 2007/3253, reg 2(1), Sch 1, paras 1, 2(5)(b); came into force 10 December 2007.

[722] Substituted by SI 2004/3379, reg 6(1), (7)(a)(ii); came into force 11 January 2005.

[723] Inserted by SI 2007/3253, reg 2(1), Sch 1, paras 1, 2(5)(c); came into force 10 December 2007.

    (b) the business to which the proposed insurance business transfer scheme relates is business which consists of the effecting or carrying out of contracts of general insurance; and

    (c) as regards any policy which is included in the proposed transfer and which evidences a contract of insurance (other than reinsurance), the risk is situated in an EEA State other than the United Kingdom.

[(5) This sub-paragraph applies if—

    (a) the authorised person concerned has received authorisation under Article 23 of the first non-life insurance directive or Article 51 of the life assurance consolidation directive from the Authority; and

    (b) the proposed transfer is to a branch or agency, in an EEA State other than the United Kingdom, authorised under the same Article.][724]

Certificates as to margin of solvency

2. - (1) A certificate under this paragraph is to be given—

    (a) by the relevant authority; or

    (b) in a case in which there is no relevant authority, by the Authority.

(2) A certificate given under sub-paragraph (1)(a) is one certifying that, taking the proposed transfer into account—

    (a) the transferee possesses, or will possess before the scheme takes effect, the necessary margin of solvency; or

    (b) there is no necessary margin of solvency applicable to the transferee.

(3) A certificate under sub-paragraph (1)(b) is one certifying that the Authority has received from the authority which it considers to be the authority responsible for supervising persons who effect or carry out contracts of insurance in the place to which the business is to be transferred that, taking the proposed transfer into account—

    (a) the transferee possesses or will possess before the scheme takes effect the margin of solvency required under the law applicable in that place; or

    (b) there is no such margin of solvency applicable to the transferee .

(4) "Necessary margin of solvency" means the margin of solvency required in relation to the transferee, taking the proposed transfer into account, under the law which it is the responsibility of the relevant authority to apply.

(5) "Margin of solvency" means the excess of the value of the assets of the transferee over the amount of its liabilities.

(6) "Relevant authority" means—

    (a) if the transferee is an EEA firm falling within paragraph 5(d) [or (da)][725] of Schedule 3, its home state regulator;

    [(aa) if the transferee is a non-EEA branch, the competent authorities of the EEA State in which the transferee is situated or, where appropriate, the competent authorities of an EEA State which supervises the state of solvency of the entire business of the transferee's agencies and branches within the EEA in accordance with Article 26 of the first non-life insurance directive or Article 56 of the life assurance consolidation directive;][726]

    (b) if the transferee is a Swiss general insurer, the authority responsible in Switzerland for supervising persons who effect or carry out contracts of insurance;

    (c) if the transferee is an authorised person not falling within [paragraph (a), (aa)][727] or (b), the Authority.

---

[724] Inserted by SI 2007/3253, reg 2(1), Sch 1, paras 1, 2(5)(d); came into force 10 December 2007.

[725] Inserted by SI 2007/3253, reg 2(1), Sch 1, paras 1, 2(5)(e)(i); came into force 10 December 2007.

[726] Inserted by SI 2007/3253, reg 2(1), Sch 1, paras 1, 2(5)(e)(ii); came into force 10 December 2007.

[727] Substituted by SI 2007/3253, reg 2(1), Sch 1, paras 1, 2(5)(e)(iii); came into force 10 December 2007.

(7) In sub-paragraph (6), any reference to a transferee of a particular description includes a reference to a transferee who will be of that description if the proposed scheme takes effect.

[(7A) "Competent authorities" has the same meaning as in the insurance directives.][728]

(8) "Swiss general insurer" means a body—

    (a) whose head office is in Switzerland;

    (b) which has permission to carry on regulated activities consisting of the effecting and carrying out of contracts of general insurance; and

    (c) whose permission is not restricted to the effecting or carrying out of contracts of reinsurance.

[(9) "Non-EEA branch" means a branch or agency which has received authorisation under Article 23 of the first non-life insurance directive or Article 51 of the life assurance consolidation directive.][729]

Certificates as to consent

3. - A certificate under this paragraph is one given by the Authority and certifying that the host State regulator has been notified of the proposed scheme and that—

    (a) that regulator has responded to the notification; or

    (b) that it has not responded but the period of three months beginning with the notification has elapsed.

Certificates as to long-term business

4. - A certificate under this paragraph is one given by the Authority and certifying that the authority responsible for supervising persons who effect or carry out contracts of insurance in the State of the commitment has been notified of the proposed scheme and that—

    (a) that authority has consented to the proposed scheme; or

    (b) the period of three months beginning with the notification has elapsed and that authority has not refused its consent.

Certificates as to general business

5. - A certificate under this paragraph is one given by the Authority and certifying that the authority responsible for supervising persons who effect or carry out contracts of insurance in the EEA State in which the risk is situated has been notified of the proposed scheme and that—

    (a) that authority has consented to the proposed scheme; or

    (b) the period of three months beginning with the notification has elapsed and that authority has not refused its consent.

[Certificates as to legality and as to consent

5A. - (1) The certificates under this paragraph are to be given—

    (a) in the case of the certificate under sub-paragraph (2), by the Authority;

    (b) in the case of the certificate under sub-paragraph (3), by the relevant authority.

(2) A certificate given under this sub-paragraph is one certifying that the relevant authority has been notified of the proposed scheme and that—

    (a) the relevant authority has consented to the proposed scheme; or

    (b) the period of three months beginning with the notification has elapsed and that relevant authority has not refused its consent.

(3) A certificate given under this sub-paragraph is one certifying that the law of the EEA State in which the transferee is set up permits such a transfer.

---

[728] Inserted by SI 2007/3253, reg 2(1), Sch 1, paras 1, 2(5)(e)(iv); came into force 10 December 2007.

[729] Inserted by SI 2007/3253, reg 2(1), Sch 1, paras 1, 2(5)(e)(v); came into force 10 December 2007.

(4) "Relevant authority" means the competent authorities (within the meaning of the insurance directives) of the EEA State in which the transferee is set up.][730]

Interpretation of Part I

6. - (1) "State of the commitment", in relation to a commitment entered into at any date, means—
  (a) if the policyholder is an individual, the State in which he had his habitual residence at that date;
  (b) if the policyholder is not an individual, the State in which the establishment of the policyholder to which the commitment relates was situated at that date.
(2) "Commitment" means a commitment represented by contracts of insurance of a prescribed class.
(3) References to the EEA State in which a risk is situated are—
  (a) if the insurance relates to a building or to a building and its contents (so far as the contents are covered by the same policy), to the EEA State in which the building is situated;
  (b) if the insurance relates to a vehicle of any type, to the EEA State of registration;
  (c) in the case of policies of a duration of four months or less covering travel or holiday risks (whatever the class concerned), to the EEA State in which the policyholder took out the policy;
  (d) in a case not covered by paragraphs (a) to (c)—
    (i) if the policyholder is an individual, to the EEA State in which he has his habitual residence at the date when the contract is entered into; and
    (ii) otherwise, to the EEA State in which the establishment of the policyholder to which the policy relates is situated at that date.
[(4) If the insurance relates to a vehicle dispatched from one EEA State to another, in respect of the period of 30 days beginning with the day on which the purchaser accepts delivery a reference to the EEA State in which a risk is situated is a reference to the State of destination (and not, as provided by sub-paragraph (3)(b), to the State of registration).][731]

PART II
BANKING BUSINESS TRANSFER SCHEMES

7. - (1) For the purposes of section 111(2) the appropriate certificates, in relation to a banking business transfer scheme, are—
  (a) a certificate under paragraph 8; and
  (b) if sub-paragraph (2) applies, a certificate under paragraph 9.
(2) This sub-paragraph applies if the authorised person concerned or the transferee is an EEA firm falling within paragraph 5(b) of Schedule 3.

Certificates as to financial resources

8. - (1) A certificate under this paragraph is one given by the relevant authority and certifying that, taking the proposed transfer into account, the transferee possesses, or will possess before the scheme takes effect, adequate financial resources.
(2) "Relevant authority" means—
  (a) if the transferee is a person with a Part IV permission or with permission under Schedule 4, the Authority;

---

[730] Inserted by SI 2007/3253, reg 2(1), Sch 1, paras 1, 2(5)(f); came into force 10 December 2007.
[731] Inserted by SI 2007/2403, reg 2; came into force 5 September 2007.

(b) if the transferee is an EEA firm falling within paragraph 5(b) of Schedule 3, its home state regulator;

(c) if the transferee does not fall within paragraph (a) or (b), the authority responsible for the supervision of the transferee's business in the place in which the transferee has its head office.

(3) In sub-paragraph (2), any reference to a transferee of a particular description of person includes a reference to a transferee who will be of that description if the proposed banking business transfer scheme takes effect.

Certificates as to consent of home state regulator

9. - A certificate under this paragraph is one given by the Authority and certifying that the home State regulator of the authorised person concerned or of the transferee has been notified of the proposed scheme and that—

(a) the home State regulator has responded to the notification; or

(b) the period of three months beginning with the notification has elapsed.

[PART 2A
RECLAIM FUND BUSINESS TRANSFER SCHEMES][732]

[Certificate as to financial resources

9A. - For the purposes of section 111(2) the appropriate certificate, in relation to a reclaim fund business transfer scheme, is a certificate given by the Authority certifying that, taking the proposed transfer into account, the transferee possesses, or will possess before the scheme takes effect, adequate financial resources.][733]

PART III
INSURANCE BUSINESS TRANSFERS EFFECTED OUTSIDE THE
UNITED KINGDOM

10. - (1) This paragraph applies to a proposal to execute under provisions corresponding to Part VII in a country or territory other than the United Kingdom an instrument transferring all the rights and obligations of the transferor under general or long-term insurance policies, or under such descriptions of such policies as may be specified in the instrument, to the transferee if any of the conditions in sub-paragraphs (2), (3) or (4) is met in relation to it.

(2) The transferor is an EEA firm falling within paragraph 5(d) [or (da)][734] of Schedule 3 and the transferee is an authorised person whose margin of solvency is supervised by the Authority.

(3) The transferor is a company authorised in an EEA State other than the United Kingdom under [Article 51 of the life assurance consolidation directive],[735] or Article 23 of the first non-life insurance directive and the transferee is a UK authorised person which has received authorisation under [Article 4 of the life assurance consolidation directive or Article 6 of the first non-life insurance directive].[736]

---

[732] Inserted by the Dormant Bank and Building Society Accounts Act 2008, s 15, Sch 2, para 5; came into force 12 March 2009.

[733] Inserted by the Dormant Bank and Building Society Accounts Act 2008, s 15, Sch 2, para 5; came into force 12 March 2009.

[734] Inserted by SI 2007/3253, reg 2(1), Sch 1, paras 1, 2(5)(g); came into force 10 December 2007.

[735] Substituted by SI 2004/3379, reg 6(1), (7)(b)(i); came into force 11 January 2005.

[736] Substituted by SI 2004/3379, reg 6(1), (7)(b)(ii); came into force 11 January 2005.

(4) The transferor is a Swiss general insurer and the transferee is a UK authorised person which has received authorisation under [Article 4 of the life assurance consolidation directive or Article 6 of the first non-life insurance directive].[737]

(5) In relation to a proposed transfer to which this paragraph applies, the Authority may, if it is satisfied that the transferee possesses the necessary margin of solvency, issue a certificate to that effect.

(6) "Necessary margin of solvency" means the margin of solvency which the transferee, taking the proposed transfer into account, is required by the Authority to maintain.

(7) "Swiss general insurer" has the same meaning as in paragraph 2.

(8) "General policy" means a policy evidencing a contract which, if it had been effected by the transferee, would have constituted the carrying on of a regulated activity consisting of the effecting of contracts of general insurance.

(9) "Long-term policy" means a policy evidencing a contract which, if it had been effected by the transferee, would have constituted the carrying on of a regulated activity consisting of the effecting of contracts of long-term insurance.

SCHEDULE 13
THE FINANCIAL SERVICES AND
MARKETS TRIBUNAL   Section 132(4)

PART I
GENERAL

Interpretation

1. - In this Schedule—
   "panel of chairmen" means the panel established under paragraph 3(1);
   "lay panel" means the panel established under paragraph 3(4);
   "rules" means rules made by the Lord Chancellor under section 132.

PART II
THE TRIBUNAL

President

2. - (1) The Lord Chancellor must appoint one of the members of the panel of chairmen to preside over the discharge of the Tribunal's functions.

(2) The member so appointed is to be known as the President of the Financial Services and Markets Tribunal (but is referred to in this Act as "the President").

(3) The Lord Chancellor may appoint one of the members of the panel of chairmen to be Deputy President.

(4) The Deputy President is to have such functions in relation to the Tribunal as the President may assign to him.

---

[737] Substituted by SI 2004/3379, reg 6(1), (7)(c); came into force 11 January 2005.

(5) The Lord Chancellor may not appoint a person to be the President or Deputy President unless that person—

[(a) satisfies the judicial-appointment eligibility condition on a 7-year basis;]738

(b) is an advocate or solicitor in Scotland of at least [7]739 years' standing; or

(c) is—

(i) a member of the Bar of Northern Ireland of at least [7]740 years' standing; or

(ii) a *solicitor of the Supreme Court of Northern Ireland* [solicitor of the Court of Judicature of Northern Ireland]741 of at least [7]742 years' standing.

(6) If the President (or Deputy President) ceases to be a member of the panel of chairmen, he also ceases to be the President (or Deputy President).

(7) The functions of the President may, if he is absent or is otherwise unable to act, be discharged—

(a) by the Deputy President; or

(b) if there is no Deputy President or he too is absent or otherwise unable to act, by a person appointed for that purpose from the panel of chairmen by the Lord Chancellor.

[(8) The Lord Chancellor may appoint a person under sub-paragraph (7)(b) only after consulting the following—

(a) the Lord Chief Justice of England and Wales;

(b) the Lord President of the Court of Session;

(c) the Lord Chief Justice of Northern Ireland.

(9) The Lord Chief Justice of England and Wales may nominate a judicial office holder (as defined in section 109(4) of the Constitutional Reform Act 2005) to exercise his functions under this paragraph.

(10) The Lord President of the Court of Session may nominate a judge of the Court of Session who is a member of the First or Second Division of the Inner House of that Court to exercise his functions under this paragraph.

(11) The Lord Chief Justice of Northern Ireland may nominate any of the following to exercise his functions under this paragraph—

(a) the holder of one of the offices listed in Schedule 1 to the Justice (Northern Ireland) Act 2002;

(b) a Lord Justice of Appeal (as defined in section 88 of that Act).]743

Panels

3. - (1) The Lord Chancellor must appoint a panel of persons for the purposes of serving as chairmen of the Tribunal.

(2) A person is qualified for membership of the panel of chairmen if—

[(a) he satisfies the judicial-appointment eligibility condition on a 5-year basis;]744

---

738 Substituted by the Tribunals, Courts and Enforcement Act 2007, s 50, Sch 10, Pt 1, para 34(1), (2)(a); came into force 21 July 2008.

739 Substituted by the Tribunals, Courts and Enforcement Act 2007, s 50, Sch 10, Pt 1, para 34(1), (2)(b); came into force 21 July 2008.

740 Substituted by the Tribunals, Courts and Enforcement Act 2007, s 50, Sch 10, Pt 1, para 34(1), (2)(b); came into force 21 July 2008.

741 Words in italics repealed and subsequent words in square brackets substituted by the Constitutional Reform Act 2005, s 59(5), Sch 11, Pt 3, para 5; date in force to be appointed: see the Constitutional Reform Act 2005, s 148(1).

742 Substituted by the Tribunals, Courts and Enforcement Act 2007, s 50, Sch 10, Pt 1, para 34(1), (2)(b); came into force 21 July 2008.

743 Inserted by the Constitutional Reform Act 2005, s 15(1), Sch 4, Pt 1, para 286(1), (2); came into force 3 April 2006.

744 Substituted by the Tribunals, Courts and Enforcement Act 2007, s 50, Sch 10, Pt 1, para 34(1), (3)(a); came into force 21 July 2008.

(b) he is an advocate or solicitor in Scotland of at least [5]⁷⁴⁵ years' standing; or

(c) he is—

    (i) a member of the Bar of Northern Ireland of at least [5]⁷⁴⁶ years' standing; or

    (ii) a *solicitor of the Supreme Court of Northern Ireland* [solicitor of the Court of Judicature of Northern Ireland]⁷⁴⁷ of at least [5]⁷⁴⁸ years' standing.

(3) The panel of chairmen must include at least one member who is a person of the kind mentioned in sub-paragraph (2)(b).

(4) The Lord Chancellor must also appoint a panel of persons who appear to him to be qualified by experience or otherwise to deal with matters of the kind that may be referred to the Tribunal.

Terms of office etc

4. - (1) Subject to the provisions of this Schedule, each member of the panel of chairmen and the lay panel is to hold and vacate office in accordance with the terms of his appointment.

(2) The Lord Chancellor may remove a member of either panel (including the President) on the ground of incapacity or misbehaviour.

[(2A) The Lord Chancellor may remove a person under sub-paragraph (2) only with the concurrence of the the the appropriate senior judge.

(2B) The appropriate senior judge is the Lord Chief Justice of England and Wales, unless—

    (a) the person to be removed exercises functions wholly or mainly in Scotland, in which case it is the Lord President of the Court of Session, or

    (b) the person to be removed exercises functions wholly or mainly in Northern Ireland, in which case it is the Lord Chief Justice of Northern Ireland.]⁷⁴⁹

(3) A member of either panel—

    (a) may at any time resign office by notice in writing to the Lord Chancellor;

    (b) is eligible for re-appointment if he ceases to hold office.

Remuneration and expenses

5. - The Lord Chancellor may pay to any person, in respect of his service—

    (a) as a member of the Tribunal (including service as the President or Deputy President), or

    (b) as a person appointed under paragraph 7(4),

such remuneration and allowances as he may determine.

Staff

6. - (1) The Lord Chancellor may appoint such staff for the Tribunal as he may determine.

(2) The remuneration of the Tribunal's staff is to be defrayed by the Lord Chancellor.

(3) Such expenses of the Tribunal as the Lord Chancellor may determine are to be defrayed by the Lord Chancellor.

---

⁷⁴⁵ Substituted by the Tribunals, Courts and Enforcement Act 2007, s 50, Sch 10, Pt 1, para 34(1), (3)(b); came into force 21 July 2008.

⁷⁴⁶ Substituted by the Tribunals, Courts and Enforcement Act 2007, s 50, Sch 10, Pt 1, para 34(1), (3)(b); came into force 21 July 2008.

⁷⁴⁷ Words in italics repealed and subsequent words in square brackets substituted by the Constitutional Reform Act 2005, s 59(5), Sch 11, Pt 3, para 5; date in force to be appointed: see the Constitutional Reform Act 2005, s 148(1).

⁷⁴⁸ Substituted by the Tribunals, Courts and Enforcement Act 2007, s 50, Sch 10, Pt 1, para 34(1), (3)(b); came into force 21 July 2008.

⁷⁴⁹ Inserted by the Constitutional Reform Act 2005, s 15(1), Sch 4, Pt 1, para 286(1), (3); came into force 3 April 2006.

PART III
CONSTITUTION OF TRIBUNAL

7. - (1) On a reference to the Tribunal, the persons to act as members of the Tribunal for the purposes of the reference are to be selected from the panel of chairmen or the lay panel in accordance with arrangements made by the President for the purposes of this paragraph ("the standing arrangements").

(2) The standing arrangements must provide for at least one member to be selected from the panel of chairmen.

(3) If while a reference is being dealt with, a person serving as member of the Tribunal in respect of the reference becomes unable to act, the reference may be dealt with by—

(a) the other members selected in respect of that reference; or

(b) if it is being dealt with by a single member, such other member of the panel of chairmen as may be selected in accordance with the standing arrangements for the purposes of the reference.

(4) If it appears to the Tribunal that a matter before it involves a question of fact of special difficulty, it may appoint one or more experts to provide assistance.

PART IV
TRIBUNAL PROCEDURE

8. - For the purpose of dealing with references, or any matter preliminary or incidental to a reference, the Tribunal must sit at such times and in such place or places as the Lord Chancellor may[, after consulting the President of the Financial Services and Markets Tribunal,][750] direct.

9. - Rules made by the Lord Chancellor under section 132 may, in particular, include provision—

(a) as to the manner in which references are to be instituted;

(b) for the holding of hearings in private in such circumstances as may be specified in the rules;

(c) as to the persons who may appear on behalf of the parties;

(d) for a member of the panel of chairmen to hear and determine interlocutory matters arising on a reference;

(e) for the suspension of decisions of the Authority which have taken effect;

(f) as to the withdrawal of references;

(g) as to the registration, publication and proof of decisions and orders.

Practice directions

10. - The President of the Tribunal may give directions as to the practice and procedure to be followed by the Tribunal in relation to references to it.

Evidence

11. - (1) The Tribunal may by summons require any person to attend, at such time and place as is specified in the summons, to give evidence or to produce any document in his custody or under his control which the Tribunal considers it necessary to examine.

(2) The Tribunal may—

(a) take evidence on oath and for that purpose administer oaths; or

---

[750] Inserted by the Constitutional Reform Act 2005, s 15(1), Sch 4, Pt 1, para 286(1), (4); came into force 3 April 2006.

(b) instead of administering an oath, require the person examined to make and subscribe a declaration of the truth of the matters in respect of which he is examined.

(3) A person who without reasonable excuse—
  (a) refuses or fails—
    (i) to attend following the issue of a summons by the Tribunal, or
    (ii) to give evidence, or
  (b) alters, suppresses, conceals or destroys, or refuses to produce a document which he may be required to produce for the purposes of proceedings before the Tribunal,
  is guilty of an offence.

(4) A person guilty of an offence under sub-paragraph (3)(a) is liable on summary conviction to a fine not exceeding the statutory maximum.

(5) A person guilty of an offence under sub-paragraph (3)(b) is liable—
  (a) on summary conviction, to a fine not exceeding the statutory maximum;
  (b) on conviction on indictment, to imprisonment for a term not exceeding two years or a fine or both.

Decisions of Tribunal

12. - (1) A decision of the Tribunal may be taken by a majority.

(2) The decision must—
  (a) state whether it was unanimous or taken by a majority;
  (b) be recorded in a document which—
    (i) contains a statement of the reasons for the decision; and
    (ii) is signed and dated by the member of the panel of chairmen dealing with the reference.

(3) The Tribunal must—
  (a) inform each party of its decision; and
  (b) as soon as reasonably practicable, send to each party and, if different, to any authorised person concerned, a copy of the document mentioned in sub-paragraph (2).

(4) The Tribunal must send the Treasury a copy of its decision.

Costs

13. - (1) If the Tribunal considers that a party to any proceedings on a reference has acted vexatiously, frivolously or unreasonably it may order that party to pay to another party to the proceedings the whole or part of the costs or expenses incurred by the other party in connection with the proceedings.

(2) If, in any proceedings on a reference, the Tribunal considers that a decision of the Authority which is the subject of the reference was unreasonable it may order the Authority to pay to another party to the proceedings the whole or part of the costs or expenses incurred by the other party in connection with the proceedings.

SCHEDULE 14
ROLE OF THE COMPETITION COMMISSION   Section 162

Provision of information by Treasury

1. - (1) The Treasury's powers under this paragraph are to be exercised only for the purpose of assisting the Commission in carrying out an investigation under section 162.

(2) The Treasury may give to the Commission—
  (a) any information in their possession which relates to matters falling within the scope of the investigation; and
  (b) other assistance in relation to any such matters.

(3) In carrying out an investigation under section 162, the Commission must have regard to any information given to it under this paragraph.

Consideration of matters arising on a report

2. - In considering any matter arising from a report made by the [OFT][751] under section 160, the Commission must have regard to—

(a) any representations made to [the Commission][752] in connection with the matter by any person appearing to the Commission to have a substantial interest in the matter; and

(b) any cost benefit analysis prepared by the Authority (at any time) in connection with the regulatory provision or practice, or any of the regulatory provisions or practices, which are the subject of the report.

[Investigations under section 162: application of Enterprise Act 2002

2A. - (1) The following sections of Part 3 of the Enterprise Act 2002 shall apply, with the modifications mentioned in sub-paragraphs (2) and (3), for the purposes of any investigation by the Commission under section 162 of this Act as they apply for the purposes of references under that Part—

(a) section 109 (attendance of witnesses and production of documents etc);

(b) section 110 (enforcement of powers under section 109: general);

(c) section 111 (penalties);

(d) section 112 (penalties: main procedural requirements);

(e) section 113 (payments and interest by instalments);

(f) section 114 (appeals in relation to penalties);

(g) section 115 (recovery of penalties); and

(h) section 116 (statement of policy).

(2) Section 110 shall, in its application by virtue of sub-paragraph (1), have effect as if—

(a) subsection (2) were omitted; and

(b) in subsection (9) the words from "or section" to "section 65(3))" were omitted.

(3) Section 111(5)(b) shall, in its application by virtue of sub-paragraph (1), have effect as if for sub-paragraph (ii) there were substituted—

"(ii) if earlier, the day on which the report of the Commission on the investigation concerned is made or, if the Commission decides not to make a report, the day on which the Commission makes the statement required by section 162(3) of the Financial Services and Markets Act 2000."

(4) Section 117 of the Enterprise Act 2002 (false or misleading information) shall apply in relation to functions of the Commission in connection with an investigation under section 162 of this Act as it applies in relation to its functions under Part 3 of that Act but as if, in subsections (1)(a) and (2), the words ["the OFT, OFCOM,"][753] and "or the Secretary of State" were omitted.

(5) Provisions of Part 3 of the Enterprise Act 2002 which have effect for the purposes of sections 109 to 117 of that Act (including, in particular, provisions relating to offences and the making of orders) shall, for the purposes of the application of those sections by virtue of sub-paragraph (1) or (4) above, have effect in relation to those sections as applied by virtue of those sub-paragraphs.

---

[751] Substituted by the Enterprise Act 2002, s 278(1), Sch 25, para 40(1), (20)(a); came into force 1 April 2003.

[752] Substituted by the Enterprise Act 2002, s 278(1), Sch 25, para 40(1), (20)(a); came into force 1 April 2003.

[753] Substituted by the Communications Act 2003, s 389(1), Sch 16, para 5; came into force 29 December 2003.

(6) Accordingly, corresponding provisions of this Act shall not have effect in relation to those sections as applied by virtue of those sub-paragraphs.

Section 162: modification of Schedule 7 to the Competition Act 1998

2B. - For the purposes of its application in relation to the function of the Commission of deciding in accordance with section 162(2) of this Act not to make a report, paragraph 15(7) of Schedule 7 to the Competition Act 1998 (power of the Chairman to act on his own while a group is being constituted) has effect as if, after paragraph (a), there were inserted

"; or

(aa) in the case of an investigation under section 162 of the Financial Services and Markets Act 2000, decide not to make a report in accordance with subsection (2) of that section (decision not to make a report where no useful purpose would be served).

Reports under section 162: further provision

2C. - (1) For the purposes of section 163 of this Act, a conclusion contained in a report of the Commission is to be disregarded if the conclusion is not that of at least two-thirds of the members of the group constituted in connection with the investigation concerned in pursuance of paragraph 15 of Schedule 7 to the Competition Act 1998.

(2) If a member of a group so constituted disagrees with any conclusions contained in a report made under section 162 of this Act as the conclusions of the Commission, the report shall, if the member so wishes, include a statement of his disagreement and of his reasons for disagreeing.

(3) For the purposes of the law relating to defamation, absolute privilege attaches to any report made by the Commission under section 162.][754]

. . .

3. - . . .[755]

Publication of reports

4. - (1) If the Commission makes a report under section 162, it must publish it in such a way as appears to it to be best calculated to bring it to the attention of the public.

(2) Before publishing the report the Commission must, so far as practicable, exclude any matter which relates to the private affairs of a particular individual the publication of which, in the opinion of the Commission, would or might seriously and prejudicially affect his interests.

(3) Before publishing the report the Commission must, so far as practicable, also exclude any matter which relates to the affairs of a particular body the publication of which, in the opinion of the Commission, would or might seriously and prejudicially affect its interests.

(4) Sub-paragraphs (2) and (3) do not apply in relation to copies of a report which the Commission is required to send under section 162(10).

---

[754] Inserted by the Enterprise Act 2002, s 278(1), Sch 25, para 40(1), (20)(b); came into force 20 June 2003.

[755] Repealed by the Enterprise Act 2002, s 278, Sch 25, para 40(1), (20)(c), Sch 26; came into force 20 June 2003.

SCHEDULE 15
INFORMATION AND INVESTIGATIONS:
CONNECTED PERSONS   Sections 165(11) and 171(4)

PART I
RULES FOR SPECIFIC BODIES

Corporate bodies

1.- If the authorised person ("BC") is a body corporate, a person who is or has been—
  (a) an officer or manager of BC or of a parent undertaking of BC;
  (b) an employee of BC;
  (c) an agent of BC or of a parent undertaking of BC.

Partnerships

2.- If the authorised person ("PP") is a partnership, a person who is or has been a member, manager, employee or agent of PP.

Unincorporated associations

3.- If the authorised person ("UA") is an unincorporated association of persons which is neither a partnership nor an unincorporated friendly society, a person who is or has been an officer, manager, employee or agent of UA.

Friendly societies

4.- (1) If the authorised person ("FS") is a friendly society, a person who is or has been an officer, manager or employee of FS.
(2) In relation to FS, "officer" and "manager" have the same meaning as in section 119(1) of the Friendly Societies Act 1992.

Building societies

5.- (1) If the authorised person ("BS") is a building society, a person who is or has been an officer or employee of BS.
(2) In relation to BS, "officer" has the same meaning as it has in section 119(1) of the Building Societies Act 1986.

Individuals

6.- If the authorised person ("IP") is an individual, a person who is or has been an employee or agent of IP.

Application to sections 171 and 172

7.- For the purposes of sections 171 and 172, if the person under investigation is not an authorised person the references in this Part of this Schedule to an authorised person are to be taken to be references to the person under investigation.

PART II
ADDITIONAL RULES

8.- A person who is, or at the relevant time was, the partner, manager, employee, agent, appointed representative, banker, auditor, actuary or solicitor of—
  (a) the person under investigation ("A");
  (b) a parent undertaking of A;

(c) a subsidiary undertaking of A;

(d) a subsidiary undertaking of a parent undertaking of A; or

(e) a parent undertaking of a subsidiary undertaking of A.

SCHEDULE 16

PROHIBITIONS AND RESTRICTIONS IMPOSED BY

[OFFICE OF FAIR TRADING][756]   Section 203(8)

Preliminary

1.- In this Schedule—

"appeal period" has the same meaning as in the Consumer Credit Act 1974;

"prohibition" means a consumer credit prohibition under section 203;

"restriction" means a restriction under section 204.

Notice of prohibition or restriction

2.- (1) This paragraph applies if the [OFT][757] proposes, in relation to a firm—

(a) to impose a prohibition;

(b) to impose a restriction; or

(c) to vary a restriction otherwise than with the agreement of the firm.

(2) The [OFT][758] must by notice—

(a) inform the firm of [its][759] proposal, stating [its][760] reasons; and

(b) invite the firm to submit representations in accordance with paragraph 4.

(3) If [the OFT][761] imposes the prohibition or restriction or varies the restriction, the [OFT][762] may give directions authorising the firm to carry into effect agreements made before the coming into force of the prohibition, restriction or variation.

(4) A prohibition, restriction or variation is not to come into force before the end of the appeal period.

(5) If the [OFT][763] imposes a prohibition or restriction or varies a restriction, [the OFT][764] must serve a copy of the prohibition, restriction or variation—

(a) on the Authority; and

(b) on the firm's home state regulator.

Application to revoke prohibition or restriction

3.- (1) This paragraph applies if the [OFT][765] proposes to refuse an application made by a firm for the revocation of a prohibition or restriction.

---

[756] Substituted by the Enterprise Act 2002, s 278(1), Sch 25, para 40(1), (21)(a); came into force 1 April 2003.

[757] Substituted by the Enterprise Act 2002, s 278(1), Sch 25, para 40(1), (21)(b); came into force 1 April 2003.

[758] Substituted by the Enterprise Act 2002, s 278(1), Sch 25, para 40(1), (21)(b); came into force 1 April 2003.

[759] Substituted by the Enterprise Act 2002, s 278(1), Sch 25, para 40(1), (21)(b); came into force 1 April 2003.

[760] Substituted by the Enterprise Act 2002, s 278(1), Sch 25, para 40(1), (21)(b); came into force 1 April 2003.

[761] Substituted by the Enterprise Act 2002, s 278(1), Sch 25, para 40(1), (21)(b); came into force 1 April 2003.

[762] Substituted by the Enterprise Act 2002, s 278(1), Sch 25, para 40(1), (21)(b); came into force 1 April 2003.

[763] Substituted by the Enterprise Act 2002, s 278(1), Sch 25, para 40(1), (21)(b); came into force 1 April 2003.

[764] Substituted by the Enterprise Act 2002, s 278(1), Sch 25, para 40(1), (21)(b); came into force 1 April 2003.

[765] Substituted by the Enterprise Act 2002, s 278(1), Sch 25, para 40(1), (21)(b); came into force 1 April 2003.

(2) The [OFT]⁷⁶⁶ must by notice—

    (a) inform the firm of the proposed refusal, stating [its]⁷⁶⁷ reasons; and

    (b) invite the firm to submit representations in accordance with paragraph 4.

Representations to [OFT]⁷⁶⁸

4.- (1) If this paragraph applies to an invitation to submit representations, the [OFT]⁷⁶⁹ must invite the firm, within 21 days after the notice containing the invitation is given to it or such longer period as [the OFT]⁷⁷⁰ may allow—

    (a) to submit its representations in writing to [the OFT];⁷⁷¹ and

    (b) to give notice to [the OFT],⁷⁷² if the firm thinks fit, that it wishes to make representations orally.

(2) If notice is given under sub-paragraph (1)(b), the [OFT]⁷⁷³ must arrange for the oral representations to be heard.

(3) The [OFT]⁷⁷⁴ must give the firm notice of [its]⁷⁷⁵ determination.

Appeals

5.- Section 41 of the Consumer Credit Act 1974 (appeals to the Secretary of State) has effect as if—

    (a) the following determinations were mentioned in column 1 of the table set out at the end of that section—

        (i) imposition of a prohibition or restriction or the variation of a restriction; and

        (ii) refusal of an application for the revocation of a prohibition or restriction; and

    (b) the firm concerned were mentioned in column 2 of that table in relation to those determinations.

SCHEDULE 17
THE OMBUDSMAN SCHEME
Section 225(4)

PART I
GENERAL

Interpretation

1.-In this Schedule—

"ombudsman" means a person who is a member of the panel; and

"the panel" means the panel established under paragraph 4.

---

⁷⁶⁶ Substituted by the Enterprise Act 2002, s 278(1), Sch 25, para 40(1), (21)(b); came into force 1 April 2003.
⁷⁶⁷ Substituted by the Enterprise Act 2002, s 278(1), Sch 25, para 40(1), (21)(b); came into force 1 April 2003.
⁷⁶⁸ Substituted by the Enterprise Act 2002, s 278(1), Sch 25, para 40(1), (21)(b); came into force 1 April 2003.
⁷⁶⁹ Substituted by the Enterprise Act 2002, s 278(1), Sch 25, para 40(1), (21)(b); came into force 1 April 2003.
⁷⁷⁰ Substituted by the Enterprise Act 2002, s 278(1), Sch 25, para 40(1), (21)(b); came into force 1 April 2003.
⁷⁷¹ Substituted by the Enterprise Act 2002, s 278(1), Sch 25, para 40(1), (21)(b); came into force 1 April 2003.
⁷⁷² Substituted by the Enterprise Act 2002, s 278(1), Sch 25, para 40(1), (21)(b); came into force 1 April 2003.
⁷⁷³ Substituted by the Enterprise Act 2002, s 278(1), Sch 25, para 40(1), (21)(b); came into force 1 April 2003.
⁷⁷⁴ Substituted by the Enterprise Act 2002, s 278(1), Sch 25, para 40(1), (21)(b); came into force 1 April 2003.
⁷⁷⁵ Substituted by the Enterprise Act 2002, s 278(1), Sch 25, para 40(1), (21)(b); came into force 1 April 2003.

PART II
THE SCHEME OPERATOR

Establishment by the Authority

2.-(1) The Authority must establish a body corporate to exercise the functions conferred on the scheme operator by or under this Act.

(2) The Authority must take such steps as are necessary to ensure that the scheme operator is, at all times, capable of exercising those functions.

Constitution

3.- (1) The constitution of the scheme operator must provide for it to have—

(a) a chairman; and

(b) a board (which must include the chairman) whose members are the scheme operator's directors.

(2) The chairman and other members of the board must be persons appointed, and liable to removal from office, by the Authority (acting, in the case of the chairman, with the approval of the Treasury).

(3) But the terms of their appointment (and in particular those governing removal from office) must be such as to secure their independence from the Authority in the operation of the scheme.

(4) The function of making voluntary jurisdiction rules under section 227[, the function of making consumer credit rules, the function of making determinations under section 234A(1)][776] and the functions conferred by paragraphs 4, 5, 7, 9 or 14 may be exercised only by the board.

(5) The validity of any act of the scheme operator is unaffected by—

(a) a vacancy in the office of chairman; or

(b) a defect in the appointment of a person as chairman or as a member of the board.

The panel of ombudsmen

4.- (1) The scheme operator must appoint and maintain a panel of persons, appearing to it to have appropriate qualifications and experience, to act as ombudsmen for the purposes of the scheme.

(2) A person's appointment to the panel is to be on such terms (including terms as to the duration and termination of his appointment and as to remuneration) as the scheme operator considers—

(a) consistent with the independence of the person appointed; and

(b) otherwise appropriate.

The Chief Ombudsman

5.- (1) The scheme operator must appoint one member of the panel to act as Chief Ombudsman.

(2) The Chief Ombudsman is to be appointed on such terms (including terms as to the duration and termination of his appointment) as the scheme operator considers appropriate.

Status

6.- (1) The scheme operator is not to be regarded as exercising functions on behalf of the Crown.

(2) The scheme operator's board members, officers and staff are not to be regarded as Crown servants.

---

[776] Inserted by the Consumer Credit Act 2006, s 61(10)(a); came into force 16 June 2006.

(3) Appointment as Chief Ombudsman or to the panel or as a deputy ombudsman does not confer the status of Crown servant.

Annual reports

7.- (1) At least once a year—
  (a) the scheme operator must make a report to the Authority on the discharge of its functions; and
  (b) the Chief Ombudsman must make a report to the Authority on the discharge of his functions.
(2) Each report must distinguish between functions in relation to the scheme's compulsory jurisdiction[, functions in relation to its consumer credit jurisdiction][777] and functions in relation to its voluntary jurisdiction.
(3) Each report must also comply with any requirements specified in rules made by the Authority.
(4) The scheme operator must publish each report in the way it considers appropriate.

Guidance

8.- The scheme operator may publish guidance consisting of such information and advice as it considers appropriate and may charge for it or distribute it free of charge.

Budget

9.- (1) The scheme operator must, before the start of each of its financial years, adopt an annual budget which has been approved by the Authority.
(2) The scheme operator may, with the approval of the Authority, vary the budget for a financial year at any time after its adoption.
(3) The annual budget must include an indication of—
  (a) the distribution of resources deployed in the operation of the scheme, and
  (b) the amounts of income of the scheme operator arising or expected to arise from the operation of the scheme,
distinguishing between the scheme's compulsory[, consumer credit][778] and voluntary jurisdiction.

Exemption from liability in damages

10.- (1) No person is to be liable in damages for anything done or omitted in the discharge, or purported discharge, of any functions under this Act in relation to the compulsory jurisdiction [or to the consumer credit jurisdiction].[779]
(2) Sub-paragraph (1) does not apply—
  (a) if the act or omission is shown to have been in bad faith; or
  (b) so as to prevent an award of damages made in respect of an act or omission on the ground that the act or omission was unlawful as a result of section 6(1) of the Human Rights Act 1998.

Privilege

11.- For the purposes of the law relating to defamation, proceedings in relation to a complaint which is subject to the compulsory jurisdiction [or to the consumer credit jurisdiction][780] are to be treated as if they were proceedings before a court.

---

[777] Inserted by the Consumer Credit Act 2006, s 61(10)(b); came into force 16 June 2006.
[778] Inserted by the Consumer Credit Act 2006, s 61(10)(c); came into force 16 June 2006.
[779] Inserted by the Consumer Credit Act 2006, s 61(10)(d); came into force 16 June 2006.
[780] Inserted by the Consumer Credit Act 2006, s 61(10)(d); came into force 16 June 2006.

PART III
THE COMPULSORY JURISDICTION

Introduction

12.- This Part of this Schedule applies only in relation to the compulsory jurisdiction.

Authority's procedural rules

13.- (1) The Authority must make rules providing that a complaint is not to be entertained unless the complainant has referred it under the ombudsman scheme before the applicable time limit (determined in accordance with the rules) has expired.

(2) The rules may provide that an ombudsman may extend that time limit in specified circumstances.

(3) The Authority may make rules providing that a complaint is not to be entertained (except in specified circumstances) if the complainant has not previously communicated its substance to the respondent and given him a reasonable opportunity to deal with it.

(4) The Authority may make rules requiring an authorised person[, or a payment service provider within the meaning of the Payment Services Regulations 2009,][781] who may become subject to the compulsory jurisdiction as a respondent to establish such procedures as the Authority considers appropriate for the resolution of complaints which—

(a) may be referred to the scheme; and

(b) arise out of activity to which the Authority's powers under Part X do not apply.

The scheme operator's rules

14.- (1) The scheme operator must make rules, to be known as "scheme rules", which are to set out the procedure for reference of complaints and for their investigation, consideration and determination by an ombudsman.

(2) Scheme rules may, among other things—

(a) specify matters which are to be taken into account in determining whether an act or omission was fair and reasonable;

(b) provide that a complaint may, in specified circumstances, be dismissed without consideration of its merits;

(c) provide for the reference of a complaint, in specified circumstances and with the consent of the complainant, to another body with a view to its being determined by that body instead of by an ombudsman;

(d) make provision as to the evidence which may be required or admitted, the extent to which it should be oral or written and the consequences of a person's failure to produce any information or document which he has been required (under section 231 or otherwise) to produce;

(e) allow an ombudsman to fix time limits for any aspect of the proceedings and to extend a time limit;

(f) provide for certain things in relation to the reference, investigation or consideration (but not determination) of a complaint to be done by a member of the scheme operator's staff instead of by an ombudsman;

(g) make different provision in relation to different kinds of complaint.

(3) The circumstances specified under sub-paragraph (2)(b) may include the following—

(a) the ombudsman considers the complaint frivolous or vexatious;

(b) legal proceedings have been brought concerning the subject-matter of the complaint and the ombudsman considers that the complaint is best dealt with in those proceedings; or

---

[781] Inserted by SI 2009/209, reg 126, Sch 6, Pt 1, para 1(2); came into force 2 March 2009.

(c) the ombudsman is satisfied that there are other compelling reasons why it is inappropriate for the complaint to be dealt with under the ombudsman scheme.

(4) If the scheme operator proposes to make any scheme rules it must publish a draft of the proposed rules in the way appearing to it to be best calculated to bring them to the attention of persons appearing to it to be likely to be affected.

(5) The draft must be accompanied by a statement that representations about the proposals may be made to the scheme operator within a time specified in the statement.

(6) Before making the proposed scheme rules, the scheme operator must have regard to any representations made to it under sub-paragraph (5).

(7) The consent of the Authority is required before any scheme rules may be made.

Fees

15.- (1) Scheme rules may require a respondent to pay to the scheme operator such fees as may be specified in the rules.

(2) The rules may, among other things—
    (a) provide for the scheme operator to reduce or waive a fee in a particular case;
    (b) set different fees for different stages of the proceedings on a complaint;
    (c) provide for fees to be refunded in specified circumstances;
    (d) make different provision for different kinds of complaint.

Enforcement of money awards

16.- A money award, including interest, which has been registered in accordance with scheme rules may—
    (a) if a county court so orders in England and Wales, be recovered *by execution issued from the county court* [under section 85 of the County Courts Act 1984][782] (or otherwise) as if it were payable under an order of that court;
    (b) be enforced in Northern Ireland as a money judgment under the Judgments Enforcement (Northern Ireland) Order 1981;
    (c) be enforced in Scotland by the sheriff, as if it were a judgment or order of the sheriff and whether or not the sheriff could himself have granted such judgment or order.

[PART 3A
THE CONSUMER CREDIT JURISDICTION][783]

[Introduction

16A.- This Part of this Schedule applies only in relation to the consumer credit jurisdiction.

Procedure for complaints etc

16B.- (1) Consumer credit rules—
    (a) must provide that a complaint is not to be entertained unless the complainant has referred it under the ombudsman scheme before the applicable time limit (determined in accordance with the rules) has expired;

---

[782] Words in italics repealed and words in square brackets substituted by the Tribunals, Courts and Enforcement Act 2007, s 62(3), Sch 13, para 134; date in force to be appointed: see the Tribunals, Courts and Enforcement Act 2007, s 148(5).

[783] Inserted by the Consumer Credit Act 2006, s 59(2), Sch 2; came into force 16 June 2006.

(b) may provide that an ombudsman may extend that time limit in specified circumstances;

(c) may provide that a complaint is not to be entertained (except in specified circumstances) if the complainant has not previously communicated its substance to the respondent and given him a reasonable opportunity to deal with it;

(d) may make provision about the procedure for the reference of complaints and for their investigation, consideration and determination by an ombudsman.

(2) Sub-paragraphs (2) and (3) of paragraph 14 apply in relation to consumer credit rules under sub-paragraph (1) of this paragraph as they apply in relation to scheme rules under that paragraph.

(3) Consumer credit rules may require persons falling within sub-paragraph (6) to establish such procedures as the scheme operator considers appropriate for the resolution of complaints which may be referred to the scheme.

(4) Consumer credit rules under sub-paragraph (3) may make different provision in relation to persons of different descriptions or to complaints of different descriptions.

(5) Consumer credit rules under sub-paragraph (3) may authorise the scheme operator to dispense with or modify the application of such rules in particular cases where the scheme operator—

(a) considers it appropriate to do so; and

(b) is satisfied that the specified conditions (if any) are met.

(6) A person falls within this sub-paragraph if he is licensed by a standard licence (within the meaning of the Consumer Credit Act 1974) to carry on to any extent a business of a type specified in an order under section 226A(2)(e) of this Act.

Fees

16C.- (1) Consumer credit rules may require a respondent to pay to the scheme operator such fees as may be specified in the rules.

(2) Sub-paragraph (2) of paragraph 15 applies in relation to consumer credit rules under this paragraph as it applies in relation to scheme rules under that paragraph.

Enforcement of money awards

16D.- A money award, including interest, which has been registered in accordance with consumer credit rules may—

(a) if a county court so orders in England and Wales, be recovered by execution issued from the county court (or otherwise) as if it were payable under an order of that court;

(b) be enforced in Northern Ireland as a money judgment under the Judgments Enforcement (Northern Ireland) Order 1981;

(c) be enforced in Scotland as if it were a decree of the sheriff and whether or not the sheriff could himself have granted such a decree.

Procedure for consumer credit rules

16E.- (1) If the scheme operator makes any consumer credit rules, it must give a copy of them to the Authority without delay.

(2) If the scheme operator revokes any such rules, it must give written notice to the Authority without delay.

(3) The power to make such rules is exercisable in writing.

(4) Immediately after the making of such rules, the scheme operator must arrange for them to be printed and made available to the public.

(5) The scheme operator may charge a reasonable fee for providing a person with a copy of any such rules.

Verification of consumer credit rules

16F.- (1) The production of a printed copy of consumer credit rules purporting to be made by the scheme operator—

(a) on which there is endorsed a certificate signed by a member of the scheme operator's staff authorised by the scheme operator for that purpose, and

(b) which contains the required statements,

is evidence (or in Scotland sufficient evidence) of the facts stated in the certificate.

(2) The required statements are—

(a) that the rules were made by the scheme operator;

(b) that the copy is a true copy of the rules; and

(c) that on a specified date the rules were made available to the public in accordance with paragraph 16E(4).

(3) A certificate purporting to be signed as mentioned in sub-paragraph (1) is to be taken to have been duly signed unless the contrary is shown.

Consultation

16G.- (1) If the scheme operator proposes to make consumer credit rules, it must publish a draft of the proposed rules in the way appearing to it to be best calculated to bring the draft to the attention of the public.

(2) The draft must be accompanied by—

(a) an explanation of the proposed rules; and

(b) a statement that representations about the proposals may be made to the scheme operator within a specified time.

(3) Before making any consumer credit rules, the scheme operator must have regard to any representations made to it in accordance with sub-paragraph (2)(b).

(4) If consumer credit rules made by the scheme operator differ from the draft published under sub-paragraph (1) in a way which the scheme operator considers significant, the scheme operator must publish a statement of the difference.][784]

PART IV
THE VOLUNTARY JURISDICTION

Introduction

17.- This Part of this Schedule applies only in relation to the voluntary jurisdiction.

Terms of reference to the scheme

18.- (1) Complaints are to be dealt with and determined under the voluntary jurisdiction on standard terms fixed by the scheme operator with the approval of the Authority.

(2) Different standard terms may be fixed with respect to different matters or in relation to different cases.

(3) The standard terms may, in particular—

(a) require the making of payments to the scheme operator by participants in the scheme of such amounts, and at such times, as may be determined by the scheme operator;

(b) make provision as to the award of costs on the determination of a complaint.

(4) The scheme operator may not vary any of the standard terms or add or remove terms without the approval of the Authority.

---

[784] Inserted by the Consumer Credit Act 2006, s 59(2), Sch 2; came into force 16 June 2006.

(5) The standard terms may include provision to the effect that (unless acting in bad faith) none of the following is to be liable in damages for anything done or omitted in the discharge or purported discharge of functions in connection with the voluntary jurisdiction—
- (a) the scheme operator;
- (b) any member of its governing body;
- (c) any member of its staff;
- (d) any person acting as an ombudsman for the purposes of the scheme.

Delegation by and to other schemes

19.- (1) The scheme operator may make arrangements with a relevant body—
- (a) for the exercise by that body of any part of the voluntary jurisdiction of the ombudsman scheme on behalf of the scheme; or
- (b) for the exercise by the scheme of any function of that body as if it were part of the voluntary jurisdiction of the scheme.

(2) A "relevant body" is one which the scheme operator is satisfied—
- (a) is responsible for the operation of a broadly comparable scheme (whether or not established by statute) for the resolution of disputes; and
- (b) in the case of arrangements under sub-paragraph (1)(a), will exercise the jurisdiction in question in a way compatible with the requirements imposed by or under this Act in relation to complaints of the kind concerned.

(3) Such arrangements require the approval of the Authority.

Voluntary jurisdiction rules: procedure

20.- (1) If the scheme operator makes voluntary jurisdiction rules, it must give a copy to the Authority without delay.

(2) If the scheme operator revokes any such rules, it must give written notice to the Authority without delay.

(3) The power to make voluntary jurisdiction rules is exercisable in writing.

(4) Immediately after making voluntary jurisdiction rules, the scheme operator must arrange for them to be printed and made available to the public.

(5) The scheme operator may charge a reasonable fee for providing a person with a copy of any voluntary jurisdiction rules.

Verification of the rules

21.- (1) The production of a printed copy of voluntary jurisdiction rules purporting to be made by the scheme operator—
- (a) on which is endorsed a certificate signed by a member of the scheme operator's staff authorised by the scheme operator for that purpose, and
- (b) which contains the required statements,

is evidence (or in Scotland sufficient evidence) of the facts stated in the certificate.

(2) The required statements are—
- (a) that the rules were made by the scheme operator;
- (b) that the copy is a true copy of the rules; and
- (c) that on a specified date the rules were made available to the public in accordance with paragraph 20(4).

(3) A certificate purporting to be signed as mentioned in sub-paragraph (1) is to be taken to have been duly signed unless the contrary is shown.

Consultation

22.- (1) If the scheme operator proposes to make voluntary jurisdiction rules, it must publish a draft of the proposed rules in the way appearing to it to be best calculated to bring them to the attention of the public.

(2) The draft must be accompanied by—
    (a) an explanation of the proposed rules; and
    (b) a statement that representations about the proposals may be made to the scheme operator within a specified time.
(3) Before making any voluntary jurisdiction rules, the scheme operator must have regard to any representations made to it in accordance with sub-paragraph (2)(b).
(4) If voluntary jurisdiction rules made by the scheme operator differ from the draft published under sub-paragraph (1) in a way which the scheme operator considers significant, the scheme operator must publish a statement of the difference.

SCHEDULE 18
MUTUALS
Sections 334, 336 and 338

PART I
FRIENDLY SOCIETIES

The Friendly Societies Act 1974 (c 46)

1.- Omit sections 4 (provision for separate registration areas) and 10 (societies registered in one registration area carrying on business in another).
2.- In section 7 (societies which may be registered), in subsection (2)(b), for "in the central registration area or in Scotland" substitute "in the United Kingdom, the Channel Islands or the Isle of Man".
3.- In section 11 (additional registration requirements for societies with branches), omit "and where any such society has branches in more than one registration area, section 10 above shall apply to that society".
4.-In section 99(4) (punishment of fraud etc and recovery of property misapplied), omit "in the central registration area".

The Friendly Societies Act 1992 (c 40)

5.- Omit sections 31 to 36A (authorisation of friendly societies business).
6.- In section 37 (restrictions on combinations of business), omit subsections (1), (1A) and (7A) to (9).
7.- Omit sections 38 to 43 (restrictions on business of certain authorised societies).
8.- Omit sections 44 to 50 (regulation of friendly societies business).

PART II
FRIENDLY SOCIETIES: SUBSIDIARIES AND CONTROLLED BODIES

Interpretation

9.- In this Part of this Schedule—
    "the 1992 Act" means the Friendly Societies Act 1992; and
    "section 13" means section 13 of that Act.

Qualifying bodies

10.- (1) Subsections (2) to (5) of section 13 (incorporated friendly societies allowed to form or acquire control or joint control only of qualifying bodies) cease to have effect.
(2) As a result, omit—
    (a) subsections (8) and (11) of that section, and

(b) Schedule 7 to the 1992 Act (activities which may be carried on by a subsidiary of, or body jointly controlled by, an incorporated friendly society).

Bodies controlled by societies

11.- In section 13(9) (defined terms), after paragraph (a) insert—

"(aa) an incorporated friendly society also has control of a body corporate if the body corporate is itself a body controlled in one of the ways mentioned in paragraph (a)(i), (ii) or (iii) by a body corporate of which the society has control;".

Joint control by societies

12.- In section 13(9), after paragraph (c) insert—

"(cc) an incorporated friendly society also has joint control of a body corporate if—

(i) a subsidiary of the society has joint control of the body corporate in a way mentioned in paragraph (c)(i), (ii) or (iii);

(ii) a body corporate of which the society has joint control has joint control of the body corporate in such a way; or

(iii) the body corporate is controlled in a way mentioned in paragraph (a)(i), (ii) or (iii) by a body corporate of which the society has joint control;".

Acquisition of joint control

13.- In section 13(9), in the words following paragraph (d), after "paragraph (c)" insert "or (cc)".

Amendment of Schedule 8 to the 1992 Act

14.- (1) Schedule 8 to the 1992 Act (provisions supplementing section 13) is amended as follows.

(2) Omit paragraph 3(2).

(3) After paragraph 3 insert—

"3A

(1) A body is to be treated for the purposes of section 13(9) as having the right to appoint to a directorship if—

(a) a person's appointment to the directorship follows necessarily from his appointment as an officer of that body; or

(b) the directorship is held by the body itself.

(2) A body ("B") and some other person ("P") together are to be treated, for the purposes of section 13(9), as having the right to appoint to a directorship if—

(a) P is a body corporate which has directors and a person's appointment to the directorship follows necessarily from his appointment both as an officer of B and a director of P;

(b) P is a body corporate which does not have directors and a person's appointment to the directorship follows necessarily from his appointment both as an officer of B and as a member of P's managing body; or

(c) the directorship is held jointly by B and P.

(3) For the purposes of section 13(9), a right to appoint (or remove) which is exercisable only with the consent or agreement of another person must be left out of account unless no other person has a right to appoint (or remove) in relation to that directorship.

(4) Nothing in this paragraph is to be read as restricting the effect of section 13(9)."

(4) In paragraph 9 (exercise of certain rights under instruction by, or in the interests of, incorporated friendly society) insert at the end "or in the interests of any body over which the society has joint control".

Consequential amendments

15.- (1) Section 52 of the 1992 Act is amended as follows.

(2) In subsection (2), omit paragraph (d).

(3) In subsection (3), for "(4) below" substitute "(2)".

(4) For subsection (4) substitute—

"(4) A court may not make an order under subsection (5) unless it is satisfied that one or more of the conditions mentioned in subsection (2) are satisfied."

(5) In subsection (5), omit the words from "or, where" to the end.

References in other enactments

16.- References in any provision of, or made under, any enactment to subsidiaries of, or bodies jointly controlled by, an incorporated friendly society are to be read as including references to bodies which are such subsidiaries or bodies as a result of any provision of this Part of this Schedule.

PART III
BUILDING SOCIETIES

The Building Societies Act 1986 (c 53)

17.- Omit section 9 (initial authorisation to raise funds and borrow money).

18.- Omit Schedule 3 (supplementary provisions about authorisation).

PART IV
INDUSTRIAL AND PROVIDENT SOCIETIES

The Industrial and Provident Societies Act 1965 (c 12)

19.- Omit section 8 (provision for separate registration areas for Scotland and for England, Wales and the Channel Islands).

20.- Omit section 70 (scale of fees to be paid in respect of transactions and inspection of documents).

PART V
CREDIT UNIONS

The Credit Unions Act 1979 (c 34)

21.- In section 6 (minimum and maximum number of members), omit subsections (2) to (6).

22.- In section 11 (loans), omit subsections (2) and (6).

23.- Omit sections 11B (loans approved by credit unions), 11C (grant of certificates of approval) and 11D (withdrawal of certificates of approval).

24.- In section 12, omit subsections (4) and (5).

25.- In section 14, omit subsections (2), (3), (5) and (6).

26.- In section 28 (offences), omit subsection (2).

SCHEDULE 19
. . .785

. . .786

PART I
. . .787

. . .788

PART II
. . .789

. . .790

SCHEDULE 20
MINOR AND CONSEQUENTIAL
AMENDMENTS   Section 432(1)

The House of Commons Disqualification Act 1975 (c 24)

1.- In Part III of Schedule 1 to the House of Commons Disqualification Act 1975 (disqualifying offices)—

(a) omit—

"Any member of the Financial Services Tribunal in receipt of remuneration"; and

(b) at the appropriate place, insert—

"Any member, in receipt of remuneration, of a panel of persons who may be selected to act as members of the Financial Services and Markets Tribunal".

The Northern Ireland Assembly Disqualification Act 1975 (c 25)

2.- In Part III of Schedule 1 to the Northern Ireland Assembly Disqualification Act 1975 (disqualifying offices)—

(a) omit—

"Any member of the Financial Services Tribunal in receipt of remuneration"; and

(b) at the appropriate place, insert—

"Any member, in receipt of remuneration, of a panel of persons who may be selected to act as members of the Financial Services and Markets Tribunal".

The Civil Jurisdiction and Judgments Act 1982 (c 27)

3.- In paragraph 10 of Schedule 5 to the Civil Jurisdiction and Judgments Act 1982 (proceedings excluded from the operation of Schedule 4 to that Act), for "section 188 of the Financial Services Act 1986" substitute "section 415 of the Financial Services and Markets Act 2000".

---

785 Repealed by the Enterprise Act 2002, ss 247(k), 278(2), Sch 26; came into force 20 June 2003.
786 Repealed by the Enterprise Act 2002, ss 247(k), 278(2), Sch 26; came into force 20 June 2003.
787 Repealed by the Enterprise Act 2002, ss 247(k), 278(2), Sch 26; came into force 20 June 2003.
788 Repealed by the Enterprise Act 2002, ss 247(k), 278(2), Sch 26; came into force 20 June 2003.
789 Repealed by the Enterprise Act 2002, ss 247(k), 278(2), Sch 26; came into force 20 June 2003.
790 Repealed by the Enterprise Act 2002, ss 247(k), 278(2), Sch 26; came into force 20 June 2003.

The Income and Corporation Taxes Act 1988 (c 1)

4.- (1) The Income and Corporation Taxes Act 1988 is amended as follows.

(2) In section 76 (expenses of management: insurance companies), in subsection (8), omit the definitions of—

"the 1986 Act";

"authorised person";

"investment business";

"investor";

"investor protection scheme";

"prescribed"; and

"recognised self-regulating organisation".

(3) In section 468 (authorised unit trusts), in subsections (6) and (8), for "78 of the Financial Services Act 1986" substitute " 243 of the Financial Services and Markets Act 2000".

(4)...[791]

(5) In section 728 (information in relation to transfers of securities), in subsection (7)(a), for "Financial Services Act 1986" substitute "Financial Services and Markets Act 2000".

(6)...[792]

The Finance Act 1991 (c 31)

5.- (1) The Finance Act 1991 is amended as follows.

(2) In section 47 (investor protection schemes), omit subsections (1), (2) and (4).

(3) In section 116 (investment exchanges and clearing houses: stamp duty), in subsection (4)(b), for "Financial Services Act 1986" substitute "Financial Services and Markets Act 2000".

The Tribunals and Inquiries Act 1992 (c 53)

6.- (1) The Tribunals and Inquiries Act 1992 is amended as follows.

(2) In Schedule 1 (tribunals under supervision of the Council on Tribunals), for the entry relating to financial services and paragraph 18, substitute—

"Financial services and markets 18 The Financial Services and Markets Tribunal."

The Judicial Pensions and Retirement Act 1993 (c 8)

7.- (1) The Judicial Pensions and Retirement Act 1993 is amended as follows.

(2) In Schedule 1 (offices which may be qualifying offices), in Part II, after the entry relating to the President or chairman of the Transport Tribunal insert—

"President or Deputy President of the Financial Services and Markets Tribunal"

(3) In Schedule 5 (relevant offices in relation to retirement provisions)—

(a) omit the entry—

"Member of the Financial Services Tribunal appointed by the Lord Chancellor"; and

(b) at the end insert—

"Member of the Financial Services and Markets Tribunal".

---

[791] Repealed by the Income Tax Act 2007, s 1031, Sch 3, Pt 1; date in force: this repeal has effect, for the purposes of income tax for the year 2007–08 and subsequent tax years, and for the purposes of corporation tax for accounting periods ending after 5 April 2007.

[792] Repealed by the Finance Act 2007, s 114, Sch 27, Pt 6(5); came into force on 19 July 2007 (date of Royal Assent of the Finance Act 2007) in the absence of any specific commencement provision.

SCHEDULE 21
TRANSITIONAL PROVISIONS
AND SAVINGS

Section 432(2)

Self-regulating organisations

1.- (1) No new application under section 9 of the 1986 Act (application for recognition) may be entertained.

(2) No outstanding application made under that section before the passing of this Act may continue to be entertained.

(3) After the date which is the designated date for a recognised self-regulating organisation—

    (a) the recognition order for that organisation may not be revoked under section 11 of the 1986 Act (revocation of recognition);

    (b) no application may be made to the court under section 12 of the 1986 Act (compliance orders) with respect to that organisation.

(4) The powers conferred by section 13 of the 1986 Act (alteration of rules for protection of investors) may not be exercised.

(5) "Designated date" means such date as the Treasury may by order designate.

(6) Sub-paragraph (3) does not apply to a recognised self-regulating organisation in respect of which a notice of intention to revoke its recognition order was given under section 11(3) of the 1986 Act before the passing of this Act if that notice has not been withdrawn.

(7) Expenditure incurred by the Authority in connection with the winding up of any body which was, immediately before the passing of this Act, a recognised self-regulating organisation is to be treated as having been incurred in connection with the discharge by the Authority of functions under this Act.

(8) "Recognised self-regulating organisation" means an organisation which, immediately before the passing of this Act, was such an organisation for the purposes of the 1986 Act.

(9) "The 1986 Act" means the Financial Services Act 1986.

Self-regulating organisations for friendly societies

2.- (1) No new application under paragraph 2 of Schedule 11 to the 1986 Act (application for recognition) may be entertained.

(2) No outstanding application made under that paragraph before the passing of this Act may continue to be entertained.

(3) After the date which is the designated date for a recognised self-regulating organisation for friendly societies—

    (a) the recognition order for that organisation may not be revoked under paragraph 5 of Schedule 11 to the 1986 Act (revocation of recognition);

    (b) no application may be made to the court under paragraph 6 of that Schedule (compliance orders) with respect to that organisation.

(4) "Designated date" means such date as the Treasury may by order designate.

(5) Sub-paragraph (3) does not apply to a recognised self-regulating organisation for friendly societies in respect of which a notice of intention to revoke its recognition order was given under section 11(3) of the 1986 Act (as applied by paragraph 5(2) of that Schedule) before the passing of this Act if that notice has not been withdrawn.

(6) Expenditure incurred by the Authority in connection with the winding up of any body which was, immediately before the passing of this Act, a recognised self-regulating organisation for friendly societies is to be treated as having been incurred in connection with the discharge by the Authority of functions under this Act.

(7) "Recognised self-regulating organisation for friendly societies" means an organisation which, immediately before the passing of this Act, was such an organisation for the purposes of the 1986 Act.

(8) "The 1986 Act" means the Financial Services Act 1986.

SCHEDULE 22
REPEALS

Section 432(3)

Chapter	Short title	Extent of repeal
1923 c 8	The Industrial Assurance Act 1923.	The whole Act.
		The whole Act.
1948 c 39	The Industrial Assurance and Friendly Societies Act 1948.	Section 8. Section 70.
1965 c 12	The Industrial and Provident Societies Act 1965.	Section 4. Section 10.
1974 c 46	The Friendly Societies Act 1974.	In section 11, from "and where" to "that society". In section 99(4), "in the central registration area". In Schedule 1, in Part III, "Any member of the Financial Services Tribunal in receipt of remuneration".
1975 c 24	The House of Commons Disqualification Act 1975.	In Schedule 1, in Part III, "Any member of the Financial Services Tribunal in receipt of remuneration".
1975 c 25	The Northern Ireland Assembly Disqualification Act 1975.	The whole Act. Section 6(2) to (6).
1977 c 46	The Insurance Brokers (Registration) Act 1977.	Section 11(2) and (6). Sections 11B, 11C and 11D.
1979 c 34	The Credit Unions Act 1979.	Section 12(4) and (5). In section 14, subsections (2), (3), (5) and (6). Section 28(2). Section 9. Schedule 3.
1986 c 53	The Building Societies Act 1986.	In section 76, in subsection (8), the definitions of "the 1986 Act", "authorised person", "investment business", "investor", "investor protection scheme", "prescribed" and "recognised self-regulating organisation". In section 47, subsections (1), (2) and (4).
1988 c 1	The Income and Corporation Taxes Act 1988.	In section 13, subsections (2) to (5), (8) and (11). Sections 31 to 36.
1991 c 31	The Finance Act 1991.	In section 37, subsections (1), (1A) and (7A) to (9). Sections 38 to 50. In section 52, subsection (2)(d) and, in subsection (5), the words from "or where" to the end.
1992 c 40	The Friendly Societies Act 1992.	Schedule 7. In Schedule 8, paragraph 3(2).
1993 c 8	The Judicial Pensions and Retirement Act 1993.	In Schedule 5, "Member of the Financial Services Tribunal appointed by the Lord Chancellor".

Index

Financial Services Law
Second Edition
Edited by **Michael Blair QC, George Walker** and **Robert Purves**

The new edition of *Financial Services Law* continues to provide an authoritative analysis of the UK regulatory regime under FSMA and the FSA handbook and rules as impacted by EC legislation, written by a team of lawyers from private practice and present or formed regulators.

This new edition includes coverage of:

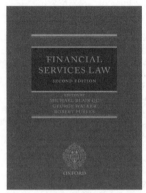

- MiFID post implementation and the Capital Requirements Directive
- The impact of the financial crisis including actual and proposed new regulation
- Islamic Financial Services
- The new Conduct of Business sourcebook (NEWCOB)
- The redrafting of the Insurance Conduct of Business Rules (NEWICOB)
- The new enforcement handbook
- New money laundering rules

March 2009
1,128 pages
Hardback
978-0-19-956418-7

Visit **www.oup.co.uk/law/practitioner**
for more information on this title and how to purchase

OXFORD
UNIVERSITY PRESS